CAMBRIDGE STUDIES IN
ANGLO-SAXON ENGLAND

22

HEATHEN GODS IN
OLD ENGLISH LITERATURE

CAMBRIDGE STUDIES IN ANGLO-SAXON ENGLAND

GENERAL EDITORS
SIMON KEYNES
MICHAEL LAPIDGE
ANDY ORCHARD

Volumes published

1 *Anglo-Saxon Crucifixion Iconography and the Art of the Monastic Revival* by BARBARA C. RAW
2 *The Cult of the Virgin Mary in Anglo-Saxon England* by MARY CLAYTON
3 *Religion and Literature in Western England, 600–800* by PATRICK SIMS-WILLIAMS
4 *Visible Song: Transitional Literacy in Old English Verse* by KATHERINE O'BRIEN O'KEEFFE
5 *The Metrical Grammar of* Beowulf by CALVIN B. KENDALL
6 *The Irish Tradition in Old English Literature* by CHARLES D. WRIGHT
7 *Anglo-Saxon Medicine* by M. L. CAMERON
8 *The Poetic Art of Aldhelm* by ANDY ORCHARD
9 *The Old English Lives of St Margaret* by MARY CLAYTON and HUGH MAGENNIS
10 *Biblical Commentaries from the Canterbury School of Theodore and Hadrian* by BERNHARD BISCHOFF and MICHAEL LAPIDGE
11 *Archbishop Theodore: Commemorative Studies on his Life and Influence* edited by MICHAEL LAPIDGE
12 *Interactions of Thought and Language in Old English Poetry* by PETER CLEMOES
13 *The Textuality of Old English Poetry* by CAROL BRAUN PASTERNACK
14 *The 'Laterculus Malalianus' and the School of Archbishop Theodore* by JANE STEVENSON
15 *The Text of the Old Testament in Anglo-Saxon England* by RICHARD MARSDEN
16 *Old English Biblical Verse* by PAUL G. REMLEY
17 *The Hymns of the Anglo-Saxon Church* by INGE B. MILFULL
18 *Scenes of Community in Old English Poetry* by HUGH MAGENNIS
19 *The Old English Apocrypha and their Manuscript Source: 'The Gospel of Nichodemus' and 'The Avenging of the Saviour'* edited by J. E. CROSS
20 *The Composition of Old English Poetry* by H. MOMMA
21 *Trinity and Incarnation in Anglo-Saxon Art and Thought* by BARBARA C. RAW

HEATHEN GODS IN OLD ENGLISH LITERATURE

RICHARD NORTH
University College London

CAMBRIDGE
UNIVERSITY PRESS

CAMBRIDGE UNIVERSITY PRESS
Cambridge, New York, Melbourne, Madrid, Cape Town, Singapore, São Paulo

Cambridge University Press
The Edinburgh Building, Cambridge CB2 2RU, UK

Published in the United States of America by Cambridge University Press, New York

www.cambridge.org
Information on this title: www.cambridge.org/9780521551830

© Cambridge University Press 1997

This publication is in copyright. Subject to statutory exception
and to the provisions of relevant collective licensing agreements,
no reproduction of any part may take place without
the written permission of Cambridge University Press.

First published 1997
This digitally printed first paperback version 2006

A catalogue record for this publication is available from the British Library

Library of Congress Cataloguing in Publication data
North, Richard, 1961–
Heathen gods in Old English literature / Richard North.
p. cm. – (Cambridge studies in Anglo-Saxon England; 22)
Includes bibliographical references and index.
ISBN 0 521 55183 8 (hardback)
1. English literature – Old English, ca. 450–1100 – History and
criticism. 2. Gods in literature. 3. Civilization, Anglo-Saxon, in literature.
4. Paganism – England – History. 5. Religion and literature.
6. Paganism in literature. 7. Anglo-Saxons – Religion.
8. Gods, Anglo-Saxon. I. Series.
PR179.G63N67 1997
829'.0938291211 – dc21   96–40353   CIP

ISBN-13 978-0-521-55183-0 hardback
ISBN-10 0-521-55183-8 hardback

ISBN-13 978-0-521-03026-7 paperback
ISBN-10 0-521-03026-9 paperback

To Inma

Contents

	Preface	page ix
	List of abbreviations	xiii
1	Nerthus and Terra Mater: Anglian religion in the first century	1
2	Ingui of Bernicia	26
3	Ingui's cult remembered: Ing and the *ingefolc*	44
4	Woden's witchcraft	78
5	'Uoden de cuius stirpe': the role of Woden in royal genealogy	111
6	Aspects of Ingui: *-geot* and Geat	133
7	The cult of Ingui in *Beowulf*	172
8	Ingui's marriage: natural phenomena	204
9	Ingui's death: the world-tree sacrifice	273
10	Paulinus and the *stultus error*: the Anglo-Saxon conversion	304
	Bibliography	343
	Index	355

Preface

'And you really think that the wooden figure . . . ?' Clarissa tailed away in query.

'Oh, a fertility god, dear', said Rose. 'No doubt of it at all. Of course, the carving's very crude. Much cruder than the few finds they've made on the Baltic coast. Due to native workmanship, no doubt with the Continental tradition almost lost. That accounts for the large size of the member, you know.' Clarissa felt that she need not have feared to finish her sentence. 'But it's an Anglo-Saxon deity all right. A true *wig*. One of the *idola* Bede was so shocked about. Or pretended to be, shall we say?'

Angus Wilson, Anglo-Saxon Attitudes

When I started working on this book some ten years ago, I had no idea what the conclusion would be or how the project would end. That it now ends with Bede and a fertility god has surprised me and may be the last straw to some of Bede's modern readers, but is a conclusion to which some entirely unforeseen implications of the evidence led me. The thrust of my arguments became clear to me only gradually and in the last three years. Nor at any time in the last decade could I have developed any of these arguments without trying them out on older and wiser scholars, whose reservations about the study of Anglo-Saxon paganism consequently gave shape to this project no less than my enthusiasm did. Their doubts were to do with the dearth of relevant material, with the Christianization of the evidence, with the problem of dating the Norse poetry on which most analogies with Old English literature depend, and with the relative unsuitability of Norse prose, which is too often held to be the equal of Norse poetry in pagan authenticity. These doubts are legitimate and well known, but the climate which they create is not

Preface

always helpful in the wider Anglo-Saxon field. Because the study of Anglo-Saxon paganism is never free of these uncertainties, many scholars find it easier to be 'sceptical' than observant about heathen gods in Old English literature. For most scholars it is easiest not to bother with this subject at all. Ours is a long and distinguished Christian tradition, in which most heathen gods were excised, transformed, filtered out or forgotten in the seventh century, some generations before the composition of the first literary evidence. There is more to say about the gods in Old Norse–Icelandic Eddic and Scaldic poetry of the tenth century, and in the mythography and saga-prose of the thirteenth century, but the picture here, though so much fuller, must usually be made clearer before it can inform Anglo-Saxon texts of the eighth to the eleventh centuries. But then not every scholar of Old English knows Old Norse, and recently it seems that even some with an interest in Anglo-Saxon paganism would rather declare Old Norse irrelevant than see the justice of any textual comparison with Old English. Heaven forbid that this vogue should become an orthodoxy. The motives for this unfashionable kind of philology have also been viewed with suspicion. What has Woden to do with Bede, Scandinavian paganism with *Beowulf*, *Hinieldus cum Christo*? Not much, it might be insisted. The romanticism of these 'pagan' enquiries, whatever their results, has proved alien to many scholars in both Anglo-Saxon and Norse fields, and there is no denying that romantic philology (no less than statistical analysis or ultraviolet photography) is a product of the modern age and would have been strange to the Christian men and women who preserved or created Old English literature, as well as to their heathen ancestors who shaped the language in which this was written. These, in short, are the reservations of most scholars concerning 'heathen gods in Old English literature'.

The simplest apology for an interest in this subject, however, is that it remains relevant to Anglo-Saxon history. Heathen religion was a political issue in seventh-century England and was still practised in some kingdoms during the lifetimes of Aldhelm and Bede. Some of its beliefs were of common ancestry with Scandinavian paganism and may have been revived when the Vikings settled in England. Norse paganism itself, first in Scandinavia and then in the countryside around the Danelaw boroughs and in Yorkshire, Cheshire, Lancashire, Cumbria and Northumberland, lived next door to the Anglo-Saxons almost from beginning to end of their history. Cognate Icelandic literature may thus be used to throw

Preface

light on the changing ideologies of the early Anglo-Saxons, particularly through the late literary traces of their gods. The arguments which do this here are written in the subjunctive mood, but also with a self-evident methodology and with the use of a probability by which it may be assumed that if the *contra* of any case had outweighed the *pro*, the argument would not have been included in the first place. As long as all the doubts are admitted and the argumentation is made clear in all places along the route of this enquiry, my conclusion at the end of the book, however unorthodox it first seems, is supported by evidence.

The writing of this book has also led me to question a number of axioms which continue to define the field of comparative Anglo-Saxon and Old Norse–Icelandic studies today. For example, it is sometimes stated by historians that pagans saw Christianity as something new; that Anglo-Saxon paganism was failing when the Roman mission reached England; that Bede would have been horrified if he had known what that paganism was; that comparative Icelandic evidence can be lightly dismissed as tenuous, without further discussion, because it is preserved in later medieval manuscripts; that most of what passes for heathen poetry there anyway is the product of learned Christian invention in twelfth- and thirteenth-century Iceland; that 'sacral kingship', in particular, is a figment of the same or a later era; that nothing can be concluded from a Norse text on pagan themes, even if it is accepted that this text predates the conversion; and that even if a motif in Norse poetry is accepted as pre-Christian, it surely had no existence prior to the late pagan poets who created it *ex nihilo*. By other scholars it is often stated that Norse gods and their roles can be fitted into a tripartite caste-system alleged to work for Indo-European mythologies as a whole; that the cult of Woden or Óðinn – a love-affair continuing to this day – was of Nordic origin and dominated the pantheons of all Germanic religions; and that Nerthus, the Old Anglian deity whose name is cited in the *Germania* of Tacitus, underwent a sex-change from female to male at a time between the first century and the ninth. The scholarship is often impressive in which these views are upheld, but in view of the rareness with which some of them are challenged, it might be said that there are other sacred cows in this field than the heifers pulling Nerthus through *Germania*.

All these views I have been obliged to revise in some way, but in doing so I have made three new arguments crucial to the conclusion of my book. I suggest that Nerthus was male, like Njǫrðr; that Baldr was derived

Preface

from the same figure as Freyr; and that Njǫrðr's wife Skaði was a Norse reflex of Terra Mater. If these innovations are accepted as a new joint premise for heathen gods in Old English literature, then our picture of Bede's knowledge may change – not to the extent that Rose Lorimer would have changed it, of course, but enough to show that Bede knew the *gens* as well as the *ecclesia Anglorum*. Lest I share the fate of Dr Lorimer, however, let me finish by urging sceptics and enthusiasts alike to read this book carefully from beginning to end.

I am grateful to my wife Inma Ridao, my father and mother Professor John and Mrs Marion North, my sisters Rachel and Julian, Mr David Ashurst, Dr Peter Heather, Dr Susan Irvine, Professor Elaine Jahner, Mr Roger Llewellyn and Ms Cath Ranzetta, Mr Timothy McFarland, Professor Janet Nelson, Dr Peter Orton, Dr Clive Tolley, Dr Elizabeth Tyler, Dr Martin Welch and Dr Bryan Wyly, among other friends and colleagues, for reading through and making comments on various passages in this book. My thanks also go to Professor Michael Lapidge, Dr Simon Keynes and Dr Andy Orchard for reading, and in Michael's case for patiently rereading and correcting, drafts of this book for the press. Thanks go to the late Jenny Potts for her meticulous copy-editing of this book. Thanks also go to my colleagues in the English Department, University College London, who supported me with a grant with which to assist the completion of this book. I acknowledge Curtis Brown on behalf of Angus Wilson for my quotation from *Anglo-Saxon Attitudes* (copyright as printed in original volumes). My debt extends further back to Sally Frank, in whose confidence I raised many questions on the subject of my doctoral thesis and to whose memory I dedicated it on her untimely death in 1985, to Professor Ray Page, my then supervisor, without whose good-humoured objections I would never have learnt to evaluate the material which I have used, and to Mrs Ursula Dronke, whose undergraduate tuition and later imaginative guidance helped generate many of the ideas contained in this book.

Abbreviations

All translations are mine unless otherwise indicated.

ABäG	Amsterdamer Beiträge zur älteren Germanistik
AF	Anglistische Forschungen
AIEW	Johannesson, Altisländisches etymologisches Wörterbuch
Akv	Atlakviða
AM	Arnamagnaean
Am	Atlamál
And	Andreas
ANEW	de Vries, Altnordisches etymologisches Wörterbuch, 2nd ed.
ANF	Arkiv för nordisk filologi
AR	de Vries, Altgermanische Religionsgeschichte, 2nd ed.
ASC	The Anglo-Saxon Chronicle, ed. Plummer and Earle, cited by volume and page number
ASE	Anglo-Saxon England
ASPR	The Anglo-Saxon Poetic Records, ed. Krapp and Dobbie
BAR	British Archaeological Reports
Bdr	Baldrs Draumar
Beo	Beowulf
BGdSL	Beiträge zur Geschichte der deutschen Sprache und Literatur [Paul und Braunes Beiträge]
CCSL	Corpus Christianorum Series Latina
CR	Codex Regius
CSASE	Cambridge Studies in Anglo-Saxon England
Dan	Daniel
Dan	Danish
Du	Dutch

List of abbreviations

EETS	Early English Text Society
El	*Elene*
ES	*English Studies*
EStn	*Englische Studien*
eWS	Early West Saxon
Ex	*Exodus*
Fáf	*Fáfnismál*
Fates	*The Fates of the Apostles*
Finn	*Finnsburh Fragment*
FJSnE	*Edda Snorra Sturlusonar*, ed. Finnur Jónsson; cited by page number
Flat	*Flateyjarbók*, ed. Unger; cited by volume and page number
Fort	*Fortunes of Men*
Fris	Frisian
GD	Saxo Grammaticus, *Gesta Danorum*, ed. Olrik and Ræder
Gen	*Genesis*
Ger	German
Germania	*The Germania of Tacitus*, ed. Robinson
Gmc	Germanic
Got	Gothic
Grím	*Grímnismál*
Gríp	*Grípisspá*
GRM	*Germanisch-romanische Monatsschrift*
Guð	*Guðrúnarkviða* (I, II, III)
Guth	*Guthlac*
Gylf	*Gylfaginning*, ed. Faulkes
Hamð	*Hamðismál*
HAR	Helm, *Altgermanische Religionsgeschichte*
Hárb	*Hárbarðsljóð*
Háv	*Hávamál*
HE	Bede, *Historia ecclesiastica*, ed. Colgrave and Mynors
HHj	*Helgakviða Hjǫrvarðssonar*
HHund	*Helgakviða Hundingsbana* (I, II)
Hym	*Hymiskviða*
Hynd	*Hyndluljóð*
ÍF	Íslenzk Fornrit
JDay	*Judgement Day* (I, II)
JMH	*Journal of Medieval History*

List of abbreviations

Jud	*Judith*
Jul	*Juliana*
Lok	*Lokasenna*
LSE	*Leeds Studies in English*
lWS	late West Saxon
Max	*Maxims* (I, II)
MÆ	*Medium Ævum*
MCharm	*The Metrical Charms*
ME	Middle English
Met	*The Meters of Boethius*
MGH	Monumenta Germaniae Historica
Auct. Antiq.	Auctores Antiquissimi
FIG	Fontes Iuris Germanici in usum scholarum separatim editi
SRG	Scriptores Rerum Germanicarum
SRM	Scriptores Rerum Merovingicarum
MLR	*Modern Language Review*
ModIce	Modern Icelandic
ModSw	Modern Swedish
MoM	*Mål og Minne*
MScan	*Medieval Scandinavia*
MSol	*Solomon and Saturn*
Neophil	*Neophilologus*
NM	*Neuphilologische Mitteilungen*
NoB	*Namn och bygd*
Norw	Norwegian
Oddr	*Oddrúnargrátr*
OE	Old English
OHG	Old High German
OIce	Old Icelandic
OrW	*The Order of the World*
OS	Old Saxon
PBA	*Proceedings of the British Academy*
Peritia	*Peritia: Journal of the Medieval Academy of Ireland*
PGmc	Proto-Germanic
Phoen	*The Phoenix*
PL	Patrologia Latina, ed. J.-P. Migne, 221 vols. (Paris, 1844–64)
PMLA	*Publications of the Modern Language Association*

List of abbreviations

PPs	The Paris Psalter
Prec	*Precepts*
RES	Review of English Studies
Ríg	*Rígsþula*
Saga-Book	*Saga-Book of the Viking Society* (formerly *Club*)
Settimane	*Settimane di studio del Centro italiano di studi sull'alto medioevo*
Sigsk	*Sigurðarkviða in skamma*
Skí	*Skírnismál*
Skj	*Den norsk-islandske skjaldedigtning*, ed. Finnur Jónsson
SnE	*Edda Snorra Sturlusonar*, vol. I, ed. Jón Sigurðsson (1848); cited by page number (text slightly normalized)
SNF	*Studier i nordisk filologi*
Soul	*Soul and Body* (I, II)
Þrym	*Þrymskviða*
Vaf	*Vafþrúðnismál*
Vsp	*Vǫluspá*
Vǫl	*Vǫlundarkviða*
Wald	*Waldere* (I, II)
Wan	*The Wanderer*
Wid	*Widsith*
ZfdA	*Zeitschrift für deutsches Altertum*
ZfdPh	*Zeitschrift für deutsche Philologie*

1
Nerthus and Terra Mater: Anglian religion in the first century

Heathen gods are hard to find in Old English literature. Most Anglo-Saxon writers had no interest in them and consequently the reaction of today's scholars to this topic can vary from polite amusement to hostility. What price a few scraps of Germanic antiquity, compared with the learned civilization for which the Anglo-Saxons were so famous? The hunt for pagan survivals might seem futile in comparison. When the italianate sculpture and latinity of Northumbria are considered, the riches of Anglo-Latin and Old English poetry, Alfred's reconstruction of Wessex, or the development of West Saxon prose through Æthelwold, Ælfric and Wulfstan, this reaction is not surprising. Names such as Tiu, Thunor, Frig and Woden do not inspire confidence alongside famous ones such as Aldhelm, Bede or Alcuin. The men represent a literature, the gods a preliterate ideology mostly of the early seventh century. The men are rooted in history, whereas the gods must be discussed with reference to later myths and folktales. Even the names of these gods are misleading: the name *Tiu* is partly based on the Old English name for 'Tuesday' and on glosses; *Thunor* is a modern personification of the Old English word for 'thunder'; *Frig* is a loan into modern scholarship from the thirteenth-century literature of Iceland; only *Woden* survives as an outright personification, and his name is mentioned only in two proverbs, in some placenames, and in regnal lists. Thus it might seem that there is little material to work with, and even less reward to be gained, from studying heathen gods in Old English literature.

I shall try a more productive approach in what follows, by treating Woden and the other aforesaid 'gods' in the sixth and seventh centuries in England as relatively minor elements within a larger natural religion of which the main concern was the renewal of the farming year. With the exception of Woden, whose literary role I shall introduce in the present chapter, I shall approach the Anglo-Saxon gods only after I have discussed *Nerthus*, an older Germanic deity whose name is cited by the Roman historian Tacitus at the end of the first century and whose worshippers are said to have included the Angles in their continental homeland. Not Woden but Nerthus, a deity whom Tacitus calls 'mother earth', is named in connection with the Angles at this early date. My method is thus to start with Tacitus and to reconsider both his idea of Nerthus and his ethnography in the *Germania* in relation to the names of Scandinavian gods in Old Norse–Icelandic poetry, in order to throw more light on the North Sea Germanic tradition from which the Angles emerged; then to apply my conclusions to passages in Old English literature, in particular to poems of an underlying Anglian dialect and provenance, in order to reconstruct the shape and development of heathen gods in England.

In this introductory chapter I shall explain how Norse evidence can be used in an enquiry into Anglo-Saxon paganism; then, after illustrating the impact of Woden on this field, I shall focus on Nerthus and attempt to show how Tacitus may have misinterpreted this deity as a northern counterpart of the goddess Cybele or Magna Mater. In ch. 2, I shall define *Ing-* as an early Germanic hypostasis of Nerthus and present the Anglian reflex of this name in *Ingui* of Bernicia. In ch. 3, I shall attempt to throw light on Ing in *The Old English Rune Poem* and on the meaning of his *incge*-prefix where it occurs in a letter from Alcuin to Speratus, in the Old English *Exodus* and in the Finnsburh Episode in *Beowulf*. In ch. 4 of this book I shall seek to explain a connection between the witchcraft associated with Nerthus's religion and the magic of Woden, a figure whose cult is likely to have been derived from that of Mercury in Roman Gaul. My conclusion concerning Woden's witchcraft in ch. 4 will be cited in ch. 5 in order to explain how Woden's role in Anglo-Saxon royal genealogy may have usurped that of Ingui or other tribal gods. In ch. 6, I shall focus on two aspects of Ingui: on the suffix OE *-geot* as an epithet of the Ing-hypostasis denoting Ingui's marriage and sacrifice; and on Geat, a politically inspired personification of *-geot* in the genealogy of King Æthelwulf of Wessex (833–58). In a further exploration of Ingui's role in *Beowulf*, in ch. 7, I shall argue that the poet of this work, representing Danish paganism as if the Danes were figures of the Old Testament, identified Ingui or Ing with the devil and either concealed other Scandinavian gods or presented them as euhemerized heroes. I shall also argue in ch. 7 that the poet of *Beowulf* was influenced by Danish legends before the Viking Age, and that Æthelwulf later owned a text of this poem from which he or his clergy took names for new West Saxon ancestors allegedly even older than Geat. In ch. 8, a discussion of animism in Anglo-Saxon England, I shall present the evidence for *numina* including Eostre, Tiu and *þunor*, as a preliminary to an attempted reconstruction of the seasonal marriage and death of the Ing-hypostasis in the old Anglian homeland on the southern border of Scandinavia. Ch. 9 concerns some Northumbrian traces of Ingui, the presumed Anglian reflex of this figure, in the language with which Christ is described in *The Dream of the Rood*. I shall conclude, in ch. 10, with a new hypothesis on the last days of Ingui in Northumbria, and on the inspired role of Paulinus in the mission that led to Ingui's defeat.

PROBLEM AND METHOD

The relics of heathen religion are not easy to identify within early Christian vernaculars.[1] Consequently there is an illusion that Anglo-Saxon paganism was weak. To quote one recent commentator: 'Why was Christianity so readily, if at times only superficially and temporarily, accepted by the English? Certainly, the inherent inadequacies of Germanic paganism, its incomplete pantheon and woefully weak and drearily fatalistic religion, had something to do with the easy and rapid spread of the gospel.'[2] The question here is well chosen, better than the statement following, which is misconceived in several ways. Firstly, no faith which is current is likely to be regarded as inadequate by its believers. Secondly, the term 'pantheon', which in any case may be wrong for a natural religion based on animism, cannot refer to a collection of gods which is incomplete. Thirdly, the idea that Anglo-Saxon paganism was fatalistic is based on an old premise that the Anglo-Saxons worshipped OE *wyrd* ('fate') as a god. Yet this premise was challenged more than half a century ago: first by B. J. Timmer, who regarded *wyrd* as a Christian literary abstraction;[3] then by Dorothy Whitelock, who thought that the impor-

---

[1] North, *Pagan Words*, pp. 1–13.
[2] Brown, *Bede the Venerable*, p. 5.
[3] B. J. Timmer, 'Wyrd in Anglo-Saxon Prose and Poetry', *Neophil* 26 (1940–1), 24–33 and 213–28; repr. in *Essential Articles for the Study of OE Poetry*, ed. J. B. Bessinger and S. J. Kahrl (Hamden, CT, 1968), pp. 124–58.

tance of this word had been 'exaggerated';[4] and then by E. G. Stanley and Gerd Wolfgang Weber, each of whom confirmed the Christian status of *wyrd* in even closer detail.[5] Lastly, as I shall try to show in my concluding chapter, the fact that Christianity sometimes spread rapidly in England does not necessarily mean that Anglo-Saxon paganism was in terminal decline, but rather that it was probably a form of animism sufficiently widespread, ingrained and powerful to swallow up a new god whenever one appeared. This idea may explain why the Anglo-Saxons converted quickly, yet also why their bishops fought with paganism into the lifetime of Bede (c. 675–735).

Between Bede and the Old Norse–Icelandic literature by which I shall eventually try to interpret parts of his *Historia ecclesiastica gentis Anglorum* (c. 732), there appears at first to be a world of difference.[6] Bede wrote biblical commentaries, theological and computistical treatises, devotional poems and letters all in Latin, had little interest in Anglian paganism and lived in Northumbria more than three hundred years before Icelandic antiquarians even began to make records of their island's pre-Christian past. Iceland, a wild volcanic outcrop in the mid-Atlantic, might also seem to be an odd and faraway place for comparison with the latinate civilization of Anglo-Saxon England. Yet Iceland, also a unique repository of learning with a vernacular literature to rival that of any country in medieval Europe, preserves the mythology by which it is possible to interpret the few but tantalizing references to heathen gods in Old English literature. Iceland was settled mostly by Norwegians in c. 890, when King Haraldr *hárfagri* ('fair-hair') of Vestfold (ruled c. 885 – c. 930) conquered western Norway and forced many dispossessed chieftains to look for new land overseas. With a general assembly in the late ninth century, constitutional reforms in 930 and 960 and Christianization *en masse* in c. 999, Iceland remained an independent republic until its

---

[4] D. Whitelock, *The Beginnings of English Society* (Harmondsworth, 1950), pp. 27–8.
[5] E. G. Stanley, *The Search for Anglo-Saxon Paganism* (Cambridge, 1975), pp. 92–4 and 95–121; G. W. Weber, *Wyrd: Studien zum Schicksalsbegriff der altenglischen und altnordischen Literatur*, Frankfurter Beiträge zur Germanistik 8 (Frankfurt, 1969), 155–8; on the agency of *wyrd* in *ealuscerwen* (*Beo* 769), see North, '"Wyrd" and "wearð ealuscerwen"', pp. 69–82.
[6] Henceforth I shall refer to *Historia ecclesiastica* in Bede's *Ecclesiastical History of the English People*, ed. and trans. B. Colgrave and R. A. B. Mynors (Oxford, 1969, repr. with corrections 1991).

annexation by Norway, which was initiated by King Hákon Hákonarson in *c.* 1262.[7] Icelandic nationalism throughout this period, from the tenth to the fourteenth century, contributed to the survival of native history, poetry and mythology in Icelandic monasteries when traditions of this kind had died out in Norway and elsewhere. Because there is a cognate relationship between the vernacular languages, poetic cultures and hence the heathen traditions of England and Scandinavia, it is possible to reconstruct the earliest English religion on the basis of analogues from Old Norse–Icelandic literature.

However, there are problems of methodology in this comparative field. Old Norse–Icelandic literature is notoriously problematic where its record of Scandinavian paganism is concerned. The historical novels or 'sagas' (*sǫgur*) for which thirteenth-century Iceland is famous provide a colourful but incidental and untrustworthy picture of heathen religion in which some authors appear to reconstruct supernatural detail on the basis of saints' lives, Irish folklore, French and German romances and even contemporary fortune-telling.[8] The true pagan cults had died out in Iceland and in Norway not long after these countries were Christianized respectively in *c.* 999 and *c.* 1030. Some poems, longer works rather than individual *lausavísur* ('loose verses'), may go back to a time in Scandinavia before the conversion. Yet it is often hard to judge whether the extant work of a poet said to have lived in the pre-Christian period is genuinely his, or is rather one of the many clever forgeries produced in Iceland in the twelfth or thirteenth centuries. There is no internal and little circumstantial evidence for the date of Norse or Icelandic poems, most of which are preserved in the sagas and other prose works written in Iceland in the thirteenth century and surviving in manuscripts datable to the fourteenth or fifteenth centuries. These poems are all stanzaic and are usually studied in two categories: as 'Scaldic' or occasional poems which named warrior–poets or *skáld* ('versifiers') composed in *dróttkvætt* ('court-metre') and in other baroque metrical forms, sometimes to commemorate gifts, sometimes to lament the dead, but most often to flatter kings and princes in Norway;[9] or as the anonymous 'Eddic' poems, or mythological and heroic ballads from the 'poetic *Edda*', most of which are found in a

---

[7] Byock, *Medieval Iceland*, pp. 52–71. On the revised date of the Icelandic conversion, see *Íslendingabók*, ed. Jakob, pp. xxix–lxi, esp. xxxv.

[8] North, *Pagan Words*, pp. 145–76.

[9] Frank, *Old Norse Court Poetry*, pp. 55–70; and Jónas, *Eddas and Sagas*, pp. 83–114.

Heathen gods

collection copied into the Codex Regius of *c*. 1270–80.[10] Each of these poems, whether Scaldic or Eddic, must be dated with probability rather than certainty, for the burden of proof now lies in showing that a Norse poem thought to be pagan is not an antiquarian forgery. Sagas in which the earlier Scaldic poems are quoted fall into two categories. First there are 'sagas of Icelanders' (*Íslendingasǫgur*), which glorify the tenth-century ancestors of the families that commissioned them, partly as a reflection of the intermittent civil war in the thirteenth century (the 'Age of the Sturlungs'), and partly in consolation for the outcome of this war, Iceland's loss of independence to Norway in *c*. 1262–4.[11] Then there are the 'kings' sagas' (*konungasǫgur*) including the 'Garland of the World' (*Heimskringla*), a collection of the lives of the kings of Norway which Snorri Sturluson (1179–1241), an Icelandic historian, landowner and politician, wrote probably in the 1220s with reference to older historical works.[12] From then on until he was assassinated by King Hákon's men in 1241, Snorri also wrote the 'prose *Edda*' in three stages: first, the *Háttatal* ('List of Metres', now known as *Edda* part III), a poem exemplifying Scaldic metres and praising the two rulers of Norway, Hákon and his father-in-law and regent Jarl Skúli, both of whom Snorri visited in 1218–20; second, the *Skáldskaparmál* ('Poetics', now *Edda* part II), a discourse with abundant quotation and paraphrase on the many types of 'kennings' or periphrases to be found in Scaldic poetry; third, *Gylfaginning* ('The Beguiling of Gylfi', now *Edda* part I), a mythography based mostly on quoted and paraphrased Eddic poems in which King Gylfi of Sweden learns of the Norse gods, their creation, adventures and destruction, apparently from three of their descendants; in addition, Snorri or a different author wrote a Prologue to this compilation in which the Norse gods are euhemerized as Trojans who migrated to northern Europe.[13]

---

[10] Jónas, *ibid.*, pp. 25–82. CR is listed as GkS 2365 quarto in Stofnun Árna Magnússonar, Reykjavík; also preserved in this library are AM 748 I and II quarto, related manuscript fragments containing *Grímnismál* and part of *Skírnismál* which are otherwise in Codex Regius. On specific items of Icelandic literature, see R. Simek, *Lexikon der altnordischen Literatur* (Stuttgart, 1987).

[11] Jónas, *Eddas and Sagas*, pp. 187–223. On the political background, see Byock, *Medieval Iceland*, pp. 31–50 and 71–102.

[12] Jónas, *ibid.*, pp. 147–78, esp. 168–78.

[13] See *Gylf*, pp. xii–xxix, and A. Faulkes, 'The Sources of *Skáldskaparmál*: Snorri's Intellectual Background', in *Snorri Sturluson: Kolloquium anlässlich der 750. Wiederkehr seines Todestages*, ed. A. Wolf (Tübingen, 1993), pp. 59–76; also U. Dronke and

This prose *Edda*, written by Snorri to keep the indigenous poetics alive in the face of ballads and romances from Europe, is the major source for Old Norse–Icelandic poetry and mythology. Only the first three books of *Gesta Danorum*, a history of Denmark written in sixteen books by Saxo Grammaticus c. 1185–1216, offer comparable mythological material; in Saxo's work, however, the Scandinavian gods live in 'Byzantium' and are cited marginally with reference to northern kings and princes. *Edda*, Snorri's name for his mythography, was erroneously given to the poems in Codex Regius when this codex was discovered in an Icelandic farmhouse in 1643: hence the distinction between 'prose *Edda*' and 'poetic *Edda*'.[14] It is also believed that Snorri wrote *Egils saga Skalla-Grímssonar*, a biography of a tenth-century Icelandic farmer, warrior and poet, probably after he had completed *Heimskringla* and following his second visit to Norway in 1237–9.[15] Snorri's *Edda* and *Heimskringla* preserve the Eddic and Scaldic poems on which I shall base fundamental arguments in this book.

These poems are assumed to come from Norway in the ninth and tenth centuries. In the case of Scaldic verse, there is Bragi's *Ragnarsdrápa* ('Poem in honour of Ragnarr') of the mid ninth century; and towards the end of that century, there is Þjóðólfr's *Ynglingatal* ('List of the Ynglingar'), which celebrates the lives and deaths of the kings of Uppsala and Vestfold, and Þjóðólfr's *Haustlǫng* ('Harvest-long [poem]'), a poem composed in return for the gift of a shield. There is also Eyvindr's *Hákonarmál* ('Lay of Hákon'), a poem composed in c. 960 in memory of King Hákon Haraldsson; Eyvindr's *Háleygjatal* ('List of the Háleygir'), a genealogical poem composed in c. 985 and apparently modelled on *Ynglingatal*; and other works associated with Hákon Jarl in the Trondheim region. The Codex Regius contains the four Eddic poems on which I shall also partly rely for pre-Christian material: *Vǫluspá* ('Sibyl's Prophecy'), in which a sibylline oracle reveals the history of the Norse gods and their world from its creation to its end; the gods' truth-game *Lokasenna* ('Loki's Flyting'), in which Loki, an *agent provocateur*, subjects

---

P. Dronke, 'The Prologue of the Prose *Edda*: Explorations of a Latin Background', in *Sjötíu Ritgerðir helgaðar Jakob Benediktssyni*, ed. G. Pétursson and Jónas Kristjánsson (Reykjavik, 1977), pp. 153–76 (also published in *Myth and Fiction*, no. III).

[14] Jónas, *Eddas and Sagas*, pp. 25–6.

[15] *Ibid.*, pp. 265–70; R. West, 'Snorri Sturluson and *Egils Saga*: Statistics of Style', *Scandinavian Studies* 52 (1980), 163–93.

each Norse god in turn to an illuminating mockery of his or her divine role; *Skírnismál* ('Lay of Skírnir'), in which, apparently for the health of the land and harvest, Freyr sends his servant Skírnir to coerce Gerðr, a giantess, into sex with Freyr; and the Gothic legend *Hamðismál* ('Lay of Hamðir'), in which the brothers Hamðir and Sǫrli try with only partial success to avenge their sister Svanhildr on the Gothic emperor Jǫrmunrekkr. These and other Eddic poems were evidently popular in the thirteenth century even while they contained living or fossilized allusions to tenth-century paganism.

For each Scaldic or Eddic poem of this kind, a tentative case for oral transmission must be made from a historically suitable date at a time between *c*. 890 and *c*. 1000, with composition usually in the Trondheim region, to the early twelfth century in Skálholt, Oddi, Þingeyrar or other ecclesiastical centres in Iceland, where these works were probably transcribed for the first time.[16] In his *Íslendingabók* ('Book of Icelanders'), which he wrote in *c*. 1125–30, Ari Þorgilsson (1067–1148) names one source, Hallr Þórarinsson, who was born in *c*. 985; in theory, with just one other such long-lived informant before Hallr, Ari's knowledge of Icelandic history could have extended as far back as the late ninth century.[17] OIce *Edda*, Snorri's name for his treatise on Scaldic and other poetry, claims the same length of oral tradition. In view of such traditions, Snorri's meaning in *edda* is more likely to be 'great-grandmother' (the literal meaning of this word) than 'poetics' (putatively derived from *óðr*, 'poem') or 'edition' (from Lat *edo* on analogy with Faroese *kredda* from Lat *credo*).[18] If the difference in age between a child and its great-grandmother is about sixty to seventy years, then with only two such periods of transmission Snorri could have access to a human chain of memory lasting nearly one and a half centuries. With three consecutive *eddur*, a family memory of this kind would have amounted to more than two centuries. This is the length of time needed to bridge the gap between the ninth century and the period of the first vernacular writing in Iceland, which probably began in *c*. 1049, when the missionary

---

[16] Jónas, *Eddas and Sagas*, pp. 89–110. See also Dronke, 'Scope of the *Corpus Poeticvm Boreale*', pp. 93–111, esp. 106 (also published in *Myth and Fiction*, no. V).

[17] *Íslendingabók*, ed. Jakob, pp. xx–xxix (Ari's sources). See also Jónas, *Eddas and Sagas*, pp. 120–4.

[18] F. Wagner, 'Que signifie le mot "Edda"?', *Revue belge de philologie et d'histoire* 18 (1939), 962–4; for *Edda* as 'edition', see A. Faulkes, 'Edda', *Gripla* 2 (1977), 32–9.

bishop Hróðólfr or Rúðólfr (who had lived in Iceland from 1030 and later died as the abbot of Abingdon in 1052) is said to have left three monks behind him in a monastery in Bœr in Borgarfjǫrðr.[19] After writing sermons (first in Latin and then in the vernacular), saints' lives and annals for three or four generations, Icelanders in the early twelfth century could thus have written down secular poems or quotations from poems which dated back to the late ninth century. In cases of this kind, the more semantic obscurity or corruption there is in a poem, the less likely is its composition in the Christian period. These are the reasons for treating the mythology in some Eddic and Scaldic poems as genuinely pre-Christian.

A controversy surrounding *Ynglingatal* well illustrates the problem of authenticity. Snorri quotes part or all of *Ynglingatal* in *Ynglinga saga*, at the beginning of *Heimskringla*, claiming that Þjóðólfr of Hvinir composed this Scaldic poem for King Rǫgnvaldr Óláfsson of Grenland (c. 850–920), an older cousin of King Haraldr hárfagri. *Ynglingatal* is thus dated to c. 890. Yet if *Ynglingatal* is Þjóðólfr's, it cannot be preserved quite as he intended it and was probably revised in the course of oral and scribal transmission. Claus Krag believes that *Ynglingatal* is not Þjóðólfr's poem, but was rather abstracted from a now-lost prose chronicle in the twelfth century. He suggests that the first four stanzas of *Ynglingatal* were contrived to represent the four elements, one stanza for each; and he cites in this poem, as further evidence of twelfth-century scholarship, the kennings for the natural elements 'fire' (*sævar niðr*, 'sea's kinsman', st. 4, and *sonr Fornjóts*, 'Fornjótr's son', st. 23) and 'water' (*Loga dís*, 'fire's ?sister', st. 9).[20] Krag points out a resemblance between these kennings and the personified names of natural elements in ch. 1 of *Orkneyinga saga* ('Saga of the Men of Orkney', c. 1200) and in a work derived from this chapter entitled *Hversu Nóregr byggðisk* ('How Norway was Settled').[21] Yet the names of the natural elements in *Orkneyinga saga*, including that of Fornjótr, were based on some mythological expressions for the sea, wind

---

[19] *Íslendingabók*, ed. Jakob, p. 18 (named in ch. 8); and *Landnámabók*, p. 65 (*Hauksbók*, ch. 21): 'En er Hróðólfr byskup fór brott ór Bœ, þar er hann hafði búit, þá váru þar eptir munkar þrír.' For the general background, see [E. O.] G. Turville-Petre, *Origins of Icelandic Literature* (Oxford, 1953, repr. and corr. 1967 and 1975), pp. 70–101, esp. 72–4.

[20] Krag, *Ynglingatal og Ynglingesaga*, pp. 47–59 and 182–200.

[21] *Ibid.*, pp. 100–4; also noted by von See, *Mythos und Theologie*, pp. 76–8. See *Orkneyinga saga*, ed. Finnbogi, pp. 3–5 and *Flat* I, 21–4.

and waves in Sveinn's *Norðrsetudrápa* ('Poem of the Northern Hunting Grounds'), a text of a poet from eleventh-century Greenland; this poem, as Krag points out, does not have the same tradition of Fornjótr as that to be found in *Ynglingatal*.[22] Therefore, as there appears to be no connection between *Ynglingatal* and ch. 1 of *Orkneyinga saga*, it seems that the kennings *sonr Fornjóts*, *Loga dís* and *sævar niðr* in *Ynglingatal* are not a sign of learned twelfth-century influence, but are rather derived from folktale motifs which Þjóðólfr considered to be a part of his mythology. Edith Marold, in her monograph on early Scaldic kennings, shows that *Ynglingatal* was probably composed by the same author as *Haustlǫng* on the evidence of a unique style of verbal metaphor that both poems share; no-one would claim that the fragmented, incomplete and semantically obscure *Haustlǫng* is a twelfth-century forgery.[23] It should be said that Krag, in his brief commentary on the poem *Ynglingatal*, shows little interest in philology and reduces rather than elucidates the many semantic problems of this poem.[24] Thus it is likely that *Ynglingatal* is largely what Snorri says it is, a poem from the reign of King Rǫgnvaldr (d. 920).

A further complication in the methodology of this book, however, is the use of *Germania* and other texts dating from the first century to the sixth. *Germania* is a brief work of ethnography on Germanic tribes which the Roman historian Cornelius Tacitus wrote for moral–patriotic reasons in *c*. 98. Towards the end of this treatise, Tacitus names the *Anglii* among

---

[22] See *Orkneyinga saga*, ed. Finnbogi, pp. x–xi; and Krag, *Ynglingatal og Ynglingesaga*, pp. 52–3.

[23] E. Marold, *Kenningkunst: ein Beitrag zu einer Poetik der Skaldendichtung*, Quellen und Forschungen zur Sprach- und Kulturgeschichte der germanischen Völker, n.s. 80 (Berlin and New York, 1983), 153–210.

[24] Krag, *Ynglingatal og Ynglingesaga*, pp. 99–142. For example, at pp. 105–6, Krag takes Dómaldi's epithet *Jóta dolgi* in *Ynglingatal* 5 ('foe of Jutes') to be 'a wholly conventional periphrasis for a Swedish king which fits the alliteration here' ('en helt konvensjonell omskrivning for en svensk konge, som passer med rimet her'); at pp. 110–11, he renders Dagr's epithet *valteins spakfrǫmuðr* in st. 8 as 'clever-performer of the slaughter-twig' ('val-tenens klokfremmer'), without attempting to explain what this might be; at pp. 70–2 and 122–3, he renders *vitta véttr* in st. 21 as 'magical being' ('trolldomsvesenet'), without analysing these unusual words; at pp. 126–7, he explains the obscure *lagar hjarta*, where Yngvarr is killed in st. 25, as an island 'which was named in the prose-text on which the poem is based' ('som har vært navngitt i prosateksten kvadet bygger på'); and at pp. 142–3 he takes st. 37, the final stanza, to be self-contained and thus 'genuinely scaldic' ('ekte skaldisk').

Nerthus and Terra Mater

nations that worship an earthmother goddess *Nerthus*. In principle, as the Anglii were ancestors of the Angles in Britain, it might be possible to use Tacitus to unravel the meanings of some cryptic references in Old English poems. Yet Tacitus is often too cryptic himself or too cursory and vague in *Germania* to be of use in this exercise, unless we read him in combination with some of the Eddic and Scaldic texts that can be identified as genuinely pre-Christian in the manner stated above. The problem with this type of source comparison is naturally that it spans more than a thousand years. This may be a leap too wide for some scholars to contemplate, although the formal relationship between two divine names, between *Nerthus* of the Anglii and *Njǫrðr* of the Norsemen, is evidence of a cultural continuity in this period sufficient to permit further comparison between Tacitus's *Germania* and pagan poems in the Old Norse–Icelandic vernacular. In these ways, Icelandic literature may be read uniquely, or in combination with Tacitus and later latinate and even hellenistic sources, to interpret the literary traces of heathen gods in Old English literature.

A final problem is that of distinguishing pristine Anglo-Saxon paganism from the hybrid variety that may have sprung into existence as soon as the Danes settled *en masse* in eastern and northern England. One way of addressing this complex question is to show how and why the god 'Baldr' is peculiar to Scandinavia. After showing, in chs. 5–6, why Baldr could not have evolved in England, I shall present Baldr in ch. 7 as a means of showing Danish influence on the poem *Beowulf*. Thereafter I shall focus specifically on Anglian England before the eighth century, concluding with a reconstruction of seventh-century Anglian paganism on the basis of Bede's account of its last days in his *Historia ecclesiastica*.

THE LITERARY CULT OF WODEN

The most striking episode in Bede's account of this Anglian paganism is his story of Coifi, the high-priest of Deira (*c.* 627). In this story Bede says that Bishop Paulinus was able to convert King Edwin and his thegns when Coifi denounced the old religion as a waste of time, rode to his own shrine at Goodmanham and threw a spear at the altar of his gods (*HE* II.13). Henry Mayr-Harting calls this dramatic gesture 'a small but highly significant pointer to the cult of Woden and the knowledge of his mythology at that time', because the Norse god *Óðinn* (whose name is cognate with OE *Uoden* or *Woden*) is known to cast a spear at his enemies on the battlefield.[25] J. M. Wallace-Hadrill says that 'Bede would hardly have known this.'[26] But not everything that Bede knew is to be found in Latin sources, nor should the devout pastoral aim be mistaken for simplicity of meaning where Bede is concerned.[27] Bede may have contrived this tale to show the Angles destroying their old shrine at Goodmanham prior to building a new church in York. Consequently we are not led to suspect 'the self-seeking pagan high priest Coifi' for more than the reasons Bede gives us.[28] Yet some difficulties of interpretation remain: namely in the obscurity of Paulinus's role at this critical moment in the conversion of the Angles; in the location of this scene in Goodmanham rather than in York; and above all, in the seemingly fortuitous resemblance between Coifi and Woden.[29]

Bede elsewhere records Woden's name as the ancestor of Anglo-Saxon kings, when he presents the house of Kent as sprung from *Uoden, de cuius stirpe multarum prouinciarum regium genus originem duxit* (*HE* I.15).[30] Later, the use of Woden's name is widespread in the Anglian collection of regnal lists. These records show that, by the early eighth century in England, a king's record of descent from Woden had become the proof of his long lineage and intermarriage with other royalty. This fiction is typical of the genealogist's trade: the metrical catalogue of names and nations in the Old English poem *Widsith* shows how simply genealogies could be created in preliterate societies; and in the Christian period the local clergy could invent some blood-lines, suppress others and alter reign lengths, all

---

[25] Mayr-Harting, *The Coming of Christianity*, pp. 22–30, esp. 26.
[26] Wallace-Hadrill, *Commentary*, p. 72.
[27] Bede's political context is illuminated by W. Goffart in 'The *Historia Ecclesiastica*: Bede's Agenda and Ours', *Haskins Society Journal* 2 (1990), 29–45, esp. 39.
[28] Brown, *Bede the Venerable*, p. 91.
[29] This resemblance between Coifi and Woden is usually taken to imply that Goodmanham 'was the main centre of Woden worship in the north of England' (C. R. Barker, *Churches of the Wolds* (Tayport and Beverley, 1982), p. 10); most recently, C. R. Davis (*Beowulf and the Demise of Germanic Legend in England* (New York and London, 1996), p. 35) also believes that the shrine in Goodmanham was 'probably Woden's' and that Coifi's Odinic spear-cast was 'apparently intended as a parody, or transference to Christ, of the ritual dedication preceding sacrifice to Woden'.
[30] *HE* I.15 (p. 50): 'from whose stem the royal kin of many provinces takes its beginning'; cf. Wallace-Hadrill, *Commentary*, pp. 23–4.

Nerthus and Terra Mater

to increase a king's prestige.³¹ Through accretion and renewal, in this way, in tribal politics of which certain oral records were probably less often forgotten than expunged, royal genealogies came to be harmonized with a deceptively patrilinear simplicity. Any myths created in the process would simplify the complexities of tribal settlement and expansion in a way that suited royal patrons. It seems that no king by the late seventh century could do without the status that descent from Woden entailed. The East Saxons never claimed Woden, but kept *Seaxneat* ('companion of Saxons') as their founder. Because the East Saxons began to lose their jurisdiction to neighbouring kingdoms even before the Anglo-Saxon conversion was complete in the second half of the seventh century, Seaxneat's name for them was perhaps a token of independence.³² In all other Anglo-Saxon kingdoms of which records have survived, Woden is claimed as a royal ancestor. Bede's record of Woden's name in his *Historia ecclesiastica* may be explained partly with reference to this political *fait accompli*; but not wholly, given that Woden was the name of a heathen god and given Bede's knowledge that some parts of England, Sussex for example, were still heathen when he was a child.

The heathen cult of Óðinn, Woden's Scandinavian counterpart, was still growing in Denmark and southern Sweden in Bede's lifetime. One and a half centuries later Óðinn seems to have figured in the ideology of the subjugation of western Norway, completed by the three-quarters Danish Haraldr hárfagri in *c.* 890.³³ Yet Haraldr's family did not claim descent from Óðinn. Haraldr's son Hákon *Aðalsteinsfóstri* ('Æthelstan's fosterson') was sent to King Æthelstan when he was a baby; the evidence concerning this young man, who would have returned to Norway from England as a Christian in *c.* 945, suggests that the men of Hálogaland eventually claimed descent from Óðinn because they wished to copy the use of Woden's name in a West Saxon regnal list brought to Norway by

---

[31] For a detailed study and reconstruction of West Saxon kings post-Cerdic, see Dumville, 'Regnal List and Chronology of Early Wessex', pp. 56–64.

[32] See Kirby, *Earliest English Kings*, p. 97; B. Yorke, 'The Kingdom of the East Saxons', *ASE* 14 (1985), 1–36, esp. 13–15; D. N. Dumville, 'Essex, Middle Anglia, and the Expansion of Mercia in the South-East Midlands', in *The Origins of Anglo-Saxon Kingdoms*, ed. Bassett, pp. 123–40, esp. 135–6.

[33] Turville-Petre, 'The Cult of Óðinn in Iceland', in *Nine Norse Studies*, pp. 1–19, esp. 15–16; originally published as 'Um Óðinsdýrkun á Íslandi', *Studia Islandica* 17 (1958), 5–25; see also Hastrup, *Culture and History*, pp. 190–1.

Heathen gods

Hákon Aðalsteinsfóstri. Hákon Jarl Sigurðarson, a ruler of the Trondheim region in the later tenth century, had himself traced from Óðinn in Scaldic poems composed in his honour in which Óðinn was also commemorated in his role as a god of poetry.[34] A tradition of praise-poetry from Hákon Jarl's late heathen enclave encouraged the growth of historiography and later antiquarian mythography in Icelandic monasteries. Even after the end of Scandinavian paganism, Óðinn's name and reputation flourished in these places. To what extent Óðinn's mystique grew in Iceland can be seen in the poem *Hávamál* and some prose works of the early thirteenth century.[35] Snorri Sturluson was fascinated by the intellectual status of this god. In his *Gylfaginning*, as well as in his *Ynglinga saga* and probably also in *Egils saga*, if this work is his, Snorri portrays Óðinn variously as witch and shaman, patron of poets, war-god and 'All-Father' (*Alfǫðr*) of the *Æsir* whom he rules. Þórr, Baldr and then Váli are Óðinn's sons; Frigg, his wife; Jǫrð his consort and Rindr, Gunnlǫð, the 'wife' of Billingr and other women his paramours.[36] Living as hostages with the *Æsir* are the *Vanir*, three fertility gods of a different tribe whose names are Njǫrðr *inn auðgi* ('the wealthy') and his children Freyr and Freyja.[37] Yet both Æsir and Vanir look to the day when together they must face the giants in Ragnarǫk, the last war in the world. Until this time, Óðinn and Freyja gather fallen warriors from innumerable battlefields for *Valhǫll* ('hall of the slain') from which these men will one day issue in their thousands to fight for the gods against the giants. Wrapped in a cloak and wandering the earth in a long hood or floppy hat, with a spear and one glowing eye, Óðinn had thus become a complex character by the thirteenth century. None the less, it was mostly Snorri's achievement to glamorize this figure beyond the status he would have had either in heathen Scandinavia in the tenth century or earlier still at the start of the seventh century in Northumbria.

---

[34] Frank, *Old Norse Court Poetry*, p. 60.
[35] All quotations from Old Norse-Icelandic non-Scaldic poetry will be taken from *Edda*, ed. Neckel and Kuhn; on Óðinn in *Hávamál*, see North, *Pagan Words*, pp. 122–44.
[36] Useful accounts in English of these Norse myths can be found in H. R. Ellis Davidson, *Gods and Myths of Northern Europe* (Harmondsworth, 1964); R. I. Page, *Norse Myths* (London, 1990); and R. Simek, *Dictionary of Northern Mythology*, trans. A. Hall (Cambridge, 1993 (first published 1984)).
[37] *Heimskringla I*, ed. Bjarni, p. 12 (*Ynglinga saga*, ch. 4). See further *Gylf*, p. 23 (ch. 23).

Nerthus and Terra Mater

Today it might be said that the literary cult of Óðinn, Woden or Wotan is still growing. It is also worth noting that the uncritical acceptance of Óðinn's pre-eminence in *Gylfaginning* as typical of his status in the pagan period often obscures rather than clarifies the many problems of Germanic mythology.[38] For example, Woden's role in genealogy was the premise of William Chaney's attempt to show that sacral kings once ruled in England as they had in Scandinavia.[39] In this study it was unfortunate that Chaney's instinct about this type of kingship was probably right, but that his premise about Woden was wrong. On one hand, it is likely that Anglo-Saxon kings mediated between gods and people for the health of land and harvest in heathen times, given the lack of evidence for a Germanic priesthood of any kind.[40] On the other hand,

---

[38] Óðinn's prominence in modern scholarship is partly due to his place in G. Dumézil's tripartite categorization of Norse divine roles: see J. Lindow, *Scandinavian Mythology: an Annotated Bibliography* (New York and London, 1988), pp. 476–7 (no. 2903) and 456–7 (no. 2801). Dumézil's three-function theory encouraged de Vries to revise his first edition of *AR* (1935–37) into its second formidable version (1956–7); [E. O.] G. Turville-Petre was likewise influenced by Dumézil in *Myth and Religion of the North: the Religion of Ancient Scandinavia* (New York, 1964); for criticism of Dumézil's presentation of Norse mythology, however, see R. I. Page, 'Dumézil Revisited', *Saga-Book* 20 (1978–9), 49–69, esp. 68. I have not found Dumézil's scheme useful to this book.

[39] Chaney, *Cult of Kingship*, pp. 7–42. Chaney's overemphasis of Woden has influenced scholars up to this day. For example, D. H. Miller states that the Frankish Merovingian kings were 'Wotanic kings' because the sculptured bull's head found in Childeric's tomb in Tournai has a solar disk between its horns, and 'Wotan was, among other things, the All-Father figure in Germanic mythology, which means that he was the solar deity as well': see 'Sacral Kingship, Biblical Kingship, and the Elevation of Pepin the Short', in *Religion, Culture and Society in the Early Middle Ages: Studies in Honor of Richard E. Sullivan* (Kalamazoo, MI, 1987), pp. 131–54, esp. 133. J. C. Russell uses Dumézil, Chaney and Miller as a basis for stating that 'Odin' was known not only to the Franks but also to the Goths as well (for which there is no evidence): see *The Germanization of Early Medieval Christianity: a Sociohistorical Approach to Religious Transformation* (Oxford, 1994), pp. 166–82, esp. 174–5. A tendency to read Woden unduly often into literary and archaeological evidence can be seen also in Wilson, *Anglo-Saxon Paganism*, pp. 33–4, 109, 117–18, 150, 168 and 179.

[40] See *HAR* II.ii, 189–90 (§126): 'Weiter ergibt sich daraus, dass eine Priesterherrschaft, eine Theokratie, wie wir sie bei vielen Völkern namentlich im Bereich des östlichen Mittelmeers kennen, bei den Germanen nicht zu erwarten ist.' Meaney ('Bede and Anglo-Saxon Paganism', pp. 18–20) bases a case for a pagan priesthood in England largely on a burial deposit in Yeavering containing a Roman surveyor's equipment.

Heathen gods

as there is no other West Germanic evidence for Woden's role in tribal genealogy, nor any Scandinavian evidence for Óðinn's genealogical role before the period of Anglo-Saxon influence on Norway, it is not clear that Woden got his place in English regnal lists from a heathen tradition. As I shall show in ch. 4, Woden's name survives in proverbs associated with magic and also in some placenames, but Woden may have meant little to most people in England up to the early seventh century, either to peasant farmers or to the advisers who could influence the election and removal of their kings according to politics or this or the next year's harvest.[41] Some nobles might have invoked Tiu and Woden for success in war, but it is unlikely that any of them took Woden for an ancestor. To heathen kings and subjects alike there were more powerful *numina* to propitiate – the natural phenomena and farming activities on which they relied for spring growth, autumn harvest and their winter lives.[42] With no popular animism of this kind, there was no loaf of bread; with no loaf, no *hlaford*; and with no lords, no kingdom. With these urgent priorities, it is unlikely that Woden, a god of magic and warfare, was regarded as the 'All-Father' in heathen times.

Instead it is likely that Germanic pagans on the Continent and in Britain knew something of an older era in which a marriage between the earth and a god other than Woden had been seasonally embodied in their ancestors' female and male rulers. *Hieros gamos* ('holy marriage') is both a heathen and a Christian idea: Bragi *inn gamli* ('the old') Boddason, a heathen poet from the mid ninth century, portrays the earth as a god's consort in the kenning *Hergauts vina* ('War-*gautr*'s girl-friend', hence 'the (Gothic) earth');[43] and Gildas in the mid sixth century describes the isle of Britain as *electa veluti sponsa monilibus diversis ornata*, shortly before he rebukes the Britons for renewing their paganism.[44] Gildas's line recalls Jerusalem being described as *paratam sicut sponsam ornatam* in Rev. XXI.2. Whether or not Gildas thought of Britain as a holy consort of Christ, his

---

[41] See S. Bassett, 'In Search of the Origins of Anglo-Saxon Kingdoms', in *The Origins of Anglo-Saxon Kingdoms*, ed. Bassett, pp. 3–27, esp. 23; and M. O. H. Carver, 'Kingship and Material Culture in Early Anglo-Saxon East Anglia', in *ibid.*, pp. 141–58, esp. 152–8.

[42] Chaney gives Woden the status of a fertility god, in *Cult of Kingship*, pp. 115–20.

[43] *Skj* B I, 2, 5.

[44] *De Excidio*, ed. Winterbottom, p. 90 (ch. 3): 'like a chosen bride decorated with many kinds of jewels'.

conceit shows that the personification of earth or its regions as a bride may be an idea no less Christian than pagan.[45]

In the course of this book I shall argue that this idea was still current in England in the early seventh century, that it was descended from the cult of Nerthus, with whom Tacitus associates the Anglii in *Germania* (ch. 40), and that it formed the core not only of Anglian natural religion, but also of a royal ideology for which the most common term is now 'sacral kingship'. The term 'sacral king' describes a king who is both married to his country and descended from a god to whom he sacrifices on behalf of his people.[46] Since the Second World War there has been a strong reaction against any idea of Germanic sacral kingship.[47] Much of the resistance to this idea is focused on the argument that pre-Christian Germanic kings believed themselves to be descended from gods, although a tradition of this kind might have evolved from an earlier topos of an engendering god made mortal flesh.[48] When the possibility of this development is acknowledged, sacral kingship becomes a more viable topic in the Anglo-Saxon field, especially if we drop Chaney's notion of 'Woden-sprung kings' and look to an aboriginal progenitor of Anglian leaders among the *Ingvaeones* in coastal Germania.[49] Woden was a war-god and so came to help the Christian cause, whereas I shall show that the Anglo-Saxon church, in its early days, may have had reason to regard *Ingui*, a reflex of Nerthus, as the devil incarnate. Around this figure the church would face its most baffling opponents in the unseen self-regenerating *numina* of an old agrarian tradition. That is why the official Christianization of England took nearly ninety years.

Pagan superstition was good enough for most people during and after this time because its mixture of temerity and magic was pragmatically adjusted to the farming year. The peasants are rarely mentioned in the

---

[45] Biblical quotations will henceforth be taken from *Biblia Sacra iuxta Vulgatam Clementinam*, ed. A. Colunga and L. Turrado, 7th ed., Biblioteca de Autores Cristianos 14 (Madrid, 1985).

[46] Definitions are reviewed in McTurk, 'Sacral Kingship in Ancient Scandinavia', pp. 139–69, esp. 156; and again in McTurk, 'Scandinavian Sacral Kingship Revisited', pp. 19–32.

[47] Cf. Baetke, *Yngvi und die Ynglinger*, pp. 139–64.

[48] Cf. von See, *Mythos und Theologie*, pp. 69–79.

[49] Chaney (*Cult of Kingship*, pp. 88–9) notes the fertility role of Freyr, Njǫrðr, Nerthus and Gefjun, but adds that 'the complications of these early agricultural and fertility cults need not envelop us here'.

Heathen gods

sources, but it can be assumed that some of their old ways continued within Christianity until these ways were given a new lease of life by the Vikings in the ninth-century Danelaw. The surviving Old English laws, charms and poems show that some Anglo-Saxon minds were crippled by paranoias linked to poverty, disease, violence, failed harvests and anything else for which doctrine rather than miracles could not provide an immediate cure. In the face of malign influences, the more divine protection the better. There may have been thousands of cults in Roman Britain.[50] *Ad Gefrin* or Yeavering in Bernicia was a Romano-British, then royal Anglian, site, while old shrines of any description were no doubt revived by new settlers.[51] Anglo-Saxon heathendom in this way was a shifting top surface, beneath which various non-Indo-European, Celtic, Roman, Mediterranean and oriental cults, including Christianity, had sedimented in slow layers.[52] Nor were the people less various themselves: 'Angles' and 'Saxons' were names for more diverse groups including Jutes, Norwegians, Suebians, Frisians and Franks, plus Romano-British in western pockets or even in towns such as London and Canterbury. In the north and north-west, in the century following the decline of Roman Britain after *c.* 410, there were Welshmen from the Elmet, Rheged and Strathclyde regions, Picts, Romans and any number of Germanic or other auxiliary units who stayed on after the Roman withdrawal from the highland zone.[53] A division of North African infantry, for example, was stationed in 253–8 at *Aballava*, now Burgh-by-Sands near Carlisle.[54] It is among a Romano-British people of these diverse origins that the ancestors of Deiran, Lindsey and Bernician Angles would have settled when they rowed up the river Humber in the fifth and sixth centuries.[55]

Angles are distinguished from Saxons by their archaeological remains,

---

[50] Henig, *Religion in Roman Britain*, pp. 217–28, esp. 225.
[51] B. Hope-Taylor, *Yeavering: an Anglo-British Centre of Early Northumbria*, Department of the Environment Archaeological Reports 7 (London, 1977), 244–78; Myres, *English Settlements*, p. 199.
[52] Henig, *Religion in Roman Britain*, pp. 36–67; see also C. Thomas, *Christianity in Roman Britain to AD 500* (London, 1981), pp. 26–34.
[53] Myres, *English Settlements*, pp. 74–83.
[54] *Notitia Dignitatum: accedunt Notitia Urbis Constantinopolitanae et Laterculi Prouinciarum*, ed. O. Seeck (Berlin, 1876), p. 212 (occidental §xl.47): 'numerus Maurorum Aurelianorum'.
[55] Myres, *English Settlements*, pp. 174–5 and 187–9; L. Alcock, 'Quantity or Quality: the Anglian Graves of Bernicia', in *Angles, Saxons and Jutes: Essays Presented to J. N. L.*

in that the Angles lived 'north of an approximate line from the mouth of the Stour on the east coast of England running almost due west to the valley of the Avon'.[56] Yet, as the Sutton Hoo grave-goods show, the Angles continued to look to Scandinavia as their cultural homeland until the seventh century.[57] Some of their older material culture relates the Angles even more closely to an area in continental Europe which John Hines defines as lying 'to the north and north-east of what appears to have been the Anglian homeland in Schleswig-Holstein and south-eastern Fyn', virtually identifiable with modern Denmark, Sweden, Norway and Finland.[58] It was from this eastern homeland, now Angeln in Germany, that the Angles brought their gods to Britain.

NERTHUS AND TERRA MATER

In his *Germania* (*c.* 98), Tacitus puts the Anglii third among seven Suebian tribes which dwell in a north-eastern region walled off by rivers and forest:

Nec quicquam notabile in singulis, nisi quod in commune *Nerthum, id est Terram matrem*, colunt eamque interuenire rebus hominum, inuehi populis arbitrantur. Est in insula *Oceani* castum nemus, dicatumque in eo uehiculum, ueste contectum; attingere uni sacerdoti concessum. Is adesse penetrali deam intellegit uectam bubus feminis multa cum ueneratione prosequitur. Laeti tunc dies, festa loca quaecumque aduentu hospitioque dignatur. Non bella ineunt, non arma sumunt; clausum omne ferrum; pax et quies tunc tantum nota, tunc tantum amata, donec idem sacerdos satiatam conuersatione mortalium deam templo reddat. Mox uehiculum et uestis et, si credere uelis, numen ipsum secreto lacu abluitur. Serui ministrant, quos statim idem lacus haurit. Arcanus hinc terror sanctaque ignorantia, quid sit illud quod tantum perituri uident.[59]

Myres, ed. V. I. Evison (Oxford, 1981), pp. 168–86; Dumville, 'The Origins of Northumbria', pp. 219–22.
[56] Hines, *Scandinavian Character of Anglian England*, p. 13.
[57] Hines, 'The Scandinavian Character of Anglian England: an Update', pp. 315–29.
[58] Hines, *Scandinavian Character of Anglian England*, p. 14; see further Myres, *English Settlements*, pp. 54–5.
[59] *Germania*, p. 317 (ch. 40): 'Nothing is worth noting about any of them individually but their common worship of *Nerthus, i.e. Terra Mater* ('earth the mother'). They believe she enters into the affairs of men as she is borne about the nations. On an island in the *Ocean* stands a chaste grove, in which a wagon, veiled with cloth, is dedicated; only the priest has leave to touch it. This man can tell when the goddess is present in

Heathen gods

With one cult spread across at least seven nations, the scale of Terra Mater's worship in this period appears to have been massive. The words *clausum omne ferrum* in this passage, furthermore, show that iron was excluded from this cult. This deduction seems to imply that Terra Mater was still worshipped as a bronze-age goddess in the first century. Lotte Hedeager's archaeological study of the Danish region in this period also shows that 'in the earliest part of the Iron Age ritual activities were normally a continuation of later Bronze-Age practice'.[60]

Nerthus has long been seen as the etymon of *Njǫrðr*, a male god and the father of Freyr and Freyja. *Nerthus*, unless it be a rare fourth-declension noun, has a masculine ending in both Latin and Germanic, as does its reflex *Njǫrðr* in Icelandic. Explanations for this subject's gender disparity vary from Nerthus's undergoing a sex-change in the first millennium AD, to Nerthus's being hermaphroditic, to Nerthus's being the female partner of a god of the same name.[61] In the first case, Eve Picard suggests that the northern Germanic tribes, in their later 'reception' of the cult of Nerthus mother earth, made this goddess male to make her physically consistent with the grammatical ending of her name.[62] In my turn, I suggest that

> her innermost shrine, and with many a show of reverence he escorts her as she is drawn along by female oxen. Happy then the days, festive the places she makes worthy with her arrival and her stay. They do not go to war, do not take up arms; all iron is locked up; then, and only then, are peace and quiet known and loved, until the same priest returns the goddess, who is satiated with her dealings with mortals, to her temple. Soon the wagon and vestments, and if you want to believe it, the deity itself are washed in a solitary lake. Slaves administer, whom the same lake swallows immediately afterwards. Hidden thus the terror, and sacred the ignorance, of what that thing may be that is only seen by those about to die.'

[60] Hedeager, *Iron-Age Societies*, pp. 77–82, esp. 78; also at 80–1: 'As a metal, bronze could be superseded by iron, but not as a symbol.' See also Hedeager, 'Kingdoms, Ethnicity and Material Culture', pp. 279–85.

[61] E. C. Polomé, 'A propos de la déesse Nerthus', *Latomus* 13 (1954), 167–200; J. Sahlgren, 'Förbjudna namn', *NoB* 6 (1918), 1–40, esp. 22–7; E. Lehmann, 'Tvekønnede frugtbarhedsguder i Norden', *MoM* (1919), 1–4; A. Kock, 'Die Göttin Nerthus und der Gott Niorþr', *ZfdPh* 28 (1896), 289–94. R. McTurk accordingly suggests that Ragnarr's grammatically feminine epithet *loðbrók* ('hairy trousers') shows that Ragnarr and his sons were devotees of a goddess descended from Nerthus: see his *Studies in Ragnars saga Loðbrókar and its Major Scandinavian Analogues*, Medium Ævum Monographs, New Series 15 (Oxford, 1991), 16–17.

[62] Picard, *Germanisches Sakralkönigtum?*, p. 164: 'die Nordgermanen hätten bei der Rezeption des Nerthuskultes den Namen der Göttin für ein Maskulinum gehalten, da in den nordischen u-Stämmen hauptsächlich Maskulina vorkämen'.

Nerthus was male, that Terra Mater was female and that Tacitus misunderstood his source. Accordingly, I shall try to show that a divine marriage between Nerthus and Terra Mater could have been seasonally enacted by human hypostases on the first-century Anglian seaboard of continental Germania.

By now it is well known that the wagon, cows and the washing of the goddess in *Germania* could have been details obtained from the ceremonies of Cybele or Magna Mater in Rome.[63] Tacitus was a priest of the *Quindecemviri* who superintended *Magna Mater* and other gods of foreign extraction.[64] As a priest, in particular, Tacitus was entitled to wash the image of Magna Mater in the river Almo on 27 March; this ritual resembles the washing of Terra Mater that he describes in the passage quoted above.[65] Yet there are two reasons why Tacitus may not have based the details of Nerthus's wagon-tour on the ritual procession of Cybele or Magna Mater. First, by writing 'Terra Mater' in ch. 40 of *Germania*, Tacitus does not give *Magna Mater* her proper name: the Roman *Tellus* or *Terra Mater* is known to have had a ceremony different from the one which Tacitus here describes.[66] Second, Tacitus must have had a Germanic source for the name *Nerthus*, which is one of only three divine names of ethnic origin in his *Germania* (the others are *Tuisto* in ch. 2 and *alci* in ch. 43). So, although Terra Mater's wagon-tour resembles the procession of Cybele, Tacitus's use of an inappropriate Roman title in *Terra Mater*, and an ethnic form in *Nerthus*, indicates that the details of Nerthus's cult as he reports them are probably not Roman, but Germanic. If Tacitus heard details of a genuinely Germanic wagon-tour, he would have been inclined to perceive this tour as if it were the same as Cybele's

---

[63] *Ibid.*, pp. 172–83, esp. 180: 'Nimmt man Tacitus' Anliegen ernst, muss man dieses Bild in seiner Gesamtheit akzeptieren und darf es nicht in "Germanisches" und "Römisches" zertrennen'; for a more straightforward view of Germanic religion in this period, see D. Timpe, 'Tacitus' *Germania* als religionsgeschichtliche Quelle', in *Germanische Religionsgeschichte*, ed. Beck, Ellmers and Schier, pp. 434–85.

[64] Syme, *Tacitus* I, 65–6.

[65] On Tacitus's priesthood, see *ibid.* I, 65–6; also on the *lavatio* of Magna Mater, see Picard, *Germanisches Sakralkönigtum?*, pp. 172–83, esp. 173–4: Picard argues that Tacitus divides the Germanic goddess into two aspects, positive (Magna Mater) and negative (Cybele).

[66] Cows were sacrificed to Tellus Mater on the Fordicidia (14 April): *HAR* I, 314–15 and 315 n. 53 (§178).

procession in Rome.[67] The consort of the Magna Mater (the Roman name for Cybele) was the castrated Attis, no longer a fertile male.[68] So, being unfamiliar with the name *Nerthus* when he heard it, but thinking already of the single Cybele, Tacitus could have mistaken *Terra Mater* as his informant's attempt to give him an *interpretatio Romana* for Nerthus.[69]

An analogue of Cybele, Magna Mater, Terra and Tellus Mater was worshipped in late fourth-century Gaul, as *Berecynthia*, in one of several hybrid Gallo-Roman cults of the Great Mother.[70] Gregory of Tours relates how Bishop Simplicius thwarted a 'countless multitude' (*vulgus innumerum*) in a festival outside Autun: 'Hanc cum in carpento pro salvatione agrorum ac vinearum suarum misero gentilitatis more deferrent adfuit supradictus Simplicius episcopus haud procul aspiciens cantantes atque saltantes ante hoc simulacrum.'[71] This festival corresponds to Cybele's *Megalensia* in Rome, which took place annually 4–10 April after sowing time and before the plebeian *Liberalia* of Ceres.[72]

The idea of a divine marriage between Nerthus and the Germanic Terra Mater is supported by some archaeological evidence. In his study on the

---

[67] *Ibid.* I, 314 (§178): 'eine *Interpretatio Romana* ... die weniger auf Erschöpfung der Kenntnis vom Wesen der Göttin als vielmehr auf der Übereinstimmung kultischer Bräuche beruht'.

[68] Vermaseren, *Cybele and Attis*, pp. 140–1; Henig, *Religion in Roman Britain*, pp. 110–11. Cybele and Attis are paralleled to some extent by the giantess Skaði and Loki, who makes her laugh by tying a rope to his testicles, the other end of which is jerked by a goat: this Norse myth is discussed by J. Lindow, with reference to Freud and folktale, in 'Loki and Skaði', in *Snorrastefna*, ed. Úlfar, pp. 130–42.

[69] *HAR* I, 315 (§178): 'Ich bin deshalb geneigt, doch anzunehmen, dass Tacitus dem Bericht seines Gewährsmannes bereits entnommen hat, Nerthus werde als mütterliche Erde verehrt'; Helm suggests a *hieros gamos* in Nerthus's procession between heaven and earth. Tacitus's informant may have been King Masyos of the Semnones, who visited Rome in 92: the Semnones are described in preferential detail in ch. 39, immediately before the account of Nerthus in ch. 40. For the record of Masyos's visit, see p. 141 n. 39.

[70] On Cybele in Gaul and in Britain, see Vermaseren, *Cybele and Attis*, pp. 131–9; and M. J. Green, *A Corpus of Religious Material from the Civilian Areas of Roman Britain*, BAR (Oxford, 1976), pp. 55–6 and fig. 15.

[71] *Liber de gloria confessorum*, PL 71, 884 (ch. 77): 'while in the wretched manner of paganism they were driving her off in a carriage for the preservation of their fields and vines, the aforesaid bishop Simplicius approached her, even as he caught sight of people not far off who were singing and dancing before this idol'.

[72] *Fasti*, ed. Schilling II, 16 (IV.357) and 117–18 (n. 125); Henig, *Religion in Roman Britain*, p. 29.

bog-people of Jutland and further south, P. V. Glob noted pictures of an earth goddess and an increase in the number of female over male representations of the human figure in late bronze-age burial deposits, adding that 'perhaps it is because of the dominating position of the goddess that Tacitus makes no mention of a male partner, essential in a ritual marriage'.[73] With respect to the phallic Broddenbjærg oakfork form from north central Jutland, Glob says that 'it is clear that the goddess had a male partner'.[74]

It may thus be appropriate to see a late literary reflex of Nerthus and Terra Mater in the marriage of Njǫrðr and Skaði in *Gylfaginning*. The word *Njǫrðr* appears to derive from *Nerthus*; and *Skaði*, a form identical with Germanic forms of *Scandinavia*, denotes the northern 'earth'.[75] Snorri illustrates the marriage of Njǫrðr and Skaði with the help of two quoted verses and says that Skaði wanted to live in the mountains, Njǫrðr by the sea; they agreed to spend nine nights in each place:

> En er Njǫrðr kom aptr til Nóatúna af fjallinu þá kvað hann þetta:
> 'Leið erumk fjǫll —   varka ek lengi á,
>   nætr einar níu:
> úlfa þytr   mér þótti illr vera
>   hjá sǫngvi svana.'
> Þá kvað Skaði þetta:
> 'Sofa ek máttigak   sævar beðjum á
>   fugls jarmi fyrir:
> sá mik vekr   er af víði kemr
>   morgun hverjan: már.'[76]

Njǫrðr hates the mountains, Skaði the sea in this verse exchange, yet this Eddic poem reveals a tradition of their marriage. I suggest that Nerthus and Terra Mater in Tacitus's *Germania* would likewise be married in communities that worked the fisheries and farms of a coastal zone.

---

[73] Glob, *Bog People*, pp. 113–32, esp. 118.   [74] *Ibid.*, p. 127.

[75] *AR* II, 335–40, esp. 338 (§561): OE *Scedeland, Scedenig, Sconeg*; OIce *Skáney*; and ModSw *Skåne*.

[76] *Gylf*, p. 24 (ch. 23): 'And yet when Njǫrðr came back to "Ships' enclosures" from the mountains, he said this: "To me the fells are loathsome – I wasn't long on them, some nine nights: the howling of wolves seemed bad to me compared to the song of a swan." Then Skaði said this: "I couldn't sleep on the bed of the sea for the shrieking of a bird: that bird, a seagull, wakes me when each morning he comes from over the ocean."'

Nerthus in this case may be linked with Tacitus's use of *Oceanus* in the passage from *Germania* quoted above.[77]

With regard to Nerthus and the *uehiculum* in ch. 40 of *Germania*, Njǫrðr is known as *vagna guð* ('god of wagons') in a Scaldic kenning cited in the principal manuscript of *Skáldskaparmál*.[78] Nerthus and Terra Mater can also be compared with Njǫrðr's son Freyr and a woman in a wagon in *Gunnars þáttr helmings*, a tale from the fourteenth-century *Flateyjarbók*.[79] Gunnarr, the apostate hero of this tale, is on the run from King Óláfr Tryggvason (*c.* 995–*c.* 1000) of Norway and hides out in a sanctuary in Sweden where there is an idol of Freyr: 'it was the peasants' belief that Freyr was alive, as in some ways it seemed he was, and they thought he would need to have marital relations with his wife'.[80] Freyr's wife gives Gunnarr permission to accompany 'Freyr and me when he makes the season better for men'.[81] From winter into spring Gunnarr leads Freyr's idol and wife in a 'wagon' (*uagn*) around the country, until a snowstorm drives the other attendants away on a mountain road. Freyr's idol rises up and wrestles with him, but Gunnarr, promising God to become Christian again, overthrows the idol. When he takes Freyr's place, joins in local festivals and makes the priestess pregnant, the Swedes take Freyr to be the father: 'the weather looked balmy and everything gave such hope of a good season that no man could have done such a thing'.[82]

Also where Nerthus's *uehiculum* is concerned, Stuart Piggott points out that a wagon heavy enough to be drawn by oxen implies a political infrastructure to provide for it.[83] Piggott puts the speed of a four-wheeled wagon of 670–700 kg drawn by two oxen at 3.2 km per hour.[84] A wagon

---

[77] *Germania*, p. 317 (ch. 40).

[78] In R; the other manuscripts have *Vana guð* ('god of the Vanir') probably in confusion with *Vana nið* ('Vanir-descendant'), the phrase following: see *SnE* 260 (ch. 6).

[79] *Germania*, p. 285; *Flat* I, 337–9 (chs. 277–8).

[80] *Flat* I, 337: 'uar þat atrunadr landzmanna at Freyr uære lifande j sumu lagi ok ætludu at hann munde þurfa at æiga hiuskaparfar vid konu sina'.

[81] *Ibid.* I, 338 (ch. 278): 'okkr Frey þa er hann gerir monnum arbot'.

[82] *Ibid.* I, 339 (ch. 278): 'uar ok uedratta blid ok allir hlutir suo aruænir at æingi madr munde sligt'.

[83] Piggott, *Waggon, Chariot and Carriage*, pp. 13–36, esp. 13–16; this inference is supported by Hedeager's conclusions on the political organization in the Danish area, in *Iron-Age Societies*, pp. 225–55.

[84] *Waggon, Chariot and Carriage*, pp. 17–18: 'a ponderous vehicle ... Speed was not a glamorous component of the early prestige of ox traction.'

of this kind would go about ten miles in a five-hour travelling day. Since Tacitus specifies *hospitia* ('places to stay') along the route of Nerthus's tour, for more than one day each time, and Nerthus's wagon crosses at least seven tribal regions there and back again, it is thus possible that this (type of) first-century procession, if circular as Tacitus says, continued for several months. Although the wagon-motif in *Gunnars þáttr* is similar to that of Nerthus and Terra Mater, it is unlikely that the literary tradition of this tale in *Flateyjarbók* was influenced by a text of Tacitus's *Germania*.[85] Rather, since one of the aims of *Gunnars þáttr* seems to be to make fun of the Swedes, it is likely that this annual tour with Freyr and his wife within a wagon was imagined on the basis of a Swedish original.[86] The woman whom *Freyr* makes pregnant may thus be adduced as a very late reflex of the *dea* ('goddess') or *numen* ('deity') by which Tacitus defines Terra Mater in the wagon at the end of her procession. A male Nerthus seems to be matched in *Gunnars þáttr* by Freyr; *Freyr* is a personification of a noun meaning 'lord'.[87] For these reasons, despite the gulf of time between *Gunnars þáttr* and *Germania*, it is possible that each summer season, as late as the first century of this era, a wagon was driven round the coasts and islands of south-eastern Jutland with a lord and lady embodying Nerthus and Terra Mater. The question that I shall address in the next two chapters is in what names Nerthus, probably a male god and the consort of the earth, is reflected in Old English literature.

---

[85] On the limited extent of the early medieval knowledge of *Germania*, see F. J. Haverfield, 'Tacitus during the Late Roman Period and the Middle Ages', *Journal of Roman Studies* 6 (1916), 196–200.

[86] See Turville-Petre, 'Fertility of Beast and Soil', pp. 244–64, esp. 249–50.

[87] *Pace* Baetke, *Yngvi und die Ynglinger*, pp. 150–1; Turville-Petre regards Freyr's earthbound fertility as a later development, in 'Fertility of Beast and Soil', p. 261.

2
Ingui of Bernicia

In this chapter, I shall use the name and role of Njǫrðr's son *'Ingvi-freyr'* to identify a corresponding Old English reflex of Nerthus: first, by arguing that the name of Nerthus's human hypostasis may be reconstructed from the stem of *Ingvaeones*, allegedly the name of one of three tribal groupings presented by Tacitus in his *Germania*; second, by presenting this *Ing*-hypostasis as an Anglian analogue of Dionysus or Liber in Graeco-Roman mythology, with a comparable fertility cult of his own; and third, by presenting the name *Ingui* in the Bernician regnal list as evidence that formerly all Anglian kings in Britain, just like the *Ynglingar* in Uppsala, claimed to be descended from this god.

ING-: HYPOSTASIS OF NERTHUS

Near the beginning of his *Germania*, Tacitus cites a tribal name of which the stem reveals the etymon of *Ingvi-* or *Yngvi-*, a prefix of Freyr:

Celebrant carminibus antiquis, quod unum apud illos memoriae et annalium genus est, Tuistonem deum terra editum. Ei filium Mannum originem gentis conditoresque Manno tres filios adsignant, e quorum nominibus proximi Oceano *Ingaeuones*, medii Herminiones, ceteri Istaeuones uocentur. Quidam, ut in licentia uetustatis, plures deo ortos pluresque gentis appellationes, Marsos Gambriuios Suebos Uandilios adfirmant, eaque uera et antiqua nomina.   (ch. 2)[1]

[1] *Germania*, p. 273: 'In ancient songs, the only kind of record or annal they have among them, they celebrate the god Tuisto born from the earth. To him they attribute a son Mannus as the origin of their people, to Mannus three sons and founders from whose names those nearest the Ocean may be called the *Ingvaeones* [for Ingaeuones], those in the middle the Herminiones, and the rest the Istaevones. With the licence of antiquity, some men assert that more sons, hence tribal titles, arose from the god [Mannus or

Ingui of Bernicia

Tacitus here refers to the *Ingaeuones*. However, Pliny's *Historia naturalis*, compiled in *c*. 50 AD after his military service in the German provinces, refers to the *Inguaeones*, with a *u*-infix after the stem. Since the later Norse forms *ingvi* or *yngvi* show that *Inguaeones* is probably the correct form, from now on I shall refer to this tribe as the *Ingvaeones*.[2]

Tacitus in *Germania* does not connect the tribes of Nerthus with the *Ingvaeones*. With his words *et haec quidem pars Sueborum* in ch. 41, Tacitus implies that the tribes of Nerthus are a subgroup of the Suebi and that consequently they all live in the remote north-east.[3] None the less, as he places Nerthus's temple *in insula Oceani* and the Ingvaeones *proximi Oceano*, it is possible to associate the shore-dwelling Ingvaeones with Nerthus without having to rationalize them as subgroups of the Suebi.[4] The name *Inguz*, a cognate simplex form, has been read in runes on a bone amulet dating from a pre-Christian time and found in a terp at Wijnaldum in modern West Friesland.[5] Extrapolating from *Ingaeuones*, therefore, *Ing-* can be regarded for the time being as an epithet for the son of Mannus the son of Tuisto who is 'born from the earth'.[6] The suffix in *Ingaeu-ones* or *Inguae-ones* appears to be derived from Greek -ων and may thus betray an origin in Greek ethnography. Taken as a whole, this tribal name seems to mean 'friends of Ing-', having its reflex in OE 'eodor *Ing-wina*' (*Beo* 1044) and 'frea *Ing-wina*' (*Beo* 1319) and OIce '*Ingunar*-Freyr' (*Lok* 43). In the two phrases from *Beowulf*, Hrothgar of the Danes appears to be 'lord of the friends of Ing-'; in the phrase from *Lokasenna*, the evidence suggests – more problematically – that Freyr takes his name from being the 'lord of a friend of Ing-' (from *Ing-*vinar-*freyr*), i.e. the

---

Tuisto]: the Marsi, Gambrivii, Suebi and Vandilii, and that these are true and ancient names.'
[2] *Secundi Naturalis Historia*, ed. Mayhoff I, 347 (IV.28). *Inguaeones* is Mayhoff's rationalization of manuscript forms as varied as *Ing\\\nes*, *Ingyaeones* and (also Tacitus's) *Ingaeuones*.
[3] *Germania*, p. 317: 'and even this part of Suebian territory'.
[4] *Ibid.*, pp. 317 and 273: 'on an island in the Ocean'; 'nearest the Ocean'.
[5] Arntz and Zeiss, *Runendenkmäler des Festlandes*, pp. 413–18, esp. 417.
[6] The brothers *Erminus*, *Inguo* and *Istio* were extracted from Tacitus's *Germania*, in a table of nations which W. Goffart traces to Constantinople in *c*. 520, in 'The Supposedly "Frankish" Table of Nations: an Edition and Study', *Frühmittelalterliche Studien* 17 (1983), 98–130, at 111 and 122–7. In the *Historia Brittonum* these names are respectively *Armenon*, *Nogue* and *Hessitio*: see *Historia Brittonum*, ed. Lot, pp. 161 (text of ch. 17) and 50–1 (source comparison).

lord of a king who worships him. On the evidence of these forms, two suggestions can be made. One is that Posidonius or an earlier Greek ethnographer hellenized an ethnic form such as *Ingua-uini-* ('friends of Ing-') through a misunderstanding, then rationalized the second element as a Greek -ων suffix. Second, since no *uini*-reflexes survive attached to *Irmin* or to a reflex of *Istaeuones*, it is possible that *Inguaeones* worked as a model for the other two and was therefore given as the first member of the hellenized triad.

In the passage quoted above, Tacitus draws his information from at least two sources. In the first, the three peoples descended from Mannus are grouped together in two ways: by alliteration, by which *Ingaeuones*, *Herminiones* and *Istaeuones* might represent the first three stressed syllables of a four-beat line, perhaps in keeping with Tacitus's attribution to Germanic *antiqua carmina*; and by the apparently Greek -ων suffixes. *Irmin-* probably reappears as OE *eormen-* ('colossal'); and as the Old Saxon *Hirmin* or *Hermis* in Widukind's ninth-century record of Charlemagne's destruction of a Saxon column, named *Hirminsuul* by other sources, near the Weser in 772.[7] While reflexes of *Ing-* and *Irmin-* thus have some claim to be simplex names, no Germanic cognate of *Ist(r)-* has yet been found.[8] Yet both *Istaeuones* and *Istriones* (a variant form in *Germania*) are reminiscent of *Ister*, the Greek name for the Danube. The evidence thus suggests that Tacitus's source for the names *Ingvaeones*, *Irminiones* and *Istaevones* was probably a Greek treatise: perhaps the lost *Historiae* of the Stoic Posidonius (*c*. 135–51 BC), either in the original or through Livy or another commentator.[9] Picard believes that Tacitus created the alliteration of this triad himself, but this creative step is less likely, given that the Germanic alliterative system, not a Latin alliterative device, is inherent in the stems *Ing-*, *Irmin-* and *Ist-* in which these names appear to make up the first three stressed syllables of a four-stressed Germanic verse line. In this way it is more likely that Tuisto's grandsons had been stylized as a triad before Tacitus, and that Posidonius or an earlier writer dignified this

---

[7] *Widukindi Gestarum Saxonicarum*, ed. Hirsch and Lohmann, pp. 20–1 (I.12); *Annales Regni Francorum*, ed. Pertz and rev. Kurze, p. 35.

[8] E. Schröder first separated 'Irmin' from *Irminsul*, in 'Irminsûl', *ZfdA* 72 (1935), 292; typically, de Vries takes *Istraz* to be a name for Wodan, in *AR* II, 35 (§367).

[9] *Cornelii Taciti De Origine et Situ Germanorum*, ed. J. G. C. Anderson (Oxford, 1938), p. xxi.

scrap of information as tribal ethnography when he inherited it from frontier Gauls or Germans.

Tacitus's second group of informants in the passage quoted above, which he calls *quidam ut in licentia uetustatis*, seems to be a rival to the tradition of the *i*-alliterating triad, since it claims the Marsi, Gambrivii, Suebi and Vandilii to be *deo ortos*, presumably from Tuisto who is the god concerned. For some Germans in the first century, therefore, an origin in Tuisto may have been a matter of political rivalry. Tracing the Suebi from Tuisto, Picard takes them (and, by implication, their cult of Nerthus) to be distinct from the Ingvaeones.[10] However, if we compare the Latin forms of the extra four tribes with the apparently Greek -ων suffixes in the *i*-alliterating triad, it seems that not only the sources but also the categories of Tacitus's information differ one from the other. Tacitus uses the word *Oceanus* rather than Lat *mare* to describe the sea at the edge of which the Ingvaeones live. As *Oceanus* is a proper noun derived from Greek mythology, it is possible that it was taken from a Greek treatise, whereas Tacitus's second group of informants do not appear to be influenced by Greek ethnography.

Pliny mixes the categories of myth and ethnography that Tacitus's sources keep distinct. Pliny presents five or six tribal groups on a par with Tacitus's initial three: Vandilii, *Inguaeones, Istuaeuones, Hermiones*, Peucini and Basternae.[11] Not one of Pliny's Ingvaeones (the Cimbri, Teutoni and Chauci) matches any of the seven Suebian tribes of Nerthus in *Germania*. Pliny's Vandilii are also more powerful than in *Germania*, whereas his Suebi are only a subgroup of the Hermiones. Yet it should be noted that from *Germania* ch. 38 onwards Tacitus uses *Suebi* as a general term for tribes east of the river Elbe.[12]

Noting this disparity between Tacitus and Pliny, Walter Baetke pointed out the lack of direct evidence for the connection of Ingvaeones or Ingaevones with Nerthus or the Norse god Ingvi-freyr, in order to disprove the existence of 'sacral kingship' in Scandinavia.[13] Yet he gave little credit to the frequency of these cognates – Got *Enguz*, Frisian *Inguz*,

---

[10] Picard, *Germanisches Sakralkönigtum?*, pp. 184–219, esp. 188.

[11] *Ibid.*, p. 192. Pliny, *Naturalis Historia*, ed. Mayhoff I, 347.

[12] Martin, *Tacitus*, pp. 49–58, esp. 53. In preparation for ch. 6, it is worth noting that among the Suebi Tacitus also includes the *Gothones* and *Semnones*. See *Germania*, pp. 315–16 and 320 (chs. 39 and 44).

[13] Baetke, *Yngvi und die Ynglinger*, pp. 139–64.

Heathen gods

Frankish and Frisian *Ingo-*, the Old English *Ingui* of Bernicia and *Ing*, Old Norse–Icelandic *Ingvi*, *Yngvi* and *Ingunar-* – – in a wide Germanic area over more than a thousand years. With respect to *Ing-*, the oldest form, Picard is probably right to doubt that either this eponym of the Ingvaeones or *Mannus* ('man') was a god.[14] The most plausible etymology is that **inguaz* meant 'man' as opposed to 'woman', just as Tocharian A *onk* and B *enkwe* mean 'man' in reflexes of a more ancient form of Indo-European.[15] So the Norse Ingvi-freyr probably got his divine status at a stage in northern history later than the first century.

As with this etymology of **inguaz*, so male sex is the overriding meaning in the case of the Broddenbjærg tree-fork. Glob identifies this tree-fork with Terra Mater's partner because of its bearded face and erect phallus.[16] Nearly a millennium after Tacitus, Adam of Bremen cites a certain *Fricco*, probably *Freyr*, as one of three gods in the temple in Uppsala, in his *Gesta Hammaburgensis Ecclesiae Pontificum* (this part written c. 1076): 'The third is Fricco, lavishing peace and pleasure on mortals, whose likeness they fashion even with a huge penis.'[17] A corroboration for this line of continuity in Germanic religion can be found in the ninth- or tenth-century tumescent bronze figure from Rällinge in Sweden, which is usually taken to be the god Freyr in *Skírnismál* as he sits watching the giantess Gerðr before sending his servant Skírnir to coerce her into his *droit du seigneur*.[18] So while *Ing-*, the etymon of *Ingvi-*freyr, was probably an epithet for a king rather than a god in the first century, these kings are likely to have been men of special calibre with whom the Ingvaeones claimed kinship.[19]

Ing- (as represented in *Ingvaeones*) and Nerthus appear in widely separated chapters of *Germania* (chs. 2 and 40, respectively).[20] If, as I have suggested, a man *Ing-* was regarded as the hypostasis of Nerthus, it is not

---

[14] Picard, *Germanisches Sakralkönigtum?*, pp. 114–27, 185–92 and 201–13.

[15] W. Krause, 'Ing', *Nachrichten der Akademie der Wissenschaften in Göttingen, philologisch-historische Klasse* 10 (Göttingen, 1944), 229–54; *ANEW* 286 (*Ingunarfreyr*) and 678–9 (*Yngvi*).

[16] Glob, *Bog People*, pp. 80–1 (penultimate plate) and 127.

[17] *Gesta*, ed. Schmeidler, p. 258 (IV.26): 'Tercius est Fricco, pacem voluptatem largiens mortalibus. Cuius etiam simulacrum fingunt cum ingenti priapo.'

[18] Graham-Campbell, *Viking Artefacts*, pp. 153 (no. 513) and 306 (illustration).

[19] There are thirty-one instances of *Freyr* where this name is used as the basis of kennings for 'man': see Meissner, *Kenningar der Skalden*, pp. 260–1 (§88).

[20] *Germania*, pp. 273 (ch. 2) and 317 (ch. 40).

clear to what extent a man entitled *Ing-* was understood to have assumed the divinity of Nerthus. A solution to this problem may be found in some classical analogues of the Old Norse–Icelandic Ingvi-freyr and, in particular, in the parallels between Freyr and Dionysus to which Ursula Dronke has alluded.[21] Dionysus, the long-haired consort of Demeter and son of Zeus by the human Semele, was the liberating agent of an ecstatic religion in which wine seasonally lowered social barriers and permitted widespread sexual indulgence.[22] Other oriental cults grew up in Rome around Adonis and Attis, human consorts of Cybele, yet Dionysus was the most prominent orgiastic god in the Graeco-Roman world. His consort Demeter was identified with Cybele at an early time, as Euripides shows when he associates the thyrsus and worship of Dionysus with 'the revels of the great mother Cybele' (τά τε µατρὸς µεγάλας ὄργια Κυβέλας).[23] Central to Euripides's play *The Bacchae* and to later Roman cults of Bacchus is the way in which Dionysus is denigrated as a newcomer in the semi-mythical story of the death of his first cousin Pentheus, the king of Thebes.[24] When Dionysus arrives from Asia, Pentheus refuses to honour him as a god. Dionysus continues to draw out Thebans of all ages into his worship on the slopes of Mount Cithaeron. Prominent among Dionysus's *maenades* are the respectable women of Thebes. A reveller whom Pentheus arrests turns out to be Dionysus himself, now transformed into a man in order to punish Pentheus. Still in disguise, Dionysus slips his iron bonds and agrees to lead Pentheus to a site where he can watch the 'band of worshippers' (θίασος) without being observed. But as Pentheus watches from a pine tree, Dionysus orders the maenads to destroy him. Pentheus is torn apart in their hands and his mother Agaue, thinking that she has dismembered a young lion, carries the head back to Thebes.

At the outset of this play, 'that I might be a supernatural being made manifest to mortals' (ἵν' εἴην ἐµφανὴς δαίµων βρότοις), Dionysus has

---

[21] Dronke, 'War of the Æsir and Vanir', pp. 223–38 (also published in *Myth and Fiction*, no. VII); this and other work on *Vǫluspá* will be available in U. Dronke, *Poetic Edda II* (Oxford, forthcoming).

[22] Dodds, *Greeks and the Irrational*, pp. 76–9 and 270–82.

[23] *Bacchae*, ed. Dodds, p. 6 (lines 78–9); the cult of Dionysus at Eleusis also came under the aegis of Demeter, goddess of the earth: see *The Bacchae*, trans. Kirk, pp. 5–6, and Dodds, *Greeks and the Irrational*, p. 76.

[24] *The Bacchae*, trans. Kirk, pp. 6–7.

already established his rituals in the east.[25] Now he will punish Pentheus and 'shall reveal to him and to all the Thebans that I was born a god'.[26] As if he is a general on campaign, Dionysus says:

> with the maenads I will join and lead an army into the field.
> For this reason I have switched into a mortal form
> and changed my shape into the constitution of a man.
>
> *(Bacchae* 52–4)[27]

This topos would be unremarkable, were it not that at least in the ἀγών between him and Pentheus in the play, Dionysus in human form has some fun with the irony of pretending to represent, not to embody, the god that he is. Thus when Pentheus asks the whereabouts of Dionysus, he answers 'with me; but you, not being pious, do not perceive him'.[28] However, Pentheus's objections are typical of the way in which ecstatic religion was perceived from the outside. This perspective, by which a god embodied in a man is understood to be a man representing the god, was realized in Ovid's version of the same story in *Metamorphoses* (book III), in which the part of Dionysus in this tale is assigned to Acoetes, a human devotee representing his master Liber (i.e. Dionysus). In the Germanic tradition of Nerthus, it appears that *Ing-* was first a functional term for a human embodiment of Nerthus, then a name for a man representing Nerthus.[29]

In Scandinavia, it seems that the Norse reflexes of *Ing-* received a **freyr*-suffix ('lord') as an epithet of political status.[30] Eventually, when **inguaz*, a human incarnation of Nerthus, came to be deified separately from this god and stylized as his son, this **freyr*-suffix would have evolved into a new god's name *Freyr* with a female adjunct *Freyja* ('lady'), and both Freyr

---

[25] *Bacchae*, ed. Dodds, p. 4 (line 22).
[26] *Ibid.*, lines 47–8: αὐτῷ θεὸς γεγὼς ἐνδείξομαι πᾶσίν τε Θηβαίουσιν.
[27] *Ibid.*, lines 52–4:
> ξυνάψω μαινάσι στρατηλατῶν
> ὧν οὕνεκ' εἶος θνητὸν ἀλλάξας ἔχω
> μορφήν τ' ἐμὴν μετέβαλον εἰς ἀνδρὸς φύσιν.
[28] *Ibid.*, p. 22 (line 502): παρ' ἐμοί σὺ δ'ἀσεβὴς αὐτὸς ὢν οὐκ εἰσορᾷς.
[29] Perhaps this man was a king such as McTurk redefines in 'Scandinavian Sacral Kingship Revisited', p. 31: 'one who is marked off from his fellow men by an aura of specialness which has [changed from "may or may not have"] its origin in more or less direct associations with the supernatural'.
[30] Green, *Carolingian Lord*, pp. 19–55.

Ingui of Bernicia

and Freyja would have been taken for the children of *Njǫrðr*. In England, two nominal reflexes of the *Ing*-hypostasis of Nerthus appear to be *Ingui* of Bernicia and *Ing* in *The Old English Rune Poem*. The evidence of these names, and of the related *incge*-form which I shall discuss in the next chapter, suggests that the cult of the Vanir (as they are known from Old Norse–Icelandic sources) was also known in pre-Christian parts of England. However, before I illustrate the genealogical roles of OIce *Ingvifreyr* and OE *Ingui*, I shall attempt to demonstrate the antiquity of the Vanir cult from which they derive by showing the classical analogues of Freyr's wagon-tour and the myth of the Æsir–Vanir cult-war.

CLASSICAL ANALOGUES OF THE VANIR

Freyr's wagon-tour

The fourteenth-century text of Freyr's tour with a woman in a wagon in *Flateyjarbók*, as we have seen, seems to confirm in some details the seasonal circuit of Nerthus and Terra Mater in *Germania* (ch. 40). I have accordingly suggested in the previous chapter that *Ing*- and a high-status woman may have travelled as the human manifestations of Nerthus and Terra Mater. In classical literature and religion, this Anglian couple appears to have analogues in the Hellenic Dionysus and Demeter and in the Roman Liber and Ceres. In Euripides's play *The Bacchae*, the seer Teiresias warns Pentheus that 'there are two things, young man, that come first among men': one is Demeter the corn-giving goddess, 'she is the earth, call her whatever name you will'; the other is her companion Dionysus, who gave men the wine that brings oblivion.[31] Dionysus and Demeter make a couple in at least five more Greek poets from the fourth century BC or earlier.[32] Liber and Ceres, the Roman counterparts, can be found giving man his corn and wine and joining in his harvest festivals in the poems of Lucretius, Vergil and Tibullus.[33] Both a literary reference and an ivory relief-carving surviving from the mid and late fourth century

---

[31] *Bacchae*, ed. Dodds, p. 12 (lines 274–5 and line 276): δύο γάρ, ὦ νεανία, τὰ πρῶτ' ἐν ἀνθρώποισι and γῆ δ' ἐστίν, ὄνομα δ' ὁπότερον βούλῃ κάλει. My translations from *The Bacchae* are based on *The Bacchae*, trans. Kirk.
[32] Merkelbach, *Die Hirten*, pp. 31–2.
[33] Lucretius, *De rerum natura* V.14–15; Vergil, *Georg* I.7; Tibullus, *Carm* II.i.3–4 and III.vii.163.

Heathen gods

respectively show that the joint cult of Ceres and Liber persisted throughout the Roman period.[34]

St Augustine records Liber's ceremonies in the Italian countryside in which the image of a phallus was drawn around in a cart and into Lavinium to ensure a good sowing.[35] Liber's festival, the Liberalia, took place on 17 March, following on from the Lupercalia on 15 February.[36] In Rome these festivals thus led up to the Megalensia of Cybele (4–10 April) and the plebeian Cerealia of Liber's companion Ceres (19 April). Ariadne, a woman whom Bacchus or Liber transforms into his divine consort, was known as *Libera* in Roman festivals.[37] Augustine reveals that the Romans call Libera *Venus* because she and Liber help the release of semen in coition: 'besides this they have women who are given over to Liber, as well as wine because wine provokes sexual desire. Thus are the Bacchanalia celebrated in the height of insanity.'[38] Libera or Venus would thus appear to denote a human form in which the earth-goddess Ceres coupled with Bacchus or Liber, god of the vine.

Tacitus alluded to two contemporary hypostases of Bacchus and Ariadne in his *Annales*, when he described the aftermath of a marriage between a consul designate and Messalina, wife of the Emperor Claudius:

Moreover, Messalina, nowhere else more wanton in her debauchery, celebrated the image of the vintage in late harvest throughout the house. The wine-press was pressed, wine-lakes flowed; and women provided with fawnskins launched an attack like the worshippers or insane ravers of Bacchus; Messalina herself, with her hair undone, was shaking a thyrsus-wand, and nearby Silius, bound up with ivy, was wearing actors' buskins and throwing back his head, while, around them, the shameless chorus roared. (XI.27)[39]

---

[34] See Merkelbach, *Die Hirten*, p. 32.   [35] *De civitate Dei*, pp. 202–3 (VII.21).

[36] *Varro: De Lingua Latina: On the Latin Language*, ed. R. G. Kent, 2 vols. (Cambridge, MA, and London, 1938–58) I, 186–8 (VI.14); *Fasti*, ed. Schilling I, 91–5 (III.17) and 156, n. 190.

[37] *Fasti* I, 91–5 (III.17).

[38] *De civitate Dei*, p. 178 (VI.ix; see also VII.iii, esp. p. 187): 'adhaec addunt mulieres adtributas Libero et uinum propter libidinem concitandum. Sic Bacchanalia summa celebrantur insania.'

[39] *Taciti Annales*, ed. Furneaux II, 45: 'at Messalina non alias solutior luxu, adulto autumno simulacrum vindemiae per domum celebrabat. urgeri prela, fluere lacus; et feminae pellibus accinctae adsultabant ut sacrificantes vel insanientes Bacchae; ipsa crine fluxo thyrsum quatiens, iuxtaque Silius hedera vinctus, gerere cothurnos, iacere caput, strepente circum procaci choro.'

Ingui of Bernicia

Tacitus portrays Silius as Bacchus, and Messalina, who later rides through Rome in a rubbish cart when the scandal is blown, as Ariadne on Naxos now deified by the god of wine. This was apparently a light-hearted human enactment of the union of Bacchus and Ariadne in Tacitus's lifetime.[40]

Ovid's version of the Theban story shows the popular riot that Liber's arrival brings, in the words of Pentheus, whom Teiresias has warned to show the god respect. The god of wine draws near:

Free-one is at hand and the acres resound with the shrieking of his festival; the crowd flows forth, matrons and young women mingled with men and the common mob and people of high estate are borne towards the unknown rites. 'What frenzy, O descendants of the Serpent, offspring of Mars, has struck your senses?' so Pentheus, 'Can bronze cymbals clashing and pipes with curving horns and the tricks of magic be so strong that men whom neither the swords nor the trumpets nor the ranks of war with javelins drawn could terrify should be bound by women's wailing and wine-maddened riots, by obscene flocks of groupies and empty tambourines?' (III.527–37)[41]

Pentheus says that King Acrisius of Argos has shut his gates to Bacchus, an example which they should follow. On this evidence it appears that Ovid's Liber, just like Euripides's Dionysus, arrives *en route* on a tour. These depictions of an ecstatic god's arrival appear to be distant analogues of Freyr's wagon-tour in Sweden and of Nerthus's procession in *Germania*.

---

[40] Plutarch says that Mark Antony was hailed as Dionysus in Ephesus and that he and Cleopatra were likened to Dionysus and Aphrodite later in Alexandria (*Life of Antony* XXIV.4–5 and XXVI.5).

[41] *Ovide: Les Métamorphoses*, ed. and trans. G. LaFaye, 2nd ed., 2 vols. (Paris, 1957) I, 86–7:

> Liber adest festisque fremunt ululatibus agri;
> Turba ruit mixtaeque viris matresque nurusque
> Vulgusque proceresque ignota ad sacra feruntur.
> 'Quis furor, anguigenae, proles Mavortia, vestras
> Attonuit mentes?' Pentheus ait 'aerane tantum
> Aere repulsa valent et adunco tibia cornu
> Et magicae fraudes ut quos non bellicus ensis,
> Non tuba terruerit, non strictis agmina telis,
> Femineae voces et mota insania vino
> Obscenique greges et inania tympana vincant?'

Translations are my own. Similar to this passage is Ovid's picture of the worship of Cybele in *Fasti*, ed. Schilling II, 9 (IV.183–7).

Heathen gods

As we shall see (below, pp. 44–8), Ing's arrival as described in *The Old English Rune Poem* may have been part of the same European tradition.

The Æsir–Vanir cult-war

Ursula Dronke, following in the path of Georges Dumézil, has shown that not only the story of *The Bacchae* but also its Indian cousins in the *Mahabharata* and *Satapatha-Brahmana* correspond to a legend in the Old Icelandic *Vǫluspá* in which the Æsir fight the Vanir for rights of sacrifice.[42] This legend is crucial to Norse mythology, because it defines a system of checks and balances in the Norse pantheon in which the antagonism between Pentheus and Dionysus seems to have an analogue in the war of the Æsir and Vanir.

Snorri briefly alludes to an Æsir–Vanir war in two places: in *Gylfaginning*, the colloquy in which a text of *Vǫluspá* is contained; and more fully in *Ynglinga saga* (ch. 4).[43] In the second case, we are told without preamble that Óðinn led an army against the Vanir. Since neither side could win, however, hostages were exchanged: Hœnir and Mímir from the Æsir; Njǫrðr, his children Freyr and Freyja, and Kvasir from the Vanir. The Vanir suspected trickery when Hœnir revealed himself unable to take part in meetings, so they cut off Mímir's head and sent it back to the Æsir: an interesting parallel to the manner in which Pentheus is returned to Thebes.[44] The wise *Kvasir* ('man of *kvass*') was more successful among the Æsir, however, for according to Snorri's later *Skáldskaparmál*, the gods jointly created him out of their spittle when they resolved the same war.[45] Kvasir was killed, his blood was mixed with honey and the mead of poetry was created. In *Ynglinga saga* Snorri says that Óðinn appointed Njǫrðr and his children as gods of sacrifice.

The Æsir–Vanir cult-war is the focus of stanzas 21–4 of *Vǫluspá*.[46] In

---

[42] Dronke, 'War of the Æsir and Vanir', pp. 236–8 (also published in *Myth and Fiction*, no. VII); G. Dumézil, *Gods of the Ancient Northmen*, trans. J. Lindow, ed. E. Haugen (Berkeley, CA, 1973), pp. 3–25.

[43] *Gylf*, p. 23 (ch. 23); *Heimskringla I*, ed. Bjarni, pp. 12–13.

[44] Cf. the courtier's fear in 'Hadet wyth an aluisch mon, for angardez pryde', in *Sir Gawain and the Green Knight*, ed. J. R. R. Tolkien and E. V. Gordon, 2nd ed. revised by N. Davis (Oxford, 1967), p. 19 (line 681).

[45] *SnE* 216 (*Bragarœður*, ch. 57); *FJSnE* 82.

[46] Dronke, 'War of the Æsir and Vanir', pp. 224–31 (also published in *Myth and Fiction*, no. VII).

Ingui of Bernicia

Vsp 21 the Vanir are imagined as newcomers on the scene; whose claim to receive divine honours leads Óðinn to attack them in 'the first war in the world' (*fólcvíg fyrst í heimi*). Humiliated there by the regenerative power of Freyja, the Æsir try to kill *Gullveig* ('Gold Brew'), her hypostasis:

> er Gullveigo   geirom studdo
> ok í hǫll Hárs   hana brendo,
> þrysvar brendo, þrysvar borna,
> opt, ósialdan,   þó hón enn lifir.   (*Vsp* 21/3–10)[47]

The Vanir send the witch Heiðr to corrupt the Æsir in their homes, rather as Dionysus casts his spell over the inhabitants of Thebes. At a loss, the Æsir go to their council to determine whether they should share tribute with the Vanir. They decide to renew the war instead. Óðinn hurls his spear into the mob, but the Vanir grow back as fast as the Æsir can kill them. Eventually the Æsir are forced to allow the compromise for which the Vanir had asked.[48] As a result of this agreement, Njǫrðr and his children live as gods among the Æsir.

This warfare between Norse gods or between their cults appears to have an analogue in Euripides's play *The Bacchae*, in which a peasant reports to Pentheus that he has seen the maenads raiding Theban villages, snatching children and cooking utensils which stick to them as if by magic and carrying fire in their hair (lines 748–64). The villagers, he says, defend themselves with weapons:

> for the men's lance-pointed missiles did not draw blood,
> rather these women loosing wands from their hands
> wounded them and turned them around in flight,
> women against men, surely not without a god of some kind!
> (*Bacchae* 761–4)[49]

---

[47] These are difficult lines; here and in the following stanza of *Vǫluspá*, I base my text and translation on those of Dronke, *ibid.*, pp. 225–6: 'they studded Gold Brew with spears and burned her in Hárr's [Óðinn's] hall, three times burned her three times reborn – often, without cease – though she yet lives'.

[48] *Bacchae*, ed. Dodds, p. 78 (note to lines 88–9).

[49] *Ibid.*, p. 32 (lines 761–4):

> Τοῖς μὲν γὰρ οὐχ ᾕμασσε λογχωτὸν βέλος,
> κεῖναι δὲ θύρσους ἐχανιεῖσαι χερῶν
> ἐτραυμάτιζον κ' ἀπενώτιζον φυγῇ
> γυναῖκες ἄνδρας, οὐκ ἄνευ θεῶν τινος.

Heathen gods

These lines are echoed not only by the attempted spear-stabbing and burning of Gullveig in Óðinn's hall, but also by Óðinn's useless spear-cast against the Vanir on the battlefield in *Vǫluspá*. In contrast, the 'ivy spear' (κίσσινον βέλος) or thyrsus of Dionysus and his μαινάδες correspond to the *tamsvǫndr* ('taming-wand') and *munir* ('(love-) impulses', cognate with *mainades*) with which Skírnir, Freyr's procurer in *Skírnismál*, threatens to make Gerðr mad when she refuses his master's love:

> Til holtz ec gecc   oc til hrás viðar,
> gambantein at geta,
> gambantein ec gat.   (*Skí* 32/1–3)[50]

Similarly, when Ovid's Dionysus the liberator uses his 'spear enveloped in vine leaves' (*hasta velata frondibus pampineis*) against sailors who wish to kidnap him in Ovid's *Metamorphoses*, its sprouting leaves soon entangle the ship and the sailors are turned into dolphins (III.667). Thus the traditions of Vanir and Bacchantes developed in different ways; but in so far as they both involve warfare by plant regeneration, they seem to have evolved from a common archetype. These classical tales of Dionysus, Bacchus or Liber help to show the antiquity of the cognate figures Ingvi-freyr of Uppsala and Ingui of Bernicia.

INGVI-FREYR OF UPPSALA

Njǫrðr and *Ingvi-freyr* are father and son in all Old Icelandic texts dating from the ninth century to the thirteenth, although their etyma in *Germania*, as we have seen, lie far apart in different chapters. Though an *Ing-*, etymon of *Ingvi*-freyr, appears to be the ancestor of a tribe in ch. 2, Tacitus shows no sign that this is also Nerthus's role in ch. 40. However, five instances of a suffix OIce *-njǫrðungar* as a synonym for 'princes' in the kennings of Scaldic poetry provide a pretext to look for a topos of royal descent from Nerthus, the etymon of Njǫrðr.[51]

Ingvi-freyr, son of Njǫrðr, is implied to be the progenitor of the

---

[50] 'To the copse I went and to a fresh tree, to get a ?newly budded branch, a ?newly budded branch I got.' This meaning of *gamban*, '?newly budded', would be in keeping not only with *hrár*, 'raw, fresh', but also with the image of Dionysus's self-regenerating thyrsus: see *Bacchae*, ed. Dodds, p. 4 (line 25). Óðinn himself uses such a *gambanteinn* to make a giant mad in *Hárb* 20: 'I tricked him out of his wits' (*ec vélta hann ór viti*).

[51] Meissner, *Kenningar der Skalden*, pp. 261–2 (§88).

Ingui of Bernicia

Ynglingar in the *Ynglingatal* of Þjóðólfr of Hvinir. In *Ynglingatal* Þjóðólfr grafts the family of his patron Rǫgnvaldr onto the stem of the more prestigious Ynglingar of Uppsala, and makes two references to Freyr as the founder of his patron Rǫgnvaldr's line: *Freys afspringr* ('Freyr's offspring') in stanza 17 and *Freys áttungr* ('Freyr's kinsman') in stanza 21. Other references to divine descent are *goðkynningr* ('of god-born kindred') in stanza 11 and *Týs áttungr* ('Týr's kinsman') in stanza 27. These claims, together with the stem of *Ynglingar*, the name of Rǫgnvaldr's forebears, show that Þjóðólfr probably wished to claim *Ingvi*-freyr as Rǫgnvaldr's most distant ancestor.

In his prologue to *Ynglinga saga*, Snorri claims that Þjóðólfr gave Rǫgnvaldr thirty forebears. However, in *Ynglingatal*, as Snorri quotes it, only twenty-seven generations can be counted including Rǫgnvaldr and Fjǫlnir, Rǫgnvaldr's first-named ancestor in stanza 1. A later poet, Eyvindr skáldaspillir (fl. 960–85) seems to have known *Ynglingatal*: for reasons of political rivalry between the Trondheim and Vestfold regions, it is assumed that he modelled his *Háleygjatal* on this poem. Though not all *Háleygjatal* has survived, AM 1 e *beta* II fol. (copied by Árni Magnússon in the library of P. H. Resen from a thirteenth-century manuscript which was later destroyed by the Copenhagen fire of 1728) contains a list of twenty-seven generations of Norwegian kings which is derived from this poem. The twelfth-century poem *Nóregs konungatal*, itself derived from the format of *Háleygjatal*, also has twenty-seven generations.[52] Given that the early ninth-century manuscripts of the Anglian collection in Britain have regnal lists structured with fourteen generations (including most recent king and founder), it seems that, with twenty-eight or twice fourteen generations in *Ynglingatal*, Þjóðólfr could arguably have made his tally by doubling a prestigious format derived from England or from elsewhere in the British Isles.[53] In this

---

[52] See A. Faulkes, 'The Genealogies and Regnal Lists in a Manuscript in Resen's Library', in *Sjötíu Ritgerðir helgaðar Jakob Benediktssyni*, ed. Einar G. Pétursson and Jónas Kristjánsson (Reykjavik, 1977), pp. 188–9; and 'Descent from the Gods', p. 99.

[53] See J. Turville-Petre, 'On *Ynglingatal*', pp. 49–50. The fourteen-generation format is discussed by Sisam in 'Anglo-Saxon Royal Genealogies', pp. 326–8, and by D. Whaley in her review of Krag (*Saga-Book* 23 (1993), 511–15, esp. 513–14), though Whaley seems not to admit the possibility of this type of Christian influence on a heathen tradition. G. Steinsland (*Det hellige bryllup*, pp. 179–88) regards Freyr as the progenitor implicit in the title of *Ynglingatal*, although, in her view, the poem (which represents a dynasty of men, not of gods) begins with Fjǫlnir.

Heathen gods

way, it may be suggested that Þjóðólfr started *Ynglingatal* with one or more stanzas on Ingvi-freyr which were subsequently lost at some point in its transmission, perhaps during the first three-quarters of the tenth century.

Ynglingatal begins without such a display of purpose or political significance as Eyvindr provides in *Háleygjatal*. In his commentary in *Ynglinga saga*, Snorri says that 'Fjǫlnir, son of Yngvifreyr' drowned when he fell into a mead-vat at a festival arranged by his friend King Fróði of Lejre. Þjóðólfr says:

> Varð framgengt, þars Fróði bjó,
> feigðarorð, es at Fjǫlni kom,
> ok sikling svigðis geira
> vágr vindlauss of víða skyldi. (*Ynglingatal* 1)[54]

The oldest prose source for the Yngling-genealogy, the *langfeðgatal*, lies at the end of a later postscript to Ari's *Íslendingabók*. This postscript, though of a sixteenth-century date, was probably copied unchanged from a list that Ari omitted in the first draft of his work.[55] In ch. 1 Ari claims that his first draft was read by three leading churchmen of his day: Sæmundr Sigfússon (1054–1123), Bishop Þorlákr of Skálholt (1086–1133) and Bishop Ketill of Hólar (1075–1145).[56] In the postscript the lineages of Þorlákr and Ketill come before Ari's and after those of the eleventh-century bishops Gizurr and Jón. Here Ari appears to have known a version of *Ynglingatal*, for, after the bishops, he derives his own paternal line from Rǫgnvaldr's ancestor King Óláfr trételgja of Vestfold. Ari's list of forefathers follows the names of *Ynglingatal* as far as Guðrøðr, before going a separate way; and follows Þjóðólfr's order up to this point, barring the sequence 'fl[i]. Dagr. fl[ii]. Alrekr. fl[iii]. Agni', where *Ynglingatal* puts Agni before Alrekr.[57] Ari's genealogy begins thus: '[i]. Yngvi Tyrkjakonungr. [ii]. Njǫrðr Svíakonungr. [iii]. Freyr. [iiii].

---

[54] *Heimskringla I*, ed. Bjarni, p. 26 (*Ynglinga saga*, ch. 11): 'It came to pass, where Fróði dwelt, that there was news of the decease which came to Fjǫlnir, and the windless wave [liquid] of the spears of curved-one [spears of the ox–head: horns] was said to furnish pyre-wood for the king'; also in *Skj* B I, 7, 1. For the sake of consistency with verse quotations from Old English and Eddic poetry, I shall set out Scaldic verse in long-line format with caesura.

[55] *Íslendingabók*, ed. Jakob, pp. 26–7. J. Turville-Petre, 'The Genealogist and History: Ari to Snorri', *Saga-Book* 20 (1978–9), 7–23, esp. 9–10.

[56] *Íslendingabók*, ed. Jakob, p. 3.   [57] *Ibid.*, p. 27, n. 3.

Fjǫlnir'.[58] Probably in the thirteenth century the anonymous author of the *Historia Norvegiae* follows Ari, but without his reference to the Turks: 'So King Ingui, whom many believe to have been the first to rule the kingdom of Sweden, begat Neorth, who indeed begat Froy; for a long time their whole posterity worshipped both of them [i.e. Neorth and Froy] as gods.'[59] Ari's allusion to the Turks was part of his contemporary learning, a topos used by his contemporary Geoffrey of Monmouth and inherited from the Frank Fredegar in the sixth century, who was apparently the first to trace his people to Troy since Vergil with Aeneas.[60]

In spite of his use of Latin learning in the formulation of *Yngvi Tyrkjakonungr*, however, Ari names his ancestors *Ynglingar*. This name was important to Ari because it connected him through his alleged ancestor Óláfr trételgja to the kings of Uppsala, the oldest known dynasty in Scandinavia. *Ynglingatal* was the title by which Ari (if not his predecessors) knew Þjóðólfr's poem. By naming his progenitor *Yngvi*, Ari rationalized a problem inherent in this title. As he could not start his list of kings with Ingvi-freyr without disposing of Njǫrðr, Freyr's father, it follows that he was obliged to invent a father for Njǫrðr using the stem of *Ynglingatal* and detaching it from *Freyr*. As the Anglo-Saxon regnal lists bear witness, it is more customary for scribal genealogists to lengthen lineages than to shorten them.[61] There is no evidence that the genealogist's trade had changed significantly by the twelfth century. Ari could thus have invented a father for Njǫrðr in order to remain consistent with the name of the dynasty he coveted for his ancestors.

---

[58] *Ibid.*, p. 27: 'I. Yngvi king of the Turks. II. Njǫrðr king of the Swedes. III. Freyr. IV. Fjǫlnir.'

[59] *Historia Norvegiae*, ed. Storm, p. 97: 'Rex itaque Ingui, quem primum Swethiae monarchium rexisse plurimi astruunt, genuit Neorth, qui vero genuit Froy; hos ambos tota illorum posteritas per longa saecula ut deos venerati sunt.'

[60] See Faulkes, 'Descent from the Gods', pp. 110–24, esp. 114. See also *Chronicorum quae dicuntur Fredegarii Scholastici Libri IV, Fredegarii et Aliorum Chronica*, ed. B. Krusch, MGH, SRM 2 (Hanover, 1888), 194–6; *The Historia Regum Britanniae of Geoffrey of Monmouth*, ed. A. Griscom, with R. E. Jones (London, New York and Toronto, 1929), pp. 223–4 (I.3); *Historia Brittonum*, ed. Lot, p. 161. The *Historia Brittonum*, fictitiously attributed to 'Nennius', was probably written in 829/30 by an author whose name does not survive: see D. N. Dumville, '"Nennius" and the *Historia Brittonum*', *Studia Celtica* 10–11 (1975–6), 78–95.

[61] Dumville, 'Kingship, Genealogies and Regnal Lists', pp. 72–104.

Yngvi or *Ingui* is not only an indeclinable prefix of the name of Freyr, whom Ari otherwise makes Njǫrðr's son, but is also a declinable synonym for 'king', a proper noun (*Ynglingatal* 11 and *HHund* I 52) and a dwarf's name (*Vsp* 16).[62] Freyr is known as *Ingvi-freyr* in Eyvindr's *Háleygjatal* 13;[63] as *Ingunar-Freyr* in *Lok* 43; and as *Ing[v]i-freyr* in *Haustlǫng* (c. 890), Þjóðólfr's other surviving poem and probably the most apposite example:

> gǫrðusk allar áttir   Ing[v]i-freys at þingi
> (vǫru heldr) ok hárar   (hamljót regin) gamlar
>
> (*Haustlǫng* 10)[64]

Þjóðólfr in this stanza describes not only the Æsir but all other categories of living things in the world as 'all the kindreds of the Ing[v]i-lord' (*allar áttir Ing[v]i-freys*), i.e. as members of the Vanir. In *Haustlǫng*, one of the oldest surviving Scaldic poems, these words appear to afford a glimpse of an even older type of paganism in which the Vanir ruled.

INGUI OF BERNICIA

An *Ingui* is presented in Ida's Bernician genealogy in the *Anglo-Saxon Chronicle* (A) for the year 547.[65] The form of *Ingui* appears to be identical with *Ingvi* or *Yngvi*, the appellative prefix of the Norse god Freyr, though Erna Hackenberg showed that *Inguec*, in the same genealogy in *Historia Brittonum*, is an earlier form.[66] In *Inguec*, however, the *Ingu*-stem is more significant than the form and meaning of the suffix *-(u)ec*, which resembles that of *Beorn-uc* closely enough to have been added to the stem by analogy at or after the time *Beornuc* was eponymized from *Bernicia*.[67] Among the

---

[62] *Skj* B I, 9 (*Ynglingatal* 11).   [63] *Ibid.*, pp. 15–16 and 61.

[64] *Ibid.*, pp. 15–16 (*Skj* A I (diplomatic text), 18: *inge freys* all manuscripts): 'All the kindreds of Ing[v]i-freyr (the divine powers looked rather ugly) deliberated at the assembly, grey-haired and old.' Without reference to Ing[v]i-freyr in *Haustlǫng* 10, Krag suggests that it was first Snorri who joined *Yngvi* to *Freyr* (*Ynglingatal og Ynglingesaga*, pp. 85–6).

[65] *MS A: a Semi-Diplomatic Edition*, ed. Bately, p. 22: 'Ida wæs Eopping, Eoppa wæs Esing, Esa Inguing, Ingui [Ingin G[N] and G[W]; Ingui BC]; Angenwiting.'

[66] *Stammtafeln*, ed. Hackenberg, pp. 109–10.

[67] *Ibid.*, p. 110. *Ingui* seems to have been modified to *Ingibrand* on analogy with *Wægbrand* in the later Anglian collection. For texts, see Dumville, 'Anglian Collection', pp. 30 (Vespasian B. vi, 109r–v), 32 (CCCC 183, 65r–67r) and 35 (Tiberius B. v, vol. I, 22v–23r).

Ingui of Bernicia

following lists of Bernician kings, the latinized version in *Historia Brittonum* is probably the oldest, though it incorporates later additions.[68] The oldest witness of the Anglian collection is London, British Library, Cotton Vespasian B. vi, a Mercian fragment from *c.* 814:[69]

Historia Brittonum	*Vespasian B. vi*	*ASC (A)*
Woden	Uoden	Woden
Beldeg	Beldæg	Bældæg
		Brand
Beornuc	Beornic	Benoc
Gechbrond	Wegbrand	
Aluson	*Ingi*brand	Aloc
	Alusa	Angenwit
Inguec	Angengeot	*Ingui*
Aedibrith	Eðilberht	
Ossa	Oesa	Esa
Eobba	Eoppa	Eoppa
Ida	Ida	Ida

Ingui is thus related to Ida in an open-vowel alliteration that is the oldest pattern in the Bernician list. In all surviving regnal lists and genealogies the Bernician legend of Ingui's (Inguec's or Ingibrand's) close ancestry of Ida seems to be older than the seventh-century extensions that introduced Beornuc (an eponym) and Woden (a god). *Ingui* is the form I shall adopt as the Anglian reflex of *Ing*- (except for references to *Ing* in *The Old English Rune Poem* in the next chapter). Given that *Ingvaeones* is presented as a term in *Germania* (ch. 2) for seaboard tribes, to which the Anglii also belonged (ch. 40), I suggest that Ingui, at the earliest stage of Anglo-Saxon history, was held to be the progenitor of all Anglian kings.

[68] *Stammtafeln*, ed. Hackenberg, p. 109.
[69] Dumville, 'Anglian Collection', pp. 24 (discussion of manuscripts) and 30–1 (texts).

3
Ingui's cult remembered: Ing and the *ingefolc*

In this chapter I shall discuss five areas of Old English literature in which it is possible to detect late reflexes of the pre-Christian cult of Ingui: in Ing in *The Old English Rune Poem*; in the various meanings and contexts of the words OE *ylfe* ('demons') and *ælfsiden* ('demonic possession'); in Alcuin's use of the name *Hinieldus*; and in the *incge*-compounds of the poems *Exodus* and *Beowulf*.

ING IN *THE OLD ENGLISH RUNE POEM*

The Old English Rune Poem is the work of one author and has been dated to the end of the tenth century.[1] In each of the twenty-nine textual divisions in this poem the name of a rune is written as a runic letter and described in a few mnemonic lines of verse. The first word of each division is also the name of the rune. *Ing* is the name of the twenty-second:

> [Ing] wæs ærest   mid Eastdenum
> gesewen secgun,   oþ he siððan est
> ofer wæg gewat,   wæn æfter ran;
> þus Heardingas   ðone hæle nemdun.   (*Rune* 67–70)[2]

---

[1] *Old English Rune Poem*, ed. Halsall. The original manuscript in which this poem was found, London, British Library, Cotton Otho B. x (165r–v), was destroyed by the fire in 1731, but had been copied by George Hickes in 1705.

[2] *Ibid.*, pp. 21–32 (text and manuscript) and 86–93 (notes): 'Ing was first seen among men with the East-Danes, until he then passed east [or MS *est* emend. *eft*: 'back again'] over the wave; his wagon ran after him: thus the Heardings gave the man his name.' With regard to Nerthus's wagon, it is worth noting that Picard, when she cites among her Ing- examples 'die schwerdeutbare Strophe' of Ing in *The Old English Rune Poem*, does so without translation and quotes only the first three half-lines: *Germanisches*

Ing's *wæn* appears to be an analogue of Nerthus's *uehiculum* and Freyr's *uagn* in *Gunnars þáttr helmings*, but strictly this *wæn* comes after his tour, since it '*æfter* ran'. Ing's tour thus seems to come before a wagon and to represent a solitary spring prelude to a joint summer procession.[3]

In the previous chapter I argued that Tacitus confused a male Nerthus with a female Terra Mater because he was predisposed to think of Cybele or Magna Mater in Rome. Yet Tacitus's vocabulary also suggests that his informant described the spring tour of a solitary god and that Tacitus conflated two types of procession into one. When Nerthus is first drawn about in *Germania*, Tacitus says: 'pax et quies tunc tantum nota, tunc tantum amata, donec idem sacerdos satiatam conuersatione mortalium deam templo reddat'.[4] If Nerthus, through his manifestation as Ing-, is taken as male and single, his *conuersatio mortalium* resembles that of Dionysus as perceived by Pentheus in *The Bacchae*, in whose phallic innuendo Dionysus proceeds 'with the favours of Aphrodite in his eye' and 'holds converse day-long and all the kindly night with young women, extending out to them his initiation into bacchic mysteries'.[5] Thus, in first-century coastal Germania, we might see Ing-, the hypostasis of Nerthus, touring the regions with a driver (*sacerdos*) in pursuit of love (*amare*) in quiet places (*pax et quies*), returning only when his appetite for social and sexual intercourse is fulfilled (*satiatam conuersatione mortalium deam*).

Tacitus was not disposed to find sexual impropriety in the subjects of *Germania*. This stricture was part of his background: the rites of Bacchus, for example, had been outlawed from Roman religion in 186 BC, when the senate purged these festivals from state cults.[6] Though Bacchus was subsequently absorbed into the cult of Liber and Ceres, Tacitus's highborn priesthood, the *Quindecemviri*, had no brief to superintend the lowly gods of Italian extraction.[7] Nor would Tacitus have taken an interest in Liber,

---

Sakralkönigtum?, pp. 192–6, esp. 193; Baetke also omitted to discuss Ing's *wæn* in connection with Ing, in *Yngvi und die Ynglinger*, pp. 141 and 154–7.

[3] *Germania*, p. 285; *Flat* I, 338–9 (ch. 278).

[4] *Germania*, p. 317 (ch. 40): 'then, and only then, are peace and quiet known and loved, until the same priest returns the goddess, who is satiated with her dealings with mortals, to her temple'.

[5] *Bacchae*, ed. Dodds, p. 12 (lines 236–8): οἰνῶπας ὅσσοις χάριτας Ἀφροδίτης ἔχων and ἡμέρας τε κ'εὐφρόνας συγγίγνεται τελετὰς προτείνων εὐίους νεάνισιν.

[6] Dumézil, *Archaic Roman Religion*, pp. 515–21.   [7] Syme, *Tacitus* I, 65–6.

since it is assumed from evidence within *Germania* that he wrote this treatise to improve his debauched contemporaries in Rome. He allows for drunkenness in Germanic men only in councils where women are not present, praises 'the harsh marriage code in this place' as one which is made sacred with the exchange of weapons, suggests that adultery is 'extremely rare in so numerous a population', says that Germanic women live 'uncorrupted by the temptations of any public shows or by the carousals of banquets', and adds that among them secret *billets-doux* are unknown.[8] If this last claim is true, it is probably because few Germans could write. Tacitus would not have been interested in associating Nerthus with the sexual licence of Germanic worshippers, if this is how Nerthus's festival was reported to him.

Yet, to the extent of four points of comparison, Tacitus's words concerning the itinerant Nerthus resemble the text and theme of *Skírnismál*, a poem probably from ninth- or tenth-century pre-Christian Norway, in which Ingvi-freyr sends his servant Skírnir to coerce a giantess Gerðr into sex. After Skírnir threatens her with a runic curse, Gerðr appoints a time and place and Skírnir relays this message to Freyr (*Ski* 41). Gerðr says:

> Barri heitir,   er við bæði *vitom*,
>   *lundr lognfara*;
> enn eptir nætr nío   þar mun *Niarða[r]* syni
> Gerðr *unna gamans*.   (*Ski* 39)[9]

The italicized Norse words recall Tacitus's *castum nemus*, *pax et quies tantum nota, tantum amata* and *Nerthus*. Though the order of these four elements in *Skírnismál* is not the same as it is in *Germania*, they resemble one another: either they go back to a common North Sea Germanic tradition, or they may be taken as four coincidences. If they derive from common tradition, then it is possible that Tacitus conflated more than one allusion

---

[8] *Germania*, pp. 294–6 (ch. 18–19): 'seuera illic matrimonia'; 'paucissima in tam numerosa gente'; 'nullis spectaculorum illecebris, nullis conuiuiorum irritationibus corruptae'.

[9] '"For Barley", as we both *know*, is the name of *a tranquil grove*. There after nine nights will Gerðr *grant pleasure* to the son of *Njǫrðr*.' The meaning of OIce *Barri* as 'for barley' (in a dative or locative case) is developed from Olsen's interpretation in 'Fra gammelnorsk myte og kultus', pp. 24–6; on the meaning 'pine-cone' in *Barri*, supported by a questionable reading of *lundr* as a pine-wood rather than as a grove, see Steinsland, *Det hellige bryllup*, pp. 92–6.

Ingui's cult remembered

to Nerthus in which (on the one hand) Nerthus's mortal form, a sacral king, toured the regions in spring or early summer, sexually coercing local women along his route, and in which (on the other hand) Nerthus and Terra Mater celebrated their marriage with a joint wagon-tour through their local provinces.

A solitary wagon-tour, dated to the eighth century in Gaul, had a male subject as its focus. Einhard, the biographer of Charlemagne, says that Childeric III, last of the long-haired Merovingian kings, was a degenerate king and had given up his power in all but name: 'Quocumque eundum erat, carpento ibat, quod bubus iunctis et bubulco rustico more agente trahebatur. Sic ad palatium, sic ad publicum populi sui conventum, qui annuatim ob regni utilitatem celebrabatur, ire, sic domum redire solebat.'[10] Piggott has suggested that Einhard borrowed the word *carpentum* from classical authors in order to ridicule a custom which he did not understand.[11] Childeric's *bubulcus agens* is reminiscent of the *sacerdos* who drives the wagon in *Germania*; as Helm pointed out, Tacitus says that no-one but the 'priest' may touch Nerthus's wagon; thus it was probably the same man who yoked the heifers to the shaft.[12] Childeric's royal ox-cart procession, given its ceremonial status, seems to belong to a Merovingian tradition, perhaps as old as the Merovingians themselves (they are first recorded in the early fifth century); Piggott has suggested that this royal procession had its origin in Nerthus's wagon-tour.[13] If so,

---

[10] *Vita Karoli Magni*, ed. Pertz and Waitz, p. 3 (i.1): 'Whenever he needed to travel, he went in a two-wheeled carriage which was drawn by yoked oxen and was driven by a cowherd in rustic style. In this manner he was accustomed to go to the palace, to go to the public assembly of his people which was celebrated annually for the running of the kingdom, and to go back home.' Childeric styled himself 'crine profuso, barba summissa' (see *ibid.*, p. 3: 'with abundant hair and flowing beard'). An intaglio portrait on the gold signet ring of Childeric I (d. 481) shows that shoulder-length hair was the style of Merovingian kings from pre-Christian times: Piggott, *Waggon, Chariot and Carriage*, p. 34.

[11] Piggott, *ibid.*: 'need not reflect ninth-century usage' ... 'overtones of effeminacy as well as display'. J. M. Wallace-Hadrill believes that this 'bullock-cart' could derive from a manuscript illustration, or be a reference to the bull-founder of the Merovingians: see Wallace-Hadrill, *The Long-Haired Kings* (Toronto, Buffalo and London, 1962), pp. 231–3, esp. 232.

[12] *HAR* I, 314 (§177).

[13] Piggott, *Waggon, Chariot and Carriage*, p. 35: 'The Franks had come south from the archaeological areas of what I have called "Cimbric wagons", ceremonial four-wheeled

it provides evidence that the ceremony of a religious procession could have been part of a political institution.

To return to *The Old English Rune Poem*, the word *hæle* in line 70 might confirm the etymology of *Ing* as an epithet for a 'man', not a god.[14] Yet the words 'first seen among men' (*ærest gesewen secgun*), which are used of Ing, suggest Nerthus's manifestation among crowds of worshippers. Ing's connection with *Heardingas* can be read as meaningful, since in the first book of Saxo's *Gesta Danorum* (*c*. 1200), a certain *Hadingus* and his wife deliver an exchange of verses which is Saxo's elaborated version of the exchange between Njǫrðr and Skaði in *Gylfaginning*.[15] The Heardings who gave Ing his name in *The Old English Rune Poem* would thus appear to be yet another name for his descendants. Since OE *heardingas* otherwise denotes Constantine's heathen enemies (Huns, Goths and Franks) in *El* 25 and 130, Maureen Halsall's 'warriors' does not do justice to this name in the *The Old English Rune Poem*.[16]

Ing's journey here starts with *ærest*; with *siððan* he moves back east (*est*) across the water. Read literally, this verse shows the beginning and end of a journey there and back that crosses either the Øresund from eastern to western Danish possessions, or the North Sea from Denmark to the Danes and Anglo-Saxons in England. In either case, Ing appears to be an Anglo-Saxon form of Ingvi-freyr with his own seaboard tour in a North Sea Germanic tradition analogous to that of Dionysus or Liber through Asia, Argos and Thebes.

ÆLFSIDEN AND THE FIEND

Ing's sexual activity while he tours through coastal Germania, if analogous to that of Dionysus in Greece, Liber in Italy or Ingvi-freyr in Norway, could have been assisted by demonic magic. In Old Norse–Icelandic poetry Ingvi-freyr's tribe are reputed to be 'wise Vanir' (*vísir vanir*) in *Vaf* 39, *Skí* 17–18 and *Sigrdrífumál* 18. This wisdom includes prophecy, for Heimdallr in *Þrym* 15 'knew the future well, just as other Vanir did' (*vissi hann vel fram sem vanir aðrir*). So Teiresias describes the

carriages known from votive bog-finds as in Dejbjerg or in graves such as Husby: the Nerthus vehicle is wholly appropriate here.'

[14] *ANEW* 286 (*Ingunarfreyr*) and 678–9 (*Yngvi*).
[15] *Gylf*, p. 24 (ch. 23); *GD*, pp. 30–1.
[16] *Old English Rune Poem*, ed. Halsall, pp. 90–1 (text) and 146–8 (notes).

cult of Dionysus: 'for that which is bacchic and that which is manic have much prophetic power'.[17] From the tenth century to the thirteenth, this magic in Icelandic literature is known as *seiðr*; the verbs *seiða* and *síða* ('to perform magic') with women and men also involve a degree of lust or carnality.[18] In *Egils saga*, for example, Gunnhildr uses her sensual magic to draw her worst enemy from Iceland to York: 'had *seiðr*-magic performed and had such a spell cast that Egill Skalla-Grímsson should never enjoy a moment's rest until she had seen him'.[19] This kind of *seiðr* represents a kind of possession and corresponds to the drawing out of Thebans to the mountainside. In the domestic part of the Æsir–Vanir cult-war, in *Vǫluspá*, Heiðr works against the Æsir to similar Dionysian effect:

> Seið hón kunni,   seið hón leikin,
> æ var hón angan   illrar brúðar.   (*Vsp* 22/5–8)[20]

That Heiðr is *leikin* probably means that she herself has been 'possessed'.[21] Here the poet puns on *seið* the accusative noun with the preterite of *síða* the verb. The effect of this pun is to make the listener pause and reconsider the meaning of the second half-line in a way that imitates the mental entrapment it describes.

Snorri defines *seiðr* in *Ynglinga saga*, where he notes that this witchcraft was left to goddesses because male Æsir thought it a matter of shame.[22] Though it could enable Óðinn, who learnt it from Freyja, to know the future, it involved *ergi*, by which Snorri could mean male homosexuality, transsexuality or cross-dressing. Not without reason in *Lokasenna*, a poem to which I shall often return, does Loki accuse Óðinn of 'practising *seiðr*-

---

[17] *Bacchae*, ed. Dodds, p. 14 (line 299): τὸ γὰρ βακχεύσιμον καὶ τὸ μανιῶδες μαντικὴν πολλὴν ἔχει.

[18] See Strömbäck, *Sejd*, pp. 17–21 (*Vsp* 22); AR I, 330–3 (§237); and F. Ström, '*Níð, ergi* and Old Norse Moral Attitudes', Dorothea Coke Memorial Lecture (London, 1974). In qualification of Strömbäck, F.-X. Dillmann excludes shamanism from *seiðr*, in 'Seiður og shamanismi í Íslendingasögum', *Skáldskaparmál: Tímarit um Íslenskar Bókmenntir Fyrri Alda* 2 (1992), 20–33.

[19] *Egils saga*, ed. Sigurður, p. 176 (ch. 59): 'lét seið efla ok lét þat seiða, at Egill Skalla-Grímsson skyldi aldri ró bíða á Íslandi, fyrr en hon sæi hann'.

[20] 'Witchcraft she had skill in, witchcraft she practised, possessed. She was always the darling of an evil bride.'

[21] Strömbäck includes possession in his interpretation, in *Sejd*, p. 20: 'she could do magic, distracted (or possessed) she performed magic' ('kunde sejd, hon sejdade förryckt (eller besatt)').

[22] *Heimskringla I*, ed. Bjarni, p. 19.

magic in the form of a witch' (*síða vitca líki*, *Lok* 24) and of dressing in women's clothes; Kormákr in the late tenth century alludes to the same myth when he says 'Yggr [Óðinn] practised *seiðr*-magic to get Rindr' (*seið Yggr til Rindar*, *Sigurðardrápa* 3).[23] OIce *seiðberendr* (perhaps 'womb-bearers'), a word which probably refers to effeminate male witches, is cited once (*Hynd* 33).[24] Elsewhere Snorri cites cults of *seiðmenn*, 'magicians', in late ninth-century Norway. One of these, Rǫgnvaldr réttilbeini, was the son of King Haraldr hárfagri, whose son Eiríkr is said to have regarded *seiðr* as a social menace and to have destroyed Rǫgnvaldr and eighty *seiðmenn* in a house in Hadeland: 'and that deed was highly praised'.[25]

There appear to have been analogues of *seiðmenn* in Anglo-Saxon paganism. A grave in Portway, Hampshire, contained the skeleton of a man at least fifty years old whose survivors appear to have buried him not only in a female dress with two brooches and a bead necklace, but also with a large flint nodule on his chest, 'one of only two bodies, out of some seventy, so treated' and perhaps in such a way as 'to prevent the ghost of the deceased from rising'.[26] Monks were also attired in long skirts; here it is worth noting Bede's story of the Battle of Chester in his *Historia ecclesiastica*. When the Welsh bishops in *HE* turn down Augustine's request for conformity with Roman observances and for cooperation in converting the English, Augustine warns them that if they refuse peace from their brethren, they will have war from their Anglian enemies. His prophecy comes true when Æthelfrith of Bernicia expands Anglian territory into Rheged and in Chester wipes out more than a thousand monks who had come from their houses in Bangor to pray for a Welsh victory. In Bede's admiring words, Æthelfrith 'made the greatest slaughter of that heretical nation'.[27] In the battle, Æthelfrith sees the monks, whose gowns would not have identified them with male warriors,

---

[23] *Skj* B I, 69.
[24] Cf. Strömbäck, *Sejd*, pp. 29–31. In Roman religion Attis and his followers the Galli were similarly human worshippers of Cybele who castrated themselves on 24 March (after the spring equinox) probably in an effort to acquire feminine powers. See Henig, *Religion in Roman Britain*, p. 110.
[25] *Heimskringla I*, ed. Bjarni, p. 139 (*Haralds saga hárfagra*, ch. 34): 'ok var þat verk lofat mjǫk'.
[26] Wilson, *Anglo-Saxon Paganism*, pp. 96–7.
[27] *HE* II.2 (p. 140): 'maximam gentis perfidae stragem dedit'.

Ingui's cult remembered

asks who they are and why they have come. Then he says: 'If they are calling on their God against us, though they bear no arms, they still fight us by pursuing us with hostile prayers.'[28] Bede thus presents Æthelfrith as if this pagan king was regarding the Bangor monks as wizards whose magic could disarm his warriors.[29]

These disparate pieces of evidence, then, may indicate that Anglo-Saxon paganism had its own analogues of Norse *seiðmenn*. This suggestion appears to receive some support from late seventh-century evidence. Bishop Aldhelm of Sherborne (d. 709) appears to show some concern about Bacchanalia in a letter to Wihtfrith, in which he asks what good comes from either studying Proserpina, or revering Hermione, 'or to record in the heroic style of epic – the high priests of the *Luperci*, who revel in the fashion of those cultists that sacrifice to Priapus'.[30] To Heahfrith, a student who had spent six years in Ireland, Aldhelm praises God for West Saxon learning now being carried out in buildings on the site of pagan shrines 'where once the crude pillars (*ermula*) of the same foul snake and the stag were worshipped with coarse stupidity in profane shrines'.[31] In *Beowulf*, *Heorot* ('stag') is the hall of King Hrothgar *se wisa frea Ingwina*, 'the wise lord of the Ingwine' (*Beo* 1319); in thirteenth-century Iceland, Snorri says that a *hjartar horn* ('stag's horn') is the weapon with which Freyr kills his opponent in Ragnarǫk.[32] It is possible, therefore, that the West Saxon stag images celebrated an archaic Saxon counterpart of Ingvi-freyr.[33] The name of this figure may have been a form of *Irmin-* or OE *eormen*, as in the Old Saxon *Hirmin-suul*, for Aldhelm

---

[28] 'Ergo si aduersum nos ad Deum suum clamant, profecto et ipsi, quamuis arma non ferant, contra nos pugnant, qui aduersis nos inprecationibus persequuntur.'

[29] Also suggested by Meaney, 'Bede and Anglo-Saxon Paganism', p. 19.

[30] *Aldhelmi Opera*, ed. Ehwald, p. 479: 'aut *Lupercorum* bacchantum antistites ritu litantium Priapo; parasitorum heroico stilo historiae caraxare'. See *Aldhelm: the Prose Works*, trans. Lapidge and Herren, pp. 154–5. Italics are my own.

[31] *Aldhelmi Opera*, ed. Ehwald, p. 489: 'ubi pridem eiusdem nefandae natricis ermula cervulusque cruda fanis colebantur stoliditate in profanis'. See *Aldhelm: the Prose Works*, trans. Lapidge and Herren, pp. 160–1. For discussion of this passage from an archaeological perspective, see J. Blair, 'Anglo-Saxon Pagan Shrines and their Prototypes', *Anglo-Saxon Studies in Archaeology and History* 8 (1995), 1–28.

[32] *Gylf*, p. 31 (ch. 36). Cf. also the stag emblem on the Sutton Hoo sceptre, illustrated and discussed in *The Making of England*, ed. Webster and Backhouse, p. 33 (no. 17).

[33] The snake images that Aldhelm describes may be thematically related to the snake which Bacchus holds aloft in the fourth-century Walbrook marble statuette, which is illustrated and discussed by Henig in *Religion in Roman Britain*, p. 119 (fig. 49).

Heathen gods

not only uses *ermula* suggestively for the snakes, but also refers to a pagan goddess named *Hermione* earlier in the same passage.

Two Old English and two Latin glosses from the early eleventh century show that states of possession were thought to be the effects of a magic equivalent to *seiðr*. The following words gloss *commitiales* ('epileptics') in Aldhelm's *De laudibus virginitatis*, in Brussels, Royal Library, 1650: Hand A glosses this word as *garritores* ('babblers') and *ylfie* ('demoniacally possessed'); Hand C, as *lunaticos* ('lunatics') and *wanseoce* ('devil-sick ones').[34] All four words are used to gloss Aldhelm's story of Victoria and Anatolia in ch. 52, in which Anatolia drives out evil spirits not only from a boy demoniacally possessed, but also from 'those possessed [with devils], epileptics and other diseased persons'.[35] *Wan-seoc* possibly contains as its first element an Old English cognate of Norse *van-* (as in *Vanir*): thus 'those made sick by the Vanir'. This word appears to be a unique variant of the more common *deofulseoc*, a word for 'possessed' and itself a gloss in an earlier passage in Aldhelm.[36] Demonic possession would describe the madness in *Skírnismál* with which Skírnir threatens the reluctant Gerðr, whom he woos on behalf of Freyr; Gerðr calls Freyr *vaningi* ('son of the Vanir') when she finally gives in (*Skí* 37); among Anglo-Saxons, therefore, the word *wan-* seems to have meant 'demon'. In ch. 7, I shall suggest that Bede attempted to allude to a form such as **uuani* (a Northumbrian cognate of OIce *vanir* and lWS *wan-*) in his use of the Latin words *vanus* and *vanitas*.

Secondly, OE *ylfi*[g]*e* seems to mean 'demoniacally possessed', given that *ælf* probably means 'demon' rather than 'elf', its whimsical modern reflex. Demons in Anglo-Saxon medicine are a subject of study in their own right, one which lies beyond the scope of this book.[37] In one set of glosses a feminine form is used for 'nymphs' (*aelfinni*), 'oreads' (*duun.aelfinni*), 'dryads' (*uudu.aelfinne*), 'hamadriads' (*uater.aefinn*[*e*]), 'maiads' (*fel-*

---

[34] Goossens, *Glosses*, p. 457 (no. 4820).

[35] *Aldhelmi Opera*, ed. Ehwald, p. 310: 'larvatos et comitiales ac ceteros valitudinarios'. See *Aldhelm: the Prose Works*, trans. Lapidge and Herren, pp. 51–8 (introduction) and 121 (text).

[36] Goossens, *Glosses*, p. 456 (no. 4815): 'devil-sick'; *deofulseocnys* occurs in *Medicina de Quadrupedibus*, ed. de Vriend, 56.3, 66.8, 172.17, 224.13 and 262.18; *deofulseoc* occurs in *The Blickling Homilies of the Tenth Century*, ed. R. Morris, EETS o.s. 73 (London, 1880), 173.28.

[37] See R. A. Peters, 'OE *ælf*, *-ælf*, *ælfen*, *-ælfen*', *Philological Quarterly* 42 (1963), 250–7; and H. Stuart, 'The Anglo-Saxon Elf', *Studia Neophilologica* 48 (1976), 313–20.

d.aelfinne) and 'naiads' (*sae.aelfinne*).³⁸ The feminine beauty of *ylfe* is apparent in *ælfscinu* ('bewitchingly bright'), an epithet with which Sarah is twice described in *Genesis A* (1827 and 2731) when Abraham tries to pass her off as his sister. In *Judith*, probably of the early tenth century, Judith dresses up as *ides ælfscinu* ('a lady bewitchingly bright') to lure the drunken Holofernes to his death (*Jud* 14). In Norse formulae such as Skírnir's being 'a son of neither elves nor Æsir nor wise Vanir' in *Skí* 18 (*álfa né ása sona né vissa vana*), the *álfar* are distinguished from the Vanir, though they have much in common. However, Freyr may equate *álfar* with Vanir when he divides the supernatural world alliteratively into 'Æsir and elves' (*æsir oc álfar*) in *Skí* 7. When Óðinn in disguise is tortured as a travelling wizard in *Grímnismál*, he tells the son of his captor in *Grím* 5 that 'the gods gave Elf-home to Freyr in the ancient days as a gift for cutting his first tooth' (*Álfheim Frey gáfo í árdaga tívar at tannfé*). Freyr and all his people may thus be seen to be connected with 'elves' or 'demons'.

Vǫlundr is a 'prince of demons' (*álfa lióði*) in stanza 10 of *Vǫlundarkviða*, a poem probably of ninth-century date which John McKinnell believes to have been composed in Scandinavian Yorkshire.³⁹ The name *Wieland*, a cognate of OIce *Vǫlundr*, was known throughout Middle German literature.⁴⁰ An English Weland-figure was celebrated in relief on the early eighth-century Franks Casket, in a story which is known both from *Vǫlundarkviða* and from *Deor* 1–6, at the moment *Welund* prepares to seduce Beadohild; there is a reference to *Weland* as a renowned smith or armourer in *Wald* I 2 and II 9 and in *Beo* 455; and *Weland* is also named as the West Saxon version of *Fabricius* in Alfred's translation of Boethius's *De consolatione Philosophiae* (II met. 7).⁴¹ Weland's name appears in two charters, one in 903 citing a *Welandes stocc* ('Wayland's post') near Princes Risborough and the other, in 955, *Welandes smiþþe* ('Wayland's smithy') on the Berkshire ridgeway.⁴² Given Freyr's association with

---

³⁸ Meritt, *Old English Glosses*, p. 61 (Leiden, Voss. Lat. quarto 106, 10r).
³⁹ J. McKinnell, 'The Context of *Vǫlundarkviða*', *Saga-Book* 23 (1990), 1–27, esp. 1–13.
⁴⁰ Gillespie, *Catalogue*, s.v. 'Wieland' (pp. 141–3).
⁴¹ *King Alfred's Boethius*, ed. Sedgefield, pp. 46 (XIX.17) and 165 (*Met* 10.33, 10.45 and 10.42).
⁴² W. de G. Birch, *Cartularium Saxonicum: a Collection of Charters Relating to Anglo-Saxon History*, 3 vols. (London, 1885–93) II, 259, 13 (no. 603); *Codex Diplomaticus Ævi Saxonici*, ed. J. M. Kemble, 6 vols. (London, 1839–48) V, 332, 23 (no. 1172); for

Álfheimr in *Grím* 5, Vǫlundr's epithet *álfa lióði* defines Vǫlundr, hence Weland, as a demon connected with the Vanir.

Christian parents may have hoped to protect their children with the *ælf*-prefix, by innoculating them with such names as *Ælf-ræd* ('demon-counsel'), *Ælf-ric* ('demon-?king') or *Ælf-giefu* ('demon-gift'), for the *ælf* was capable of malign effects on personal health. In *The Charm for a Sudden Stitch*, the poet warns against 'esa gescot oððe hit wære ylfa gescot' ('a shot from spirits or it might be a shot from demons', *MCharm* 4.23); then of 'hægtessan gescot' ('witch-shot', *MCharm* 4.24). In the first instance, the only attested simplex of OE *ese* ('spirits'), cognate with OIce *Æsir*, probably survives through an association with the more durable *ylfe*. The phrase *Satanae diabulus aelfae* ('devil of the elf Satan') from an eighth-century Worcester prayer-book shows that 'elf' could be used as an epithet of Satan.[43] Bede associates possession with the fiend, when he tells a story of a man who was often afflicted 'by an unclean spirit' (*ab inmundo spiritu*), was cured and from that time onwards suffered no more afflictions 'from the ancient enemy' (*ab antiquo hoste*).[44] Demonic possession and its cause are the subject of a remedy in *The Christian Ritual against Elves* (in *Lacnunga*, following an Irish incantation against venom):

Þis is se halga drænc *wið ælfsidene 7 wið eallum feondes costungum*: writ on husldisce, 'In principio erat uerbum' usque 'non conprehenderunt', et plura 'et circumibat iesus totam galileam docens' usque 'et secuti sunt eum / turbe multe'; 'Deus in nomine tuo' usque in finem; 'Deus misereatur nobis' usque in finem; 'Domine deus in adiutorium'.[45]

Here the reader must recite John I.1–5; Matt. IV.23–5 and Ps. LIII (LIV), which, as Grattan and Singer note, was used at the beginning of

---

dates, see P. H. Sawyer, *Anglo-Saxon Charters: an Annotated List and Bibliography*, Royal Historical Society, Guides and Handbooks, 8 (London, 1968), 161 (no. 367) and 204 (no. 564).

[43] Quoted by Sims-Williams, *Religion and Literature*, p. 54: 'The word for the pagan Germanic sprite may be included to reinforce the Christian demonology.'

[44] *HE* III.11 (pp. 248–50).

[45] *Lacnunga*, ed. and trans. Grattan and Singer, pp. 108–9: 'This is the holy drink *against demon-magic and against all the temptations of the fiend*: write on the plate for the eucharist "In the beginning was the word" until "comprehended it not", and again "And Jesus went round all Galilee teaching" as far as "and there followed Him / great crowds", "God in Thy name" until the end, "God have mercy upon us" until the end, "Lord God to our aid" until the end.'

Ingui's cult remembered

the ritual *De exorcizandis obsessis a daemonio*.[46] Jesus thus protects the patient against the devil and his possession. All temptations, but especially demonic possession, are indicated in *ælfsiden*. As 'demon-magic', *ælfsiden* also occurs in *Leechdoms* in a recipe 'against each ?witch or demon magic' ('wið ælcre leodrunan 7 wið *ælfsidenne*').[47] In a third medical context, a doctor is urged to make a potion 'wið ælfe and wiþ uncuþum *sidsan*', which seems to mean 'against a demon and against an unknown ?*influence*'; here the unique OE *sidsa* is associated with the word *ælf* and may also be cognate with OIce *seiðr*.[48] In short, OE *ælf-siden* shows the malign influence of *ylfe* in its first element; in its second, a plausible Old English cognate of OIce *seiðr*.

Grattan and Singer claimed that 'the Teutonic peoples originally knew nothing of *possession* by demons'.[49] Yet this is precisely the force of Skírnir's threat to tame Gerðr to his *munir*, to make her a *maenad*, in *Skírnismál*: 'with a taming wand I will tame you, girl, through my "(love) impulses"' ('tamsvendi ec þik drep, enn ec þic temia mun, mær, at mínom *munom*', Skí 26/1–3).[50] So, too, *The Christian Ritual against Elves* can be read as a deliberate reversal of Ing's wild progress through the tribes of coastal Germania. This is true if we consider the text from the Gospel of Matthew that the patient is urged to recite:

Et abiit opinio eius in totam Syriam, et obtulerunt ei omnes male habentes, variis languoribus, et tormentis comprehensos, et qui daemonia habebant, et lunaticos, et paralyticos, et curavit eos: et secutae sunt eum turbae multae de Galilaea, et Decapoli, et de Ierosolymis, et de Iudaea, et de trans Iordanem.[51]

---

[46] *Ibid.*, p. 109.   [47] *Leechdoms*, ed. Cockayne I, 138 (LXIV).

[48] *Ibid.* II, 296–7 (LXV). There is an informative note on OE *sidsa* in P. Kitson, 'From Eastern Learning to Western Folklore', in *Superstition and Popular Medicine in Anglo-Saxon England*, ed. D. G. Scragg (Manchester, 1989), pp. 57–71, esp. 68 n. 28.

[49] *Lacnunga*, ed. Grattan and Singer, p. 56 (their italics).

[50] Freyr's and Skírnir's *munir* occur six times in this poem (Skí 4/6, 24/3, 26/3, 35/9, 35/10 and 40/6). OIce *munir* recalls the cognate Greek μαντική with which, according to Teiresias, Dionysus fills the body of his worshippers: see *Bacchae*, ed. Dodds, p. 14 (lines 299–300); see also *The Bacchae*, trans. Kirk, pp. 51–2. On OIce *munr* and Greek μένος, see North, *Pagan Words*, pp. 29–31.

[51] Matt. IV.24–5 (quoted here up to the end of the verse): 'and his fame spread into all Syria, and they brought to him everyone who had something wrong, whether people taken ill with different diseases or deformed, those who had demons, lunatics and people paralysed, and he cured them: and many crowds followed him from Galilee, the Ten Towns, Jerusalem, from Judaea and from across the Jordan'.

Heathen gods

The general motifs are similar: Jesus proceeding in triumph around a shoreline accumulating huge crowds of tormented and possessed people from regions of which the varied names add to his fame. But there the resemblance ends. As Dionysus, Ingvi-freyr or Ing might have possessed ordinary people with his socially disruptive *ælfsiden*, so Jesus heals all of them and destroys every trace of Satan along the way. In England it must be assumed that the first Christian missionaries attempted to do likewise, for the figure feared in this charm as the *feond* is possibly a reflex of Ing or Ingui himself, the alleged ancestor of King Ida and the human incarnation, later the euhemerized reflex, of Nerthus. So it was no doubt Ingui whom the Anglo-Saxon church first identified with Satan. That may explain why Alcuin compares Hinieldus with Belial and why, in addition, the poets of *Exodus* and *Beowulf* seem to ascribe Ingui to their lost kinsmen in Germania.

'QUID HINIELDUS CUM CHRISTO?'

Writing from Francia in *c.* 796 to a friend in England whom he names 'Speratus', Alcuin turns to the theme of Doomsday and the necessity of living a religious life. Then, in the context of some sharp moral advice, he adds: 'Verba Dei legantur in sacerdotali convivio. Ibi decet lectorem audiri, non citharistam; sermones patrum, non carmina gentilium. Quid Hinieldus cum Christo?'[52] The same *Hinieldus* occurs as *Ingeld*, a Heathobard, in *Beo* 2064; and as *Ingellus*, a Dane, in Saxo's *Gesta Danorum*.[53] In these contexts Beowulf predicts and Saxo relates a common story in which Ingeld is provoked to re-open a feud with the family of his new bride. In his reference to Hinieldus, Alcuin was probably alluding to St Paul's advice to Christians never to consort with pagans: 'What meeting can Christ have with Belial? What can a believer have to do with an unbeliever? What pact then can God's temple have with idols?'[54] Yet it is odd that Alcuin chooses Hinieldus

---

[52] *Epistolae*, ed. Duemmler, pp. 181–4, esp. 183: 'Let God's words be read in priestly assembly. There it is the reader who should be heard, not the harper; the sermons of the Fathers, not the songs of pagans. What has Ingeld to do with Christ?'

[53] *GD*, pp. 165–80; *History of the Danes*, trans. Fisher and ed. Ellis Davidson I, 175–95; II, 102–7.

[54] II Cor. VI.15–16: 'Quae autem conventio Christi ad Belial? Aut quae pars fideli cum infideli? Qui autem consensus templo Dei cum idolis?'

to match Belial (also a name for wickedness in Deut. XIII.13). One reason for this choice may lie in the Scandinavian provenance of Ingeld, four years after the sack of Lindisfarne; another, in the form of Hinieldus's name, the first element of which, as *hini*-, derives from OE *in(c)ge*, an adjectival referent of Ingui (the Anglo-Saxon cognate of Ingvi-freyr).[55] Also important is the name of Hinieldus's father: Froda in *Beo* 2025 and Frotho in Saxo's tale of Ingellus. In the Old Norse *Skírnismál*, 'inn *fróði* afi' is the epithet with which Freyr is introduced, as 'the wise/fertile grandfather [or "heir"]' (*Skí* 1 and 2); and the epithet by which he has been identified with Saxo's Frotho.[56] In this respect it would not be the legend of Ingeld but the connotation of his and his father's names that led Alcuin to typify Hinieldus as 'this lost heathen lamenting in hell'.[57]

Alcuin's reference to Hinieldus is not found in all manuscripts of this letter.[58] The addressee, *Speratus*, was formerly identified with Abbot Hygebald of Lindisfarne, to whom Alcuin addresses three letters by name, one to him individually and two to him as the leader of his community.[59] Recently, however, Donald A. Bullough has made a good case for the recipient of this letter being Bishop Unuuona (OE *un-wana*, 'not lacking') of Leicester, who flourished in *c.* 796.[60] It thus seems that there were not only Vikings attacking Lindisfarne in 793, but also Danes in peaceful contact with the Mercians at about the same time, from whom a story about the Danish *Ing[v]i-[v]aldr* the human son of *Fróði* was in general circulation. Ingui's adjectival prefix *in(c)ge-* also occurs in *Exodus* and *Beowulf*. In the course of this book I hope to show evidence of Danish influence on *Beowulf*.

---

[55] Ball, 'Incge Beow. 2577', pp. 403–10.
[56] *AR* II, 182–6. Baetke argues against identifying Fróði with Freyr, the man with the god: *Yngvi und die Ynglinger*, p. 87. On the other hand, Schier finds these figures sufficiently close to identify one with the other: 'Freys und Fróthis Bestattung', p. 407.
[57] *Epistolae*, ed. Duemmler II, 183: 'ille paganus perditus plangit in inferno'.
[58] W. F. Bolton, *Alcuin and Beowulf: an Eighth-Century View* (London, 1979), pp. 101–3.
[59] *Epistolae*, ed. Duemmler II, 54–7.
[60] This letter is not preserved in the same collection as the others; *Speratus* as 'longed-for' is strictly closer to *Unuuona*, as 'not lacking', than to *Hygebald*, as 'powerful of mind'; and *sacerdotali convivio* is more likely to denote a priestly than a monastic community. See Bullough, 'What has Ingeld to do with Lindisfarne?', pp. 101–2 and 122–5.

Heathen gods

INGE IN *EXODUS*

My point of departure in *Exodus* is Nicholas Howe's reading of this poem as a historical allegory in which the Israelites on their way to Canaan represent the Anglo-Saxon settlers of Britain, the land of their future conversion.[61] I shall suggest that the Egyptians in *Exodus* are imagined not only as pagans, but also as if they were Ingui's worshippers left behind on the mainland. This identification is mostly achieved by the poet's use of four *inge*-compounds.

The notion of this poem as historical allegory is new to *Exodus* scholarship. Until recently, *Exodus* was discussed chiefly as an example of spiritual allegory, Old Testament *figura* for the New. In this case Moses and the Israelites, as they escape from Egypt across the Red Sea to Canaan, would be thought to prefigure good souls passing from the world through the waters of baptism to Heaven. Figural readings are encouraged by the well-known injunction towards the end of *Exodus* to unlock the meaning of this work *gæstes cægon* ('with the keys of the spirit', *Ex* 525). But otherwise, as Malcolm Godden says, the poet's method is 'highly oblique and allusive, almost in the manner of an extended riddle'.[62] This quality has led Roberta Frank to claim that *Exodus* was influenced by Norse Scaldic poetry.[63] Tom Shippey has argued that 'the concern for human motivation on a realistic level is markedly alien to the type of commentary most practised by Augustine and his followers'.[64] Figural readings of the biblical Exodus lay in the poet's tradition, but so vivid is the *Exodus* poet's narrative that it seems to be detail rather than symbol that preoccupies him: for instance, the martial displays of Israelites and Egyptians, an unwarranted scene of the aftermath of battle in *Ex* 162–9, the bloody turmoil as the Red Sea engulfs Pharaoh and his men, and the plundering of the dead on the far shore. Thus there is much in the imagery of *Exodus* to support Shippey's view that 'there were pressures at work other than those of faithful translation or dogmatic relevance'.[65]

---

[61] Howe, *Migration and Mythmaking*, pp. 73–107.
[62] Godden, 'Biblical Literature: the Old Testament', pp. 206–26, esp. 217.
[63] R. Frank, 'What Kind of Poetry is Exodus?', in *Germania: Comparative Studies in the Old Germanic Languages and Literatures*, ed. D. G. Calder and T. C. Christy (Wolfboro, NH, and Woodbridge, 1988), pp. 191–205.
[64] T. A. Shippey, *Old English Verse* (London, 1972), pp. 136–43, esp. 140–1.
[65] *Ibid.*, p. 138.

One of these pressures may have been the poet's need to vindicate his ancestors.

Only Howe has made sense of the metamorphosis of the pillar of cloud with which God guides Moses towards the Red Sea, into a 'roof-beam' (*bælc*, Ex 73), 'holy net' (*halig nett*, Ex 74), then a 'sail' (*segl*), with 'mastropes' (*mæstrapas*) and a 'sailyard' (*seglrod*, Ex 80–3), then a 'tent' (*feldhus*, Ex 85).[66] The journey from Egypt is described as a voyage over the sea: 'a sail guided the journey, seamen went after on the flood-way' (*segl siðe weold, sæmen æfter foron flodwege*, Ex 105–6). Why the sail and flood-way in a desert? Why does the poet refer to the pursuing Egyptians as 'landsmen' (*landmen*, Ex 179), in contrast to the Jews above as 'seamen' (*sæmen*)? Howe suggests that the poet's nautical imagery is due to his 'desire to incorporate, in as striking a fashion as possible, the Anglo-Saxon migration into Biblical history'.[67] Where the cloud's image shifts to that of a sail we are thus led to think not only of the twelve tribes of Israel crossing the Red Sea, but also of the early Germanic tribes as they migrated to Britain. This identification can be traced to Pope Gregory's letter to Mellitus in 601 (preserved in Bede's *HE*), in which he praises God's initial toleration of old animal sacrifice in the Jews as the method to follow in converting the Anglo-Saxons.[68] Howe's idea of political allegory in *Exodus* finds further Christian justification in the cross-symbolism of 'tree of glory' (*wuldres beam*, Ex 567) or pillar of fire that leads the Jews to victory. The Anglo-Saxons who preached to the Germans in the eighth century knew that it was only through their ancestors' arrival and conversion in Britain that they were not still pagan themselves. Others less fortunate had been left behind. 'Take pity upon them', says Boniface of the Old Saxons in a letter to the English in *c*. 738, 'for they themselves are saying: "We are of one blood and one bone with you"'.[69] So if the poet of *Exodus* presents the flight from Egypt as the migration of the Anglo-Saxons to Britain, the land of their future salvation, he thereby vindicates the paganism of his ancestors.

Any discussion of *Exodus* is vitiated by the miscopied form of the only

---

[66] Howe, *Migration and Mythmaking*, pp. 73–107.
[67] *Ibid.*, pp. 92–8, esp. 98. [68] *HE* I.30 (p. 108).
[69] *Sancti Bonifatii et Lullii Epistolae*, ed. M. Tangl, MGH, Epistolae Selectae 1 (Berlin, 1916), 75: 'Miseremini illorum, quia et ipsi solent dicere: De uno sanguine et de uno osse sumus.'

surviving text.⁷⁰ This poem was probably copied into the Junius Book at the end of the tenth century (after *Genesis* and before *Daniel*) from a deficient exemplar by a scribe who seems to have garbled it further. As *Genesis* in the same codex contains an interpolation of a poem on Satan originally in Old Saxon (*Gen* 235–851), so parts of *Exodus* might look extraneous. Two leaves are missing in the middle of the gathering in *Ex* 141–2, and following *Ex* 445 the manuscript has two blank sides between which a leaf has been excised. The end of *Exodus* is also lost, with the present text ending in the middle of a word. Thus emendation is often necessary in *Exodus*. This is twice the case with the *inge-* compounds found there, of which as many as four may survive: *ingehere* (emended from MS *ingere*, *Ex* 33), *ingefolca* (*Ex* 142), *ingemen* (*Ex* 190), and *ingeþeode* (emended from MS *incaþeode*, *Ex* 444).

Another occurrence of the word *ingeþeode*, in the Paris Psalter, helps us to grasp something of its meaning. There is first an exhortation to praise the Lord over the extent of the world from sunrise to sunset (Ps. CXII, 3.1–2); then a declaration of God's authority:

> He is ofer ealle   ingeþeode
> se heahsta   hæleða cynnes,
> is ofer heofenas eac   ahafen his wuldur.   (*Ps* CXII.4)⁷¹

This corresponds to the Latin of the Vulgate: 'Excelsus super omnes *gentes* Dominus, Et super caelos gloria eius' (Ps. CXII.4).⁷² Here, as in the Vulgate sources of MS *incaþeode* (*Ex* 444), probably Gen. XV.5, XVII.4–8 and XXII.16–19, the Latin correlate of *ingeþeode* is (*omnes*) *gentes*. To Rosier, and to Howe after him, the *in-ge-* prefix means 'native', the Egyptians being (in Howe's words) 'natives of this earth and not of heaven'.⁷³

---

[70] *Exodus*, ed. Tolkien, pp. 33–6, 47–8 and 68–9; *Exodus*, ed. Irving, pp. 1–12; also edited in *Exodus*, ed. P. J. Lucas (London, 1973, revised (and updated) edition 1994). The emendations suggested by Lucas, in particular, have not been followed in this book.

[71] 'He is over all the *nations*, the highest over the tribe of men, and also over the heavens his glory is raised.'

[72] Ps. CXII.4: 'High is the LORD above all *nations*, his glory above the heavens.'

[73] J. L. Rosier, '*Icge Gold* and *Incge Lafe* in *Beowulf*', PMLA 81 (1966), 342–6. See also Howe, *Migration and Mythmaking*, pp. 94–5. OIce usage also shows that *út* and *útan* mean 'west' and 'back east' in Atlantic sailing terminology: this may imply that OE *inn* in *Exodus* and *Beowulf* means 'in the east' in addition to its other senses.

Ingui's cult remembered

This is a suitable reading of *inge-* in *Exodus*, but not only for the reasons given by Rosier and Howe. The poet's interest in the *in-*adverb is clear enough in his 'land–sea' distinction between Egypt and Israel, and in *oht inlende* (*Ex* 136), Pharaoh's 'pursuit from inland' after the Israelites have fled. Yet with morphological rather than textual argument, Ball shows that *incge* (as in *incge laf*, *Beo* 2377) is cognate with the first element of *Ingvi-freyr*.[74] Spellings of *inge-* are various, but the *c* of MS *incapeode* in *Exodus* may have an *incgepeode as its source. Ball translates this and the other *inge-* prefixes in *Beowulf* and *Exodus* as 'immense/mysterious/sublime', without further reference to Ingvi-freyr. His reluctance to face the question of a semantic relationship between *ingvi* and *incge* was wise enough in its time. Yet, taking account of Howe's suggestion that the Israelites in *Exodus* are an allegorical representation of the first Anglo-Saxons, it should now be possible also to interpret the Egyptians as the pagans of continental Germania.

In *Exodus* the Egyptians are first known as *Faraones cyn, Godes andsacan* ('Pharaoh's kin, God's enemies', *Ex* 14–15), whom Moses *gyrdwite band* ('bound with rod-torment', *Ex* 15). Egyptians, furthermore, are *wraðe* ('fierce ones', *Ex* 20), and *feond* ('fiends', *Ex* 22). Their treasure taken (Ex. XII.35–6), their first-born slain (Ex. XII.28–30), the Egyptians lose the gold off their idols:

> feond [MS *freond*] wæs bereafod,
> hergas on he[a]lle.   Heofon[g] þider becwom,
> druron deofolgyld.   (*Ex* 45–7)[75]

This poet makes much of Pharaoh's gods in Exodus, to whom the Lord only briefly refers in announcing the slaying of the first-born: 'et in cunctis diis Aegypti faciam iudicia'.[76] Yet if altars are despoiled with such abandon in this garbled passage, who is the *feond* in their midst? The answer to this question probably lies in the four *inge-*compounds of this poem.

(a) inge[he]re

By telling Moses something of His mystery, God enables him to take his host out of Egypt:

---

[74] Ball, 'Incge *Beow.* 2577', pp. 403–10.
[75] 'The fiend was plundered, altars in the hall. Lamentation came there, idols crashed.'
[76] Ex. XII.12: 'and I will make judgement on all the gods of Egypt'.

Heathen gods

> Þa wæs inge[he]re   ealdum witum
> deaðe gedrecced,   drihtfolca mæst;   (Ex 33–4)[77]

The Israelites leave Egypt and the pillar of cloud is transformed into a mast with sails, leading them all forward through four camps, until suddenly the Egyptians are heard to be in pursuit.

(b) yrfeweard ingefolca

Just as the poet reminds us of Egyptians breaking the vows made by *se yldra cyning* ('the older king', *Ex* 141), the text runs out, resuming after a lacuna with some ambiguity:

> Þa wearð yrfeweard   ingefolca,
> manna æfter maðmum,   þæt he swa micles geðah. (*Ex* 142–3)[78]

A man's earthly rather than heavenly riches are imagined with *manna æfter maðmum* in these lines. Thus the *yrfeweard* who inherits them is probably the younger Pharaoh. Although the word *yrfeweard*, as 'guardian of the inheritance' or even 'cattle-guardian' (*orf*), might refer to Joseph, the phrase *ealles þæs forgeton* ('they forgot all of this') makes better sense of the Egyptians in the next line if these words refer to the older Pharaoh's prosperity in Egypt (Gen. XLVII.20), rather than to Joseph's in Goshen (Gen. XLV.16–20 and XLVII.3–6). Since the detritus of Pharaoh's drowned armies is washed up in the end of *Exodus* as *Iosepes gestreon* ('Joseph's treasure', *Ex* 588), it seems that the poet, in the lines now lost to us here, wanted to make Joseph the creator of the younger Pharaoh's wealth.

(c) ingemen

In keeping with the plural of 'ingefolca' (*Ex* 142), Pharaoh's army is composed of more than one kin-group: *cyningas and cneowmagas on þæt ea*[*l*]*de riht* ('kings and kinsmen according to the ancient law', *Ex* 185–6), each of whom leads out every male he can find. The Egyptians are thus imagined as a horde of different kin-groups:

[77] 'Then was Ingui's army afflicted with ancient torments, the greatest of military peoples, with death.'
[78] 'It was then that the inheritor of Ingui's peoples came to prosper so much in his inheritance of the treasures of men.'

Ingui's cult remembered

> Wæron ingemen ealle ætgædere,
> cyningas on corþre.   (*Ex* 190–1)[79]

This reference to Ingui's people resembles Þjóðólfr's comprehensive terminology for the Norse gods gathering in *Haustlǫng*: 'all the kindreds of the Ing[v]i-lord deliberated at the assembly' (*gǫrðusk allar áttir Ing[v]ifreys at þingi*, st. 10).[80] Since the compound *inge-men* is varied by *cyningas*, Rosier's translation of *inge-* as 'native' seems to be justified as far as it goes. Finn at the end of the Finnsburh Episode in *Beowulf* is slain as *cyning on corþre* ('a king among his retinue', *Beo* 1153), just before the Scyldings carry off *eal ingesteald eorðcyninges* ('all the Ingui-treasure of the earth-king', *Beo* 1155). In this part of *Beowulf*, as in *Exodus*, *inge-* seems to denote inner privacy, in contrast with its expansive sense in *ingefolc* and *ingeþeode* (*omnes gentes*). On the other hand, if the homophones *in-ge-* and *incge* had long been confused by the time *Exodus* and *Beowulf* were written, it is still possible that 'innermost, native' in *in-ge-* was regarded as the true meaning of *incge*, the epithet of an old god whose descendants are not only the poet's *ingemen* and *ingeþeode* but chiefly the Pharaoh himself. To the extent that Egypt represents the eastern parts of Germania in *Exodus*, Ingui was the devil identified with them, as he may be in the tradition of Ing's section in *The Old English Rune Poem*. By the same token, Pharaoh would be a sacral king also regarded as Ingui's descendant. Used only of the Egyptians, *inge-* thus alludes to at least three things: to the relative placing of the Egyptians in the poet's topography, to the universal *gentes*, and to the *gentes* which worshipped Ingui in Germania.

(d) oð Egipta ingeðeode

It is probably to vindicate his ancestors that the poet of *Exodus* digresses on Noah, Abraham and Isaac in Moses's past (*Ex* 357–445) and on Solomon in Moses's future (*Ex* 389–96). Until the publication of Irving's edition of *Exodus* in 1953 it was still common to regard this passage as an interpolation.[81] It can be justified, however, as the poet's attempt to record the deep faith of Noah (*treow, Ex* 366); of Abraham (*wær, Ex* 421; *treow, Ex* 425); and of Solomon, whose construction of a temple probably represents the future Christian *civitas Dei*. The triumph of Abraham's

---

[79] 'Ingui's men were all together, kings in the retinue.'
[80] *Skj* B I, 15–16.   [81] *Exodus*, ed. Irving, pp. 8–9.

Heathen gods

descendants is thus confirmed only in terms of God's devotion to his tribe. *He að swereð, engla Þeoden* ('He swears an oath, the King of Angels', *Ex* 431), says the voice of Glory. The sons of Abraham will be more numerous than stones on earth or stars in heaven or sand on the seashore:

> 'ac hie gesittað, be sæm tweonum
> oð Egipta ingeðeode [MS *incaþeode*],
> land Cananea, leode þine,
> freobearn fæder, folca selost' (*Ex* 442–5)[82]

Ingeðeode is the fourth and last *inge-* compound in the surviving poem. The climactic speech in which it occurs is probably drawn from Gen. XXII.16–18 (supported by Gen. XV.5, XVII.4–8 and XXXII.12) in which the Lord makes a crucial distinction between Jew and gentile. If *Exodus* were read as a biblical story at face value only, 'gentile' would be a reasonable translation of *ingeðeode*. However, in the light of Howe's case for historical allegory in *Exodus*, 'gentile', 'native' or 'innermost' do not go far enough. God assures the Israelites in *Exodus* a glorious future *oð Egipta ingeðeode* (*Ex* 443). The Egyptians are thus excluded from glory, as in Gen. XXII.18; and if *Exodus* is read as historical allegory, the Anglo-Saxons are promised victory on condition that they too stay separate from *ingeðeod*, the pagans left behind on the mainland.

INCGE IN BEOWULF

Hrothgar frea Ingwina

As we have seen, one of the many epithets in *Beowulf* for King Hrothgar of the Danes is *eodor Ingwina* ('prince of the Ingwine', *Beo* 1044); another is *se wisa frea Ingwina* ('the wise lord of the Ingwine', *Beo* 1319). *Ingwine*, which seems to mean 'friends of Ing' and to reflect *Ingvaeones*, is found only in these two instances, which occur each on either side of one of the most dramatic sequences in the poem: the festivity following Beowulf's victory over Grendel, the singing of the Danish Finnsburh epic in Heorot, and Grendel's mother's unexpected attack on the hall. Why the poet of *Beowulf* should have wished to characterize Hrothgar with an Ing-

---

[82] 'But they will occupy Canaan between the seas right up to the Ingui/gentile nation of the Egyptians, your people, the free-born children of their father, the best of tribes [MS *break*].'

appellative before and after this varied sequence may thus be connected with the oath sworn on *i[n]cge gold* in the intervening 'Finnsburh Episode' (*Beo* 1063–160).

What happens where in Finnsburh

There are six cases in the Finnsburh Episode in which Old English words or phrases correspond with texts derived from the Old Icelandic tradition of Ingvi-freyr. Either these manifest the poet's allusion to Ingui in the Finnsburh story, or they must be regarded as six coincidences.

The Finnsburh Episode is a complex narrative, told in a highly allusive style, and apparently constituting the second part of a tale, the first part of which survives separately in the so-called *Finnsburh Fragment*. In my interpretation of this tale, a band of Scyldings stays in Frisia as a component of the 'Half-Danes', a mercenary group of Danes, Hocings, Secgan and Jutes, if not other tribes. The Half-Danes are suddenly attacked in the night by King Finn of the Frisians, their host and employer, who appears to send not only Frisians against the Half-Danes, but also a group of Jutes settled in Frisia. After five days' fighting the Half-Danish leader Hnæf is killed. Finn now makes peace with the survivors, led by Hengest, Hnæf's Jutish lieutenant. After a winter darkened by the memory of slaughter, Hnæf's Scylding kinsmen with Hengest's help kill Finn in revenge, ransack his kingdom and sail home with Hildeburh, Finn's queen and their Danish kinswoman.[83]

When Finn has killed Hnæf after five days of fighting, he sets about rebuilding his army with survivors from both sides (his collective *folc* in *Finn* 9). The Danes among the Half-Danes are welcome to stay. At the same time the possibility of their vengeance for Hnæf is obstructed by Finn's *weotena dom* ('council of wise men', *Beo* 1098), who devise a four-clause oath for Hengest and Finn to swear jointly: (1) Finn 'renounces feud' or 'flyting' (with *unflitme*, *Beo* 1097) with Hengest and his men for his own losses; (2) no man in any party shall break the 'pact' (*wære*, *Beo*

---

[83] See North, 'Tribal Loyalties', pp. 13–43; also in R. North, 'Kening Finn en it Ferdrach fan Finnsboarch', *Us Wurk* 38 (1989), 1–11; see also Tolkien, *Finn and Hengest*, ed. Bliss; *Finnsburh*, ed. Fry; J. F. Vickrey, 'The Narrative Structure of Hengest's Revenge in *Beowulf*', *ASE* 6 (1977), 91–103; A. G. Brodeur, 'Design and Motive in the *Finn* Episode', *Essays and Studies: University of California Publications in English* 14 (1943), 1–42, and 'The Climax of the *Finn* Episode', pp. 285–361.

1100) in word or deed; (3) no surviving member of Hnæf's Half-Danes shall 'ever complain with malicious skill' (*þurh inwitsearo æfre gemænden*, *Beo* 1101) about their leader's death; and (4) no Frisian shall allude to the past murders concerning a loss of his own 'with savage speech' (*frecnen spræce*, *Beo* 1104), on pain of execution by Finn's sword.

Hengest is thus made the leader of the Half-Danes, yet subject in his turn to Finn for as long as he stays in Frisia. Thereby Finn ensures that should the Danes and any others try to break the oath themselves, they must fight Hengest and his Jutish followers in addition to Finn's retinue. As the Danes have no hope of succeeding in this enterprise, they are forced to acquiesce in a peace with Finn, whom they have a duty to kill. Finn, in this ruthless way, has managed to fill his depleted army with Hnæf's band of Half-Danes minus Hnæf.

Finn's motive for killing his brother-in-law has never been considered, partly because most scholars have taken him for an innocent. But he would have cause to remove Hnæf as a potential usurper of his kingdom if he responded to the Half-Danes with the same suspicion that Kentish Britons once entertained of their Germanic mercenaries.[84] Once Hnæf is dead, Finn is free to negotiate with the Half-Danes in the person of Hengest, their Jutish spokesman.

Hengest has long been identified with Hengistus, who played a central part in the eighth- and ninth-century legends of the Jutish settlement of Kent in Bede, the *Historia Brittonum* and *The Anglo-Saxon Chronicle*.[85] Bliss (editing Tolkien) pointed out that Hengistus is not said to be a Jute in any of these sources.[86] On the other hand, Hengistus is not said to belong to any other tribe either. His identification with Jutes in Kent, and thus that of Hengest with the *Eote* in the Episode, is the best possibility. The *Eote* are mentioned four times in this episode, in *Beo* 1072, 1088, 1141 and 1145. What this word means is partly a phonological problem: for 'Jutes' a WS *Yte* or weak *Ytan* would be

---

[84] North, 'Tribal Loyalties', pp. 16–17.

[85] De Vries identifies Hengest with his namesake of the legend of the Jutish settlement of Kent (though Hengistus is nowhere said to be a Jute or anything else): 'Die beiden Hengeste', *ZfdA* 72 (1953), 125–43, esp. 137–8. A. G. van Hamel, however, distinguishes two Hengests: 'Hengest and his Namesake', *Studies in English Philology: a Miscellany in Honor of Frederick Klaeber*, ed. K. Malone and M. B. Ruud (Minneapolis, MN, 1929), pp. 159–71.

[86] Tolkien, *Finn and Hengest*, pp. 168–80.

Ingui's cult remembered

expected in *Beowulf* rather than the Anglian *Eote*, which is unusual; its dative should be *Eotum* rather than the *Eotenum*, strictly 'giants' from *eoten*, governed by *mid* in *Beo* 1145. It is possible that the *-n* infix in the dative *Eotenum* was added on analogy with *Eotena*, genitive of both 'Jutes' and 'giants' in *Beo* 1072, 1088 and 1141, but this explanation is not convincing. Kaske read 'giants', hence 'enemies', in all three instances of *Eote* or *Eotan*, arguing that the Danes started the feud with Finn by using this nickname to insult the Frisians. His evidence is the poetic licence catalogued in Snorri's *Skáldskaparmál* to indicate 'men' with synonyms for gods and giants, the latter as a term of insult.[87] However, as this argument does not explain the coincidence between Hengest and the legendary Hengistus, we should not exclude 'Jutes' in the meanings of these four forms in the Episode.[88]

Tolkien first suggested that there were Jutes on the Frisian side in Finnsburh, because of the resemblance of *Garulf*, the first attacker on Hnæf's hall in the *Fragment* (*Finn* 31), and *Gefwulf*, who is said to rule the *Yte* in *Wid* 26.[89] A new piece of evidence for this hypothesis can be found in the topographical meaning of *inne* later in the Episode: Hengest staying in Frisia to remember 'Eotena bearn inne' ('the sons of giants/ Jutes in this country', *Beo* 1141).[90] In this way, I suggest that the poet of *Beowulf* alludes to Jutes settled in Frisia and to Hengest and his kin, whom he makes both 'Jutes' and 'giants' at the same time: 'Jutes' imagined as a crowd of uncanny people grown out of an archaic race of 'giants'. The potential ambiguity in the oblique forms *Eotenum* once and *Eotena* three times would be enough, perhaps, to help the conflation of *eotenas* and Anglian *Eote* at a semantic level. Thus Hengest and his Jutes would resemble the OIce *jǫtnar*, 'giants', in qualities of remote antiquity, wisdom and malice.

The only innocent in this story is Hildeburh, on whom the poet of *Beowulf* focuses in the aftermath of the Frisian night-time attack. In the morning Hildeburh's son and brother lie dead before her, her former *worolde wynne* ('worldly joys', *Beo* 1080). What has happened? As ever, the poet's lines are densely allusive, but they can be explained if we suppose a conflict of interests between Hildeburh and Finn:

---

[87] Kaske, 'The Finnsburh Episode in *Beowulf*', p. 289.
[88] North, 'Tribal Loyalties', pp. 36–7.   [89] Tolkien, *Finn and Hengest*, pp. 33–4.
[90] North, 'Tribal Loyalties', pp. 18–19.

Heathen gods

> Ne huru Hildeburh   herian þorfte
> Eotena treowe;   (*Beo* 1071–2)[91]

The effect of *huru* is to stress the name of Hildeburh with which it alliterates; not just to intensify an awareness of her suffering described in the lines to come, but in conjunction with the litotes of *ne herian þorfte*, to imply that if not Hildeburh herself, someone else had cause to praise the pledges of the Jutes. Of the two men in previous lines, Finn is the more likely candidate. By the implication of *ne huru Hildeburh*, therefore, Finn needed to praise the pledges, that is to test the loyalty of the Jutes on his side. Hence I suggest that the Jutes in Frisia had put aside their kinship with Hengest and his followers and had chosen to make *treowe* to Finn instead. Perhaps, also in this case, the phrase *Eotena bearn inne* in *Beo* 1141 can be read with emphasis on every word: it was the 'sons of Jutes in this country' who had forgotten their ancestors, betrayed their cousins who had not, and deserved death from Hengest as a result. Thus Hengest and the Scyldings have separate motives for breaking the treaty which Finn's council has devised.

After the oath is sworn and the dead of both sides burnt on a pyre, Finn seems to let most of his Frisian fighters go home to their 'heaburh' ('settlement-mounds' or *terpen*, *Beo* 1125–7).[92] Though Hengest is also free to leave Frisia with his Jutes and any other mercenaries willing to sail with him, he chooses to stay and thus refrains from casting lots:[93]

>   Hengest þa gyt
> wælfægne winter   wunode mid Finne
> [ea]l unhlitme   (eard gemunde)

---

[91] 'Nor did Hildeburh, at any rate, have any need to praise the pledges of the Jutes.'

[92] On *terpen* and on the geography of this (then undyked) region, see H. Halbertsma, *Terpen tussen Vlie en Eems*, 2 vols. (Groningen, 1963) II, 159–207. In the last few years, excavations of the *terp* at Wijnaldum in W. Friesland have produced a fibula and other evidence that this was a high-status site. For a report on this dig with illustrations, and a less convincing attempt to connect *Finn* with *Winiwald* (> *Wijnaldum*) by *Finwald, see Zijlstra, 'Onderzoek Wijnaldum', pp. 17–22.

[93] Gildas says that the 'Saxons' (*Saxi*) who invaded Kent followed the 'omen and auguries' (*omine auguriisque*) that foretold 'according to a sure portent among them' (*certo apud eum praesagio*) that they would live for three hundred years in the new 'homeland' (*patria*) to which their prows headed: *De Excidio*, ed. and trans. Winterbottom, p. 97. In keeping with this legend, I suggest that OE *hlitm* means literally 'casting lots' in *Beo* 1129.

Ingui's cult remembered

> þeah þe he meahte   on mere drifan
> hringedstefnan;   (*Beo* 1127–31)[94]

Hengest has a homeland in mind – Britain – but as autumn gives way to winter, winter to spring, another question takes precedence:

>   he to gyrnwræce
> swiðor þohte   þonne to sælade,
> gif he torngemot   þurhteon mihte,
> þæt he Eotena bearn   inne gemunde.   (*Beo* 1138–41)[95]

Hengest thus wants revenge on the Jutes who fought for Finn against him and against the other Jutes among the Half-Danes. This and not Hnæf's death is probably his 'injury', the first element of *gyrnwræce* (*Beo* 1138). Thus he hopes that while keeping to the word of his oath, he may, without exposing himself, induce the Frisians to break it themselves. This is the only way in which he is prepared to break Finn's treaty and 'remember the sons of the Jutes in this country': to kill them. But Finn has frightened his men into silence with the sword; hence the impasse. Finn's terms are neatly devised, and Hengest is caught by them:

> Swa he ne forwyrnde   woroldrædenne,
> þonne him Hunlafing   hildeleoman,
> billa selest,   on bearm dyde,
> þæs wæron mid Eotenum   ecge cuðe.   (*Beo* 1142–5)[96]

Hengest thus agrees to a Danish plan by which he makes over his command to one of Hnæf's Scylding kinsmen. Elsewhere I have drawn attention to four instances in Scandinavian and Old English literature where a vassal enters the service of his master by taking his proffered sword.[97] Here it

---

[94] 'Hengest still lived with Finn, through a winter stained with slaughter, without casting lots (he had a homeland in mind), al(?)-though he could sail his ring-prowed ship(s) on the ocean.'

[95] 'He thought more strongly of revenge for his injury than of the sea-road: if he could bring about a furious encounter in such a way that he might remember the sons of the Jutes in this country.'

[96] 'So he did not oppose "world rule", when the son of Hunlaf placed a battle-flash, best of blades, into his lap. Its edges were famous among the Jutes [giants].'

[97] North, 'Tribal Loyalties', pp. 29–30. I would here like to correct a mistake I made in these pages: Beowulf himself receives a sword not from Hrothgar, as I said, but from his uncle Hygelac on his return to Geatland (*Beo* 2194).

seems that Hengest enters the service of the son of Hunlaf, one of Hnæf's Scylding kinsmen. If he lets the Scyldings take his command from him in this way, it can only be to relieve himself of liability for the oath. The fact that he, rather than the Danes, swore this oath with Finn (*Beo* 1096–7) suggests that Hunlafing and his family were not liable themselves: the oath, which goes with Hengest's former position, was therefore made null and void. What is missing in Finn's calculations was an awareness of Hengest's private desire for revenge – not on him, but on the Jutes on the Frisian side.

From the beginning the Danes have moved inexorably closer to their objective: first, by getting common quarters with their Jutish allies (*þæt hie healfre geweald wið Eotena bearn agan moston*, *Beo* 1087–8); second, by persuading Hengest there to let them break his oath (*swa he ne forwyrnde*, *Beo* 1142); and third, by using Hengest to reach Finn and kill him in the midst of his retinue. Two other Scyldings, Guthlaf and Oslaf, put the rest of their plan into action: singing of their earlier adventures on the sea to the whole company in Finn's hall, they surreptitiously rouse their own men, begin to recount their story in Frisia (the theme forbidden to them), and taunt the Frisians for their share of misery (*ætwiton weana dæl*, *Beo* 1150). Finn's hall erupts into violence: 'within the breast a turbulent fury could not be contained' (*ne meahte wæfre mod forhabban in hreþre*, *Beo* 1150–1). Hengest now fails to help Finn as his oath demands, but sides unexpectedly with the Danes. On the Danish signal it is probably Hengest who puts Finn to the sword (*Beo* 1152). Finn dies as a 'king among his retinue' (*cyning on corþre*, *Beo* 1153). If no Dane could go near him, then it seems that Finn had come to trust Hengest closely enough, over the winter, for Hengest to be able to stab him without warning on behalf of the Danes, and with their sword. The story ends with the abduction of Hildeburh and the looting of Finn's treasure.

að *and* i[n]cge gold

This reading of the Finnsburh Episode raises some important questions. Why does the oath apparently enable Finn to trust Hengest with his life even to the extent of sending his Frisian fighters home? In the *Historia Brittonum* it is *Hengistus* who arranges a treacherous attack on Vortigern in his hall while their men celebrate *perpetua amicitia* ('everlasting friend-

Ingui's cult remembered

ship').⁹⁸ How, if this is our Hengest, could he break this agreement but still refuse to break the treaty in Finnsburh?

Vortigern was a Christian, Finn and Hengest certainly not (Christ is nowhere mentioned in *Beowulf*). The oath that binds Finn and Hengest to a *fæste frioðuwære* ('firm contract of peace', *Beo* 1096), at least in pretence, would probably be sworn with reference to whichever cult their two leaders had in common. Hence Hengest might break faith with Vortigern, but not with Finn.

Finn's oath is of abiding importance, as was any in Anglo-Saxon times, when perjury was a crime. In the Anglo-Saxon laws *mansworan* ('oath-breakers') are reviled with the same terms as witches, murderers and whores: they must be exiled and the land purged of them.⁹⁹ Penalties are unknown for pagan defaulters, Frisians or others, though in the *Vita S. Wilfridi* of Stephen of Ripon, written between 710 and 720, when Duke Ebroin of the Franks tries to persuade King Aldgisl of the Frisians to break his oath to Bishop Wilfrid and kill him, Aldgisl tears up the letter and says: 'Thus may the Creator (*Creator*) of all things rend and destroy the life and kingdom of him who perjures himself before his god and does not keep the pact he has made! Thus may he tear him to pieces and burn him to ashes!'¹⁰⁰ In that Aldgisl, if this story is true, must have meant a deity other than God by his *Creator*, probably a local reflex of Nerthus, there seems to be a connection between heathen cults and the keeping of one's oath in pre-Christian Frisia.

Finn's pagan oath-ritual is prominent in the Episode: *að wæs geæfned* ('the oath was performed', *Beo* 1107). Fry keeps *að*, the reading of the manuscript, but the commoner reading is *ad* ('pyre'), hence 'the pyre was made ready', because the funeral coincides with the peace ceremony.¹⁰¹ The only instance of a *bær*, 'pyre' being 'prepared' with *geæfnan* is in Beowulf's own funeral (*Beo* 3105–56). As the text makes good sense without emendation, therefore, the transmitted *að* deserves to stay. Oaths are mandatory in *Lex Frisionum*, in which there are five allusions to

---

⁹⁸ *Historia Brittonum*, ed. Lot, p. 97 (ch. 23).
⁹⁹ Liebermann, *Gesetze der Angelsachsen* II, 580–1 (*Meineid*).
¹⁰⁰ *Vita S. Wilfridi*, ed. Levison, pp. 163–263, esp. 220 (ch. 27): 'Sic rerum Creator regnum et vitam in Deo suo periurantis pactumque initum non custodientis scindens destruat et consumens in favillam devellat!'
¹⁰¹ *Finnsburh*, ed. Fry, p. 41.

Heathen gods

swearing oaths on 'saints' relics'.[102] The pre-Christian oath in the Finnsburh Episode is probably sworn on precious symbols too:

> Að wæs geæfned ond i[n]cge gold
> ahæfen of horde.   (Beo 1107–8)[103]

ingesteald

If both *i[n]cge gold* (*Beo* 1107) and *ingesteald* (*Beo* 1155) are thus connected with this god, as seems likely, the gold in Finn's hoard on which Finn and Hengest seem to swear an oath is 'Ingui's gold' (compare *i[n]cge gold* with *hæðen gold*, 'heathen gold', which describes the Dragon's hoard in *Beo* 2276). In the *Germania* of Tacitus, the Frisians are said (ch. 35) to live to the west of the region in which Tacitus houses the Anglii and other Nerthic tribes (ch. 40), and Tacitus lists them neither there nor among the Ingvaeones (ch. 2).[104] Yet, as we have seen, a runic inscription dedicated to *Inguz*, a name which reflects the first element of Tacitus's form *Ingaeuones* or *Inguaeones*, was found in the *terp* at Wijnaldum in West Friesland.[105] In addition, two people in the early tenth-century *Vita S. Vulframni*, a victim of sacrifice and a king's messenger, are both named *Ingomarus*.[106] It appears, therefore, that the Frisians knew the Ing-hypostasis by the early eighth century, if not earlier, and probably earlier than the composition of *Beowulf*.

---

[102] *Lex Frisionum*, ed. and trans. Eckhardt and Eckhardt, pp. 44, 52, 54, 56 and 58.

[103] 'The oath was performed and *Ingui*'s gold lifted out of the hoard.' On *incge* for MS *icge*, see Ball, 'Incge *Beow.* 2577', pp. 409–10. On Freyr's *ingvi*-appellatives, see *AR* I, 367 (§259) and II, 177 (§457).

[104] *Germania*, pp. 273 and 317.

[105] P. C. Boeles, 'Zu den friesischen Runendenkmälern', in *Berichte zur Runenforschung*, ed. H. Arntz, 3 vols. (Giessen, 1939–42) III, 116–22, esp. 119; a fuller description of this amulet can be found in Arntz and Zeiss, *Runendenkmäler des Festlandes*, pp. 413–18, esp. 417; a diagram of the amulet with the runic inscription *Inguz* is in Zijlstra, 'Onderzoek Wijnaldum', p. 59.

[106] *Vita S. Vulframni*, ed. Levison, pp. 657–73, esp. 666 (ch. 7) and 670 (ch. 10). The name *Ingomer/Ingomar*, of the first son of Clovis and Clothild, shows that *ingo-* was a high-status prefix also in Merovingian names. See *Gregorii Historiae*, ed. Krusch and Levison, p. 75 (II.29).

Ingui's cult remembered

Folcwaldan sunu

Finn's father is *Folcwalda* ('ruler of the people', *Beo* 1089 and *Wid* 27). This epithet is identical with the first element of *fólcvaldi goða* ('ruler of the host of gods', *Skí* 3), which is an epithet reserved for Freyr. *Folcwalda* resembles furthermore the phrase *fólkum stýrir* ('he leads peoples', *Húsdrápa* 7) which celebrates Freyr in Baldr's funeral (*Skj* B I, 129, 7). Freyja is reputed to rule (with *ráða*, 'to rule') a place named *Fólcvangr* ('field of the host', *Grím* 14). Some further evidence may be mentioned here. The common word *friðu* in *frioðuwære* ('contract of peace') is cognate with OIce *friðr* in *frið at kaupa* ('to buy a love-contract', *Skí* 19) and in *ár ok friðr* ('peace and plenty'), which is characteristic of the peaceful reigns of Njǫrðr and Freyr in *Ynglinga saga* (chs. 9–10).[107] Of Freyr it is also said in *Gylfaginning* (ch. 24) that 'it is good to invoke him for peace and plenty' (*á hann er gott at heita til árs ok friðar*).[108] Secondly, when the Danes sack Finnsburh they make off with *eal ingesteald eorðcyninges* (*Beo* 1155). Finn's *ingesteald* is unparalleled, but probably meant 'native treasure' to contemporaries before any denotation of 'Ingui's treasure' occurred to them. On the other hand, *ingesteald* could also be taken as the wealth of Njǫrðr and Freyr, proverbial in *Gylfaginning* (chs. 23–4), especially in the line immediately following the extract with *ár ok friðr* above: 'he [Freyr] also rules the wealth of men' (*hann ræðr ok fésælu manna*). The reference to Finn as *eorðcyning* ('earth-/mortal king', *Beo* 1155), could thus parallel the tribute which was loaded into Freyr's mound for three years after his death in *Ynglinga saga* (ch. 10).[109]

swyn ealgylden

Part of the armour placed on Hnæf's funeral pyre is a *swyn ealgylden, eofer irenheard* ('a pig all-golden, a boar iron-hard(?-ened)', *Beo* 1111–12). Bronze and iron boar images were plentiful in Celtic, Roman and Germanic Britain, in which it is possible that a boar-cult associated with Anglo-Saxon counterparts of Ingvi-freyr was identified with earlier Romano-British cults.[110] The *swyn ealgylden* in *Beo* 1112 may be the

---

[107] *Heimskringla I*, ed. Bjarni, pp. 22–5.   [108] *Gylf*, p. 24.
[109] *Heimskringla I*, ed. Bjarni, pp. 24–5.
[110] J. Foster, *Bronze Boar Figurines in Iron Age and Roman Britain*, BAR 39 (Oxford, 1977), 26–8.

Heathen gods

image of a boar on a helmet, as is the case with two Anglian finds, namely the boar image on the Benty Grange helmet and possibly also the unattached Guilden Morden boar image.[111] Whether or not this Frisian *swyn* image is on a helmet, however, the Finnsburh Episode is paralleled in three Old Icelandic sources. First, in the thirteenth-century prose accompanying the poem *Helgakviða Hjǫrvarðssonar*, a work which is probably Norwegian and of the eleventh century, a ceremony is reported (between *HHj* 30 and 31) at which Heðinn swears an oath to Sváva, his brother Helgi's wife: 'In the evening solemn vows were made. A boar was led forward, men laid their hands on him, and then, with a toast with the poet's cup, men made a solemn vow.'[112] Two variant passages in the thirteenth-century *Heiðreks saga ok Hervarar* show the interwoven traditions of sacred pig, gold, winter festival and the councils of wise men. In one passage (ch. 10), it is said that:[113]

Heiðrekr konungr blótaði Frey; þann gǫlt er mestan fekk, skyldi hann gefa Frey; kǫlluðu þeir hann svá helgan, at yfir hans burst skyldi sverja um ǫll stórmál, ok skyldi þeim gelti blóta at sonarblóti; jólaaptan skyldi leiða sonargǫltinn í hǫll fyrir konung ok lǫgðu menn þá hendr yfir burst hans ok strengja heit.[114]

In the other version (ch. 9), it is said that King Heiðrekr:

lét ala gölt mikinn. Hann var svá mikill sem öldungar þeir, er stærstir váru, ok svá fagr, at hvert hár þótti ór gulli vera. Konungrinn leggr hönd sína á höfuð geltinum, en aðra á burst ok sverr þess, at aldri hefir maðr svá mikit af gert við hann, at eigi skuli hann hafa réttan dóm spekinga hans, en þeir tólf skulu gæta galtarins.[115]

[111] Wilson, *Anglo-Saxon Paganism*, pp. 109–10; Wilson attributes the boar images on helmets to Woden.
[112] 'Um qveldit óro heitstrengingar. Var fram leiddr sonargǫltr, lǫgðo menn þar á hendr sínar, oc strengðo menn þá heit at bragafulli.'
[113] *Heiðreks saga*, ed. Jón, pp. 54–5.
[114] 'King Heiðrekr worshipped Freyr; he was obliged to give Freyr the biggest boar he had; they considered the boar to be so holy that in all cases of great importance oaths would be sworn over its bristles, and this was the boar that was sacrificed at the pig-sacrifice; at Yule eve this porker would be led into the hall and before the king; men laid hands on its bristles and made vows.'
[115] *Heiðreks saga*, ed. Turville-Petre and Tolkien, p. 36: 'had a great pig bred, one as huge as the largest bulls, and so beautiful that each hair seemed made of gold. The king puts one hand on the pig's head and the other on his bristles, and swears this, that no matter what a man has done against him, he will get true justice from the king's wise men, and these twelve would watch over the pig.'

Ingui's cult remembered

King Heiðrekr's *réttr dómr spekinga* ('council of wise men') resembles Finn's *weotena dom* of the same meaning (*Beo* 1098), with whom the *sapientes*, to whom part of the *Lex Frisionum* is ascribed, may be culturally related.[116] In addition, Freyr's 'boar' is known from *Gylfaginning* (ch. 49), as *Gullinbursti* ('Golden-Bristles'), the pig that in Snorri's version draws Freyr in a cart to Baldr's pyre in a wild procession of Norse gods.[117] Snorri quotes Úlfr Uggason's *Húsdrápa* (*c.* 985):

> Ríðr á borg til borgar   boðfróðr sonar Óðins
> Freyr ok fólkum stýrir   fyrst ok gulli byrstum. (*Húsdrápa* 7)[118]

This matches the Episode in two details besides the *folc*-epithet already noted: in the pyre and the golden boar.

incge laf *and* ecge mid eotenum cuðe

There is evidence in *Beowulf* that the poet knew of Ingui's sword, comparable to the sword which Freyr gives to his servant Skírnir in *Skí* 9: this sword can be seen in *incge laf* ('Ingui's heirloom', *Beo* 2577), the blade which let Beowulf down in his fight against the Dragon because it *bat unswiðor* ('bit less strongly', *Beo* 2587). Kaske compared also Hengest's blade whose *ecge* ('edges') were *mid eotenum cuðe* ('known among the giants/ Jutes', *Beo* 1145) with Freyr's sword.[119] Skírnir describes the sword as 'that sword which fights by itself against the race of giants' (*þat sverð, er sialft vegiz við iotna ætt*, *Skí* 8).

Swa he ne forwyrnde woroldrædenne

Not only the cult and name but also the epithet of Ingui seem to be mentioned in this story. At first sight the meaning of *woroldræden* (*Beo* 1142) might be left as 'choice of the world' or something similar.[120] Yet the Old Icelandic cognate of *woruld* is associated with Freyr in a story in

---

[116] *Lex Frisionum*, ed. and trans. Eckhardt and Eckhardt, p. 35.
[117] *Gylf*, pp. 46–7.
[118] *Skj* B I, 129, 7: 'Freyr the battle-fertile rides first to the pyre of Óðinn's son on his boar (and he leads peoples), on his boar with bristles of gold.'
[119] Kaske, 'The Finnsburh Episode in *Beowulf*', p. 295.
[120] North, 'Tribal Loyalties', pp. 28–9; on *woroldræden*, see Tolkien, *Finn and Hengest*, pp. 131–2; and Brodeur, 'The Climax of the *Finn* Episode', pp. 313–30.

Ynglinga saga (ch. 10) in which the Swedes kept the mortal Freyr in his mound when they knew he was dead, believing that the good times would last 'for as long as Freyr was in Sweden, and they would not burn him, but called him "god of the world" (*veraldargoð*), and worshipped him mostly for peace and prosperity ever after'.[121] In the fourteenth-century *Flateyjarbók*, the same epithet is found in Óláfr Tryggvason's tale of Freyr to the heathens of the Trondheim region, whose Swedish neighbours 'called him "god of the world" (*veralldar gud*) and worshipped him a long time'.[122]

Further evidence appears in a Lappish reflex of a Scandinavian loanword: *Veralden Rad*, a deity in eighteenth-century Lappish superstition known as 'world ruler'.[123] In this name an archaic second vowel is preserved and *-en* is a native genitive suffix on a par with the ending of OIce *veraldar*. This evidence is late, but given that the plural *ráð* ('ruling powers') denotes 'gods' in Eyvindr's *Hákonarmál* 18, it is likely that Lappish *Veralden Rad* was a loan from a Norse *veraldar ráð* in pre-Christian times. OIce *ráða* is also used of Freyr in Snorri's definition of this god: 'hann *rœðr* fyrir regni ok skíni sólar ok þar með ávexti jarðar' ('he *rules* over rain and sunshine and along with them the growth of the earth').[124] These elements are seemingly cognate with those of the unique OE *woroldrǣden* in the Finnsburh Episode.

Given these three parallels, *woroldrǣden* would appear to be a loan-translation from a contemporary Danish *veraldar ráð* by which the poet of *Beowulf* referred to Ingui, the Anglo-Saxon counterpart of Freyr, as 'world rule'. In another way this compound can perhaps be read as 'condition of the world', a violent repudiation of the *worolde wynne* ('joys of the world', *Beo* 1080) that were Hildeburh's before her brother and son lay dead before her. However, this sense could also be included in the meaning of *woroldrǣden*, a word which seems to be an informed periphrasis for Ingui, a powerful heathen god common to Danes, Frisians

---

[121] *Heimskringla I*, ed. Bjarni, p. 25: 'meðan Freyr væri á Svíþjóð, ok vildu eigi brenna hann ok kǫlluðu hann veraldargoð, blótuðu mest til árs ok friðar alla ævi síðan'.

[122] *Flat* I, 403 (ch. 323): 'kǫlludu hann veralldar gud; ok blotudu hann langa æfui'.

[123] Other terms, with Norse forms italicized, are as follows: '*Veralden Rad*ien', 'Chierva *Rad*ien', '*Ver alld*en-Ollma', 'Maylmen*rad*ien'. All names mean 'World Ruler'; I take this information from Tolley, 'Germanic and Finnic Myths', pp. 110–11; see also Tolley, 'Oswald's Tree', pp. 161–2.

[124] *Gylf*, p. 24.

and Jutes. Why Hengest should fear his oath can thus be explained if we accept the presence of Ingui in this *Episode* here and in the *i[n]cge gold* on which Hengest swore the oath. For it is shown in *Flateyjarbók* and in the late thirteenth-century *Hrafnkels saga Freysgoða* that the 'stallion' signified in OE *hengest*, OIce *hestr*, was another sacred animal of Freyr.[125] Hengest would thus have cause to fear an oath made on *i[n]cge gold*, if the cult of Ingui was invested in his name.

CONCLUSION

The classical and Old Norse–Icelandic evidence cited so far in chs. 2–3 suggests that a certain *Ing-* was the first-century hypostasis of Nerthus and that *Ingui* was the Anglian reflex of this god. Given that spring in the antique Roman and Norse calendars was the time of sowing and of the orgiastic tour of a phallic god such as Liber or Ingvi-freyr, Ing in *The Old English Rune Poem* may reflect the existence of similar spring festivals also in pre-Christian England. The widespread evidence of *ylfe* in the Anglo-Saxon tradition, together with the association of *ælfsiden* with Satan in *The Christian Ritual against Elves* and that of *Hinieldus* with Belial in Alcuin's letter to Speratus, shows that the early Anglo-Saxon church may have identified Ingui or Ing with the devil. Finally, I suggest that the roles of *ingefolc* in *Exodus* and *i[n]cge gold* in *Beowulf* represent the attempt of Anglian poets to attribute Ingui or Ing and his type of paganism to their lost kinsmen in continental Germania. The figure with whose help the church overcame this 'god of the world' in England will be the subject of the next two chapters.

[125] *Flat* I, 400–1 (ch. 322); *Hrafnkels saga*, ed. Jón, pp. 100 (ch. 3) and 123 (ch. 6). In ch. 3 of this saga, Hrafnkell swears an oath by his god Freyr and keeps this even to the price it demands, 'in the belief that nothing comes of men who let their own sworn oaths rebound on them' (*við þann átrúnað, at ekki verði at þeim mǫnnum, er heitstrengingar fella á sik*); when he throws Hrafnkell's horse Freyfaxi from a cliff into a pool in ch. 6, Þorkell makes clear on whose account the animal is destroyed: 'It will be appropriate that he [Freyr] who owns him takes him back' (*mun þat makligt, at sá taki við honum, er hann á*).

4
Woden's witchcraft

The formal kinship between OE *Woden*, OHG *Uuodan* and OIce *Óðinn* provides a basis for attempting to explain the Anglo-Saxon Woden with reference to Óðinn, his better documented Scandinavian counterpart. So far Óðinn has not figured prominently in my picture of Ingvi-freyr and the Vanir. Yet in Old Norse–Icelandic literature Óðinn is bound to the Vanir in a relationship in which their antagonism and cooperation are curiously mixed. This chapter is an attempt to show a connection, through Óðinn, between Woden and the witchcraft of 'Vanir' cults. I shall first suggest that the gods Woden and Óðinn both derive from Mercury; then, after discussing the evidence in *Vǫluspá* of the ancient cult-war between Óðinn and the Vanir, I shall cite more evidence from which it may be deduced that Óðinn derives part of his magic from these gods; finally, I shall discuss Woden's witchcraft in *The Nine Herbs Charm* and in the Exeter Book *Maxims*. My conclusion will be that Woden had his own role as the father of dead kings in an Anglo-Saxon 'hall of the slain'. This conclusion is supported by what at first seems to be a far-flung variety of sources, but none the less, it may help to explain how Woden got his role as the father of English kings.

THE CULT OF WODEN IN ENGLAND

The Germanic cult of Woden, Uuodan or Óðinn probably originated as the cult of Mercury in Roman Gaul. Through warfare and trade between the Gauls, Romans and Germanic tribes, Mercury, a god of travel and trade in this and other worlds, seems to have crossed the Rhine into northern Germania and spread into the North Sea coastal area, England and southern Scandinavia by the end of the fifth

Woden's witchcraft

century.¹ *Wodanaz (henceforth *Wodan*) would have been the ethnic name for this imported foreign god.² The association of the Norse god Óðinn with runes would thus appear to reflect the derivation of this god from the figure of Mercury *inventor artium*, which is Caesar's term for Mercury among the early Gauls in *c*. 54 BC:³

Deum maxime Mercurium colunt. Huius sunt plurima simulacra, hunc omnium inventorem artium ferunt, hunc viarum atque itinerum ducem, hunc ad quaestus pecuniae mercaturosque habere vim maximam arbitrantur. Post hunc Apollinam et Martem et Iovem et Minervam.⁴

In *Germania* (ch. 9), Tacitus follows Caesar's first sentence almost word for word (*deorum maxime Mercurium colunt*) and adds that Mercury is offered human sacrifice.⁵ But these words were not Caesar's; Caesar borrowed them from Herodotus's comment on the Thracian princes who worshipped Hermes and also claimed descent from this god.⁶ That Caesar did not copy the Thracian claim of divine descent, however, may show that he knew that Mercury was not taken for an ancestor in Gaul. There is no evidence that *Uuodan* had this role in southern Germanic territory when he was cited as a god of the *Suaevi* at Bregenz (near Lake Constance) in the early seventh century.⁷ That *Uoden* emerges as an ancestor a century later in Bede (*HE* I.15), then in the Anglian regnal lists of the later eighth century, is thus a mystery peculiar to the Anglo-Saxons.

Some English placenames show that Woden was probably worshipped as a god by the Anglo-Saxons, mostly in southern England, in the early

---

¹ Helm, *Wodan*, pp. 60–71.
² *Ibid.*, pp. 13–16; *AR* II, 27–9 (§§361–2).
³ Bremmer, 'Hermes–Mercury and Woden–Odin', pp. 409–19, esp. 418–19.
⁴ *C. Iuli Caesaris Commentariorum Libri VII de Bello Gallico*, ed. R. Du Pontet (Oxford, 1900) VI.17 (no page nos.): 'Most of all they worship the god Mercury. There are many images of him, and they say that he is the discoverer of all arts, the ruler of roads and journeys, and they believe that he has the greatest power in getting wealth, and for merchants. After him come Apollo, Mars, Jupiter and Minerva.'
⁵ *Germania*, p. 284: 'of their gods they worship Mercury most of all'.
⁶ *Herodoti Historiae*, ed. C. Hude, 3rd ed. (Oxford, 1927) V.7 (no page nos.): 'they worship Hermes most among their gods' (σέβονται Ἑρμέην μάλιστα θεῶν).
⁷ *Ionae Vitae Sanctorum*, ed. B. Krusch, MGH, SRG 37 (Hanover and Leipzig, 1905), 213 (*Vita Columbani*, I.27).

Heathen gods

seventh century.[8] Woden's cult in England at this time was probably a late reflection of the influence of this god in the previous four centuries over western and southern regions of continental Germania. Although a belief in Woden may have been dying out in England by the beginning of the eighth century, the memory of this figure did not disappear.[9] *Uoden* is not only copied by Bede into a royal genealogy (*HE* I.15), but may be concealed (as part of an indigenous motif) in Bede's story of Cædmon the cowherd from the monastery of Whitby (*c*. 657–80), whom a dream-visitant miraculously inspired to compose a creation-hymn in the cowbyre where he slept (*HE* IV.24).[10] The speaker of *Vǫluspá*, a heathen creation-poem probably composed in Iceland in *c*. 1000, refers to a request from Óðinn to sing a creation poem:

> vildo, at ec, Valfǫðr, vel fyrtelia
> forn spiǫll fira, þau er fremst um man.   (*Vsp* 1)[11]

OIce *Valfǫðr* ('Father of the Slain') is one of many by-names attributed to Óðinn in Eddic and Scaldic poetry, in which Óðinn was regarded as the Norse god of secrets of the dead and also the god of poetry. Was Uoden implicit in a similar guise in the composition of Cædmon's *Hymn*? A prominent theme of Bede's story is the rare creation genre by which Cædmon first raised himself above his fellow peasants and ensured that 'he could never compose any kind of frivolous or utterly empty poem'.[12] As in the story of the vision of King Edwin (*HE* II.12), Bede does not say

---

[8] Gelling, *Signposts to the Past*, pp. 154–61 (esp. 160: distribution map): Wansdyke (Wilts.), Wednesbury (Staffs.), Wednesfield (Staffs.), Wensley (Derby.), *Woddesgeat* (Wilts.), *Wodnesbeorg* (Wilts.), *Wodnesdene* (Wilts.), *Wodnesfeld* (Essex), *Wodneslawe* (Beds.) and Woodnesborough (Kent). See further M. Gelling, *Place-Names in the Landscape: the Geographical Roots of Britain's Place-Names* (London, 1984); and Wilson, *Anglo-Saxon Paganism*, pp. 5–21, esp. 16–20.

[9] See Philippson, *Germanisches Heidentum*, pp. 146–56; Meaney, 'Woden in England', p. 106; cf. *Corpus Glossary*, ed. Lindsay, p. 114.197 (*Mercurium: Woden*).

[10] The St Petersburg text is quoted, edited and discussed by E. G. Stanley, 'New Formulas for Old: *Cædmon's Hymn*', in *Pagans and Christians*, ed. Hofstra, Houwen and MacDonald, pp. 131–48, esp. 132–3. A Latin source for this motif of poetic inspiration through a dream is discussed in Clemoes, *Interactions of Thought and Language*, pp. 242–3, n. 26.

[11] 'You wanted me, Father of the Slain, to recount in a good manner the ancient stories of men, those that I remember from furthest back'; see North, *Pagan Words*, pp. 15–26.

[12] *HE* IV.23 (p. 414): 'nil unquam friuoli et superuacui poematis facere potuit'.

who this apparition was at the moment he appears. I suggest that Bede's reticence in the story of Cædmon is careful, rather than careless, and shows that Bede may have adapted a story which he inherited with the surviving *Hymn*, in which a British–Anglian poet had been invited to transfer the source of his poetic gift to God, by first detaching it from Uoden.

The Christian position with Woden in later Anglo-Saxon England was politically rather than spiritually ambiguous. Towards the end of the Anglo-Saxon period, Ælfric, adapting a passage on Mercury in Martin of Braga's *De correctione rusticorum*, characterized a Danish Mercury in his *De falsis diis*:

> Sum man wæs gehaten Mercurius on life,
> se wæs swiðe facenfull and swicol on dædum,
> and lufode eac stala and leasbregdnyssa.   (lines 133–5)[13]

Ælfric in *De falsis diis* also explains that mountain sacrifices are offered to Mercury, as if Mercury were the Scandinavian Óðinn: in stanza 30 of the Old Norse poem *Atlakviða*, which is datable to the late ninth or early tenth century, the phrase *Sigtýs berg* ('Victory-Týr's mountain') appears to contain an allusion to mountains as Óðinn's place of worship. Then Ælfric names the Norse god:

> Ðes god wæs [a]rwyrðe betwyx eallum hæþenum,
> and he is Oðon gehaten oðrum naman on Denisc.
>   (lines 139–40)[14]

Elsewhere Ælfric also alluded to *Oðon*, an anglicized form of *Óðinn*, in his description of Mercury as one of the forms in which the devil appeared to St Martin of Tours in his cell.[15] Neither Ælfric nor Wulfstan, who abbreviated *De falsis diis* into a homily of his own, brings the Old English name *Woden* into his discussion of Mercury, or of the English form of *Mercurii dies*. To Pope, Ælfric's modern editor, this omission is 'a deliberate reticence' which can be explained by Ælfric's reluctance to

---

[13] *Homilies of Ælfric*, ed. Pope II, 684: 'There was a man called Mercury in his life who was very full of crime and treacherous in his deeds and also loved stealing and dishonesty.'

[14] 'This god was venerated among all heathens and by another name he is called "Oðon" in Danish.'

[15] *Ælfric's Lives of Saints*, ed. Skeat II, 265, line 715 (XXXI.xxiv).

imply that his own ancestors were heathens like the Danes.[16] By witholding the Old English form of *Oðon* in *De falsis diis*, however, Ælfric may also be refraining from informing his readers that Oðon was the same figure from whom his patrons Æthelweard (d. 1000) and Æthelmær (d. 1017), not to mention King Æthelræd (978–1016), could claim descent.[17]

Æthelweard himself, in his Latin translation of an early *Chronicle* text, partially anglicizes *Óðinn*, whose Scandinavian cult he cites as contemporary, as *Vvothen* three times and *Vuoddan* and *Wothen* each once.[18] Another allusion to the Norse Óðinn is probably contained in *The Old English Rune Poem*:

> [Os] byþ ordfruma   ælcre spræce,
> wisdomes wraþu   and witena frofur
> and eorla gehwam   eadnys and tohiht.   (*Rune* 10–12)[19]

The Old Icelandic Rune Poem is more explicit with this runic symbol: '*Áss* is the ancient "god" and warrior–prince of Ásgarðr and lord of Valhǫll'.[20] Maureen Halsall doubts that *os* refers to Óðinn in *The Old English Rune Poem*, for she says that a Christian poet could not 'knowingly assist in reinforcing the reputation of the Germanic pantheon'.[21] Yet if Ælfric or Æthelweard had no intention of glorifying *Oðon* by recording his name, it is unlikely that the anonymous poet of *The Old English Rune Poem* was intending to corrupt Christians by hinting at Woden's legendary status with a pun on the Latin and Anglo-Saxon meanings (respectively, 'mouth' and 'heathen god') of the word *os*. Elsewhere I have suggested that Woden is latent as the patron of the *anhaga* in *The Wanderer*, corresponding to Mercury in his role as the friend of Ulysses in *De consolatione Philosophiae* (IV, met. 3), of which treatise *The Wanderer* may be a riddle with 'Boethius' as its solution.[22] Whatever the date of *The Wanderer*, at any rate, any

---

[16] *Homilies of Ælfric*, ed. Pope II, 715.
[17] Johnson, 'Euhemerization versus Demonisation', pp. 59–61.
[18] *Chronicle of Æthelweard*, ed. Campbell, pp. 7, 9, 17, 25 and 33.
[19] *Old English Rune Poem*, ed. Halsall, p. 86: '"mouth/*Áss*" is the point of every utterance, support of wisdom and comfort of wise men and the blessedness and hope of each nobleman'.
[20] Quoted *ibid*., p. 184: '(óss) er aldingautr ok ásgarðs jöfurr/ok valhallar vísi'.
[21] *Ibid*., pp. 109–11.
[22] North, 'Boethius and the Mercenary', pp. 95–7.

superstitious belief in Woden in England had probably waned by the tenth century.

ÓÐINN AND THE VANIR

The witchcraft of the Germanic Mercury appears to be associated with 'Vanir' deities in Old High German and Old Norse–Icelandic sources. Firstly, there is an isolated reference to Uuodan's medicinal skill in *The Second Merseburg Charm*, in a German manuscript from the first part of the tenth century:

> Phol ende Uuodan   vuorun zi holza;
> dû uuart demo balderes volon   sîn vuoz birenkit;
> thû biguolen Sinhtgunt,   Sunna era suister;
> thû biguolen Friia,   Volla era suister;
> thû biguolen Uuodan,   sô hê uuola conda:
> sôse bênrenkî   sôse bluotrenkî,
> sôse lidrenkî;
> bên zi bêna,   bluot zi bluoda,
> lid zi geliden,   sôse gelîmida sîn![23]

The word *phol* may mean 'foal', as in *volon* on line 2, yet these two words are spelt differently and the phrase *demo balderes* seems to refer to one of two riders. As Freyr's horse is called 'Bloody-Hoof' (*Blóðughófi*) in the fifteenth-century *Alsvinnsmál*, it is possible that Phol, the *balder* in *The Second Merseburg Charm*, refers to an Old High German version of Freyr.[24] It is, first, the named female deities that heal the injured horse in this poem; not Uuodan, whose role is apparently to follow these deities. Secondly, witchcraft is a distinctive feature of Óðinn, whose many magic skills Snorri describes in the first few chapters of *Ynglinga saga*. In stanzas

---

[23] AR I, 169 (§451): 'Phol and Wodan went to the wood. Then was wrenched the foot of the lord's foal. Then Sinhtgunt made a charm, [and] her sister Sunna; then Friia made a charm, [and] her sister Volla; then Wodan made a charm, as he well knew how: as for bone wrench, so for blood wrench, so for limb wrench; bone to bone, blood to blood, limb to limbs, so let them be limed together!'

[24] AR II, 171–2 (§§452–3); *Edda*, ed. Neckel and rev. Kuhn, p. 320. For theories connecting Phol to Freyr (and Baldr) via Fulla and Freyja, see F. Genzmer, 'Die Götter des zweiten Merseburger Zauberspruchs', *ANF* 63 (1948), 55–72; and F. R. Schröder, 'Balder und der zweite Merseburger Zauberspruch', *GRM* 34 (1953), 161–83; Green (*Carolingian Lord*, pp. 15–17) only hints at the possibility of this identification.

138–45 of *Hávamál*, which Snorri does not quote but may have known, there is evidence that magic was not thought to be Óðinn's aboriginal property, but that Óðinn learned his secrets from the giants in the world of the dead. By hanging himself in *Háv* 138–9, Óðinn apparently intended to die and return from the world of the dead.[25] This shamanistic journey appears to be described in the following stanzas, at the heart of *Hávamál*:[26]

> Veit ec, at ec hecc   vindgameiði á
>   nætr allar nío,
> geiri undaðr   oc gefinn Óðni,
>   siálfr siálfom mér,
> á þeim meiði,   er mangi veit,
>   hvers hann af rótom renn.
>
> Við hleifi mic sældo   né við hornigi,
>   nýsta ec niðr;
> nam ec upp rúnar,   œpandi nam,
>   fell ec aptr þaðan.   (*Háv* 138–9)[27]

It is hard to exclude the possibility of influence from the story of Christ's crucifixion on these lines.[28] Yet it is likely that this influence, if it was made, would have augmented a sacrificial motif already existing within a heathen cult. When the poet of *Baldrs Draumar*, a work probably of twelfth-century date, stylizes the same journey as Óðinn's ride to Niflhel on Sleipnir, Óðinn's eight-legged horse, he calls Óðinn *gautr* ('sacrificed-victim', *Bdr* 2), an epithet which has nothing to do with Christianity.[29] In *Hávamál*, Óðinn learns nine great chants from his mother's (presumably dead) brother, drinks from the precious mead (*Háv* 140) and begins to 'grow teeming and be fertile and wise' (*frævaz oc fróðr vera*, *Háv* 141). This adjective *fróðr* may show that Óðinn's cult had appropriated an

---

[25] R. Pipping, 'Oden i galgen', *SNF* 18 (1928), 1–13; A. G. van Hamel, 'Óðinn Hanging on the Tree', *Acta Philologica Scandinavica* 7 (1932), 260–88.

[26] North, *Pagan Words*, pp. 122–44, esp. 132–8.

[27] 'I know that I hung on the windy branch for nine whole nights, wounded with a spear and given to Óðinn, myself to myself, on the branch that no-one knows from whose roots it runs. They revived me neither with a loaf nor with a horn; I peered down; I took up runic staves, screaming I learnt runic secrets; I fell back from there/then.'

[28] See Bremmer, 'Hermes–Mercury and Woden–Odin', pp. 411 and 418.

[29] On the meaning of this word, see Kuhn, 'Gaut', pp. 417–33 (repr. in his *Kleine Schriften* II, 364–77).

epithet of Ingvi-freyr, who is elsewhere named *inn fróði afi* ('the wise-fertile grandfather' (or 'heir'), *Skí* 1 and 2). Óðinn thus appears to need the help of the Vanir in order to return from the world of the dead.

Óðinn also learns part of his witchcraft from the Vanir in Snorri's account of him in *Ynglinga saga*. Having described the Æsir–Vanir peace-agreement and the variety of Óðinn's magic in earlier chapters of this saga, Snorri writes that Freyja 'was the first to teach *seiðr*, common among the Vanir, to the Æsir'.[30] It is the power of *seiðr* (with which, as we have seen, OE *-siden* is cognate) that forces the Æsir to terms with the Vanir in the first war of the world (*Vsp* 21–4). Snorri also focuses on Óðinn's use of *seiðr* in gaining powers and bringing good or bad fortune to men: 'And yet so much perversity accompanies this magic when it is performed that men did not think it a matter of no shame to engage in it, and this skill was taught to goddesses.'[31] Here it is worth noting that in *Vsp* 28–9 Óðinn cannot divine the future himself but must get this knowledge from a sibyl. Óðinn's link with the Vanir is also implicit in the late tenth century in Kormákr's tag 'Yggr practised *seiðr* to get Rindr' (*seið Yggr til Rindar, Sigurðardrápa* 3).[32] This is a story that Saxo narrates most fully as Othinus's desperate attempt in a woman's costume to seduce Rinda after the death of Balderus, his son, in order to beget another son to avenge Balderus on his slayer Hotherus.[33] As we shall see, Óðinn uses *seiðr* to regenerate not only himself, but also kings and princes from the dead. In the meantime, however, I shall use the Norse tradition of Óðinn's witchcraft to throw light on Woden's role in *The Nine Herbs Charm* and in the Exeter Book *Maxims*.

'ÞA GENAM WODEN VIIII WULDORTANAS'

The Nine Herbs Charm is a text which embodies Hellenistic Greek and Latin medicine, Roman plant-names and Irish magic, not excluding Germanic lore which may be either Anglo-Saxon or Norse in origin.[34] I quote the text from Grattan and Singer:

---

[30] *Heimskringla I*, ed. Bjarni, p. 13 (*Ynglinga saga*, ch. 4): 'kenndi fyrst með Ásum seið, sem Vǫnum var títt'.
[31] *Ibid.*, p. 19 (ch. 7): 'En þessi fjǫlkyngi, er framið er, fylgir svá mikil ergi, at eigi þótti karlmǫnnum skammlaust við at fara, ok var gyðjunum kennd sú íþrótt.'
[32] *Skj* B I, 69.   [33] *GD*, pp. 70–1.
[34] *Lacnunga*, ed. Grattan and Singer, pp. 23–79, esp. 52–62.

Heathen gods

> Þis is seo wyrt ðe wergulu hatte;
> ðas onsænde seolh ofer sæs hrygc
> ondan attres oþres to bote.
> Ðas VIIII magon wið nygon attrum.
> Wyrm com snican, toslat he *m*an [MS *nan*];
> ða genam woden VIIII wuldortanas,
> sloh ða þa næddran, þæt heo on VIIII tofleah.
> Þær geændode æppel 7 attor,
> þæt heo næfre ne wolde on hus bugan.
> Fille 7 finule, fela mihtigu twa,
> þa wyrtu gesceop witig drihten,
> halig on heofonu[m], þa he hongode;
> sette 7 sænde on VII worulde
> earmum and eadigum eall[um] to bote. (*MCharm* 2.27–40)[35]

Grattan and Singer note that chervil and fennel, said specifically to have been created by the hanging Lord, are the only plant-names of Latin origin among the nine; the 'seven worlds' to which the Lord sends these two (or perhaps the seven other plants), refer to the planets, 'an intrusive idea in a Northern Pagan setting'.[36] Nine plant-names can be seen before Woden appears with his nine *wuldortanas* ('glory-twigs') to defeat the serpent. With reference to the fruit-bearing boughs of Tacitus's *Germania*, inscribed with runes in divination, Grattan and Singer take Woden's *wuldortanas* to be emblems of fate.[37] However, the context of *The Nine Herbs Charm* suggests instead that *wuldortanas* is a collective name for the plants whose names lie immediately before. The *wyrm* ('serpent'), as it

---

[35] *Ibid.*, pp. 151–5 ('3' written as 'g'): 'This is the root which is called Wergule (crab-apple). This a seal sent over the sea's back as a cure for the malice of another poison. These nine herbs against nine poisons. A serpent came [fol. 161a/161b] sneaking up, he tore in two a man; then Woden took nine glory-twigs, then struck the adder, so that she flew into nine parts. There apple and poison brought it about that she would never move into a house. Chervil and fennel, two many-powered ones, these roots a wise Lord creàted, holy in heaven, when he hung; he established them and sent them into seven places in the world as a remedy for all men, poor and rich alike.'

[36] *Ibid.*, p. 155, nn. 1 and 2.

[37] *Ibid.*, pp. 54 and 151 (plant-names according to Entry LXXIX): Mugwort; Waybroad; Stune; Stithe; Attorlothe; Maythe; Wergule; [Fille]; [Fennel]. *Germania*, p. 285 (ch. 10): 'they slice into strips a branch cut down from a nut-bearing tree' (*uirgam frugiferae arbori decisam in surculos amputant*).

toslat ('tore in two') a man, may be reminiscent of the dragon *Níðhǫggr* ('Malice-Striker') in *Vǫluspá*; and of the *naðr fránn, neðan frá Niðafiǫllom* ('glittering adder, from down below the mountains of his ?descendants', *Vsp* 66), that sucks the blood from corpses in the world of the dead (*Vsp* 39). It is appropriate that the cure for snake-bite should come from the same region.

Though the hanging Lord is a Christian motif, the Lord's creation of herbs on the gallows is reminiscent of Óðinn's acquisition of *rúnar* in *Hávamál*: Óðinn *nam upp rúnar* in his nine nights of death in *Háv* 139, while Woden *genam VIIII wuldortanas* (*MCharm* 2.32), presumably from nine worlds of the dead. This is not to say that the hanging Lord of *The Nine Herbs Charm* was understood to be Woden rather than Christ – far from it; but I suggest that the continuing need to practise herbal magic within Christianity led this poet to characterize Christ's sacrifice as if it were Woden's, because the extraction of curative herbs from Hell does not appear to be a biblical motif.

The motif of *wyrtu gesceop* (*MCharm* 2.37) is paralleled in the Circe episode of the Homeric *Odyssey*. There we see Hermes appearing on Circe's isle to save Odysseus from the potions with which Circe has already bewitched Odysseus's men. When Odysseus relates this story to Alcinous in Phaeacia, he says that 'golden-wanded Hermes' ('Ερμείας χρυσόρραπις) intercepted him on the way to Circe's house.[38] Hermes at first merely warns Odysseus by reminding him of the danger from Circe, who has turned his crew to swine. Then he offers to help, giving Odysseus immediately 'a lucky herb' (φαρμακον ἐσθλὸν, *Od*. X.288). If Odysseus throws this herb into Circe's potion, he will stay immune from its effects when she strikes him 'with her long staff' (περιμήκεϊ ῥάβδῳ, *Od*. X.293). Odysseus must then threaten to kill her with his sword, then give in to her next request, to sleep with her, only after exacting from her 'the great oath of the blessed ones' (μακάρων μέγαν ὅρκον, *Od*. X.299) that she will do no further harm to him.

> Thus having spoken, straightaway the slayer of Argus
> furnished me with a herb that he had pulled from the earth,
> showing me its properties. It had a black root, but its flower

---

[38] *The Odyssey of Homer*, ed. W. B. Stanford, 2 vols. (New York, 1959) I, 158 (X.277).

Heathen gods

looked like milk: 'Mandrake' the gods call it. To dig it up
is dangerous for mortal men, but the gods can do anything.

(*Od.* X.302–6)[39]

Mortals risk their lives digging up the moly because this root lies buried
in the world of the dead. Only Hermes the psychopomp here in Homer,
Óðinn the shaman in *Hávamál* and, by implication, the Lord in the
manner of Woden in *The Nine Herbs Charm* can return from the world of
the dead with their secrets. Though the word *genam* is linked with Woden
in this Old English text, *nam* and *nam upp* with Óðinn in *Háv* 139, in *The
Nine Herbs Charm* Woden does no more than use the medicine that only
Christ has the privilege of bringing into the light of day.

'WODEN WORHTE WEOS'

Woden and idols

Woden is contrasted with God the Creator in a metrically anomalous line
in the second section of *Maxims I*. Following the statement that the
eucharist (the body and blood of Christ) is for a holy man, sin for a
heathen, the poet says:

> Woden worhte weos,   wuldor alwalda,
> rume roderas;   þæt is rice god,
> sylf soðcyning,   sawla nergend.   (*Max I*, II, 132–4)[40]

The poet proceeds to show how God gave us everything we need in order
to live and how at the end he will rule all mankind. Then the Lord's rule
is re-affirmed: 'Þæt is meotud sylfa' ("The Lord himself is this').

E. A. Philippson first noted that the lines from *Maxims I* are modelled
on Ps. XCV.5.[41] Jerome's Psalter *iuxta Hebraeos* at this point reads *Omnes*

---

[39] *Ibid.* I, 158:

"Ὣς ἄρα φωνήσας πόρε φάρμακον ἀργεϊφόντης
ἐκ γαίης ἐρύσας, καί μοι φύσιν αὐτοῦ ἔδειξε.
ῥίζῃ μὲν μέλαν ἔσκε, γάλακτι δὲ εἴκελον ἄνθος·
μῶλυ δέ μιν καλέουσι θεοί· χαλεπὸν δέ τ' ὀρύσσειν
ἀνδράσι γε θνητοῖσι· θεοὶ δέ τε πάντα δύνανται.

[40] 'Woden made idols, the Almighty [made] glory, the roomy heavens; this is a powerful
god, himself the true king, healer of souls.'

[41] Philippson, *Germanisches Heidentum*, p. 154.

enim dii populorum [sc. sunt] sculptilia, Dominus autem caelos fecit ('For all the gods of the gentiles [are] carved things, the Lord however made the heavens'). The Roman version is the same, though it reads *daemonia* ('demons'), in variation of *sculptilia* ('carved things'). Ps. XCV.5 was probably one of the first biblical texts to be preached to the heathen Anglo-Saxons, for Pope Gregory, instigator of the Anglo-Saxon conversion, assumed that they worshipped idols in his letters to Mellitus and Æthelberht (*HE* I.30 and 32). Pope Boniface, when he wrote to Edwin of Northumbria in *c.* 625, entreated him to renounce idols and believe in the Trinity, and then quoted Ps. XCV.5 in the Roman version. Boniface's message against idolatry was doubtless repeated many times in the seventh and eighth centuries in England.

Idolatry is a theme in *Juliana*, a poem with a runic acrostic in its final lines attributing its authorship to 'Cynewulf'. Juliana is martyred after refusing to worship the Roman gods:

> Næfre þu gelærest   þæt ic leasingum,
> dumbum ond deafum   deofolgieldum,
> gæsta geniðlum   gaful onhate,
> þam wyrrestum   wites þegnum,
> ac ic weorðige   wuldres ealdor
> middengeardes   ond mægenþrymmes.   (*Jul* 149–54)[42]

Ælfric's Life of St Eugenia also incorporates the Roman Ps. XCV.5 with the Old English words *Ealle þære hæðenra godas syndon deofla. and dryhten soðlice heofonas geworhte* ('All the gods of the heathen are devils and the Lord truly made the heavens', lines 38–9).[43] Similarly, the Paris Psalter:

> Syndon ealle hæþenu godu   hildedeoful;
> heofonas þænne worhte   halig drihten.   (PPs 95.5)[44]

R. L. Ramsay concluded that the poetic psalms (51–150) of the Paris Psalter are not connected with the Latin text written in the same codex, and that they seem to render 'an early and distinctively Anglian type of

---

[42] 'You will never teach me to promise tribute to lies, deaf and dumb images of devils, the enemies of the spirit, the worst servants of torment; but I will adore the king of glory and of the earth and of the heavenly host.'
[43] *Ælfric's Lives of Saints*, ed. Skeat, p. 26.
[44] 'All heathen gods are devils of battle; then the holy Lord made the heavens.'

the Roman version'.⁴⁵ If so, *hildedeoful* possibly rendered *daemonia* rather than *sculptilia*. Accordingly *hilde-* is the poet's addition, in alliteration with *hæþenu*.

What Anglian tradition conceived of demons as 'devils of battle'? Audrey Meaney takes Woden's making of *weos* in *Max I* (II, 132a) to be a confusion with his likely former status as an idol, but a parallel can be found in an eleventh-century gloss on the Roman Ps. XCV.5 in the 'Salisbury Psalter' (Salisbury Cathedral 150), which reads 'ealle godas ðeoda *woddreamas* drihten witodlice heofenas worhte'.⁴⁶ Here *woddream* is a variant of OE *wodendream* ('fury'). Furthermore, in his *Gesta Danorum*, Saxo states that the god Othinus restored a desecrated statue of himself and 'by amazing craftsmanship made it respond with a voice to human touch'.⁴⁷ In the light of this late Danish parallel to *Max I* (II, 132a) and the relatively frequent reference to the Roman *daemonia* in Old English versions of Ps. XCV.5, I suggest that the words *Woden worhte weos* allude to an Anglian legend in which 'Woden made demons' by conjuring idols into life.

Óðinn and 'tree-men'

In an early, probably tenth-century, part of *Hávamál* is a stanza (*Háv* 49) in which the speaker gives his clothes to two wooden men in a field. I suggest that this stanza has a twofold meaning: clothes make a man; and less obviously, Óðinn's gift of armour conjures an idol into a demon. In order to sustain this reading of *Háv* 49 it will be necessary to make a long detour through various Old Icelandic material.

The god Óðinn appears to be the speaker characterized in stanzas 13–14 and 96–108 of *Hávamál*; these characterizations occur without explicit directions in the text; therefore, in the absence of a more suitable candidate for the narration of a specific, rather than generalized, incident in *Háv* 49, it is plausible to take the narrator of this stanza as Óðinn.⁴⁸

---

⁴⁵ R. L. Ramsay, 'The Latin Text of the Paris Psalter: a Collation and some Conclusions', *American Journal of Philology* 41 (1920), 147–76, esp. 174 and 176.

⁴⁶ Meaney, 'Woden in England', p. 110; *The Salisbury Psalter*, ed. C. Sisam and K. Sisam, EETS o.s. 242 (London, 1959), 212: 'all gods of the nations [are] *furies*, the Lord indeed made the heavens'.

⁴⁷ *GD*, p. 25 (I.vii): 'etiam mira artis industria ad humanos tactus vocalem reddidit'.

⁴⁸ See North, *Pagan Words*, pp. 122–44, esp. 139–43.

Woden's witchcraft

Stanza 49 follows a stanza on the theme of giving; but the generosity its poet describes could be called eccentric:

> Váðir mínar   gaf ec velli at
> tveim trémǫnnom;
> reccar þat þóttuz,   er þeir rift hǫfðo,
> neiss er nøcqviðr halr.   (Háv 49)[49]

From the theme of human wretchedness at the end of the stanza the poet leads into *Háv* 50, colouring this new theme with an image of a solitary tree or post on a *þorp* ('?mound'). *Mínar* in *Háv* 49 is Óðinn's possessive term and from *váðir mínar* we should therefore understand 'Óðinn's clothes'. In *Akv* 8, the words *váðir heiðingja* ('heathranger's coat') indicate that *váðir* could appear in ninth- to tenth-century Norway (where it is most likely *Atlakviða* was composed), not as a general term for 'clothes' but as a figurative word. Therefore in a part of *Hávamál* which is taken to be of the tenth century, *váðir mínar* can also be understood as a kenning: 'Óðinn's clothes'.[50] The one example of *váðir* qualified by an Óðinn-term signifies 'protective armour': Eyvindr skáldaspillir's *váðir Váfaðar* ('Swinging One's [Óðinn's] clothes', *Hákonarmál* 5).[51] The formulaic pairs *vápn oc váðir* (*Háv* 41) and *wæpen ond gewædu* (*Beo* 292) also point to a common Germanic association of terms. *Herewædu* occurs at *Beo* 1897, and *guðgewædu* six times (with no extant Old Icelandic counterpart).[52] Because it is most likely that Eyvindr skáldspillir in the tenth century borrowed the first line of *Háv* 76 (or 77) for that of his *Hákonarmál* 21, his poem and at least parts of *Hávamál* may have similar frames of reference. Thus *váðir mínar* in *Háv* 49 was probably understood as a kenning for armour.

---

[49] 'I gave my clothes to two wooden men on the field; they seemed princes when they had some clothing: a naked man is ashamed.'

[50] *Hávamál*, ed. Evans, pp. 13–14. OIce *váð* or (mostly) plural *váðir* or *væðr* means 'clothes' in Eddic poetry: *matar oc váða þǫrf* ('need of food and clothing', *Háv* 3); *biartar váðir* ('bright clothes', *Sigsk* 49); *Amma bió til váðar* ('Amma made cloth', *Ríg* 16).

[51] *Skj* B I, 57; cf. Einarr Helgason's *váðir Heðins* in *Vellekla* 30 ('Heðinn's clothes', *ibid*. B I, 122); ?Hallfreðr's *væðr Hǫgna* ('Hǫgni's clothes', *ibid*. B I, 148, 1, 7); and *væðr Hamðis* of Arnórr Þórðarson ('Hamðir's clothes', *ibid*. B I, 314, 3, 14) and of Guðmundr Oddsson (*ibid*. B II, 91, 2, 3).

[52] *Beo* 227, 2617, 2623, 2730, 2851 and 2871; cf. *hervæðir* ('warclothes', in Eyvindr's *Hákonarmál* 4, *Skj* B I, 57); in Arnórr (*ibid*. B I, 311, 3, 2); and in *Heiðreks saga* (*ibid*. B II, 272, V, 9).

Heathen gods

If *váðir mínar* refers to 'Óðinn's armour', what does *ript* mean? There is an implication of fine material in the eleventh-century instances of *ript*: where the churl's wife 'is put under a bridal veil' (*settiz undir ripti*, *Ríg* 21); where Sigurðr 'enfolds' Guðrún in his arms 'in the bedlinen' (*sveipr í ripti*, *Sigsk* 8); and where Brynhildr asks for her pyre to be decked in 'well-dyed French cloth' (*valaript vel fáð*, *Sigsk* 66).[53] Thus *ript* refers to fine clothing suitable for a *rekkr* ('nobleman'). *Rekkar*, as Hans Kuhn observed, when qualified by a word or name for a king, has a predominantly military sense: *Níðaðar reccar* ('Níðaðr's warriors', *Vǫl* 29); *ræsis reccar* ('the prince's warriors', *HHj* 18); *þjóðans reccar* ('the chieftain's warriors', *Guðrúanrkviða* I, 19).[54] Snorri says that Hálfr's followers were *Hálfs rekkar* ('Hálfr's warriors'), 'and warriors are defined with their name' (*ok af þeirra nafni eru rekkar kallaðir hermenn*).[55] Relevant, too, is Gunnarr's *reccar óneisar* ('unashamed warriors', *Akv* 17), the Burgundian men-at-arms he could have chosen to bring with him to Atli's court.

The other instance of *velli at*, probably from eleventh-century Norway, supports an active rather than static sense: *varð fyr Helga Hundingr konungr hníga at velli* ('King Hundingr did fall in the field before Helgi', *HHund* II, 10, eleventh century). *Vǫllr* is also used of Surtr's doomsday battleground against the gods (*Vaf* 18) and of the plain in the first war between the Æsir and Vanir (*Vsp* 24). Anne Holtsmark points out that *at* in *velli at* means 'at, to, towards; against, by', and cites *kom þar at húsi* ('he came there to a house', *Ríg* 2).[56] Thus *velli at* in *Háv* 49 could be translated 'by, at the field' or 'for use on the field', suggesting a military context for *reccar*.

Óneiss occurs five times in Old Norse–Icelandic literature. Like *óargr* ('uncowardly, brave'), *óneiss* celebrates a warrior's courage by litotes, apparently meaning 'courageous' in all places, including in *óneiss sem*

---

[53] Cf. OE *rift* in Hessels, *An Eighth-Century Latin–Anglo-Saxon Glossary*, pp. 72 (*laena*) and 89 (*palla*); *Épinal-Erfurt Glossary*, ed. Pheifer, p. 42 (*palla*); and Oliphant, *Harley Latin–Old English Glossary*, p. 32 (*biuligo*). Isidore reveals that *rept* was the Visigothic term for 'coverings of shoulders and chest down to the navel, and so heavy with twisted hairs that they repel the rain' (*velamina humerorum et pectoris usque umbilicum, atque intortis villis adeo hispida ut imbrem respuant*): *Isidori Hispalensis Episcopi Etymologiarum sive Originum Libri XX*, ed. W. M. Lindsay, 2 vols. (Oxford, 1911), II. xix. 13. 4 (no page nos.).

[54] H. Kuhn, 'Altnordische *rekkr* und Verwandte', *ANF* 58 (1944), 105–21, esp. 117.

[55] *SnE* 528 (ch. 65); *FJSnE* 186.

[56] A. Holtsmark, 'Kattar sonr', *Saga-Book* 16 (1963), 144–55, esp. 146–7.

kattar sonr ('courageous as a cat's son'), a phrase which Holtsmark discussed in detail when suggesting an eleventh-century date for *Helgakviða Hundingsbana I*.[57] The simplex *neiss* occurs in poetry only in *Háv* 49 and in the phrase *nœktr ok neiss* ('naked and ashamed') once in prose.[58] ME *nais* is derived from a Danish form of *neiss* and is associated with 'naked' in both instances: *nakid and nais* in the early fourteenth-century *Northern Homilies* (1), *Sermons on the Gospel*, and *nars* [*nais*] *and naked* in *Cursor Mundi* 989.[59] Related to *neiss*, but with Icelandic pre-aspiration, is probably *hneistr* ('stripped'), from *(h)neisa*, as in *hneist* ('stripped'), which describes the idol of Þorgerðr Hǫlgabrúðr, stripped and flayed of vestment by a Christian zealot in *Óláfs saga Tryggvasonar*.[60] The words 'neiss er nǿcqviðr halr' in *Háv* 49 could thus convey an image of a man, or here a tree-man, stripped of clothing.

If *Háv* 49 means more than 'clothes make a man', its meaning is that Óðinn, the speaker, clothes two wooden men with the armour and finery worn by noblemen, thus restoring them from a state of stripped abandon (*neiss er nǿcqviðr halr*) to make them once more *reccar óneisir* such as the Burgundian cohorts cited by Gunnarr (*Akv* 17). At a deeper level of meaning, Óðinn arms two idols and brings them to life as demons of battle: 'I gave my gear to two wooden men (*tveim trémǫnnom*) for use on the field; they seemed warriors when they had some clothing; a naked man is ashamed.'

Elsewhere the word *trémaðr* ('tree-man') occurs in the prose and verses of *Ragnars saga Loðbrókar*; with one verse also preserved in *Hálfs saga*; and twice in *Flateyjarbók*.(chs. 173 and 323).[61] Icelandic evidence even as late

---

[57] *Ibid.*, pp. 148–55. Other examples of OIce *óneiss* are: *lýðar óneisir* (*Akv* 12), *reccar óneisir* (*Akv* 17) *konir óneisir* (*HHund* I, 23), *konung óneisan sem kattar son* (*H Hund* I 18), *iǫfur óneisinn* (*Guð* III, 4).

[58] *Barlaams saga*, ed. Keyser and Unger, p. 62 (ch. 63).

[59] *English Metrical Homilies*, ed. J. Small (Edinburgh, 1862), p. 52; *Cursor Mundi*, ed. R. Morris, EETS o.s. 57 (London, 1874), 64.

[60] *Flat* I, 408 (ch. 326). However, G. Holm suggests that *neiss* is related to *nið* ('contumely'): 'Ordet fvn. *(h)neisa*, f., sv. *nesa*', in *Festskrift til Ludvig Holm-Olsen*, ed. B. Fidjestøl (Øvre-Ervik, 1984), pp. 152–61.

[61] *Fornaldarsögur*, ed. Guðni I, 284–5 (*Ragnars saga Loðbrókar*, ch. 20); II, 96–7 (*Hálfs saga*, ch. 2); *Flat* I, 213–14 (ch. 173) and 401–3 (ch. 323). Thematically related to *trémaðr* is *tréguð* ('wooden god') in *Barlaams saga*, ed. Keyser and Unger, p. 62 (ch. 167); *skurðgoð* ('carved god(s)') in *Gammel norsk Homiliebog*, ed. C. R. Unger (Christiania [Oslo], 1864), p. 209, and in *Stjórn*, ed. Unger, p. 101.

as the fourteenth-century *Flateyjarbók* is admissible, if it can be argued that the tradition expressed is more likely to be indigenous than borrowed from outside Scandinavia. In the first example, Ǫgmundr the Dane puts in at Munarvág in Sámsey, and goes ashore with his men.[62] Some men get fresh water, others go into the wood: 'they found an ancient wooden man (*trémann fornan*), a hundred and forty feet high and grown over with moss, and yet they saw all his features; and now they discussed to themselves who would have worshipped this great god'.[63] The *trémaðr* answers their questions with three verses:

> Þat var fyr löngu   er í leið megir
> Hæklings fóru   hlunnalungum
> fram um salta   slóð birtinga,
> þá varðk þessa   þorps ráðandi.
>
> Ok því settumk   sverðmerðlingar
> suðr hjá salti,   synir Loðbrókar;
> þá vark blótinn   til bana mönnum
> í Sámseyju   sunnanverðri.
>
> Þar báðu standa   meðan strönd þolir,
> mann hjá þyrni   ok mosa vaxinn;
> nú skýtr á mér   skýja gráti,
> hlýr hvárki mér   hold né klæði.[64]

When King Óláfr Tryggvason converts the heathens of Trøndelag in *Flateyjarbók*, he tells them a story about the idol of Freyr hitherto worshipped in this province. This idol, he claims, was once one of two 'tree-men' (*tremenn*) the Swedes made when Freyr died, which they put

---

[62] *Fornaldarsögur*, ed. Guðni II, 96–7.
[63] *Ibid.*: 'ok þar fundu þeir einn trémann fornan, ok var fertugr at hæð ok mosa vaxinn, ok sá þó öll deili á honum, ok ræddu nú um með sér, hverr blótat mundi hafa þetta it mikla goð'.
[64] *Ibid.*: 'That was a long time ago that the sons of Hæklingr sailed on a journey with the ships of the roller forward over the salty tracks of sea-trouts: then I became ruler of this mound. And for this they set me, famous swordsmen, sons of Loðbrók, south by the salt sea: then sacrifice was made to me to bring about the deaths of men, in the southern part of Sámsey. There they ordered me to stand as long as shore endures, a man among thorns and overgrown with moss; now the tears of clouds shoot down at me, neither flesh nor clothes protect me.'

into his burial mound, 'because they thought Freyr would find it fun to play with them'.⁶⁵ Later, he says, these wooden men frightened tomb-robbers and thus prevented them from leaving with their booty. The Swedes took the statues out and sent one of them to the Trondheim region, keeping the other at Uppsala. Both statues were then worshipped as Freyr himself.

In another story, Hákon Jarl arranged Þorleifr Jarlaskáld's death when it became clear that Þorleifr had cursed him with itching-sickness. On this errand Hákon did not send a human retainer, but a *trémaðr*:

Heitir nú á fulltrúa sína Þorgerði Hǫrgabrúði ok Irpu systur hennar at reka þann galdr út til Íslands at Þorleifi ynni at fullu, ok fœrir þeim miklar fornir ok gekk til fréttar. En er hann fekk þá frétt er honum líkaði, lét hann taka einn rekabút ok gera ór trémann. Ok með fjǫlkynngi ok atkvæðum jarls en trǫllskap ok fítonsanda þeirra systra lét hann drepa einn mann ok taka ór hjartat ok láta í þenna trémann. Ok fœrðu síðan í fǫt ok gáfu nafn ok kǫlluðu Þorgarð ok mǫgnuðu hann með svá miklum fjandans krapti, at hann gekk ok mælti við menn. Kómu honum síðan í skip ok sendu hann út til Íslands, þess ørendis at drepa Þorleif jarlskáld. Gyrði Hákon hann atgeir þeim er hafði tekit ór hofi þeirra systra ok Hǫrgi hafði átt. (ch. 7)⁶⁶

Þorgarðr carries out his mission in Þingvellir and runs Þorleifr through with his halberd on meeting him. This monster then disappears into the ground, whereupon the dying Þorleifr speaks the following verse:

> Hvarf inn hildardjarfi —   hvat varð af Þorgarði?
> villumaðr á velli —   vígdjarfr refilstíga.

⁶⁵ *Flat* I, 401–3 (ch. 323): 'þuiat þeir hugdu at honum mundi gaman þikia at læika ser at þeim'.

⁶⁶ *Eyfirðinga sǫgur*, ed. Jónas, pp. 226–7 (*Þorleifs þáttr Jarlsskálds*): 'He called on his close friend Þorgerðr Hǫrgi's-bride and Irpa her sister to cast a spell towards Iceland that might have a full effect on Þorleifr, performed great sacrifices in their honour and consulted an oracle. And when he got the oracle he wanted, he had a piece of driftwood taken and out of it he had a wooden man made. And with the earl's magic and his prayers and the monstrous witchcraft and python's breath of those sisters, he had a man killed and his heart taken out and put into this wooden man. And then they dressed him in clothes, gave him a name, called him "Þorgarðr" and empowered him with so much demonic strength that he walked and talked with men. They put him then into a ship and sent him out to Iceland with a mission to kill Þorleifr Poet-of-Earls. Hákon armed him with the halberd that he had taken out of the temple of those sisters, the halberd that had once been Hǫrgi's.'

Heathen gods

Farit hefir Gautr at grjóti   gunnelds inn fjǫlkunni,
síðan mun hann í helju   hvílast stund ok mílu.[67]

Though not Þorleifr's, this verse is likely to be older than the fourteenth-century prose which contains it. Þorleifr's description of his killer differs from what the prose has led us to expect, since Þorgarðr's independence seems greater: he is 'magically skilled' (*fjǫlkunni*) and a 'heretic' (*villumaðr*, which occurs also in *Maúmets villumenn* ('Muhammad's heretics') in at least three thirteenth-century sources).[68] *Gautr* in the kenning *inn fjǫlkunni Gautr gunnelds* is an appellative of Óðinn (*Grím* 54); Óðinn is associated with magic (*Ynglinga saga*, ch. 7); *refilstígar* ('serpentine paths') occurs elsewhere apparently once, in *Gylfaginning*, where Gylfi, arriving at Ásgarðr, uses this word of himself: 'he said his name was Gangleri, that he had come by serpentine paths' (*hann nefndisk Gangleri ok kominn af refilstígum*).[69] Furthermore *Gangleri* is another of Óðinn's names (*Grím* 46), and *refill* ('serpent') is the type of animal into which Óðinn transforms himself in order to slip through a channel in a wall of rock and come out where Gunnlǫð keeps the mead of poetry (*Háv* 106 and *Skáldskaparmál*, ch. 6). Though the (probably thirteenth-century) poet of the above verse in *Þorleifs þáttr* was first and foremost conveying the pagan wizardry of Þorgarðr as he killed and then vanished, he seems to show with *Gautr* and *refilstígar* that Óðinn inspired this kind of magic.

Let us now compare these instances of *trémaðr*. In five ways, the image of clothed statues in *Háv* 49 appears to be connected with other myths and may have an antecedent in common with some or all of them. Firstly, the statue in *Ragnars saga Loðbrókar* complains of no clothing (and no flesh) in rainy weather, while the two wooden men in *Háv* 49 have no clothes until they are given them; Þorgarðr is given clothes in *Flateyjarbók*. Secondly, in Þorleifr's verse the whereabouts of Þorgarðr are *á velli*; the two wooden men in *Háv* 49 are *velli at*. Thirdly, there are two wooden men in Óláfr's story in *Flateyjarbók*; and two in *Háv* 49. Fourthly, Þorgarðr is dressed in clothes to carry out a murder; when the Sámsey

---

[67] *Ibid.*, p. 226: 'The daring man in battle (what became of Þorgarðr?) infidel on the field, daring in combat, disappeared by serpentine paths; the Gautr of the battlefire, skilled in magic, has gone a mile into rock, and after this he'll have to dwell some time in hell.'

[68] *Orkneyinga saga*, ed. Finnbogi, p. 225 (ch. 88); *Barlaams saga*, ed. Keyser and Unger, p. 146; *Stjórn*, ed. Unger, p. 21.

[69] *Gylf*, pp. 7–8 (ch. 2).

trémaðr says that he was worshipped *til bana mönnum* ('?for the death of men'), he finishes by lamenting his nakedness: this may imply that honouring him is giving him clothes, after which he can do murder for those who honour him. Fifthly, the god Óðinn is suggested in the dying verse of Þorleifr in *Gautr inn fjǫlkunni* and *refilstígar*. In these five ways the image of clothed *trémenn* in *Háv* 49 appears to be connected with other myths and may have an antecedent in common with some or all of them. It thus seems to be part of Óðinn's magic to bring idols to life by giving them armour and clothing.

OIce véar-vé *and* OE weos

Neuter OIce *vé* is cognate with masculine OE *weoh*. *Weos* (from **weohas*) is the plural of *weoh* (also spelt *weh*, *wih* and *wig*), which glosses *uana* ('empty, vain things') in an eleventh-century text of Caelius Sedulius's *Carmen paschale*.[70] *Weoh* describes the monstrous idol made for Nebuchadnezzar (*Dan* 170, 201 and 207); an idol for which St Bartholomew is killed (*Fates* 48); and one of the idols worshipped by the Roman heathen Eleusius (*Jul* 23), an idol which is also described as a *hæðenweoh* ('heathen idol', *Jul* 51).[71] In placenames, *weoh* is associated either with *-leah* ('grove') or *-dun* ('down') in about half its instances; it is never attached to a god's name, indicates a shrine smaller than OE *hearh* and is found in Anglian, Saxon and Jutish areas of England.[72] David N. Wilson suggests that *weoh* and *hearh* may not have been attached to a specific god's name because they denoted shrines including more than one god.[73] In Denmark, however, all placenames ending in **-vé* are attached to reflexes of Óðinn, including the modern *Odense* (from *Óðins-vé*, 'Óðinn's sanctuary').[74]

---

[70] Meritt, *Old English Glosses*, p. xv (§28).

[71] Though simplex OE *weoh* is not found outside glosses in prose, its prose compounds are numerous: *wigbed* ('altar'), *wigbora* ('standard bearer', related to Lat *vexillum*), *wiggild* ('idol'), *wigsmiþ* ('maker of idols'), *weohsteall* ('apse', as in OIce *véstallr*), and *wigweorþung* ('honour to idols'). There is no OE verbal cognate of OIce *vígja*, OHG *wîhian* and Got *weihan* ('to consecrate').

[72] Gelling, *Signposts to the Past*, pp. 154–61.

[73] Wilson, *Anglo-Saxon Paganism*, p. 16.

[74] See K. Hald, 'The Cult of Odin in Danish Place-Names', in *Early English and Norse Studies Presented to Hugh Smith in Honour of his Sixtieth Birthday*, ed. A. Brown and P. Foote (London, 1963), pp. 99–109, esp. 107.

Heathen gods

OIce *vé* can refer to the sanctuary of an individual god, ruled by him or her with or without smaller gods: Víðarr and Váli, who build their *vé goða* ('sanctuary of the gods', *Vaf* 51) in the restored world, following the war of the end of the world; Heimdallr in Himinbjǫrg, *enn þar Heimdall qveða valda véom* ('and there they say Heimdallr rules the holy places', *Grím* 13); and Skaði, who tells Loki, in *Lokasenna*, that *frá mínom véom oc vǫngom scolo þér æ kǫld ráð koma* ('from my holy places and hillsides cold counsels shall always come for you', *Lok* 51). *Vé* can refer to the sanctuary of all the gods, ruled by Óðinn and others: *hofslǫnd ok vé banda* ('temple-lands and sanctuaries of powers', *Vellekla* 15); *vé heilagt* ('holy sanctuary', *Hynd* 1); and in *Gylfaginning*, the Æsir's *vé ok griðastaðir* ('sanctuaries and places of refuge', *Gylf*, p. 29). *Vé* seems to connote a holy place inhabited by one or more gods; or, in a collective ritual sense, may denote the gods themselves. *Vé* may even connote the activity of sacrificing to these gods. In the *Sturlubók* recension of *Landnámabók*, for example, there is an account of a fanatic who settled in Iceland in the mid tenth century: 'Geirr het maðr ágætr í Sogni; hann var kallaðr Végeirr, því at hann var blótmaðr mikill; hann átti mǫrg bǫrn. Vébjǫrn Sygnakappi var elztr sona hans ok Vésteinn, Véþormr, Vémundr, Végestr ok Véþorn, en Védís dóttir' (ch. 149).[75] That *vé* in Végeirr's children's names was taken to indicate 'sacrificing' shows that the sense of 'holy place and idols' was probably included in this word during the tenth century in Scandinavia.

The weak adjectival form *Véi* was used to refer to one of Óðinn's brothers.[76] The plural form is *véar*, which is either weak or strong (if strong, it is an exact cognate of OE *weos*). *Véar* occurs in *Hymiskviða*, where the gods wait for a drink from Ægir's kettle: 'en *véar* hverian vel scolo drecca ǫlðr at Ægis eitt hǫrmeitið' ('and *the holy ones* must be drinking ale well [meaning unknown] at Ægir's place', *Hym* 39). As OE *weos* appears to share the masculine rather than neuter gender of OIce *véar*,

---

[75] *Landnámabók*, ed. Jakob, pp. 188–9: 'There was a wealthy man in Sogn called Geirr ('spear'); he was called Vé-Geirr because he was a great sacrificer; he had many children. Vé-bjǫrn ("-bear") Champion of the men of Sogn was his eldest son, and there was Vé-steinn ("-stone"), Vé-þormr ("-comfort"), Vé-mundr ("-hand, sword"), Vé-gestr ("-guest") and Vé-þorn ("-thorn")' and a daughter Vé-dís ("-lady").'

[76] *AIEW* 713 (*Véi*); see also M. Cahen, *Le Mot Dieu en vieux Scandinave* (Paris, 1921), p. 24; W. Baetke, *Das Heilige im Germanischen* (Tübingen, 1942), pp. 80–122; *Véi*, Óðinn's brother, appears in *Gylf*, p. 11 (ch. 6) and in *Heimskringla I*, ed. Bjarni, pp. 12 and 14 (*Ynglinga saga*, chs. 3 and 5).

the meaning of *weos* is consistent not with holy places or 'sanctuaries', but with the manifestations of gods inside them. In Christian eyes such idols were inevitably 'demons'.

In Scandinavia the words *véar* or *vé* kept a broader connotation of idols within sanctuaries. The second word, in particular, occurs in the *Vellekla* (*c.* 985) of Einarr *skálaglamm* ('cup-tinkle'), verses of which are preserved in *Fagrskinna*, a history of Norway probably written in 1220–30. According to the prose of *Fagrskinna*, the sons of Eiríkr *blóðøx* ('bloodaxe') accepted baptism in their youth, but forced no-one into Christianity in Norway after Hákon Aðalsteinsfóstri's death in *c.* 960, when they took the name of king; however, 'they then destroyed temples and sacrifice' (*þá brutu þeir niðr hof ok blótskap*).[77] When Hákon Jarl succeeded and began to sacrifice again, the old religion was restored:

> Ok herþarfir hverfa   (Hlakkar móts) til blóta
> (rauðbríkar fremsk rœkir   ríkr) ásmegir (slíku).
> Nú grœr jǫrð sem áðan –   aptr geirbrúar hapta
> auðrýrir lætr áru   óhryggva vé byggva.   (*Vellekla* 16)[78]

The greatest problem of interpretation in this stanza of *Vellekla* lies in making a correct arrangement of words in the second half of the stanza. Finnur Jónsson paraphrased as follows: 'the generous man allows the warriors happy once more to inhabit the temples of the gods' (*auðrýrir lætr áru geirbrúar aptr óhryggva byggva hapta vé*).[79] Bjarni followed Finnur but otherwise tried to make sense of these lines by weakening *geirbrúar áru* ('heralds of the spearbridge', hence 'shield's heralds') or 'warriors', into 'men'; he also makes *byggva* ('to build', 'to inhabit') imply 'to visit'.[80] Turville-Petre, followed by Ström, translated 'again the destroyer of the

---

[77] *Ágrip*, ed. Bjarni, p. 98 (*Fagrskinna*, ch. 14).

[78] Text and translation based on Davidson, 'Earl Hákon and his Poets', p. 304: 'And the Æsir's sons, useful to an army, return to the sacrifices, the mighty tender of the board of Hlǫkk's meeting [battle] wins fame with this. Now the earth grows as before-again the diminisher of wealth allows the sorrow-free heralds of the spear-bridge [shield] to inhabit the holy places of gods.'

[79] *Skj* B I, 119–20: 'den gavmilde mand lader krigerne igen glade befolke gudernes templer'.

[80] *Heimskringla I*, ed. Bjarni, p. 242 (*Óláfs saga Tryggvasonar*, ch. 16): 'the generous prince allows men once more to sit happy in the gods's temples' 'hinn gjǫfuli hǫfðingi lætur menn aftur sitja glaða í hofum goðanna'.

wealth of the spear-bridge allows the merry messengers of the gods to inhabit the temples'.[81]

The problem in *Vellekla* 16 is that of deciding whether *geirbrúar* should qualify *áru* (Finnur, Bjarni and Davidson) or *auðrýrir* (Turville-Petre and Ström); or, in other words, whether 'heralds of the spearbridge [warriors]' inhabiting gods' shrines is more or less strange than 'destroyer of the wealth of the spearbridge', hence Hákon diminishing wealth in the form of shield-ornaments (in which case it is *hapta árar* ('heralds of the gods') who inhabit the holy places). *Auðrýrir* as ('diminisher of wealth') can denote 'king' independently of a qualifier, just as *gullsendir* ('gold-deliverer', *Vellekla* 33); furthermore, 'warriors' in *geirbrúar áru* is corroborated by *herþarfir ásmegir* in the same stanza, which must mean 'sons of the Æsir useful to an army'. So the first option seems preferable, the 'heralds' being understood as manifestations of gods, hence idols, in holy places. 'Sorrow-free' seems better for *óhryggva* because 'glad' does not capture the litotes of a construction that tells us that Hákon's war-idols are happy to be restored to worship. Correspondingly, the statue in *Ragnars saga* looks like an old idol that is *hryggr*, his poem the lament of an idol waiting in vain to be brought to life.

The idols of Hákon Jarl would thus have been imagined as war-demons or beings of which the Þorgarðr of *Flateyjarbók* is a fourteenth-century derivation. In Þorkell Gíslason's *Búadrápa*, however, it is the goddess Þorgerðr who fights for Hákon in the battle of Hjǫrungavágr: 'with sharp arrows she decided to shoot from her fingers' (*ǫrum réð sér snǫrpum af fingrum skjóta*).[82] This motif is probably related to Einarr's unusual *herþarfir ásmegir* dwelling in and making up the *hapta vé* of Hákon Jarl.

Armed idols in a temple were described by Bishop Thietmar of Merseburg in a record in *c*. 1014 of the destruction of a Slavic temple at Riedegost in 1005. According to Thietmar, the temple was decorated on the outside with splendidly carved images of gods and goddesses, while 'inside are statues of gods each inscribed with a name, awe-inspiringly clad in helmets and breastplates'.[83] One might also compare Adam of Bremen's later description of the heathen temple at Uppsala in Sweden,

---

[81] Turville-Petre, *Scaldic Poetry*, pp. 61–2; Ström, 'Poetry as an Instrument of Propaganda', pp. 450–1. See also Davidson, 'Jarl Hákon and his Poets', p. 304.

[82] *Skj* B II, 538, 10; Þorgerðr similarly causes a hailstorm to thwart the fleet of Hákon's viking enemies in the twelfth-century *Jómsvíkingadrápa* (ibid. B II, 7, 32).

[83] *Thietmari Merseburgensis episcopi chronicon*, ed. R. Holzmann, MGH, SRG n.s. 9 (Berlin,

with its statues of Thor, Wodan and Fricco [Freyr].[84] Thor sat on a couch in the centre with a sceptre, the others on either side, much as the poet of *Vǫluspá* describes Þórr rising up to slaughter the giant who had asked for Freyja: 'he seldom stays sitting when he's heard of such a thing' (*hann sialdan sitr, er hann slíct um fregn, Vsp* 26).[85] Adam says that the Swedes carve Wodan 'armed, just as our people are used to portraying Mars', and 'that [his name] means Fury. He wages wars and gives a man courage against his enemies.'[86] There is no suggestion in this passage that Adam's informant's informants considered the idols of Thor or Wodan to be anything other than gods.

From the evidence of Hákon's *herþarfir ásmegir* ('sons of the Æsir useful to an army') it seems that temples could also house the lesser deities. These *geirbrúar árar* ('heralds of the spearbridge [warriors]') in *Vellekla* 16 appear to be ready for wars in contemporary Norway, though their counterparts in the Þórr fragment of Þorbjǫrn *dísarskáld* ('poet of the female deity') fight in Ragnarǫk: *Þórr hefr Yggs með árum Ásgarð of þrek varðan* ('Þórr has strongly defended Ásgarð with the heralds of Yggr [Óðinn]').[87] Thus I suggest that Einarr's *geirbrúar árar* and Þorbjǫrn's *Yggs árar* are pre-Christian images of the demons characterized as *trémenn* in *Flateyjarbók* and *Ragnars saga Loðbrókar*. Óðinn's scarecrows in *Háv* 49 seem to fall within the same tradition, for they appear to be two *trémenn* that he brings magically to life by giving them his armour and clothing.

The next question is who Óðinn's *trémenn* are. Nordal considers *Háv* 49 to be an analogue of the story of Askr and Embla in *Vsp* 17–18, two trees which the gods Óðinn, Hœnir and Lóðurr make into man and woman.[88] Snorri may have known *Háv* 49, particularly the words *váðir* and *ript*, because when he paraphrased *Vsp* 17–18 in *Gylfaginning*, he added *klæði* ('clothes') to the gifts that Askr and Embla, as *tré tvau* ('two trees'),

---

1955), 302 (VI.17): 'interius autem dii stant manu facti, singulis nominibus insculptis, galeis atque loricis terribiliter vestiti'.

[84] *Gesta*, ed. Schmeidler, pp. 257–9.

[85] So Dala-Guðbrandr and other heathens regarded their Þórr-idol as the god himself, capable of movement (*ef hann kǫmr á þingit*), eating bread and meat (*fjórir hleifar brauðs ... hvern dag ok þar slátr við*) and inspiring fear (*yðr skjóti skelk í bringu*): see *Heimskringla I*, ed. Bjarni, p. 187 (*Óláfs saga Helga*, ch. 112).

[86] *Gesta*, ed. Schmeidler, p. 258 (IV.26): 'armatum, sicut nostri Martem; solent'; 'id est furor, bella gerit hominique ministrat virtutem contra inimicos'.

[87] *Skj* B I, 135.   [88] *Vǫluspá*, ed. Sigurður, p. 34.

receive.[89] On the other hand, Óðinn's wooden figures in *Háv* 49 are both *reccar*, not male and female. Gro Steinsland suggests that the *trémenn* or *reccar* in *Háv* 49 are two humanoid deformities waiting to be made man and woman, because Þórr mockingly refers to a dwarf as *reccr* in *Alvíssmál* 5.[90] Yet, like Sigurður Nordal, she does not explain for what purpose a female dwarf should be stylized as male in *Háv* 49.

I suggest, instead, that Óðinn's *reccar* in *Háv* 49 are his two lieutenants in Valhǫll. In *Hyndluljóð*, a fourteenth-century text embodying older material, these men are named Hermóðr and Sigmundr. This poem begins in the underworld, with Freyja rousing a sibyl from the dead to ask her for knowledge of the future:

> nú er rǫcr rǫcra, ríða við scolom
> til Valhallar oc *til vés* [MS *véss*] *heilags*.
>
> Biðiom Heriafǫðr í hugom sitia!
> hann geldr oc gefr gull verðugom;
> gaf hann Hermóði hiálm oc brynio,
> enn Sigmundi sverð at þiggia. (*Hynd* 1/5–8 and 2)[91]

Endowed with weapons in their lives and represented after their deaths as idols in sanctuaries of various kinds, Hermóðr and Sigmundr would be as likely as any other *einherjar* ('individual warriors') to be candidates for the *trémenn* decked with armour and clothing in *Háv* 49. Their mission is to fight for Óðinn in Ragnarǫk.

A place in Valhǫll is also the honour accorded to the former Christian Hákon Aðalsteinsfóstri in Eyvindr's *Hákonarmál*. After his death in the battle of Storð against the sons of Eiríkr blóðøx, Hákon is described preparing to lead his army to Óðinn's hall of the slain. Óðinn calls on two lieutenants, Bragi and Hermóðr, to receive Hákon when he gets there. Bragi promises 'the peace-terms of Einherjar' (*Einherja grið*) to Hákon and his men. Hákon's weapons and armour have been broken to pieces and he

---

[89] *Gylf*, p. 13 (ch. 9).

[90] G. Steinsland, 'Antropogonimyten i *Vǫluspá*: en tekst- og tradisjonshistorisk analyse', *ANF* 98 (1983), 80–107, esp. 92–104; cf. *Hávamál*, ed. Evans, pp. 93–5.

[91] 'Now is the Day of Judgement! We must ride to Valhǫll and to the holy sanctuary. Let's bid the Father of Armies be in good cheer! He gives and pays out gold to worthy ones; he gave Hermóðr a helmet and a coat of mail, and gave Sigmundr the present of a sword.' I am grateful to Hilda Ellis Davidson for the reference to the parallel in *Hyndluljóð*.

makes a request for some new gear (this may also be a request implicit in the deliberately broken spear-shafts and blunted spear-heads found mostly in both cremation and inhumation burials in pagan England).[92] Hákon makes his request as follows:

> 'Gerðar órar',   kvað enn góði konungr,
> 'viljum vér sjálfir hafa.
> Hjálm ok brynju   skal hirða vel.
>   Gótt es til gǫrs at taka.'
>
> Þá þat kynndisk,   hvé sá konungr hafði
>   *vel of þyrmt véum*,
> es Hákon báðu   heilan koma
>   ráð ǫll ok regin.   (*Hákonarmál* 17–18)[93]

These lines are an uncompromising statement of Hákon's devotion to the heathen gods of Norway. How might Hákon's request for weapons have been answered, unless affirmatively? If it is true that he 'respected the gods or sanctuaries' (*vel of þyrmt véum*) in his lifetime, perhaps he had done so by arming the *vé* (a neuter plural form indicating both male and female 'idols'), as Hákon Jarl would do later in *c*. 985. Eyvindr's meaning is clear. Whatever the priests had taught him in England, Hákon 'went among heathen gods' when he died (*fór með heiðin goð*, *Hákonarmál* 24): Óðinn made King Hákon one of the *vé*.

OE *WEOS*: REGENERATION OF DEAD KINGS

Royal apotheosis was a topos in Britain before the Germanic settlement. Tacitus in his *Agricola* shows a native Briton referring to Julius Caesar as 'Julius the god' (*divus Iulius*), while coin legends with the words *salus Augusti* help to show that the cult of the imperial *numen* was standard in large Romano-British towns.[94] A first-century temple in Colchester, one

---

[92] Wilson, *Anglo-Saxon Paganism*, p. 123.
[93] *Heimskringla I*, ed. Bjarni, pp. 194 and 196–7 (*Hákonar saga góða*, ch. 31): '"We ourselves want", said the good king, "our own weapons. Helmet and coat of mail must be carefully kept. It is good to take to one's gear." Then it was made known how this king *beautifully respected the sanctuaries*, when all the deciding powers bade Hákon be welcome.'
[94] *Agricola*, in *Taciti Opera Minora*, ed. H. Furneaux, ed. and rev. J. G. C. Anderson, 2nd ed. (Oxford, 1922), p. 13 (ch. 15).

Heathen gods

of the biggest of its kind, had an altar which was built to rival Augustus's altar in Lyon (c. 12 BC) and his *Ara Ubiorum* in Cologne (c. 9 BC), where the loyal Germanic Ubii had also coupled Augustus's name with the goddess *Dea Roma*.[95] The Libyan-born emperor Septimius Severus (193–211), not long after he defeated the Caledonians near Carlisle, met an Ethiopian soldier bearing him a crown of cypress boughs; Severus dismissed him because he took fright at the man's colour and the cypress, to him both omens of the underworld; as he was going, the Ethiopian said sardonically: 'you have been all things, you have conquered all things, now, O conqueror, be a god!'[96] Severus died not long after and the exhortation became true. These references reveal a topos of royal apotheosis in Roman Britain before the coming of the Angles.

Given that Mercury was probably introduced into Germania from Roman Gaul across the Rhine frontier in the first century BC, the late role of Óðinn as *valfǫðr* can be correlated with that of Hermes the 'psychopomp'. A mass-sacrifice of war-captives made by the Hermunduri to Mercury and Mars in AD 59, in combination with the names of battle-goddesses from second-century Germanic votary inscriptions, shows that Woden's continental ancestor was probably believed to convey, then later to receive, warriors into a realm of the dead from at least the first century onwards.[97] It is likely that the Germanic word for this realm was cognate with OIce *hel* ('underworld'), rather than with OIce *Valhǫll* ('hall of the slain'), a later formation: in *Atlakviða*, probably from late ninth-century Norway, *valhǫll* is used of an earthly hall in *vín í valhǫllo* ('wine in the choice hall', *Akv* 2); while cognates of *hel* in all Germanic languages indicate only the abode of the dead.[98]

In Germanic England, joints of meat and other foodstuffs buried alongside men, women and children in a large number of heathen graves seem to show that the Anglo-Saxons believed in an afterlife where this

---

[95] See Henig, *Religion in Roman Britain*, pp. 69–76, esp. 69–70.

[96] *Scriptores Historiae Augustae ab Hadriano ad Numerianum*, ed. H. Jordan and F. Eyssenhardt (Berlin, 1864), p. 136 (*Severus Imperator*, ch. 22): 'totum fuisti, totum vicisti, iam deus esto victor'.

[97] *Taciti Annales*, ed. Furneaux II, 228 (XIII.57). On likely Germanic battle-goddesses from the first and second centuries, see Gutenbrunner, *Götternamen*, pp. 99–105: Baudihillia (no. 32), Harimella (no. 65), Hariasa (no. 64), Vihansa (no. 115), Vagdavercustis (no. 104).

[98] See G. Neckel, *Walhall: Studien über germanischen Jenseitsglauben* (Dortmund, 1913), p. 51.

food could be eaten: this type of deposit resembles the Norse topos of feasting in Valhǫll (*Grím* 18, 23 and 25).[99] Where a place for fighting in the underworld is concerned, there is also the evidence of weapon deposits buried alongside Anglo-Saxon noblemen in heathen graves.[100] About 47 per cent of discovered male skeletons from early Anglo-Saxon cemeteries were buried with weapons; Heinrich Härke imputes this statistic solely to symbolism and the need of Anglo-Saxon families to display their wealth and status; yet this theory does not explain how these families had once imagined the hereafter whereby they now wished to impress each other.[101] Thus the ideology of a warrior's paradise cannot be excluded from these early English weapon-graves.

There may also be literary allusions to a 'valkyrie' tradition native to Anglo-Saxon England. First, in BL, Harley 585, of a tenth- to eleventh-century date, *The Charm for a Sudden Stitch* (against elfshot) begins with a description of supernatural spirits who are heard *ða hy ofer þone hlæw ridan* ('when they rode over the barrow'). Barrow-burials became common in England in the seventh century, possibly 'to emphasize ties to ancestors, symbolized by the barrows'.[102] The speaker of this *Charm* then says that he

>   stod under linde,   under leohtum scylde,
>   þær ða mihtigan wif   hyra mægen beræddon
>   and hy gyllende   garas sændan;   (*MCharm* 4.7–9)[103]

Though it is not clear what the poet takes these women to be, their female sex, riding in flight and throwing spears suggest that they were imagined in England as female beings analogous to the later Norse *valkyrjur*.[104] Second, with reference to a similar tradition, flying bees are

---

[99] Wilson, *Anglo-Saxon Paganism*, pp. 97–100.

[100] *Ibid.*, pp. 115–23.

[101] H. Härke, 'Changing Symbols in a Changing Society: the Anglo-Saxon Weapon Burial Rite in the Seventh Century', in *The Age of Sutton Hoo*, ed. Carver, pp. 149–65, esp. 150–5.

[102] Wilson, *Anglo-Saxon Paganism*, p. 70.

[103] Trans. based on *Lacnunga*, ed. Grattan and Singer, pp. 174–5: '[I] stood under the linden [shield], under a light shield, where the mighty women got ready their powers, and yelling, they sent spears.' On the use of language to perform magic in this spell, see Clemoes, *Interactions of Thought and Language*, pp. 109–10.

[104] On the role of women in the magic of this period, see A. L. Meaney, 'Women, Witchcraft and Magic in Anglo-Saxon England', in *Superstition and Popular Medicine in Anglo-Saxon England*, ed. D. G. Scragg (Manchester, 1989), pp. 9–40, esp. 16–17; see

described as *sigewif* ('victory-women') in *A Charm for a Sudden Swarm* in CCCC 41 (*MCharm* 8.9). In addition, a description of a raven over the Egyptian army as *wonn wælceaseg* ('dark one choosing the slain') in *Ex* 164 may have been influenced directly by the Old Norse Valhǫll topos. OE *wælceaseg* is an adjective cognate with the noun OIce *valkyrja* ('chooser of the slain') from which Wulfstan borrowed *wælcyrie* apparently for a human 'sorceress' in his *Sermo Lupi ad Anglos*.[105] OE *wælcyrie* (with *gydene*, 'goddess') glosses *ueneris* in Oxford, Bodleian Library, Digby 146 (an early eleventh-century manuscript of Aldhelm's *De laudibus virginitatis*).[106] This instance may represent a loan or loan-translation of OIce *valkyrja*; on the other hand, *wælcyrge* glosses the names of classical furies in glossary I in Cotton Cleopatra A. iii and in the older *Corpus Glossary*; in the former, *wælcyrge* also glosses *Bellona*; these glosses appear to show an Anglo-Saxon conception of *wælcyrge* that was independent of contemporary Scandinavian influence.[107]

The Scandinavian evidence suggests that mortal kings whom Óðinn's valkyries summoned to Valhǫll were thereafter held to be minor gods. As we have seen, this is the case with Hákon Aðalsteinsfóstri in *Hákonarmál* and with Eiríkr blóðøx in *Eiríksmál*; it was also true of King Erik of Sweden, according to Rimbert's *Vita S. Anskarii* (c. 875), in which the gods of Birka generously agreed 'to receive Erik, once a king of yours, unanimously into our guild that he may be accounted one of the gods' (ch. 26).[108] Adam of Bremen, who used Rimbert as a source, also refers to 'Hericus' in his comment on Uppsala: 'They also worship gods made out

---

also H. Damico, 'The Valkyrie Reflex in Old English Literature', in *New Readings on Women in Old English Literature*, ed. H. Damico and A. Hennessey Olsen (Bloomington and Indianapolis, IN, 1990), pp. 176–90.

[105] *Homilies of Wulfstan*, ed. Bethurum, p. 273.

[106] A. S. Napier, *Old English Glosses Chiefly Unpublished* (Oxford, 1900), p. 115 (no. 4449).

[107] See the entry in the 'First Cleopatra Glossary' (Cotton Cleopatra A. iii), in *Vocabularies*, ed. Wright and Wülcker, pp. 347.32 (*Allecto: wælcyrige*), 360.3 and 417.12 (*Herinis: wælcyrge*); see also the 'Third Cleopatra Glossary', in *ibid.*, pp. 527.17 (*Bellona: wælcyrge*). See also *Corpus Glossary*, ed. Lindsay, pp. 68.351 (*Eurynis: walcyrge*), 89.87 ([*H*]*Erinis: walcrigge*) and 176.159 (*Tisifone: uualcyrge*).

[108] *Vita S. Anskarii*, ed. Waitz, p. 56: 'Ericum quondam regem vestrum nos unanimes in collegium nostrum asciscimus, ut sit unus de numero deorum.'

Woden's witchcraft

of the men whom they honour with immortality on account of their monstrous deeds.'[109]

While Rimbert shows that apotheosis was an option for some Scandinavian pagan kings, *Hákonarmál* and *Eiríksmál* provide evidence that this deification of royal ancestors would usually come about through death in combat. In the first century AD, Nerthus could not pass by, Tacitus says, unless 'they do not go to war, do not take up arms; all iron is locked up'.[110] The evidence of gravegoods and settlement layouts in the southern Jutish area suggests that large-scale warfare became more common there in the first and second centuries of this era.[111] Presumably the poets of Germanic *carmina antiqua* in this period would find a poetic topos through which to present their slain kings' continuity in the hereafter: gradually a Valhǫll quarter of *hel* would evolve as a distinct place with a name of its own. There were many wars in early northern history.[112] Of the 540 (or 640) doors in Valhǫll counted in *Grím* 23, each one spills forth 800 (or 960) *einherjar* who daily train for Ragnarǫk; each man who falls in the day's fighting is revived in the evening, according to Snorri in *Gylfaginning* (ch. 41), who quotes Eddic lines in which the *einherjar* 'decide whom to slay and [then] ride from the battle, sit together with each other once more reconciled' (*val þeir kiósa ok ríða vígi frá, sitia meirr um sáttir saman*, Vaf 41). To go by *Hákonarmál* of c. 960 and by the probably later *Eiríksmál*, in which Eiríkr is preceded by no fewer than eight brothers, the welcoming of newly deceased warriors and kings to Valhǫll was a regular business.[113] These poems probably reflect a common Germanic ideology that was also inherited by the earliest English kings.

The etymology of OIce *Áss* ('god'), cognate with OE *ese* (*MCharm*

---

[109] *Gesta*, ed. Schmeidler, p. 259: 'colunt et deos ex hominibus factos, quos pro ingentibus factis immortalitate donant'.

[110] *Germania*, p. 317 (ch. 40): 'non bella ineunt, non arma sumunt; clausum omne ferrum'.

[111] Hedeager, 'Kingdoms, Ethnicity and Material Culture', pp. 285–7; *Iron-Age Societies*, pp. 133–4, 170–3 and 229–38.

[112] 'Kingdoms, Ethnicity and Material Culture', pp. 287–92.

[113] Von See argues plausibly that *Eiríksmál* is an imitation of *Hákonarmál*, in 'Zwei eddische Preislieder', pp. 107–17; repr. in his *Edda. Saga. Skaldendichtung*, pp. 318–28 and 522–5 (addendum). E. Marold argues that *Hákonarmál* reflects the Christian-influenced world of Trondheim, *Eiríksmál* the more heathen Danish court, in 'Das Walhallbild in den Eiríksmál und den Hákonarmál', *MScan* 5 (1972), 19–33.

4.23), shows that the Germanic etymon of *Æsir* appears to have connoted deified mortals at an earlier time: PGmc **ansuz*, etymon of OIce *áss* (and of OE *os*), is usually defined as 'breath' or 'spirit' (cognate with OIce *ǫnd*).[114] This etymology suggests that the meaning of *áss* evolved from 'ghost', signifying 'ancestor', to 'god'; a trace of this development may be preserved in lines in which a sibyl tells Óðinn that the hall of Niflhel is prepared for Baldr's arrival, with *'ásmegir í ofvæni'* ('the sons of the *Æsir* in anxious expectation', *Bdr* 7).

Norse evidence suggests that the precedent for the regeneration of dead nobles lay in *seiðr*, a word which, as we have seen, is probably cognate with OE *-siden*. Ursula Dronke has shown how *seiðr* works in the Æsir–Vanir war in *Vǫluspá*: faster than the Æsir can kill their Vanir opponents, the Vanir conjure their own rebirth on the battlefield: 'Vanir by a war charm were live and kicking on the plains' (*knátto vanir vígspá vǫllo sporna*, *Vsp* 24).[115] This *vígspá* constitutes the *seiðr* that Óðinn must learn, once the war is resolved and the Vanir become teachers of the Æsir. In *Gylfaginning* Snorri paraphrases and quotes lines which show an equal division of the slain between Óðinn and Freyja, with 'half the slain she chooses' (*hálfan val hón kýss*, *Grím* 14).[116] *Godan* (Woden) and *Frea* similarly discuss apportioning victory or death to the Vandals and Winnili in an anecdote in the *Historia Langobardorum* of Paulus Diaconus in the late eighth century.[117] These references may reveal Freyja to be the archetypal *valkyrja*. Only with Freyja's witchcraft, in this way, can Óðinn regenerate fallen kings for Valhǫll, half of whose number must go to her embrace as if for the teacher's fee: the sibyl Hyndla reminds Freyja of the time 'when you have your man in the company of the slain' (*er þú hefir ver þinn í valsinni*, *Hynd* 6). Similarly, only with the witchcraft of the goddesses Þorgerðr and her sister Irpa can Hákon Jarl create a demon from a tree and a man's heart in *Þorleifs þáttr*. The sum of this Norse evidence suggests that the *seiðr*-magic of the Vanir was regarded from the earliest time as instrumental in the regeneration and subsequent deification of kings who fell in battle.

[114] *AIEW* 25 (*an-*); *ANEW* 16 (*áss*).
[115] Dronke, 'War of the Æsir and Vanir', pp. 226 and 230–1 (also published in *Myth and Fiction*, no. VII). Dronke compares OIce *vǫllo sporna* with the idiom in *Oddr* 8: *knátti mær oc mǫgr moldveg sporna* ('daughter and son began to kick at the earth-road [were born]').
[116] *Gylf*, p. 24 (ch. 24).   [117] *Historia Langobardorum*, ed. Waitz, pp. 52–6.

Óðinn illustrates another use of *seiðr* when he begets Váli to avenge the death of Baldr. When Loki induces Hǫðr to throw the mistletoe-spear that kills Hǫðr's brother Baldr, Óðinn seduces Rindr to beget Váli, a new son; this boy grows to manhood in one day and avenges Baldr on Hǫðr. There is an allusion to this myth in *Vsp* 32–3. Saxo reveals that Othinus has to dress up as a female physician to get near Rinda, whom he seduces in her bed only on the fourth attempt.[118] In *Gylfaginning*, Snorri probably suppresses this undignified epilogue to the story of Baldr's death. Yet we have seen that Kormákr alludes to this story with a tag that says 'Yggr practised *seiðr* to get Rindr' (*seið Yggr til Rindar*).[119] Loki also accuses Óðinn of 'practising witchcraft' (*síða*) and travelling 'in the shape of a witch' (*vitca líki*, *Lok* 23), not long before he taunts Frigg, his next victim, with the memory of his (Loki's) part in Baldr's death (*Lok* 28). If Loki's taunt against Óðinn and Frigg, Baldr's parents, is to be read as pointed rather than as broadly offensive, it seems that Óðinn must become a *seiðmaðr*, a man with a woman's procreative powers, in order to produce Váli.[120]

OIce *Váli* appears to mean 'little member of the Vanir' (from *wanila). De Vries suggests that *váli* means 'little warrior' (from *waihalaR), in support of his idea that Baldr's death represents a mock-stabbing initiation rite in an Odinic *Männerbund*; with no initial diphthong in the stem of *wanila, however, the phonology of *wanila > váli is easier to explain than that of *waihalaR > váli.[121] With Váli, Óðinn's use of *seiðr* to beget a new brother for Baldr marks the crucial contribution of the Vanir. The manner of Váli's birth, the replacing of Baldr, resembles the resurrection of dead warriors in Valhǫll. In both cases it is the power of *seiðr* that enables Óðinn to bring warriors to life, whether by reincarnating a prince in a rapidly growing baby one day old (Baldr and Váli), or by regenerating him from a dead king in Valhǫll (the *einherjar*).

A family relationship between Óðinn and the *einherjar* is implicit in

---

[118] *GD*, pp. 70–1.   [119] *Skj* B I, 69, 3.

[120] A similar motif may be contained in the second birth of Dionysus, when Zeus sews this baby into his thigh: *Bacchae*, ed. Dodds, p. 23 (lines 526–7): 'Come, twice-born, pass into this male womb of mine' (Ἴθι, Διθύραμβ᾽, ἐμὰν ἄρσενα τάνδε βᾶθι νηδύν).

[121] *Wanila with loss of *n* and compensatory lengthening of the first syllable; see E. Sievers, 'Grammatische Miscellen 8. Altnordische Váli und Beyla', *BGdSL* 18 (1894), 582–4, esp. 582–3; *pace* de Vries, 'Mythos von Baldrs Tod', pp. 48–9 and *ANEW* 641 (*Váli*).

Heathen gods

Óðinn's epithets *Valfǫðr* ('father of the slain', *Vsp* 1), and *Heriafǫðr* ('father of armies', *Grím* 25 and *Hynd* 2 (emended from MS *Herians fǫðr*)). Snorri explains this relationship when he names Óðinn 'Father of the slain (*Valfǫðr*), because his adopted sons are all those who fall in battle'.[122] This father–son relationship may have started as adoptive, but I suggest that it was as old as the earliest Germanic ideology of a warrior-paradise. It explains how, in pre-Christian England, any number of successful warriors with no name or background, but with this ideology in their children's minds, might have been claimed as Woden's sons when they were dead. It is thus possible that the earliest churchmen used this adoptive kinship with Woden as a substitute for their patrons's older ideology of descent from Ingui or another genuinely tribal god.

CONCLUSION

Woden's role in *Woden worhte weos* (*Max I* II, 132a) may now be explained as follows. Two Valhǫll-demons named in an Old Norse–Icelandic source are the prototypical *einherjar* Sigmundr and Hermóðr, to whom Óðinn in their lifetimes gave weapons and coats of mail (*Hynd* 1–2). In the riddle in *Háv* 49 both appear to be stylized as 'tree-men' or idols receiving armour from the speaker Óðinn. 'Tree-men' are further associated with funeral mounds in *Ragnars saga Loðbrókar* and in Óláfr Tryggvason's tale of Freyr in *Flateyjarbók*. In these sources and in *Þorleifs þáttr Jarlsskálds*, Þorgarðr and the other idols of Hákon Jarl appear to be late versions of the *herþarfir ásmegir* ('the kinsmen of the Æsir necessary to an army') that are said to fill the temples of Norway in Einarr's *Vellekla* (stanza 16). To the extent that Óðinn immortalizes dead warrior kings by regenerating them in Valhǫll, he is imagined as the father of such *ásmegir*, who, by living within Hákon Jarl's *vé*, count as minor gods (*vé* or *véar*) themselves. These uses of *vé* in *Hákonarmál* 17–18, *Vellekla* 16 and *Hyndluljóð* 1–2, together with the deification of Hákon Aðalsteinsfóstri and King Erik of Sweden, show the possibility of an indigenous Anglian Valhǫll in *Woden worhte weos*, in which, with witchcraft taught him by the Vanir, 'Woden made demons' out of dead kings on Anglian battlefields who then became his sons.

---

[122] *Gylf*, p. 21 (ch. 20): 'Valfǫðr, þvíat hans óskasynir eru allir þeir er í val falla.'

5

'Uoden de cuius stirpe': the role of Woden in royal genealogy

Woden is known as the ancestor of kings in Anglo-Saxon royal genealogy. This chapter is an attempt to show with what ecclesiastical justification this role could have been adapted from the mythological status of Woden as a witch or necromancer. I shall begin by showing how Woden probably usurped Seaxneat in West Saxon genealogy in the late seventh century; how Bede or his predecessors may have rationalized the dynastic status of Woden, a former heathen god, by implying his equivalence to Jacob, father of the twelve tribes of Israel; and how Bede's inheritors, in turn, seem to have positioned Woden in the regnal lists as the Abraham of the Anglo-Saxon past. Then I shall try to show how the West Saxons could have been responsible for Óðinn's ancestral role in the influential *Háleygjatal* (*c*. 985). Last of all, I shall explore what connection, if any, there is between Woden's Bernician son *Bældæg* and Óðinn's son *Baldr*; in the process of this discussion I shall argue that Baldr's name is derived from an epithet of Ingvi-freyr.

WODEN IN ANGLO-SAXON ROYAL GENEALOGY

Anglo-Saxon royal genealogies are found in the *Anglo-Saxon Chronicle* in the entries for the years 547, 560 and 855; and also in the more important regnal lists. This material is various and palaeographically difficult. Though Erna Hackenberg's presentation of the evidence is still useful, Kenneth Sisam gave a more detailed picture of Anglo-Saxon royal genealogies by producing a chronology of regnal lists and genealogies and the alterations which they underwent.[1] Thus Sisam identified a stage in

---

[1] *Stammtafeln*, ed. Hackenberg; Sisam, 'Anglo-Saxon Royal Genealogies', pp. 287–348,

which Woden, later the son of Frealaf, became the founder of all Anglian and Anglian-dominated tribes; then a stage in the later eighth century in which the Lindsey Angles extended Woden's line back to Geot, whose name was spelt *Geat* by the West Saxons; later, probably in the reign of King Æthelwulf, a West Saxon extension of Geat's line back to Sceldwea the son of Sceaf(a); then a crucial extension in which probably King Alfred had Sceldwea descend from Noah in the entry for 855, thus linking the house of Wessex with 'Adam primus homo; et pater noster est Christus, amen.'[2]

The West Saxon extension from Geat to Noah was neither immediate nor straightforward. Æthelweard took the West Saxon kings no further back than *Scef* when he translated a (lost) text of the *Anglo-Saxon Chronicle* into Latin. In this respect, it is likely that the text with which Æthelweard worked contained no extension further back than Scef, otherwise Æthelweard would have included it.[3] Since Scef is provided with ancestors in all extant versions of the *Anglo-Saxon Chronicle*, the vernacular text which Æthelweard translated was probably older than the common archetype.[4] In the æ-*Chronicle* and later, Sceaf(ing) was made a son of Noah. With correction of an omission in *Chronicle* A, the most fully extended West Saxon line descends thus, with the names of relevant figures italicized: Noah – *Sceaf* or Bedwig Sceafing – (three generations) – Heremod – *Sceldwea* – *Beaw* – Tætwa – *Geat* – (five generations) – *Woden* – Bældæg – (seven generations) – Cerdic – Cynric – Ceawlin – (four generations) – Ine brother of Ingild; Ingild – (three generations) – Ecgberht – Æthelwulf, whose death in 858 is the pretext for the whole record under year 855.

Not all of these names are gods whom the clergy euhemerized. Woden is the well-known Germanic *Mercurius*; Geat's name is apparently derived from that of the progenitor of the Goths; Sceaf, Sceldwea and Beaw are personifications of 'sheaf', 'shield' and 'barley'. Royal ancestors thus grew

---

esp. 308–14. For a more detailed study of the oldest *Chronicle* version in the Annals of St. Neots, see C. Hart, 'The East Anglian Chronicle', *JMH* 7 (1981), 249–82.

[2] *MS A: a Semi-Diplomatic Edition*, ed. Bately, p. 46.

[3] Meaney, 'Scyld Scefing Again', p. 13: 'shorter genealogies are earlier than longer ones: once a prestigiously long set of ancestors has been claimed, none of them is likely to be discarded deliberately – only by accidental omission'.

[4] A. L. Meaney, 'St. Neots, Æthelweard, and the Anglo-Saxon Chronicle', *Studies in English Prose*, ed. P. Szarmach (Albany, NY, 1986), pp. 193–245.

'Uoden de cuius stirpe'

more fantastic the further back in time the genealogists chose to invent them. That it was probably the bishops rather than the kings of Wessex who did so may be inferred from the work of Janet Bately, whose study of *Chronicle* vocabulary shows that not Alfred but his clergy ordered or dictated the compilation of the *Chronicle* even in the writing that began *c*. 892.[5]

It is with Woden and Frealaf that the Anglian collection ends, even if in the table below the case of Lindsey shows that at least one regnal list, by the end of the eighth century, had been extended further back. By this time, *G[i]ut(a)* in the *Historia Brittonum* or the Lindsey *Geot* had become WS *Geat*, eponym of the Goths and Geats.[6] Dumville's text of these lists is as follows:[7]

Deira	Bernicia	Mercia	Lindsey Geot	East Anglia
Frealaf	Frealaf	Frealaf	Frealaf	Frealaf
Uoden	Uoden	Woden	Uuoden	Uoden
Uegdæg	Beldaeg	Weoðulgeot	Uinta	Caser

Essex in a manuscript not belonging to the Anglian collection tells a different story: Seaxnet – Gesecg – Ants[ecg].[8] *Seaxneat* ('companion of the Saxons') is identical with OS *Saxnôt*, one of three deities whom converted Old Saxons were asked to renounce in a baptismal formula from the ninth century (*Wodan, Thunaer ende Saxnôt*). Because the name *Saxnôt* seems to allude to the Saxon tribes, Saxnôt or Seaxneat seems more likely than Wodan or Thunaer to be the god from whom all Saxons claimed descent. Tacitus states that the *Herminiones* were descended from Mannus and Tuisto in *Germania*; since it is known that the Old Saxons worshipped an *Irmin*-figure in their *Hirminsul*-shrine on the Weser, it is possible that Irmin-, a pillar-deity, became identified with Seaxneat at a time when the Saxons, unmentioned in *Germania*, arrived in the northern parts of Germany.[9]

---

[5] See J. Bately, 'The Compilation of the Anglo-Saxon Chronicle, 60 BC to A.D. 890: Vocabulary as Evidence', *PBA* 64 (1978), 93–129, esp. 127–9.

[6] For distribution, see Sisam, 'Anglo-Saxon Royal Genealogies', p. 308, n. 3; and Dumville, 'Anglian Collection', pp. 48–9.

[7] Dumville, *ibid.*, pp. 24 (dating) and 30–1 (text).

[8] Dumville, 'West Saxon Regnal List: Manuscripts and Texts', p. 32.

[9] *Germania*, p. 273 (ch. 2); *Widukindi Gestarum Saxonicarum*, ed. Hirsch and Lohmann, pp. 20–1 (I.12); *Annales Regni Francorum*, ed. Pertz and rev. Kurze, p. 35. See Tolley's discussion in 'Oswald's Tree', pp. 158–61.

Seaxneat survives only in the house of Essex, though his name suggests that he had once been taken as the founder of all Saxon kingdoms. Thus Woden's dynastic role was probably created by Angles rather than Saxons. Dumville, following a hint in Sisam's study, suggests that two Southumbrian king-lists were made on Northumbrian models at this time: the Kentish, upon the marriage of Edwin of Deira with Æthelburh daughter of Æthelberht (thus before 619–27); the West Saxon, either upon the baptism of King Cynegils *c.* 636 at which Oswald of Bernicia stood sponsor, or the marriage of King Aldfrith (685–705) to the sister of Ine of Wessex before the end of the seventh century.[10] The date for this transformation can be narrowed still further if the East Saxon conversions are taken into account. King Sæberht led the East Saxons into baptism in 604, but his sons reacted and drove Mellitus out on their father's death *c.* 616. Only after Wulfhere became king of Mercia in 659 did pressure come from outside to restore the East Saxons to Christianity; yet after the plague of 664 they apostatized again. Given that Seaxneat survived as the East Saxon royal forebear, it is likely that the political pressure to swap him for Woden had eased by the second half of the seventh century. Essex was never powerful in relation to its neighbours, so its kings could not have destroyed counter-propaganda in regnal lists outside their territory, if that had existed. The lack of any evidence, therefore, that Woden not Seaxneat was the forebear of East Saxon kings means that probably no attempt was made to install Woden in the royal genealogy of Essex. Sæberht thus kept Seaxneat as his ancestor when he was baptized because he had no reason to do otherwise. For these reasons, the ideology that gave Woden his dynastic role would have flourished at a time after 604 and before *c.* 650, and probably not long after a prominent Anglian king, by dying in battle, became the first 'son' of Woden to be entered into written record.

WODEN AND JACOB

In their choice of Woden, in particular, all royal families in the Anglian collection and West Saxon regnal lists reflect the power of Northumbria in the seventh century. All houses in the extant Anglian or Anglian-

---

[10] Dumville, 'Kingship, Genealogies and Regnal Lists', pp. 78–81; see also Sisam, 'Anglo-Saxon Royal Genealogies', p. 302.

dominated tradition conceive of Woden (rather than Frealaf, a later accretion) as an ultimate ancestor, and all Anglian kings descend each from a particular son, beneath which point no one house shares an ancestor with another. The artificiality of this numbering suggests that one Anglian house, possibly Oswald's Bernicia after his succession *c.* 633, sanctioned the re-ordering of other pedigrees as the statement of its hegemony over them. As shown below, the Kentish kings were now alleged to descend from Uegdaeg, the Deiran son of Uoden (Vespasian B. vi, 109r–v); the West Saxons from Bældæg, the Bernician son of Woden (CCCC 183, 65r–67r).[11] For their part, the eastern Angles claimed descent from Woden through an even more illustrious ancestor:

Deira/Kent	*Wessex/Bernicia*	*Mercia*	*East Anglia*
Frealaf	Frealaf	Frealaf	Frealaf
Uoden	Woden	Woden	Woden
Uegdaeg	Bældæg	Weoðulgeot	Caser

A picture of alliances could be read from these genealogies, with all Anglian houses making themselves known as sons of Woden. Yet even given the euhemerism which was popular in the early Middle Ages, it is still not clear how Woden's popularity was justified in ecclesiastical documents or how Bede records widespread royal descent from Woden in *HE* I.15 as a matter of course.[12] It is true that in England Woden may have been largely forgotten after the eighth century, as Meaney supposes.[13] Yet some English placename evidence, which occurs nearly exclusively outside the Anglian region of England, shows that the early Saxons and at least some Mercian Angles probably worshipped Woden as a god.[14] Though Woden's aristocratic status may have endeared him to the early missionary clergy in England, the witchcraft of Woden god of poetry, psychopomp or shaman, would not. Thus by the time *Oðon* had been established in the Danelaw for a century or more, Ælfric, adapting Martin of Braga's *De correctione rusticorum*, decries Mercury as 'very full of

---

[11] Dumville, 'Regnal List and Chronology of Early Wessex', pp. 29–34.

[12] On the development of euhemerism in early medieval Europe, see Faulkes, 'Descent from the Gods', pp. 106–10.

[13] Meaney, 'Woden in England', pp. 105–15; in reply to J. S. Ryan, 'Othin in England: Evidence from the Poetry for a Cult of Woden in Anglo-Saxon England', *Folklore* 74 (1963), 460–80.

[14] Gelling, *Signposts to the Past*, pp. 154–61, esp. 160 (distribution map).

crime and treacherous in his deeds' (*swiðe facenfull and swicol on dædum*).[15] However, given that Woden had once been worshipped in England, it is still necessary to give an account of the ecclesiastical sanction for Woden's place not only in regnal lists and royal genealogies, but more importantly in the *Historia ecclesiastica* of Bede, whose anti-secular tendencies Wormald has so well illustrated.[16]

By the early eighth century Woden was probably isolated from the more pernicious legends, though his status as a euhemerized war-god remains in the *Chronicle*'s suggestive placing of Ceawlin's battle in 592 (Laud): 'mycel wæl geweard on Brytene þes geares æt Wodnes beorge'.[17] This sentence appears to refer to a ritual analogous to the sacrifice of defeated Chatti to Mercury and Mars by the Hermunduri in AD 59.[18] As Wallace-Hadrill showed, the Anglo-Saxon church probably tolerated Woden for political reasons, in that any noble family's claim to be descended from Woden defined its royal status.[19] In Wallace-Hadrill's view, seventh- and eighth-century churchmen would idealize a king as a secular arm of the church, identifying his military aims with their own. The warlike kings of the Jews were thus the ideals on which the church could style its own kings in an age of conquest and expansion.

Bede's admiration for the pagan Æthelfrith is vindicated, in this way, when he compares Æthelfrith to Saul, 'except of course that he was ignorant of the faith'.[20] Besides trying to exterminate the Welsh, whose failure to convert his ancestors Bede had not forgiven, Æthelfrith is admired for having overrun Welsh lands to make them fit for English settlement: 'To whom could deservedly be applied that which the patriarch [Jacob] said, blessing his son in the aspect of Saul: "Benjamin shall ravin as the wolf; in the morning he shall devour the prey, and in the evening he shall divide the spoil."'[21] Here Bede uses St Paul's

---

[15] *Homilies of Ælfric*, ed. Pope II, 684 (line 134).
[16] Wormald, 'Bede, "Beowulf" and Conversion', pp. 58–63.
[17] *ASC* I, 21: 'a great slaughter of Britons took place this year at Woden's hill'.
[18] *Taciti Annales*, ed. Furneaux II, 228 (XIII.57).
[19] Wallace-Hadrill, *Early Germanic Kingship*, pp. 72–97, esp. 94–7; Dumville, 'Kingship, Genealogies and Regnal Lists', pp. 78–9.
[20] *HE* I.34 (p. 116): 'excepto dumtaxat hoc, quod diuinae erat religionis ignarus'; cf. the saving ignorance of Danish heathens at the close of the first numbered manuscript section of *Beowulf* (lines 50–2).
[21] 'Cui merito poterat illud, quod benedicens filium patriarcha in personam Saulis dicebat, aptari: "Beniamin lupus rapax; mane comedet praedam et uespere diuidet spolia."'

interpretation of Gen. XLIX.27 to look to Æthelfrith's barbaric example as but the prelude to the great missionary work of his descendants.[22] Yet there is one further aspect to this use of scripture. As Saul was descended by blood from Benjamin and Jacob, so it is possible to look for Æthelfrith's Bernician ancestors in the corresponding places: Bældæg thus answering for Benjamin, Woden for Jacob.

This identification could have been made as early as 655, as a result of a letter written in this year by Pope Vitalian to King Oswiu of Northumbria, in which Vitalian praised Oswiu's desire to strengthen the Anglo-Saxon church and quoted from Isaiah, particularly from verse XL.6: 'Parum est ut mihi sis seruus ad suscitandas tribus Iacob et Israel conuertendas. Dedi te in lucem gentium, ut sis salus mea usque ad extremum terrae.'[23] Also, as we have seen in Howe's interpretation of *Exodus*, it is likely that some Angles, perhaps the Northumbrians, had already identified their Germanic settler ancestors with the Jews in their journey from Egypt to the Holy Land. As the father of Israel's twelve tribes, Jacob was never far away:

> 1.   Alleluia.
> In exitu Israel de Aegypto,
> Domus Iacob de populo barbaro,
> 2. Facta est Iudaea sanctificatio eius,
> Israel potestas eius.
> 3. Mare vidit, et fugit;
> Iordanis conversus est retrorsum.   (Ps. CXIII.1–3)[24]

An existing Woden–Jacob correspondence could have enabled Bede to refer to Uoden by name in *HE* I.15.

WODEN AND ABRAHAM

A different scriptural ideology, later than Bede's, may be inferred from the late eighth-century regnal lists of the Anglian collection, in which

---

[22] Wallace-Hadrill, *Commentary*, pp. 47–8, esp. 48.

[23] *HE* III.29 (p. 318): 'It is a little thing for you to be my servant in reviving the tribes of Jacob and turning back Israel. I have given you as a light for the nations, that you may be my salvation until the ends of the earth.'

[24] 'Alleluia. In Israel's leaving Egypt, the House of Jacob leaving a people of foreign speech, Judaea was made his sanctuary, Israel was made his dominion. The sea looked on and fled; Jordan was turned back.'

Heathen gods

Wecta (Kent) or Wegdæg (Deira and Kent), Bældæg (Bernicia and Wessex), Weoþolgeot (Mercia), Winta (Lindsey) and Caser (East Anglia) are all alleged to be sons of Woden. As Sisam noted, these pedigrees number fourteen generations (including Woden), a sign of clerical influence, for St Matthew numbers fourteen generations from Abraham to David, then fourteen to Jeconiah at the Babylonian Captivity and fourteen again to Jesus (Matt. I.17).[25] In this context, it is possible that, after Bede, Woden was sanctioned in regnal lists as a counterpart of Abraham, a more ancient figure than Jacob. This claim to greater antiquity would be in keeping with the general backwards extension of royal genealogies throughout the Anglo-Saxon period.

WODEN GOES TO NORWAY

Power in England eventually moved south out of Northumbria, passing from Ecgfrith to the Mercians at the battle of the Trent in 670; later, after the reign of Offa, from Mercia to Wessex in Æthelwulf's victory in the battle of *Ellandun* c. 825.[26] Though the West Saxons struggled with Viking armies for the remainder of the ninth century, Alfred regained and fortified Wessex, his children Edward and Æthelflæd won territory in the Danelaw and Æthelstan, son of Edward, consolidated his family's expanded power by defeating a Scottish–Norse alliance in the battle of *Brunanburh* in c. 937. Æthelstan by this time had fostered Hákon, the baby son of King Haraldr hárfagri of Norway. It was probably following *Brunanburh* and with some financial support from Æthelstan's brothers, that Hákon sailed to Trondheim to claim his father's kingdom. There he managed to supplant his older half-brother Eiríkr blóðøx, who became a king of York in vassalage to Æthelstan's brothers Edmund and Eadred, until he was killed in the battle of Stainmoor in 954. Given Hákon's upbringing, it is likely that the priests and adventurers he brought from England carried a West Saxon regnal list as documentary proof of the status of this house now dominating the English scene.

In their half-fabulous way, *Ágrip*, *Fagrskinna* and Snorri's *Hákonar saga*

---

[25] Sisam, 'Anglo-Saxon Royal Genealogies', pp. 326–8; Dumville, 'Kingship, Genealogies and Regnal Lists', pp. 89–90.
[26] Kirby, *Earliest English Kings*, pp. 95–8 and 189–91.

góða show that Hákon failed to convert the heathens of Norway.[27] Yet for more political than spiritual reasons Hákon's West Saxon pedigree was not forgotten. As Joan Turville-Petre and Klaus von See have indicated, Hákon *Aðalsteinsfóstri* ('Æthelstan's foster-son') could have stabilized his family's claims to Norway by grafting his mother's *Hlaðajarla*-dynasty onto the politically mature stem of the house of Wessex; i.e. onto the family tree of Woden.[28] This would be a late example, albeit through Christian literate means, of Wodan's northward migration from the south.

The anglicized Hákon soon went native and abandoned the Christian mission, probably to keep his power over the men of the Trondheim region. The length of Hákon's reign in his part of Norway (*c.* 947–60) suggests that he established himself by this move. Yet Hákon's nephews, the sons of Eiríkr blóðøx, took Hákon's life and kingdom in *c.* 960 in the Battle of Storð. Haraldr gráfeldr Eiríksson is then said to have ruled Norway under the supervision of his widowed mother Gunnhildr. Their rule lasted until another Hákon appeared on the scene. This man, the clever Hákon Sigurðarson of Hlaðir, contrived two murders to return to Norway while he was in exile in Denmark: that of Haraldr gráfeldr himself at the hands of King Gull-Haraldr, with whom Hákon was staying; then Gull-Haraldr's death in battle by the sword of Haraldr gráfeldr's uncle, Haraldr Gormsson. The surviving Haraldr drove the remaining sons of Eiríkr blóðøx from Norway in *c.* 970 and put Hákon in power over Hálogaland and seven districts south of the Trondheim boundary. Hákon in this way remained a Danish vassal for four years until he joined Haraldr Gormsson in a war against Otto II of Saxony. Otto's generals defeated both kings, but let them live, forcibly baptizing Hákon, who none the less cast off his new faith on the way home and seceded from the Danes. To avoid pirates or Danish capture on the way, he is said to have disembarked in Göteland and taken his depleted force back

---

[27] *Ágrip*, ed. Bjarni, pp. 7–11 (chs. 5–6) and 74–95 (*Fagrskinna*, chs. 6–13); *Heimskringla I*, ed. Bjarni, pp. 150–97 (*Hákonar saga góða*, chs. 13–18).

[28] Turville-Petre, 'On *Ynglingatal*', pp. 48–67, esp. 63; Von See, *Mythos und Theologie*, pp. 69–79, esp. 78. H. Kuhn also suggested that 'eine Erhöhung Odins' in Norway could have come about as a result of contact with England, in 'Die Religion der nordischen Völker in der Wikingerzeit', in *I normanni e la loro espansione in Europa nell'alto medioevo*, *Settimane* 16 (1968), 117–29, esp. 125; and Steinsland (*Det hellige bryllup*, p. 87) suggests that Eyvindr skáldaspillir chose Óðinn over Freyr for Hákon's ancestor.

overland to Trøndelag. Here he took the archaic title *jarl* and re-established a provincial style of leadership in reaction to Haraldr Gormsson the Danish *konungr*.

The zenith of Hákon Jarl was yet to come. In *c.* 985 he is said to have earned the epithet *inn ríki* ('the powerful') after defeating an invading Danish fleet in the battle of Hjǫrungavágr. For a while his part of Norway was pagan once more; harvests were good and heathen sacrifices were renewed; the last flame of paganism burned all the brighter for a number of distinguished court poets, including Eyvindr skáldaspillir Finnsson, Hallfreðr vandræðaskáld Óttarsson, Tindr Hallkelsson, Einarr skála-glamm Helgason, and Eilífr Goðrúnarson. Yet the high quality of the surviving work of these poets conceals the eccentricity of Hákon's experiment. Norway and its northern ruler were politically insignificant and Hákon Jarl's political reaction, however Eyvindr and the younger poets began to stylize it into a theology, would survive no longer than he did. When his luck ran out, Hákon was murdered by a slave while on the run from his countrymen in 995 following one attempt too many to take a farmer's wife as his temporary concubine.[29] With indifference to the genealogical claims of *Háleygjatal*, the men of Trondheim replaced Hákon Jarl with Óláfr Tryggvason, an adventurer from the rival dynasty of Vestfold.

It was in honour of Hákon Jarl that Eyvindr composed the *Háleygjatal*, probably soon after the victory against the Danes and Jómsvikings in Hjǫrungavágr. Daphne Davidson, in her edition of this and three other poems of the same reign, confirms what has long been accepted: that true to his epithet *skáldaspillir* ('plunderer of poets', hence 'plagiarist'), Eyvindr modelled his *Háleygjatal* ('list of kings of Hálogaland') on the older *Ynglingatal* of Þjóðólfr of Hvinir. As Davidson has suggested in her edition of *Háleygjatal* and other poems, the Hlaðajarlar probably wanted to rival the Vestfold kings; hence the position of Óðinn as the god-founder of Hákon Jarl's line in opposition to the pre-eminent Ingvi-freyr, father of the Swedish kings and the smaller kings of Vestfold.[30] The West Saxon Woden was probably pressed into this service in the 950s, about two generations before Óðinn emerged at the head of *Háleygjatal*.

Eyvindr skáldaspillir was the last Norwegian skáld of distinction in

---

[29] *Ágrip*, ed. Bjarni, p. 16 (ch. 12).
[30] Davidson, 'Earl Hákon and his Poets', p. 57.

heathen Scandinavia. His father Finnr skjálgi was a chieftain from Hálogaland; his mother a grand-daughter of King Haraldr hárfagri of Vestfold. If not from his own family, in this way, Eyvindr is likely to have inherited from Sigurðr Jarl Hákonarson, his patron Hákon Jarl's father, some knowledge of the West Saxon house which had fostered Hákon Haraldsson some sixty years before. It was Haraldr hárfagri's ally Sigurðr Jarl who gave the child the *Hákon* name from his own family, before Haraldr sent his baby son to Æthelstan. It was the same Sigurðr who helped to establish Hákon Aðalsteinsfóstri in the Trondheim region and who was therefore in a position to learn the pedigree of King Alfred of Wessex.

Unlike the older *Ynglingatal* on which Eyvindr probably based his work, the *Háleygjatal* of Eyvindr survives with its opening stanza intact. In *Háleygjatal* 1 he asks for a hearing 'while I trace his [Jarl Hákon's] lineage in the cauldron, in the liquid of the cargo of gallows [Óðinn's poetry], back to the gods' (*meðan hans ætt í hverlegi galga farms til goða teljum*). He describes a union between Óðinn and Skaði which begot *Sæmingr* ('son of the Lapp') at the head of Hákon's family:

> Þann skjaldblœtr   skattfœri gat
> Ása niðr   við Jarnviðju,
> þás þau mær   í Manheimum
> skatna vinr   ok Skaði byggðu.   (*Háleygjatal* 3)[31]

Eyvindr's pedigree for his patron Hákon Jarl is complicated by the contradictions of Snorri, the leading commentator. Alluding to *Háleygjatal* in the prologues to *Óláfs saga Helga* and *Heimskringla*, the larger kings' sagas, Snorri takes Sæmingr to be son of Ingunar-Freyr, the son of Njǫrðr.[32] Quoting the first stanza of this poem later in *Ynglinga saga*, however, Snorri gives Sæmingr as the offspring of Óðinn and Skaði, after Skaði divorced Njǫrðr.[33] Óðinn is Sæmingr's father in a more complicated text, the prologue to Snorri's *Edda*, in which either Snorri or another author derived the Æsir from Troy.[34] The author of this prologue made

---

[31] 'The kinsman of the Æsir, worshipped with a shield, begot that tribute-bringer with Iron-wood giantess, when the glorious pair, the friend of warriors and Skaði, lived in the homes of "Man" [?man/?love].'
[32] *Heimskringla II*, ed. Bjarni, p. 421; and *Heimskringla I*, ed. Bjarni, p. 4.
[33] *Heimskringla I*, ed. Bjarni, p. 21.
[34] Faulkes, 'Descent from the Gods', pp. 96–102.

Óðinn an *Alfǫðr* ('all-father') of a further four productive sons: Veggdegg, father of the German East Saxons, Beldegg or Baldr, of Westphalia, Siggi, of France and of the Vǫlsungs, and Skjǫldr, of the Goths, Jutland and Denmark.[35]

In *Háleygjatal* Eyvindr may also have conflated *Sceldwea* with Woden in his unparalleled compound *skjaldblœtr* ('worshipped with a shield'). If it is true that Eyvindr grafted the relatively undistinguished Háleygir on Woden, the ancestor of a West Saxon stem, it was Sceldwea whom the West Saxons by the time of Æthelstan counted as one of the oldest indigenous members of their line. The etymology of *Sceldwea* or *Scyldwa* is uncertain, though the Anglian stem-vowel of its first form suggests that this name is at least as old as the eighth century. The form *Sceldwea* probably influenced Eyvindr's *skjaldblœtr* (*Háleygjatal* 3) in the tenth century, even before the Icelanders appropriated this name from West Saxon documents in the twelfth or thirteenth: *Skuld*, modelled on IWS *Scyld*, is thus re-identified with the Danish *Skjǫldr* when he is assimilated into the Trojan pedigree in the prologue to *Gylfaginning*.[36]

In the Trondheim region in the late tenth century, as Davidson has shown, Eyvindr probably exploited the ambiguity of epithets to have Hákon Jarl descend from both Freyr and Óðinn; possibly there is an allusion to Freyr and Freyr's legendary wealth in *skattfœrir* ('tribute-bringer'), the title by which Eyvindr refers to Óðinn's son and Sæmingr's father. Adam of Bremen, nearly a century later, seems to have indicated Freyr and Skaði when he refers to Hákon Jarl as 'that most cruel man descended from the kin of Ingunar and the blood of giants'.[37] Thus Eyvindr would have replaced Hǫlgi, Njǫrðr or Freyr with Óðinn; and Snorri, taking this tendency further and comparing Eyvindr's account with *Skírnismál* and *Lokasenna*, 'may have cut Freyr/Yngvifreyr out of Eyvindr's genealogy and attempted to "correct" Eyvindr's poem in one of his prose versions of it'.[38] Davidson follows Ström in taking Skaði to be a winter aspect of Freyja (though perhaps Freyja should be regarded as the human hypostasis of Skaði), but she also regards *Jarnviðja* as a reference to the half-monstrous ancestry of the men of Hálogaland which is also

---

[35] *Gylf*, pp. 5–6.   [36] *Ibid.*, p. 6.

[37] *Gesta*, ed. Schmeidler, p. 84 (II.xxv): 'Haacon iste crudelissimus ex genere Ingunar et giganteo sanguine descendens.'

[38] Davidson, 'Earl Hákon and his Poets', pp. 58–64, esp. 60–1. This problem is discussed at greater length in Steinsland (*Det hellige bryllup*, pp. 216–19).

hinted at in a similar picture of the men of nearby Hrafnista in *Egils saga Skalla-Grímssonar*.[39] Elsewhere in *Háleygjatal*, Eyvindr describes Hákon's ancestors as *Freys áttungr*, 'Freyr's kinsman' (of Hákon Grjótgarðsson, *Háleygjatal* 8), or *Týs áttungr*, 'Óðinn's/Týr's kinsman' (Sigurðr Jarl, *Háleygjatal* 11). Therefore, as he indicates in stanza 1, it seems that Eyvindr wished to obscure Freyr's role in his patron's lineage by gathering or syncreting as many other names as possible for his patron's supernatural forebears: Skaði, Njǫrðr, Freyja, giants and Lapps; but no-one greater than Óðinn.

The increasing use of Óðinn as a founder of Scandinavian dynasties, both Norwegian and Icelandic, can probably be traced to the influence of West Saxon texts in twelfth-century Iceland: Ælfric's *De falsis diis* was translated into *Um þat hvaðan ótrú hófst* at this time, and a list of West Saxon kings similar to that of Cotton Tiberius A. iii., fol. 178, was incorporated into the early thirteenth-century *Breta sǫgur*, a translation of Geoffrey of Monmouth's *Historia regum Britanniae* (c. 1135).[40] Óðinn's great popularity with Snorri was probably a consequence of his status as the intellectual god of poetry. Yet, as a passage in Paulus Diaconus's *Historia Langobardorum* shows, with Godan's unwitting gift of victory to the Winnili (forebears of the Langobards), Woden could already be claimed as a patron by Germanic tribes in older heathen times.[41] In Scandinavia, as *Grímnismál* shows, Óðinn seems to have appropriated the roles of many other gods long before the earliest Old Norse–Icelandic records were written down. Óðinn's adoption of the role of Skaði's husband was probably the latest addition to an old syncretic tendency. Thus Eyvindr, in *Háleygjatal* 14, alludes to Norway as if the land were Óðinn's enormous bride now lying under the embrace of Hákon Jarl, Óðinn's descendant through his union with the even bigger *Skaði*, whose name is an ethnic form of *Scandinavia*. This union is reported in *Háleygjatal* 4, where Eyvindr says that 'many sons did the Snowshoe-goddess [Skaði] conceive by Óðinn' (*sunu marga Ǫndurdís við Óðni gat*).

As we have seen in ch. 1, Skaði's husband in a verse exchange preserved in *Gylfaginning* is properly Njǫrðr.[42] Though the name of the local

---

[39] *Egils saga*, ed. Sigurður, pp. 3–4 (ch. 1).
[40] Faulkes, 'Descent from the Gods', pp. 97–9.
[41] *Historia Langobardorum*, ed. Waitz, pp. 52–6.
[42] *Gylf*, p. 24 (ch. 23); Snorri describes Skaði's marriage to Njǫrðr in *SnE* 212–14 (*Bragarœður*, ch. 56); *FJSnE* 81.

Heathen gods

goddess Þórgerðr *Hǫlga-brúðr* ('bride of Hǫlgi') suggests that some Háleygir continued to trace themselves back to Gerðr and Freyr (or a male eponym), it seems likely that when Woden was placed at the head of the Háleygir in the late 940s, he took a dynastic role which had been Freyr's and thereby took most of Freyr's position as the husband of Norway. As Þjóðólfr shows in *Haustlǫng*, it was already Óðinn's role a century earlier to beget Þórr on Jǫrð: Þórr is both *grundar sveinn* ('ground's lad') and *Óðins burr* ('Óðinn's boy') in this poem.[43] So the Norwegian subjects of Hákon Aðalsteinsfóstri, once they had followed the West Saxon precedent with Woden and had made Óðinn into the father of human dynasties, may have been encouraged to go further and give Óðinn the place of Freyr or Hǫlgi as Norway's divine husband. From *Háleygjatal* onwards, there is barely a hint in the Old Norse–Icelandic tradition that any god other than Óðinn had married the earth to beget kings.

BÆLDÆG AND BALDR

As we have seen, *Bældæg* ('pyre-day') is the name of Woden's son in the Bernician and West Saxon regnal lists.[44] Jan de Vries accordingly suggested that the Norse god *Baldr* got his name and role as Óðinn's son from an OE *Bealdor*, which had been personified from OE *bealdor* ('lord') on the model of *Bældæg*.[45] This theory is unsound, however, because no Anglian or native West Saxon personification of OE *bealdor* can be traced. Æthelweard presents a *Balder* in *Bældæg*'s place in Kings' Æthelwulf's genealogy in his *Chronicon* (*c*. 975), but in his case this name is most likely to be a product of contemporary Danish or Norwegian influence.[46] Anthony Faulkes notes that a dynasty is traced from *Balldr* the son of *Óðinn* in AM 1 f. fol., fol. 13 (which Ketill Jörundarson copied in the early seventeenth century from a continuation of the thirteenth-century fragment AM 162 m fol., which was originally part of another manuscript, AM 764 quarto); but otherwise Baldr is not portrayed as a progenitor.[47] Baldr's dynastic role in this manuscript was probably

---

[43] *Skj* B I, 18, 19.   [44] Dumville, 'Anglian Collection', pp. 24 and 30–1.
[45] *AR* II, 233 (§488): 'Man kann ja auch das Verhältnis so erklären, dass nach dem Vorbild dieser *dæg*-Namen das mythologische Wort *Bealdor* umgebildet wurde.'
[46] *Chronicle of Æthelweard*, ed. Campbell, p. 7.
[47] Faulkes, 'Descent from the Gods', p. 105.

influenced by that of *Beldegg*, a form which is given as a variant of *Baldr*'s name in the prologue to *Gylfaginning* and is clearly based on *Bældæg* in a borrowed West Saxon regnal list.[48] There is thus no evidence that an Anglo-Saxon counterpart of the god Baldr was known in England by an Old English cognate of Baldr's name.

The background of Baldr, whose name is cognate with OE *bealdor*, is as follows. Snorri states Baldr's status as the son of Óðinn and Frigg in *Gylfaginning* (chs. 22 and 49); this position is already implicit in *Haustlǫng* 16, *Lok* 27, *Vsp* 33 and *Bdr* 3. In Old Norse–Icelandic mythology Baldr is a dying god, for he is killed when Loki tricks Baldr's blind brother Hǫðr into spearing Baldr with a spear tipped with mistletoe. In outline this story resembles the death of warriors on the battlefield, killed by the spears of Óðinn's valkyries, especially since the names *Baldr* and *Hǫðr* appear to mean 'prince' and 'battle' respectively. Yet Baldr represents a tradition separate from the *einherjar* of Valhǫll, in that he is a god to start with, while any deified warriors are not; and in that he dies in tragic circumstances in an apparent emulation of the death of Jesus Christ.

Most references to Baldr are datable to the period after the conversion of Scandinavia and are scattered widely throughout the Eddic corpus; Baldr is the chief subject of *Baldrs Draumar*, a poem probably of the eleventh or twelfth century; the fullest account of Baldr, Snorri's in *Gylfaginning* (ch. 49), is of the early thirteenth century. Snorri says that when Baldr dreams of his imminent death one night, Frigg exacts oaths from all phenomena of creation not to harm him, with the exception of mistletoe, which she regards as too young to swear the oath. The Æsir then test Baldr's new strength by pelting him with all kinds of missiles. Loki finds out about the mistletoe, arms Baldr's blind brother Hǫðr with a mistletoe point and persuades him to shoot. Baldr falls dead. While Óðinn foresees the resulting end of the world, the ever-resourceful Æsir ask another son of Óðinn, Hermóðr, to ride to the goddess Hel and negotiate for Baldr's release. Meanwhile Baldr's funeral takes place, Óðinn places him on his pyre, whispers a secret message into his ear and orders him to be pushed out to sea in his burning ship. Having stayed with Baldr overnight in the underworld, Hermóðr puts the question to Hel, who promises to release Baldr if all creation weeps for him. The Æsir pass

---

[48] *Gylf*, p. 5 (prol. ch. 10): 'Óðinn's second son was named Beldegg, whom we call Baldr' (*annarr son Óðins hét Beldegg, er vér kǫllum Baldr*).

on her instructions, but lose Baldr in the end when the giantess Þǫkk, Loki in disguise, refuses to weep for his return. Baldr stays in the world of the dead.

The name *Baldr*, as we have seen, was probably personified from a Norse epithet cognate with OE *bealdor* meaning 'lord' or 'prince'.[49] Beowulf is called *winia bealdor* ('prince/lord of friends', *Beo* 2567); likewise King Hreðel, who dies of grief, as *sinca baldor* ('lord of treasures', *Beo* 2428); Holofernes, before and after his death at the hands of Judith, is successively *gumena baldor* ('lord of men', *Jud* 9), *wigena baldor* ('lord of fighters', *Jud* 49) and *rinca baldor* ('lord of warriors', *Jud* 338); St Juliana when she fights the devil is *mægþa bealdor* ('prince of virgins', *Jul* 568); the Lord, remembered as the youthful Christ, is *þeoda baldor* ('Lord of nations', *And* 547); Abraham calls King Abimelech *gumena baldor* ('prince of men', *Gen* 2694); David is *wigona baldor* ('prince of fighters', *El* 344); and Guthlac's servant recalls Guthlac as *beorna bealdor* ('lord of soldiers', *Guth* 1358) after his death. Six out of eight instances thus show that the referent of OE *bealdor* is expected to die before his time; and since Abimelech is threatened with death by the Lord in Gen. XX.3, only David in *Elene* appears to be an exception. Though the extant Anglo-Saxon poets never personify *bealdor*, which was not used with the meaning of its Norse cognate, it appears that the Old English word connotes a hero (or heroine) whose days are numbered.

The earliest surviving cognate of OE *bealdor* and OIce *Baldr* appears in a third- or fourth-century inscription found among sixteen votary dedications, eight on each of two tablets, from Roman Utrecht: [*vota erc*]*oul*[*eo*] *macusa*[*n*]*o, baldruo, lobbo*[*no*] *sol*[*verunt*] *decur*[*iones*] ('the decurions have made their offerings to Ercouleus [Hercules] the Powerful, the *baldruus* and *lobbonus*').[50] In order to throw some more light on the meaning of *bealdor* and *Baldr*, it will be necessary to discuss the words *baldruus* and *lobbonus* in this inscription.

---

[49] Green, *Carolingian Lord*, pp. 21–33. Green's discussion includes a refutation of H. Kuhn's idea that 'brightness' rather than 'lord' or 'prince' is the underlying meaning of *baldr*: see Kuhn, who otherwise identifies the Merseburg *balder* with Phol, in 'Es gibt kein balder "Herr"', in *Erbe der Vergangenheit: Germanistische Beiträge: Festgabe für Karl Helm zum 80. Geburtstage 19. Mai 1951*, ed. L. Wolff (Tübingen, 1951), pp. 37–45 (repr. in his *Kleine Schriften* II, 296–326).

[50] Gutenbrunner, *Götternamen*, pp. 58–9 (date), 63–5 (discussion) and 218–20 (text); Gutenbrunner takes *Baldruus* to be identical with the Norse *Baldr* (p. 62).

'Uoden de cuius stirpe'

Lobbon(n)us, a form apparently related to the name of a Celtic god, is in all sixteen inscriptions in which he is otherwise hailed as *deus* ('god'), *deus aeques* ('horseman god') and *genius sanctus Bataborum* ('holy guardian spirit of the Batavi').[51] Germanic cognates or reflexes of the Utrecht *lobbon-* appear to be OE *lufu* ('love'), OIce *lyf* ('herbal medicine') and *Lofn*, the last a synonym for 'woman' in scaldic kennings and the name of the eighth of Snorri's *ásynjur* ('goddesses').[52] Snorri says that Lofn is so generous that 'she gets leave from All-father [Óðinn] or Frigg for people's union, between men and women, though it may previously have been forbidden or absolutely refused'.[53] With a dative masculine ending in the Utrecht inscription, *lobbonus* thus seems to be an epithet of Hercules indicating urgent human union. This interpretation is also in keeping with a classical tale in which *Heracles* made all fifty daughters of King Thespius pregnant, either in fifty nights or in one.[54] D. H. Green identifies *Ercouleus* in the Utrecht inscription with a Germanic Donar or Þórr, but this claim is still open to doubt:[55] both Hercules and Freyr are associated with the boar, the horse and apples of eternal youth; Hercules's weapon is a wooden club, Þórr's an iron hammer; since Freyr's is a stag's horn, and lust is not documented as characteristic of Þórr, the formula *Ercouleus macusanus baldruus lobbonus* in the Utrecht votary inscription is more likely to refer to a Lower Rhineland conception of Ingvi-freyr.

The old etymology of Indo-European *$bhel$, the stem of *baldr*, is 'to swell (with vigour or strength)'; the etymology of Gmc *$balþs$, etymon of OE *beald*, OIce *ballr* and ModE *bold*, is 'swollen', slowly developing into 'powerful'; thus Green suggests that the Old English and Norse *baldr* appellatives 'go back to an Indo-European root meaning "virile"'.[56] A word *magusanus* ('?powerful') is otherwise used as an epithet of Hercules in fifteen inscriptions.[57] In the light of these connections, *Baldr* appears to be derived from an epithet indicating fertile physical power. Thus the

---

[51] *Ibid.*, pp. 218–20.
[52] *Ibid.*, pp. 65–9; Meissner, *Kenningar der Skalden*, p. 407 (x. 9).
[53] *Gylf*, p. 29 (ch. 35): 'hon fær leyfi af Alfǫður eða Frigg til manna samgangs, kvenna ok karla, þótt áðr sé bannat eða þvertekit'.
[54] *Pausaniae Graeciae Descriptio*, ed. H. Hitzig and H. Bluemner, 3 vols. (Leipzig, 1896–1910) III, 356–7 (IX. xxvi. 6); *Pausanias: Description of Greece*, trans. A. R. Shilleto, 2 vols. (London, 1886) II, 191.
[55] Green, *Carolingian Lord*, pp. 12–13.
[56] *Ibid.*, pp. 5–9, esp. 9; for other interpretations, see also *ANEW* 24 (*ballr*).
[57] Gutenbrunner, *Götternamen*, pp. 220–1.

Heathen gods

Batavian Hercules *macusanus*, *baldruus* and *lobbonus*, god of horsemen, may be identified with Freyr *inn þroski* ('the vigorous') in *Skí* 38, in Freyr's role as the imminent sexual partner of Gerðr. Since *baldruus* is only found in the Utrecht inscription, *baldruus* may have been a relatively new epithet for the Freyr-hypostasis in the third or fourth century.

Two other Germanic instances, both involving horses, suggest that Baldr and Freyr share a common origin in a figure probably related to Lobbonus *deus aequites*. First, there is Týr's definition of Freyr in *Lok* 37: 'Freyr er beztr allra *ball*riða ása gǫrðom í' ('Freyr is the best of all *bold*-riders in the courtyards of the Æsir'). An OIce *baldriði* occurs in *Akv* 21. Second, as we have seen in the previous chapter, an OHG *balder* whose foal injures his hoof in *The Second Merseburg Charm* may be Freyr by another name, whose horse is named *Blóðughófi* ('bloody-hoof') in *Alsvinnsmál*.[58] In addition, Baldr and Freyr resemble one another in two other ways. First, Saxo says that Balderus, before dying at the hands of Hotherus, was made so ill by phantoms of Nanna, the nymph over whom they were at war, that he could no longer walk and 'for this reason began to make it his custom to measure out his journeys in a chariot or carriage'.[59] This wagon-tour resembles Freyr's in *Gunnars þáttr helmings*. Second, of all Norse gods only Baldr and Freyr appear to live mortal lives: Baldr is struck dead by Hǫðr's shaft of mistletoe (*Vsp* 32), then sent down in a burning ship and kept by the goddess Hel;[60] according to Saxo, who tells a partly euhemerized version of this story, Balderus is killed by Hotherus and then buried in a mound; while the Old Norse–Icelandic Freyr was once a baby (*Grím* 5), has his youth to look back on (*Skí* 5) and when he dies of old age is also interred in a mound.[61] On the evidence of the Utrecht inscription, *The Second Merseburg Charm* and this later

---

[58] *AR* II, 171–2 (§§452–3). *Edda*, ed. Neckel and rev. Kuhn, p. 320. Green shows this parallel (*Carolingian Lord*, pp. 15–17), but stops short of using it to identify Baldr with Freyr. For an attempt to connect this *balder* with Baldr, see S. Gutenbrunner, 'Der zweite Merseburger Zauberspruch im Lichte nordischer Überlieferung', *ZfdA* 80 (1944), 1–5.

[59] *GD*, p. 67 (III.ii): 'Quamobrem biga raedave emetiendorum itinerum consuetudinem habere coepit.' H. R. Ellis Davidson believes that Saxo confused Balderus with Frø (Freyr) at this point: see *History of the Danes*, ed. Fisher and Ellis Davidson II, 54–5, n. 25.

[60] *Gylf*, p. 47.

[61] *GD*, p. 66 (III.ii); see also *Heimskringla I*, ed. Bjarni, pp. 24–25 (*Ynglinga saga*, ch. 10); and *Flat* I, 401–3 (ch. 323).

Scandinavian material, the Norse god Baldr seems to have developed as a variant of Ingvi-freyr, his name being a personification of a Freyr-epithet that included Freyr's sexual power and Freyr's death.[62]

In different ways, the poets of *Vǫluspá*, *Hákonarmál* and *Eiríksmál*, as well as Saxo Grammaticus in *Gesta Danorum*, appear to exploit the resemblance between Baldr's death and that of the *einherjar* destined for Valhǫll on the battlefield. In *Vǫluspá* Baldr's death may be a sacrifice which is necessary for the renewal of growth in the world.[63] Though Loki is the instigator, probably from a very early time, Ursula Dronke notes that he refuses as Þǫkk to weep for Baldr's return because to do so would annul the sacrifice.[64] In a cyclical chronology within *Vǫluspá*, it also seems that the poet imagines Baldr as a recyclable god:

> bǫls mun allz batna,   Baldr mun koma;
> búa þeir Hǫðr oc Baldr   Hroptz sigtóptir,
> vé [MSS *vel*] valtíva.   (*Vsp* 62)[65]

By 'coming' rather than 'coming back' in this stanza, *Baldr* appears to be used as an epithet, not a name. Yet with Baldr and Hǫðr dwelling in 'victory-settlements' here and with Frigg's weeping for Baldr as a 'grief of the hall of the slain' (*vá Valhallar*, *Vsp* 33), the Icelandic poet also seems

---

[62] F. Detter suggested an equivalence between Freyr and Baldr in 'Der Baldermythus', *BGdSL* 19 (1894), 495–516; F. R. Schröder puts Baldr among the Vanir and postulates a Germanic origin for his story at least as old as farming in northern Europe, in 'Balder-Probleme', *BGdSL* 84 (1962), 319–57, esp. 345–55; without going so far, K. Schier concludes that Freyr belongs to the category of dying god, in 'Freys und Fróthis Bestattung', pp. 407–9; mostly with reference to Saxo's Baldr story, H. A. Molenaar identifies Baldr with Freyr, though he regards the Baldr–Freyr division of functions as a reflection of a death–life dichotomy between respectively the Æsir and Vanir: 'Óðinn's Gift: Betekenis en Werking van de Skandinavische Mythologie' (Ph.D. dissertation, University of Leiden, 1985), pp. 125–39.

[63] Dronke, 'War of the Æsir and Vanir', pp. 223–38 (also published in *Myth and Fiction*, no. VII). Parallels between Baldr and Near Eastern 'dying gods' (such as Tammuz) are illustrated by K. Schier, in 'Balder', *Reallexikon der germanischen Altertumskunde*, ed. H. Beck (Berlin and New York, 1976) II, 2–7.

[64] Loki's *felix culpa*? See Dronke, 'War of the Æsir and Vanir', p. 232, n. 38: 'it is as if only he knew the value of Baldr's death'.

[65] 'All horror will be mended, Baldr will come; the two of them Baldr and Hǫðr will inhabit the victory-settlements of *Hroptr* [?concealer], sanctuaries of choice/slaughter-deities'. OIce *vel* in the *Hauksbók* form, *vel valtívar*, seems to be a later rationalization of *vé*.

to stylize Baldr's death as that of a Valhǫll-hero on the battlefield. Likewise, with a combination of sacrificial and battlefield motifs, but with a military emphasis contrary to that of *Vǫluspá*, Eyvindr skáldaspillir emphasizes the warlike aspect over the sacrificial aspect of the death of Hákon Aðalsteinsfóstri in Storð by likening Hákon to Baldr in *Hákonarmál*:

> Mun óbundinn   á ýta sjǫt
> Fenrisulfr of fara,
> áðr jafngóðr   á auða trǫð
> konungmaðr komi.   (*Hákonarmál* 20)[66]

In *Eiríksmál*, which may have been composed in imitation of *Hákonarmál* in the eleventh century, Óðinn asks Bragi why Valhǫll shakes as if with the din of a thousand men.[67] Hinting that Eiríkr blóðøx is coming (after his death in Stainmoor in 954), Bragi replies:

> Braka ǫll bekkþili   sem myni Baldr koma
> eptir í Óðins sali.[68]

In the next stanza Óðinn denounces the idea of Baldr's return as a *heimska* ('folly'), because he expects Eiríkr, a greater hero; yet here Bragi seems to refer to a Norse tradition in which *Baldr* has become a name for the epitome of princes killed in war. Lastly, Saxo, in his late twelfth-century *Gesta Danorum*, relates the death of the *semideus* ('half-god') *Balderus* whom the more virtuous *Hotherus* stabs with a magic sword that he took from the satyr Mimmingus in the last of three wars over the nymph Nanna. In Saxo's narrative *Balderus* ('prince') and *Hotherus* ('battle') have a story which is entirely consistent with the meaning of their names. More so than in any other source, therefore, Saxo's tale of Balderus emphasizes the military aspect within a combination of warlike and sacrificial aspects of the *baldr*-hypostasis.[69]

In this way, with his historical origin apparently in Ingvi-freyr and

---

[66] *Heimskringla I*, ed. Bjarni, pp. 193–7, esp. 197 (*Hákonar saga góða*): 'unbound the wolf of Fenrir will go to the dwellings of men, before equally good a man of king's family comes to the path of riches [?Norway]'.

[67] Von See, 'Zwei eddische Preislieder', pp. 107–17.

[68] *An Introduction to Old Norse*, ed. E. V. Gordon, 2nd ed. rev. A. R. Taylor (Oxford, 1957), p. 148: 'All the benchboards are cracking, as if Baldr were coming back into Óðinn's halls.'

[69] *GD*, pp. 63–9 (III.i–vii).

with his mythical reincarnation in Váli, the Norse Baldr may show how a regular sacrifice and renewal of the Ing-hypostasis was thought to be carried out with the same magic as the *vígspá* ('war-spell') that regenerates dead Vanir in the Æsir-Vanir cult-war in *Vǫluspá*. As suggested in the previous chapter, the rapid growth of Váli and the physical regeneration of dead warriors in Valhǫll in *Vsp* 24 appear to have a common origin in Vanir *seiðr*. So, as connoted by the Batavian word *baldruus*, an early Germanic *baldr*-epithet may have defined the death of the Ing-hypostasis, whether this was imagined as a death by sacrifice or as a death in war. In what circumstances the name *Baldr* was developed from a cognate of *baldruus*, will be the subject of a study within the next chapter. What is clear at this stage, however, is that, before Scandinavian influence induced Æthelweard to change the West Saxon name *Bældæg* to *Balder* in his *Chronicon* in the later tenth century, no Baldr figure could have been known in England as *Bældæg*, nor as an entity separate from Ingui, the Anglian cognate of Ingvi-freyr.[70]

CONCLUSION

Óðinn's dynastic role in *Háleygjatal* was the last development in the political career of Woden, an Anglo-Saxon god. Outside England Woden's Germanic counterparts were probably never progenitors of kings or tribes, though Óðinn's *Valfǫðr* and *Heriafǫðr* epithets in *Grímnismál* suggest that Óðinn was known in Scandinavia as the adoptive father of kings, princes or warriors slain in battle. His son *Baldr* seems not to have been imagined on the basis of Woden's son *Bældæg* in the Bernician regnal list, but to have been personified from an epithet of Ingvi-freyr at a stage long before the composition of the written evidence. Through an indigenous Anglian *Valhǫll* topos, it is possible that Woden was taken into the forefather's role in Britain very early, probably because the first bishops who gave their kings new authority here welcomed Woden's military cult and could excuse him in their own terms; perhaps, as I have suggested, with reference to Old Testament patriarchy. A legend of the Anglo-Saxon conquest of Britain lasted into the tenth century and beyond: Bede presents an almost Trojan image of collapse and invasion in Kent and elsewhere, issuing from his reference to Uoden in the first book

[70] *Chronicle of Æthelweard*, ed. Campbell, p. 7.

Heathen gods

of his *Historia*;[71] and in the *Chronicle* poem *The Battle of Brunanburh* (c. 937), without mention of Woden, Æthelstan's eulogist ends up commemorating the original 'Angles and Saxons' (*Engle and Seaxe*) who as 'proud smiths of war, men keen for fame, obtained their homeland' (*wlance wigsmiþas, eorlas arhwate eard begeatan, The Battle of Brunanburh* 70–3). When, in Northumbria and elsewhere, the turbulence of the fifth and sixth centuries had been simplified with an anachronistic image of royal ancestry, Bede or his predecessors could thus have sanctioned Woden as the pan-Anglian counterpart of Jacob; and with a more political purpose two or three generations later, in the Anglian collection of regnal lists, Bede's Southumbrian successors could have reconstructed Woden as the Abraham of their past; in the tenth century it seems that the West Saxon Woden was exported into Norway where he gave the native Óðinn a new dynastic role. In the light of these developments, it appears that the cult of Woden in Anglo-Saxon England got an extra lease of life from Christian hands.

---

[71] *HE* I.15 (p. 50). The scarcity of grave-weapons in the continental Germanic sites may show that this image of violent conquest was exaggerated: see J. Hines, 'The Military Contexts of the Adventus Saxonum: Some Continental Evidence', in *Weapons and Warfare in Anglo-Saxon England*, ed. S. C. Hawkes, Oxford University Committee for Archaeology, Monograph 21 (Oxford, 1989), 25–48, esp. 44–5.

6
Aspects of Ingui: -*geot* and Geat

By the early eighth century the Anglo-Saxon church was relatively secure. Woden had been euhemerized during the initial phases of Christianization in Northumbria and Mercia, and churchmen north and south of the Humber were free to extend a search for ancestors beyond him. One name that the genealogists of Lindsey created (possibly at the end of the eighth century) was *Geot*, a name which was later copied as *Geat* in West Saxon royal genealogy probably in the early ninth century. *Geot* furthermore is related to -*geot*, a suffix found in three older names in the Anglian collection of regnal lists. This chapter is an attempt to demonstrate both the semantic development of these forms and the contemporary impact of *Geat* in the reign of Æthelwulf of Wessex (*c.* 839–58).

To explain the background of -*geot*, *Geot* and *Geat*, it will be necessary to show how *Gapt*, the Gothic cognate, could have evolved into a proper noun from Got *gáut*, an epithet of *Enguz* (a figure whose name derives from a stem such as that of the first-century *Ingvaeones*). I shall then suggest that the Anglian suffix -*geot* may be derived in parallel fashion from an ancient epithet of *Ingui* or *Ing*, the Old English cognate of *Enguz*; and that the name *Geot* and its derivative *Geat*, on the other hand, were coined in politically motivated attempts to connect the ancestors of Anglo-Saxon kings with the Goths and Lombards. In a corollary to this enquiry, with an argument which prepares the ground for my discussion of Ingui in chs. 8 and 9 of this book, I shall suggest that Baldr developed as a god unique to Scandinavia as a result of a Gothic–Arian syncretism of Enguz with Christ. In the remainder of the present chapter, I shall argue that the poem *Deor* was written as a satire on the political use to which King Æthelwulf may have put his alleged descent from Geat when he

Heathen gods

arranged his marriage with Judith, daughter of King Charles the Bald of West Francia, in *c*. 855–6.

ANGLIAN -*GEOT* AND GEOT

The first two forms to consider in this enquiry are -*geot*, the second element of Anglian compound names, and *Geot*, a ninth-century simplex indicating an ancestor of Woden.[1] The suffix -*geot* appears (variously spelt) in three manuscripts containing Anglian regnal lists: in Angen*geot*, which is listed six places below Woden (and two below *Ingi*brand) in the first Bernician list (*I Bernicia*) and five places below Woden in the first Mercian list (*I Mercia*) in Vespasian B. vi, 109r–v; in Sig*geot*, four places below Woden in the Deiran list (*Deira*) in CCCC 183, 65r–67v; and in Weoðul*geot*, one place below Woden in the first Mercian list (*I Mercia*) in Tiberius B. v, vol. I, 22v–23r.[2] In Vespasian B. vi, an extension shows a simplex *Geot* five places above Woden in the Lindsey regnal list.[3] When the West Saxons transcribed *Geot* as WS *Geat*, this figure took up a standard position in their royal genealogy. The following table, with columns in order of chronology from left to right, shows the history of the relationship between Geat and Woden in Anglo-Saxon royal genealogy:[4]

Historia Brittonum	Lindsey	ASC (A) 855	Asser
G[i]uta[5]	Geot(ing)	Geat	Geata
Folcpald	Godulf	Godwulf	Godwulf
Fran	Finn	Finn	Finn
Freudulf	Frioðulf	Friþuwulf	Frithuwulf
Frelab	Frealaf	Frealaf	Frealaf
		Friþuwald	Frithowald
Uuoden	Uoden	Woden	Uuoden

The *Historia Brittonum* also presents *Geta* as a king who 'was, as they say, the son of a god' (*fuit, ut aiunt, filius dei*), although it is also made clear that Geta was not thereby the God of gods, 'but is one of their idols

---

[1] See Dumville ('Anglian Collection', p. 48) on the development of *geot* from **gaut*: *Geot* is derived from *gaut-*, with **au* becoming OE **æu* becoming Southumbrian *æo/eo*: these changes identify *Geot* with PGmc *Gaut* (> OE *Geat*).

[2] *Ibid.*, pp. 30–7.   [3] *Ibid.*, p. 31.

[4] Sisam, 'Anglo-Saxon Royal Genealogies', p. 312; *Historia Brittonum*, ed. Lot, pp. 171–2.

[5] On the form *G[i]uta*, see Sisam, *ibid.*, pp. 308–9.

Aspects of Ingui

which they themselves used to worship' (*sed unus est ab idolis eorum, quod ipsi colebant*).⁶ In addition, Asser, in his biography of King Alfred, cites as the ancestor of Æthelwulf, Alfred's father, a certain 'Geata whom the pagans quite recently worshipped as a god' (*Geata, quem Getam iamdudum pagani pro Deo venerabantur*).⁷ In this context, Asser's form *Geata* seems to be influenced by *Geta*, the name of a slave in a comedy of Terence: the name from which Asser made this form was probably *Geat* in a version of the *Anglo-Saxon Chronicle*. All forms, *-geot*, *Geot* and *Geat*, are cognate with *Gapt*, a Gothic name which throws light both on the meaning of *geot* and on the reason for the creation of *Geot* and *Geat*.

GAPT AND THE ANSES

Gapt is the name given to the founder of the Ostrogothic Amali in the *Getica* or *Origo Gothica* (XIII.79), which the historian Jordanes, a Goth, wrote c. 551 apparently as an abridgement of the now lost *Historia Gothorum* (c. 520–5) of the Roman senator Cassiodorus.⁸ It has been suggested that *Gapt* is a Latin transcription either of a Greek upper-case spelling or of a Greek pronunciation of Got *gáut-*.⁹ In the light of this morphology, *Gapt* is probably cognate both with *Gausus*, which is the name given to the founder of the Lombards in the mid seventh-century prologue to the *Edicta* of Rothari;¹⁰ and with *-geot*, *Geot* and *Geat* in Anglo-Saxon regnal lists. Though it seems likely that the name *Gapt* was

---

⁶ *Historia Brittonum*, ed. Lot, p. 172.
⁷ *Asser's Life*, ed. Stevenson and rev. Whitelock, pp. 3 and 160–1.
⁸ *Getica*, ed. Mommsen I, 76; on the dating of this work, see S. Barnish, 'The Genesis and Completion of Cassiodorus' Gothic History', *Latomus* 43 (1984), 336–61. On Cassiodorus's anachronistic use of 'Ostrogoths' and 'Visigoths' of Goths in the period before the transdanubian migration of c. 376, see Heather, *Goths and Romans*, pp. 1–67, esp. 51–2.
⁹ *Getica*, ed. Mommsen I, 143; disputed by R. Much, 'Gapt', *ZfdA* 41 (1896), 95–6; supported by Moisl, 'Anglo-Saxon Royal Genealogies', pp. 219–23. Got *gáut-* represents the stem of the preterite singular of Got *giutan* (II), of which *gutaneis*, the masculine nominative plural past participle meaning 'men poured open', appears to be the etymon of *Gothones* in Tacitus's *Germania*; other derivatives are probably the *Gutar* of Gotland and the *Gautar* of the province of Göteland with whom the *Geatas* of *Beowulf* are synonymous. The *h* in Tacitus's spelling of *Gothones* may have been inserted on analogy with *Otho*, the name of an emperor in AD 69; or it may be the addition of a medieval scribe.
¹⁰ F. Beyerle, *Die Gesetze der Langobarden* (Weimar, 1947), p. 4.

135

taken from a Greek source, Cassiodorus probably based other genealogical elements of his new Gothic history on what he could learn from his Amal patron, Theoderic (493–526).[11] In the genealogy of Ostrogothic kings in *Getica*, there are seventeen generations from Gapt to Theoderic's successor, Athalaric (526–34), which matches the seventeen from Aeneas to Romulus.[12] Accordingly, it has been suggested that Cassiodorus positioned Gapt on a par with Aeneas, son of Venus and the mortal Anchises, in order to give his patrons a status equal to that of the Roman emperors.[13]

Anses is apparently Jordanes's name for the ancestors of Theoderic and Athalaric: the Ostrogoths, having seized great wealth in their rout of the Romans in the reign of Domitian (81–96), 'iam proceres suos, quorum quasi fortuna vincebant, non puros homines, sed *semideos* id est *Ansis* vocaverunt' (*Getica* XIII.78).[14] *Semidei* ('half-gods') is a learned compound which indicates an attempt to euhemerize the old gods: apparently Cassiodorus wished to claim with this word that the old Gothic gods were really men whose subjects wrongly worshipped them as divine.[15] The vernacular name for these old gods, *Anses* (from Got **anseis*), has a surviving late Gothic cognate in *Aza*, the name for the Gothic A-rune in Vienna, Nationalbibliothek, lat. 795 (s. ix¹), fol. 20v;[16] and is cognate with OE *ese* in *esa gescot* ('a shot from the spirits', *MCharm* 4.23); these forms are also related to OIce *Áss* (sg.) and *Æsir* (pl.), the name of the leading Norse gods.[17] The older meaning of *Æsir*, perhaps 'spirits' indicating deified ancestors, may show that either Cassiodorus, a Roman

---

[11] On Cassiodorus's sources, see Heather, 'Cassiodorus and the Rise of the Amals', pp. 107–16.

[12] H. Wolfram, 'Gotische Studien III', *Mitteilungen des Instituts für österreichische Geschichtsforschung* 84 (1976), 239–61, esp. 247–51; see also H. Wolfram, 'Theogonie, Ethnogenese und ein kompromittierter Grossvater im Stammbaum Theoderichs des Grossen', in *Festschrift für Helmut Beumann zum 65. Geburtstag*, ed. K.-U. Jäschke and R. Wenskus (Sigmaringen, 1977), pp. 80–97, esp. 81–2.

[13] N. Wagner, 'Bemerkungen zur Amalergenealogie', *Beiträge zur Namenforschung* n.s. 14 (1979), 26–43, esp. 27–9; Wolfram, *History of the Goths*, pp. 3–14; Heather, 'Cassiodorus and the Rise of the Amals', p. 109.

[14] *Getica*, ed. Mommsen I, 142 (Gapt's family tree) and 76 (text): 'now called their chiefs, through whose good fortune as it were they were winning, not wholly men, but half-gods, that is to say "Ansis"'.

[15] Cf. von See, *Mythos und Theologie*, pp. 69–79, esp. 77.

[16] Unterkircher, *Alkuin-Briefe*, pp. 19–21.   [17] *AIEW* 25 (*an-*); *ANEW* 16 (*áss*).

Aspects of Ingui

consulting Goths, or Jordanes, himself a Goth, glossed *semideos* with *id est Ansis* in order to offer a vernacular justification for euhemerism with a word for 'ancestral spirits'.[18]

Jordanes says that 'Gapt was the first of these heroes, as they [the Goths] themselves relate in their tales' (*Getica* XIV.79).[19] Thus, as Hermann Moisl points out, Jordanes treats Gapt 'not as a god, but as a man who had been deified'.[20] In this way Jordanes probably considered the Anses, to whom his Gapt belongs, as Gothic counterparts of (Livy's) early heroes of Rome. Yet the evidence for the development of *Gapt* and *Anses* may show that there had been a categorical difference at a stage earlier than the fifth century between the Gothic words from which these two names derive: whereas Got *anseis appears to denote men deified after they die, Got *gáut-* and its Germanic cognates, as I now hope to show, may have described a man who is hallowed as divine while still alive.

The Norse forms cognate with *Gapt* are OIce *gautr* (an epithet used of Óðinn) and *Gautr* (one of Óðinn's names): in the first case, an Icelandic poet, probably in the thirteenth century, used *gautr* to describe Óðinn as he prepares to visit the world of the dead in *Bdr* 2 and 13; and in the second, at the end of *Grímnismál*, part if not all of which was probably composed in Norway in the late ninth or tenth century, Óðinn says that *Gautr* is his name among the gods (*Grím* 54).[21] These instances are taken from Eddic verse. The identification of Gautr with Óðinn is less clear in Scaldic poetry, however, for here *Gautr*, just like the names of other Norse gods, can also work as the basis of a kenning for a warlike man.[22] Thus in *Sonatorrek*, an elegy datable to *c*. 960, Egill Skalla-Grímsson imagines that his son Bǫðvarr would have grown, if he had not drowned, 'unz her-Gauts hendr of tœki', which arguably (with *hendr* as accusative) means 'until he

---

[18] On Gothic paganism as the worship of tribal ancestors, see Thompson, *The Visigoths in the Time of Ulfila*, pp. 55–63.

[19] *Getica*, ed. Mommsen I, 76: 'Horum ergo heroum, ut ipsi suis in fabulis referunt, primus fuit Gapt.'

[20] Moisl, 'Anglo-Saxon Royal Genealogies', p. 221; see Wolfram, *History of the Goths*, pp. 29–34.

[21] *AR* II, 41–2 (§372). De Vries also notes a profusion of Oden-prefixes in theophoric placenames in Göteland, where there were probably *Gautr*-prefixes earlier; cf. his earlier *Religionsgeschichte* (1st ed.) I, 170 (§148).

[22] In twenty-two instances: see Meissner, *Kenningar der Skalden*, p. 261 (§88).

might have attained the hands of war-*Gautr* [warrior]'.²³ Here Óðinn does not appear to be synonymous with Gautr.

It is also unlikely that any counterparts of Óðinn and Gautr were taken as synonymous in old east Germanic religion, for Helm found no proof that 'Wodan' was known as *Gapt* or indeed known among the Goths at all.²⁴ An Odinic ideology of warfare in the hereafter, such as that of the Norse Valhǫll, may never have been part of Gothic paganism: Gothic burial deposits, from beginning to end of Gothic history, are distinguished from those of western Germanic peoples by their entire absence of weapons.²⁵ In this way, Gothic paganism seems to be truer to the archaic picture of Norse gods that we have seen (in ch. 2) in the late ninth-century *Haustlǫng*, in which the meaning of Þjóðólfr's expression for all categories of men and gods derives from 'kindreds of the Ing[v]i-lord' (*áttir Ing[v]i-freys*).²⁶ If we take this kenning as representative of an earlier stage in Norse religion, it would be correct to identify both the divine epithet *gautr* and the god's name *Gautr* with the Vanir at a time before the oral composition of the surviving Old Norse–Icelandic evidence.²⁷ No close Gothic cognate of OIce *vanir* survives, but as *Gapt* is cognate with OIce *gautr* and *Gautr*, it is possible that this figure was likewise considered as a god of the Vanir type.²⁸

This inference is supported by a kenning in Bragi's *Ragnarsdrápa* of the mid ninth century. In stanza 5 of this poem, Bragi appears to allude to 'Gautr' in a role as the husband of the *Gothic* earth in the kenning *harðir herðimýlar Hergauts vinu* ('the hard strength-pellets of war-Gautr's girl-friend', hence 'stones').²⁹ Where the king Jǫrmunrekkr orders the destruction of his attackers Hamðir and Sǫrli with the stones of 'war-

---

²³ *Egils saga*, ed. Sigurður, p. 250: 'unz hann hefði fengið hermanns hendur (hefði verið orðinn fullröskur til víga)'; also edited in *Skj* B I, 35, 11.

²⁴ Helm, *Wodan*, pp. 45–7; *HAR* II.i, 37–8 (§20); followed by Wolfram, *History of the Goths*, pp. 106–12, esp. 110–11, and 421–2, n. 481.

²⁵ Wolfram, *ibid.*, pp. 111 and 418, n. 442.   ²⁶ *Skj* B I, 16, 10.

²⁷ So K. Helm, in 'Spaltung, Schichtung und Mischung im germanischen Heidentum', in *Vom Werden des deutschen Geistes: Festgabe Gustav Ehrismann zum 8. Oktober 1925 dargebracht von Freunden und Schülern*, ed. P. Merker and W. Stammler (Berlin and Leipzig, 1925), pp. 1–20, esp. 18; see also *HAR* II.i, 32–3 (§19).

²⁸ *HAR* II.i, 34 (§19). The stem of Got *unwunands* ('unconcerned') represents the only extant Gothic cognate of OE *wine*, OIce *vinr* and *vanir*, and Lat *Venus*: *AIEW* 132 (*uen-*); *ANEW* 664 (*vanr*) and 666 (*vinr*).

²⁹ *Skj* B I, 2, 5.

Aspects of Ingui

Gautr's girl-friend', Bragi's kenning shows that Jǫrmunrekkr uses his maternal ancestor, the earth, to defeat the magic of Guðrún, who (as Jǫrmunrekkr reveals) seems to have equipped her sons with magically immune coats of mail (*Hamð* 25). In this kenning, the earth's husband appears to be a figure named *-gautr* which, as we have seen, is not necessarily identical with Óðinn. In chs. 1 and 2 I have tried to show that the sexual union of Ingvi-freyr of the Vanir with Gerðr is a hypostatic version of the marriage of Njǫrðr with Skaði, and that these stories represent the oldest extant example of a Germanic topos of *hieros gamos*. In keeping with this topos, therefore, the role of *-gautr* in Bragi's kenning as the husband of the land of the Goths would appear to denote a variant of Njǫrðr's marriage with Skaði or of Ingvi-freyr's union with Gerðr.

GOTHIC PARALLELS FOR THE RELATION OF *-GEOT* TO INGUI

The Old English cognates of OIce *gautr* and *Ingvi* are respectively *-geot* and *Ingui* or *Ing*. Both *-geot* and *Ingui* (or *Ingi*-compounds) are found in the Anglian collection of regnal lists. To suggest the possibility of a further thematic connection between these words, however, it is necessary to trace a relationship between their Gothic cognates, respectively *gáut-* (> *Gapt*) and *enguz* or *inggws*.

Enguz is one of a set of Gothic rune-names written in a unique hand on 20v of Vienna, Nationalbibliothek, lat. 795 (s. ix¹), a codex that belonged to Archbishop Arno of Salzburg, a pupil of Alcuin (20r contains an Anglo-Saxon runic alphabet); these rune-names, written in the third of three columns on the left side of the folio, were apparently meant to correspond with symbols of cursive and classical Gothic Roman alphabets written in the first and second columns respectively; though René Derolez believes that these entries were written in the tenth century, the view expressed by the editor, Franz Unterkircher, is that a scribe filled in 20v in *c.* 799.[30] *Enguz* is also cognate with the stem of the *Ingvaeones* (to whom Tacitus alludes in ch. 2 of *Germania*) and with *Inguz* of the *terp* in Wijnaldum.[31]

A second and older piece of evidence for a Gothic *Ing*-hypostasis is

---

[30] Unterkircher, *Alkuin-Briefe*, pp. 10–13 and 20v; R. Derolez, *Runica Manuscripta: the English Tradition* (Bruges, 1954), pp. 52–63, esp. 58.

[31] Arntz and Zeiss, *Runendenkmäler des Festlandes*, p. 417; Zijlstra, 'Onderzoek Wijnaldum', pp. 17–22.

provided by a (damaged) runic inscription on a golden neck-ring found in the Pietroasa hoard in Walachia (near *Turris*, a Roman camp in former Gothic Romania) and datable to the third or fourth century.[32] C. J. S. Marstrander normalized this inscription (*gutaningwahailag*), as *gutan[i] ingwa hailag* ('holy to Inggws of the Goths').[33] Got *gutani* in this inscription is an acceptable variant spelling of *gutané* ('of the Goths').[34] Marstrander's closely argued reading is less well known than *gutan[i] iowi hailag* ('holy to the Jupiter of the Goths'), although it is not clear why a writer of this *iowi* inscription should refer to a Gothic god with a kenning of which the base was a Roman name.[35] The Pietroasa inscription has also been read as *gutani o[þal] wi[h] hailag* ('property of the Goths. I am invulnerable').[36] It is simplest, however, to follow Marstrander and read *gutan[i] ingwa hailag*, for this reading of the Pietroasa inscription ('holy to Inggws of the Goths') presents the least difficulty of interpretation. 'Inggws of the Goths' appears to refer to Inggws as a figure known to a number of tribes of whom the Goths acknowledge themselves as only one group of worshippers: *gutani inggws* may thus have denoted *gáut-* or the form from which Jordanes's *Gapt* is probably derived. No doubt because *Ingwa* in this reading conflicted with the idea of Gautr as an ancient incarnation of Óðinn, Jan de Vries dismissed it out of hand, although in the first edition of his *Religionsgeschichte* he briefly acknowledged that the meaning of *Gautr*, which is related to the class II strong verb *gjóta* ('to

---

[32] See M. Rusa, 'Der Schatz von Pietroasele und der zeitgenössische historische Kontext', *Zeitschrift für Archäologie* 20 (1986), 181–200, esp. 181–8.

[33] C. J. S. Marstrander, 'De Gotiske Runeminnesmerker', *Norsk tidsskrift for sprogvidenskap* 3 (1929), 25–175, esp. 40 (date), 39–65 (discussion) and 63 (conclusion); Helm supports Marstrander and notes that *inggws* represents an older form of *enguz* (*HAR* II.i, 42).

[34] On Got *gutans*, see J. Wright, *Grammar of the Gothic Language* (Oxford, 1910), p. 142 (§302); on the variation of long *i*, *ei* and *é*, see *ibid.*, p. 6 (§5).

[35] R. Loewe, 'Der Goldring von Pietroasa', *Indogermanische Forschungen* 26 (1909), 203–8; followed by Wolfram, *History of the Goths*, pp. 109–10. On the Goth Fravitta and his followers, however, who became Roman pagans in *c.* 382, see Thompson, *The Visigoths in the Time of Ulfila*, p. 105.

[36] *Runendenkmäler des Festlandes*, p. 96, n. 4. See further T. Capelle, who suggests that the Pietroasa ring was a heathen oath-ring, in 'Zum Runenring von Pietroassa', *Frühmittelalterliche Studien* 2 (1968), 228–32, esp. 231; Capelle's theory would be no less viable if he read *ingwa* instead: *incge* is associated with *að* in 'að wæs geæfned ond i[n]cge gold ahæfen of horde' (*Beo* 1107–8).

Aspects of Ingui

pour'), suggested the fertility of a phallic god such as Freyr.[37] Although there is no other evidence of such a character for Gautr, some connection between *gjóta* and Enguz, Inguz, Ingvi or Ingui seems clear. It is possible, therefore, that the *gáut-* and *gutans* forms by which the Goths gave themselves their name denoted a ritual aspect of Enguz.

A first-century analogue of *gutaneis* ('the poured ones'), a form such as that on which Tacitus's *Gothones* was probably based, appears in a passage in *Germania* in which the Semnones are said to sacrifice a man in a sacred grove. Tacitus presents the Semnones not only as Suebi, like the Gothones and Anglii and other tribes, but also as the oldest and most famous Suebi of all, saying that their antiquity is proved by their religion: 'Stato tempore in siluam auguriis patrum et prisca formidine sacram nominis eiusdem sanguinis populi legationibus coeunt *caeso*que publice *homine* celebrant barbari ritus horrenda primordia' (ch. 39).[38] Tacitus's information in the passage was probably up-to-date, for it is likely that his informant was King Masyos of the Semnones, who visited Emperor Domitian (81–96) in Rome in 92, when Tacitus was praetor.[39]

This passage is an old showcase for the dispute over sacral kingship. F. R. Schröder identified the victim in the grove with *Helgi* ('the holy one') of the Eddic Helgi-Lays, as a king both representing a god such as Freyr and ending up sacrificed to him.[40] Rejecting the idea that this victim represented a fertility god, Otto Höfler made Wodan the god honoured by the Semnones in this affair.[41] Elsewhere in *Germania* Tacitus attributes

---

[37] On *Gaut*, see de Vries, *Religionsgeschichte* (1st ed.) I, 199–200 (§175).

[38] *Germania*, pp. 315–16: 'At a set time, nations of the blood of the same name gather in their deputations in a wood hallowed by the auguries of their fathers and by the terror of the ancients; and celebrate the hair-raising opening of their barbaric rite by having *a man* publicly *cut open*.'

[39] For the visit of Masyos (and the seeress Veleda) to Rome, see *Dio's Roman History*, ed. and trans. E. Cary, based on H. B. Foster, 9 vols. (London and New York, 1925) VIII, 346 (LXVII.5, 3).

[40] F. R. Schröder, *Germanentum und Hellenismus: Untersuchungen zur germanischen Religionsgeschichte*, Germanische Bibliothek (II Abteilung) 17 (Heidelberg, 1924), 39–42; and *Ingunar-Freyr* (Tübingen, 1941), p. 48.

[41] O. Höfler, 'Das Opfer im Semnonenhain und die Edda', in *Edda, Skalden, Saga. Festschrift zum 70. Geburtstag von Felix Genzmer*, ed. H. Schneider (Heidelberg, 1952), pp. 1–67, esp. 59–60; followed by de Vries, in *AR* II, 32 (§366); and by K. Hauck, in 'Lebensnormen und Kultmythen in germanischen Stammes- und Herschergenealogien', *Saeculum* 6 (1955), 186–223, esp. 194. The Helgi connection is rejected by Picard (*Germanisches Sakralkönigtum?*, pp. 132–41), but she does not explain how

Heathen gods

victims to Mercury 'whom on certain days they are not ashamed to honour with human victims also'.[42] Yet Mercury's name is not cited in ch. 39 of *Germania*; nor is the example of the Chatti, whom their victorious enemies the Hermunduri sacrificed to Mercury and Mars after a battle in A.D. 59, relevant here, for these tribesmen were not victims chosen at a set time, but warriors captured in battle.[43] In this way it seems better to leave Wodan out of the *Semnonenhain*.[44]

More straightforwardly, Lat *caesus* in *caeso homine* appears to be a translation of Gmc **gutans*, for the use of *caedere* ('to cut') seems to be technical; and OE *geotan* ('to pour, cut open') is a ritual act in *Juliana*, where the poet, adapting the Latin *Passio S. Iulianae*, tells us that the emperor, as the persecutor of Christians, 'poured on the grassy plain the blood of holy ones' (*geat on græswong haligra blod*, lines 6–7). Also relevant to this discussion is OE *getan* ('to make pour'), which occurs in a scene in *Beowulf* in which King Ongentheow of the Swedes, having surrounded Hæthcyn's 'Geats' (*Geatas*) in Raven's Wood, threatens 'to cut them open with the edges of a sword' (*meces ecgum getan*) in the morning, some on the gallows, for the pleasure of birds (lines 2939–41). In this way, Schröder's idea appears to fit most closely the expression *caesus homo* in Tacitus's account of the Semnones: *caesus* appears to render *gutans*; and *Gapt* or a form such as *gáut-* appears to be the name of 'Inggws of the *gutaneis*', a god of the Goths to whom a neck-ring was considered holy in the Pietroasa hoard in the late fourth century. Before *Gautr* became a byname of Óðinn in Scandinavia, *gautr* may thus have been an epithet for Ingvi-freyr that denoted the sacrificial death of this god. The early role of Ingvi-freyr, in this way, would be not only to marry an embodiment of the land (for example, the Gothic earth in Bragi's kenning *hergauts vina* cited above in *Ragnarsdrápa* 5, and Gerðr in *Skírnismál*), but also to be sacrificed when his purpose was fulfilled.[45] In England, correspondingly,

---

Fjǫtrlundr ('fetter-grove') in *HHund* II, 30 is not descended from a tradition of a fettered grove such as that of the Semnones.

[42] *Germania*, p. 284 (ch. 9): 'cui certis diebus humanis quoque hostiis litare fas habent'.

[43] *Taciti Annales*, ed. Furneaux II, 228 (XIII.57). Varus's officers were also sacrificed, to whom Tacitus does not say, in the groves of Teutoburger Wald in AD 15: see *ibid.* I, 233 (I.61).

[44] So Helm, in *HAR* I, 308 (§174) and *Wodan*, p. 32.

[45] H. Kuhn defines *gaut-* largely as a sacrificial epithet, in 'Gaut', pp. 417–33 (repr. in his *Kleine Schriften* II, 364–77).

Aspects of Ingui

the compound-base -*geot*, surviving as a fossil in Bernician and Mercian *Angengeot* ('joy-sacrificed'), Deiran *Siggeot* ('victory-sacrificed') and Mercian *Weoðulgeot* ('wandering-sacrificed'), may reflect a legend of Ingui's marriage and death in the tradition of seventh-century Anglian royal families.[46]

INGUI AND THE ARIAN–GOTHIC ORIGIN OF BALDR

In so far as the Scandinavian heathens knew of a sacrificed god in the Viking Age, this was not Ingvi-freyr (cognate with Enguz, Inggws or Ingui), but Baldr (plus Óðinn, a shaman). However, it is possible to reconstruct something of the evolution of Baldr from Ingvi-freyr as a process that would have been complete by the time the earliest extant Norse poetry was composed. I have suggested in chs. 4–5 that OE *bealdor* and OIce *Baldr* are cognate with *baldruus*, apparently a Batavian epithet in the third or fourth century for Hercules (a Roman version of the Ing-hypostasis). In the following presentation of Norse and east Germanic material, it will appear that *Baldr*, the Norse cognate of *baldruus*, was used as the name of a new god separate from Ingvi-freyr at the end of a semantic development which, centuries earlier, had affected a Gothic form of *baldruus* (used as an epithet of Enguz, varying Got *gáut*-). In Old English literature, where the *geot*-suffix may reflect the sacrificial epithet of Ingui in royal names, it will thus appear that the presence or absence of a loan or loan-translation of *Baldr* may be used as a limited means of distinguishing Norse-influenced Anglo-Saxon paganism from an older Anglian religion of the seventh and early eighth centuries.

A thematic connection between the Norse names Baldr and Gautr appears in the Eddic poems *Hamðismál* (probably of the late ninth century) and *Baldrs Draumar* (probably of the eleventh or twelfth century). As a simplex, OIce *baldr* ('lord') occurs only once in Old Norse poetry, when the poet of *Hamðismál*, retelling a story derived from a Gothic tradition, calls the Gothic king Jǫrmunrekkr *baldr í brynio* ('a warlord in his coat of mail') at the moment he orders his men to stone Hamðir and Sǫrli to death (*Hamð* 25);[47] in the next stanza Hamðir uses the Norse adjectival counterpart of Got **balþs* ('bold') in a proverb, when

[46] Dumville, 'Anglian Collection', pp. 23–50, esp. 30–1 (Vespasian B. vi, 109r–v), 32–4 (CCCC 183, 65r–67v) and 35–7 (Tiberius B. v, vol. I, 22v–23r).

[47] Green (*Carolingian Lord*, pp. 6–7) defends *baldr* as a noun rather than as an adjective in

143

he accuses Sǫrli of having loosed evils upon them: 'opt ór þeim belg bǫll ráð koma' ('often out of the bag *bold* counsels come', *Hamð* 26).[48] *Baldr*, about to die in *Baldrs Draumar*, suffers *ballir draumar* ('bold dreams') before his death (*Bdr* 1); Óðinn is named *gautr* ('sacrificial victim') in *Bdr* 2, when he saddles his horse Sleipnir for a journey to the underworld. In the first case Jǫrmunrekkr is a royal descendant of *Gautr* preparing to die; while, in the second, *gautr* appears to refer to a candidate for sacrifice who makes the journey into the world of the dead. Both contexts in *Hamðismál* and *Baldrs Draumar* thus show a traditional association, albeit unclear, between OIce *ballr/baldr* and *gautr*.

As we have seen, the Gothic cognates of OIce *gautr* are *Gapt* (from *gáut-*) in *Getica* and *gutans* in the Pietroasa neck-ring inscription. The Gothic cognate of OIce *ballr* and *baldr*, on the other hand, appears to be *baltha* (Got *balþa*, from **balþs*), which occurs only in *Getica*. In this treatise Jordanes uses Lat *audax* to define *baltha*, when he says that it was the Gothic leader Alaric 'to whom befell a nobility second to the Amali and an amazing origin from the nation of the Balthi, [and] who among his people had formerly taken the name *Baltha*, that is "the bold" (*audax*), on account of the boldness of his courage'.[49] Wolfram derives the *balth-* stem here from *Baltia* (an island mentioned by Pliny the Elder) which he regards as the ancient homeland of the *Balthi*.[50] Yet this theory is weakened by Peter Heather's conclusion that Cassiodorus backdated the

---

this context. There are forty instances of *Baldr* in which this name works as the basis for kennings for 'man': see Meissner, *Kenningar der Skalden*, pp. 260–1 (§88).

[48] U. Dronke emends to 'opt ór [rau]ðom belg' and translates 'from a bleeding bag often bold counsels come', noting the proverbial status of this image in Old Norse: *Poetic Edda I*, pp. 166 (text) and 237 (note). Adjectival *ballr* is also found in *Hym* 17 and *Sigsk* 37. Wolfram says that 'there is much to support the notion that the Greuthungian king sacrificed himself at the moment of defeat', in *History of the Goths*, pp. 86–9, esp. 89. Unfortunately H. Wolfram provides no support for this theory in his earlier reference, in 'Theogonie, Ethnogenese und ein kompromittierter Grossvater im Stammbaum Theoderichs des Grossen', in *Festschrift für Helmut Beumann zum 65. Geburtstage*, ed. K.-U. Jäschke and R. Wenskus (Sigmaringen, 1977), pp. 80–97, at 82 ('Ermanarichs Selbstopferung an seinen namengebenden Gott – von Ammianus Marcellinus als Selbstmord berichtet').

[49] *Getica*, ed. Mommsen I, 95: 'cui erat post Amalos secunda nobilitas Balthorumque ex genere origo mirifica, qui dudum ob audacia virtutis Baltha, id est audax, nomen inter suos acceperat'. Got **balþs* may also be reconstructed from Wulfila's adverb *balþaba* ('bravely'): see *ibid*. I, 147.

[50] *History of the Goths*, p. 32.

Aspects of Ingui

existence of the Visigothic and Ostrogothic tribes anachronistically into the fourth century before the Gothic migration across the Danube in 376.[51] In this way, it is more likely that Alaric's epithet *baltha* meant 'the bold', just as Jordanes said it did.

Got *balþa*, then, is probably evidence for a lost nominal Gothic cognate of the Batavian *baldruus*. Where there was a connection between Alaric's *balþa*-epithet and divine power may be inferred from the claim of Socrates Scholasticus, a contemporary Christian historian writing in Greek, that Alaric was driven to make war on Rome by a personal god or demon. In the words of Socrates (*c.* 380–439), Alaric explains to an old man (in 410) that he had not wanted to attack Rome, 'but someone troubles me each day, tormenting me'.[52] In addition, when Stilicho's panegyrist Claudian (*c.* 370–404), a pagan of Greek origin, claimed a victory for Stilicho against Alaric outside Pollentia (*c.* 402), he gave Alaric some Vergilian lines in which the Goth declares that neither dreams nor augury but 'a clear voice openly issuing from a grove' (*clara palam vox edita luco*) urged him to proceed to Rome.[53] It is possible, therefore, that Alaric believed himself to be guided by his god, and that this god was associated with his epithet, Got *balþa* ('the bold').[54]

In the previous chapter, I have argued on the basis of some Norse evidence that the Batavian noun *baldruus* (cognate with Got *balþa*) denoted an aspect of the Ing-hypostasis (i.e. an early Germanic analogue of Ingvi-freyr). In the light of this argument and of the discussion above, I shall now argue that nominal forms of the Gothic words *balþa* and *gáut-*

---

[51] Heather, *Goths and Romans*, pp. 28–33; *pace* Wolfram (*History of the Goths*, p. 145), who regards the Balthi as a kin-group which had stayed intact from the early fourth century.

[52] Socrates, *Historiae*, p. 757 (*Socratis scholastici Historia*, VII.10): ἀλλά τις καθ' ἑκάστην ὀχλεῖ μοι βασανίζων. Sozomenos repeats Socrates (*Hermiae Sozomeni Historia*, ibid., p. 1609 (IX.6)): 'but someone is constantly troubling him inside and constraining him' (ἀλλά τις συνεχῶς ἐνοχλῶν αὐτὸν βιάζεται). On these and other ecclesiastical authors, see Heather, *Goths and Romans*, pp. 81–3.

[53] *De Bello Gothico, Claudii Claudiani Carmina*, ed. T. Birt, MGH, Auct. Antiq. 10 (Berlin, 1892), 279 (V.545). See further Wolfram, *History of the Goths*, pp. 150–61, esp. 151–2; on the history and reliability of these sources, see Heather, *Goths and Romans*, pp. 80–1 and 208–18.

[54] Cf. Einarr's phrase *at mun banda* ('at the prompting of divine powers') in *Vellekla*, where he describes his patron Hákon Jarl's divine guidance in war (North, *Pagan Words*, pp. 26–33, esp. 32).

were both used to describe Enguz until the Goths were converted to Christianity in the fourth century.

A sketch of the history of the Gothic conversion will make this argument clearer. The Tervingi began to raid into Dacia from over the Danube from 238 onwards and in these territories became one of the first Gothic groups to encounter Christianity.[55] In 332 they were romanized by Emperor Constantine I (306–37), who levied about 3,000 of their men into his army with a *foedus* ('treaty').[56] The Tervingi and other *foederati* had reason to be impressed by Constantine's military skill, for Constantine had already fought his way into power from York to Nicomedia. In his lifetime Constantine blended Christianity with a sun-cult and had himself portrayed on coin reliefs as Jupiter, his son as Bacchus; however, there is also a contemporary story of his and his army's vision in 312, before his battle for Rome against Maxentius, of the cross above the sun in the noon sky with the legend 'conquer by this' (τούτῳ νίκα).[57] This story is testimony to the widespread belief at this time in the military power of Christianity. Eventually some Tervingi became Arian Christians in Constantine's later years; in addition, the Arian bishop Wulfila began to convert some Goths in lower Moesia by the Black Sea and to translate parts of the Bible into Gothic in 341–60.[58]

With the accession of the Arian Valens (364–78) to the eastern empire the accord reached between Constantine and the Tervingi fell apart. Valens made war on the Tervingi in 367–9, but this war seems to have ended in stalemate, with the Goths as pagan as before and now determined to resist Christianity as an instrument of Roman power.[59] In his discussion of the ensuing anti-Christian purges of 369–72, Heather suggests that the Tervingi had been 'afraid that Christianity would

---

[55] Summarized by Kuhn, 'Die gotische Mission', pp. 50–65, esp. 51–2 (repr. in his *Kleine Schriften* IV, 201–22, esp. 202–3).

[56] *History of the Goths*, pp. 59–64, esp. 61–2.

[57] On Constantine's vision, see Eusebius Pamphilus, *Vita Constantini et Panegyricus atque Constantini ad Sanctorum Coetum Oratio*, ed. F. A. Heinichen (Leipzig, 1869), p. 28 (I.28.2); on Constantine's sun-cult, see Henig, *Religion in Roman Britain*, pp. 214–15; on Constantine and his son as Jupiter and Bacchus, see V. J. Hutchinson, *Bacchus in Roman Britain: the Evidence for his Cult*, 2 vols. BAR, British Series, 151 (Oxford, 1986) I, 113.

[58] Wolfram, *History of the Goths*, pp. 75–85; *AR* II, 406–15 (§§599–604); on Wulfila's Arianism, see Thompson, *The Visigoths in the Time of Ulfila*, pp. 94–132, and Heather and Matthews, *Goths in the Fourth Century*, pp. 135–41, esp. 140–1.

[59] Heather, 'The Crossing of the Danube', p. 295.

Aspects of Ingui

undermine that aspect of Gothic identity which was derived from a common inherited religion'.[60] So the Tervingi may have been alarmed by the Arian Christ because they took him for the '*Inggws* of the Romans', a Roman counterpart of their own tribal god (*Inggws gutané*), who might too easily change them and all the Goths into Romans. Athanaric, the reactionary *iudex* ('judge') of the Tervingi north of the Danube frontier at this time, is an important figure in the survey of evidence for Enguz.[61] The historian Sozomenos says that Athanaric undertook a persecution when some Christians in the Gothic camp stayed away from a pagan festival: 'It is said that when those whom Athanaric had commanded to do this were leading about the place a certain wooden image placed on a covered wagon, they passed by the tent of Christian converts and ordered these men to do obeisance and make offerings to it' (VI.37).[62] Sozomenos gives no indication here of this idol's name or sex, what the draught animals were or the time of year, but he says that those who refused Athanaric's offer were burned alive in their tents. Helm suggests that this violence occurred in a seasonal procession of which Sozomenos revealed as much as he knew.[63] Sozomenos also associates this incident with the persecution of 347/8, but it is more likely to have happened at the outset of Athanaric's anti-Christian purges of 369–72 which followed his treaty of independence from Valens. Four points of comparison in this passage (the wagon, its coverings, the deity and its circuit) show that the procession of this Gothic idol may be claimed as a reduced fourth-century analogue of Nerthus's tour in *Germania*, of Freyr's in *Gunnars þáttr helmings*, and of Ing's in *The Old English Rune Poem*.[64] If these motifs are taken to have a common origin, then the wooden idol would thus have represented the *Inggws gutané* to whom the Pietroasa neck-ring was

---

[60] *Ibid.*, p. 316.

[61] Wolfram (*History of the Goths*, p. 94) suggests that Lat *iudex* translated Got *kindins* (Burgundian *hendinos*), which would have meant 'representative of the kindred'. Heather (*Goths and Romans*, p. 98) thinks that either *kindins* or *þiudans* could have been understood.

[62] *Historiae*, p. 1406 (*Hermiae Sozomeni Historia*): Λέγεται γὰρ ὥς τι ξόανον ἐφ᾽ ἁρμαμάξης ἑστὼς, οἵ γε τοῦτο ποιεῖν ὑπὸ Ἀθαναρίχου προσετάχθησαν, καθ᾽ ἑκάστην σκηνὴν περιάγοντες τῶν Χριστιανίζειν καταγγελλομένων, ἐκέλευον τοῦτο προσκυνεῖν, καὶ θύειν.

[63] *HAR* II.i, 59–62 (§32).

[64] *Germania*, p. 285; *Flat* I, 337–9 (chs. 277–8); *Old English Rune Poem*, ed. Halsall, pp. 21–32.

inscribed, i.e. *gáut-* (later *Gapt*), the divine ancestor whose mediator among the Tervingi was Athanaric.[65]

In 376 a civil war broke out between Athanaric and two rival Terving leaders, Fritigern and Alavivus, over the Terving policy towards the Huns, who were now invading from the rear; when these rival Tervingi took refuge with Valens, he gave them asylum in the empire, but on condition that they converted by treaty to Christianity.[66] Thousands of Goths, in this way, not only of the Terving confederation but also some of the Greuthungi, crossed the Danube into Thrace. A further war broke out after this river-crossing, in which Fritigern eventually routed and killed Valens outside Hadrianople in 378, but later died himself. The western emperor Gratian and Valens's eastern replacement Theodosius I seem then to have decided on a policy of appeasement towards the Tervingi. By now Athanaric was old and had lost most of his support, but Theodosius invited him to Constantinople, where Athanaric's father had once been held as a hostage;[67] Athanaric arrived on 14 January 381.[68] Jordanes says that Athanaric, amazed at the size of this city and the power of its ruler, said 'Truly the emperor of the Romans is a god upon earth (*deus terrenus*); and any man who raises his hand against him is guilty of his own blood' (XXVIII.143).[69]

With these words Athanaric appears to have undergone both a political and religious conversion and to have believed that Theodosius, as *deus terrenus*, was the true incarnation of Inggws to whom the Goths must now pay homage. It is possible that Cassiodorus based this opinion of Theodosius on Roman documents containing the emperor's own propaganda, but no version of this speech is found in other sources.[70] Theodosius seems to have cultivated the allegiance of Gothic troops: Zosimus gives an account of barbarian federates serving under Theodosius in the 380s, who 'had golden neck-rings given to them by the emperor for their personal adornment'.[71] Thus it is possible that the Tervingi in

---

[65] Wolfram (*History of the Goths*, p. 69) implies that Gapt was this idol.
[66] Heather, 'The Crossing of the Danube', pp. 313–15.
[67] Heather, *Goths and Romans*, p. 99.   [68] *Ibid.*, pp. 165–71, esp. 167.
[69] *Getica*, ed. Mommsen I, 95 (XXVIII): '"deus," inquit, "sine dubio terrenus est imperator et quisquis adversus eum manu moverit, ipse sui sanguinis reus existit"'.
[70] See Wolfram, *History of the Goths*, pp. 131–5, esp. 132.
[71] *Zosimi Comitis et Exadvocati Fisci Historia Nova*, ed. L. Mendelssohn (Leipzig, 1887), p. 197 (IV.40): ἦν δὲ περιαυχένια χρυσᾶ παρὰ βασιλέως αὐτοῖς δεδομένα πρὸς

Aspects of Ingui

381 perceived Theodosius to be a 'lover of peace and of the Gothic race' (*amator pacis generisque Gothorum*), as Cassiodorus described him more than a century later in *Getica* (XXIX.146).[72] In addition, an obit for 3 November in a sixth-century Gothic calendar shows that Emperor 'Constantine', a mistake for Constantius II (350–61), was called *þiudans* ('ruler of the people').[73] Given these epithets for Roman emperors from a Gothic tradition, the simplest reading *gutan[i] ingwa hailag* on the Pietroasa neck-ring, and the possibility that this and other neck-rings were issued by Roman emperors, I suggest that Athanaric accepted Theodosius as the '*Inggws* of the Romans'.

I shall now argue that the first Goths to convert to Arianism, with an awe of the Roman empire similar to that attributed in this passage to Athanaric, would have accepted Christ as a past incarnation of Enguz. Athanaric died on 25 January 381, less than two weeks after arriving in Constantinople.[74] Yet when his treaty with Theodosius was ratified a year later in 382, the Tervingi and other groups under this new Roman *foedus* became a new nation and were converted to Arianism *en masse*.[75] E. A. Thompson, followed by Heather, suggests that the Tervingi, in due course, preserved their Arian Christianity in order to remain free of imperial control.[76] Yet some Goths other than Athanaric must have admired and even emulated the prestigious Roman power. When the heathen Radagaisus of the Greuthungi invaded Italy in 405–6, some Arian Tervingi probably joined his

κόσμον. On the status of Zosimus (*c*. 500) as a derivative historian, see Heather, *Goths and Romans*, pp. 76–8. It is possible that the Pietroasa neck-ring (15.2cm in diameter and 1.2 cm thick) and seven others originally found in the same hoard, not to mention two others from separate finds, belonged to Gothic soldiers in Roman service.

[72] *Getica*, ed. Mommsen I, 96.
[73] 'Kustantei(n)us þiudanis', in Heather and Matthews, *Goths in the Fourth Century*, pp. 128–30, esp. 129.
[74] See E. Gibbon, *The Decline and Fall of the Roman Empire*, ed. D. A. Saunders with an introduction by C. A. Robinson, Jr (first published 1776–88) (Harmondsworth, 1985), p. 542: 'As temperance was not the virtue of his nation, it may justly be suspected that his mortal disease was contracted amidst the pleasures of the Imperial banquets.' For more sober interpretations of Athanaric's death, see Wolfram, *History of the Goths*, pp. 132–3, and Heather, *Goths and Romans*, p. 154.
[75] On the terms of this treaty, see Wolfram, *History of the Goths*, p. 133; Heather, *Goths and Romans*, pp. 157–65.
[76] Thompson, *The Visigoths in the Time of Ulfila*, pp. 109–17; Heather, *Goths and Romans*, p. 328.

Heathen gods

forces;[77] and when this invasion was defeated, the surviving Greuthungi in turn swelled out Alaric's Terving army in 408;[78] heathen and Arian Goths began to mingle in this way. What was the consequence of a scaled-down Arian creed being passed back further over Balkan, Carpathian and Alpine frontiers to barbarian admirers of the Roman empire? Inevitably, as Alaric's Arian Tervingi rejected the consubstantiality of Father and Son, so they bestowed Constantine's old image of a conquering Christ on heathen Greuthungi, Vandals, Gepids, Lombards, Burgundians, Alemans, Alans, Heruli and initially Franks, not as the divine, but as the subordinate human son of God.[79]

This suggested assimilation of Arian Christianity into Gothic paganism would not have been new. North of the Danube, even before the Terving persecution presumably of 369–72, Bishop Wulfila already seems to have reacted to a syncretism of this kind among the Moesian Tervingi in his Gothic Bible translation of the 340s. The fragments of Wulfila's work that survive are translations of the gospels and parts of the Old Testament; yet the Cappadocian historian Philostorgius claims that Wulfila, his older contemporary, refrained from translating the Book of Kings so as not to inflame the warlike spirits of his people.[80] Green, in his study of these gospel translations, shows that Wulfila never used Got *drauhtins* (cognate with OE *dryhten* and OIce *dróttinn*) for 'Lord', but usually *frauja* (cognate with OE *frea* and OIce *Freyr*); never *háilags* for 'holy', but always *weihs*.[81] In other words, Wulfila would have chosen terms which, on the one hand, emphasized a peaceful rather than military aspect of Christ, and which, on the other, attempted to keep him distinct from a native dying god. Yet, as the rout of Valens shows, the warlike

---

[77] A. Schwarcz, 'Reichsangehörige Personen gotischer Herkunft: Prosopographische Studien' (unpublished Ph.D. dissertation, University of Vienna, 1984), p. 188.

[78] Heather, *Goths and Romans*, pp. 213–14; Wolfram, *History of the Goths*, p. 169.

[79] On the Goths and their literal perception of Arian theology, see Thompson, *The Visigoths in the Time of Ulfila*, pp. 119–26.

[80] Wolfram, *History of the Goths*, p. 75.

[81] On Wulfila's vocabulary, see Green, *Carolingian Lord*, pp. 265–98, esp. 267–9. On OE *weos*, see pp. 97–103, where I have concluded that OIce *vé* (cognate with Got *weihs*) seems to indicate a mortal who becomes deified, OIce *heilagr* (cognate with Got *háilags*) a deity who is born mortal; cf. S. Flowers, *Runes and Magic* (New York, 1986), p. 126: 'A thing is *wihaz* in so far as it belongs to, or has been made a part of the numinous, "otherly" realm (in a state of sacrality), and it is *hailagaz* as far as this power resides in it and streams forth from it.'

Aspects of Ingui

tendency that Wulfila tried to dampen among the Goths flared up among most of them in the end. So it is possible that where Gothic pagans first understood the existence of a human son of God from Wulfila and other Arian missionaries, they began to imagine Christ's death with a latitude reflecting the premature ways in which their own kings died; and thus accepted Arianism because they imagined Christ as a Roman incarnation of Enguz who died in battle.

Arianism was condemned by a synod called by Theodosius in Constantinople in 381 (the Second Ecumenical Council), but as the second canon of the same synod decreed that churches among barbarian congregations should continue to be governed by local precedent, this heresy remained unchecked among the Goths and Vandals, spread through them into Italy, Aquitaine, Spain and North Africa and did not die out until the end of the sixth century.[82] During this period the Catholic clergy deplored Arianism as a Christian–pagan or Christian–secular blend. Thus, in a letter of May 382, Ambrose of Milan attacked an Arian priest named Julian Valens for wearing a Gothic habit unsuitable for Christians, 'unless, perhaps, that is how the priests of Gothic idolatry are used to presenting themselves' (as Heather points out, 'Ambrose may provide a glimpse into the Gothic world where pagan forms affected the new religion').[83] In the 440s, Salvian of Marseilles castigated the barbarism of Arian Christianity and supposed that 'the most barbarous rites of Scythians and Gepids bring the name of Our Lord Saviour into cursing and blasphemy'.[84] In the 470s, Bishop Sidonius Apollinaris of Clermont complained that King Euric of Visigothic Toulouse was so embittered by even the sound of the Catholic name 'that you might wonder whether he is head of his nation or of his sect'.[85] Fourthly, as late as *c.* 570, Bishop

---

[82] Wolfram, *History of the Goths*, pp. 84–5.

[83] *De fide* (II.XVI), cited in Heather, 'The Crossing of the Danube', p. 314: 'nisi forte sic solent idolatrae sacerdotes prodire Gothorum'. Heather also believes (pers. comm.) that Ambrose referred to rings as the heathen feature of Julian's priestly habit.

[84] *Salviani Presbyteri Massiliensis Libri qui supersunt*, ed. K. Halm, MGH, Auct. Antiq. 1 (Berlin, 1877), 52 (*De gubernatione Dei*, IV.81–3): 'Scytharum aut Gepidarum inhumanissimi ritus in maledictum atque blasphemiam nomen domini inducunt'; *Scythi* probably means 'Goths', given that *Chuni* is Salvian's word for 'Huns' in his earlier discussion in *ibid.*, p. 49 (IV.67).

[85] *Epistulae et Carmina*, ed. Luetjohann, p. 109 (VII.vi): 'ut ambigas ampliusne suae gentis an suae sectae teneat principatum'; Wolfram, *History of the Goths*, pp. 197–202, esp. 199.

Heathen gods

Gregory of Tours recorded a dispute between himself and Agilan, an envoy whom King Leuvigild of Visigothic Spain sent to King Chilperic of the Merovingian Franks; after failing to understand Gregory's arguments on the consubstantiality of Father and Son, Agilan asked Gregory not to blaspheme against Arianism, saying that the Visigoths allow Christians to believe in whatever doctrine they wish to follow: 'Indeed, in our vernacular speech we say that no harm is done if a man passing pagan altars and the church of God should worship at both.'[86] In response, Gregory rebuked Agilan as 'a defender of pagans' (*gentilium defensor*) and as 'a promoter of heretics' (*hereticorum adsertor*) at one and the same time.

On the basis of this enduring Catholic propaganda, it may be inferred that in the fourth century, some two centuries before Gregory, Gothic Arian converts had begun to stylize Christ with the epithets of Enguz, their native dying god: in particular, with a nominal form of the adjective represented in Got *balþa*. I suggest that the Scandinavian *Baldr* was born when the heathen admirers of the romanized Gothic kingdoms, in the following centuries, took this Arian–Gothic Christ as a new god of their own. Until the arrival of an Arian Christ in their lives, most heathen Goths worshipping Enguz would have no cause to give his *balþa* aspect a personification of its own; but the more they began to admire the Arian Christ and the military power of the empire behind him, the more the *balþa* aspect of Enguz would have become important in its own right. In this way a new dying god, one separate from Enguz, may have been introduced into the eastern Germanic hinterland. If the western Heruli, on their way back to Denmark, from where they came, helped to bring Wodan to southern Scandinavia towards the end of the fifth century, as Helm suggests, then it is also possible that they introduced a *balþa* image of Christ; for some Heruli were Arians too.[87] In *c.* 890, after nearly four centuries of silence, *Baldr* emerges in a kenning for Þórr's brother (*Baldrs barmr*, 'Baldr's bosom-sibling'), hence son of Óðinn, in Þjóðólfr's *Haustlǫng*; in *c.* 985 Baldr is called *heilagt tafn* ('holy sacrifice') in Úlfr Uggason's *Húsdrápa*; and in *c.* 1000, Baldr is described *blóðugr tívurr* ('blood-stained sacrifice') in *Vsp* 31.[88]

---

[86] *Gregorii Historiae*, ed. Krusch and Levison, p. 251 (V.43): 'Sic enim vulgato sermone dicimus, non esse noxium, si inter gentilium aras et Dei ecclesiam quis transiens utraque veneretur.'

[87] Helm, *Wodan*, pp. 70–1; Kuhn, 'Die gotische Mission', pp. 60–5.

[88] *Skj* B I, 15, 5; 17, 16; and 130, 14. M. Olsen suggests that the Baldr tradition evolved

Aspects of Ingui

As more Goths became Christian, it is possible that they personified Enguz as *Gáut-*, identified him with their euhemerized ancestors, the **anseis*, and later forgot him almost completely. Thus, by the time of Athalaric (526–34), the name *Gapt* had been drawn from a Greek source (Theoderic was educated in Constantinople) and had become a proper noun which was suitable to be deployed in a regnal list to represent the ultimate Ostrogothic 'ancestor' as a counterpart of Augustus's forebear Aeneas. Historical parity, if not yet kinship with the Romans, would be achieved in this way. In remote Norway and Sweden, however, the *gautr*-epithet seems to have been employed separately as a synonym for Óðinn, a self-sacrificing god to whom the name *Gautr* would better apply once *Baldr* had displaced Freyr in the role of dying god. Baldr became a member of the Æsir and as the centuries passed, Ingvi-freyr lost virtually all his claim to the sacrificial motif. So Baldr would have evolved as a god peculiar to Scandinavia.[89]

With this hypothesis, I suggest that a form of Christ was adopted into east Germanic paganism early and thence passed back to Scandinavia before any official attempts at conversion there were made. There is no hint of this development in Anglo-Saxon England, where no Anglian or unadulterated Anglo-Saxon personification of OE *bealdor* can be traced. In this way, the presence or absence of 'Baldr' in Anglo-Saxon records may be used to distinguish traces of imported Danish from indigenous Anglian paganism. In the latter religion, more crucially, it appears that Ingui and *-geot* referred at one time to a native Anglian 'dying god'.

GEAT AND THE GOTHS IN *DEOR*

Whatever the reason for the creation of the simplex forms *Geot* and *Geat*, there is little doubt that these forms were constructed on the basis of the suffix *-geot* in older Anglian names. In England, simplex *Giuta* appears in *Historia Brittonum* in c. 829–30, *Geot* in the mid eighth-century Lindsey

from a parody of Christianity: 'Om Balder-digtning og Balder-kultus', *ANF* 40 (1924), 148–75, esp. 171–3.

[89] There is no evidence that a god Baldr was cultivated outside Scandinavia: see K. Helm, 'Balder in Deutschland?', *BGdSL* 67 (1944), 216–27; less plausibly, S. Gutenbrunner suggested that the Baldr stanzas *Vsp* 59–64 were derived from a Gothic 'Vorstufe' (in which Baldr was modelled on a Dacian Mithras), in 'Balders Wiederkehr: Südostgermanisches in der Vǫluspá?', *GRM* 37 (1956), 62–72, esp. 66–7.

Heathen gods

regnal list and *Geat* in ninth-century West Saxon genealogy. There is no way of telling if Geot/Geat was adopted in England as the ancestor of Anglo-Saxon kings in emulation of Gapt or the cognate Lombard *Gausus*, though Anglo-Saxon nobles could have learned of the Goths from their journeys to Rome from as early as the mid seventh century.[90] Probably as a result of some Anglo-Saxon knowledge of Lombardic and Carolingian Italy, if not directly from a reading of *Getica*, both the author of *Historia Brittonum* and Bishop Asser, in the early and late ninth century respectively, presented *Geat* not only as the ancestor of the West Saxons, but also as the deified founder of the Goths.[91] It is probably in connection with both these roles that Geat appears in *Deor*.

Geat and Mæthhild

Outside Anglo-Saxon genealogies Geat appears once only, as the subject of an allusion in the poem in the Exeter Book now named *Deor*. Elsewhere I have tried to suggest that the story of Geat and Mæthhild in *Deor* is the poet's prelude to two allusions concerning Theoderic and Ermanaric, with the implication that Geat founded the Ostrogothic family of Amal kings.[92] The context in which Geat appears in *Deor* is best quoted and translated here:

> We þæt Mæðhilde   monge gefrugnon,
> wurdon grundlease   Geates frige,
> þæt hi[m] seo sorglufu   slæp ealle binom.   (*Deor* 14–16)[93]

I shall now argue that the story contained in *Deor* 14–16 has common ancestry with the fabliau-style narrative of stanzas 96–102 of *Hávamál*; and that this *senex amans* narrative was written as part of a satire against King Æthelwulf of Wessex.

Many scholars regard the story of Geat and Mæthhild in *Deor* 14–16 as

---

[90] On these journeys, see Mayr-Harting, *The Coming of Christianity*, pp. 120–1.

[91] On the manuscript tradition of *Getica*, see Heather, 'Cassiodorus and the Rise of the Amals', pp. 110–16, esp. 111, n. 29. Heather believes on the evidence of *Widsith* (pers. comm.) that a manuscript of *Getica* was in circulation in ninth-century England.

[92] North, '*Jeux d'Esprit* in "Deor" 14–16', pp. 19–23; the conclusion of this argument is based on R. North, 'King Æthelwulf and the Goths in "Deor"', *ABäG* 40 (1994), 7–20.

[93] 'We heard this of Mæthhild's love-bartering (Geat's loves went without fulfilment) that this sorrowful love deprived him completely of sleep.'

Aspects of Ingui

a melancholy legend, in keeping with the view that *Deor* is a sombre poem. None the less, the story of Geat and Mæthhild in *Deor* may be meant to be diverting rather than moving. Within *Deor* 14–16 the poet may have made reference to both the dynastic reputation and the pagan cult of Geat. The scribe of the Exeter Book divided his text unevenly into six sections resembling stanzas. In each of the first five, allusion is made to an ancient legend in which one or more persons suffer: Welund, enslaved by Nithhad (*Deor* 1–6); Beadohild, whose brothers Welund kills and whom Welund rapes (*Deor* 8–12); Geat (*Deor* 14–16); King Theodric and his reign, subject of the briefest allusion (*Deor* 18–19); and the suffering subjects of King Eormanric (*Deor* 21–6). That the sorrow in each case passed is indicated in a refrain at the end of each section: *Þæs ofereode, þisses swa mæg* ('That passed over, so can this', *Deor* 7, 13, 17, 20, 27 and 42). By withholding the implication of *þisses*, the poet keeps his readers in suspense until the last section, in which his persona 'Deor' reveals his own misfortune: he was once the poet of the Heodenings, dear to their lord; now he has fallen from favour and another poet, Heorrenda, has taken the position and estates which were formerly his; but even this sorrow will pass.

With its refrain the scheme of *Deor* is tightly controlled, while the unique format of its written 'stanzas' suggests a coherent work of a date not far removed from the date of the exemplar of the one scribe of the Exeter Book proper (fols. 8–130). So it is possible that *Deor* was first composed in the corresponding West Saxon dialect.[94] In keeping with the refrain of *Deor*, the opaque lines on Geat and Mæthhild would be expected to refer to a sorrow that only time will heal. It is in keeping with this expression of optimism that I translate *Deor* 14–16 as above.

The one emendation needed for this reading is MS *hi* to *him* in *Deor* 16: 'þæt hi[m] seo sorglufu slæp ealle binom'. *Beniman*, of which 'binom' ('deprived') in this line is the third person singular preterite, always takes the dative of the deprived person and the accusative of the thing of which he is deprived. As 'seo sorglufu' is the subject of this line, then 'slæp', a masculine noun, must be the object of 'binom'. The person whom sorrowful love deprives of sleep is likely to be indicated in the pronoun *hi*, which must therefore be emended to a dative case *hi[m]*. *Ealle* would either have to be emended to *ealne* in agreement with *slæp*, thus 'of all

[94] *Deor*, ed. Malone, pp. 18–19.

sleep', or left unchanged as an adverbial use of the instrumental of *eall*. MS *hi* emended to *hi[m]* ('him') probably refers to Geat in the preceding line. *Hi* with a suspension mark for *him* occurs frequently in the Exeter Book, with the exception of *The Gifts of Men* 99, where in 'þæt hi[m] æfre anum ealle weorþen' ('that to him alone all things might ever happen'), *hi* occurs without its suspension mark. It is therefore possible that the scribe who wrote both *The Gifts of Men* 99 and *Deor* 16 left out a mark in each case because of the proximity of *ealle* in the second half of either line. Thus the sense of *Deor* 16 is probably that a sorrowful love, the sorrow of which resulted from something earlier, deprived Geat of a whole night's sleep.

The parallel needed for this reading of *Deor* 14–16 is a tale in *Hávamál* in which either the wife or the daughter of an unknown Billingr keeps the god Óðinn awake all night with a false promise of sex (stanzas 96–102).[95] Óðinn begins by repeating critical words of the conversation: *Billings mær* promised to let him into her room later in the evening when no-one would see them. He waited in the reeds, crept up to her house and found the hallway lined with guards, spears ready and torches burning; he retreated, waited till dawn and stole back past the sleeping retinue; but the 'wife' of Billingr was gone, a bitch tied to the end of her bed in mockery. In epilogue, Óðinn says:

> háðungar hverrar   leitaði mér it horsca man,
> oc hafða ec þess vætki vífs.   (*Háv* 102/7–9)[96]

Elsewhere I have tried to show that *Háv* 96–102 was composed as a part of the last contribution to the *Hávamál* compilation, thus more plausibly in an Icelandic monastery at the end of the twelfth or the beginning of the thirteenth century.[97] The purpose of this fabliau-type narrative in *Hávamál*, which is placed into Óðinn's mouth as *Hávi* ('the High One'), is to contrast his first failure with his consequent success in love; and by

---

[95] This theory is developed from an idea which occurred independently to U. Dronke (pers. comm.) and D. E. M. Clarke, in *The Hávamál*, ed. Clarke (Cambridge, 1923), p. 111. For the theory that 'Billings mær' is the wife of another man, see Sigurður Nordal, 'Billings mær', in *Bidrag till nordisk filologi tillägnade Emil Olson* (Lund, 1936), pp. 288–95.

[96] 'The clever mistress sought every humiliation for me, and I got nothing of that woman at all.'

[97] North, *Pagan Words*, pp. 122–44.

Aspects of Ingui

adding the gain of the Mead of Poetry, to exalt Óðinn's status from human to god, prior to his supernatural role in the main body of this long gnomic poem. Though Óðinn's failure to seduce the wife of Billingr is close to the old myth of Óðinn's barely successful union with Rindr to beget Váli, here in *Hávamál* it is first presented as a farcical illustration of a sorrow sometimes having comic overtones. Such may also be the motivation for a comic element in *Deor*, the narrative allusions of which are otherwise sombrely connected with violent incidents in Germanic legend, perhaps as native counterparts to Boethius's metrical allusions to the *Odyssey* and other material in his *De consolatione Philosophiae*.[98]

Mæðhild is not a form that appears elsewhere, but could be an Old English variant of the popular continental name *Mechthildis*.[99] Kemp Malone and Kevin Kiernan have found different analogues of *Mæðhild* in *Deor* 14–16. Malone first identified Geat and Mæthhild with Gaute and Magnild of a nineteenth-century Norwegian ballad; and with Gauti and Magnhildur of a ballad from Iceland of the same time.[100] In the Norwegian version, Gaute marries Magnild, who then tearfully foresees her own death in the Vending river. As they cross a bridge over the river one day, Magnild falls into it and drowns. Her husband draws her out again by the skill of his harp, alive, in the Norwegian version; in the Icelandic version, dead. Thus Malone translates: 'we learned that, [namely] Mæðhild's moans, [they] became numberless, [the moans] of Geat's lady, so that distressing love robbed her of all sleep'.[101]

Malone gets 'moans' by emending *monge* to *mone, assuming that the *-ge* in *monge gefrugnon* was a dittograph, and reading 'moan' into an otherwise unattested OE *man separate from *man* ('crime'). Malone's interpretation of *frige* as the genitive singular of feminine *freo* ('lady') is unlikely to be right, since *freo* occurs only at *Gen* 457 and is presumably a loan from OS *frî*. Malone's revised argument does not bear much scrutiny. Since Norman questioned the relevance of these Scandinavian ballads to Geat and Mæthhild, there appears to be a difficulty in reconciling narrative outlines; though the names are the same, the English and Scandinavian stories are probably not; and more than one story may be

---

[98] For another poem of the Exeter Book that may have been styled on Boethius's treatise, see North, 'Boethius and the Mercenary', pp. 71–98.

[99] There are about thirty entries in E. Förstemann, *Altdeutsches Namenbuch*, 3 vols. (Bonn, 1900–16) I, 1083–4.

[100] *Deor*, ed. Malone, pp. 8–9. [101] *Ibid*.

acted out by a pair of famous names.¹⁰² These ballads might confirm that two or more legends circulated in northern Europe concerning a couple whose counterparts in *Deor* were Geat and Mæthhild.

Kiernan has proposed a new interpretation of Geat and Mæthhild in the light of Malone's discovery of these ballads; despite Norman's sceptical comments, Kiernan paraphrases *Deor* 14–16 as '"Geat's grieving love rescued his wife unharmed from Death"'; his literal translation is as follows: 'We that about Mæðhild many learned; became bottomless Geat's sexual passions, so that her grieving love [of Geat's] the sleep of death (or the slippery place) all deprived'.¹⁰³ However, Malone's emendation of *monge* to **mone* should not be 'now generally accepted', as Kiernan says. Nor can *slæp* in its more conventional sense bear the second reading which Kiernan puts on it: Geat rescues Mæthhild from her *slæp* as a 'sleep of Death', and thus the poem renders a Germanic version of the legend of Orpheus and Eurydice known from the *De consolatione*. The theme of this text is similar to that of *Deor*, Kiernan makes no emendations, and thus his idea would be attractive were it not for the lack of parallels for 'the sleep of Death' motif in *slæp* and the inherent weaknesses of Malone's revised theory.

MS *monge* is better left without emendation. In this case it might be *mon(i)ge*, as in 'many of us have heard'. But, as Joyce Hill points out, 'the position of *monge* makes it likely that it is not in apposition to *we*, but is the object of *gefrugnon* and the key noun in introducing the Mæðhild allusion'.¹⁰⁴ A noun *monge*, as Malone proposed in his first and second editions of *Deor*, might be the dative singular of a neuter prefixless variant of *gemang* ('sexual intercourse'). OE *mong* is not recorded with this meaning in Old English sexual euphemisms, though *(ge-)mengan* occurs as the verbal form of *gemang*.¹⁰⁵ A sense 'commerce' in *mong*, the Middle English reflex, is easier to find than the sexual connotation suggested by Malone, though both senses are probably intended in *Of Arthour and Merlin*: 'An hore strong, Þat wiþ harlotes made hire *mong*' (c. 1425).¹⁰⁶

---

[102] F. Norman, '*Deor* and Modern Scandinavian Ballads', *London Mediæval Studies* 1.2 (1938), 165–78, esp. 175–6.

[103] K. Kiernan, 'A Solution to the Mæðhild–Geat Crux in *Deor*', *ES* 51 (1975), 97–9; and Kiernan, '*Deor*', *NM* 79 (1978), 333–40, esp. 337.

[104] *Heroic Poems*, ed. Hill, p. 42.

[105] J. Coleman, 'Sexual Euphemism in Old English', *NM* 93 (1992), 93–8, esp. 94.

[106] *Of Arthour and Merlin*, ed. O. D. Macrae-Gibson, EETS n.s. 268 (1973), 60 (lines

Malone's first translation of *Deor* 14–16 was 'we learned that: Geat's boundless passion and the (love) commerce of Mæðhild came to pass, so that sorrow-love deprived them of all sleep'.[107]

Where Geat's 'love' is concerned, the poet of *Deor* thus uses three terms, one on each line of his allusion in *Deor* 14–16: *mong*, *frige* and *sorglufu*. OE *frige* denotes a man's sexual 'love' in the other instances: *Jul* 103, *El* 341, *Christ* 37 and typically:

> ond sio weres friga   wiht ne cuþe,
> ne þurh sæd ne cwom   sigores agend
> monnes ofer moldan.   (*Christ* 419–21)[108]

I shall provide a fuller discussion of *frige* in ch. 8, with regard to an image of *grund*- as Geat's divine consort. Within this discussion *Deor* 15 occurs in parenthesis: line 14 is apposed to 16 by repetition of *þæt* at 16 (cf. *Deor* 35–6; *Beo* 415–17 and 809–12). *Grundlease* at *Deor* 15 appears to mean 'limitless' and is translated so in Joyce Hill's edition of this poem.[109] With the sense 'bottomless', *grundleas* describes Tartarus, and is used of a wave in *Whale* 46, and yet helps to translate Boethius's *fluctus*, 'wave' (II, met. 4) and *avaritia*, 'greed' (II, pr. 5), which is rendered *grundleas gitsung* ('unfulfilled, insatiable greed') in Alfred's West Saxon *De consolatione*.[110] This sense would help to render *Deor* 15 'Geat's loves went without fulfilment'.

Geat's only role in the *Anglo-Saxon Chronicle* is as an ancestor of West Saxon kings. In Britain, Geat's name was probably known widely in connection with the Goths, if not directly from Jordanes, then from tales descended from *fabulae* of Gapt the progenitor such as those Jordanes cites as a source for his royal genealogy in *Getica* ('Gapt, who begat

---

773–4): 'a strong whore who carried out her commerce with young men'. *Middle English Dictionary*, ed. H. Kurath and S. M. Kuhn (Chicago, 1954–), s.v. 'mong'.

[107] *Deor*, ed. Malone (1st ed.), pp. 8–9; F. Norman based 'affair' on Malone's first translation of *monge*, in '*Deor*: a Criticism and Interpretation', *MLR* 32 (1937), 374–81, esp. 380.

[108] 'And she [Mary] knew nothing of a man's love, nor through seed of man did the Owner of Victory come over the earth.'

[109] *Heroic Poems*, ed. Hill, p. 63.

[110] *Boethius: the Theological Tractates*, ed. and trans. H. F. Stewart, E. K. Rand and S. J. Tester, Loeb Classical Library (Cambridge, MA, and London, 1978), pp. 198–9 and 120–1; *King Alfred's Boethius*, ed. Sedgefield, p. 159.15; also edited in *Met* 7.15.

Hulmul').[111] In Scandinavia, the god Óðinn appropriated the role and presumably some of the legends previously attributed to Gautr. Thus the story of Geat and Mæthhild in *Deor* 14–16 can be read as an older analogue of a tale in the Norse–Icelandic *Hávamál* 96–102 in which an unnamed, but possibly married, woman tricks Óðinn into waiting up all night long for sex. Though Óðinn and *Billings mær* came to enact this story in *Hávamál*, I suggest that the names they had respectively displaced continued as the subjects of a variant legend which Malone discovered in the nineteenth-century ballads of Gauti and Magnhildur. What these ballads show, with regard to *Deor* 14–16, is the possibility that the poet got his story of Geat and Mæthhild from a contemporary Scandinavian source. Whether or not Geat's story in *Deor* has this provenance, however, it is worth noting that Geat is a name derived from an aspect of Ingui or Ing; that the tale of Geat and Mæthhild and its Scandinavian variants are the only surviving narratives in which Geat appears; and that Geat's attempt to make love to a woman resembles in outline the frustrated love of Freyr for Gerðr in *Skírnismál*.

To conclude, Geat's story in *Deor* appears to go as follows. Mæthhild negotiates the time and place of a secret affair (*mong*: line 14) with Geat. She eludes him, however, bringing his sexual love (*frige*: line 15) to an insatiable level over the period of one night. So Mæthhild gives Geat's lust the dignity of a sorrow (*sorglufu*: line 16) which deprives him of sleep completely. In this way, the poet in these lines appears to mock Geat as a failed lover. Let us now consider the wider implications of this reading in *Deor*.

Æthelwulf and Judith

With the exception of Deor at the end, the heroes in this poem are all related to the Goths. Widia, to whose begetting the poet alludes in *Deor* 1–12, was a Gothic hero celebrated by the Amali in the fifth century whom Jordanes knew as *Vidigoia* and 'whose reputation in this nation is great'.[112] Theodric, who rules for thirty winters in *Deor* 18–19, is probably Theoderic the Ostrogoth, prefect of the western Roman empire for about thirty-three years (493–526) and later celebrated as Dietrich

---

[111] *Getica*, ed. Mommsen I, 76: 'Gapt, qui genuit Hulmul'.
[112] *Ibid*. I, 65: 'quorum in hac gente magna opinio est'.

von Bern.[113] Eormanric is probably Ermanaric, who probably committed suicide in the face of Hunnish invasions, just before the Gothic tribes crossed the Danube in *c.* 376;[114] elsewhere in Old English poetry, Eormanric is mentioned prominently in *Wid* 111 and is called *wraþ wærloga* ('a savage magician') in *Wid* 8–9; Jǫrmunrekkr, his counterpart in the Norse *Hamðismál*, survives an attempt on his life, but not mutilation, by the two brothers who came to avenge his murder of their sister (his wife). Eormanric is the subject of the *Deor* poet's last narrative allusion before he reveals his own fictitious name as 'Deor'.

Deor is ambivalent towards the Goths in his poem. After Eormanric, in particular, the implication of the refrain is that this early Gothic empire *ofereode* ('passed over') because it was wiped out by the Huns. Later Theoderic would rule for thirty-three years, but in 552 General Narses killed Totila and drove the last Ostrogoths out of Italy.[115] Geat's role in *Deor* 14–16, as I have interpreted it, seems tarnished by the implication that he is a *senex amans*. Even the great Widia's conception comes about through bitterness and suffering. Although all of these figures have some connection with the Goths, Deor's treatment of his figures is by turns oblique, irreverent, suggestive and defamatory.

In Anglo-Saxon literature outside *Deor*, Geat appears only as an ancestor of the kings of Wessex. No-one seems to have asked why King Ecgberht of Wessex, or his son Æthelwulf, should have sanctioned a record of their descent from the Goths, who were an east Germanic people. Nor has this predilection for Geat's role as a West Saxon ancestor, written in the *Chronicle* genealogy for the year 855, been connected with King Æthelwulf's journey to Rome in the same year.

Æthelwulf's purpose in going to Rome partly concerned his son Alfred, whom he took with him in 853. The letter of Pope Leo IV (847–55) to Æthelwulf, if genuine, suggests that Alfred was decorated as a consul on his first papal visit.[116] Asser, on the other hand, repeats the

---

[113] *Deor*, ed. Malone, pp. 9–13; E. Marold, 'Wandel und Konstanz in der Darstellung der Figur des Dietrich von Bern', in *Heldensagen und Heldendichtung im Germanischen*, ed. H. Beck, Ergänzungsbände zum Reallexikon der Germanischen Altertumskunde 2 (Berlin and New York, 1988), 149–82.

[114] Wolfram, *History of the Goths*, pp. 86–9; *Poetic Edda I*, ed. Dronke, pp. 192–204.

[115] On the history of Ermanaric, see Wolfram, *History of the Goths*, pp. 353–61, esp. 360.

[116] *Alfred the Great*, trans. Keynes and Lapidge, p. 232; my translations are based on their text, pp. 66–110. For a theory (since revised by the author) that Pope Leo's letter was

Anglo-Saxon Chronicle in stating that Leo ordained and anointed Alfred as king, received him as an adopted son and confirmed him.[117] Æthelwulf might have hoped that his other sons would perceive his visit as the confirmation of Alfred's claim to Wessex. The fact that Alfred had been sent to Rome once, if not twice, may support Asser's claim that Æthelwulf loved Alfred *plus ceteris filiis*, 'more than his other sons' (ch. 11).

If descent from Geat was a crucial part of West Saxon royal genealogy, Asser gives Alfred better continental connections than his half-brothers, relating him to the Goths not only through Æthelwulf, whose genealogy he quotes in the first chapter, but also through his mother Osburh, the daughter of Oslac, Æthelwulf's butler: 'Qui Oslac Gothus erat natione; ortus enim erat de Gothis et Iutis, de semine scilicet Stuf et Wihtgar.'[118] Asser thus connects Oslac with the Jutes on Wight and with Cerdic, the first West Saxon invader. But why is Oslac called *Gothus*? Jutes and Goths may have been confused in the vernacular and in the 'Gothi et Iuti' of his Latin, Asser seems to regard them as close if not identical. Keynes and Lapidge refer to a possible confusion of forms in the voyage of Ohthere added to the Alfredian translation of Orosius's *Historia adversus paganos*, where *Gotland* is usually thought to have been written for Ohthere's Old Norse *Jótland* ('Jutland'); rather than for *Gaut(a)land* ('Göteland'), as is more likely in what appears to be the transcription of an occasionally garbled interview.[119] With *Gothus*, therefore, Keynes and Lapidge believe that 'Asser was probably trying to convey the information that Oslac was of ultimately Danish extraction.' In a similar vein, Janet Nelson argues that Alfred had Asser connect his mother Osburh with the Goths so as to claim a solidarity with Danes inside and outside his kingdom.[120] Yet this idea would depend on contemporary Danes considering themselves to be of Gothic descent, for which there is no evidence.[121] Thus while Asser

a forgery, see J. Nelson, 'The Problem of King Alfred's Royal Anointing', *Journal of Ecclesiastical History* 18 (1967), 145–63, esp. 160–2.

[117] *Asser's Life*, ed. Stevenson and rev. Whitelock, p. 7 (ch. 8).

[118] *Ibid.*, p. 4 (ch. 2): 'Which Oslac was a Goth by race; for he was descended from the Goths and Jutes, particularly from the seed of Stuf and Wihtgar.'

[119] *The Old English Orosius*, ed. Bately, pp. 16.11 and 196; *Alfred the Great*, trans. Keynes and Lapidge, pp. 229–30 (n. 8).

[120] Nelson, 'Reconstructing a Royal Family', pp. 48–51.

[121] There is no evidence, for example, in twelfth-century Danish chronicles. See *Historiae Danicae*, ed. Gertz I, 14 (*Chronicon Roskildense*), 43–4 (*Chronicon Lethrense*), 96–7 (Sven

Aspects of Ingui

showed Osburh's Kentish connections with *Iuti*, with *Gothus* it is possible that he was trying to be faithful to an older account of Alfred's maternal ancestry which reinforced the place of the Goths in Æthelwulf's genealogy.[122] Yet, where the Goths are concerned, in another part of *De rebus gestis Ælfredi*, Asser tries to make sense of Geat, eponym of the Goths, by identifying him with *Geta*, a slave in an early Roman comedy by Terence (ch. 1). So it seems that the political reasons for demonstrating Alfred's kinship with the Goths had been lost by the 890s.

It was probably to his father Æthelwulf that Alfred, the force behind Asser's contemporary biography, owed the ideology if not the understanding of his alleged Gothic descent. To Æthelwulf some forty years earlier, Alfred's audience with Pope Leo was probably a necessary stage in the continuing growth of West Saxon influence at home and abroad. Who better to meet the heir of St Peter than a kinsman on both sides of Italy's past temporal rulers, the Goths and Lombards, whose mantle Charlemagne had adopted? Having been feted by King Charles the Bald, grandson of Charlemagne, on his trip to Rome, Æthelwulf married Judith his daughter on the way home. Thus he joined his kingdom with the rising house of the most prestigious nation in Europe.[123]

But when Æthelwulf returned to Wessex in 856, he did not get the reward he might have expected for his year's dynastic work in Italy and western Francia. A rebellion had broken out in his absence. Writing in c. 893, Asser provided differing versions of what happened when Æthelwulf came home. Some of his informants blamed Æthelwulf's bishop and ealdorman, some the king's son the 'grasping' (*pertinax*) Æthelbald. But the coup was real enough, despite Asser's effusions: when Æthelwulf returned, he only retained eastern Wessex, the lesser part of his kingdom. This uprising seems to have resulted from Æthelwulf's marriage with Judith. Nelson's view is that the Æthelwulf–Judith alliance principally served Charles, who found himself in a stronger position to propose the

---

Aggesen's *Brevis Historia Regum Dacie*), 142–3 (*Genealogia Regum Dacie*); 159, 161, 167, 175, 176–7 and 186 (*Series et Genealogiae Regum Danorum I–VII*).

[122] For a theory that Osburh's father may have had family connections in Kent while Æthelwulf was sub-king there in the mid 830s, see Nelson, 'Reconstructing a Royal Family', p. 56.

[123] On the tripartitite *imperium Christianum* of the grandsons of Charlemagne, still an item in the 860s, see T. Reuter, *Germany in the Early Middle Ages c. 800–1056* (London and New York, 1991), pp. 70–7.

match to his guest when Æthelbald usurped the throne of Wessex in 856; though she notes that 'Æthelwulf needed an infusion of Carolingian wealth and prestige.'[124] In return, Charles would have had the prospect of a grandson ruling Wessex. It was probably to this end that Bishop Hincmar of Rheims consecrated and anointed Judith queen when she married Æthelwulf in 856. M. J. Enright, similarly, suggests that Æthelwulf and Charles decided to ally their families in this way only when Æthelwulf heard of his son's revolt, though he notes that friction had probably developed between father and son after their joint defeat of the Vikings at *Aclea* in 851, and adds that the marriage 'may have been the proximate cause for bringing the rebellion to a head'.[125] Yet the order of these events is uncertain and Enright dismisses too lightly the old view that at least part of the reason for this marriage was to build an alliance against the Danes.[126] Nor is it plausible that Æthelwulf had so little part in planning his marriage in 855 that he waited nearly a year in Rome before considering the matter for the first time.

It is therefore more likely that Æthelwulf had worked for this alliance while abroad in Rome and Francia. In Wessex the resentment felt by his son and others may have grown from the time Æthelwulf left England in 855. Nelson shows that Æthelwulf probably had to spurn Osburh, Æthelbald's (and Alfred's) mother, to marry Judith.[127] Asser says that Æthelbald, Bishop Ealhstan of Sherborne and Ealdorman Eanwulf of Somerset 'are said to have plotted' (*coniurasse referuntur*) to prevent Æthelwulf from being received in his kingdom again.[128] If Bishop Ealhstan was involved, this was a serious conspiracy: an 'Ealhstan' is named in *The Anglo-Saxon Chronicle* as Æthelwulf's companion in Ecgberht's conquest of Kent after the battle of *Ellandun* in *c*. 825.[129] As Alfred was about seven years old in 855, he could not have helped his father until he became Asser's chief informant many years later. Although Alfred, through Asser, seems to suppress present conflicts within his

---

[124] Nelson, *Charles the Bald*, p. 182.
[125] M. J. Enright, 'Charles the Bald and Aethelwulf of Wessex: the Alliance of 856 and Strategies of Royal Succession', *JMH* 5 (1979), 291–314, esp. 296.
[126] *Ibid.*, pp. 291–3; Nelson, *Charles the Bald*, pp. 180–9.
[127] So Nelson, in 'Reconstructing a Royal Family', pp. 54–6.
[128] *Asser's Life*, ed. Stevenson and rev. Whitelock, p. 10 (ch. 12).
[129] *ASC* I, 61 (823 (= 825)).

Aspects of Ingui

family, he sanctions a record of them in the previous generation.[130] Asser thus favours Æthelwulf in this past conflict and presents his loss of the Wessex heartland as due to 'the indescribable forbearance of the father' (*ineffabili patris clementia*, ch. 12). Perhaps Asser also exaggerates when he writes that 'the entire nation' (*tota illa gens*) would have ejected Æthelbald from his part of the kingdom 'had Æthelwulf allowed it' (*si ille permitteret*). Æthelwulf ruled a smaller kingdom for two years and died in 858, having made a will with instructions to divide Wessex among his surviving sons. Æthelbald ruled all Wessex after him 'for two and a half unrestrained years' (*effrenisque duobus et dimidio annis*, ch. 17), in which increasing Viking raids on England may have diverted West Saxon attention away from Europe.

What did Æthelbald think of his father's bigamy in western Francia and Italy in 855–6? Asser's denunciations of Æthelbald offer some help in finding an answer. Asser hints that Æthelbald was forced to compromise with Æthelwulf 'by common agreement of all the nobles' (*omnium astipulatione nobilium*, ch. 12). Though Æthelbald probably had to conspire with a bishop and ealdorman to try to usurp his father's power, Asser singles him out as the sole cause of the revolt: 'Many also attribute it solely to the insolence (*insolentia*) of this king, because this king was as stubborn (*pertinax*) in this affair as he was in many other perversities (*in multis aliis perversitatibus*), so we have heard from the report of certain men' (ch. 12).[131] Thus I suggest that *Deor* was written in *c*. 855–6 as a reflection of Æthelbald's 'insolent', 'stubborn' and 'perverse' attitude to his father.

To many it may seem surprising to look for political allegory in *Deor*. This poem is mostly read as sad and full of depressed wisdom, though the cryptic brevity, variously sectioned form and final pun on the poet Deor's name in *Deor* are not quite in keeping with this idea. Part of the problem is the lack of criteria with which to judge the poet's skill, if *Deor* is to be read as a sombre work. *Deor*'s refrain suggests change, the instability of the world, through which the poet's persona hopes eventually to win back his fortune. Yet change is presented in some stories more clearly than in others. The poet alludes variously to Germanic legends, swiftly in the

---

[130] Nelson, 'Reconstructing a Royal Family', pp. 62–3.
[131] *Asser's Life*, ed. Stevenson and rev. Whitelock, pp. 11–12: 'Multi quoque regali solummodo insolentiae deputant, quia et ille rex in hac re et in multis aliis perversitatibus pertinax fuit, sicut quorundam hominum relatu audivimus.'

Heathen gods

case of Geat and Theodric, but with *longueurs* in the case of Welund's suffering and the oppression of Eormanric's subjects. The first case suggests the concise brevity of a mature poetic tradition for which certain heroic topoi seem to be overfamiliar, rather than fresh. The second might just as easily be evidence of inferior workmanship. Both drawbacks occur in Deor's reflection on God's various apportioning of *wislicne blæd* ('assured glory') and *weana dæl* ('a number of miseries') in *Deor* 34. These lines may have been inspired by passages in the *De consolatione Philosophiae*, but if so, they are cursory and lack Boethius's conclusion. In this respect, my earlier reading of Geat as a *senex amans* in *Deor* 14–16 looks less out of place. The legend to which these lines allude was probably old, but as Mæthhild is an Old English form of a name later associated with France, Geat's failure to beget an heir on her could now have been read as the first Gothic attempt to marry a Frank, an overture which failed.

This reading could have mocked Æthelwulf's dynastic pretentions with Judith. Asser says that Æthelwulf broke with West Saxon custom when he made Judith queen beside him and called her *regina* ('queen'), rather than *regis coniunx* ('king's wife').[132] Keynes and Lapidge note that Asser's statement about West Saxon royal custom at this time appears to be accurate.[133] In this context, Æthelwulf placed great value on his marriage with Judith. As Æthelbald married Judith when Æthelwulf died two years later, he probably admired her Carolingian and Lombard lineage as much as his father had done. Thus it was probably not Judith's later eminence in Wessex, but the possible consequences of her union with Æthelwulf that led Æthelbald to revolt. Father and son were political rivals, and if *Deor* was written as a satire on the Goths in West Saxon genealogy, then the three-line comedy of Geat and Mæthhild could have drawn attention to an impending marriage between Æthelwulf and Judith, a marriage that Æthelbald wanted to fail.

Deor starts with the union of another couple, Welund and Beadohild: 'Welund him be w*ifmen* [MS *wurman*] wræces cunnade' ('Welund got to know exile through a *woman*') in *Deor* 1.[134] With this line the poet of

---

[132] *Ibid.*, p. 12 (ch. 13).

[133] *Alfred the Great*, trans. Keynes and Lapidge, pp. 235–6; this view is qualified by Nelson, in 'Reconstructing a Royal Family', pp. 54–5.

[134] As OE *wyrm* occurs seven times in the text before *Deor* in the Exeter Book, *Soul and Body* II (lines 22, 67, 79, 106, 110, 117 and 119), MS *wurman* may have been miscopied from *wifmen. I am grateful to Ursula Dronke for this suggestion.

Aspects of Ingui

Deor avoids an epic opening which he uses elsewhere, thereafter building slowly from *gefrugnon* in *Deor* 14, through *monegum cuþ* in *Deor* 19, to *geascodan* in *Deor* 21. As Welund and Beadohild between them fill two sections out of six in *Deor*, their story may be deemed essential to the rest of the poem. The theme of this story is not only change, but the mythical birth of Widia, a Goth, from misery, murder and an act of rape. With Mæthhild's *mong* and the sleepless Geat, thereafter, we are invited to think of the failure of an old Goth to consummate a marriage. In Theodric's two lines, *Mæringa burg* is probably a place (perhaps Ravenna), but can also mean 'citadel of famous men' as I have shown elsewhere, the pun being made with *þæt wæs monegum cuþ* ('that was known to many', *Deor* 19).[135] Theodric's well-known thirty years is thus all we have of him in *Deor*. But Theoderic was an Arian and had imprisoned and executed Boethius in 524; given the wretched circumstances in which Boethius portrayed himself in book I of his *De consolatione*, Theoderic's reputation in later Christian Europe might not be described as fame but rather as infamy.[136]

The colourful history of Ermanaric, the last Goth to be mentioned in *Deor*, is entirely lacking in the six lines that end the speaker's bare sequence of narrative allusion. However, Eormanric's *wylfen geþoht* ('wolvish intention', *Deor* 22) must be connected with his story, in that his disaster ensues when he decides to marry again (in *Hamðismál*, Jǫrmunrekkr marries the young Svanhildr, whose execution shortly thereafter, on suspicion of adultery with Randvér, Jǫrmunrekkr's son by a previous marriage, is later avenged by her half-brothers Hamðir and Sǫrli). Perhaps *wylfen geþoht* is also a pun on *Æþel-wulf* ('noble-wolf'). What is not in short supply in *Deor* is an impression of Eormanric's tyranny as a ruler:

> Sæt secg monig   sorgum gebunden,
> wean on wenan,   wyscte geneahhe
> þæt þæs cynerices   ofercumen wære.
>   Þæs ofereode,   þisses swa mæg!   (*Deor* 24–7)[137]

---

[135] See North, '*Jeux d'Esprit* in "Deor" 14–16', p. 23.

[136] Fifteen Latin versions survive from Anglo-Saxon libraries: see Gneuss, 'Preliminary List of Manuscripts', pp. 1–60 (nos. 12, 23, 68, 193, 408, 533, 671, 776, 823, 829, 886, 887, 899, 901 and 908).

[137] 'Many a man sat bound with sorrows, expecting misery, constantly wishing that that kingdom might be over and done with. That passed over, so can this!.'

With *þæs ofereode* each time, the refrain captures unsettling images: a cripple suffering exile; a young woman discovering pregnancy; an old man made sleepless by his failure to secure a sexual bargain; a long-established emperor achieving notoriety rather than fame; another tyrant's oppressive reign that everyone hopes will end and does end when he makes a foolish marriage.

From Æthelbald's point of view, these images would probably fit his father Æthelwulf in 856: the year in Italy away from his kingdom; his interest in the daughter of Charles the Bald; and through Geat, his pretensions in claiming kinship with the *Gotena rice*, as well as the imminent loss of his power. If Asser exaggerated when he implied of Wessex that 'tota illa gens' would have supported Æthelwulf against his son when he returned, then the opposing view may have been more explicit in Eormanric's subjects wishing for their king's complete destruction.

A satirical reference to Æthelwulf's prospective courtship with Judith may be the subject of Deor's allusion to himself in the last passage of all. Deor does not reveal why his loyal master stripped him of his estates and gave them to Heorrenda, a skilled poet. Deor only names his former role as *Heodeninga scop* ('court poet of the Heodenings', *Deor* 36). This title suggests that a certain *Heoden* is the name of the king who replaced Deor with Heorrenda. Although no analogue of the name *Deor* has been identified, Heoden and Heorrenda have counterparts in a story common to Old Icelandic and Middle High German literature. According to Snorri, who wrote a *précis* of a story that he quotes from Bragi's *Ragnarsdrápa* (stanzas 7–11), Heðinn steals princess Hildr away from her country while her father King Hǫgni is away.[138] Hǫgni pursues Heðinn to the isle of Hoy in Orkney, where Hildr attempts to make peace between them with the offer of a golden necklace. When Hǫgni refuses this compensation, he and his *de facto* son-in-law fight an endless battle known to Snorri as the *Hjaðningavíg* ('battle of the Hjaðningar'), one which is doomed to start afresh each day when Hildr, here gifted with a form of *seiðr* (regenerative magic of the Vanir), revives all dead combatants on either side. Bragi referred to a depiction of this story on the shield for which he composed the *Ragnarsdrápa*. Many lines in this poem are obscure, including Bragi's reference to Hjarrandi:

---

[138] *SnE* 432–4 (ch. 50) (*FJSnE* 153–5); *Flat* I, 279–83 (chs. 233–6).

Aspects of Ingui

> allr gekk herr und hurðir   Hjarranda fram kyrrar
> reiðr af Reifnis skeiði   raðaralfs mari bráðum.   (11/5–8)[139]

It is impossible to judge Hjarrandi's role in these lines, quite apart from Bragi's understanding of his kinship with Heðinn. Snorri, and consequently the writers of two fourteenth-century *fornaldarsǫgur*, present Hjarrandi as Heðinn's father.[140] With Hithinus and Hoginus, furthermore, Saxo tells a late twelfth-century Danish version of this story, but without Hiarrando, to whom he gives a different story in *Gesta Danorum*.[141]

More relevant to *Deor* than these analogues is *Kudrun* (*c*. 1230–40), the German version of this tale, in which King Hetele von Hegelingen abducts the young Kudrun from her absent father. Hetele enlists the help of Wate and Hôrant, the last a king of Denmark, kinsman of Hetele and a skilful musician:

> Dô sich diu naht verendet   und ez begunde tagen,
> Hôránt begunde singen,   daz dâ bî in den hagen
> geswigen alle vogele   von sînem süezen sange.
> die liute, die dâ sliefen,   die [en]lâgen dô niht [ze] lange.
> ('Wie suoze Hôrant sanc', VI.379–82)[142]

After Hôrant charms the maiden and her mother with his master's praises, Wate helps Hetele and Kudrun to escape by sea. Hôrant was well known in Middle High German poetry.[143] Another version of this story was probably known to Geoffrey Chaucer: once in *Troilus and Criseyde*, where to the young Criseyde, shortly to be inveigled into bed with Troilus, Pandarus 'tolde tale of Wade' (III.614); and less clearly in *The Merchant's Tale*, where the aged January, discussing marriage with his

---

[139] *Skj* B I, 3, 11: 'The whole army of the ?necklace-demon of the ?quiet race-course [?Heðinn] went enraged forward beneath the quiet doors of Hjarrandi [?shields] out of the swift steed of Reifnir [sea-king's horse: ship].'

[140] *SnE* 432 (marked for p. 423; see also *FJSnE* 154); *Fornaldarsögur*, ed. Guðni and Bjarni I, 373 (*Sǫrla þáttr*), II, 207 (*Göngu-Hrólfs saga*) and III, 312 (*Hjarrandahljóð*, name of a dance with singing, in *Bósa saga*).

[141] *GD*, p. 138; *History of the Danes*, trans. Fisher and ed. Ellis Davidson I, 149.

[142] *Kudrun*, ed. K. Bartsch, rev. with an introduction by K. Stackmann, 5th ed. (Wiesbaden, 1980), p. 80: 'When the night came to an end and it began to dawn, Hôrant began to sing so well that all the birds in the hedgerows fell silent at his sweet song. Those people who were sleeping, they did not lie down too long!'

[143] Gillespie, *Catalogue*, s.v. 'Hôrant' (pp. 80–1).

friends, disdains 'thise olde wydwes', who 'konne so muchel crafte on Wades boot' (lines 1423–4).[144] Chaucer thus seems to regard Wade as a resourceful aider and abettor of illicit unions: Pandarus helping Troilus to compromise Criseyde, in the first instance; and widows stage-managing their own elopements in the second.

Similarly, in ninth-century Wessex, Heorrenda could have been regarded as Heoden's ally in stealing a foreign princess from her father. If so, the point of his inclusion in *Deor* might finally become clear; it is not what Heorrenda did to replace Deor that matters; but what he is going to do that makes this *leoðcræftig monn* ('man skilled in poetry') the new poet of the Heodenings in *Deor* 40. In keeping with his negative appraisals of old men looking forward to wedlock with young princesses, therefore, Deor yields the task of securing a new bride for his master to a man better suited to the job. Where Heorrenda *londryht geþah* ('received [Deor's] titles to land') in *Deor* 40, I suggest that this poet alludes to Æthelwulf's second decimation of land in 854. Keynes and Lapidge show that the *Anglo-Saxon Chronicle* and certain charters are probably more reliable sources than Asser in recording Æthelwulf's grant of a tenth part of his disposable lands either directly to the church, or to the church through lay beneficiaries.[145] Æthelwulf's second grant to the church, the year before his departure to Rome, was thus a gift to the papal see, whose approval of Æthelwulf, registered in the likely fiction of Pope Leo's adoption of the young Alfred, would have helped Æthelwulf's match with Judith. To the extent of these implicit manoeuvres, Deor's loss of position to an instrument of Heoden's forthcoming elopement could have mocked the gift of various West Saxon *londryht* to the church before Æthelwulf's departure to Rome. Deor's name is punned with *dyre* in 'Drihtne dyre. Me wæs Deor noma' ('Dear to my lord. "Dear" was my name') in the same line (*Deor* 37). The past tense shows that the king in this case takes Deor's personal worth as lightly as he does his wealth. So the bond between king and subject is broken in the interests of a foreign cause.

---

[144] *The Riverside Chaucer: Based on the Works of Geoffrey Chaucer edited by F. N. Robinson*, ed. L. D. Benson (Oxford, New York and Toronto, 1987), pp. 522 ('told a tale of Wade') and 146 ('these old widows' who 'know so much skill in the matter of Wade's boat').

[145] *Alfred the Great*, trans. Keynes and Lapidge, pp. 232–4. For a study of the Second Decimation Charters, see also S. Keynes, 'The West Saxon Charters of King Æthelwulf and his Sons', *English Historical Review* 109 (1994), 1109–49.

Aspects of Ingui

Satire should not be ruled out as a possible genre in Old English poetry. As Michael Herren has shown, it is possible that Walahfrid Strabo satirized Theoderic when he sought to amuse the Frankish court in his poem *De imagine Tetrici* in 829.[146] One generation before Æthelwulf's reign in Wessex, therefore, a precedent for using the Goths in political satire existed in a Carolingian Latin form. Thus I take Geat's comedy with Mæthhild to be one of several oblique references to Æthelwulf's marriage with Judith on his return from Rome in 856.

CONCLUSION

In this chapter I have attempted to show that *Gapt* of the Amali and *Gausus* of the Lombards were names derived from Got *gáut-*; and that *gáut-* was an epithet denoting a ritual aspect of Enguz, a god whose name identifies him not only with Ingvi-freyr but also with Ingui or Ing. On analogy with this argument, I have suggested that the *geot*-suffix in Anglian royal names, an Old English cognate of *Gapt*, was derived from an epithet of Ingui (denoting Ingui's marriage and sacrifice) within heathen Northumbria and Mercia. As a corollary to my argument on Got *gáut-* and Enguz, I have suggested that Baldr, a god peculiar to Scandinavia, developed from an Enguz-influenced conception of the Arian Christ which was assimilated back into east Germanic paganism in the fifth and sixth centuries, whence this figure was passed on into Danish and Norse paganism more than three centuries before the first attempts at Christianization in Scandinavia. In other words, Baldr, Gautr and Freyr may all descend from aspects of Nerthus, an ancient figure whose Anglian reflexes appear to be Ingui, Ing and OE *-geot*. Finally, I have attempted to show that the *geot*-suffix was personified as *Geot* or *Geat* in England in an attempt to connect Anglo-Saxon kings with the Italian Goths and Lombards; and that *Deor* was written as a satire of Æthelwulf because Æthelwulf used the name of Geat in his genealogy to help arrange a prestigious match with Judith, a great-grand-daughter of Charlemagne.

---

[146] M. W. Herren, 'Walahfrid Strabo's *De Imagine Tetrici*: an Interpretation', *in Latin Culture and Medieval Germanic Europe*, ed. North and Hofstra, pp. 25–41; Nelson suggests (*Charles the Bald*, p. 86) that Charlemagne's son Louis the Pious is favourably compared with the grasping Theoderic in this poem.

7

The cult of Ingui in *Beowulf*

It seems to be a truth universally acknowledged that the poet of *Beowulf* 'may have known that his heroes were pagans, but he did not know much about paganism'.[1] In this chapter, however, I shall argue that the poet of *Beowulf* knew more about the paganism of his heroes than he chose to reveal. Where Ingui or Ing is concerned, the *incge*-vocabulary cited in ch. 3 already suggests that the poet of *Beowulf* was familiar with traditions that appear elsewhere only in relation to Ingvi-freyr in Old Norse–Icelandic literature. Where I have said in ch. 3 and elsewhere that this poet hints at gods or cults for which the major evidence is to be found only in Scandinavian sources, it might be objected that there is no evidence in *Beowulf* that the poet knew about Ingui or other heathen gods. Yet it is obvious that the same argument might be used to show that the poet of *Beowulf* knew little of the Old Testament other than the Creation (*Beo* 91–8), Cain and Abel (*Beo* 107–8) and the Flood (*Beo* 1689–91), and nothing at all of Christ, whose name appears nowhere in *Beowulf*. Clearly, therefore, this poet knew more about some things than he had reason to reveal; and given that this Anglo-Saxon chose Scandinavian heroes as his theme in *Beowulf*, it is likely that he knew something about their gods and religion to supplement his knowledge of their histories, families and tribal affiliations. It is true, on the other hand, that *Beowulf* 'should be considered for what it is and not as a quarry for hints about heathen practice, which in any case would be more likely to relate to Scandinavia than to England'.[2] My enquiry in this present chapter attempts to identify words and motifs of a pre-Christian Germanic origin

[1] Wormald, 'Bede, "Beowulf" and Conversion', p. 66.
[2] Wilson, *Anglo-Saxon Paganism*, pp. 2–3.

in *Beowulf* mostly in order to throw more light on the poem itself. It is thus possible to read *Beowulf* as a reflection of a period before the Viking Age in which a Christian Anglian poet reinforced his knowledge of his own pre-Christian society with information gleaned from contemporary Danish mythology. It would have been no idle exercise for this poet to gather myths and legends about Danish or Geatish paganism, for the religion of Beowulf and of the other people whose lives he wished to commemorate in *Beowulf*, far from being irrelevant to the meaning of this poem, may have confronted him with the most important question of all: can these heathens be saved?

HEATHEN RELIGION IN *BEOWULF*

The poet of *Beowulf* loses little time in addressing the question of the religious status of the Danes, the first heathens in his poem. At first, early in the poem and before the first numbered manuscript section, he seems to allude to Danish beliefs as being suspended in a state of ignorance. When the Danes push the dying Scyld in his funeral boat out to sea:

> Men ne cunnon
> secgan to soðe,   selerædende [MS seleræðenne],
> hæleð under heofenum,   hwa þæm hlæste onfeng.
>
> (*Beo* 50–3)[3]

With the present tense of *cunnon*, rather than *cuðon*, furthermore, the poet may allude to contemporary Danes whose own speculations about the divine world would have produced more tangible results in his own lifetime: myths, idols and pagan shrines. Some friendly contact between Anglo-Saxons and Danes before the Viking Age can be assumed on the evidence of two letters by Alcuin: one, in 793, in which he rebukes King Æthelred of Northumbria for having a Danish haircut;[4] and the other, in *c*. 796, in which he castigates the community of Speratus (probably Bishop Unuuona of Leicester) for taking an interest in secular songs and in particular songs concerning *Hinieldus* or Ingeld, whom Saxo presents as

---

[3] 'Men do not know how to say in truth, hall counsellors, heroes under the heavens, who received that cargo.'

[4] *Epistolae*, ed. Duemmler, pp. 42–4, esp. 43. See also Bullough, 'What has Ingeld to do with Lindisfarne?', pp. 93–125.

Heathen gods

a Danish king.[5] Sam Newton has argued against contemporary Scandinavian influence on *Beowulf*, mainly by highlighting the differences between the *Scyldingas* in Beowulf and the *Skjǫldungar* in Old Norse–Icelandic literature.[6] The weakness of this argument, however, is that the Norse tradition of the Skjǫldungar had two or three centuries in which to develop from older legends which may have been closer to the stories in *Beowulf*.[7] As there is archaeological evidence of Anglo-Scandinavian trade before the Viking Age, it is hard to believe that there was no poetic exchange between Danes and Anglo-Saxons in the same period.[8] An investigation into the date and provenance of *Beowulf* lies beyond the scope of this book. However, as Peter Clemoes argued, there are several good reasons for supposing that *Beowulf* was written in eighth-century Mercia.[9]

Although the Danes of two centuries earlier, such as those portrayed in *Beowulf*, were as heathen as the Danes contemporary with the poet of this work, Klaeber imagined that King Hrothgar of the Danes 'is throughout depicted as a good Christian'.[10] This optimistic view is belied, however, by an early illustration of paganism in this poem which is seemingly at odds with the picture of Danish ignorance in lines 50–3: the Danish recourse to devil-worship when all else against Grendel fails:

> Hwilum hie geheton æt hærgtrafum
> wigweorþunga, wordum bædon,
> þæt him gastbona geoce gefremede
> wiþ þeodþreaum. Swylc wæs þeaw hyra,
> hæþenra hyht; helle gemundon
> in modsefan, Metod hie ne cuþon,
> dæda Demend, ne wiston hie Drihten God,
> ne hie huru heofena Helm herian ne cuþon,

---

[5] *Epistolae*, ed. Duemmler, pp. 181–4, esp. 183. On Ingellus, see *GD*, pp. 165–80.
[6] *Origins of Beowulf*, pp. 20–7 and 64–71.
[7] For a study of the differing aims of the authors of *Beowulf* and of *Skjǫldunga saga* and related Scandinavian texts, see R. North, 'Saxo and the Swedish Wars in *Beowulf*', in *Saxo Grammaticus: tra storiografia e letteratura*, ed. C. Santini (Rome, 1992), pp. 175–88.
[8] See Hines, *Scandinavian Character of Anglian England*, pp. 270–85; and 'The Scandinavian Character of Anglian England: an Update', pp. 315–29.
[9] P. Clemoes, 'Style as the Criterion for Dating the Composition of *Beowulf*', in *The Dating of 'Beowulf'*, ed. C. Chase (Toronto, 1981), pp. 173–85; and *Interactions of Thought and Language*, pp. 3–67, esp. 53–8.
[10] *Beowulf*, ed. Klaeber, p. 135 (note to lines 175–88).

The cult of Ingui in Beowulf

> wuldres Waldend.   Wa bið þæm ðe sceal
> þurh sliðne nið   sawle bescufan
> in fyres fæþm,   frofre ne wenan,
> wihte gewendan!   Wel bið þæm þe mot
> æfter deaðdæge   Drihten secean
> ond to Fæder fæþmum   freoðo wilnian!   (Beo 175–88)[11]

Hrothgar's worship of a *gastbona* ('soul-slayer') is presented unequivocally in these lines. This passage occurs just before the third numbered manuscript section of this poem. As it thus occurs early in *Beowulf*, and possibly in a deliberately climactic position, this passage effectively gives Christians advice on how to proceed with the Danes and other heathens in the rest of this poem.

Some early guidance is necessary for the Christian audience or readers of *Beowulf*, because Hrothgar and other heathens in this poem appear to praise God without restraint. Christ is nowhere mentioned in this poem, but rarely does Hrothgar offer comment without appearing to honour God: of Beowulf's timely arrival in Denmark, he says 'holy God sent him to us through His kindness' (*hine halig God for arstafum us onsende*, Beo 381–2); of an end to Grendel's crimes, 'God can easily put an end to the deeds of that mad attacker' (*God eaþe mæg þone dolsceaðan dæda getwæfan*, Beo 478–9); when Grendel's death is announced, 'God can always make wonder after wonder, Shepherd of glory' (*a mæg God wyrcan wunder æfter wundre, wuldres Hyrde*, Beo 930–1) and to Beowulf, 'may the All-Ruler repay you with advantage' (*Alwalda þec gode forgylde*, Beo 955–6); God is 'Ruler of glory' (*wuldres Waldend*) for granting wisdom and favour to successful men (Beo 1752). In particular, *wuldres Waldend* appears in the poet's praise of God on line 17, in the Danish inability to praise God on line 183 and, apparently without contradiction, in Hrothgar's praise of God on line 1752.

Although these invocations might reassure us, they appear none the

---

[11] 'Sometimes they offered at temple altars honours to idols, asked in words that the soul-slayer might extend help to them against the calamities of their nation. Such was their custom, hope of heathen men; they were mindful of hell in their hearts, they did not know the Measurer, Judge of deeds, nor did they know of the Lord God, nor did they know how to praise the Helm of heaven, Ruler of glory. Woe for them who through a dangerous violence must thrust their souls into fire's embrace, who must not expect comfort, change in any way! Well it will be for them who after their dying day will be allowed to seek the Lord and ask for protection from the Father's embrace!'

Heathen gods

less to be the poet's Christian adaptation of heathen points of reference. Martin of Braga (the bishop who wrote *De correctione rusticorum*, a treatise against Iberian superstitions, in 572) stated that the first men knew their Creator before they lost this knowledge and became pagans; this work, had it been known by the poet of *Beowulf*, would have given him the licence to grant Hrothgar's distant ancestors some original knowledge of the God whom *Beowulf*'s heathens frequently seem to praise.[12]

A spiritual salvage operation probably older than *Beowulf* can be seen in Bede's tale of the unnamed thegn in Edwin's court in *c.* 627, who remarks how the sparrow flying in and out of the bright hall in the winter night is like the pagan in relation to the question of his origin and destiny: 'of what went before this life or of what follows, we know nothing' (*HE* II.13).[13] Bede's attribution of philosophy, or at least of an awareness of ignorance, in this passage to an untutored pagan in Edwin's court resembles the almost Christian guise in which the poet of *Beowulf* presents Hrothgar in Heorot; but it was probably a moral fiction, given Bede's vivid demonstration with the scene at Goodmanham in the same chapter that the Angles still worshipped *idola* ('idols').[14] A story in the *Vita S. Gregorii Magni*, written before *Historia ecclesiastica* by the anonymous author of Whitby in *c.* 704–10, throws some light on what Bede may have done to exonerate Edwin and his family from the true implications of their paganism. This story appears to take place on a Sunday not long before Edwin and other Deirans are successfully baptized by Paulinus:

Cum stipatus ad eclesiam rex prefatus ad caticuminum eorum qui adhuc erant gentilitati non solum, sed etiam et non licitis stricti coniugiis, cum illo festinavit ab aula ubi prius adhuc utrumque emendandum hortati sunt ab illis, dum quedam stridula cornix ad plagam voce peiorem cantavit.[15]

---

[12] *Opera*, ed. Barlow, pp. 159–203, esp. 186.

[13] *HE*, p. 184: 'quid autem sequatur, quidue praecesserit, prorsus ignoramus'. D. K. Fry suggests that Edwin's thegns had learnt some of the psalms by this time, in 'The Art of Bede: Edwin's Council', in *Saints, Scholars and Heroes: Studies in Medieval Culture in Honour of Charles W. Jones*, ed. M. H. King and W. M. Stevens, 2 vols. (Collegeville, MN, 1979) I, 191–207.

[14] *HE*, p. 182.

[15] *Vita S. Gregorii*, ed. Colgrave, p. 97 (ch. 15): 'The aforesaid king, thronged about, was then hurrying to church with Paulinus to the catechizing of those who were still as yet bound not only to heathendom but also to unlawful wives, from a hall in which these men had been urged by both Edwin and Paulinus to put both matters right, when

The cult of Ingui in Beowulf

The reaction of the Angles is instantaneous:

Tunc omnis multitudo regia que adhuc erat in platea populi, audiens avem, stupore ad eam conversa subsistit, quasi illud 'canticum novum carmen Deo nostro' non esset vero futurum in eclesia, sed falso ad nihil utile.[16]

It is worth drawing further attention to the relevant words of Ps. XXXIX which the author of *Vita S. Gregorii Magni* quotes in the passage above and which, so it seems from his story, were about to be taught to Edwin's kindred while they were catechized in church. The Lord, in the words of this psalm, has led David up out of the mire of a horrible pit and placed his feet on stone:[17]

> 4. *Et immisit in os meum canticum novum,*
> Carmen nostro Deo,
> Videbunt multi, et timebunt,
> Et sperabunt in Domino.
> 5. *Beatus vir* cuius est nomen Domini spes eius,
> Et non respexit in *vanitates* et *insanias falsas.*
>
> (Ps. XXXIX.4–5)[18]

The reason why Paulinus chose this psalm is clear from the words of verse 4, by which the heathen Angles may be taught to sing to a new tune. Thereafter in verse 5, however, it is also possible that *beatus vir* seemed a good rendering of *aeduuini* ('blessed friend', a Northumbrian cognate form of lWS *eadwine*), which was the name of the Deiran king who had renounced his paganism; that *insanias falsas* seemed to Paulinus to be a good Latin reference to an Anglian form of *ælfsiden* ('demon-magic', i.e.

---

some crow sang forth in a hoarse voice from a less propitious quarter of the sky.' My translation is based not on Colgrave but on that in *English Historical Documents, I: c. 500–1042*, ed. D. Whitelock, 2nd ed. (London and New York, 1979), pp. 747–59, esp. 748–9 (no. 152).

[16] *Vita S. Gregorii*, ed. Colgrave, p. 97 (ch. 15). 'Then all the royal household which was still in the main street, hearing the bird, halted and turned to it in stupor as if that "new song" in the church was not to be "Praise to Our God" but falsely was to be for no good purpose at all.'

[17] Perhaps he word *petra* in this psalm indicated the construction of the first York Minster, which would have been completed by this time.

[18] 'And he has put into my mouth a new song, Praise to our God: many shall see, and many shall fear, and many shall hope in the Lord. Blessed is the man whose hope is the name of the Lord and who has not looked back upon vanities and false attacks of madness.'

Heathen gods

possession by devils); and that *vanitates* ('vanities', 'idols'), in particular, seemed to be an ideal name, almost a homophone, for a form of OE *wan-* in *wanseoc* ('devil-sick'). The compound *wanseoc*, in particular, contains both the form of *vanitates* and the meaning of *insanias falsas*, the phrase adjacent to this word in Ps. XXXIX.5. Thus it is likely that the gods worshipped by Edwin and the northern Angles were known as **uuani* in the Deiran vernacular and shared not only the name but also the orgiastic character of the OIce *Vanir*.

There appear to be two pointed instances of Lat *vanitas* or *vanus* in Bede's works. Firstly, Bede uses 'superstitio *uanitatis*' ('superstition of vanity') to describe the religion which Coifi casts aside when he sets out to destroy the heathen shrine in Goodmanham (*HE* II.13).[19] Secondly, Bede, when he gives the Angles' name for April in ch. 15 of *De temporibus*, says that '"Easter-month", which is now understood as the paschal month, formerly got its name from a goddess of theirs whom they used to call *Eostre* and in whose honour they used to celebrate festivals in that month.'[20] Easter Sunday in 627 was the day on which Edwin was baptized. At the end of this chapter, after defining *Blodmonath* as the 'month of sacrifices' (*mensis immolationum*) in which the Angles slaughtered excess livestock 'to their gods' (*diis suis*), Bede then gives thanks to Jesus 'qui nos *ab his vanis* avertens tibi sacrificia laudis offerre donasti'.[21] If Bede chose Lat *vanitas* and *vani dii* with a Northumbrian homophone in mind, it appears that he reveals more explicitly than the author of the Whitby *Vita* that the Deirans used **uuani* to describe their old gods of whom Ingui, as we have seen in chs. 1–3, was probably the name of the devil incarnate.[22] If heathen *festa* and *gaudia* had been held in the honour of *vani dii* in the month of April, as Bede's words seem to imply, then it is likely that these festivals were characterized by the type of sexual licence which we have already seen

---

[19] *HE*, p. 182.

[20] *Bedae Opera de Temporibus*, ed. Jones, pp. 211–13, esp. 212 (*De mensis Anglorum*): 'Eosturmonath, qui nunc paschalis mensis interpretatur, quondam a dea illorum quae Eostre vocabatur, et cui in illo festa celebrabant, nomen habuit.'

[21] *Ibid.*, p. 213: 'Who, turning us away from these vain [gods], have granted us to offer sacrifices with praises to you.'

[22] Elsewhere Bede uses this word conventionally of the defeated Pelagian heresy (*convincitur vanitas*, *HE* I.17) and uses *vanus* of the earthly glory despised by Aidan (*HE* III.17). See Jones, *Concordance to Historia Ecclesiastica*, s.v.v. 'vanitas' and 'vanus' (p. 553).

(in ch. 2) in the analogous traditions of Dionysus or Liber and of the Old Norse Ingvi-freyr. In this light, Paulinus's injunction against the 'unlawful unions' (*inlicita coniugia*) of Edwin's royal kinsmen, probably formerly of Edwin himself, appears to refer to royal concubines, rather than to singly wedded wives with whom the church forbade wedlock on the grounds of consanguinity.[23]

If we return to the textual comparison between the crow in the *Vita S. Gregorii* and the sparrow in Bede's tale of Edwin's counsellors, we see that in the *Vita*, Paulinus has the crow, the bird whose augury threatens to annihilate his teaching of Ps. XXXIX to Edwin's royal household, shot down and kept until the end of the service, whereupon he brandishes it before the court and tells Edwin's men that 'since that insensate bird did not know how to avoid death for itself, still less might it foretell men anything of the events to come' (ch. 15).[24] Bede's unnamed thegn presents the image of the sparrow flying in and out of the brightly lit hall in the winter night as a metaphor for pagans who necessarily live without answers to questions of their origin and destiny: 'of what went before this life or of what follows, we know nothing' (*HE* II.13). Bede's Latin is more elegant than that of the anonymous author of Whitby; yet Wallace-Hadrill says of Bede's style in this passage that 'the Latin reads like his own';[25] in this case, it seems that Bede adapted a story about augury in Edwin's court, partly with reference to the sparrow in Ps. LXXXIII.4 (*Etenim passer invenit sibi domum*), in order to give Edwin's prophesying bird a symbolic rather than literal role to play.[26] With his Deiran thegn's 'beautiful words on the nature of human life', Bede seems to save Edwin and other Deiran worshippers of Ingui and *vani dii* from the punishment of knowing what they were doing.[27] The noble words of Hrothgar, and of some other heathens in *Beowulf*, may be seen in the same light.

[23] As suggested by Colgrave, in *Vita S. Gregorii*, pp. 148–9, n. 59. In chs. 8 and 10, I shall suggest that Edwin, too, had had *inlicita coniugia* before Paulinus baptized him in 627.

[24] *Ibid.*, p. 98: 'etiam sibi ipsi avis illa insensata mortem cavere cum nescisset, immo hominibus nihil profuturum prenuntiet'.

[25] Wallace-Hadrill, *Commentary*, p. 71.

[26] Ps. LXXXIII.4: 'Etiam passer invenit sibi domum, Et turtur nidum sibi, ubi pollat ponos suos: Altaria tua, Domine virtutum, Rex meus, et Deus meus'; discussed by Meaney, 'Bede and Anglo-Saxon Paganism', pp. 22–3; and by Page, 'The Evidence of Bede', pp. 110–11.

[27] Brown, *Bede the Venerable*, p. 91.

Heathen gods

The poet's picture of Danish idolatry is thus the poet's warning within the first 200 lines of *Beowulf* from then on to take each heathen intuition of 'God' as the poet's moral translation of a historically misguided religion. So when Hrothgar warns against 'the accursed spirit' (*werga gast*) in *Beo* 1747, as the 'the killer very near, who shoots with crimes from his arrow-bow' (*bona swiðe neah, se þe of flanbogan fyrenum sceoteð, Beo* 1743–4), the resemblance of his words to Ps. X.3 and Ps. XVII.14–15 shows the poet's effort to rehabilitate a heathen view into one of our own.[28] Thereby Hrothgar is shown in the best possible light as a pagan finding his own way to God. There are several such people in *Beowulf*: Hrethel 'chose God's light' (*Godes leoht geceas, Beo* 2469) when he died; Hama chose 'eternal counsel' (*ecne ræd, Beo* 1201); and Hrothgar (unwittingly emulating Luke X.42) urges Beowulf to choose 'the better course' (*þæt selre*), or 'eternal counsels' (*ece rædas, Beo* 1759–60). Yet the Danes, Frisians, Jutes, Geats and others in this poem remain heathens to a man. Until they are converted, the poet's implication is that all heathens in *Beowulf*, Hrothgar included, must honour the devil as their god.

Since Hrothgar worships the *gastbona* in lines 175–83, it appears that *Ingui* or *Ing* is the name of the devil in *Beowulf*, for this name, cognate with OIce *Ingvi-freyr*, is implicit in Hrothgar's *Ingwine*-epithets, the first of which comes before and the second of which comes after the Finnsburh Episode and the arrival of Grendel's Mother (*eodor Ingwina*, 'prince of the Ingwine', *Beo* 1044; and *se wisa frea Ingwina*, 'the wise lord of the Ingwine', *Beo* 1319). The fact that Hrothgar is named *eodor Ingwina* just after he gives Beowulf 'eight stallions' (*eahta mearas, Beo* 1035) also suggests that Hrothgar worships a version of Ingvi-freyr.[29]

There are other traces of Ingui in this poem, some of which I have discussed above in ch. 3 (*incge laf*, Beowulf's sword in *Beo* 2577; *i[n]cge gold*, Finn's gold in *Beo* 1107; and *woroldræden*, Hengest's god in *Beo* 1142); others I shall discuss below in connection with Beow(ulf) and Scyld Scefing, Hrothgar's grandfather and great-grandfather. Hrothgar's connection with Ingui in this poem seems to be clear. Yet although the poet of

---

[28] See M. Atherton, 'The Figure of the Archer in *Beowulf* and the Anglo-Saxon Psalter', *Neophil* 77 (1993), 653–7.

[29] As Childeric I probably did: excavations have revealed twenty-one horses buried along with Clovis's pagan father Childeric in 481/512: see J. Werner, 'Childerichs Pferde', *Germanische Religionsgeschichte*, ed. Beck, Ellmers and Schier, pp. 229–69; on horses and the cult of Ingvi-freyr, see *AR* II, 188–91 (§§463–4).

The cult of Ingui in Beowulf

Beowulf reveals this king's status as *se wisa frea Ingwina* (*Beo* 1319), he does not emphasize the possibility that Hrothgar believes in his descent from this god. I shall suggest below that the poet of *Beowulf* distances Hrothgar from the satanic patron of the *Ingwine* by detaching Hrothgar from Heremod in the royal genealogy with which the poem opens (the Danish tradition that survives in Saxo's *Gesta Danorum* presents a royal line extending from a Heremod-figure to the Scyldings without a break).[30] As *Hermóðr* is named as Óðinn's Valhǫll lieutenant in *Hákonarmál* 14 and *Hynd* 2, it is likely that *Heremod* in England was regarded as a deified mortal, a Valhǫll demon, in the (Danish) source from which the poet of *Beowulf* took him. Therefore, by separating Scyld, Hrothgar's grandfather, from Heremod, and by obscuring Hrothgar's relationship with the god implicit in *Ingwine*, this poet seems keen to save Hrothgar from the damnation of claiming descent from the devil to whose idol he makes offerings in *Beo* 176. Elsewhere, in contrast, by calling Finn of Frisia *Folcwaldan sunu* in *Beo* 1089, this poet appears to show no hesitation in making Finn a son of Ingvi-freyr *fólcvaldi goða* (*Skí* 2). This partial obfuscation of Danish error, a 'less than full logic', in Peter Clemoes's words, shows the poet's preeminent sympathy for Hrothgar and the Danes.[31]

EUHEMERIZED GODS IN *BEOWULF*

The presence of Ingui's name in compounds and periphrases of *Beowulf* serves to emphasize the absence of other Germanic gods in this poem. For example, there are only hints of Woden: perhaps the god of the *eald æscwiga* ('an old spear-fighter', *Beo* 2042), who seems to be an Odinic hypostasis known as 'Starkaðr' in Scandinavian analogues, and whose incitement of the Heathobards to end their marriage-alliance with the Danes Beowulf predicts to Hygelac when he comes home to Geatland in *Beo* 2032–69;[32] in King Hrethel's apparent rejection of an Odinic pattern of revenge on Hæthcyn for the death of Herebeald in *Beo* 2464–9;[33] and possibly in Ongentheow's threat to sacrifice Hæthcyn's defeated Geatish soldiers by hanging them on the trees of *Hrefnesholt* ('raven's wood') in *Beo* 2939–41.[34]

---

[30] *GD*, p. 11.   [31] Clemoes, *Interactions of Thought and Language*, pp. 50–2, esp. 51.
[32] See North, 'Boethius and the Mercenary', pp. 76–80.
[33] See North, *Pagan Words*, pp. 55–62.
[34] Cf. the mass sacrifice of war-captives to Mercury and Mars in AD 59, in *Taciti Annales*, ed. Furneaux II, 228 (XIII.57).

Heathen gods

Otherwise, the poet's image of heathen religion, where he allows this religion to be seen, seems confined to the necessarily Christian antagonism between God and the devil. Other 'heathen gods' in *Beowulf*, that is to say names whose etyma were probably the object of cults in the heathen Germanic period, appear in this poem as euhemerized mortal heroes. I shall now attempt to illustrate the background of these figures, whose names are *Scyld Scefing*, *Beow*, *Hama*, *Hæðcyn* and *Herebeald*.

Scyld Scefing

Scyld Scefing is the hero whose unexpected arrival ends a period of Danish crisis caused by the exile and death of Heremod. In the first 52 lines of *Beowulf*, the poet describes Scyld's arrival as a baby in a boat from the sea, his growth and success as king of the Danes, his son 'Beowulf' and his death and departure to the sea whence he came.

This Danish hero *Beowulf* (not to be confused with either the Geatish hero by that name or the title of this poem), his father *Scyld* and his presumed grandfather *Scef* are represented not only in *Beowulf*, but also in West Saxon royal genealogy in which Æthelwulf extended his royal line further back beyond Geat to include *Beaw* and his father *Sceldwea* son of *Sceaf*. Thereafter, probably before *c*. 892, it seems that Alfred connected Sceaf with Noah and himself thereby with Adam and God. Kenneth Sisam showed the stages of this backwards extension in Asser's early *Chronicle* source and in all versions of the *Chronicle* except Æthelweard's Latin translation of *c*. 975, in which the extension goes no further than Beo – Scyld – Scef.[35] Æthelweard's vernacular version of the *Chronicle* is lost, but, as Audrey Meaney points out in her study of the relationship between these genealogies, Æthelweard is not likely to have discarded a set of ancestors further back than Scef if he had known of one: therefore his source can be deduced to be earlier than the common archetype of *The Anglo-Saxon Chronicle*; in the following argument I shall use Meaney's terms, which are 'æ' for this common *Chronicle*-archetype and 'pre-æ' for Æthelweard's source.[36] Descending to Geat from Noah, the final king-lists of æ and pre-æ versions compare with that in the opening lines of *Beowulf* as follows:

---

[35] Sisam, 'Anglo-Saxon Royal Genealogies', pp. 297–8 and 307–22.
[36] Meaney, 'Scyld Scefing Again', p. 13; see also A. C. Murray, '*Beowulf*, the Danish Invasions, and Royal Genealogy', in *The Dating of 'Beowulf'*, ed. Chase, pp. 101–12.

The cult of Ingui in Beowulf

Beowulf[37]	Æthelweard	ASC (BC) s.a. 855
		Noe
Scef(ing)	Scef	Sceaf(ing)
		Bedwig
		Hwala
		Hraðra
		Itermon
		Heremod
Scyld	Scyld	Scyldwa[38]
Beow(ulf)	Beo	Beaw
(Healfdene)	Tetuua	Tætwa
(Hrothgar)	Geat	Geat

The vernacular chronicles connect Æthelwulf and his West Saxon dynasty with Adam through Sceldwea, Sceaf and Noah. As regards the peculiar formulation and role of *Scyld Scefing* in *Beowulf*, Meaney suggests that the West Saxon genealogy in Æthelweard's pre-æ source influenced the poet of *Beowulf*. From this conclusion it could be argued that *Beowulf* was not composed before the late ninth century.[39]

As Meaney shows, the genealogy that Æthelweard presents in the late tenth century looks suspiciously like the one we can derive from *Beowulf*. Æthelweard's three generations ancestral to the house of Wessex are *Beo* the son of *Scyld* the son of *Scef*. These forms are very close to *Scyld Scefing* (*Beo* 4), less so to *Beowulf* son of Scyld (*Beo* 18), although the very late tenth-century spellings of the *Beowulf* manuscript (Cotton Vitellius A. xv) could explain the similarity of these forms with Æthelweard's. The vernacular *Chronicle* versions give the weak form *Sceldwea* or *Scyldwa* and not *Scyld*. Æthelweard's text appends a note to Scef:

Ipse Scef cum uno dromone advectus est in insulam oceani que dicitur Scani, armis circundatis, eratque valde recens puer, et ab incolis illius terrae ignotus. Attamen ab eis suscipitur, et ut familiarem diligenti animo eum custodierunt, et post in regem eligunt; de cuius prosapia ordinem trahit Æðulf rex.[40]

---

[37] Sisam, 'Anglo-Saxon Royal Genealogies', p. 315.
[38] *MS A: a Semi-Diplomatic Edition*, ed. Bately, p. 46 (*Sceldwea*).
[39] Meaney, 'Scyld Scefing Again', pp. 13–22.
[40] *Chronicle of Æthelweard*, ed. Campbell, p. 33 (translation mine): 'This Scef was carried in a ship to an ocean island which is called Scani, with weapons put about him, and he was a boy mightily fresh [very young], and unknown by the inhabitants of this island. But yet he is raised by them, and they took care of him with a loving heart as one of

Heathen gods

From the present tense of *trahit*, a *terminus ad quem* for the vernacular text underlying this passage can be deduced in Æthelwulf's death in 858.

The most obvious match between *Beowulf* and the story in Æthelweard lies in the names common to both. Yet some complication arises in the fact that *Beowulf*'s Scyld enjoys the success that in Æthelweard's source is given to his father Sceaf. Accordingly, Meaney suggests, because the poet of *Beowulf* transferred the foundling legend from Sceaf to Scyld Scefing, from father to son, he must have taken the family line from Æthelweard's Old English source.[41] Thus the *Beowulf* prologue would have 'one clear source which provides one clear *terminus post quem*: the genealogy of Æthelwulf from the pre-æ *Chronicle* translated by Æthelweard, which *could* not have been fabricated before 858, and probably *was* not before Alfred's reign'.[42]

As Meaney points out, it is strange that *Beowulf* shows a foundling progenitor with a father named. In the dynastic context of *Beowulf*, Scyld's name *Scefing* must mean 'son of Sceaf'. Meaney's case rests on this peculiarity, for she holds it to be 'very unlikely that Scyld and Sceaf (who did not belong to the same tradition) could anywhere have been brought into contact as father and son except in an artificial genealogy such as Æthelwulf's'.[43] This is where the case for *Beowulf*'s debt to the pre-æ king-list is first called in doubt. Given that the Scyld–Sceaf link in the pre-æ genealogy was artificial, where did the artifice come from?

David Dumville has shown that the cryptic brevity of royal genealogies may be read as the final stage of successful politics, pointing out in his study on kingship and regnal lists that 'ideology is an essential part of the genealogist's trade', and that the royal pedigrees that have survived from the early Middle Ages 'may seek to conceal, rather than merely to convey, information'.[44] In this way, the pre-æ genealogy contained in Æthelweard's *Chronicon* does not make clear why names derived from such objects of complementary though antithetical cultural function as 'sheaf' and 'shield' should be related respectively as father and son. The ideology implicit in the West Saxon genealogy was hidden by the time Æthelweard translated it; or, as regards the Sceaf–Scyld combination, lost in the myths of an extinct folklore. Meaney rules out 'popular tradition' as a

---

the household, and then chose him for king; from whose stock King Æthelwulf takes his line.'

[41] Meaney, 'Scyld Scefing Again', pp. 20–1.   [42] *Ibid.*, p. 37.   [43] *Ibid.*, p. 20.
[44] Dumville, 'Kingship, Genealogies and Regnal Lists', p. 72.

respectable source for *Scyld Scefing* in *Beowulf* because she must argue for a pre-æ king-list as that source. But even if the *Beowulf* poet borrowed from a pre-æ *Chronicle*, as Meaney believes, a pre-æ manuscript tradition would have to rely at one stage on an oral source of some kind. The fact is that no other text, not even in the Danish histories, can be found in which true counterparts of Scyld and Sceaf are connected in any way. For his part in Æthelweard's genealogy, Scef, if not his grandson Beo, seems to belong to a distinctly English context: the only surviving meaning of OIce *skauf* ('fox-brush') is figurative, unlike that of its cognate OE *sceaf*, nor is there a Scandinavian myth of a sheaf in a shield or the Æthelweardian sheaf in a boat.

These details are crucial, because it must be ultimately a Danish and not an English tradition from which the poet of *Beowulf* derived not only the Scylding line from Healfdene downwards, but also his quotation of Scyld in the earlier sequence *Scef- – Scyld – Beowulf*. Scef and Scyld may thus come from different traditions, probably English and Danish respectively. Furthermore, it is likely that these names were linked in mythical, hence poetic, sources which Æthelwulf and his bishops may have consulted in their need to give Æthelwulf historically convincing ancestors.

In *Beowulf* Scyld arrives to rule Denmark after the death in exile of Heremod, to whom he appears to be unrelated. Scyld probably comes from a Danish tradition, in that as *Scioldus* or *Skiold*, his name is preserved in Danish sources. Saxo Grammaticus places Scioldus third after Dan and Lotherus in the first book of his *Gesta Danorum*.[45] *Dan* is the forefather of the Danes, *Lotherus* is a king whose career resembles that of Heremod in *Beo* 901–15. Though Lotherus, like Heremod, robs his subjects of life and wealth and dies in a popular uprising, his name is distinct from Heremod's. The lack of any formal relationship between *Lotherus* and *Heremod* probably shows that Saxo wrote this part of *Gesta Danorum* without reference either to a text of *Beowulf* or to any eleventh- or twelfth-century chronicles in which Heremod's paternity of *Scyldwa* (i.e Scyld) was preserved as part of a royal West Saxon genealogy. Lotherus's name in Old Icelandic appears to be *Lóðurr*, the otherwise unknown god in *Vǫluspá* (*c*. 1000) who helps Óðinn and Hœnir to make man and woman out of the inanimate Ascr and Embla (*Vsp* 17–18). With reference

---

[45] *GD*, pp. 10–11; *History of the Danes*, trans. Fisher and ed. Ellis Davidson I, 14–15.

to this myth, Lotherus has a more appropriate name than Heremod for the role of a dynastic forebear.

In Saxo's *Gesta*, Scioldus is the son and heir of Lotherus and takes care to avoid what Saxo calls 'all traces of paternal contagion' (*cuncta paternae contagionis vestigia*). This precaution suggests that Saxo had reason to deplore Lotherus and therefore cited his relation to Scioldus with reluctance. Thus in the opening lines of *Beowulf*, in which there is no apparent relation between the decadent Heremod and his foundling successor Scyld, it is more likely that the early English poet broke an existing relationship of father and son than that Saxo invented the Lotherus–Scioldus relationship only to deplore it. To this extent, while Scyld's name may be taken from a Danish tradition, his pristine arrival from the sea would seem to be the innovation of the poet of *Beowulf*.

That Scyld's foundling-motif is an innovation in *Beowulf* can also be deduced from its absence in the Scioldus narrative in Sven Aggesen's twelfth-century Danish chronicle.[46] No reference to Skiold at all, furthermore, can be found in the *Chronicon Lethrense* (*c*. 1170), though its anonymous writer records Dan as the founder of the Danes.[47] The absence of a Skiold in this native Lejre tradition to which the historical Hrothgar belonged can be taken as a third sign of the change made to Scyld's history in *Beowulf*, for the poet of this work has made Hrothgar the great-grandson of Scyld, who is proper to Scedenig (i.e. Skåne).

Where Scyld's name does occur in Danish sources, however, a Danish military context appears alongside him. Thus both Saxo and the poet of *Beowulf* use Scyld's name as a generic term for Danish kings: Saxo says that Scioldus's warlike skill was so impressive, 'that from him the other kings of the Danes were named "Scioldungs" (*Scioldungi*) by common title';[48] and even the decadent Heremod, the forerunner of Scyld in *Beowulf*, is said to rule the 'hereditary land of the Scyldings' (*eþel Scyldinga*, *Beo* 913). Secondly, Saxo describes Scioldus as physically grown by the age of fifteen, precocious and brave, the winner of victories against Alemannic tribes. Sven Aggesen, too, celebrates Skiold's valour, though making him the first ruler of the Danes. Sven reads Skiold's destiny into his name: 'and as we allude to his title, the reason he was created with such a name was

---

[46] *Historiae Danicae*, ed. Gertz I, 96–7 (*Brevis Historia Regum Dacie*).
[47] *Ibid.* I, 43–4 (*Chronicon Lethrense*).
[48] *GD*, p. 11: 'ut ab ipso ceteri Danorum reges communi quodam uocabulo Scioldungi nuncuparentur'.

that he guarded uncommonly well all boundaries of the kingdom with the protection of his royal defence'.[49] These descriptions broadly agree with what the *Beowulf* poet tells us of Scyld. Sven adds that kings were named *Skioldunger* after Skiold 'in the Icelandic manner' (*modis Islandensibus*); Skiold's heirs were Frothi and his son Haldanus. Saxo's form *Scioldungi* and Sven's form *Skioldunger* effectively rule out the possibility that either of these authors made use of a text or digest of *Beowulf*, for these forms rather imply a familiarity with Icelandic manuscripts or contact with Icelanders, in whose tradition Skjǫldr is represented in a form not influenced by the WS *Scyld*: Arngrímr Jónsson's Latin abstract of the lost *Skjǫldunga saga* (*c.* 1200) shows *Skioldus* to be the progenitor of the Danes in keeping with their *Skjǫldung*-name;[50] and *Skjǫldr* is mentioned in the prologue to Snorri's *Gylfaginning* (in his *Edda*), where he is the son of Óðinn: a late innovation and perhaps the first time Skjǫldr gets the warlike father he deserves.[51] The author of this prologue knew some West Saxon royal genealogy (though not *Beowulf*), for he blends West Saxon royal ancestors with Scandinavian gods and heroes. Thus, with a lineage similar to the extant pedigrees of the *Anglo-Saxon Chronicle*, but in the genealogical style of family sagas, descent in the *Gylfaginning* prologue starts from *Tror* (*er vér kǫllum Þór*, 'whom we call Þórr'), eventually reaching Sescef (probably from OE *se Scef*); the sequence is then Beðvig – Athra – Annan – Itrmann – Heremóð – Scialdun (probably for *Scialdua*) 'whom we call Skjǫldr, his son Biaf, whom we call Bjár'; so on down to *Voden* ('whom we call Óðinn'). That the author of this prologue fails to associate *Biaf* with its cognate OIce *bygg* and later makes Óðinn the father of Skjǫldr shows that he had imperfect understanding of the West Saxon king-list and failed to assimilate it completely into his Scandinavian history.[52]

In short, neither Saxo nor Sven nor the *Skjǫldunga saga* abstract nor the author of the prologue of Snorri's *Gylfaginning* knows a version of the

---

[49] *Historiae Danicae*, ed. Gertz I, 96: 'et ut eius alludamus vocabulo, idcirco tali functus est nomine, quia universos regni terminos regie defensionis patrocinio affatim egregie tuebatur'.

[50] *Arngrimi Jonae Opera Latine Conscripta*, ed. Jakob Benediktsson, Bibliotheca Arnamagnæana, 9 vols. (Copenhagen, 1950) I, 148–9 and 333–4.

[51] *Gylf*, pp. 5–6.

[52] On the Icelandic use of Latin and West Saxon genealogies, see Faulkes, 'Descent from the Gods', pp. 97–105.

story of Scyld's arrival as a foundling or a story of his connection with Sceaf. Yet stories of Scyld or Skiold are common to both Anglo-Saxon and Scandinavian traditions in which this name connects Skiold with warfare, signifies, as Sven recognized, 'shield' and connotes warlike precocity and strength. Other than this common tradition, however, there appears to be no written Anglo-Saxon or Scandinavian authority for the descent of Sceldwea/Scyld from Sceaf in *Beowulf*, in Æthelweard's *Chronicon* and in the surviving versions of the *Anglo-Saxon Chronicle*.

Scyld's descent from Scef is more clearly presented in the source for Æthelweard's *Chronicon* than in the formulation *Scyld Scefing* in *Beo* 4. In the *Chronicle*, the descent of *Beaw* (Æthelweard's *Beo*) from *Sceldwea* (Æthelweard's *Scyld*) is just as hard to account for as *Sceaf(a)*'s role as Sceldwea's father. In none of the Scandinavian sources, except the *Gylfaginning* prologue's half-assimilated loan from England, is a cognate of *Beow* ('barley') to be found as the son of Sceldwea. In fact it is *Sceaf(a)*, not *Sceldwea*, that is better suited to be the father of *Beaw*: quite simply, a 'sheaf' is better suited than a 'shield' to produce 'barley'. Given the name, an agrarian context is obvious for Sceaf(a) and Beaw in which Sceldwea is not only an irrelevant but also an unauthorized intruder. This pattern is also true of the relationship inherent in *Scyld Scefing* in *Beowulf*. What comes across as 'artificial' in this family is not Scyld's relationship with Sceaf, but the fact that he is in the picture at all.

In this respect it is inevitable that at least two traditions are involved in Æthelweard's pattern *Scef – Scyld – Beo*. First there is confirmation in Danish sources that Scyld was known as the progenitor of Danish kings. Second, we have what must be an Anglian popular tradition, the barley from the sheaf. What could be more important to the creation of a poem or a kingdom than a loaf of bread? If today's consumers find nineteenth-century vegetation myths unworthy of modern scholarship, let them study OE *hlaford* ('loaf-ward') and *hlæfdige* ('loaf-kneader'), the meanings of which indicate that the Anglo-Saxons gave social status to the making and keeping of bread. In both *Beowulf* and Æthelweard's *Chronicon*, the association of *Scef* with *Beo* is easier to explain than the relationship of either with *Scyld*. No explanation of this artificial relationship is given in Æthelweard's *Chronicon*, where Scef's connection with Scyld is recorded without comment. Reading Æthelweard, William of Malmesbury in the twelfth century seems to have re-invented the sheaf-phenomenon in his own tale of Sceldius son of Sceaf: 'because a handful of corn was placed by his head while he slept, he was named "Sheaf"'.[53] But neither Æthelweard nor William gives any reason for the connection between a sheaf and a shield.

For an idea of how this 'artificial' relationship was created, we must turn to *Beowulf*, for if *scefing* does not necessarily mean 'son of Sceaf' there, this context is worth studying further. Swords can be named with a so-called patronymic *-ing* ending: *Hrunting* (*Beo* 1457, 1490, 1659 and 1807), *Nægling* (*Beo* 2680) and the Old Norse *Tyrfingr*, a leitmotiv in the late thirteenth-century *Hervarar saga ok Heiðreks*.[54] In these cases, a new sword is descended from an old one in that the swordsmith welds an old blade on to a new hilt. This relationship could have been imagined on the basis of the patrilinear descent of kings, if the swords were personified (which, given the fact that the swords are named, they probably were). Yet the *-ing* suffix can be found with wider application: not every *Scylding*, for example, is the son of the eponymous ancestor Scyld. Most Scyldings are more properly members of the larger family group – *Beowulf Scyldinga* is an example of this wider sense in *Beo* 53. Similarly, a suffixed *scefing* indicates that *scyld* is not a descendant, but is a less specific relative of *sceaf*. That the shield in question 'belongs to the sheaf', therefore, is also a viable reading of *Scyld Scefing* in *Beowulf*.

One tradition in which we can find a *scyld–sceaf* association is the account of an Anglo-Saxon boundary dispute recorded in the thirteenth-century *Chronicon de Abingdon*. This is the story of a protracted dispute between the abbot and monks of Abingdon and the men of Oxfordshire over possession of a river meadow. The abbot is said to have turned to 'divine mercy' (*clementia divina*) for a resolution:

Quod dum servi Dei propensius actitarent, inspiratum est eis salubre consilium et (ut pium est credere) divinitus provisum. Die etenim statuto mane surgentes monachi sumpserunt scutum rotundum, cui imponebant manipulum frumenti, et super manipulum cereum circumspectæ quantitatis et grossitudinis. Quo accenso scutum cum manipulo et cereo, fluvio ecclesiam præcurrenti committunt, paucis in navicula fratribus subsequentibus. Præcedebat itaque eos scutum et quasi digito demonstrans possessiones domui Abbendoniæ de jure adjacentes nunc huc, nunc illuc divertens; nunc in dextra nunc in sinistra parte fiducialiter eos præibat, usquedum veniret ad rivum prope pratum quod Beri vocatur, in quo

---

[53] *De Gestis Regum Anglorum*, ed. W. Stubbs, 2 vols. (London, 1887) II, 121: 'posito ad caput frumenti manipulo, dormiens, ideoque Sceaf nuncupatus'.

[54] *Heiðreks saga*, ed. Turville-Petre and Tolkien, pp. 1, 6–7, 17–19, 50–2, 55–6 and 66.

cereus medium cursum Tamisiæ miraculose deserens se declinavit et circumdedit pratum inter Tamisiam et Gifteleia, quod hieme et multociens æstate ex redundatione Tamisiæ in modum insulæ aqua circumdatur.[55]

Sisam reserved an appendix to his pioneering study of royal genealogies for a discussion of this Abingdon text. Generally, he dismissed its relevance to the *Scyld Scefing* formulation in *Beowulf*, which, like Meaney after him, he seemed to regard as a later construction.

However, although it is likely that the motives of these monks were acquisitive, this likelihood does not alter the date and authenticity of the ritual details. That the shield was rounded, as were all Anglo-Saxon shields before the Norman invasion, is only one argument for the story's pre-Norman origin; another is the form *Gifteleia*, which conforms with *Gifetelea*, the oldest extant spelling for Iffley in 1004.[56] Sisam doubts that 'this late story can be converted into evidence that the early Anglo-Saxons knew of two closely associated personages or spirits, an English Sceaf and an English Scyld'.[57] The important difference between *Beowulf* and this account, as Sisam points out, is the lit taper, which is found neither in *Beowulf*'s Scyld Scefing nor in Æthelweard's Scef; nor in the twelfth-century account of William of Malmesbury, which Sisam shows to be derived from Æthelweard.[58] However, the Abingdon *scutum cum manipulo et cereo* can be shown to correspond to a phenomenon *scyld scefing* with the

[55] *Chronicon Monasterii de Abingdon*, ed. J. Stevenson, 2 vols. (London, 1858) I, 88–9: 'Which case while the servants of God were more readily busy in pleading, a healthful course of action was inspired in them and (which it is pious to believe) divinely provided. Indeed on the day decided, rising in the morning, the monks obtained a round shield, in which they placed a sheaf of corn, and over the sheaf they placed a wax taper of a considered quantity and size. When this has been lit, they commit the shield with the sheaf and taper to the river which runs by the church, with a few brothers following in a boat. Thus the shield preceded them, and as if with a finger pointing out the lawful possessions of the House of Abingdon which lay close by, turning one moment here, one moment there; one moment to the right-hand side, the other to the left, the shield went faithfully before them until it came to the bank near the meadow which is called Beri, in which the taper, wondrously deserting the middle course of the Thames, swerved aside and circled the meadow between the Thames and Iffley, which owing to the flood of the Thames in winter and frequently in summer the water surrounds in the manner of an island.'

[56] Later spellings are *Givetelei* (Domesday Book), *Iuittelai* (1165), *Ghyftele* (1234), *Yveteleg* (1236): see *The Concise Oxford Dictionary of English Place-Names*, ed. E. Ekwall, 4th ed. (Oxford, 1960), s.v. 'Iffley'.

[57] Sisam, 'Anglo-Saxon Royal Genealogies', p. 343.   [58] *Ibid.*, pp. 319–20.

minimum two details required to make one the analogue of the other. When Scyld departs this life, the poet of the *Beowulf* prologue says:

> Him ða Scyld gewat   to gescæphwile
> felahror feran   on Frean wære;
> hi hyne þa ætbæron   to brimes faroðe,
> swæse gesiþas,   swa he selfa bæd.   (Beo 26–9)⁵⁹

The imagery of these lines is ambiguous: either a funeral in keeping with ship-burials before the Viking Age, or an allusion to an Anglo-Saxon ritual similar to that which was later written down in the *Chronicon de Abingdon*, in which Scyld might also be taken for a humble object granted living agency by God to show His special favour for the Danes. If *scyld scefing* could thus refer to a ritual combination of objects, as in the Abingdon story, then it is the shield that does service for the sheaf. The poet of *Beowulf*, focusing on 'shield', may thus have combined a Danish genealogy with a ritual image from Anglo-Saxon superstition. With knowledge of a ritual involving a sheaf and a shield, the poet would thus give Scyld, an ancestral king, a myth of origin and departure necessary to detach him from the bad king Heremod.

In this way, if it is accepted that the poet of *Beowulf* combined a Danish legend with a motif from early English superstition, then it is likely that he, and not the writer of the pre-æ *Chronicle* genealogy inherited by Æthelweard, created the artifice of Scyld's relationship with Scef.⁶⁰ It is less complicated to assume that *Beowulf*, with its play on historical persons and crop phenomena, influenced the pre-æ source of Æthelweard's *Chronicon* genealogy. Later, when Alfred extended Æthelwulf's lineage further back to Noah, it is possible that he took the necessary authority for the crucial Noah–Sceaf(a) link likewise from a manuscript of *Beowulf*.⁶¹ If a certain *Scyld Scefing* arrived in a boat sent

---

⁵⁹ 'Scyld departed then at the fated hour, to sail very vigorous into the keeping of the Lord; him then they carried to the current of the sea, sweet companions, as he himself requested.'

⁶⁰ R. Fulk reaches a similar conclusion by suggesting that *Beow* (i.e. 'Beowulf') was an early English analogue of OIce *Ber-gelmir*, a 'barley' giant *á lúðr um lagiðr* ('laid inside a bread-bin') in *Vaf* 35: see his 'An Eddic Analogue to the Scyld Scefing Story', *RES* 40 (1991), 313–22.

⁶¹ On the possibility that Alfred knew *Beowulf* in some form, see Lapidge, '*Beowulf*, Aldhelm, the "Liber Monstrorum" and Wessex', pp. 184–7 (followed by Newton, in *Origins of Beowulf*, pp. 71–6); and P. Clemoes, 'King Alfred's Debt to Vernacular

from God in *Beowulf*, then Sceaf and Scyld could be listed as father and son in a genealogy, the former as one of Noah's (younger) sons. Even later would come the ABC *Chronicle* interpolation of a Heremod–Bedwig line below Sceaf(a) and above Sceldwea. In this case, a tenth-century West Saxon who read *Beowulf* with even less discrimination than his forebears but with greater need to make the post-Noah chronology plausible, could have taken *Scyldwa* (i.e. Scyld) to be the decadent Heremod's son, and Heremod's eldest ancestor to be the son of Sceaf.

A second indication that Æthelweard's source borrowed from a text of *Beowulf* is the placename *Scani* in Æthelweard's passage on Scyld. Though *Scani* is a tenth-century form, it is traceable to the late ninth century, if compared with OE *Sconeg*, the placename given in the Alfredian *Orosius* (I.i);[62] if *Beowulf* is to be dated in the late ninth century or after, *Scedelandum in* (Beo 19) and *Scedenig* (Beo 1686) must be considered conscious archaisms, for these forms are older than either *Sconeg* or *Scani*.

A third indication of a borrowing from *Beowulf* into Æthelweard's source may be seen in Æthelweard's rationalization of the foundling motif. Æthelweard lists Scef as the father of Scyld and tells of Scef's coming in a boat: this construction is more rational than that of the *Beowulf* poet, for Æthelweard's Scef is a foundling without a father, unlike Scyld in *Beowulf*, whose father is implicitly Scef.

Fourthly, as Meaney has noted, Æthelweard's Scef has weapons around him when he arrives as a foundling, but not when he departs this life; unlike Scyld Scefing in *Beowulf*, whose funeral boat is bedecked with weapons and treasures. Æthelweard's words *armis circundatis* for the weapons around the baby Scef match not only the meaning but also the oblique case of the *hildewæpnum and heaðowædum, billum ond byrnum* that are laid about the dying Scyld in Beo 39–40 ('battle-weapons and war-clothes, blades and mail-coats'). By endowing Scef with weapons when he is a baby, not when he dies, Æthelweard's source appears to rationalize another problem in *Beowulf*, in which the poet says:

> Nalæs hi hine læssan   lacum teodan,
> þeodgestreonum,   þon þa dydon,

Poetry: the Evidence of *ellen* and *cræft*', in *Words, Texts and Manuscripts: Studies in Anglo-Saxon Culture presented to Helmut Gneuss on the Occasion of his Sixty-Fifth Birthday*, ed. M. Korhammer (Woodbridge, 1992), pp. 213–38.

[62] *The Old English Orosius*, ed. Bately, p. 16.24.

The cult of Ingui in Beowulf

> þe hine æt frumsceafte   forð onsendon
> ænne ofer yðe   umborwesende.   (*Beo* 43–6)[63]

The contradiction apparent in this part of *Beowulf* is that Scyld had arrived with treasures, yet was *feasceaft funden* ('found destitute') on his arrival in *Beo* 7. This use of *feasceaft* must be translated as 'destitute of friends' if it is not to contradict the meaning of *Beo* 43–6. Yet *feasceaft* is ambiguous in the meaning of its elements: 'destitute', yet also 'with no shaft': the condition of a seed threshed from a sheaf of corn. The otherwise common compound *frumsceaft* in *æt frumsceafte*, when the unnamed guardians of Scyld sent him forth 'in the beginning' (*Beo* 45), might also hint at a cornstalk before growing: 'at the first-shaft'. This semantic ambiguity appears to represent the poet's play on the personification of agrarian phenomena. There is no such licence in the *Scef* passage in the *Chronicon*, in which Æthelweard's source seems to have rationalized the apparent contradictions with Scyld Scefing in *Beowulf*.

A fifth trace of Æthelweard's source's debt to *Beowulf* may be found in his expression *valde recens* ('very young') in the description of Scef's pristine state, for the literal meaning of this phrase is 'exceedingly fresh'. This Latin phrase resembles OE *felahror*, the attribute of the dying Scyld as he departs this life in *Beowulf*, which Klaeber, without noting any connection with *valde recens*, translated as 'very vigorous, strong' (*Beo* 27).[64] *Felahror* is more provocative in its context in *Beowulf*, as a word for the dying Scyld, than *valde recens* in Æthelweard's story of the young boy Scef. Yet if we imagine the dying Scyld with the full-grown attributes of a *sceaf* ('sheaf of corn'), then the contradiction in *Beowulf* disappears. No *sceaf* appears in the panegyric of Scyld's ascendancy in *Beo* 4–11, but the poet gives Sceaf's son *Scyld* ('shield') both agrarian and military attributes: ultimately all the tribes paid Scyld tribute, but, as if he is a seed from a cornsheaf, Scyld *weox under wolcnum, weorðmyndum þah* ('grew under the clouds, received honours', *Beo* 8).[65] At the same time, however, this poet's play on sheaf imagery is not the most obvious part of his portrait of Scyld; and it is thus more likely to be Æthelweard's source that

---

[63] 'Not at all did they adorn him with gifts, with treasures of their people, lesser than did those who sent him forth in the beginning [first-shaft] of [his] creation, alone over the wave when he was a child.'

[64] *Beowulf*, ed. Klaeber (5th ed.), p. 328.

[65] Noted in Meaney, 'Scyld Scefing Again', p. 20.

Heathen gods

rationalized a peculiar use of *felahror* in *Beowulf*, than the poet of *Beowulf* who took liberties with the odd hyperbole of a vernacular version of *valde recens* in a pre-æ Old English *Chronicle* text. In these five ways, it appears that the first manuscript section of *Beowulf* (lines 1–52) is one piece with the rest of the poem, and that this poem is older than the vernacular *Chronicle* which Æthelweard used as the source for his *Chronicon*.

Beow

Scyld's son is named *Beowulf*, as opposed to Æthelweard's *Beo* and the *Beaw* of *The Anglo-Saxon Chronicle s.a.* 855. Meaney speaks for many others in taking the form *Beowulf* 'simply as scribal error' for *Beow* ('barley'), or a related form, which is the more fitting name within a dynastic context involving *Sceaf*. Scyld's son Beow or Beaw would correspond to Scioldus's son *Frotho* ('fertile') in Saxo's genealogy in *Gesta Danorum*;[66] as argued above in ch. 3, Frotho appears to be a Danish hypostasis of the Norse god Ingvi-freyr.

The italicized words describing Beow(ulf) in the following passage may hint that the poet of *Beowulf* was familiar with the terminology of the Old Norse–Icelandic Ingvi-freyr. God heard the dolour of the Danes and apparently through human agents sends them Scyld and his descendants:

> him þæs Liffrea,
> wuldres Wealdend   woroldare forgeaf,
> Beow(ulf) wæs breme   (blæd wide sprang)
> Scyldes eafera   Scedelandum in.   (*Beo* 16–19)[67]

Beow(ulf)'s heroic career is described with agrarian imagery in this passage. *Blæd* may have a long vowel, meaning 'fame', yet with a short vowel may also mean 'blade', in which case the image of a leaf springing wide is more properly an allusion to growing barley. With this type of alternation between person and phenomenon in the figures Scyld Scefing and Beow(ulf), the poet of *Beowulf* displays the natural phenomena on

---

[66] *GD*, p. 11.
[67] 'To them because of this the Life-Lord, Ruler of glory, gave prosperity of the world, Beowulf was renowned – glory/leaf sprang wide – Scyld's offspring within the lands of Scania.'

The cult of Ingui in Beowulf

which the Danes rebuild their lives after the bad king Heremod, even while he attributes the Danish recovery to *God* in *Beo* 13.

Yet by celebrating God as *Liffrea* in this passage, in the context of growth and fertility in Scandinavia, the poet of *Beowulf* appears to assume the existence of a *'frea* of death' antithetical to God. In that OIce *Freyr* only became a proper noun in Scandinavian languages, it is worth noting that the poet of *Beowulf* could not have used OE *frea* in this way unless his work had been influenced by a Danish tradition.[68] The purpose of this use of language in *Beowulf* would be to hint at Danish paganism from the perspective of the Danes. Similarly, the *woroldar* that God gives the Danish Beow(ulf) may contain a secondary meaning: usually this word denotes secular property, as opposed to church possessions, when it does not refer to 'worldly honour' or vanity; however, *woroldar* in this passage from *Beowulf* may refer to Freyr and Njǫrðr. Corresponding to the second element of OE *woroldar*, OIce *ár ok friðr* ('prosperity and peace') are the typical gifts of Freyr and Njǫrðr in *Gylfaginning* and *Ynglinga saga*.[69] In the latter historical work, Snorri says that the Swedes refused to burn Freyr when they knew he was dead, but worshipped him instead as *veraldargoð* ('god of the world of men').[70] Although there is no source earlier than Snorri in which *veraldar goð* is recorded, *woroldare forgeaf* may thus hint that the Danes in *Beowulf* attribute their prosperity to a god such as Freyr.

This possibility is strengthened by the fact that *Byggvir* ('barley-man'), an Old Norse–Icelandic cognate of OE *Beow*, appears in *Lokasenna* as Freyr's devoted servant. When challenged by Loki in this poem, Byggvir says:

> Veiztu, ef ec øðli ættac sem Ingunar-Freyr,
> oc svá sæl[l]ict setr,
> mergi smæra mølða ec þá meinkráco
> oc lemða alla í lið.   (*Lok* 43)[71]

Loki then mocks Byggvir as a little thing 'which I can see wagging its

---

[68] On the development of this proper noun as unique to Scandinavia, see Green, *Carolingian Lord*, pp. 19–55.
[69] *Gylf*, p. 24 (ch. 24). *Heimskringla I*, ed. Bjarni, pp. 22–5 (*Ynglinga saga*, ch. 10).
[70] *Ibid.*, ed. Bjarni, p. 25.
[71] 'You know, if I had estates like Ingunar-Freyr, and such prosperous pasture-land, I would grind this evil crow finer than marrow and I would lam him in every limb.'

Heathen gods

tail and sniffling like a parasite' at Freyr's ear (*er ec lǫggra séc, oc snapvíst snapir, Lok* 44). In mocking Byggvir and then linking him also with garrulous drinking, Loki returns this personified 'barley-man' back to the cereal phenomenon suggested by his name. These stanzas refer to the aftermath of a good harvest, to the grinding of corn on large estates and to a barley wreath of some kind on the head of Ingunar-Freyr. As we have seen, these images are also the likely outcome of *Skírnismál*, in which OIce *barr* ('barley', 'pine-cone') is likely to be Freyr's son on Gerðr when the two figures couple in the grove named *Barri* ('for barley'). It is therefore possible that an ideology of this kind was implicit in the opening fifty-two lines of *Beowulf*, in which OE *beow* is apparently personified as *Beow(ulf)* ('barley'), the son of *Scyld Scefing* ('shield, son of sheaf').

In conclusion, *Beowulf* probably served as an important name-source for the clergy's backwards extension of royal genealogy in Wessex in the middle of the ninth century. Faced with the ever-increasing difficulty of extending their king's genealogy further back, Æthelwulf's clergy at this time seem to have turned in the end to their own traditions of Beow and Scyld Scefing, to the authority that *Beowulf* provided in the search for Germanic ancestors older than *Geat* (discussed in the previous chapter).

Hama

After the Lay of Finnsburh in Heorot and Wealhtheow's ensuing speech to Hrothgar, Beowulf is presented with a cup of mead, friendly words, two arm-bracelets, garments and rings and the biggest necklace of which the poet has ever heard:

> Nænigne ic under swegle   selran hyrde
> hordmaðum hæleþa,   syþðan Hama ætwæg
> to þære byrhtan byrig   Brosinga mene,
> sigle ond sincfæt;   searoniðas fleah
> Eormanrices,   geceas ecne ræd.   (*Beo* 1197–1201)[72]

Hama's flight from Eormanric, the emperor of the Goths to whom also the poet of *Deor* alluded (lines 22–7), is known in fuller detail in a number of mainly German analogues: elsewhere *Hama* appears in *Wid*

---

[72] 'Nor have I heard of any better hoard-treasure of men beneath the sun since Hama carried off the necklace of the Brosings to the bright city – he fled the crafty enmities of Eormanric, chose eternal counsel.'

The cult of Ingui in Beowulf

124–9 as the companion of *Wudga* (or Widia, the son of Weland) within Eormanric's *innweorud* ('inner retinue') from which he is later exiled; this figure is also known as *Hame* or *Heime* in versions of the same story in medieval German literature and as *Heimir* in versions of this story in *Vǫlsunga saga* (ch. 24) and *Þiðreks saga af Bern* (a Norwegian translation of a lost Low German romance).[73] The native Scandinavian analogue of *Hama* is *Heimdallr*, the name of a Norse god: *Hama*'s theft of the *Brosinga mene* in *Beowulf* closely resembles a story about *Heimdallr* and Freyja's *Brísingamen*. This story is the first scene presented in *Húsdrápa*, a poem which the Icelander Úlfr Uggason composed c. 985 to commemorate a sequence of mythological carvings on some new kitchen panels in Hjarðarholt in Iceland.[74] Snorri, when he quotes this stanza in *Skáldskaparmál*, tells us that Heimdallr wrestled with Loki successfully for possession of the *Brísingamen*, which he then gave to Freyja.[75] In Úlfr's baroque Scaldic diction:

> Ráðgegninn bregðr ragna   rein- at Singasteini
> frægr við firna slœgjan   Fárbauta mǫg -vári;
> móðǫflugr ræðr mœðra   mǫgr hafnýra fǫgru,
> kynnik, áðr ok einnar   átta, mærðar þáttum.   (*Húsdrápa* 2)[76]

This narrative is only a distant analogue of Hama's story in *Beowulf*, for Úlfr does not appear to have euhemerized its protagonists, either Loki or Heimdallr. Nor is Úlfr concerned with the moral dimension of his story, unlike the poet of *Beowulf*, whose leading preoccupation in lines 1197–1201 seems to be Hama's choice of a religious, possibly Christian, life. This *ecne ræd* of Hama comes closer, instead, to Heimir's decision towards the end of *Þiðreks saga* (ch. 429) to serve in the monastic life for a while.[77] In this way, Hama is fully integrated into the human cast of the

---

[73] Gillespie, *Catalogue*, s.v. 'Heime' (pp. 64–6, esp. 65).
[74] Schier argues that this stanza refers to a creation-myth, in 'Húsdrápa 2', pp. 577–88.
[75] *SnE* 268 (ch. 16); *FJSnE* 99–100.
[76] *Skj* B I, 128: 'Straightforward in counsel, the land-guardian of the powers [Heimdallr] wrests the Singa-stone away from the crime-cunning son of Fárbauti [Loki], famous for doing so; strong in heart, the son of eight and one mothers [Heimdallr] is first to take possession of the dazzling sea-kidney. I proclaim this in tales of glory.' On Heimdallr, see below, pp. 280–7, and Pipping, 'Eddastudier I', pp. 7–52, and 'Eddastudier II', pp. 120–30.
[77] *Þiðreks saga af Bern*, ed. Guðni Jónsson, 2 vols. (Reykjavik, 1951) II, 581: 'hann þjónar í þessu munklífi um hríð' ('he serves in this monastic life for a while').

Heathen gods

legends in the background of *Beowulf*, and there is no trace in this poem of his provenance in any pantheon of Germanic gods.

Herebeald and Hæthcyn

Beowulf mentions Herebeald in passing when he reminisces over King Hrethel and Geatish history before their first war with the Swedes. Hrethel loved his daughter's child Beowulf as he did his own sons Herebeald, Hæthcyn and Hygelac. But a bed of death was spread for Herebeald, the oldest:

> syððan hyne Hæðcyn   of hornbogan,
> his freawine   flane geswencte,
> miste mercelses   ond his mæg ofscet,
> broðor oðerne   blodigan gare.   (*Beo* 2437–40)[78]

No compensation can be paid nor violence offered, because Hæthcyn is the brother of Herebeald, who thus stays 'a prince unavenged' (*æðeling unwrecen*). Then Beowulf produces a puzzling image of the nature of Herebeald's death:

> Swa bið geomorlic   gomelum ceorle
> to gebidanne,   þæt his byre ride
> giong on galgan;   þonne he gyd wrece,
> sarigne sang,   þonne his sunu hangað
> hrefne to hroðre,   ond he him helpe ne mæg
> eald ond infrod   ænige gefremman.   (*Beo* 2444–9)[79]

Elsewhere I have tried to show that the poet's focus in these lines is on old King Hrethel of the Geats.[80] By rejecting violent revenge for one son against another, and then by dying in extreme suffering, Hrethel both avoids a precedent which is contained in the surviving Norse material in Óðinn's revenge on Hǫðr, and follows unwittingly the example of Christ.

---

[78] 'When Hæðcyn afflicted him, his friend and lord, with an arrow from a horn-shaped bow, missed his mark and shot his kinsman dead, one brother to another with the blood-stained spear.'

[79] 'It is miserable for an old man to suffer in this way, that his boy should ride young on the gallows; then may he make a poem, a sorrowing song, when his son hangs to the joy of the raven, and he cannot help him, old and very wise, cannot help him at all.'

[80] North, *Pagan Words*, pp. 55–62.

The cult of Ingui in Beowulf

The poet's epithets for Hrethel are Odinic, for the phrase *gomel ceorl* in *Beo* 2444 recalls a verse quoted by Snorri in *Gylfaginning* in which a hag named Þǫkk ('grace') ends the Æsir's hopes of regaining Baldr from the dead by refusing to weep for him:

> Þǫkk mun gráta   þurrum tárum
> Baldrs bálfarar.
> Kyks né dauðs   nautka ek *karls* sonar:
> haldi Hel því er hefir. [81]

The use of *gomel ceorl* in *Beo* 2444 thus recalls Þǫkk's reference to Óðinn as *karl* in this stanza quoted in *Gylfaginning*. Furthermore, *Wedra helm* ('helm of Weather-Geats', *Beo* 2462) recalls Óðinn's names *Hiálmberi* ('Helmet-bearer', *Grím* 46) and *Viðrir* ('Wutherer, storm-blower', *Lok* 26; cf. *Viðurr*, *Sonatorrek* 1). With the implication of OE *giedd* in the words 'þonne he gyd wrece' ('then may he make a poem', *Beo* 2446), Hrethel even composes an elegy in memory of his son, a cathartic option to which Óðinn's gift of *geð* entitles Egill Skalla-Grímsson in 'Sona-tor-*rek*' ('hard vengeance of sons').[82] Yet this option fails to work in Hrethel's case, and in the poet's words 'Godes leoht geceas' ('he chose God's light', *Beo* 2469), Hrethel dies of grief. By preferring extreme suffering and death to an Odinic model of paganism in this way, Hrethel follows a Christian example without knowing Christ. Also without knowing why, Beowulf shows in Hrethel how a pagan might be saved.

There is no *Godes leoht* for Herebeald, however. Beowulf suddenly typifies the dead Herebeald as a man hanging from the gallows. Dorothy Whitelock pointed out that in law a hanged man was a criminal for whom no vengeance could be taken.[83] Thus Beowulf's image would show how powerless Hrethel is to avenge one son on another. Yet Whitelock did not explain why Hæthcyn's 'arrow' (*flan*, *Beo* 2438) becomes a 'bloodstained spear' (*blodig gar*) two lines on. As Beowulf's simile is constructed

---

[81] *Gylf*, p. 48 (ch. 49): 'Þǫkk will weep with dry tears for Baldr's funeral pyre. I got no profit from the *old man's* son either alive or dead: let Hel keep what she has!'

[82] For discussion of this passage with reference to OE *giedd wrecan*, see North, 'Pagan Inheritance of Egill's *Sonatorrek*', pp. 161–7.

[83] D. Whitelock, 'Anglo-Saxon Poetry and the Historian', *Transactions of the Royal Historical Society*, 4th ser., 31 (1949), 79–94, esp. 87–91; also published in Whitelock, *From Bede to Alfred: Studies in Early Anglo-Saxon Literature and History* (London, 1980), pp. 198–204.

to allow us for a moment to see Herebeald on the gallows, stabbed with a spear, it is not Anglo-Saxon law but Norse mythology that makes the image fully intelligible. The evidence for the hanging and piercing of Baldr is scant and fragmentary. Where his sacrifice is concerned, the stabbing of Baldr is common to all versions of this story; but his hanging, as a ride to Hel on a gallows-horse, appears only in the kenning 'sea-Sleipnir', with which Úlfr Uggason described Baldr's funeral ship (*haf-Sleipnir*, *Húsdrápa* 14). Also, when Hermóðr, who rides down to the Gjǫll river on the way to negotiate for Baldr's release from the dead, meets Móðguðr, a monstrous woman guarding the bridge, she tells him that 'Baldr had ridden at that time over the Gjǫll bridge';[84] the image of Baldr riding is also contained in Loki's taunting words to Frigg in *Lokasenna* that 'you will never again see Baldr *riding*' ('*ríða* sérat Baldr', *Lok* 28), because Loki contrived his death. In Herebeald's case, the helpless father must endure 'that his boy should *ride* young on the gallows' ('þæt his byre *ride* giong on galgan', *Beo* 2445–6); and stranger still, that 'the *riders* sleep, heroes in darkness' ('*ridend* swefað, hæleð in hoðman', *Beo* 2457–8). The plural in this use of *ridend* has never been satisfactorily explained, but this form now seems to be in keeping with Móðguðr's report in *Gylfaginning* that 'five companies of dead men rode over the bridge' in company with Baldr the day before Hermóðr's arrival.[85] In addition, the 'darkness' in *hoðma* (*Beo* 2458) resembles the 'dark and deep valleys' (*døkkva dala ok djúpa*) through which Baldr must ride on his way to the Gjǫll bridge in *Gylfaginning*. Though Beowulf portrays Herebeald as dead in the ground, in this way he also seems to stylize Herebeald's death as a hanging, piercing and riding with other dead heroes to hell. Heathen despair is revealed in Beowulf's picture of father and son, for if Hrethel through terminal suffering chooses the light of God's hope, the price is the ride to hell of his son, who is never to be seen again.

This neutrality of the *Beowulf* poet towards Herebeald is striking if we compare it to the sympathetic view of Baldr in Old Norse–Icelandic sources. In Icelandic literature, in *Vsp* 62, Baldr appears to be presented as the heathen forerunner of Christ prior to the Lord's coming in the (probably accreted) stanza in which 'He who rules all' (*sá er ǫllu ræðr*, *Vsp* 65) comes to rule the reborn world; for his own part, Snorri never fails to

---

[84] *Gylf*, p. 47: 'Baldr hafði þar riðit um Gjallar brú.'
[85] *Ibid*., 'riðu um brúna fimm fylki dauðra manna'.

present Baldr and his death in a Christian style; and in the late thirteenth-century *Brennu-Njáls saga*, Baldr's hypostasis Hǫskuldr Hvítanessgoði, when slain sowing a spring field, becomes a version of Christ and Baldr in one.[86] Where Baldr is the villain, not the hero, of the piece, however, is to be found in the Danish tradition: Saxo in his *Gesta Danorum* makes clear that Balderus's death occurs at the hand of Hotherus as a result of Balderus's immoral infatuation for Nanna, a forest nymph. As Saxo's morals in his *Gesta* were firmly based on those of the Fathers, his rejection of Balderus may be contrasted with the general sympathy for Baldr in Icelandic literature.

In three respects, the poet of *Beowulf* in his treatment of Herebeald seems to share Saxo's Danish tradition of the *Baldr* story: first, with Hrethel's passive death so close to that of Christ, there is no sign in *Beowulf* that Herebeald might be imagined as a heathen forerunner or counterpart of Christ; second, no Loki figure emerges in either account, in contrast with the role of Loki as the instigator of Baldr's death in *Vǫluspá* and in other Icelandic sources; and third, both Hæthcyn and Herebeald are euhemerized, just as Saxo's mortals Hotherus and half-god Balderus are. As we have seen in ch. 5, no native use of OE *bealdor* ('lord, prince') survives with the personification of its Old Norse cognate *Baldr*; and there is no evidence that *Bældæg* was taken as Baldr's English counterpart until Danish or Norwegian influence persuaded Æthelweard to change his form of *Bældæg* to *Balder* in his *Chronicon* (*c*. 975).[87] Thus the stem of *Here-beald* (*Beo* 2434 and 2463) seems to have been borrowed from a specifically Danish form of *Baldr* with a prefix alliteratively housing him in the Geatish dynasty of Hrethel and Hygelac. In turn, with Hæthcyn's epithet '*heaðorinc*' ('*battle-warrior*', *Beo* 2466), the poet seems to be aware that the *Hæð-* prefix means 'battle' as an Old English loan of *Hǫðr*, the name of the hapless perpetrator. In this way, it seems that the poet of *Beowulf* borrowed his story of Herebeald from a Danish legend about Baldr, possibly so as to help him present the lives of Scandinavian heathens in the pattern of their own mythology.[88] Thus Herebeald's accidental death, imagined for a moment as an Odinic sacrifice with gallows, spear and 'riding' in the darkness,

---

[86] North, *Pagan Words*, pp. 171–5.

[87] *Chronicle of Æthelweard*, ed. Campbell, p. 33; for the same identification in the prologue to *Gylfaginning* in the thirteenth century, see *Gylf*, p. 5 (prol.): 'Beldegg, er vér kǫllum Baldr'.

[88] For a suggestion that *ealuscerwen* (*Beo* 769) refers to a specifically Danish tradition

becomes an *exemplum* of the futility of life without Christ. It is the *exemplum* provided by Hrethel, his grieving father, that shows the audience of *Beowulf* how a heathen might be saved.

CONCLUSION

The commemoration of Germanic heathens in verse can never have been a simple matter for a Christian poet in Anglo-Saxon England. Lest this difficulty be forgotten in the case of *Beowulf*, it is worth remembering that not even Beowulf's salvation –

                  him of hræðre gewat
   sawol secean   soðfæstra dom.   (*Beo* 2819–20)[89]

– is a foregone conclusion by the end of the long elegy that now bears his name. In view of the poet's uncertainty about the fate of heathens in the world to come, it seems reasonable to suppose that he insured the souls of Beowulf and the other heroes in this poem by making their religious status comparable with that of the tribes of Israel in the Old Testament. Accordingly, when this poet grafted Scandinavian history on to the stem of Genesis and apparently translated the heathen invocations of Hrothgar and Beowulf into pieties of the Judaic moral system, he inevitably refocused the diversity of Germanic pre-Christian beliefs into a binary opposition between the Lord and the devil. This limiting transformation would have given the poet of *Beowulf* little scope to reveal the colour and detail of his heroes' religious lives: Ingui appears to be the god of Hrothgar, Finn, Hengest and Beowulf, yet also their potential *gastbona*, the devil himself; but there are only a few hints of Woden; and the reflexes of other heathen cults, Beow, Scyld, Heremod, Hama, Hæthcyn and Herebeald, have been euhemerized as mortal heroes by the time they appear in *Beowulf*, either in the tradition from which they were taken, or by the poet himself.[90]

---

    analogous to the image of Urðr, Verðandi and Skuld carving men's fates onto a piece of wood in *Vsp* 20, see North, '"Wyrd" and "weard ealuscerwen"', pp. 69–82.

[89] 'The soul passed out of his breast to seek the judgement of the righteous'. See further Fred C. Robinson, 'The Tomb of Beowulf', in *The Tomb of Beowulf and Other Essays on Old English* (Oxford, 1993), pp. 3–19.

[90] On the myths of Baldr, the *Brísingamen* and Ragnarǫk in *Beowulf* (whereby Beowulf's fight with the Dragon is presented in the manner of Þórr's against the World-Serpent), see U. Dronke, '*Beowulf* and Ragnarǫk', *Saga-Book* 17 (1968), 302–25 (also published in *Myth and Fiction*, no. XI).

The cult of Ingui in Beowulf

In this chapter I have attempted to show that the poet of *Beowulf* used contemporary Danish legends of Ingvi-freyr, Óðinn, Skjǫldr, Hǫðr and Baldr to supplement whatever literary remains there were concerning Ingui and other superstition in his native Anglian heritage. This poet probably had little left to work with from his own pre-Christian culture, and so imported Scyld from a Danish genealogy in order to construct an origin myth for the eponym of Hrothgar's Scyldings. This mythography, whereby the poet of *Beowulf* detached Hrothgar's family from Heremod, would have effectively concealed Hrothgar's connection with the name and heathen culture implicit in *Ingwine* ('friends of Ing'), another name for his Danish subjects. I have also argued that the names Beaw, Sceldwea and Sceaf were taken from a text of *Beowulf* in the reign of Æthelwulf of Wessex (839–58) in an attempt to extend the West Saxon line further back beyond Geat. To make a new case for this loan from *Beowulf* into Æthelwulf's genealogy, I have attempted to re-affirm through Scyld Scefing that the opening fifty-two lines of *Beowulf* are not an added prologue but are rather one piece with the rest of the poem. Later, in late ninth-century Wessex, King Alfred (871–99) may have used a text of *Beowulf* to complete a process which had started in seventh- and eighth-century Northumbria: then, an older correspondence of Woden with Jacob, or with Abraham; now, the true kinship of God's chosen people with English kings. This process of genealogical transformation could never have taken place if the poet of *Beowulf* had not attempted to exonerate Danish credulity by illustrating the agrarian pattern of its birth, in particular by personifying *beow*, *scyld* and *sceaf* in the opening lines of his poem.

8

Ingui's marriage: natural phenomena

The intention of this chapter is to offer a hypothesis on Ingui's marriage, on the ideological roots of Anglian kingship as these appear within the marriage of Nerthus and Terra Mater in Tacitus's *Germania* (ch. 40). The way towards this hypothesis will be marked out with studies on the members of Ingui's family: Anglo-Saxon words for natural phenomena, including *geofon* ('sea'), *þunor* ('thunder'), *wuldor* ('glory'), *geunnan* ('to yield, grant'), *frige* ('love') and *eorþan modor* ('mother earth'). These terms have cognates, respectively, in the names of the Norse gods *Gefjun* and *Gefn*, *Þórr*, *Ullr*, *Iðunn* and *Frigg*. I shall begin with an attempt to discover why the common Germanic etyma of these words should have become abstractions in Old English vocabulary and yet personified gods in Old Norse–Icelandic poetry. In the course of this chapter I shall attempt to establish the place of Nerthus and Terra Mater at the heart of an old Germanic family of natural elements or *numina* of sea, sky and earth from which both above categories of words (Anglo-Saxon abstractions and Norse gods) developed. Then, as a prelude to my discussion in the next chapter of an Anglian dying god in *The Dream of the Rood*, I shall attempt to reconstruct the ideology of Nerthus's seasonal marriage and sacrifice in the old Anglian homeland.

ANGLO-SAXON ANIMISM

Anglo-Saxon animism was first described more than three centuries after Christianization, in language which was based on the text of *De correctione rusticorum*, a treatise which Bishop Martin of Braga wrote in 572 against the local pagans of Spain. In this treatise, Martin says that mankind forgot the Creator after the Flood and worshipped 'created things' (*creaturae*) instead: 'some worshipped the sun, others the moon or stars, others fire, others the deep waters or springs of waters, believing not that all of these things were made by God for the use of men, but that these things were originally gods themselves'.[1] These words equipped Christian ministers with a vocabulary for dealing with similar problems throughout Europe until the thirteenth century. Pirmin of Reichenau studied under Bishop Fructuosus of Braga and could have taken Martin's treatise to Germany in the first half of the eighth century.[2] According to Pirmin, 'once again forgetting the Creator of the world, God, men began to worship created things and perform many other acts, which to relate is a long matter'.[3] It is thought that Ælfric was influenced by Martin's treatise in his homily *De falsis diis* at the end of the tenth century.[4] Ælfric says that after the Flood, men took to natural religion:

Hi namon þa [to wisdome] þæt hi wurþodon him for godas þa sunnan and þonne monan, for heora scinendan beorhtnysse, ond him lac offrodan, and forletan heora Scyppend. Sume men eac sædan be þam scinendum steorrum þæt hi godas wæron, and wurþodan hy [georne]. Sume hi gelyfdon on fyr for his færlicum bryne, sume eac on þa eorðan, for þon þe heo ealle þing afet. Ac hi mihton tocnawan, gif hi cuðan þæt gescead, þæt se is ana God þe hi ealle gesceop.[5]

Wulfstan adapted Ælfric's text in the early eleventh century and part of a thirteenth-century Icelandic homily on pagan gods, *Um þat hvaðan ótrú*

---

[1] *Opera*, ed. Barlow, pp. 159–203, esp. 159 (date), 166–7 (on Pirmin) and 186 (text): 'Alii adorabant solem, alii lunam vel stellas, alii ignem, alii aquam profundam vel fontes aquarum, credentes haec omnia non a deo esse facta ad usum hominum, sed ipsa ex se orta deos esse.'

[2] R. McKitterick, *The Frankish Kingdoms under the Carolingians 751–987* (London and New York, 1983), p. 42.

[3] *Die Heimat des hl. Pirmin, des Apostels der Alamannen*, ed. G. Jecker (Münster W., 1927), pp. 34–73, esp. 36 and 88 (note): 'obliviscentes iterum homines mundi deum, ceperunt colere creaturas et multa alia opera facire [*sic*], que dinumirare longum est'.

[4] *Homilies of Ælfric*, ed. Pope II, 667–724; For parallel texts of Martin and Ælfric, see Johnson, 'Euhemerization versus Demonisation', pp. 63–9.

[5] *Homilies of Ælfric*, ed. Pope II, 680–1: 'Then they held it wise to worship as gods the sun and the moon because of their shining brightness, and dedicated to them offerings and abandoned their Creator. Some men also said of the shining stars that they were gods and eagerly worshipped them. Some of them believed in fire because of its swift burning, some in water too, and they worshipped these as gods. Some believed in the earth, because she nourishes all things. But they could have recognized, if they had known discernment of this, that only he who made all these things is God.'

hófst ('On whence unbelief began'), seems also to derive from Ælfric's *De falsis diis*.[6] The debt of each of these writers to Bishop Martin's *De correctione rusticorum*, plus the need of each to establish a text of his own, suggests that the animism which Martin describes was widespread and long-lasting.

'Animism' is an old and broad anthropological term for the worship of natural elements, features and processes as individual divinities and powers. E. B. Tylor, the pioneer in this field in the last century, perceived that animism 'at once develops with and reacts upon mythic personification, in that early state of the human mind which gives consistent individual life to phenomena that our utmost stretch of fancy only avails to personify in conscious metaphor'.[7] Natural religions were studied in the last century, in places as diverse as Africa and the plains of Dakota, by Europeans whose established Christian certainties prevented them from finding any coherence in the paganism that they beheld, and who thus defined natural religion as a chaos of superstitions rather than as an ordered system of belief.[8] This is also how the worship of created things is described in Anglo-Saxon penitentials;[9] and how Archbishop Wulfstan presented *deofolgyld* ('idolatry') in the law-code which he wrote in Cnut's reign (1016–35) for subjects of a mixed Anglo-Saxon and Scandinavian background:

Hæðenscipe byð, þæt man deofolgyld weorðige, þæt is þæt man weorðige hæðene godas & sunnan oððe monan, fyr oððe flod, wæterwyllas oððe stanas oððe æniges cynnes wudutreowa, oððon wiccecræft lufige oððon morðweorc gefremme

---

[6] *Homilies of Wulfstan*, ed. Bethurum, pp. 221–4; *Hauksbók*, ed. Egill Jónsson and Finnur Jónsson (Copenhagen, 1892–6), pp. 157–8; see further A. R. Taylor, '*Hauksbók* and Ælfric's *De Falsis Diis*', *LSE* n.s. 3 (1969), 101–9.

[7] Tylor, *Primitive Culture* I, 285–326, esp. 287.

[8] See E. E. Evans-Pritchard, *The Institutions of Primitive Society* (Oxford, 1954), p. 1; W. Müller, 'The "Passivity" of Language and the Experience of Nature: a Study in the Structure of the Primitive Mind', in *Myths and Symbols: Studies in Honor of Mircea Eliade*, ed. J. M. Kittigawa (Chicago, 1969), pp. 227–39, esp. 230–8; J. R. Walker, *Lakota Belief and Ritual*, ed. R. J. De Mallie and E. A. Jahner (Lincoln, NA, and London, 1980), pp. 65–171, esp. 72–3.

[9] See *Die Canones Theodori*, ed. Finsterwalder, p. 264 (II.cxvi); *Die altenglische Version des Halitgar'schen Bussbuches*, ed. Raith, p. 29 (II.xxii); *Councils and Synods*, ed. Whitelock, pp. 319–20 (*Canons Enacted Under King Edgar*, XVI) and 463 (*The Northumbrian Priest Law*, LIV).

Ingui's marriage

on ænigne wisan, oððon on blote oððon fyrhte, oððon swylcra gedwimera ænig þingc dreoge.[10]

The paganism in this law-code is quite remote from Snorri Sturluson's formal guide to the pagan gods in *Gylfaginning*, for Wulfstan shows non-Christian beliefs to be a disorderly heap of abuses bereft of any intelligible form or purpose. Yet this disparity is not surprising, for Wulfstan's text, unlike Snorri's, shows a struggle between Christian doctrine and living animism.

Wulfstan's definition of this animism as *deofolgyld* occurs in the early eleventh century near the end of the Anglo-Saxon period. How animism was imagined not by churchmen, but by the earliest Anglo-Saxon heathens, is another question which may be answered with reference first to classical *numina*, then to the equivalent Norse *bǫnd* ('bonds') in a Germanic tradition that extends from Tacitus to the Icelandic sagas. The personification of abstract concepts is a crucial topic in the pre-Christian religions of Tacitus's own Roman heritage. Some classical scholars admit that demonic beings and abstracts were probably perceived as having the same status in Greek and Roman religions, but show an uncertainty therein as to whether abstract words such as ἐρώς ('love') and φόβος ('fear') developed from the names of deities;[11] or whether deities of this kind had once been personified from abstract words for concepts or natural phenomena.[12] As there is no general agreement in this area, it may be best to take these alternative models of divine–abstract transformation as having been concurrent at any time. Thus Peter Dronke, in a study on the goddess Natura in the late classical period, concluded that 'Gods may become abstractions, and abstractions can be genuinely

---

[10] Liebermann, *Gesetze der Angelsachsen* I, 312–13 (*Cnut's Laws* (1016–35), §5): 'Heathendom is worshipping devil-idols, that is to say the worshipping of heathen gods and sun and moon, fire or flood, water wells or stones or forest-trees of any kind, or the loving of witchcraft or the committing of murders in any way, either in sacrifice or from bringing into fear, or doing anything so deluded as this.'

[11] F. Stössl, 'Personifikationen', *Paulys Real-Enzyclopädie der classischen Altertumswissenschaft, Neue Bearbeitung*, ed. G. Wissowa and W. Kroll (Stuttgart, 1894–1972), XIX.1, 1042–58, esp. 1044; P. Kretschmer, 'Dyaus, Ζεύς, Diespiter und die Abstrakta im Indogermanischen', *Glotta* 13 (1924), 101–13, esp. 102–7.

[12] H. Usener, 'Keraunos', *Rheinisches Museum für Philologie* 60 (1905), 1–30, esp. 14; K. Reinhardt, *Vermächtnis der Antike* (Göttingen, 1960), pp. 7–40.

Heathen gods

deified.'[13] In this way, many Greek and Roman pagans might have conceived of persons and phenomena simultaneously, entertaining what Peter Dronke has called 'a two-way passage between divine (or daimonic) beings and personifications'.[14]

There are cases of this 'two-way passage' in ancient Greek and Latin sources: in the *Iliad*, the river Axius transforms itself into a man to protect his grandson in battle against Achilles (*Il.* XXI.136–213); in the *Odyssey*, Odysseus persuades an estuary in Pheaecia to halt his current and carry him to a good shore (*Od.* V.444–53); and the river Tiber, in the *Aeneid*, promises help to Aeneas in a dream, appearing to him as an old man rising from the water and festooned with sedge and poplar leaves (*Aen.* VIII.31–76). In the Latin language Vergil's word *numen* (for the 'power' of this deity in *Aen.* VIII.78) eventually came to mean the 'deity' itself.[15] Tacitus refers to a *numen* presiding over the grove of the Semnones and calls the Germanic Terra Mater a *numen* when she is washed in her shrine in *Germania* (chs. 39 and 40).[16] With this name both types of classical deity, Olympians and abstract or natural forces, were still worshipped with their own images and shrines in the fourth and fifth centuries, the era of Neo-Platonic paganism.[17] St Augustine in the early fifth century thus cites goddesses such as Victoria, Virtus, Fides, Fortuna, besides the negative Pavor, all of which had altars in his lifetime.[18] At least three more patristic writers confirm the worship of abstract *numina*. Lactantius, converted possibly at the end of the third century, advised that even virtues besides vices should not be given temples, 'but are worthy of being located in the breast and understood inwardly there, that they be not false if located outside the man'; neither Mens, Virtus, Pietas nor Fides should be externalized, 'for the virtue must be cultivated, not the virtue's image, and cultivated not with any sacrifice or incense or solemn prayer, but only with desire and supplication'.[19] In the early

---

[13] P. Dronke, 'Bernard Silvestris, *Natura* and Personification', *Journal of the Warburg and Courtauld Institutes* 43 (1980), 16–31, esp. 30.

[14] *Ibid.*, pp. 29–30.

[15] Dumézil, *Archaic Roman Religion*, pp. 18–31, esp. 29; see also Henig, *Religion in Roman Britain*, pp. 76–9.

[16] *Germania*, pp. 317–18.

[17] Dumézil, *Archaic Roman Religion*, pp. 397–406; see also Henig, *Religion in Roman Britain*, pp. 76–9.

[18] Augustine, *De Civitate Dei*, pp. 188–9 (VII.iii).

[19] *L. Caeli Firmiani Lactanti Opera Omnia*, ed. S. Brandt and G. Laubmann, 2 vols.

fourth century, Arnobius of Sicca, another convert, referred to Pietas, Concordia and Salus, saying that 'we feel and we perceive that none of them have the force of numinous power or can be contained in any form of their own kind; but manly quality is contained in the form of a man, health in the form of a healthy man, honour in that of an honourable man'.[20] Paulinus of Nola, when he wrote on this theme to his brother in the early fifth century, asked how divine power could be accorded to abstractions such as *fors* ('chance') or *fatum* ('fate'), for these lacked the Creator's *nomen* or *numen* (the reading is unclear) and were not even created things: 'from practising an ancient error through their ignorance of God, men, poor of reason, fashion hollow names (*nomina*) as if they were also numinous powers (*numina*) into embodied form, with foolish imagination; and more foolishly accord what they have fashioned the honour due to gods'.[21] Paulinus also noted that images of Spes, Nemesis, Amor, even Furor, were all worshipped as gods. All the above prose writers cited use *numen* to describe such personified abstracts, with Paulinus in his letter playing rhetorically on the similarity of *numen* to *nomen*.

The ancient Germanic counterparts of these Greek and Latin *numina* must be inferred from the comparison of references in classical sources with a number of colourful figures in Old Norse–Icelandic literature. Here, the names of many Norse Æsir, such as *Þórr* ('Thunder'), *Ullr* ('Brilliance') or *Frigg* ('Love'), indicate the type of natural phenomena from which early Germanic gods developed. It is accepted that the myths of the *Æsir* even in *Gylfaginning* 'are, at least in part, the development of stories told to account for natural phenomena, which were later, in some cases, identified with stories about Trojan heroes'.[22] In *Germania*, Tacitus

(Vienna, 1890–3) I, 74–5 (*De falsa religione* I.20.18): 'sed intra pectus collocandae sunt et interius conprehendae, ne sint falsae, si extra hominem fuerint collocatae'; 'virtus enim colenda est, non imago virtutis, et colenda est non sacrificio aliquo, aut ture aut precatione sollemni, sed uoluntate sola atque proposito'.

[20] *Arnobii Adversus Nationes: Libri VII*, ed. C. Marchesi (Turin, 1934), p. 204 (*Disputationes adversus gentes* IV.2): 'nihil horum sentimus et cernimus habere vim numinis neque in aliqua contineri sui generis forma, sed esse virtutem viri, salutem salvi, honorem honorati'.

[21] *Sancti Pontii Meropii Paulini Epistulae*, ed. W. von Hartel (Vienna, 1894), pp. 117–18 (*Ad Jovium*): 'ab usu erroris antiqui ob ignorantiam dei rationis inopes cassa nomina tamquam ideo numina quoque sint, in speciem corporatam stultis cogitationibus fingunt stultiusque quam finxerunt, donant honore diuino'.

[22] Faulkes, 'Pagan Sympathy', pp. 303–4.

reveals the Germanic worship of natural phenomena in the first century, when he identifies Germanic cults of established Roman gods (Mercury, Mars, Hercules, Isis), but then announces that the Germans do not think it proper for the gods to dwell in shrines or images: 'they hallow the groves and woods and call by the names of gods that hidden thing which they see in reverence only' (ch. 9).[23] A Germanic deity is also said to be present in the grove of the Semnones: 'Est et alia luco reuerentia: nemo nisi *uinculo ligatus* ingreditur, ut minor et potestatem numinis prae se ferens. Si forte prolapsus est, adtolli et insurgere haud licitum: per humum euoluuntur' (ch. 39).[24] In the same passage, Tacitus, or his informant (who may have been King Masyos of the Semnones), called the divinity of this grove *regnator omnium deus* ('the god who rules all'). Eve Picard shows that this phrase is probably influenced by the Roman cult of Jupiter Latiaris.[25] However, as the stem of *regnator* resembles the sound of PGmc *ragan- (the etymon of OIce rǫgn/regin and OE regen-), it is possible that the words on which this apparent identification with Jupiter was based referred to 'gods' in general.

The chains in this grove appear to have been a symbol of divine power.[26] It can be no coincidence, therefore, that the Norse gods, in the Eddic and Scaldic poetry of Norway and Iceland, are known as *bǫnd* ('bonds'), *hǫpt* ('chains'), as well as *regin* or *rǫgn* ('rulers'), *goð* ('gods') and *ráð* ('counsels').[27] Walter Baetke concluded that these neuter plural nouns were all Germanic counterparts of Lat *numina*, which mean 'gods'.[28] Although these words are frequent in Old Norse–Icelandic poetry, their

[23] *Germania*, p. 285: 'lucos ac nemora consecrant deorumque nominibus appellant secretum illud quod sola reuerentia uident'. For documentation of Tacitus's debt to Greek and Latin ethnography, see Picard, *Germanisches Sakralkönigtum?*, pp. 131–83.

[24] *Germania*, p. 316: 'In the grove there is yet another form of worship: no-one may go in unless *being bound with a chain* he acknowledges himself less important and the *numen* powerful. If by chance he falls, it is completely forbidden that he rights himself or rises: these people roll themselves out over the ground'.

[25] Picard, *Germanisches Sakralkönigtum?*, pp. 131–58.

[26] *AR* II, 13 (§§241–2).

[27] For instances, see Dronke, 'Eddic Poetry as a Source', pp. 657–67 (also published in *Myth and Fiction*, no. IV); and E. Marold, 'Die Skaldendichtung als Quelle der Religionsgeschichte', in *Germanische Religionsgeschichte*, ed. Beck, Ellmers and Schier, pp. 685–719, esp. 705–9. Picard (*Germanisches Sakralkönigtum?*, pp. 157–8) suggests that Tacitus based the *uincula* in this passage on a line in Lucretius's *De rerum natura*.

[28] Baetke, 'guð in den altnordischen Eidesformeln', *BGdSL* 70 (1948), 351–71, esp. 362–3.

Old English analogues are few and far between. With *regen-*, cognate with OIce *regin* or *rǫgn*, the poet of *Exodus* personifies 'old age or early death' (*yldo oððe ærdeað*) as *regnþeofas* ('?demon-thieves') in *Ex* 539. A 'council of natural powers' is perhaps the meaning of the more obscure *Regenmælde* in the first line of *The Nine Herbs Charm*; whereas OE *regen* in *rondas regnhearde* ('shields ?Reginn-hardened') in *Beo* 326 seems to derive from a cognate of OIce *Reginn*, the name of a smith and the mentor of Sigurðr Sigmundarson. There is no Anglo-Saxon evidence that 'chains' became a metonymous substitute for 'gods' or 'devils' in pre-Christian England, though chains and devils are associated in descriptions of hell such as in *Genesis B*, and again when the saint in the Old English *Guthlac* tells the homeless demons hovering about Crowland that Jesus 'made you captive and drove you into *fetters* under a close bondage' ('eow gehynde ond in *hæft* bidraf under nearone clom', *Guth* 597–8).

In Icelandic paganism, on the other hand, the *bǫnd* became permanent guardians of the country. One anonymous verse of the Icelandic conversion period claims defiantly that 'the bonds will stay in the land' (*bǫnd munu vera í landi*).[29] A lampoon, ascribed to an anonymous Icelander in the tenth century, announces that the steward of the king of Denmark, a sexual deviant, is 'worthy of being driven out by the bonds of the mountain-hall' (*rækr bǫndum bergsalar*).[30] The *bǫnd* could also live in the sea, for when Steinunn *skáldkona* ('woman poet') said that Þórr had smashed the missionary Þangbrandr's ship in a storm, she added that 'the bonds have driven the beach-hawk [ship] aground' (*bǫnd rǫku val strandar*).[31] These references to *bǫnd* can be grouped with some late thirteenth-century church prohibitions that forbade Icelanders to believe in the *landvættir* ('creatures of the country') whom they held to live in groves, mounds or waterfalls.[32] OIce *landvættir* appears to be a prose equivalent of *bǫnd*. In the Icelandic *Landnámabók* ('Book of Settlements'), a great sacrificer named Þorsteinn rauðnefr was said to worship the waterfall with offerings of food.[33] In the same compilation, the opening entry of the Norwegian laws of Úlfljótr states that ships should not sail within sight of land with grinning dragonheads on their prows, 'in such a

---

[29] *Skj* B I, 169.
[30] *Heimskringla I*, ed. Bjarni, p. 270 (*Óláfs saga Tryggvasonar*, ch. 33).
[31] *Skj* B I, 128. Also edited in Turville-Petre, *Scaldic Poetry*, pp. 65–7, esp. 66.
[32] Ólafur Briem, *Heiðinn Siður á Íslandi* (Reykjavik, 1945), pp. 71–90, esp. 75–6.
[33] *Landnámabók*, ed. Jakob, p. 358 (*Sturlubók*, ch. 355 and *Hauksbók*, ch. 313).

way that the spirits of the land took fright' (*svá at landvættir fælisk við*).³⁴ In keeping with this belief, Egill Skalla-Grímsson is said to have frightened the *landvættir* of Norway with a grinning horse's head on a pole, in order to force them to drive King Eiríkr and Queen Gunnhildr out of Norway; this the *landvættir* did.³⁵ In *Landnámabók*, men with second sight are said to see *landvættir* following men to local assemblies and on hunting and fishing trips.³⁶ In *Óláfs saga Tryggvasonar* (ch. 33), Snorri says that the *landvættir* of Iceland take on the shapes of a dragon, serpents, toads, adders, birds of prey, a boar, and mountain giants, when they repel a magician scouting for a potential Danish invasion. Just like the *bǫnd*, the *landvættir* were thought to influence the movements of men.

There is nearly a thousand years and miles between these Norse *bǫnd* or *landvættir* and the *uincula* and other cryptic references of Tacitus. Yet it is plausible that particularly the concept of gods as 'bonds', obligation or constraint, as common to both cultural records, implies some connection and continuity of Germanic tradition in that intervening period. Probably through contact with the devotees of Roman gods such as Mercury, Mars, Hercules and Isis, the Germanic ancestors of Anglo-Saxons and Scandinavians came to worship some gods as personifications. However, it is likely that early Germanic religion consisted for the most part of a pantheism in which divine beings were rarely distinguished from natural phenomena.

Relatively few literary reflexes of this animism appear to survive in Anglo-Saxon records. In the beginning of *Beowulf*, as we have seen, it is possible to see the *feasceaft* Scyld Scefing putting to shore both as a baby and as a shield bearing a seedling, growing 'under the clouds' both as a prince and as a shaft growing under the sky (*weox under wolcnum*, *Beo* 7–8), then floating out to sea both as a dying king in his ship and as a ripe sheaf of corn in a shield (*Beo* 26–31). In the Exeter Book *Maxims*, frost freezes, fire melts wood, earth grows and ice hardens apparently with the autonomy of living things; the poet of *Maxims* imputes the agency of these phenomena to 'God of many powers' (*felameahtig god*, *Max I* II 75). In the Exeter Book *Riddles*, phenomena such as wind, an onion, a nightingale and many other things speak with human voices; if the creatures in these riddles derive their first-person narratives from prosopopoeia, an influence which Marie Nelson has shown to be likely, this was a

---

³⁴ *Landnámabók*, ed. Jakob, p. 313 (*Hauksbók*, ch. 307).
³⁵ *Egils saga*, ed. Sigurður, p. 171 (ch. 57).
³⁶ *Landnámabók*, ed. Jakob, pp. 330 (*Sturlubók*, ch. 329) and 331 (*Hauksbók*, ch. 284).

device in popular demand.[37] This device is also present in the first-person statements of lifeless artefacts that speak of their origins: swords, rings, combs or jewels; or as the Alfred jewel says 'Alfred had me made' (*Aelfred mec heht gewyrcan*).[38] Each of the above examples from the Christian period probably derives from a subculture of animism in whose pre-Christian form a vast number of gods had been worshipped both as personified beings and as natural or abstract phenomena at one and the same time.

It is thus likely that the names of most Anglo-Saxon gods were words whose meanings might shift freely between one perspective and the other. In the case of Norse gods, this double perspective within their names narrowed almost exclusively into personifications, probably because Germanic paganism survived into the eleventh century in Norway, more than three centuries longer in Scandinavia than it did in England or Germany; in the case of Old English words for abstractions or natural phenomena, the potential of each word to be personified into a name was probably destroyed in the process of Christianization in the seventh century, along with their tangible embodiments, heathen idols and shrines. For this reason, it would be an anachronism to look for a pantheon in seventh-century England matching Snorri's gods in *Gylfaginning*. Even after a century or so, the Anglo-Saxon conversion was too sudden and perhaps too unexpected to allow for a development of the Norse kind. With OE *þunor* and other words surviving in Old English literature, the implication is quite the reverse. Thunder may have been worshipped in an English temple or grove until the local king or bishop burned its anthropomorphic idols and scourged its personality out of each convert's mind. Yet if *þunor* was still the common word for a phenomenon that brings rain, the bishop must have sanctioned the survival of this word as a thing, though he censored *þunor* as a person. Accordingly, the homilists who described popular animism in western Europe presented *numina* such as *þunor* as *creaturae*, manifestations of one Creator rather than as living autonomous beings. In the next three sections I shall discuss the evidence for this and other Anglo-Saxon *numina* associated with the sea, the sky and the earth.

[37] *The Old English Riddles of the Exeter Book*, ed. C. Williamson (Chapel Hill, NC, 1977), pp. 23–8, esp. 26–7. See also Nelson, 'Rhetoric of the Exeter Book Riddles', pp. 425–8; Schlauch, '*The Dream of the Rood* as Prosopopoeia', pp. 23–34; and Clemoes, whose terminology is different, in *Interactions of Thought and Language*, pp. 98–101.

[38] See *The Dream of the Rood*, ed. Swanton, p. 66.

Heathen gods

SEA *NUMINA*

In this section I shall use Norse and other cognates to discuss Nerthus and the Old English terms *geneorð*, *garsecg*, *mægðegsa* and *geofon* as words derived from *numina* associated with the sea.

Old Anglian Nerthus *and OE* geneorð

As we have seen in *Germania* (ch. 40), Tacitus shows that the ancestors of the Angles worshipped a god called *Nerthus*. Two possible Old English reflexes of this name are *geneorð*, which glosses *contentus* ('happy', 'eager', 'strained') in the Corpus glossary (CCCC 144); and *ginehord*, which glosses *contentus* in the Erfurt glossary.[39] Ferdinand Holthausen suggested that these forms are two spellings of one Old English adjective cognate with the Old Anglian *Nerthus* and its later Norse cognate *Njǫrðr*.[40] Against this connection, H. D. Meritt proposed that OE *geneorð* in *contentus:geneorð* was miscopied from *gecneord*, which had glossed *intentus* ('strained', 'eager'); and that *ginehord* was written for OE *gine hord* ('ample supply').[41] Holthausen's theory is less ingenious than Meritt's, but even if Holthausen were to be preferred, the paucity of these references is striking: OE *geneorð* and *ginehord* would appear to be the only surviving reflexes of *Nerthus* in Anglo-Saxon dialects.

Early Germanic *Nerthus* is thought to be cognate with the Celtic *nertos* ('strength'); from this formal relationship it might be argued that there was a Celtic substratum in this part of continental Germania.[42] In this way it is not clear that *Nerthus* was exclusively the name for a personification. In his account of Nerthus of the Anglii and other tribes, as I have suggested above, Tacitus may have projected Cybele on a sacred marriage between Nerthus and Terra Mater and thus taken *Terra Mater* as an

---

[39] *Corpus Glossary*, ed. Lindsay, p. 44.666; *Épinal-Erfurt Glossary*, ed. Pheifer, pp. lxiii, 16.276 (*Erf.*) and 78 n.

[40] F. Holthausen, 'Wortdeutungen', *Indogermanische Forschungen* 48 (1930), 254–67, esp. 267. OE *neorxnawang* ('paradise'), which Holthausen also connects with OIce *Njǫrðr*, is unlikely to be a cognate form.

[41] H. D. Meritt, *Some of the Hardest Glosses in Old English* (Stanford, CA, 1968), pp. 78–80.

[42] Celtic *nertos* was the first non-Germanic cognate of OIce *Njǫrðr* to be identified, according to de Vries (*AR* II, 163–4 (§448) and *ANEW* 410–11 (*Njǫrðr*)).

Ingui's marriage

interpretatio Romana for *Nerthus*. Enacted by human hypostases, this marriage would be a northern Germanic analogue of the union of Dionysus with Demeter or that of Liber with Ceres.[43] Besides the Ing-hypostasis, who, as I have suggested, seems to be the man in this marriage, Tacitus may refer to a human in the part of Terra Mater; for when Terra Mater is returned to the temple, Tacitus says: 'Soon the wagon and vestments, and if you want to believe it, the deity itself are washed in a solitary lake' (ch. 40).[44] As something palpable must have been washed where this *numen* was, Terra Mater may have been embodied by a woman or an object of some kind. In this way, both Nerthus and Terra Mater may have been names for abstract and physical phenomena which were represented by human persons.

There are a few instances of OIce *Njǫrðr* as a word denoting an abstract or phenomenon in the Norse tradition. Njǫrðr is mostly a firm personification with a story of his own: Snorri calls Njǫrðr 'third member of the Æsir' (*hinn þriði áss*), though he notes that Njǫrðr was a hostage whom the Vanir sent to the Æsir with his children Freyr and Freyja; Njǫrðr was married to the giantess Skaði to compensate her for the death of Þjazi, her father, whom the Æsir killed in *Skáldskaparmál*; Njǫrðr lives in '?ships' enclosure' (*Nóatún*) and 'controls the motion of wind and moderates sea and fire' (*ræðr fyrir gǫngu vinds ok stillir sjá ok eld*); he governs fishing and journeys at sea and is perpetually wealthy.[45] In Scaldic poetry, there are sixty-one examples of kennings for 'man' in which *Njǫrðr* is used as the base-element; and five examples in which the base-element includes the suffix *-njǫrðungar*, a derivative of this god's name.[46] In this and the other respects, Njǫrðr is distinctly a person.[47]

In a few other examples, however, the word OIce *njǫrðr* is used not as a name, but as a phenomenon apparently meaning either 'strength' or the 'sea'. The first meaning is apparent in either *njarðgjǫrð* or *njarðráð* (the construction is ambiguous), which occurs once, in *Þórsdrápa*, a poem probably composed for Hákon Jarl by Eilífr Goðrúnarson in *c*. 985. Here

---

[43] Picard, *Germanisches Sakralkönigtum?*, pp. 40–5 and 131–83; Martin, *Tacitus*, pp. 49–58, esp. 50; Syme, *Tacitus* I, 46–8, 127–9 and 174; on the problems of identifying Nerthus's tribes, see Picard, *ibid.*, pp. 190–1.
[44] *Germania*, p. 317: 'Mox uehiculum et uestis et, si credere uelis, numen ipsum secreto lacu abluitur.'
[45] *Gylf*, p. 23 (ch. 23). [46] Meissner, *Kenningar der Skalden*, pp. 261–2.
[47] *AR* II, 173–8 (§§454–6) and 203–4 (§471).

Þórr and his servant Þjálfi struggle across the river Vimur to reach the mountain home of the giant Geirrøðr. Suddenly they are deluged by a river flowing from the vulva of a urinating giantess. Of Þórr, the poet says:

> Harðvaxnar leit herðar hall-lands of sik falla
> (gatat) mar njótr (in neytri) njarð- (-ráð fyr sér) -gjarðar;
> þverrir lét, nema fyrri Þórns, barna sér Marnar,
> snerriblóð, til, svíra, salþaks megin vaxa. (Þórsdrápa 7)[48]

Snorri preserves this verse in *Skáldskaparmál*, with a prose account of the same story, in which he says Þórr used his 'belts of power' (*megingjarðar*) to cross this river halfway (ch. 18); with these gloves in *Gylfaginning*, Þórr 'girds himself [. . .], then his divine strength doubles in size' (ch. 21).[49] In this way Snorri appears to see an equation of *njarð*- (in the compound *njarðgjǫrð*) with *megin*.[50] E. A. Kock suggests that Eilífr meant *njarð-ráð* ('strength-counsel').[51] Whichever the option, *njarð*- appears to have little personal sense consistent with Njǫrðr.

In *Lokasenna*, secondly, Loki mocks Njǫrðr by alluding to the ocean, a phenomenon connoted by Njǫrðr's name, as if it were Njǫrðr himself:

> Hymis meyiar hǫfðo þic at hlandtrogi
> oc þér í munn migo. (*Lok* 34)[52]

---

[48] *Skj* B I, 141: 'He saw the *ocean* of the rock-terrain fall over his hard-grown shoulders; *strength-belt*'s user could not get for himself *plans* more profitable than this: the diminisher of Mǫrn's children [giants] said that unless Þorn's swift-flowing neck-blood [river] dried up, his power would grow to the roof of heaven itself.' Davidson provides an excellent discussion of Þórsdrápa in 'Earl Hákon and his Poets', pp. 522 and 533.

[49] *SnE* 286 (also *FJSnE* 106); *Gylf*, p. 23: 'spennir þeim um sik [. . .] þá vex honum ásmegin hálfu'.

[50] In support of this reading (with tmesis), see K. Reichardt, 'A Contribution to the Interpretation of Scaldic Poetry: Tmesis', in *Old Norse Literature and Mythology: a Symposium*, ed. E. C. Polomé (Austin, TX, 1969), pp. 200–26, esp. 212–13; Davidson suggests that tmesis here would represent the sudden violence of Þórr's loss of his divine strength, in 'Earl Hákon and his Poets', p. 544.

[51] See E. A. Kock's reading *gatat meir njótr in neytri njarðráð fyr sér gjarðar*, in *Notationes Norroenae, Lunds Universitets Årsskrift* 21 (1924), 93–4 (§449): 'now the girdle-clad one knew furthermore of no better plan for himself' (*numera visste sig den jördelklädde icke någon bättre råd*). This form *njarðráð* would be conceptually close to Lappish *Veralden rad*, which I have quoted in ch. 3.

[52] '[The giant] Hymir's daughters used you as a urine-trough and pissed into your mouth.'

Ingui's marriage

Here Loki seems also to refer to Njǫrðr as the ocean into which the rivers of Norway flow. This sense in the stem of *Njǫrðr* may also be intended in *Fjǫlsvinnsmál*, a poem of the fifteenth century, in which *njarðlásar níu* ('nine strength-locks') are said to enclose a magic sword (stanza 25).[53] Although *njarð-* is probably used to alliterate with *níu* in this stanza, it is inconsistent with Njǫrðr's person and it may express a notion of magical strength. Both uses of the *njarð*-prefix express an abstract phenomenon. Both Njǫrðr and the sea are meant in *njarðarvǫttr*, which survives in three examples and means 'sponge' (literally 'glove of Njǫrðr'): this is the sea, identical with Njǫrðr, infiltrating the holes of the sponge material.[54] The use of the placename *Njarðvík* ('Njǫrðr-creek') in Iceland is probably due to the scarcity of natural harbours on the southern Icelandic coast and to the enduring importance of fish in this island's economy. In all these cases, *njarð-* expresses a concept of 'divine strength' which is associated with the ocean. On the evidence of this meaning in OIce *njarð-*, as well as through Njǫrðr's mythical association with the sea, it is possible that the Anglii used *nerthus* metonymously to describe the phenomenon *Oceanus*, Tacitus's word for the sea which lies nearby;[55] and that through the Angles, in particular, Nerthus's denotation survived in a rare adjectival derivative: OE *geneorð* ('content').

OE garsecg *and* mægðegsa

OE *garsecg* (?'spear-man') is unparalleled in other early Germanic vernaculars, but occurs about ninety times in the Old English corpus.[56] In most cases this word denotes the sea as a totality: *garsecges deop* ('ocean's deep', *Ex* 281), *garsecges gin* ('ocean's abyss', *Ex* 431), *garsecges begang* ('compass of the ocean', *And* 530), *garsecges grundas* ('ocean bottom', *OrW* 70-1). When Beowulf recalls that he and Breca *on garsecg ut aldrum neðdon* ('risked our lives out on the ocean', *Beo* 537-8), he also seems to mean the open sea beyond the reach of land. With *hlymmeð*, this word also 'roars' in

---

[53] R. C. Boer, *Die Edda: mit historisch-kritischem Commentar*, 2 vols. (Haarlem, 1922) I, 294.
[54] *Máríu saga*, ed. C. R. Unger (Christiania [Oslo]), 1871), p. 643 (l.23); *Heilagra Manna Sǫgur*, ed. C. R. Unger, 2 vols. (Christiania [Oslo], 1877) II, 662.26 (*Vitae Patrum* II); *SnE* II (Copenhagen, 1852), p. 168 (*The Third Grammatical Treatise*, §16).
[55] *Germania*, p. 317 (ch. 40).
[56] DiPaolo Healey and Venezky, *Microfiche Concordance*, s.v. 'garsecg' (etc.).

Heathen gods

St Andrew's description of the sea to his helmsman (*And* 392–3); 'resounded' on the shore earlier with *hlynede* (*And* 238); is the medium through which the 'hornfish' glides (*And* 371) and Beowulf's ship sails (*Beo* 515); and with *garsecg wedde* ('ocean went mad', *Ex* 490), the Red Sea falls on the Egyptian army in *Exodus*.

Sweet suggested that *garsecg* developed in metathesis from *gasric* ('roaring-kingdom'), a form which occurs on the Franks Casket.[57] Another idea is that the etymon of OE *garsecg* was rationalized from the second element of Welsh *mor-gaseg* ('sea-breaker').[58] However, as the second element of the Welsh compound, when a simplex, is unmutated *caseg*, this explanation seems unlikely. There is little in Snorri's mythography to justify in *garsecg* as 'spear-man' an Old English counterpart of Ægir, whose wife's instrument is a net, not a spear or trident.[59] If the word *garsecg* means 'spear-man', it seems to have been coined as a reverential periphrasis for the sea in order to evade the offence of a direct description.[60]

An ideology of OE *gar-secg* as 'spear-man' may be detected in an anecdote about Saxon pirates in *c.* 480; Bishop Sidonius of Clermont wrote to Namatius of the Visigothic navy, warning him that Saxon pirates were said to have no fear of the sea, even in rough weather:

mos est remeaturis decimum quemque captorum per aquales et *cruciarias poenas* plus ob hoc tristi quod superstitioso ritu necare superque collectam turbam periturorum mortis iniquitatem sortis aequitate dispergere. Talibus se *ligant* votis, victimis solvunt. Et per huiusmodi non tam sacrificia purgati quam sacrilegia polluti religiosum putant caedis infaustae perpetratores de capite captivo magis exigere tormenta quam pretia.[61]

---

[57] H. Sweet, 'Old English Etymologies', *EStn* 2 (1879), 312–16, esp. 315.
[58] W. J. Redbond, 'Notes on the Word "Gar-secg"', *MLR* 27 (1932), 204–6.
[59] *SnE* 338 (ch. 33); *FJSnE* 121.
[60] On Norse taboos at sea indicated in deliberately evasive or periphrastic vocabulary, adduced to explain the development of Scaldic diction, see R. Perkins, 'Rowing Chants and the Origins of *Dróttkvæðr háttr*', *Saga-Book* 21 (1984–5), 155–221, esp. 168.
[61] *Epistulae et Carmina*, ed. Luetjohann, pp. 132–3 (VIII.vi): 'It is their custom, before returning home, to kill one in ten of their prisoners with the *penalty* of drowning in the deep or *crucifixion*, in a rite that is the sadder for deriving from superstition; and thus to distribute the iniquity of this death to a gathered crowd of the doomed with the impartiality of lots. By such promises they *bind* themselves, by such victims they loose themselves. Nor so much purged by such sacrifices as polluted by such sacrilege, the perpetrators of that unhallowed slaughter think it is a religious duty [lit. binding]

Ingui's marriage

Sidonius puns and contrasts not only with *mortis iniquitatem sortis aequitate*, but also with *se ligant votis, victimis solvunt*.[62] By this rhetoric Sidonius may have stressed how irrational this horror seemed to him. But by the same token, the attributed 'bonds' of obligation were reasonable to the Saxons. By alluding to the death of the Saxons' captives as 'the penalties of crucifixion' (*cruciariae poenae*), Sidonius may show that hanging and spear-stabbing was the method of their sacrifice to a sea-god;[63] this deduction, in turn, may explain how the Anglo-Saxons could later name the sea metonymously as a 'spear-man' (OE *garsecg*).

The sea is accredited lifelike quality elsewhere in the Exeter Book *Maxims*; a seaman will return, the poet says:

> Hwonne him gebyre weorðe,
> ham cymeð, gif he hal leofað,   nefne him holm gestyreð,
> mere hafað mundum mægðegsan wyn.   (*Max I* II, 104–6)[64]

The words *mægðegsan wyn* have been translated not only as 'joy of the terror of nations' but also as 'joy of the viking', hence 'ship'; but this reading is strained, for it disregards two things: the sailor as the subject of the first half of this sentence, who is therefore likely to be the object of the second half and referent of the kenning; and the widespread use of reverential or superstitious periphrases in sea terminology, by which *mægðegsa* is more likely to denote the sea than a seafarer. In addition, the syntax of the above lines shows that words *him* and *wyn* in *Max I* II, 105–6 are the objects of verbs whose subject is the sea (either *holm* or *mere*). The sea in these lines may also be imagined as a sexually demanding female, in that it 'restrains' (*gestyreð*) and 'holds in its arms' (*hafað mundum*) the sailor whose life is threatened by drowning. This sexual interpretation of the sea's hold over her man is supported by a parallel use

---

for them to exact torture rather than rewards from [lit.] the captive's head.' Sidonius also cites Saxon 'archipiratae' in a panegyric written at about the same time: *ibid.*, p. 212.

[62] Variant *eligunt* (found in five manuscripts (MTCFP)) for *ligant* (found in one (L)), though *ligant* is preferred because of its rhetorical antithesis to nearby *solvunt*: see *ibid.*, pp. 132–3.

[63] Wilson (*Anglo-Saxon Paganism*, p. 28) suggests that these rites could have been ancestral to Saxons who settled in Britain.

[64] 'When he gets a following wind, he comes home, if he is alive and in good health, unless ocean restrains him, [unless] sea holds in [her] arms the joy of the terror of nations.'

of *gestyran* in *Genesis B*: where Satan's demon, urging Eve to eat the forbidden fruit, tells her that she can 'govern Adam again' (*Adame eft gestyran*), if she has his will and he trusts her words (*Gen* 568). In this context the *mægðegsan wyn* is also an appropriate kenning for 'man' on analogy with the late ninth-century kenning *flaums-Foglhildar munr* in *Ragnarsdrápa* 6 ('desire of current-bird-*hildr*', hence 'Swan-hildr's desire', hence 'Jǫrmunrekkr');[65] and with OIce *Friggiar angan* ('joy of Frigg', hence 'Óðinn') in *Vsp* 53. If *mægðegsan wyn* were ever imagined as these Icelandic kennings are, then it is possible that the poet of *Maxims* portrays the sea as a rapacious female being.

In this light, OE *mægðegsan wyn* would resemble Rán, an Icelandic sea-goddess. *Rán* the goddess is declined as a feminine noun; her abstract perspective *rán* ('robbery') is neuter. Rán and her husband *Ægir* ('water-man', cognate with OE *æg-*) are described holding parties for the Æsir and, on a regular basis, for drowned sailors under the sea. At such a party the Æsir admit that Rán 'owned the net with which she fished in all men who went down at sea'.[66] In *Eyrbyggja saga* the brother-in-law of Snorri goði drowns with his crew before Yuletide and yet comes home, dead and waterlogged, into his own party. People welcome the apparition, believing 'that if men drowned at sea visited their own funeral feast, they must have received a good welcome at Rán's place'.[67] In keeping with her name, therefore, it is Rán, rather than Ægir, who is believed to gather in drowned men. This is borne out in the image of a ship, in the probably eleventh-century *Helgakviða Hundingsbana* I, as a 'beast of roaring waters' (*giálfrdýr*) that 'twists violently out of the hands of Rán' (*snøriz ramliga Rán ór hendi*, HHund I. 30). Helgi Hjǫrvarðsson, hero of another poem which is datable to the eleventh century, taunts a giantess by saying that she lay in wait at the mouth of the fjord, ready to drown his ship along with 'the prince's soldiers that you would give to Rán' (*ræsis recca er þú vildir Rán gefa*, HHj 18). Though the instances of Rán so far cited probably date to the Christian period, Rán plays a major role in the pre-Christian elegy *Sonatorrek* (c. 960), in which the poet, Egill Skalla-

---

[65] *Skj* B I, 2.
[66] *SnE* 338 (ch. 33): 'átti net, þat er hon veiddi í menn alla þá er á sæ kómu'; *FJSnE* 121.
[67] *Eyrbyggja saga*, ed. Einar Ólafur Sveinsson and Matthías Þórðarson, ÍF 4 (Reykjavík, 1935), p. 148 (ch. 54): 'at þá væri mǫnnum vel fagnat at Ránar, ef sædauðir menn vitjuðu erfis síns'.

Ingui's marriage

Grímsson, appears to blame her and other Icelandic sea *numina* for the drowning of his son:

> Grimmt vǫrum hlið,   þats hrǫnn of braut
> fǫðurs míns   á frændgarði;
> veitk ófullt   ok opit standa
> sonar skarð,   es mér sær of vann.
>
> Mjǫk hefr *Rán*   ryskt um mik,
> emk ofsnauðr   at ástvinum;
> sleit *marr* bǫnd minnar ættar,
> [snaran] þǫtt   af sjǫlfum mér.
>
> Veizt, ef þá sǫk sverði of rækak,
> vas *ǫlsmíð*[r]   allra tíma;
> *hroða vágs brœðr* ef vega mættak,
> fórk andvígr   ok *Ægis mani*.   (*Sonatorrek* 6–8)[68]

Earlier, Egill sums up his loss with the verb *ræna* ('rob') in 'mik hefr marr miklu *ræntan*' ('Ocean has *robbed* me of much', *Sonatorrek* 10). Though in stanzas 22–4 Egill appears to charge Óðinn, his patron, with the ultimate responsibility for Bǫðvarr's death, he appears to blame aspects of the sea (italicized above) including *Rán* as an activity as well as a being. In his view of the sea as the robber of his son, Egill alternates between describing the sea as a person and as a phenomenon. A late Anglo-Saxon reflex of a figure such as Rán is possibly to be seen in OE *mægðegsa* in the Exeter Book *Maxims*; on the other hand, it is not possible to judge the nature of the sea *numen* in whose honour the kenning OE *garsecg* may have been coined.

OE geofon

In this section I shall suggest that OE *geofon*, cognate with the *Gabiae* on Germanic votary inscriptions and the Icelandic goddesses *Gefjun* and

---

[68] *Egils saga*, ed. Sigurður, pp. 246–56: '[6] Cruel to me was the gap that *Wave* broke in my father's family enclosure; I know it stands open and unfilled, the son's breach which *Sea* has made for me. [7] *Robbery* has shaken me hugely, I am too much stripped of loving friends; *Ocean* cut the bonds of my family, the [strong] strand of me myself. [8] You know that if I could avenge this injury with a sword, *Ale-brewer's* days would be over; if I could fight *Wave-pusher's brothers*, I would go against them and *Ægir's sweetheart*.' On the genre of Egill's poem, see North, 'Pagan Inheritance of Egill's *Sonatorrek*', pp. 147–67; and *Pagan Words*, pp. 39–62, esp. 56–60.

Gefn, denotes the phenomenal perspective of an Anglo-Saxon sea *numen*. Simplex *geofon* ('sea') occurs twenty times in Old English poetry and twice in compounds: *geofonflodas* ('floods of ocean'), which are said to obey God's commands in the Prayer of Azariah (*Azarias* 125); and *geofonhus*, Noah's 'sea-house' or Ark (*Gen* 1321). The grammatical gender of *geofon* appears to be either masculine or neuter. *Geofones stream* denotes the ocean twice in the Vercelli Book (*El* 1200 and *And* 852), and elsewhere *geofenes begang* (*Beo* 362) and *geofones gong* (*Phoen* 118) mean the 'compass of the sea'. *Geofones stæð* ('sea's shore') occurs twice (*Ex* 581 and *El* 227). With the words *geofon geotende* ('cascading sea') the poet of *Beowulf* alludes to the Flood (*Beo* 1690) and the poet of *Andreas* describes a sea both in its normal state (*And* 393) and as it drowns Mermedonians (*And* 1508). The sea wells up with waves (*geofon yþum weol*, *Beo* 515), recedes at St Andrew's command (*geofon swaðrode*, *And* 1585), and is covered with foam (*gifen bið gewreged, fam gewealcen*, *Riddles* 2.34). The Mermedonians in *Andreas* die *on geofone* (*And* 1531 and 1615), but later Andrew revives 'those whom the sea had killed earlier' (*þa ær geofon cwealde*, *And* 1624). Andrew's boat 'glides on the sea' (*glideð on geofone*, *And* 498). The sea can be made cruel in *geofon on grimmum sælum* (*Max I* I, 51); and in *geofon deaðe hweop*, it menaces an army with death (*Ex* 448). Only Christ may see the bottom of the sea, *grundas in geofene* (*Solomon and Saturn* 10). Finally, Beowulf claims that Grendel's mother will not be safe anywhere:

> ne on foldan fæðm,   ne on fyrgenholt,
> ne on gyfenes grund,   ga þær he[o] wille!   (*Beo* 1393–4)[69]

From these examples it is clear that *geofon* describes all aspects of the ocean, sometimes as if the ocean is a living creature.

OE *geofon* appears to be related to the stem of OE *giefan* ('to give');[70] just as OIce *Gefn*, a name for the goddess Freyja, appears to be related to

---

[69] 'Neither in earth's embrace, nor in mountain woods, nor on the ground-bed of ocean, go where she will!'

[70] OS *geban* (*Heliand* 2936 and 4315) is useful for reconstructing the morphological development of OE *geofon* ('sea'). OE **gefon*, with weakening of the final unstressed vowel, would become **gefen*; then after West Saxon palatal diphthongization, **giefen*, a word which was written as monophthongized *gifen* or lWS *gyfen* (cf. *gyfen*, 'given', varying *giefen*); where the back vowel in the second syllable stayed longer, as in OS *geban* and eWS **gefon*, back mutation of *e* in the first syllable produced *geofon* (later *geofen*). Cf. E. Sievers, *An Old English Grammar*, trans. A. S. Cook, 3rd ed. (London, 1903), p. 67 (§104.2).

OIce *gefa* ('to give');⁷¹ in addition, OIce *Gefjun* derives (with *i*-mutation) from *gabi- plus an *-on/-un* suffix which is used to denote a feminine abstract derived from a verb: *Gefjun* is thus the gerund of *gefja ('to give'). Where the *gabi-stem is concerned, second- and third-century Roman inscriptions yield a group of *matronae* ('mothers'), ten times called *Gabiae* ('givers'), two examples being apposed to *Iunones* ('Junos') in the dative; the *Deae Garmangabi* ('?colossal-giving goddesses') once; and once, the *matronae Alagabiae* ('all-giving mothers'), also in the dative.⁷² In *Friagabi* (?'love-givers') this stem appears just once, in an inscription at Housesteads on Hadrian's wall, with a prefix ancestral to the name *Frigg* and the sexual role of Freyja.⁷³ All these forms – OE *geofon* and OIce *Gefjun* and *Gefn* – seem to have developed from *numina* such as the old Germanic *gabiae* ('givers').

Jakob Grimm was probably the first to suggest a connection between OE *geofon* and OIce *Gefjun*, but he did not go into the morphology of these words.⁷⁴ Nor did the other scholars who proposed or rejected a link between OE *geofon* and OIce *Gefjun*.⁷⁵ However, R. E. Zachrisson, who listed ten English river-names descended from OE *Gifel* ('Yeovil', cognate with OIce *gjǫfull*, 'giving'), adduced Danish and Swedish placename evidence (*Gevninge* in Denmark and lake *Gävjan* in Sweden) and related all these names not only to OE *geofon* and *Gifel* but also to OIce *Gefjun* and *Gefn*: 'The fact that the name of Gefion is etymologically related, or very nearly so, with numerous words used to denote the sea, lakes, rivers,

---

[71] A. M. Sturtevant, 'Regarding the Old Norse Name Gefjun', *Scandinavian Studies* 24 (1952), 166–7.

[72] Gutenbrunner, *Götternamen*, pp. 202 (*Alagabiae*) and 213–14 (*Gabiae* and *Garmangabi*); also in A. Riese, *Das Rheinische Germanien in den antiken Inschriften*, 2 vols. (Leipzig, 1892–1914) II, 325 and 329.

[73] Gutenbrunner, *Götternamen*, p. 213; see *AR* II, 316–17 (§540): 'die huldreich gebende' (*Fria-gabi*).

[74] J. Grimm, *Deutsche Mythologie*, 4th ed., 3 vols. (Berlin, 1876) II, 735–6.

[75] W. Müller ('Gefjon', *ZfdA* 1 (1841), 95–6) and Philippson (*Germanisches Heidentum*, pp. 124 n. and 179) were in favour of a connection. Other scholars were against one: S. Bugge, 'Etymologische Studien über germanische Lautverschiebung', *BGdSL* 12 (1887), 399–430, esp. 417–18; Jente, *Die mythologischen Ausdrücke*, pp. 111–12; and de Vries, *ANEW* 160 (*Gefjon*). A. Kock presupposed that the chaste goddess *Gefion* developed her name from OIce *geð-fión (literally 'lust-hate'): see 'Zum altnordischen Sprachschatz', *ZfdA* 40 (1896), 196–206, esp. 196–7.

or islands seems also to support Grimm's theory that she was a sea-goddess.'[76]

Does OE *geofon* also derive from a sea *numen*? The personification of this word in the above instances and in particular the alliterative collocations *grundas in geofene* (*Sat* 10) and *gyfenes grund* (*Beo* 1394) are reminiscent of Snorri's story of *Gefjun* in both *Gylfaginning* (ch. 1) and *Ynglinga saga* (ch. 5). In this story, the Norse goddess Gefjun receives plough-land from King Gylfi of Sweden as a reward for entertaining him, changes her four sons into oxen, yokes them into a plough-team and then drags the earth out of Mälar in Sweden and settles it down as the Danish island of Zealand: 'there Gefjun put the land' (*þar setti Gefjun landit*).[77] This tale appears to personify longshore drift, a natural phenomenon whereby the sea erodes earth from one shore, to deposit it, as silt, on another. Snorri quotes a stanza from Bragi's mid ninth-century *Ragnarsdrápa*, his source in both prose contexts:

> *Gefjun dró frá Gylfa*   glǫð djúprǫðul óðla,
> svát af rennirauknum   rauk, Danmarkar auka.
> Báru øxn ok átta   ennitungl, þars gingu
> fyr vineyjar viðri   vallrauf, fjǫgur haufuð. (*Ragnarsdrápa* 13)[78]

Both names, *Gylfi* and *Gefjun*, may be linked to natural phenomena. Gylfi cedes his kingdom to Óðinn in *Ynglinga saga* (ch. 5), and he is said to be the fourth son of Hálfdanr Gamli later in *Skáldskaparmál*.[79] Yet Gylfi is

---

[76] R. E. Zachrisson, 'Topographical Names Containing Primitive Germanic *geb-*', *NoB* 14 (1926), 51–64, esp. 63.

[77] *Gylf*, p. 7 (ch. 1). On Gefjun, see also Tolley, 'Germanic and Finnic Myths', pp. 119–21.

[78] *Skj* B I, 3, 13; also *Gylf*, p. 7 (ch. 1); my text is from *Heimskringla I*, ed. Bjarni, p. 15 (*Ynglinga saga*, ch. 5): 'Gefjun drew, gleaming, *from Gylfi* the deep-sea sun [jewel] of his estates, to the increase of Denmark, in such a way that steam came from her driven beasts. The oxen bore eight forehead moons [eyes] and four heads, when they trod ahead of her broad seawall-/choice-battle-spoil of a grassy island.' My reading *óðla* ('estates') for MS *aupla* is in keeping with A. Holtsmark, *Studier i norrøn diktning* (Oslo, 1956), pp. 164–8 and *Studier i Snorres Mytologi* (Oslo, 1964), pp. 69–71; and with Frank, *Old Norse Court Poetry*, pp. 103–8. For an interpretation of this stanza based on Gefjun as a ritual prostitute, see V. Kiil, 'Gevjonmyten og *Ragnarsdråpa*', *MoM* (1965), 63–70.

[79] *SnE* 516 (ch. 64); *FJSnE* 181. On Snorri's use of this poem, see M. Clunies Ross, 'The Myth of Gefjun and Gylfi and its Function in *Snorra Edda* and *Heimskringla*', *ANF* 93 (1978), 149–65.

also a 'sea-king' (*sækonungr*) in the *Þulur*;[80] and the kenning 'estates of Gylfi' (*Gylfa grundar*) denotes the sea in the twelfth-century *Placítúsdrápa*, as do 'fields of Gylfi' (*Gylfa láð*) in a thirteenth-century *lausavísa*.[81] The sea-kenning 'current of Gylfi' (*Gylfa rǫst*) of an eleventh-century verse of Þórðr Særeksson better resembles Old English collocations with *-stream* (mostly *eagorstream*).[82] OIce *Gylfi* is formally related to *gjálfr* ('roar, swell'). Gylfi's name suggests that he rules the sea and is the sea. *Gefjun*, in this case, appears to lift up a clod of Swedish earth from *Gylfi* which she then gives to the Danes.

Otherwise both OE *geofon* and OIce *Gefjun* connote the sea in its harsh aspect. As we have seen, OE *geofon* drowns Noah's contemporaries (*Beo* 1690) and St Andrew's enemies (*And* 1508), wells up with rage (*Beo* 515), kills Mermedonians (*And* 1624) and threatens and kills Egyptians (*Ex* 448). Yet the most fully developed example occurs in *Maxims I*, in which, having said that a man must govern his *strongan mode* ('unruly heart'), the poet depicts the human mind as a rough sea:

> Storm oft holm gebringeþ,
> *geofen in grimmum sælum*; onginnað grome fundian
> fealwe on feorran to londe, hwæþer he fæste stonde.
> Weallas him wiþre healdað, him biþ wind gemæne.
>
> (*Max I* I, 50–3)[83]

Thereafter the calm sea is compared with warring nations which have agreed to peace after negotiation.

These Old English lines may be compared with a verse-sequence in *Lokasenna* in which, first of all, Loki insults Gefjun following her attempt to pacify him in the growing row that he is causing in Ægir's doomed party:

> Þegi þú, Gefion! þess mun ec nú geta,
>   er þic glapþi at geði:
> sveinn inn hvíti, er þér sigli gaf,
>   oc þú lagðir lær yfir.   (*Lok* 20)[84]

---

[80] *Skj* B I, 658, IV, 1.   [81] *Ibid.* I, 615, 35; II, 47, 4.

[82] *Ibid.* I, 303, 1; cf. Tindr Hallkelsson's tenth-century *Roða rǫst* ('current of Roði', 'sea-king'), in *ibid.* I, 136, 1.

[83] 'A storm often produces an ocean, *a sea in cruel moods*; the angry, tawny ones begin from far out to hasten to land, and yet he stands fast. Walls keep them back, the wind is shared by both of them.'

[84] 'Be quiet, Gefjun! I'll mention that man now, the one who fooled you in your affections: that white boy who gave you a jewel, and you laid your thigh over his.'

Heathen gods

A small digression is necessary to make the mythological meaning of this stanza clear, before we proceed to examine the phrase *Gefion at gremi* in *Lok* 21 which so obviously resembles *geofen in grimmum sælum* in *Max I* I, 51. Firstly, in *Lok* 20 the words *sveinn inn hvíti* ('that white boy') probably describe the Norse god Heimdallr, who is named as *hvíti Áss* ('the white god') in *Gylfaginning* (ch. 27) and *hvítastr Ása* ('whitest of the gods') in *Þrym* 15. This colour in *Lok* 20 may particularly refer to the arctic seal, in whose shape, in another poem, Heimdallr wrestles with Loki for possession of a jewel.[85] This story is presented in *Húsdrápa* 2, which I have quoted and discussed in the previous chapter.[86] In *Lok* 20, therefore, it is possible that Loki is referring to a story in which Heimdallr, having wrested from him a jewel of some kind in an underwater struggle, gave it to Gefjun (identifiable here with Freyja as Gefn) in exchange for sex. The force of this insult of Loki's may be judged in the next stanza, in Óðinn's warning to Loki not to anger Gefjun:

> Œrr ertu, Loki, oc ørviti,
> er þú fær þér *Gefion at gremi*. (*Lok* 21)[87]

In these cryptic lines, it is possible to see Gefjun portrayed rather as the *geofen in grimmum sælum* ('sea in cruel moods') in *Max I* I, 51: that is, as the personified sea in the midst of a storm. Both OE *geofon* and *Gefjun–Gefn* may thus descend from *gabia*, a Germanic sea *numen* whose name denoted 'giving'.

SKY *NUMINA*

Having finished with sea *numina*, we may proceed to sky *numina*, of which there are several surviving reflexes in Old English literature. In this section I shall use Norse and other cognates to discuss the Old English names *Eostre* ('Easter'), *eorendel* ('morning star'), *Tiu/Tig*, *þunor* ('thunder') and *wuldor* ('glory').

---

[85] The *seolh ofer sæs hrycg* ('seal over the sea's back') in *The Nine Herbs Charm* (*MCharm* 2.26), which sends the crab-apple as a cure for poison, may represent an allusion to this story: *Lacnunga*, ed. and trans. Grattan and Singer, pp. 151–5.

[86] *Skj* B I, 128. On Heimdallr, cf. Pipping, 'Eddastudier I', pp. 7–52, and 'Eddastudier II', pp. 120–30.

[87] 'You are mad and out of your wits, Loki, to bring *Gefjun into a rage* against you.'

Ingui's marriage

Bernician Eostre

In his *De temporum ratione*, Bede throws some light on spring festivals in pre-Christian Northumbria:

*Rhed*monath a dea illorum *Rheda*, cui in illo sacrificabant, nominatur; *Eostur*monath, qui nunc paschalis mensis interpretatur, quondam a dea illorum quae *Eostre* vocabatur, et cui in illo festa celebrabant, nomen habuit, a cuius nomine nunc paschale tempus cognominant, consueto antiquae observationis vocabulo gaudia novae solemnitatis vocantes.[88]

Unusually, Bede cites the names of heathen gods in this passage – Rheda and Eostre – and refers to Anglian heathen festivals which were celebrated in April. It is worth noting that Rheda and Eostre do not have Norse counterparts. However, Bede may have known some details of the pre-Christian religion in Northumbria, for the *modranect* ('night of the mothers', 25 December) cited by Bede earlier in the same chapter appears to be a genuine reflex of the *matres* or *matronae* that were worshipped by Germanic auxiliaries in the Roman empire.[89] *Rheda* and *Eostre* could thus have reflected the names of Anglian *matres* that were worshipped in March and April respectively.[90]

The etymology of *Rheda* is not clear, for *rede*, as 'March', apparently means 'fierce' in the Old English *Metrical Calendar*.[91] However, this later sense probably came about in association with *Mars*; as 'triumph', OE *hreð* in *Rheda* suggests either the time following the spring equinox at which day becomes longer than night, or the return of vegetation after winter. The word *Eostre* is cognate with OE *east* from whence Ing comes in *The Old English Rune Poem*:

---

[88] *Bedae Opera de Temporibus*, ed. Jones, pp. 211–13, esp. 212 (*De mensis Anglorum*, ch. 15): '*Rhed*-month is named after a goddess of theirs called *Rheda* to whom they used to sacrifice in that month; *Eostur*-month, which is now understood as the paschal month, formerly got its name from a goddess of theirs whom they used to call *Eostre* and in whose honour they used to celebrate festivals in that month, by whose name they now recognize the passover, thus naming the joys of a new ceremony with the customary title of an old observance.' See also Wilson, *Anglo-Saxon Paganism*, pp. 35–6.

[89] *Bedae Opera de Temporibus*, ed. Jones, p. 212; on *matres*, see Gutenbrunner, *Götternamen*, pp. 116–34.

[90] Meaney, 'Bede and Anglo-Saxon Paganism', pp. 2–8.

[91] Page, 'The Evidence of Bede', p. 126.

Heathen gods

>[Ing] wæs ærest   mid *East*denum
>gesewen secgun,   oþ he siððan *est*
>ofer wæg gewat,   wæn æfter ran;
>þus Heardingas   ðone hæle nemdun.   (*Rune* 67–70)[92]

Here, with *Eastdenum* and MS *est*, Ing's journey starts and ends 'east' across the water, suggesting the arrival of increased sunlight after the spring equinox consistent with the months of March and April, when, as Bede implies, the Angles once celebrated *festa* and *gaudia* in honour of Eostre. With the words *gaudia novae solemnitatis*, Bede implies that Good Friday and the resurrection replaced a pagan festival.[93] In ch. 10, I shall suggest that Edwin's conversion took place amid a Deiran pagan festival at Goodmanham.

OE eorendel

Cognate with *Eostre* are the first elements of three Germanic forms: OE *eorendel*; the Norse *Aurvandill*, whose story is evidence of a connection between gods and constellations in Norse mythology; and *Orendel*, a hero whose adventures take place in the Orient, in a twelfth-century Middle High German romance of that name.[94] There are six surviving instances of OE *eorendel* (variants *oerendil*, *earendil* and *earendel*). In two of these instances, *eorendel* glosses Lat *aurora* ('dawn'); in two more, Lat *iubar* ('radiance').[95] In one more example, in *Christ* 104–7, Jesus is invoked as 'morning star, brightest of angels' (*earendel, engla beorhtast*), sent over the earth for men, as well as being the 'true sun's ray, dazzling over and above

---

[92] *Old English Rune Poem*, ed. Halsall, pp. 21–32: 'Ing was first seen among men with the *East*-Danes, until he then passed *east* over the wave; his wagon ran after him: thus the Heardings gave the man his name.'

[93] The *gaudia* of *Eostre* would have coincided approximately with the Greco-Roman *Megalensia* (after sowing on 4–10 April) and the *Cerealia* soon after. See *Fasti*, ed. Schilling II, 16 (IV.357) and 117–18 (n. 125); Henig, *Religion in Roman Britain*, p. 29; *Liber de gloria confessorum*, PL 71, 884 (ch. 77).

[94] Gillespie, *Catalogue*, s.v. 'Ernthelle' (pp. 39–40).

[95] J. Stevenson, *The Latin Hymns of the Anglo-Saxon Church*, Surtees Society 23 (Durham, 1851), 1–147: *aurora cursus provehit, aurora tota prodeat* glossed as *dægrima rynas upalymþ, eorendel eall forðstæppe* (no. 2.15.8) and *auroram totam spargit* as *eorendel eallunga geondstret* (no. 2.30.1); *Corpus Glossary*, ed. Lindsay, p. 102.521 (*Iubar: earendel*); *Épinal-Erfurt Glossary*, ed. Pheifer, pp. 30.554 (*Erf.: iuuar: leoma uel oerendil*) and 40.761 (*Ép.: iuuar: leoma uel earendil*).

Ingui's marriage

the stars' (*soðfæsta sunnan leoma, torht ofer tunglas*), whose light brightens each season. Here the poet, without an exact regard for astronomy, seems to combine both the morning star (i.e. Venus as it rises a little before the sun at certain times) and the sun's rays in the person of Jesus. In *Christ* 104, *earendel* probably denotes the 'morning star'; and in the tenth-century *Blickling Homilies*, John the Baptist at his birth is called both 'the new morning star' (*se niwa eorendel*) and 'the ray of the true sun' (*se leoma þære soþan sunnan*), in as much as he is the harbinger of Jesus.[96] In this case, *eorendel* seems to have described a planet, probably Venus, preparing the way for the sun.[97]

Some astronomical significance survives in Aurvandill, a Norse cognate of OE *eorendel*. The tale of Aurvandill, which appears in Snorri's epilogue to his summary of Þórr's duel with the giant Hrungnir in *Skáldskaparmál*, does not appear in Þjóðólfr's late ninth-century *Haustlǫng*, the source that Snorri quotes for his summary. In this tale Þórr kills Hrungnir but returns home to Þrúðvangar to have a sherd from the giant's whetstone removed from his head, where it has lodged in the duel. A seeress arrives named *Gróa* ('grove'), who is the wife of Aurvandill. Gróa chants spells over Þórr until he feels the stone coming loose:

then he wanted to repay *Gróa* ('grove') for her healing and to make her glad, told her these tidings, that he had waded south across *Élivágar* ('Snow-storm-waves') and had carried Aurvandill in a basket on his back south from Giant-home, and as proof, one of his toes had been sticking out of the basket and was frozen, so that Þórr broke it off and cast it up into the heavens and made out of it the star called *Aurvandilstá* ('Aurvandill's toe'). Þórr said it would not be long before Aurvandill was home.[98]

---

[96] *The Blickling Homilies of the Tenth Century*, ed. R. Morris, EETS 73 (London, 1880), 161–9, esp. 163.30 (*The Nativity of St John the Baptist*).

[97] At other times, setting a little after the sun, Venus also counts as the evening star. Mercury is the other possible morning or evening star that at certain times rises before the sun or sets after it. See J. D. North, *The Fontana History of Astronomy and Cosmology* (London, 1994), pp. 25–8.

[98] *SnE* 276–8 (ch. 17): 'þá vildi hann launa Gró lækningina, ok gera hana fegna, sagði henni þau tíðindi, at hann hafði vaðit norðan yfir Élivága, ok hafði borit í meis á baki sér Örvandil norðan ór Jötunheimum, ok þat til jartegna, at ein tá hans hafði staðit ór meisinum, ok var sú frerin, svá at Þórr braut af, kastaði upp á himin, ok gerði af stjörnu þá, er heitir Örvandils-tá. Þórr sagði, at eigi mundi langt til, at Örvandill mundi heim koma'; *FJSnE* 104.

Gróa rejoices, forgets the spells and the stone remains in Þórr's head: hence the story. But it is worth assembling the details on which this folktale is ultimately based, for it points to an astronomical allegory of some kind in which Aurvandill may have been imagined as a constellation (such as Orion), his toe as a star (such as Rigel). Elsewhere in *Skáldskaparmál* Snorri mentions a motif similar to *Aurvandilstá* in Skaði's compensation for the death of her father Þjazi: not only did the Æsir allow her to marry one of their number, but Óðinn 'took Þjazi's eyes and threw them up into the heavens and made two stars out of them'.[99] Although OE *earendel*, stylized as St John the Baptist in the *Blickling Homilies*, appears to have been imagined as a planet, not a star or constellation, it might be inferred from the Icelandic myth of Aurvandill that OE *earendel* was personified as a heavenly body in heathen times.

OE Tiu *and* Tig

The names OE *Tiu* and OIce *Týr* survive as proof of a formal Germanic counterpart of Greek *Zeus* and the first element of Lat *Dies-pater* ('father of day').[100] A Gothic *Týz* can also be assumed from the runic letter of that name surviving in the two Gothic alphabets of the early ninth-century Vienna, Nationalbibliothek, lat. 795 (s. ix^1).[101] Týz is probably the 'Mars' whom Jordanes says to have sprung from the Goths and 'whom the Goths have always appeased with the harshest adoration (his victims were the dead bodies of captives), thinking it proper to appease a leader of wars with the out-pouring of human blood' (*Getica* V.41).[102] Although the name of OE *Tiu*, OIce *Týr* and Got *Týz* probably means 'daylight', this

---

[99] *SnE* 214 (*Bragarœður*, ch. 56): 'tók augu Þjaza; ok kastaði upp á himin, ok gerði af stjörnur ii'; *FJSnE* 81. Compare Hermes throwing up the eyes of Argus to make them into stars.

[100] Kretschmer, 'Dyans, Ζεύς, Diespiter und die Abstrakta im Indogermanischen', *Glotta* 13 (1924), 101–13.

[101] See Unterkircher, *Alkuin-Briefe*, pp. 19–21.

[102] *Getica*, ed. Mommsen I, 64: 'quem Martem Gothi semper asperrima placavere cultura (nam victimae eius mortes fuere captorum), opinantes bellorum praesulem apte humani sanguinis effusione placandum'. The fact that these captives were sacrificed is not sufficient reason, in my view, to take Jordanes's Mars as a reference to a Gothic Wodan, for which, as Helm has made clear (*Wodan*, pp. 45–7), there is no evidence.

Ingui's marriage

god appears to have been identified with Mars rather than *Jupiter* in other ancient Germanic *Tuesday* calques of Lat *Martis dies*.[103]

In England there is a possibility, which I shall argue below, that OIce *Týr* was understood in *The Old English Rune Poem*. *Tig*, an unadulterated Anglo-Saxon form, stands for Mars in the story of Sextus in *The Old English Martyrology*: 'þone Syxtum nedde Decius se casere Tiges deofolgilde'.[104] This figure is probably represented in numerous *T*-runes, all but one in Kent, on weapons and other burial artefacts; and in particular, in two runic inscriptions with *TIU*: one stamped onto three urns in the fifth-century cemetery at Spong Hill; and the other apparently in bindrune minuscule on a seventh-century spearblade in Holborough, Kent.[105] In addition, the name *Tiu* survives in Old English glosses;[106] and in four placenames: Tysoe (Warwickshire), *Tislea* (Hampshire) and *Tyesmere* (Worcester) and possibly in *Tuesnoad* (Kent).[107]

Little is known of the Norse Týr except what Snorri tells us in *Gylfaginning*, in a tale in which Týr places his hand in the young Fenriswolf's mouth as a forfeit, should the Æsir break their oath to the wolf and chain his paws; the Æsir do so and Týr loses his hand.[108] Snorri also presents Týr as the boldest and bravest of the Æsir, the patron of warriors in battle, while in *Lokasenna*, Loki seems to taunt the one-armed Týr by saying that he could never keep two fighting men apart.[109] In Old Norse–Icelandic poetry *Týr* occurs twenty-one times as the base element in kennings for 'man' and sometimes for 'god'.[110] In an anglicized form,

---

[103] WFris *tiisdei*, Ger *dienstag*, Du *dinsdag*, Dan, Norw and Sw *tisdag*; ModIce *þriðjudagur* ('third day') is an ecclesiastical innovation of the eleventh century.

[104] *Das altenglische Martyrologium*, ed. G. Kotzor, Abhandlungen der Bayerischen Akademie der Wissenschaften, philosophisch-historische Klasse, n.s. 88, 2 vols. (Munich, 1981) II, 172 (lines 8–9): 'the emperor Decius constrained Sixtus to the idolatry of Tig'.

[105] Wilson, *Anglo-Saxon Paganism*, pp. 115–17 and 146–50.

[106] *Corpus Glossary*, ed. Lindsay, p. 111.49 (*mars martis: tiig*); *Épinal-Erfurt Glossary*, ed. Pheifer, p. 35.663 (*Ép.Erf.: mars martis: tiig*).

[107] Tysoe appears to mean 'Tig's spur of land': see Gelling, *Signposts to the Past*, p. 161; see also Wilson, *Anglo-Saxon Paganism*, p. 13. Týr's name survives in Iceland only in *Týrsengi*, probably formed after the conversion, near Snæfellsnes: see Svavar, 'Átrúnaðr og örnefni', p. 244.

[108] *Gylf*, pp. 28–9 (ch. 34).

[109] Perhaps because he has only one hand with which to do so: see M.-E. Ruggerini, *Le invettive di Loki* (Rome, 1979), p. 64.

[110] Meissner, *Kenningar der Skalden*, p. 262 (§88).

the Norse *Týr* is probably to be found in *The Old English Rune Poem*, in which the poet says, for the *T*-rune:

> [Tir] biþ tacna sum;   healdeð trywa wel
> wiþ æþelingas;   a biþ on færylde
> ofer nihta genipu;   næfre swiceþ. (*Rune* 48–50, sect. xvii)[111]

In this verse a tenth-century English poet could have neutralized Týr, a heathen god, by identifying him with a planet such as Mars;[112] although, with *trywa* and *æþelingas*, he may have kept Týr's role as a patron of warriors. The evidence suggests that, although an indigenous Anglo-Saxon Tiu probably died out in the seventh century, a Scandinavian Týr was brought by the Danes into England in the ninth or tenth century.

OE þunor *and* Thunor

Tiu and OE *þunor* are both found in theophoric placenames with the suffix *-leah* ('grove') in fields and clearings in Saxon and Jutish areas of England (see below). In this respect it is interesting that Týr and Þórr, the Icelandic cognates of Tiu and *þunor*, are presented as friends in *Hymiskviða*, a poem probably composed in Iceland in the early eleventh century. In this poem Ægir refuses to serve the gods with beer until Þórr, the god who has just insulted him, brings him a cauldron big enough for all. No god can offer Þórr such a kettle:

> unz af trygðom   Týr Hlórriða
> ástráð mikit   einom sagði:
>
> 'Býr fyr austan   Élivága
> hundvíss Hymir,   at himins enda;'
> (*Hym* 4/5–8 and 5/1–4)[113]

Hymir is Týr's father and has a cauldron miles deep. Although there is no other reference to Týr's descent from giants in the Old Icelandic corpus,

---

[111] '"Tir", "fame/Týr", is a distinguished sign; keeps pledges well with princes; is always on course over the clouds of night; never betrays you.' For the text, see *Old English Rune Poem*, ed. Halsall, p. 90.

[112] See *ibid.*, pp. 135–7.

[113] 'Until from the pledges [he had made] Týr said a great piece of loving counsel to Hlórriði [Þórr] alone: "East of Snow-storm waves there dwells the dog-clever Hymir, at heaven's end."'

Ingui's marriage

this detail about Týr in *Hymiskviða* resembles the fact that *Zeus*, the Greek cognate of *Týr*, was said to be the son of a titan (Cronos) in Greek mythology. Týr's role in *Hymiskviða* is to guide Þórr to Hymir, then to accompany him home when Þórr's contests with the giant are over. His relationship with Þórr, in the 'pledges' and 'love' that he has for Þórr 'alone', is more intriguing, where their connection may derive from that of 'light' and 'thunder', two phenomena of the sky. Several details in the lines above and elsewhere in *Hymiskviða* suggest a cosmology of sorts, with Hymir at the end of heaven 'east' of the Milky Way; and Týr's grandmother perhaps part of the galaxy with a mass of stars as her 'nine hundred heads' (*hǫfða hundruð níu*, Hym 8). To cover the distance in one day, furthermore, Þórr must drive out of Ásgarðr in his goat-drawn chariot, with Týr inside. It is possible that the association of *Tiu* and *þunor* in English-*leah* placenames reflects a comparable association of sky *numina* in Anglo-Saxon England.

Forest clearings were apparently named in association with 'thunder' in the early seventh century in at least nine places in Saxon and Jutish England: Thunderfield (Surrey), Thunderley (Essex), Thundersley (Essex), *Thunorslege* (Sussex), *Thunreslau* (Essex), *Thunresfeld* (Wiltshire), *Thunreslea* (Hampshire; two examples), *Thunoreshlæw* (Thanet in Kent), and perhaps also Thurstable (Essex).[114] Gelling's view is that in England Tiu, *þunor* and the Woden placenames are found outside centres of population and that they probably survived because each was in a no-man's land where the missionaries could not easily reach them.[115] It is worth noting that all these names lie outside Anglian regions of the country.

Although no *þunor* placenames are recorded in Anglian territory, there is some limited evidence that Angles celebrated their own thunder *numen*. The swastikas on carpet pages in the Durrow and Lindisfarne Gospels may have been derived from symbols associated with a god of

---

[114] Gelling, *Signposts to the Past*, p. 161; Wilson, *Anglo-Saxon Paganism*, pp. 11–12. Þórr's connection with house-pillars, with *þunres stapol, a form taken to underlie the modern name Thurstable, is discussed by Turville-Petre in 'Thurstable', in *Nine Norse Studies*, pp. 20–9; *Þóris stapol, a hybrid form proposed by L. Bronnenkant, in 'Thurstable Revisited', *Journal of the English Place Name Society* 15 (1983), 9–19, is somewhat less likely, in that *stapol*, its older second element, is unlikely to have been a functional term at the time of any (presumably eleventh-century) Danish settlement in Essex.

[115] Gelling, *Signposts to the Past*, p. 159.

Heathen gods

thunder, for this interpretation has been made of the swastika-symbols found on artefacts in sixth- and seventh-century graves in Yorkshire, and in Kent, in which the placename *Thunoreshlæw* ('thunder's barrow') appears to reveal an association between graves and a thunder *numen*.[116] Secondly, Jacqueline Simpson has suggested that the whetstone on the Sutton Hoo sceptre hints at a myth analogous to Þórr and Hrungnir's whetstone.[117] In combination, and by analogy with the Norse cults of Ingvi-freyr and Þórr respectively, the stag and whetstone on this sceptre could show that the ruler buried or commemorated at Sutton Hoo, probably Anglian, divided his attention between his ancestors on one hand and the common people on the other.[118] However, since no imported Þórr placename survives from Anglian territory in Danish or hybrid Anglo-Danish form, it seems that the Angles had no *þunor* sites on which predominantly Þórr's name could be imposed. Although the Angles could probably personify the phenomenon of thunder, this distribution of the evidence suggests that the Angles, in contrast to the Saxons and Jutes in southern Britain, did not reserve groves or fields specifically for *þunor*.

The Corpus Glossary uses *ðuner* to translate Jupiter, a personified Roman god equivalent in power to the Norse god Þórr;[119] while the evidence of other glosses and of passages in the works of Ælfric and Wulfstan suggests that Þórr was worshipped in the Danelaw as a god equal to Jupiter.[120] A thunder-god had probably been worshipped in Germany three centuries earlier, where two *vitae* of St Boniface show the bishop and future martyr in *c.* 723–34 attempting to cut down an oak in Gaesmere, Hesse, a tree which the pagans of that area had called 'the oak of Jove' (*robor Iobis*).[121] Ælfric in his *De falsis diis* states that Jove or Jupiter was the son of Saturn, and then proceeds to give him Þórr's name as that of a contemporary Danish incarnation:

---

[116] Wilson, *Anglo-Saxon Paganism*, pp. 115, 118–19 and 142–4.
[117] Simpson, 'The King's Whetstone', pp. 96–101.
[118] Webster and Backhouse, *The Making of England*, p. 33 (no. 17).
[119] *Corpus Glossary*, ed. Lindsay, p. 101.479 (*Iovem: ðuner*).
[120] See the entry in the 'First Cleopatra Glossary', in *Vocabularies*, ed. Wright and Wülcker, p. 425.36 (*Ioppiter: þunor, oððe ður*); see also the 'Third Cleopatra Glossary', in *ibid.*, pp. 526.20 (*Ioppiter: þunor*) and 437.16 (*Latona: þures modor*). Cf. *Latona* with OIce *Hlǫðyn* ('earth' = Þórr's mother).
[121] *Vitae S. Bonifatii*, ed. Levison, pp. 31 (of Willibald) and 135 (of Otlohus).

Ingui's marriage

> Þes Iouis is arwurðast ealra þæra goda
> þe þa hæþenan hæfdon on heora gedwylde;
> and he hatte Þór betwux sumum þeodum,
> þone þa Deniscan leoda lufiað swiðost.[122]

Ælfric refrains from connecting Þórr with OE *þunor* in this passage, just as we have seen him omitting to identify *Oðon* with Woden, although he reveals his knowledge of Þor's relationship to Oðon:

> Nu secgað þa Deniscan on heora gedwylde
> þæt se Iouis wære, þe hi Þór hatað,
> Mercuries sunu, þe hi Oðon hatað.[123]

Ælfric proceeds to treat the Danish belief that Þor is Oðon's son as proof that Danish paganism is inauthentic, because Latin books say that Saturn, not Mercury, was the father of Jupiter. Wulfstan adapted this text of Ælfric in his own early eleventh-century homily *De falsis deis*.[124] Ælfric also alluded to Þor in his description of Jupiter as one of the forms in which the devil appeared to St Martin of Tours in his cell.[125] Both Ælfric and Wulfstan show the Norse god Þórr to be fully personified and at the top of his pantheon. Yet there is no evidence that OE *þunor* had the same status in England before the Viking Age.

A sketch of Þórr is necessary before we proceed to three further instances of OE *þunor* in OE *þunorrad*, in *Thunor* of Kent (a legendary figure associated with *Thunoreshlæw*) and in the phrase *se ðunor mid ðære fyrenan æcxe*. Þórr is the son of Óðinn by the earth, the husband of *Sif* ('family'), whose son by a different father is *Ullr* ('brilliance').[126] Forms of

---

[122] *Homilies of Ælfric*, ed. Pope II, 683 (lines 122–5): 'This Jove is the most honoured of all the gods that the heathens had in their folly; and among some nations he was called "Þór", whom the Danish people love the most.'

[123] *Ibid.* (lines 141–4): 'Now the Danish people say in their folly that this Jove, whom they call "Þór", was the son of Mercury, whom they call "Óðon".'

[124] *Homilies of Wulfstan*, ed. Bethurum, pp. 221–4 (XII).

[125] *Ælfric's Lives of Saints*, ed. Skeat II, 218–313 (XXXI.xxiv), esp. 265 (lines 713–19).

[126] OE *sib* ('family') is cognate with OIce *Sif* and *sif*. Unusually, a personification of OE *sib* is twice evident in *Beowulf*, in *Beo* 2016–18 and 2599–661. In the first case, Beowulf recalls Wealhþeow carrying out her duties in the feast at Heorot: 'Hwilum mæru cwen, friðusibb folca flet eall geondhwearf, bædde [MS] byre geonge' ('At times a queen renowned, contract-*Peace* of the nations, moved through the hall, urged on the young boys'); in the second, when Beowulf needs help against the dragon, his retinue flees to the woods, all of them but Wiglaf: 'Hiora in anum weoll sefa wið

Heathen gods

Þórr ('thunder') appear in a great variety of Norse placenames, personal names and literary references in Norway and Iceland throughout the Viking Age. No ancient kings claimed descent from Þórr, and judging by his popularity in Icelandic placenames as against the absence of Óðinn there, in particular, it is likely that Þórr was a god mostly for men and women of republican politics. None the less, even kings and earls celebrated Þórr in the last centuries of pre-Christian religion.[127] In *c.* 1076 Adam of Bremen described him as one of three deities in the temple at Uppsala, the others being Wodan and Fricco: 'so Thor, as the most powerful of them, has a chair in the middle of their dining hall'.[128] Earlier in his book Adam had said that an English preacher named Wulfred in 1030 'began to profane an idol of the people named Thor which stood in the assembly of the heathens', whereupon he was lynched by the crowd.[129] Without doubt Þórr was the most popular god of the Viking Age, even if the aristocratic preoccupation with Óðinn, reflected disproportionately in the Eddic and Scaldic court-poetry that has survived, made Þórr the butt of satire: 'Óðinn gets the earls, those who fall in battle, while Þórr gets the race of thralls.'[130] Yet Adam of Bremen shows what Snorri and his poetic sources do not, that Þórr was the pre-eminent Norse god and had a wide range of functions: 'Thor', Adam's informant told him, 'watches over us in the sky and governs thunder and lightning, winds and showers, fair weather and the fruits of the earth.'[131] Representing worship rather than artistic licence, in this way, Adam's account of winds and storms is more faithful to the meaning of *Þórr* than the stylization of most

sorgum; *sibb'* æfre ne mæg wiht onwendan þam þe wel þenceð' ('In one of them the mind welled up with sorrows: for the man who thinks according to what is proper, *Family* cannot be turned away'). The first instance recalls the Norse Sif as she serves beer in the hall of Ásgarðr (*SnE* 270 (ch. 17); *FJSnE* 101). In the second, the poet of *Beowulf* seems to conceive of *sibb* as a person making active demands on the young Wiglaf. Both instances may indicate that the poet of *Beowulf* was in a position to imagine sixth-century Scandinavia on the basis of his knowledge of contemporary Danish legends.

[127] See McKinnell, *Both One and Many*, p. 74.
[128] *Gesta*, ed. Schmeidler, p. 258 (IV.26): 'ita ut potentissimus eorum Thor in medio solium habeat triclinio'.
[129] *Ibid.*, p. 122 (II.62): 'ydolum gentis nomine Thor in concilio paganorum cepit anathematizare'.
[130] 'Óðinn á iarla, þá er í val falla, enn Þórr á þræla kyn' (*Hárb* 24).
[131] *Gesta*, ed. Schmeidler, p. 258: 'Thor presidet in aere, qui tonitrus et fulmina, ventos ymbresque, serena et fruges gubernat.'

Ingui's marriage

surviving vernacular references, in which Þórr defends the Æsir and mankind against the giants with iron gloves, a belt of strength and a throwing hammer with which he smashes their skulls. Yet even in this equipment there is a suggestion of a god hurling thunderbolts that remains consistent with the earliest Germanic loan-translation of Lat *Iovis dies* into various Germanic *Thursday* forms.[132]

If we proceed to the three further instances of OE *þunor*, firstly OE *þunorrad* may be evidence that a Saxon motif of a thunder-god in his chariot survived the Anglo-Saxon conversion as a figure of speech for 'clap of thunder'. *Þunorrad* ('thunder-riding') appears in descriptions of the Last Days in Old English homilies, but its meaning also recalls the image of Þórr driving his goat-drawn chariot across the sky, an image which appears in *Haustlǫng*, in *Hymiskviða*, in *Þrymskviða* and in Snorri's tale of Þórr and Útgarða-Loki in *Gylfaginning* (ch. 44).[133] In *Gylfaginning* Snorri describes 'driving-Þórr' (*Ǫku-Þórr*) driving his chariot to the house of Þjálfi and Rǫskva.[134] Þórr is not found in the poetry with the *Ǫku*-prefix, but with *aka* ('to drive') below, this image is at least as old as a stanza in *Haustlǫng*:

> Knáttu ǫll, en, Ullar,   endilág, fyr mági,
> grund vas grápi hrundin,   ginnunga vé brinna,
> þás hofregin hafrar   hógreiðar fram drógu
> (seðr gekk Svǫlnis ekkja   sundr) at Hrungnis fundi.
>
> (*Haustlǫng* 15)[135]

In prose word-order the penultimate line is *hafrar drógu hofregin hógreiðar fram*; MSS *hofregin* denotes Þórr as a 'temple-power' and the second

---

[132] WFris *tjongersdei*, Ger *donnerstag*, Du *donderdag*, Dan, Norw and Sw *torsdag*; but ModIce *fimmtudagur* ('fifth day').

[133] For example, three instances in the Vercelli collection: *The Vercelli Homilies and Related Texts*, ed. D. G. Scragg, EETS o.s. 300 (Oxford, 1992), 56.41 (II) and 359.190-1 (XXI) (*þunorrada cyrm*, 'the roar of thunders'); 256.84 (XV) (*bioð þonne swiðe mycele þunerrade 7 mycle ligitta*, 'there will then be great thunders and great lightning'); cf. Philippson, *Germanisches Heidentum*, pp. 136–41, esp. 137–8.

[134] *Gylf*, p. 37 (ch. 44).

[135] *Skj* B I, 17, 15: 'All the sanctuaries of falcons [skies] did burn before the kinsman of Ullr [Þórr], and yet the ground back below him was driven with hail and snow, when the goats drew the temple-power [Þórr] of the easy-riding-chariot forward to his meeting with Hrungnir, at the same time the widow of Svǫlnir [Óðinn's widow: earth] split in two.'

element of 'hóg-reið' as 'easy- *riding-chariot*' is cognate with that of 'þunor-rad'; this suggests that OE *þunor* could have been personified in the Old English language before *þunorrad* entered prose usage in tenth-century sermons on the Last Days. The word *þunorrad* is not found in Old English poetry; since it is likely that most surviving Old English poetry is of Anglian origin (transmitted in West Saxon form), it is possible that OE *þunorrad* was not an Anglian figure of speech, but rather a West Saxon one.

Secondly, some further evidence of a seventh-century Jutish cult of OE *þunor* is reflected in the tale of 'Thunor' in six of the eleven surviving versions of the early medieval legend of St Mildthryth. In the beginning of this legend, it is said that St Domneva, the mother of Mildthryth, founded the abbey of Minster-in-Thanet in compensation for the deaths of two young Kentish princes, her brothers, whom Thunor, a thegn of King Ecgberht, had murdered. David Rollason has dated the oldest version of this story to the second quarter of the eighth century.[136] *St Mildryð*, a vernacular version of this legend which is preserved in Cotton Caligula A. xiv (121v–124v), is a West Saxon fragment which 'may have served as a homily' before 1035.[137] In this version, Æthelred and Æthelberht, the two sons of Eormenred (a son of Eadbald), are entrusted on their father's death to the care of their cousin, King Ecgberht, the son of Eorcenberht (also a son of Eadbald). Although Ecgberht's court is Christian, the virtue of Æthelred and Æthelberht is said to become irksome to Thunor, to whom Ecgberht has entrusted the boys and who 'was afraid that if they lived longer, they would become dearer to the king than he was'.[138] In secret Thunor begins to hate the boys and warns Ecgberht that they will deprive him and his heirs of their kingdom; then Thunor 'straightaway martyred them at night within the king's high hall, as secretly as he could'.[139] Ecgberht, learning of the deed through the miraculous appearance of a beam of light, has Thunor questioned as to the whereabouts of Æthelred and Æthelberht and says 'that Thunor

---

[136] Rollason, *Mildrith Legend*, pp. 16–17.
[137] Normalized from *Leechdoms*, ed. Cockayne III, 422–8; see Rollason, *Mildrith Legend*, pp. 11 and 29–31, esp. 31.
[138] 'Ondrædde he him, gif hi leng lifedon þæt hi wurdon þam cynge leofran ðonne he.'
[139] 'He hi on niht sona gemartirode innan ðæs cyninges heahsetle, swa he dyrnlicost mihte.'

Ingui's marriage

should tell him for the sake of his friendship'.[140] When Thunor admits that he has killed the boys, Ecgberht knows that he has angered God and orders an immediate meeting of councillors and thegns. On the advice of these men and with the support of Archbishop Deusdedit, Ecgberht commands his cousins's sister Eafe (or Domneva) to be brought from Mercia to receive adequate compensation for her brothers. With God's aid she chooses compensation on the isle of Thanet, taking from the king eighty hides of land. The means by which she chooses the land is the subject of the rest of the extant story. A party which turns out to include not only Ecgberht and Domneva, but also Thunor the disgraced thegn, is said to cross from the mainland to Thanet, whereupon the king stipulates that the wergild will be no more than the distance that her pet hind can run. The hind runs ahead; they follow:

oð þæt hi comon to ðære stowe þe is nu gecwedon 'Þunores hlæwe'. 7 he ða se Þunor to ðam cyninge aleat, 7 he him to cwæð: "Leof, hu lange wylt ðu hlystan þyssum dumban nytene, þe hit eal wyle þis land utan beyrnan? Wylt ðu hit eal ðære cwenon syllan?" 7 ða sona æfter þyssum wordum se eorðe tohlad . . .[141]

Here the text runs out, though its writer probably intended that the martyrdom of SS Æthelred and Æthelberht should lead into the founding of the convent in which St Mildthryth, announced at the start as the second daughter of Domneva, is to spend the rest of her life. There is also a late West Saxon additional note in *The Anglo-Saxon Chronicle* (A) for the year 640 concerning Eormenred's sons, 'those who were later martyred by Thunor'.[142]

It seems likely that the martyrdom of SS Æthelred and Æthelberht came about as a result of a political rivalry between the two branches of Eadbald's descendants, for the focus of this part of St Mildthryth's legend is not on Domneva, but on King Ecgberht and his cousins.[143] Bede says that Oswiu of Northumbria consulted Ecgberht on the consecration of Wigheard as the new archbishop of Canterbury; Ecgberht was thus

---

[140] 'Þæt he be his freondscipe hit secgan sceolde.'

[141] 'Until they came to that place which is now called "Thunor's barrow". And he then, this Thunor, bowed down to the king and said to him: "Sire, how long will you listen to this dumb beast that will run around all this land? Do you want to give it all to the queen?" As soon as he spoke these words the earth split asunder . . .'

[142] *MS A: a Semi-Diplomatic Edition*, ed. Bately, pp. 28–9 (the addition made in 'hand 18c'): 'þa syððan wurðan gemartirode of Ðunore'.

[143] So Kirby, *Earliest English Kings*, pp. 42–4.

regarded as a protector of Christendom by 664, the year in which Deusdedit, the previous archbishop, died.[144] Yet who, if not Ecgberht, had been guilty of the martyrdom of SS Æthelred and Æthelberht? Thunor the evil thegn thus appears to be a figment of Ecgberht's defence, created to clear the king of serious guilt. The name *Thunor* seems to have been taken from the first element of the placename *Thunoreshlæw*, which lay beneath Minster-in-Thanet and indicates a 'barrow' or 'mound' belonging to a personified thunder *numen*. In this respect, Thunor, the figure apparently created in the early eighth century to exonerate King Ecgberht from the murder of his cousins, may reflect the failure of a heathen reaction to Christianity in Kent within the first half of the seventh century. Bede celebrates Eorcenberht after the death of his father Eadbald as the king who 'was the first among English kings to order idols to be abandoned and destroyed in all his kingdom', when he succeeded Eadbald in *c.* 640.[145] Thus a Kentish cult of *þunor*, a *numen* which could have been worshipped both as a phenomenon and as a person, may be represented in the name and role of Thunor in the legend of St Mildthryth.

A third instance of OE *þunor*, in which there is probably Norse influence, appears in the prose dialogue between Solomon and Saturn, interpolated in the poem of that theme in CCCC 422 probably in the tenth century. In this poem Solomon includes thunder as one of God's agents assisting the Pater Noster against the devil: 'seo liget heo bærneð and tacnað and se regn hit ufan wyrdeð and ða genipu hit dweliað and *se ðunor hit ðrysceð mid ðære fyrenan æcxe* and hit drifeð to ðære irenan ræccenteage ðe his fæder on eardað, Satan and Sathiel.'[146] Although the author of this conceit equipped the thunder with an axe rather than with a hammer such as that of Þórr, it is still likely that he did so with the Scandinavian Þórr in mind. According to the *Þórsdrápa* of Eilífr Goðrúnarson, Þórr sets out to fight the giant Geirrøðr in his mountain cave, armed with his strength-belt and gloves, but without the hammer for which he is otherwise so famous; after overcoming a swollen torrent,

---

[144] *HE* III.29 (p. 318).

[145] *HE* III.8 (p. 236): 'primus regum Anglorum in toto regno suo idola relinqui ac destrui . . . praecepit'. Also in *ASC* I, 27 ((E) 639): 'wearp ealla þa deofelgyld on his rice'.

[146] *Solomon and Saturn*, ed. Menner, p. 169: 'the lightning she burns and marks it and the rain injures it and the mist leads it astray and *the thunder thrashes it with the axe of fire* and drives it to the iron chain in which its father dwells, Satan along with Sathiel'.

Ingui's marriage

giants and Geirrøðr's daughters, Þórr faces the old giant himself. Geirrøðr hurls a red-hot iron bolt at Þórr, which Þórr, now wearing his iron gloves, catches and returns (stanzas 15–17), fatally for Geirrøðr. Then, in stanza 19, Þórr appears 'with a bloody hammer' (*með dreyrgum hamri*). Though Snorri in *Skáldskaparmál* explains that Þórr set out to Geirrøðr's cave to recover his hammer, both Margaret Clunies Ross and Roberta Frank are probably right to infer aetiology in this tale: an explanation of how Þórr got his hammer and learnt to use it.[147] The story of Þórr and Geirrøðr was unusually popular in Scandinavia, to judge from its motif's survival in eight separate versions.[148] On this evidence, the Old English conceit of thunder thrashing the devil with the axe of fire could have been formed from a story of Þórr hurling a red-hot bolt at a giant. As the manuscript containing the dialogue between Solomon and Saturn is dated to the late tenth century, the Old English prose text possibly shows the influence of Scandinavian paganism on indigenous Anglo-Saxon superstition associated with OE *þunor*.[149]

From this discussion of placenames, glosses and other vocabulary, it is reasonable to suppose that there were prominent cults of OE *þunor* in Saxon and Jutish England, as well as a later imported Scandinavian cult of Þor in northern England which may have influenced the use of OE *þunor* in the tenth-century prose dialogue between Solomon and Saturn in CCCC 422. These are the scraps of evidence for the worship, occasional personification and Scandinavian revival of an Anglo-Saxon thunder *numen*. It is worth reiterating, however, that the Angles, whom we have seen to be worshippers of *vanitates* or **uuani* in the previous chapter, do not seem to have given OE *þunor* a priority over other *numina*.

OE wuldor

The following discussion provides evidence of a 'brilliance' *numen* in the pre-Christian use of OE *wuldor*, a word with which Anglo-Saxon

---

[147] M. Clunies Ross, 'An Interpretation of the Myth of Þórr's Encounter with Geirrøðr and his Daughters', in *Speculum Norroenum*, ed. Dronke *et al.*, pp. 370–91, esp. 383; R. Frank, 'Hand Tools and Power Tools in Eilífr's *Þórsdrápa*', in *Structure and Meaning*, ed. Lindow, Lönnroth and Weber, pp. 94–109, esp. 107; *Þórsdrápa* has most recently been edited by Davidson, in 'Earl Hákon and his Poets', pp. 520–7, nn. 528–665.

[148] McKinnell, *Both One and Many*, pp. 57–86, esp. 59–60.

[149] *Solomon and Saturn*, ed. Menner, pp. 1–5 (manuscripts) and 8–10 (prose dialogue).

Heathen gods

Christians later made their standard translation of Lat *gloria*. OE *wuldor* (also spelt *wuldar, wulder, wuldur*) glosses or translates Lat *gloria* just over 900 times.[150] *Wuldor* also glosses *mirabilia* thirteen times,[151] *gratia* five times[152] and *doxa* twice.[153] Of these minor variants, *mirabilia* and *doxa* are synonymous with *gloria*; and *wuldor* glosses *gratia* with the help of other words (*ðonc* and *gefea*) corresponding more closely to the Latin sense of *gratia* in the Anglian dialects of the Lindisfarne and Rushworth Gospels. The evidence that *wuldor* means 'glory' is therefore almost unanimous. Most of *wuldor*'s compounds are of the type *wuldres cyning*, denoting God in one of his aspects. That *wuldor* still captures the less specific sense of 'brilliance' in *gloria* can be seen from the use of *wuldortorht weder* ('brilliant-bright weather', *Beo* 1136), to celebrate the arrival of spring after a harsh winter; and from *wuldorgim* ('glory-jewel', *Riddles* 84.26) which appears to refer to the sun. *Wuldor* never appears as a poetic synonym for the sun itself, even in *Christ*, where the Lord *wuldre scineð of his heahsetle hlutran lege* ('shines with glory, with pure fire, from his highseat', lines 1334–5). More particularly, in *swegles wuldor* ('sun's glory') in *Jud* 341, *wuldor* is seen as the brilliance of the sun. This word is often used to describe heaven, as in *wuldres leoht* ('light of glory') in *Sat* 140 and 555–6, yet *wuldor* never appears to be synonymous with God.

Two Norse cognates of OE *wuldor* are OIce *Ullinn* and *Ullr* (both in placenames). Elsewhere, *Ullr* is a minor heathen god in the Old Icelandic tradition who receives a brief notice in *Gylfaginning*:

Ullr heitir einn, sonr Sifjar, stjúpsonr Þórs. Hann er bogmaðr svá góðr ok

---

[150] DiPaolo Healey and Venezky, *Microfiche Concordance*, s.v. 'wuldor' (etc.).

[151] *The Tiberius Psalter*, ed. A. P. Campbell (Ottawa, 1974) [from Cotton Tiberius C. vi], pp. xvi–vii (gloss of s. xi^{med}), 14 (Ps. IX.2); *The Vitellius Psalter*, ed. J. L. Rosier (Cornell, 1962) [from Cotton Vitellius E. xviii], pp. xiv (gloss of s. xi^{med}), 14 (Ps. IX.2), 57 (Ps. XXV.7), 96 (Ps. XXXIX.6), 180 (Ps. CIV.2), 188 (Ps. CVI.8); *The Salisbury Psalter*, ed. C. Sisam and K. Sisam, EETS o.s. 242 (London, 1959), 11 (gloss *c*. 1100) 231 (Ps. CVI.31), 255 (Ps. CXVIII.37); G. Oess, 'Der altenglische Arundel-Psalter', *AF* 30 (1910), 3, 160 (Ps. XCV.3), 162 (Ps. XCVII.1), 180 (Ps. CVI.31), 226 (Ps. CXLIV.5).

[152] *The Gospel According to Saint Luke*, ed. W. W. Skeat (Cambridge, 1874), pp. 49 (Li Ru IV.32) and 67 (Li VI.32); *The Gospel According to Saint John*, ed. W. W. Skeat (Cambridge, 1878), p. 15 (Li Ru I.16).

[153] J. Zupitza, 'Altenglische Glossen zu Abbos Clericorum decus', *ZfdA* 31 (1987), 1–27 (gloss of s. xi/xii), 18.524).

Ingui's marriage

skíðfœrr svá at engi má við hann keppask. Hann er ok fagr álitum ok hefir hermanns atgervi. Á hann er gott at heita í einvígi.[154]

Þjóðólfr calls Þórr 'Ullr's kinsman' (*Ullar mágr*) in *Haustlǫng*, as if these gods represented thunder and brilliance, respectively, in the late summer sky:

> Knáttu ǫll, en, Ullar,   endilág, fyr mági,
> grund vas grápi hrundin,   ginnunga vé brinna
>
> (*Haustlǫng* 15)[155]

However, the scarcity of instances of *Ullr* in Old Norse–Icelandic literature shows that his cult was probably ancient and may have been displaced before *Haustlǫng* was composed in the late ninth century.[156] One similarity which emerges between OIce *Ullr* and OE *wuldor* is that the collocation with which Snorri describes Ullr, *fagr álitum* ('fair in feature'), is built around OIce [*v*]*litir* ('colours'), with which OE *wlite* ('brightness') is cognate. *Wlite* was used twenty times to alliterate with *wuldor* in various collocations; and *wuldre gewlitegian* ('to radiate with glory') is also a popular combination (*Az* 187, *And* 543 and 669, *MCharm* 11.26). This combination also appears in *Azarias*, where the angel speaking to Daniel and Azarias in the furnace, invulnerable to the flames, is described as *wlitescyne wer in his wuldorhoman* ('a radiant shining man in his glorious body', *Az* 51); and later, as if the quality of *wuldor* protected his *homa* ('skin') from fire: *ne mæg him bryne sceþþan wlitigne wuldorhoman* ('nor can burning harm his radiant glorious body', *Az* 176). Snorri's words *fagr álitum* thus reveal that *Wullr* or *Wullinn* was linked with *wlitir* in a lost poetic source. Although the Old English instances of this alliterative pair are used in an exclusively Christian way, its use in a common Germanic past indicates that the association of radiance with *wuldor* is ancient.

---

[154] *Gylf*, p. 26 (ch. 31): 'Ullr is the name of another god, the son of Sif and stepson of Þórr. He is such a good bowman and so good on skis that no-one can match him. He is also fair in feature (*fagr álitum*) and has the accomplishments of a warrior. He is good to call on for single combat.'

[155] *Skj* B I, 17, 15: 'All the sanctuaries of falcons [skies] did burn before the kinsman of Ullr [Þórr], and yet the ground back below him was driven with hail and snow.' Other instances of Ullr's relation to Þórr are contained in the kennings *Ulls mágr* (Eysteinn Valdason, a poem on Þórr, *c*. 1000, *Skj* B I, 131, 3) and *Ullar gulli* ('nurturer of Ullr', in Eilífr's *Þórsdrápa* 18, *Skj* B I, 143).

[156] See also Tolley, 'Germanic and Finnic Myths', pp. 121–5.

Heathen gods

OE *wuldorgeflogene* in *The Nine Herbs Charm* may be connected with Ullr's role as the 'bowman' (*bogmaðr*) of the Æsir. As if from a bow, the *wuldorgeflogene* ('glory-flown things') appear to be shot out of the sky as poisons against which the poet's nine herbs or *wuldortanas* ('glory-twigs') operate (*MCharm* 2.45). *Wuldorgeflogene* and *wuldortanas* are two specialized *wuldor*-compounds. Out of the twenty-nine other extant types, the most popular, with nineteen instances, is *wuldorbeag*: this word occurs in late prose and describes the Saviour's *corona* or *stephanus*, his 'ring of glory'. The once attested *Ullar hringr* ('ring of Ullr'), on which Guðrún Gjúkadóttir in *Akv* 30 reveals that her husband Atli swore oaths of fellowship with her brothers, looks similar to OE *wuldorbeag*, but sheds no light on the origin of this compound.[157]

One implication of *Max I* II, 132–3 (*Woden worhte weos, wuldor alwalda, rume roderas*), other than that which I have suggested in ch. 4, is that the heathen god Woden had no claim to create or possess OE *wuldor*.[158] This implication would be unremarkable were it not that Woden and *wuldor* are associated elsewhere, in *MCharm* 2.32, where Woden strikes the malevolent adder with nine *wuldortanas* ('twigs of glory'). How Woden may have acquired *wuldor* in pre-Christian Anglo-Saxon mythology may be seen in an analogue in Saxo's *Gesta Danorum*, in which the god Othinus is exiled and briefly replaced by *Ollerus* (cognate with *wuldor*), who arrives to rule 'Byzantium' in his place. This tale, a digression within Saxo's long narrative of Othinus's revenge for Balderus, appears between Othinus's seduction of Rinda and the execution of vengeance on Hotherus by Bous, their resulting son. After Balderus's death, Othinus disguises himself as a female physician, at great cost to his dignity, in order to seduce the unwilling Rinda. As a result of the shame incurred, the gods force Othinus to leave, 'perceiving that Othinus by these various flaws to his honour had stained the glory (*gloria*) of his godhead'.[159] Othinus is stripped of his worship and outlawed. So that this exile would not force the gods to abandon public cults, however, they

---

[157] On OE *wuldorbeag*, see J. Kirschner, *Die Bezeichnungen für Kranz und Krone im Altenglischen* (Munich, 1975), pp. 258–61. For a discussion of 'Ullr's ring' in the context of Saxo's tale of Othinus and Ollerus, see *Poetic Edda I*, ed. Dronke, pp. 64–5.

[158] 'Woden made idols [demons], the Almighty [made] glory, the roomy heavens.'

[159] *GD*, pp. 72–3, esp. 72: 'Othinum variis maiestatis detrimentis divinitatis gloriam maculasse cernentes'; my translation is based on *History of the Danes*, trans. Fisher and ed. Ellis Davidson I, 78–9.

Ingui's marriage

make a certain *Ollerus* into their king, substitute-pontiff and a god. The gods give Ollerus the name of Othinus to spare him 'the invidiousness of being a new man' (*invidia novitatis*).[160] Ollerus rules the gods for ten years until they take pity on Othinus and restore him 'from the filth of his wretchedness to the brightness (*fulgor*) of his former days'.[161] Some gods, however, believed at this time that Othinus had bought his way back in. Driven from Byzantium by Othinus, Ollerus goes to Sweden, where he bids for the restoration of his fame 'as if in a new world' (*veluti novo quodam orbe*); but he fails, and later the Danes kill him. Saxo concludes with a tale of how Ollerus could cross the sea on a bone; and how when Othinus recovered his divine honours: 'tanto opinionis *fulgore* cunctis terrarum partibus *enitebatur*, ut eum perinde ac redditum mundo *lumen* omnes gentes amplecterentur, nec ullus orbis locus extaret, qui numinis eius potentiae non pareret.'[162] With *gloria*, *fulgor*, *lumen* and *enitebatur* in this tale, Saxo reiterates words which translate the phenomenon contained in Ollerus's name.

Saxo might have read about Ullr in Icelandic sources now lost to us.[163] None the less, his story of Ollerus seems to have been shaped by a tradition peculiar to Denmark. The Danish murder of Ollerus after his loss of prestige in Norway and Sweden tallies with the evidence of placenames, the distribution of which indicates that an ancient Scandinavian cult of Ullr or Ullinn remained in Norway and Sweden but disappeared in Denmark.[164] Secondly, Saxo's statement that Ollerus received the name of Othinus shows that the Danish cult of Ullr was probably assimilated into that of Óðinn, whose own importance in the western and central Danish tradition is witnessed in the modern *Odense* ('Óðinn's sanctuary', from *Óðins-vé*), capital of Fyn. It is possible that Ullr lost his name and role to Óðinn, a new rival, when the cult of Wodan

---

[160] *GD*, p. 72.   [161] *Ibid.*, p. 73: 'squaloris deformitatem pristino fulgoris'.

[162] *Ibid.*: 'he *shone* in all parts of the earth with such great brightness of renown that all the nations embraced him on his return like the *light* returned to the universe, nor was there any place in the world which did not pay homage to his numinous power'.

[163] Bjarni Guðnason has shown that Saxo is truthful in his introduction about his use of Icelandic poems and sagas, particularly in the genealogy of Danish kings and the legend of Starcatherus. See Bjarni, 'The Icelandic Sources of Saxo Grammaticus', in *Saxo Grammaticus: a Medieval Author between Norse and Latin Culture*, ed. K. Friis-Jensen (Copenhagen, 1981), pp. 79–93, esp. 83–91.

[164] *AR* II, 154–8 (§§444–5).

Heathen gods

spread into Denmark probably in the early sixth century.[165] Similarly, the compound *wuldortanas* shows that OE *wuldor* was an aspect of Woden in *The Nine Herbs Charm*, and that the poet of *Maxims I* wished in part to repudiate this idea by associating *wuldor* with the Almighty rather than with Woden in *Max I* II, 132–3 (*Woden worhte weos, wuldor alwalda*). In these instances, the alliteratively convenient *Woden–wuldor* combination may reflect a period in England in which Woden, on analogy with the situation in Denmark, appropriated this sky *numen's* role as one of his own.

EARTH *NUMINA*

So far, in this chapter, I have illustrated the role and status of natural phenomena in Anglo-Saxon paganism with a discussion of sea *numina* (Old Anglian *Nerthus* and OE *garsecg*, *mægðegsa* and *geofon*) and sky *numina* (Bernician *Eostre*, OE *eorendel*, *Tiu/Tig*, *þunor* and *wuldor*). In what follows, I shall use Norse and other cognates to define the Old English terms *firgen-*, *frige*, *eorðan modor* and *geunnan* as words derived from *numina* associated with the earth.

There is surprisingly little evidence for Anglo-Saxon earth-worship in Old English texts, although some early Germanic evidence may be inferred from Tacitus's statement that *Terra Mater* was worshipped by the Anglii and other nations in north-eastern Germania.[166] It also appears that Germanic auxiliaries worshipped their homelands while on service in Roman Britain, for a votary inscription from third- or fourth-century Carlisle shows that the homesick Batavi (whose Hercules *macusanus baldruus lobbonus* I have attempted in ch. 5 to identify as an analogue of Ingvi-freyr) inscribed offerings to *Terra Bataborum* ('Earth of the Batavi'), presumably while they served on the Pictish frontier.[167] Tacitus also says that the Ingvaeones, Herminiones and Istaevones descend through *Mannus* ('man') from Tuisto, whom his sources name *deus terra editus* ('a god born from the earth').[168] An implication of this statement is that one of Tacitus's informants believed that all Germanic tribes descended from the earth.

A version of this ideology may have persisted until the eleventh

---

[165] On the likely period of Wodan's entry into Denmark, see Helm, *Wodan*, pp. 70–1.
[166] *Germania*, p. 317 (ch. 40). [167] Gutenbrunner, *Götternamen*, p. 229.
[168] *Germania*, p. 273 (ch. 2).

Ingui's marriage

century in England, as a native subculture influenced by Latin learning. There are at least two pieces of vernacular evidence: *eorðu bearn* ('sons of earth') is a variant of *ealda bearn* ('sons of men') in nine out of seventeen vernacular texts of *Cædmon's Hymn* (*c*. 657–80);[169] and the eleventh-century poet of the *Æcerbot* Charm, in his ritual to make an unfruitful field fertile, refers to the earth as *fira modor* ('mother of men', *MCharm* 1.68) and prays to her with *eorðan ic bidde* ('to earth I pray', *MCharm* 1.29). It is impossible to rule out either a Germanic or a Latinate source for the topos of earth the mother, which must have been widespread in Europe and which is probably the cause of a prescription of forty days of bread and water, in at least three Anglo-Saxon penitentials, for dragging one's sick child through a furrow.[170] Ælfric was probably borrowing from Martin of Braga when he said in his *De falsis diis* that postdiluvian men believed in the earth 'because she feeds all things';[171] the author of the *Gylfaginning* prologue reiterates this topos when he says that men, having perceived that the earth had life of her own, 'gave her a name and traced their lineages back to her'.[172] In these sparse references, the topos of 'earth the mother', whether of Germanic or Latin origin, is attested from beginning to end of the Anglo-Saxon period. The following Old English words – *firgen-*, *frige*, *eorþan modor* and *geunnan* – show aspects of this phenomenon.

OE firgen-

The Old English *firgen-* ('mountain') developed from a form cognate with OIce *Fjǫrgyn*, a synonym for the earth and also a name for the mother of

---

[169] D. K. Fry, 'Cædmon as Formulaic Poet', in *Oral Literature: Seven Essays*, ed. J. J. Duggan (Edinburgh, 1975), pp. 41–61.

[170] *Die Canones Theodori*, ed. Finsterwalder, pp. 310–11 (IV.xv.2); *Die altenglische Version des Halitgar'schen Bussbuches*, ed. Raith, p. 55 (IV.16); *Councils and Synods*, ed. Whitelock, pp. 319–20 (*Canons Enacted Under King Edgar*, XVI) and 463 (*The Northumbrian Priest Law*, LIV). Also in Ælfric's *De auguriis*, in *Ælfric's Lives of Saints*, ed. Skeat, p. 374 (lines 148–50); see A. L. Meaney, 'Ælfric's Use of his Sources in his Homily on Auguries', *ES* 66 (1985), 477–95, esp. 487. The power of earth is also invoked in *MCharm* 7.14–15 and in *MCharm* 8.46.

[171] *Homilies of Ælfric*, ed. Pope II, 680–1: 'forþon þe heo ealle þing afet'.

[172] *Gylf*, p. 3: 'gáfu þeir henni nafn ok tǫlðu ættir sínar til hennar'. Faulkes shows that this tradition derives from learned sources and finds no evidence that the descent of men from the earth was a popular tradition in the north, despite noting Tuisto in Tacitus's *Germania*. See Faulkes, 'Pagan Sympathy', pp. 289–90.

Heathen gods

Þórr.[173] OIce *firgen-* survives in *firgengæt* ('mountain goats') in eight glosses of *ibices*; and as *firginbucca* ('mountain buck') in one more.[174] In poetry *firgenstream* ('mountain river') occurs six times;[175] *fergenberig* ('earth's mountain'), *fyrgenbeamas* ('mountain trees'), *fyrgenholt* ('mountain wood') and *fyrgen hæfde* ('?head of the mountain') occur once each.[176] *Firginbucca*, which renders *capra silvatica* ('wood-goat') in the early twelfth-century *Medicina de quadrupedibus*, is further qualified in the Old English translation of this text as *wudubucca oððe gat* ('wood-buck or goat').[177] *Wudu-* is linked with *firgin-* here, as are *holt* ('wood') and *beamas* ('trees') with *fyrgen* respectively in *Beo* 1393 and 1414–15. In keeping with these associations, it seems that 'wood' formed part of the idea of *firgen-*.

The Norse cognate of OE *firgen-* denoted both a person and phenomenon in, respectively, OIce *Fjǫrgyn* and *fjǫrgyn* (or contracted *fjǫrn*). The second category denotes the 'earth' or 'ground' on to which Borgny says that she followed her friend Oddrún at birth (*á fjǫrgynio*, *Oddr* 11); *fjǫrgyn* seems to mean 'mountain' in *ǫrgildir als hrynbeðs fjǫrgynjar*, a complicated kenning in an anonymous verse probably later than the tenth century ('favourable giver of the serpent of roaring bed of the ?mountain: of the tribute of the valley-river: of gold', hence: 'generous man').[178] The use of phenomenon, as against person, in the Icelandic word is thus rare, but survived beyond the end of the pagan period in Scandinavia.

Formally cognate with OE *firgen-* and OIce *Fjǫrgyn* is OIce *fjǫrg*, a neuter plural apparently meaning 'gods' and a variant of other names for

---

[173] The common etymon appears to be **firgunj-*. See *Épinal-Erfurt Glossary*, ed. Pheifer, p. lxiv (§45); and *AIEW* 551–2.

[174] *Corpus Glossary*, ed. Lindsay, p. 91.12 (*ibices: firgingaet*); *Latin–Anglo-Saxon Glossary*, ed. Hessels, p. 64.12 (*ibices: firgingat*); *Épinal-Erfurt Glossary*. ed. Pheifer, p. 30.560 (*Ép. Erf.: ibices: firgingaett*); F. Holthausen, 'Die Leidener Glossen', *EStn* 50 (1916), 327–40, esp. 329; *Vocabularies*, ed. Wright and Wülcker, 423.11 and 428.37; E. Steinmeyer and E. Sievers, *Die Althochdeutsche Glossen*, 5 vols. (Berlin, 1879–1922) I, 496.32–3 (Job CCIX).

[175] *Beo* 2128, 1359, *And* 390 ('firigendstream'), *Max* II, 47, *Rid* 10.2 and *Phoen* 100.

[176] *Frank's Casket* 1.1; *Beo* 1414; *Beo* 1393; *MCharm* 4. 27.

[177] *Medicina de Quadrupedibus*, ed. de Vriend, pp. 252–3.

[178] *Skj* B I, 174, 5. This meaning is consistent with the Gothic neuter noun *faírguni* ('mountain'), which matches *Fjǫrgyn* with the same *i*-mutation of *-uni* and the loss of the final vowel. See *Vergleichendes Wörterbuch der gotischen Sprache*, ed. S. Feist (Leiden, 1939), s.v. 'faírguni' (pp. 138–9).

numina such as *bǫnd* and *hǫpt*. *Fjǫrg* occurs in *fjǫrgvall* ('earth-walls'), Gefjun's word apparently for the cliffs on which *Loptr* ('air') or Loki will be baffled (*Lok* 19); and *fjǫrg* occurs in *fjarghús* ('?earth-house'), apparently a shrine which Guðrún burns down along with Atli's hall (*Akv* 42). Bishop Wulfila's Got *faírhus*, for Greek *kosmos* ('world'), shows the connection between human and universal life.[179] This also seems to be the property of the *Ala-ferhui-ae* (?'those who give complete life-power'), the *matres* to which three late classical dedications have been found in Jülich in the lower Rhineland.[180] OE *firgen-* and OIce *Fjǫrgyn* thus seem to have developed from a word for a (divine) person or phenomenon 'filled with life'.

A classical analogue of this conceit shows Atlas, the titan who holds up the sky in North Africa, as partly mountain, partly man. Atlas is described from both perspectives when his grandson Mercury sweeps by him on his way to Carthage in Vergil's *Aeneid*:

> and now, as he flies, he makes out
> the summit and hard sides of tough Atlas, who balances
> the heavens on his peak, Atlas, whose pine-forested head,
> encircled constantly with black clouds, is driven by the wind
> and rain, whose shoulders are covered by the fanned snow,
> while streams plummet down the old man's chin
> and his beard bristles, freezing in the ice.
>
> (*Aen.* IV.246–51)[181]

The same topos may thus be found in the late compound MS *firgen hæfde* ('?head of the mountain'), which occurs three lines before the end of *For a Sudden Stitch* (line 27). *Hymiskviða*, a poem probably composed in Iceland in the eleventh century, shows Hymir as both a giant and a mountain: 'glaciers shook, when he came in, the chin-forest of the man was frozen'

---

[179] *Ibid.*, s.v.: 'faírhus' (p. 139).
[180] Gutenbrunner, *Götternamen*, p. 202; AR II, 293 (§524): 'die reichlich Lebenskraft schenkenden'.
[181] *Vergilii Opera*, ed. Mynors, pp. 183–4:
    iamque uolans apicem et latera ardua cernit
    Atlantis duri caelum qui uertice fulcit,
    Atlantis, cinctum adsidue cui nubibus atris
    piniferum caput et uento pulsatur et imbri,
    nix umeros infusa tegit, tum flumina mento
    praecipitant senis, et glacie riget horrida barba.

(glumðo iǫclar, var karls, er kom, kinnscógr frǿrinn, Hym 10). Here it is worth noting that *Fjǫrgynn*, a grammatically masculine form, is the name of a giant and the parent of the goddess Frigg.[182] In Old English literature, not only *firgenheafod*, but also the other compounds *firginbucca*, *firgenholt* and *firgenbeamas* appear to derive from an Anglo-Saxon tradition of common ancestry with this titan of Old Icelandic mythology.

OE eorþan modor *and* geunnan *in Æcerbot*

Towards the end of *Æcerbot*, an early eleventh-century charm for unfruitful land, the farmer whose field suffers from infertility was recommended to place *uncuð sæd* ('seed of unknown origin') on his plough and beg the eternal Lord for growth with these words:

> Erce, Erce, Erce,   *eorþan modor*,
> *geunne* þe se alwalda,   ece drihten,
> æcera wexendra   and wridendra,
> eacniendra   and elniendra,
> sceafta hehra,   *scirra wæstma*,
> and þæra bradan   berewæstma,
> and þæra hwitan   hwætewæstma,
> and ealra   eorþan wæstma.   (*MCharm* 1.51–8)[183]

The words italicized in the above passage are words of common ancestry with, respectively, *Terra Mater* in Tacitus's *Germania* (ch. 40), the Norse goddess *Iðunn* in *Haustlǫng* and *Lokasenna* and Freyr's mediator *Skírnir* in *Skírnismál*. There is another reference to mother earth and two more instances of OE *geunnan* in *Æcerbot*. The farmer went on to say '*geunne* him ece drihten' ('may the eternal Lord yield to him', that is, to the farmer) the safety of the plough (*MCharm* 1.59). Then, after finishing this poem,

---

[182] Masculine *Fjǫrgynn* is probably not a primary formation, but formed on feminine *Fjǫrgyn*: see *AR* II, 334–5 (§560); see earlier J. de Vries, 'Studiën over germaansche mythologie I: Fjǫrgynn', *Tijdschrift voor nederlandsche taal- en letterkunde* 50 (1931), 1–25, esp. 23; see further F. R. Schröder, 'Erce und Fjǫrgyn', in *Erbe der Vergangenheit: Germanistische Beiträge: Festgabe für Karl Helm zum 80. Geburtstage*, ed. L. Wolff (Tübingen, 1951), pp. 25–36, esp. 28.

[183] '"Acre", "Acre", "Acre", *Mother Earth*, may the All-wielding eternal Lord *make you yield* growing fields and sprouting fields, pregnant growing and striving fields, high haulm-shafts and *bright crops*, and the *broad crops of the barley* and the white crops of the wheat, and all the fruits of earth.'

Ingui's marriage

driving his plough and cutting the first furrow, the farmer was asked to say:

> Hal wes þu, *folde,   fira modor!*
> Beo þu growende   on godes fæþme,
> fodre gefylled   firum to nytte.   (*MCharm* 1.68–70)[184]

The farmer then had to take a loaf made from *ælces cynnes melo* ('any kind of meal'), of which the dough had been kneaded with milk and holy water, and to put it beneath the furrow, singing:

> Ful æcer fodres   fira cinne,
> beorhtblowende,   þu gebletsod weorþ
> þæs haligan noman   þe ðas heofon gesceop
> and ðas eorþan   þe we on lifiaþ;
> se god, se þas grundas geworhte,   *geunne* us growende gife,
> þæt us corna gehwylc   cume to nytte.   (*MCharm* 1.75–80)[185]

Then the farmer recited prayers, ending with the Pater Noster, which he was recommended to recite three times.

Firstly, both *eorþan modor* (*MCharm* 1.51) and *folde fira modor* (*MCharm* 1.68) resemble Terra Mater, the earth-goddess whom the continental Anglii appear to have worshipped in the first century AD. As T. D. Hill has shown, pagan superstition in *Æcerbot* seems to be blended with the number of the four gospels; furthermore, in Eccl. XL.1, the yoke is said to be heavy on the sons of Adam 'from the day of their leaving the womb of their mother to the day of their burial in the mother of all' (*A die exitus de ventre matris eorum usque in diem sepulturae in matrem omnium*).[186] Although a connection between the farming cultures represented in *Germania* and *Æcerbot* may seem less likely than an influence on the charm from this or another ecclesiastical source, the conception of the *folde fira modor* in this charm as lying *on godes fæþme* ('in the embrace of God') is not part of Christian doctrine and brings *Æcerbot* closer to *Skírnismál* and to other

---

[184] 'May you be well, *earth, Mother of men*! May you be growing in the embrace of God, filled with food for benefit of men.'

[185] 'Acre full of food for the family of men, bright-blossoming, you be blessed with the holy name of him who made heaven and the earth we live in; that God who made these farming grounds, *may he make yield* for us a gift of growing so that each grain of corn may come to be of benefit for us.'

[186] T. D. Hill, 'The "Æcerbot" Charm and its Christian User', *ASE* 6 (1977), 213–21, esp. 218.

pre-Christian poems that reflect a common Germanic tradition of the earth.

Secondly, the three uses of *geunnan* in *Æcerbot* may be compared with OIce 'Ið-*unn*' in *Haustlǫng* and '*unna* gamans' in *Skírnismál*. Iðunn, a Norse goddess and the wife of Bragi in *Lokasenna*, is the keeper of the apples of perpetual youth. Snorri in *Skáldskaparmál* says that Loki, having sneaked Iðunn into the kingdom of Þjazi the giant, whose people need her for their health and rejuvenation, is forced to bring her home again. In Þjóðólfr's *Haustlǫng*, the source that Snorri quotes, this story begins when Þjazi turns himself into an eagle and surprises Óðinn, Hœnir and Loki one day as they prepare to eat a roasted ox. Loki strikes Þjazi with a staff, but finds the staff stuck to the eagle and himself hanging on for dear life when the disguised giant flies up into the sky. Þjazi agrees to spare Loki provided that he bring Iðunn to the world of the giants:

> Sér bað sagna hrœri   sorgœra[n] mey fœra,
> þás ellilyf ása,   áttrunnr Hymis, kunni;
> brunnakrs of kom bekkjar   Brísings goða dísi
> girðiþjófr í garða   grjót-Níðaðar síðan.
>
> Urðut bjartra borða   byggvendr at þat hryggvir;
> þá vas Ið- með jǫtnum   -*unnr* nýkomin sunnan;
> gǫrðtusk allar áttir   Ing[v]i-freys at þingi
> (váru heldr) ok hárar   (hamljót regin) gamlar.
>
> (*Haustlǫng* 9–10)[187]

In Snorri's prose version of this story, Loki brings Iðunn back by flying into Þjazi's compound as a falcon, carrying Iðunn as a nut in his beak and flying back to Ásgarðr with Þjazi in hot pursuit. The Æsir burn bonfires over which Þjazi is killed when his wings catch fire.

Norse cognates of OE *geunnan* are thus represented in *Haustlǫng*, *Skírnismál* and *Lokasenna*. A digression will be necessary to make the

---

[187] My text is based on Finnur, *Skj* B I, 14–18 (*Skj* A I, 16–20): '[9] To him the kin-branch of Hymir bade the mad with pain rouser of tales bring the girl who knew the age-medicine of the Æsir; the thief of the gods's Brising girdle later got the lady of the brook of the well-spring's cornfield [Iðunn] into the courtyards of the rock-Níðaðr. [10] Those who dwelt in the bright table-tops did not become downcast at this; this was when *Again-yielder/wave* was newly come from the south into the giants; all the kindreds of the Ingvi-lord (the powers were more ugly of skin than ever) were deliberating in the assembly, grey-haired and old.'

Ingui's marriage

implications of this Norse material clearer, however, before it is possible to suggest the heathen ideology implied in *geunnan* and in other words in *Æcerbot*.

First, the *ið*-prefix in 'Ið-unn', the divine name cognate with OE *geunnan*, is taken by de Vries to be cognate with Lat *iterum* ('again'); *-unn* is related to *unna* ('yield'); thus Iðunn's name could have been coined with the meaning 'yielding again'.[188] Also, in that Þjóðólfr splits Iðunn's name into its elements in *Haustlǫng* 10, part of his aim may be to show the meanings 'again' (as in OIce *eð* and *endr*) and 'yield' (as in *unna*). Both this effect and Jan de Vries's etymology of *Ið-unn* suggest that Iðunn's job was to regenerate all forms of life on a cyclical basis: the meaning of OIce *ið-unn* thus suggests that Iðunn's role was to represent the fertile quality which the earth must have if it is to bring forth life. In *Skí* 39 and 40, OIce *unna* ('yield') is further used of Gerðr, the future consort of Ingvifreyr: Gerðr is a giantess, daughter of Gymir and object of Freyr's lust; Freyr sends his messenger Skírnir to arrange the time and place of a meeting so that Freyr can consummate his *mikinn móðtregi* ('great grief of heart', *Skí* 4) by coupling with Gerðr in a grove. Although scholars have developed sociological and historical perspectives on this poem, the vocabulary of *Skírnismál* is so loaded with hints of natural processes that its primary meaning must inevitably be agrarian: this poem reflects a drama enacted by the persons of Freyr, Skírnir and Gerðr through which difficult land is prepared for planting and harvest.[189] As Gerðr's name appears to be related to *garðr* ('farm'), or more closely to *gerði* ('fenced-off field'), Gerðr may be taken in this poem to represent a plot of land, and her male partner Freyr to represent the lord of the natural world.[190]

In three places in *Skírnismál*, Gerðr is endowed with the cyclical

---

[188] *AR* II, 334 (§559): 'die Erneuende, Verjüngende'; *ANEW* 283 (*Iðunn*). The *ið*-prefix may have an etymon in an antique inscription dedicated to the '*Id*bangabis' or '*Id*iangabis' in Hagen, Bonsdorf Pier in the lower Rhineland: see Gutenbrunner, *Götternamen*, p. 218.

[189] Olsen, 'Fra gammelnorsk myte og kultus', pp. 17–36; Dronke, 'Art and Tradition', pp. 250–68 (also published in *Myth and Fiction*, no. IX); see also L. Motz, 'Gerðr: a New Interpretation of the Lay of Skírnir', *MoM* 3–4 (1981), 121–36. S. A. Mitchell focuses on the use of *Skírnismál* 'as a charter for human behavior for the resolution of conflict', in '*Fǫr Scírnis* as Mythological Model: *frið at kaupa*', *ANF* 98 (1983), 108–22, esp. 118.

[190] On the 'small, well-defined fields which were under permanent cultivation' in the early iron age, see Hedeager *Iron-Age Societies*, pp. 217–19.

phenomenon which Iðunn represents. In the first case, Gerðr's *iðunn* aspect is implicit in Skírnir's frustrated attempt to give her 'epli elli*lyfs*' (*Skí* 19–20, emended from MS *ellifo*); the compound *ellilyf* ('apples of age-medicine') is associated with Iðunn in *Haustlǫng* 9. With these apples Gerðr becomes the 'perpetual yielder' on which nature's regeneration depends; if she refuses, she becomes like a thistle swollen with seeds, a symbol of an ill-kept field (*Skí* 31). Second, Gerðr hears outside the commotion of Skírnir's arrival and bids the servant give him a drink: 'though I am afraid that it may be my brother's killer here outside' (*þó ec hitt óomc, at hér úti sé minn bróðurbani*, *Skí* 16). This *bróðurbani* motif probably survives in *Skírnismál* because it supports the theme of the giant-god enmity in this story; but it also resembles Loki's accusation against Iðunn in *Lokasenna*:

> Þegiðu, Iðunn!   þic qveð ec allra qvenna
>   vergiarnasta vera,
> síztu arma þína   lagðir, ítrþvegna,
>   um þinn bróðurbana.   (*Lok* 17)[191]

Since Þjóðólfr presents Iðunn as an aspect of Freyja in *Haustlǫng* 9 (in *Brísings goða girðiþjófr*, 'the thief of the gods' Brísing girdle', a kenning for Loki), and since Loki accuses Freyja of incest with her brother Freyr in *Lok* 32, it follows that Iðunn's lover is a new 'brother' replacing an older one whom he has killed.[192]

The third instance in *Skírnismál* in which the poet endows Gerðr with the phenomenon of *iðunn* appears to be contained again in Gerðr's own words, when she says that after nine nights she 'will *grant* pleasure to the son of Njǫrðr' ('mun Niarðar syni Gerðr *unna* gamans', *Skí* 39). *Barri* ('?for barley', *Skí* 39) is the name of the grove in which Gerðr arranges to meet Freyr. Given that Gerðr says this is the name 'which we both know' (*er við bæði vitom*, *Skí* 39 and 41), her words probably show that her

---

[191] 'Be quiet Iðunn! I say that you of all women have been the most eager for a man, since you laid your splendid-washed arms about your brother's killer.'

[192] See Dronke, 'Scope of the *Corpvs Poeticvm Boreale*', pp. 98–101 (also published in *Myth and Fiction*, no. V); however, Steinsland (*Det hellige bryllup*, p. 89) regards *bróðurbani* as no more than a general designation for an enemy of Gerðr's family now courting Gerðr: 'the killing/marriage polarity is a literary motif well-known elsewhere which reflects a key issue of northern social problematics' ('polariteten drap-ekteskap er forøvrig et velkjent litterært motiv som rommer en kjerne av nordisk sosial problematikk').

Ingui's marriage

encounter with Freyr is repeated year after year. That Skírnir repeats Gerðr's use of *unna* to Freyr in *Ski* 41 shows that Gerðr has taken the regenerative quality of Iðunn necessary for a successful planting and harvest: necessary, that is, if the society which supported *Skírnismál* was not to die in a famine.

How relevant to *Æcerbot*, a late Anglo-Saxon charm, is this picture in *Skírnismál* of Skírnir endowing Gerðr with the phenomenon of Iðunn at the bidding of Freyr? The implication of the name *Skírnir* ('brightener') is that the fields will be *skírr* ('bright') through Skírnir's mediation between his god and the earth. It is possible that a Christian adaptation of the theme of *Skírnismál* is traceable in the formula *scirra wæstma* ('bright crops') in *MCharm* 1.55, in the image of the *fold* lying *on godes fæþme*, and in the invocation to the Lord (with three uses of *geunnan*) to make the now fertile field 'yield' a harvest. Because this agrarian theme of *hieros gamos* survives in this late Anglo-Saxon text, it may be taken as one of the most vital elements of the natural religions on which Anglo-Saxon paganism was based.

OE frige *and* Geates frige

The Norse cognates of OE *frige* ('love') and *freon* ('to love') are respectively *Frigg* and *frjá*.[193] No nominative singular OE **frigu* is extant, though *frige*, *friga* and *frigum* survive in oblique cases. The oldest analogue of these words occurs in a third-century Roman dedication in Housesteads by Hadrian's Wall, to (*inter alia*) the *dea Fria-gabi*, whose name appears to mean 'love-giver'.[194] A *Frea* appears as the wife of *Godan* (Woden) in the brief tale to which Paulus Diaconus alluded in the *Gesta Langobardorum* in the eighth century.[195] A personified *Friia* also appears in association with Uuodan in *The Second Merseburg Charm*; and in *Gylfaginning*, Frigg is named as the chief of Óðinn's many consorts.[196] OE *frige*, however, reveals no association with Woden, nor any other sign of mythic origins. This

---

[193] On the nuances of the participial noun *freond*, see A. L. Meaney, 'The *Ides* of the Cotton Gnomic Poem', *MÆ* 48 (1979), 23–39; repr. in *New Readings on Women in Old English Literature*, ed. H. Damico and A. Hennessey Olsen (Bloomington and Indianapolis, IN, 1990), pp. 158–75.

[194] Gutenbrunner, *Götternamen*, p. 213; *AR* II, 316–17 (§540).

[195] *Historia Langobardorum*, ed. Waitz, pp. 52–6.

[196] *AR* I, 169 (§451); *Gylf*, pp. 29 and 47.

word, in *frigedæg*, was used to render Lat *Venus* in *Veneris dies*.[197] When Ælfric cited Venus in *De falsis diis*, he did not refer to her vernacular form as OE *frige*:

Sum wif hatte Uen[us], seo wæs Ioues dohter, swa fracod on galnysse þæt hire fæder hi hæfde, ond eac hire broðor, and oðre gehwylce, on myltestrena wisan; ac hi wurðiað þa hæþenan for [halige] gydenan, swa swa heora godes dohter.[198]

Instead, when Ælfric offered a vernacular name for Venus, he cited the cognate Danish name:

Ðone sixtan dæg hi gesetton þære sceamleasan gydenan Uen[us] gehaten, and *Fric*[g] on Denisc.[199]

Ælfric's choice of Danish *Frigg* in this matter may be consistent with his tendency to avoid West Saxon cognates of Danish forms.[200] Ælfric further alludes to Fricg as one of the shapes in which the devil appears to St Martin of Tours in his hermit's cell: 'sometimes as Venus the foul goddess whom men call Fricg'.[201]

There is no evidence that Ælfric knew the name of *Freyja*, a goddess whose predominantly sexual role seems to have been borrowed from Frigg in the surviving Old Norse–Icelandic literature. The semantic history of OIce *Freyja* is related to that of *Frigg*, although these words are of different origin: *Freyja*, which is related neither to OIce *Frigg*, nor to OHG *Friia* nor to Lombardic *Frea*, is a by-form of *Freyr* ('lord'), a word which is related to Lat *primus* ('foremost').[202] Yet it seems that the Norse epithet *freyja was established as *Freyja*, a divine name for the sister and sexual partner of Freyr or Ingvi-freyr, at least partly through the influence

---

[197] Jente, *Die mythologischen Ausdrücke*, pp. 107–9 (§72) and 110–11 (§75); Philippson, *Germanisches Heidentum*, pp. 164–5 and 179–80. ModE *frig* is probably not related to *Frigg* despite present-day formal resemblance (*OED*, s.v. *frig*).

[198] *Homilies of Ælfric*, ed. Pope II, 685 (lines 150–5): 'There was a woman called Venus, she was the daughter of Jove, so criminal in her wantonness that her father had her, and so did her brother and others just the same, in the manner of a prostitute; and yet the heathens honour her as a [holy] goddess and as their god's daughter.'

[199] *Ibid.*, p. 685 (lines 176–7): 'The sixth day [Friday] they established for the shameless goddess called Venus and in Danish "Fricg".'

[200] See further Johnson, 'Euhemerization versus Demonisation', pp. 59–61.

[201] *Ælfric's Lives of Saints*, ed. Skeat II, 265 (lines 716–17): 'hwilon on ueneris þære fulan gyden þe men hatað fricg'.

[202] *AIEW*, pp. 545–8 and 567–8.

Ingui's marriage

of the West Germanic names cognate with OIce *Frigg* and OE *frige*. Although Frigg was probably known in Danish parts of England, it is likely that a goddess by the name of Freyja was not: no form of *Freyja* survives in the *Gesta Danorum* of Saxo Grammaticus, for whom *Frigga* represented the goddess of sex and prostitution; that *Freyja* is extant only in Old Norse–Icelandic literature, which derives from the language, shows that she was probably developed in the West Norse regions of Scandinavia. In this case, an apparent allusion to Freyja in Laʒamon's *Brut* of the late twelfth or early thirteenth century may be traceable to Norwegian rather than to Danish influence. In the *Brut*, Laʒamon (whose name is probably derived from the Danish form of *lǫgmaðr*, 'law-man') attributes the following words to the Germanic invaders of Kent:

> ʒeʒt we habbeð anne læuedi, þe hæh is 7 mæhti;
> heh heo is 7 hali. hired-men heo luuieð
> for þi heo is ihate *Fræa*, wel heo heom dihteð. (*Brut* 6944–6)[203]

This passage appears to contain the first and last reference to Freyja's name in Old and Middle English literature.

Not Freyja, then, but Frigg (anglicized as Fricg) was probably understood to embody the characteristics of a love-goddess in Danish-occupied parts of England from the ninth to the tenth centuries. During this period it is unlikely that any personification of *frige*, the Old English cognate of this name, survived the eradication of Anglo-Saxon gods in the seventh century. However, there is some evidence in *weres frige*, the collocation in which OE *frige* is usually contained, that OE **frigu* in the pagan period could have denoted a *numen* which represented both a phenomenon and a personification of 'love'. The four surviving instances of OE *weres frige* are used to suggest male insemination: first, a prophecy of Moses that Jesus will be born 'swa þæs modor ne bið wæstmum geeacnod þurh *weres frige*' ('in such a way that his mother will not be increased with growth through *a man's love*', *El* 340–1); second, Mary becomes pregnant 'butan *weres frigum*' ('without *a man's love*', *Christ* 378);

---

[203] *Laʒamon: Brut: Edited from British Museum MS. Cotton Caligula A.IX and British Museum MS. Cotton Otho C.XIII*, ed. G. L. Brook and R. F. Leslie, 2 vols., EETS 250 and 277 (Oxford, 1963–78) I, 360 [Cotton Caligula A. ix]: 'Yet we have a lady who is high and mighty; high she is and holy, household-men love her; for this reason she is called "Frææ" (*Frea* in the other surviving manuscript); she adorns herself well for them.'

third, Mary *'weres friga* wiht ne cuþe, ne þurh sæd ne cwom sigores agend monnes ofer moldan' ('knew nothing of *a man's love*, nor through seed of man did the Owner of Victory come to earth', *Christ* 419–21); and fourth, Juliana's father urges his daughter to yield to a potential heathen husband by asking her not to renounce 'þæs *weres frige*' ('this *man's love*', *Jul* 103).

In all these examples the association of OE *frige* and *were* appears to have common ancestry with a cognate association between OIce *Frigg* and *verr*. Loki defines Frigg as '*æ vergiǫrn*' ('always eager for a *man*', *Lok* 26) and Óðinn, her husband, is described as '*Friggjar frumverr*' ('first *man of Frigg*') in a satirical verse which is ascribed to Hallfreðr vandræðaskáld, but which, since it is a single *lausavísa* ('loose verse') in a dominant prose context, is more likely to have been forged in the twelfth century.[204] These instances of OE *weres frige*, on the one hand, and of OIce *Friggjar verr*, on the other, show two different perspectives of an early Germanic *numen*: one, 'love' as an abstract state within a man; the other, as the personification of that abstract into an epithet or title for the female consort of a god.[205]

Elsewhere I have suggested that the Old English line 'wurdon grundlease Geates frige' (*Deor* 15), translated as 'Geat's love-consorts went without Ground', would mean that Geat found no 'love', i.e. no human representation of the earth, in which he could be fulfilled.[206] If it can be shown that the poet of *Deor* plays on words, on the one hand, and that, on the other, Anglo-Saxons of the ninth century or earlier knew both of Geat's former divinity and of an agrarian tradition whereby God married the earth to beget provender, then it is possible that the poet of *Deor* made a punning reference to an idea that the foremost consort among Geat's *frige* ('loves') was the *grund-* ('Ground') on which he hoped to establish his royal line. Puns are not strange to *Deor*, as shown by the proper noun on which the modern title is based, since the poet 'Deor' claims that he was *dyre* ('dear') to his lord (*Deor* 37); another pun is in *Mæringa burg* ('citadel of famous men') with *þæt wæs monegum cuþ* ('that was known to many', *Deor* 19). These puns support a reading of *grundlease* in *Deor* 15 as 'without fulfilment' and yet 'without Ground'.

Secondly, the idea that God could marry the earth 'mother of men' to

[204] *Skj* B I, 158, 7.
[205] See Lactantius's words above in *De falsa religione* (I.xx.18), quoted above, p. 208.
[206] North, '*Jeux d'Esprit* in "Deor" 14–16', pp. 22–3.

Ingui's marriage

beget food is the message of the *Æcerbot* Charm (*MCharm* 1.68–70) which I shall discuss below: purely as a fertility motif, this idea does not appear to be Christian. As regards the heathen status of 'Gapt' in Jordanes, both the author of the *Historia Brittonum* and Asser claim that in earlier times 'Geat' had been wrongly worshipped as a god.[207] Furthermore, Þjóðólfr's kenning for Þórr, 'Ground's lad' (*grundar sveinn*, *Haustlǫng* 19), shows that *grund* could describe the earth as a mother in the Old Norse tradition.[208] Of all Norse poets whose verse survives, only Bragi in *Ragnarsdrápa* seems to allude to Gautr specifically in his role as the husband of the Gothic earth in the kenning *Hergauts vina* ('War-Gautr's girl-friend');[209] this kenning is reminiscent of the elements in *wurdon grundlease Geates frige* ('Geat's love-consorts went without Ground', *Deor* 15). With Geat trying to win Mæthhild as his consort, this line in *Deor* is unique in Old English literature in hinting at the personification of plural OE *frige* in *Geates frige* as a number of women representing different regions of the earth.

IDEOLOGICAL ROOTS OF ANGLIAN KINGSHIP

Was Geat's type of *droit du seigneur* a feature of Edwin's kingship before his baptism in 627? As we have seen in the previous chapter, the author of *Vita S. Gregorii* tells a story in which Paulinus, apparently before Edwin's baptism, ordered Edwin's royal kinsmen to abandon their 'unlawful unions'; Edwin before his baptism may have been as guilty of this promiscuity as they were. The final aim of this chapter will be to throw light on the promiscuity which, as this story seems to show, was an important element of heathen Anglian kingship.

To trace the development of this feature of Anglian paganism, I shall consider the *Germania* of Tacitus in the light of Old Norse–Icelandic evidence in order to identify a pattern by which a continental Anglian Ing-hypostasis, in his seasonal role as the husband of different regions of the earth, may have acted as the human focus of the natural elements of sea, sky and earth whose various Anglo-Saxon reflexes I have discussed above. The religion of the continental Anglii, as Tacitus treats it in the *Germania*, may arguably be explained with reference to the diverse Norse reflexes of Nerthus that I have already discussed with respect to Njǫrðr

---

[207] *Getica*, ed. Mommsen I, 76; *Historia Brittonum*, ed. Lot, pp. 171–2; *Asser's Life*, ed. Stevenson and rev. Whitelock, pp. 3 and 159–61.
[208] *Skj* B I, 18, 19.   [209] *Skj* B I, 2, 5.

Heathen gods

(ch. 1 and this chapter), Ingvi-freyr (chs. 1–3 and 7), Baldr (chs. 4–6) and Gautr (ch. 6). The Scandinavian evidence now cited will focus on 'sacral kingship' and on the relation between Skaði, Njǫrðr and Baldr. On the strength of this evidence, I shall propose a new hypothesis concerning the ideology, but not necessarily the first-century history, of Terra Mater, Nerthus and Tuisto as these gods were known by the Anglii. I shall conclude that the Ing-hypostasis, a man worshipped as the god Nerthus, married Terra Mater, made her fields fertile and then died in the autumn to make way for a new incarnation of Nerthus in the spring.

Old Norse–Icelandic evidence for 'sacral kingship'

Ingvi-freyr is named *afi* (a word which means both 'heir' and 'grandfather') in the expression *inn fróði afi* ('the wise/fertile grandfather', *Skí* 1 and 2). *Skírnismál* does not appear to be an occasional poem, for there is no celebration of a patron and the mythological figures in this poem show no sign of royal status; yet the word *afi* in Freyr's initial epithet appears to be an allusion to the ancestral role which may be otherwise seen in the tradition of *Ynglingatal*.[210] In addition, Þjóðólfr's words for the world, 'all the kindreds of the Ingvi-lord' (*allar áttir Ing[v]i-freys* in *Haustlǫng* 10), provide further corroboration that Freyr was formerly regarded as the ancestor of gods and men.

As we have seen in ch. 5, however, Ingvi-freyr does not appear to have kept his role as the god from whom Norse kings claimed descent: in *c*. 985, about a century after *Ynglingatal* and *Haustlǫng*, Eyvindr skáldaspillir traced Hákon's ancestry back chiefly to Óðinn (*Háleygjatal* 3); as the earth is also Óðinn's wife, Eyvindr says that it is Hákon Jarl

> þeims alt austr   til Egða býs
> brúðr Val-týs   und bœgi liggr.   (*Háleygjatal* 15)[211]

How and why Eyvindr could allude to Óðinn in the combined role of earth's husband and human forebear may be seen in the fact that Óðinn's

---

[210] See Schier, 'Freys und Fróthis Bestattung', pp. 389–409. This is the only dynastic reference in the poem. Though Steinsland (*Det hellige bryllup*, pp. 87–171) argues that *Skírnismál* celebrates kingship, her interpretation underemphasizes the agrarian elements which this poem shares with *The Charm for Unfruitful Land*.

[211] *Skj* B I, 62: 'under whose arms Slaughter-týr's [Óðinn's] bride is lying, all the way to the dwelling of the men of Agðir'.

Ingui's marriage

begetting of Þórr on Jǫrð was already a widespread motif in Scandinavia; it has been thought that Woden was introduced as a royal ancestor to Trondheim from Wessex by Hákon Aðalsteinsfóstri half a century before *Háleygjatal*; therefore, it seems that Óðinn usurped the place of Njǫrðr as Skaði's husband and that of Hǫlgi as the father of the Háleygir. Through *Háleygjatal* and other poems in Trondheim, the introduction of the West Saxon Woden into Norwegian genealogy was probably the first stage in the creation of Óðinn's dynastic role as it is represented in the Prologue to *Gylfaginning*.

The consort of this progenitor god (whether Freyr or Óðinn) was the earth: her role in the surviving Old Norse–Icelandic literature is a complex affair, for her name changes according to what offspring she bears and to whom. Where earth produces nations, her name can be *Skaði*, which, as we have seen, is identical with Germanic forms of the name *Scandinavia*.[212] Where the earth produces 'barley' (*barr*), her name appears to be Gerðr and the husband Freyr. Where she produces gods, earth is Fjǫrgyn, mother of Frigg, the mother of Baldr; with Óðinn earth is a strictly female Fjǫrgyn, otherwise Hlǫðyn, Grund or Jǫrð, the mother of Þórr, the peasant god from whom no kings descend. Finally, when the earth was imagined as the mother of kings, as with the Ynglingar or Háleygir, her husband was stylized as Ingvi-freyr or a later eponym such as Hǫlgi; while her name could easily vary in keeping with whichever political heartland was stylized as a royal patron's ancestral mother.[213]

Up in western Norway and Trøndelag at the end of the heathen period in Scandinavia, the ancient ideology of the marriage of Njǫrðr and Skaði, or of the marriage between a male god and the earth, seems to have been reflected in the reign of Hákon Jarl, a very late example of a Germanic 'sacral king'. There is a story about Hákon in the fourteenth-century *Færeyinga þáttr* in which he prostrated himself with tears before his idol-queen Þorgerðr *Hǫrða-brúðr* ('bride of the men of Hordaland') in return for a bracelet with which to reward one of his retainers.[214] It is more likely that this scene, which shows the intensity of Hákon's relationship with Þorgerðr, descends from an anecdote than that it is a late extrapolation

---

[212] *AR* II, 335–40 (§561: p. 338).
[213] So Steinsland, *Det hellige bryllup*, pp. 176–9. Hǫlgi's name is found in *Brennu-Njáls saga*, ed. Einar Ólafur Sveinsson, ÍF 12 (Reykjavik, 1954), p. 214 (ch. 88): *hǫlda-*, *hǫrða-* and *hǫlga-brúðr* are all forms of this name; see also *Flat* I, 213 (ch. 173).
[214] *Flat* I, 122–50, esp. 144–5 (ch. 114).

from the poetry of his reign. The evidence of twelfth-century prose, furthermore, suggests that Hákon, to enjoy a physical union on his ancestor's behalf with his tutelary earth-goddess, looked for her local representatives in women of flesh and blood. After his victory against the Danes in Hjǫrungavágr, Hákon seems to have spent the last ten years of his reign enforcing a *droit du seigneur* on his subjects' wives and daughters; sailing round the inlets of western Norway, sending his slaves at each stop to fetch a woman from the local farm, keeping her with him for a week or two, then sending her home, 'and no distinction was made or difference as to whose wife, whose sister or whose daughter these women might be'.[215] In time the resentment grew and the kinsmen of one Guðrún *lundasól* ('sun of the groves') overpowered Hákon's slaves, hounded Hákon to his death and elected Óláfr Tryggvason as their king.

At first, Hákon's liberties might appear to be no more than what Andrew Hamer characterizes, as 'cynical and violent sexual attacks on his women subjects'.[216] Yet the *Hákonardrápa* of Hallfreðr vandræðaskáld (c. 985) suggests that these coercions took place with a basis in royal ideology, as Hákon's political enactment of a role analogous to that of Freyr in *Skírnismál*.[217] Though Hallfreðr and his colleagues gave Óðinn the ancestor's role that an earlier poet such as Þjóðólfr would have given Hǫlgi or Ingvi-freyr, the four stanzas quoted below from *Hákonardrápa* emphasize the role of Hákon Jarl as a sacral king who renewed the life of local fields by inseminating the women whom he chose to represent them.

These coercions appear to have been stylized as if Hákon's servants were 'Skírnir' and Guðrún lundasól were the local 'Gerðr'. In the following stanzas from *Hákonardrápa*, Hallfreðr characterizes three figures: Hákon Jarl, as a seducer from the high seas, offering a woman a necklace; Norway, as if this country were a gullible peasant wife receiving these

---

[215] *Ágrip*, ed. Bjarni, p. 16 (*Ágrip*, ch. 12): 'ok var engi kvenna munr í því gǫrt ok engi grein, hvers kona hver væri eða systir eða dóttir'; also in *Heimskringla I*, ed. Bjarni, pp. 290–1 (*Óláfs saga Tryggvasonar*, ch. 44) and 293–5 (ch. 48); and *Flat* I, 216 (ch. 175) and 233–4 (ch. 189).

[216] Hamer, 'Death in a Pig-Sty', p. 58.

[217] This motif of *droit du seigneur* is also represented in the sexual peregrination of Rígr, who founds three orders of society (thrall, churl and earl) in *Rígsþula*; this twelfth- or thirteenth-century poem, edited in U. Dronke, *The Poetic Edda II: Mythological Poems* (forthcoming), may reflect an ancient caste-pattern from the pre-Christian period.

Ingui's marriage

jewels; and Óðinn, as the 'third party' (*Þriði*), Norway's 'furnace-eyed' husband (*Báleygr*):[218]

> Sannyrðum spenr sverða   snarr þiggjandi viggjar
> barrhaddaða byrjar   biðkván und sik Þriðja.
>
> Því hykk fleygjanda frakna   (ferr jǫrð und menþverri
> ítr) eina at láta   Auðs systur mjǫk trauðan.
>
> Ráð lukusk, at sá síðan   snjallráðr konungs spjalli
> átti einga dóttur Ónars,   viði gróna.
>
> Breiðleita gat brúði   Báleygs at sér teygða
> stefnir stǫðvar Hrafna   stála ríkismálum.   (*Hákonardrápa* 3–6)[219]

These lines appear to confirm several thirteenth-century references to the sexual coercions that were alleged to lead to Hákon's downfall.[220] None the less, by giving mythological status to Hákon's seduction of other men's wives (*biðkván Þriðja, brúðr Báleygs*), sisters (*Auðs systir*) and daughters (*Ónars einug dóttir viði gróin*), Hallfreðr appears to elevate his ruler's habitual coercion of female subjects into an ideology of kingship.[221]

Hákon's prolific enactment of his marriage with Þorgerðr is essentially the same as the ideology of *Skírnismál* as this is represented in the activity of Freyr with Gerðr. In *Hákonardrápa* 3, Hallfreðr makes at least three allusions to the myth presented in *Skírnismál*:

---

[218] Noted by Davidson, in 'Earl Hákon and his Poets', p. 462.

[219] Text and translation based on Davidson (*ibid.*, pp. 449 and 491–515): '[3] With the vindicating words of swords [battle] the bold accepter of the stallion of the following wind [Hákon] entices under him the barley-haired waiting wife of Third-One [Óðinn]. [4] For this reason I think that the one who makes spears fly (splendid Earth moves down under the necklace-diminisher) is extremely reluctant to leave the sister of Wealth alone. [5] The union was consummated so that afterwards the eloquent-in-counsel friend of a king took possession of Ónarr's forest-grown(/grown-up-in-the-backwoods) only daughter. [6] The steerer of the harbour's steeds [Hákon Jarl] has had success in drawing to him the broad-featured bride [Norway] of Furnace-Eye [Óðinn] with the imperial words of steel [battle].' See also *Skj* B I, 147–8, 3–6.

[220] Hamer, 'Death in a Pig-Sty', pp. 55–69, esp. 56.

[221] Was this type of kingship practised by the Merovingian Childeric I (d. 481)? See *Gregorii Historiae*, ed. Krusch and Levison, p. 61 (II.12): 'Childericus vero, cum esset nimia in luxoria dissolutus et regnaret super Francorum gentem, coepit filias eorum stuprose detrahere. Illique ob hoc indignantes, de regno eum eiecerunt.'

Heathen gods

> Sannyrðum spenr *sverða*   snarr þiggjandi *viggjar*
> *barr*haddaða byrjar   biðkván und sik Þriðja.[222]

Hákon Jarl can thus be seen as luring the woman of 'barley' through his emissary on Freyr's 'horse' with Freyr's 'sword'.[223] Also, when Hákon seduces Norway as if she is Óðinn's '*breiðleita brúði*' ('broad-featured bride'), as we have seen (*Hákonardrápa* 5), Hallfreðr's vocabulary recalls the '*bradan* berewæstma' (*broad* crops of the barley') whose growth an English farmer hopes to see in *Æcerbot* (*MCharm* 1.55).

Close to Hákon Jarl in this behaviour is King Haraldr hárfagri, whose children named in *Heimskringla* number twenty-two and whose conquest of the rest of Norway is said to have started when a certain Gyða refused to leave home with his servants until he had first made himself a king like those of Denmark and Sweden.[224] In this light, *Hákonardrápa* 3–6 may show Hákon's artificial revival of an archaic custom: how, in his later years, this reactionary *jarl* built his counter-theology against Christendom, looked back into his past for ritual precedent, then revived the sexual prerogative of an old institution: the seasonal circuit of a man descended from a god whose popular representative and mediator he must be for the health of land and harvest.[225]

Needless to say, the 'dying' role of a sacral king was not revived by Hákon Jarl. The pattern of this role, as we have seen, is implicit in two poetic allusions to women welcoming their brothers' killers (Gerðr in *Skí* 16 and Iðunn in *Lok* 17); and it may also be found in the story of Dómaldi, an ancient king of Sweden and descendant of Ingvi-freyr, who is

---

[222] Davidson, 'Earl Hákon and his Poets', p. 449: 'With the vindicating words of *swords* [battle] the bold accepter of the *stallion* of the following wind [Hákon] entices under him the *barley*-haired waiting wife of Third-One [Óðinn].'

[223] *Barr* can also mean 'pine-cone', but is clearly related to *Barri*. Davidson (*ibid.*, pp. 467–8) sees other resemblances between Hákon Jarl in this poem and Freyr in *Skírnismál*; Steinsland, who also sees resemblances, argues that they are not intended to connote a fertility myth in *Hákonardrápa* (*Det hellige bryllup*, p. 123).

[224] *Heimskringla I*, ed. Bjarni, p. 96 (*Haralds saga hárfagra*, ch. 3): herein Haraldr's named children are Álǫf, Hrœrekr, Sigtryggr, Fróði, Þorgils (by Gyða); Guthormr, Hálfdanr svarti, Hálfdanr hvíti, Sigurðr (by Ása); Eiríkr blóðøx (by Ragnhildr); Óláfr Geirstaðaálfr, Bjǫrn, Ragnarr (by Svanhildr); Dagr, Hringr, Guðrøðr skíri, Ingigerðr (by Áshildr); Sigurðr hrísi, Hálfdanr háleggr, Guðrøðr ljómi, Rǫgnvaldr réttilbeini (by Snæfríðr).

[225] For a valuable discussion of the critical heritage on this subject, see McTurk, 'Sacral Kingship in Ancient Scandinavia', pp. 139–69.

Ingui's marriage

said to have been sacrificed in a famine to ensure the regeneration of his country. This story survives in *Ynglingatal*, thereafter in *Historia Norvegiae* of the late twelfth or thirteenth century and in Snorri's *Ynglinga saga*.[226] According to Snorri, Dómaldi's stepmother puts a curse on him by which he develops 'ill luck' (*ógæfa*). The question is whether or not this ill luck is fatal to the crops. When Dómaldi inherits the kingdom of Sweden from his father Vísburr, the Swedes suffer famine. In the first autumn the Swedes sacrifice their oxen; in the second, human beings; in the third, they converge on Uppsala, sacrifice their king and redden the altar with his blood. Snorri quotes Þjóðólfr:

>   Hitt vas fyrr,   at fold ruðu
>   sverðberendr   sínum dróttni,
>   ok landherr   af lífs vǫnum
>   dreyrug vápn   Dómalda bar,
>   þás árgjǫrn   Jóta dólgi
>   Svía kind   of sóa skyldi.   (*Ynglingatal* 5)[227]

Because it counts as the oldest datable Norse reference to sacral kingship, this stanza has become a focal point in the dispute over whether or not this institution existed. Does the story to which Þjóðólfr alluded describe the renewal of royal sacrifice in an emergency? It seems that it does, because the famine required it. In *Ynglingatal* 5, Þjóðólfr's heathen Swedes are 'eager for crops' (*árgjǫrn*) and in this emergency 'had to sacrifice' (or 'sow') their king into the earth to get them (*of sóa skyldi*). In the *Historia Norvegiae* Dómaldi's sacrifice is stylized differently: 'They offered a victim to the goddess Ceres by hanging Domald for the fertility of the crops.'[228] Here the name *Ceres* may be connected with Þjóðólfr's *ár* ('harvest'). Dómaldi is not sacrificed at a mandatory time, but to the extent that the king is sacrificed, Dómaldi's story is, in Lars Lönnroth's words, 'a tragic myth dealing with the mystery of growth and vegetation'.[229]

---

[226] *Heimskringla I*, ed. Bjarni, pp. 30–2 (*Ynglinga saga*, chs. 14–15).

[227] *Ibid.*, p. 32: 'It happened before that sword-bearing men reddened the earth with their lord, and the land-army bore its weapons bloody from Dómaldi lacking in life, when eager for a harvest the race of the Swedes had to sacrifice the enemy of the Jutes' (also edited in *Skj* B I, 8, 5).

[228] *Historia Norvegiae*, ed. Storm, p. 98: 'Domald Sweones suspendentes pro fertilitate frugum deae Cereri hostiam obtulerunt.'

[229] L. Lönnroth, 'Dómaldi's Death and the Myth of Sacral Kingship', in *Structure and Meaning*, ed. Lindow, Lönnroth and Weber, pp. 73–93, esp. 83.

Heathen gods

In Dómaldi's case, however, different narrative purposes are served by Þjóðólfr, Snorri and the *Historia Norvegiae*. For his own part Þjóðólfr sardonically presents this death as one of many untimely ends suffered by the unfortunate kings of Sweden. Thus, as Lönnroth points out, it would be absurd to use *Ynglingatal* as proof that Swedish kings were regularly sacrificed for prosperity.[230] But that is also because there are more appropriate hints of a repeating pattern of sacrifice in *Skírnismál* and *Lokasenna*. The burden of proof in this case lies not with vindicating 'sacral kingship' in the story of Dómaldi in *Ynglingatal*, but in showing that the hungry condition (*árgjǫrn*) and the sacrificial obligation (*sóa skyldi*) of the Swedes are unrelated there and that the murder of Dómaldi in this late ninth-century poem may be classified as entirely separate from the harvest of his land.

The conclusion to be drawn from these traditions of Hákon Jarl and Dómaldi is that the ancestral figure which these traditions reflect had been a man held to be divine: not only as the male consort of various women representing regions of his country, but also as a seasonal king who would be replaced by another in the same role. In chs. 2–6, I have referred to this figure as the 'Ing-hypostasis'. The next section attempts to identify the ancient Germanic topos from which the institution of Dómaldi's sacrifice developed as a contingent response to an emergency.

Marriage and death of the Ing-hypostasis

To summarize the tenth-century evidence for the death of earth's husband: before Gerðr meets Skírnir, the emissary of Freyr in *Skírnismál*, she fears that he is the man who killed her brother (*Skí* 16); Iðunn, according to Loki's accusation in *Lok* 17, embraces her brother's killer with 'splendid-washed arms' (*arma ítrþvegna*) after she meets him; while in *Hákonardrápa* 4, Hallfreðr appears to allude to this bathing motif in the expression, 'splendid Earth moves down under the necklace-diminisher' (*ferr jǫrð und menþverri ítr*). Iðunn may be identified as an aspect of Gerðr, as a personification of the phenomenon of earth when it is sown. Iðunn's brother was her old husband; now she has a new one, also her brother; with luck, the process will go on. In this way, the inference from *Lok* 17

---

[230] *Ibid.*, p. 92.

Ingui's marriage

and *Skí* 16 is that each incarnation of Freyr who comes to replace the one before him must be destroyed in turn by his successor.

Baldr's role as a 'dying god' fits into this pattern, particularly in Saxo's version of the Baldr myth in *Gesta Danorum*, in which, as *Balderus*, the reflex of the Ing-hypostasis in Saxo's tradition eventually dies in battle against *Hotherus* in a struggle to possess the nymph Nanna (after which Hotherus is killed in turn by Bous, a new brother). As I have attempted to show in ch. 5, there is probably a history of semantic development with Baldr's name from an epithet indicating a 'swollen' or fertile prince.[231] In ch. 6, I have suggested that *Baldr* may have evolved as a Gothic–Arian name for Christ, borrowed into eastern Germanic paganism as an offshoot of Enguz; as the cult of Baldr grew in Scandinavia, Ingvi-freyr would then have lost his claim to be the dying god. Although Baldr is presented as an *áss*, not as a *vaningi*, a connection between him and Freyr remains visible in *Gesta Danorum*, in which Saxo inserts a reference to Frø's human sacrifices in Uppsala even while he tells the story of Balderus ('indeed, by undertaking to sacrifice victims of the human race, [Frø] dedicated foul offerings to the powers above').[232] Saxo also says, as we have seen in ch. 5, that Balderus, before his death, 'began to make it his custom to measure out his journeys in a chariot or carriage'.[233] This wagon-tour resembles Freyr's in *Gunnars þáttr helmings*.[234] Baldr and Freyr both die. Although, in *Gylfaginning*, Baldr is sent to Hel in a blazing ship, the interment of Balderus in a mound in Saxo's account resembles the burial of Freyr in a mound in Snorri's *Ynglinga saga* and in *Flateyjarbók*.[235] Just as Baldr has a human death, Freyr is the only Norse god with a childhood or adolescence: Óðinn relates that 'the gods gave Elf-home to Freyr in the ancient days as a gift for cutting his first tooth' (*Álfheim Frey gáfo í árdaga tívar at tannfé*, *Grím* 5); and Skírnir claims that he and Freyr were 'young together in ancient days' (*ungir saman í árdaga*, *Skí* 5).[236] From ancient times,

---

[231] Green, *Carolingian Lord*, pp. 21–33.
[232] *GD*, p. 66: 'siquidem humani generis hostias mactare aggressus, foeda superis libamenta persoluit'.
[233] *Ibid.*, p. 67: 'biga raedave emetiendorum itinerum consuetudinem habere coepit'.
[234] *Germania*, p. 285; *Flat* I, 337–9 (chs. 277–8).
[235] *Heimskringla I*, ed. Bjarni, pp. 24–5 (*Ynglinga saga*, ch. 10); and *Flat* I, 401–3 (ch. 323).
[236] This boyish conception of Freyr also concurs with the Greek image of Dionysus; see *The Bacchae*, trans. Kirk, pp. 61–2 (lines 451–60).

therefore, it seems that Baldr, the Ing-hypostasis, was intended to grow, couple and die not as god, but as the human (later deified) incarnation of Njǫrðr.

A story in *Skáldskaparmál* makes a link between Baldr and Njǫrðr clearer. Following the killing of Þjazi at the end of his prose version of *Haustlǫng* 1–13, Snorri adds a sequel in which Skaði, whom he calls this giant's daughter, armed herself and came to Ásgarðr looking for revenge. The Æsir offered her compensation: 'hit fyrsta at hon skal *kjósa sér mann* af Ásum, ok *kjósa at fótum* ok sjá ekki fleira af. Þá sá hon eins manns fætr forkunnar fagra, ok mælti: þenna kýs ek, fátt mun ljótt á Baldri; en þat var *Njörðr* ór Nóatúnum.'[237] Skaði's demand is that the Æsir make her laugh: as if he were Attis to her Cybele, Loki does so by tying one end of a rope to a goat's beard and the other to his testicles, then falling into her lap while the goat tugs the other way, whereupon 'peace was then made with her on behalf of the Æsir'.[238] More crucially in this story, however, it seems that Baldr must represent the god Njǫrðr in human flesh, when Skaði marries Njǫrðr.

There is an embellished Danish analogue of Skaði's marriage with Njǫrðr in Saxo's story of Hadingus in the first book of *Gesta Danorum*.[239] In Saxo's tale, Harthgrepa, a giantess from Sweden, nurses the hero Hadingus when he is a child, seduces him with promises in verse to shrink from her unwieldy size in order to enjoy his embrace, then disappears from the story. As she says, 'I am used to frightening the fierce when I am bigger, and I seek copulation with men when I am smaller.'[240]

[237] *SnE* 212–14 (*Bragarœður*, ch. 56): 'the first offer was that she should *choose a man* for herself from the Æsir and *choose him by the feet* and not see any more of him. It was then that she saw a man's feet exceptionally beautiful and said: "This man I choose, little there will be that's ugly in *Baldr*." And yet it was *Njǫrðr* of ?Ships'-Enclosures'; *FJSnE* 81 (ch. 3). Italics my own.

[238] *SnE* 214 (ch. 56): 'var þá gjör sætt af Ásanna hendi við hana'; *FJSnE* 81.

[239] *Gylf*, p. 24 (ch. 23); *GD*, p. 30; *History of the Danes*, trans. Fisher and ed. Ellis Davidson I, 170–5 and II, 99–102.

[240] *GD*, p. 22: 'maiore feroces territo, concubitus hominum breuiore capesso'. H. Ellis Davidson traces this motif to Lady Philosophy at the start of the *De consolatione Philosophiae* of Boethius, but this attribution does not explain why the motif was necessary for Hadingus's marriage with Harthgrepa: *History of the Danes*, trans. Fisher and ed. Ellis Davidson II, 30. G. Dumézil interprets the motif of *hieros gamos* in Hadingus and Harthgrepa, but does not follow the implication of Harthgrepa's changing stature: *From Myth to Fiction: the Saga of Hadingus*, trans. D. Coltman (Chicago and London, 1973), pp. 58–72.

Ingui's marriage

Hadingus later wins a woman named Regnilda by killing the giant who had courted her. When Regnilda is given leave by her father to choose her husband, rather like Skaði, she 'examined the group of young men gathered in the banquet by the very inquisitive fondling of their bodies'.[241] Regnilda thus finds the ring that she had inserted into Hadingus's leg a little earlier in this tale. Later, Hadingus and his second partner Regnilda exchange Saxo's translated version of the verses between Njǫrðr and Skaði that Snorri quotes in *Gylfaginning*.[242] It seems, therefore, that Harthgrepa and Regnilda represent respectively phenomenal and personal aspects of a being which is an analogue of Skaði. Hadingus is also probably to be seen as a euhemerized version of Njǫrðr because he later establishes sacrifices to Frø in Sweden.

If we apply the implications of the meanings of their names to the meaning of this story, Skaði's choice of Njǫrðr in *Skáldskaparmál* may not be the accident that Snorri takes it to be. When Skaði looks for Baldr and finds Njǫrðr, she gets Baldr, the man whom she wants. As phenomena rather than persons, the land of 'Scandinavia' would look for Njǫrðr's human incarnation as a husband with whom to spend a limited time. As Njǫrðr's personal manifestation would be the human lord of a dynasty descended from him, this figure is quite literally **freyr* ('lord'). The story of Skaði's choice of a husband is thus a rehearsal of *Skírnismál* from the earth's point of view. Skaði names her choice *baldr* because, in the *baldruus* phase of the meaning of Baldr's name, he is a 'swollen' male, a strong but replaceable human incarnation of Njǫrðr.

Some trace of Ingvi-freyr's motif of marriage and sacrifice in the *Germania* can be found in the name of *Tuisto*. Tuisto is said to be the father of Mannus, the father of three tribes of which the form *Ingaeuones* or *Inguaeones* suggests an *Ing*-hypostasis in its stem.[243] The name *Tuisto* led R. M. Meyer to suggest that Tuisto is identical with the titan Ymir, who produces his own offspring by himself at the outset of the Norse creation-myth; Julius Pokorny glossed *Tuisto* as 'hermaphrodite' ('Zwitter'), because the Gothic participle *twisstandands* is used to render the Greek infinitive ἀποτάσσεσθαι ('to part', thus 'to separate').[244] However, this

---

[241] *GD*, p. 30: 'contractam conuiuio iuuentutem curiosiore corporum attrectatione lustrabat'.
[242] *Gylf*, p. 24 (ch. 23).
[243] *Germania*, pp. 96 and 273.
[244] R. M. Meyer, 'Beiträge zur altgermanischen Mythologie', *ANF* 23 (1907), 245–56,

Heathen gods

meaning of *twisstandands* is figurative ('standing apart, away'), while a simpler literal meaning of *tuisto* may be 'two-standing' or 'standing twice'.[245] If, as Pokorny shows, *Tui-* or *Tuis-* is cognate with 'twice', *ston-* with 'stand', then it is simpler to explain *Tui(s)-stonem* literally as 'feet': the characteristic by which Skaði chooses Njǫrðr; or by which Terra Mater might choose her 'twice-standing' husband Nerthus. As *terra editus* ('born from the earth'), Tuisto would be a man whose feet are imagined as the roots of a growing tree. So the Broddenbjærg oak-fork sculpture (a man with erect penis and bearded face) was contrived to stand with no more than two roots in the mud.[246]

Tacitus, who makes Tuisto father of Mannus, the father of the Ingvaeones, probably relied on a Greek ethnographer who had taken the form *Tuisto*, perhaps through *Tiuaz*, to be a Germanic corruption of Zeus, a prolific father of half-mortal Dionysus, Hercules and others. More than a thousand years later in *Skáldskaparmál*, it is perhaps because Skaði is the earth, the mud itself, that she cannot see more than the feet of the man whom she finds to be Njǫrðr. So, in this case, in the ideology of the Anglii in the first century, earth the mother (*terra mater*) would join with the ocean (*Nerthus*) by choosing for her female incarnation (*dea* or *numen*) a seasonal husband (*Ing-*), one man (*Mannus*) from among many, by the soles of his feet (*Tuisto*): Tuisto = Mannus = Ing-.

The final points of a hypothesis on Nerthus and Terra Mater can now be laid out. This is a three-dimensional jigsaw puzzle for which, I admit, my solution is incapable of proof. None the less, the fragmentary evidence leads me to the following reconstruction of the ideology from which Edwin's Anglian kingship and the cult of Ingui may be taken to descend:

1 At sowing-time before winter in coastal Germania, Terra Mater marries Nerthus.
2 Terra Mater finds Nerthus in his human shape (*Mannus*) from among the *Ingvaeones*, an aboriginal royal tribe, by the soles of his feet (*Tuisto*).

---

esp. 246–8; Pokorny, *Indogermanisches etymologisches Wörterbuch* I, 230–2 (*sich trennen*); see also *AR* II, 363–4 (§573); this idea has gained widespread acceptance.

[245] Pokorny, *ibid.* I, 220 (*duis*, 'twice') and 1004 (*sta-*, 'stand'). Variant readings are *tuisconem* and *bistonem*; for a justification of *tuistonem*, however, see Robinson, *Germania*, pp. 96 and 273.

[246] Described in Glob, *Bog People*, p. 127.

Ingui's marriage

3 In order to mate with *Ing-*, Terra Mater is represented by a woman (*dea*) from the same royal tribe.
4 As if reborn after a long winter, Ing- appears for the spring sowing, tours the tribes and through the summer sows his own seed in as many women as require it for the fertility of local fields.
5 Ing- and the *dea* become political mediators between the gods and their people.
6 In harvest time Ing- and the *dea* travel round the seven tribes in a state wagon, in a popular celebration of the abundance of ale, barley and the fruits of the earth.
7 Returning to Terra Mater's sanctuary, the *numen* is washed by attendants,
8 while Ing-, worn out and now to be thrown away, is killed by next year's *Mannus* whom Terra Mater has chosen while Ing- and the *dea* were touring in the wagon.
9 The queen embraces her new man, after which her servants are drowned to keep the nature of Ing-'s regeneration a secret.[247]

CONCLUSION

Nerthus of the Anglii, later Ing or Ingui or other reflexes whose names have not survived, was probably worshipped at the heart of a number of pre-Christian religions in Anglo-Saxon England. Since heathens seemed to regard all natural phenomena as living things, it is worth reiterating that all creatures subject to the ageing process are described as 'kindreds of the Ingvi-lord' (*áttir Ing[v]i-freys*) towards the end of the ninth century in Norway in *Haustlǫng* 10; in the light of this analogue, it seems reasonable to suppose that all phenomena in pre-Christian England, especially those of sea, sky and earth whose traces have been illustrated in this chapter, likewise constituted, whenever personified, the members of Nerthus's family. The seasonal marriage of Nerthus and Terra Mater would have encouraged the renewal of all these natural phenomena. Although this seasonal 'sacrifice', if ever historical, had probably ceased before the Angles settled in Britain, it is possible that the Angles

---

[247] Cf. *Germania*, p. 317: 'Arcanus hinc terror sanctaque ignorantia, quid sit illud quod tantum perituri vident.' Iðunn lays her 'arma ítrþvegna' around her 'bróðurbani' (*Lok* 17); Nerthus's slaves are drowned; and Glob (*Bog People*, pp. 61–74) notes that there were women and children among the bodies unearthed in the Jutland peat-bog.

Heathen gods

preserved legends of Ingui's role as a 'dying god' after the demise of this role as a political institution.[248] In the next chapter I shall discuss the reflections of this seasonal sacrifice in the Anglian vocabulary with which Christ's death is described in *The Dream of the Rood*.

[248] Glob (*ibid.*, pp. 39–44, esp. 42) notes that the Grauballe man, aged at least thirty and one among several men with uncalloused hands, had eaten a meal with no less than sixty-three varieties of grain prior to the cutting of his throat and burial in a Jutland peat bog in 210 × 410 AD: 'The condition of the skin-lines on the hand made it possible to infer that the Grauballe man had never had to do any heavy or rough manual work.'

9

Ingui's death: the world-tree sacrifice

In the previous chapter I have proposed a hypothesis regarding the old Anglian homeland in which *Ing-*, a seasonally returning figure from which the Bernician name *Ingui* was later derived, was married before the spring to a woman representing the earth and was killed in the autumn by his replacement for the following year. The pattern of this suggested ideology is of course far removed from the story of Christ's works and crucifixion as this story is told in the gospels and in later commentaries and other literary adaptations. Yet there is reason to believe that the poet of *The Dream of the Rood*, which is probably derived from a Northumbrian original composed at the beginning of the eighth century, described the crucifixion using words with which an Anglian myth of Ingui may once have been told. The disparate Scandinavian mythology on which I have attempted to reconstruct the basis of a myth of Ingui's death will again be put into service in this chapter. Firstly, I shall argue that the description of the cross in *The Dream of the Rood* is partly based on the image of an Anglian 'world tree' analogous to the role of Yggdrasill in the Old Norse–Icelandic cosmos. Secondly, on the basis of the mythology of Baldr, I shall argue that the image of Christ's death was constructed in this poem with reference to an Anglian myth of Ingui's sacrifice on the world tree. In particular, I shall suggest that the poet of the Northumbrian work from which *The Dream of the Rood* is derived used the language of this myth of Ingui in order to present the Passion to his newly Christianized countrymen as a story from their native tradition.

THE CROSS AS A TREE

Early Christians faced a moral dilemma where the nature of the cross was concerned. The cross was not the object of any widespread cult until the fourth century, when it is alleged that Constantine beheld it in a vision in 312 and his mother Empress Helena discovered it in Jerusalem in 326. Thereafter the cross remained an important part of Christianity until the incipient iconoclasm of the eighth century, when this symbol seemed in Christian eyes to be too close to an idolatrous image. Defining the nature and purpose of the cross, however, remained important in patristic writing, where its obvious uses in conversion, preaching and state ceremony made it a symbol of redemption, the Christian's personal token of faith and his or her means of achieving grace. The cross has these and other roles in *The Dream of the Rood*, a poem surviving in the late tenth-century Vercelli Book.[1] In this poem the cross appears to a man in a midnight dream-vision, tells him (and us) the story of the Passion from its own uniquely dramatic point of view and delivers a sermon on Doomsday and the role of the cross in Christian redemption. Consequently the Dreamer reveals to us his (and thus our) moral transformation and his desire to seek the cross 'alone more frequently than all men' (*ana oftor þonne ealle men*, *Dream* 128).

Prosopopoeia is the technique by which the cross speaks in the first person in *The Dream of the Rood*. This technique is most common in Anglo-Saxon riddles, where a wide range of inanimate objects may speak as living things. Prosopopoeia with the cross occurs throughout the period and from one end of the country to the other: 'I [lifted up] a powerful king' ([*Ahof*] *ic riicnæ kyniNGc*), says the Ruthwell stone cross of *c.* 700 on the north-west border of Northumbria, in one of four runic passages that may or may not be extracts from an early eighth-century version of *The Dream of the Rood*;[2] and the eleventh-century inscription on the Brussels cross-reliquary pre-empts a riddle with a solution: 'Rood is my name' (*Rod is min nama*). Hwætberht, abbot of Wearmouth–Jarrow, composed cross-riddles in *c.* 716, as did the Mercian Tatwine, who was archbishop of Canterbury in 731–4.[3] *Riddles* 30, 55 and 67 of the late tenth-century Exeter Book have also been interpreted as the cross. Prosopopoeia could be a poet's licence to dramatize the crucifixion. Yet identifying prosopopoeia and its likely origin in Latin rhetorical training in early English monasteries is only half the story.[4] Why was this device

---

[1] *The Dream of the Rood*, ed. Swanton, pp. 1–9, esp. 5.
[2] *Ibid.*, pp. 9–42, esp. 32. The corresponding line is *Dream* 44.   [3] *Ibid.*, pp. 66–7.
[4] Nelson, 'Rhetoric of the Exeter Book Riddles', pp. 425–8; Schlauch, '*The Dream of the Rood* as Prosopopoeia', pp. 23–34.

so popular? There are too many poems in which inanimate objects want us to guess their names, too many cases of prosopopoeia in Anglo-Latin and Old English riddles, for this question not to deserve an answer.

One fact worth noting in connection with the common word OE *rod* ('tree', 'cross') or with other Old English words such as *gealga* ('gallows'), *beam* ('beam') or *treow* ('tree'), is that their use is standard, whereas that of *cruc*, a Latin loanword for the 'sign of the cross', is rare.[5] Pope Gregory's letter to Mellitus in 601 asks him not to tear heathen shrines to the ground, but to reconsecrate them for Christian use so that the converted people 'may hasten more readily to their accustomed places'.[6] So it is interesting that the common Old English words for the essential elements of Christian worship, baptism (*fulwiht*), altar (*wigbed*) or vestments (*godweb*), are native terms, while words for the agents of worship, such as priest (*preost*), church (*cirice*) and godfather (*cumpæder*) derive from Greek or Latin. It may be no coincidence that there appear to be no records of a Germanic priesthood in an untranslated vernacular source.[7] Native words for the cross such as *rod* appear to have described the sacrifice on Calvary well enough in the first vernacular sermons. Lat *arbor* ('tree') was in any case a standard metonym for the cross.[8] Yet if the Vikings, two or three centuries later, had reason to accept a new word *kross* with the concept of Lat *crux*, along with *kyrkja* ('church'), why did the Anglo-Saxons fail to make a regular use of this Latin word in England in the seventh century? In Scandinavia, in these intervening centuries, Germanic paganism had clearly changed. In seventh-century England, the evidence of *fulwiht* and other native terms suggests that *rod*, *gealga*, *beam* or *treow* were thought to be adequate to render 'cross' on their own. It is therefore likely that a tree-persona was part of that Anglo-Saxon superstition which preceded Christianity.

There are references to tree- or pillar-worship in Germanic areas of

---

[5] On these and other words for Christian worship, see *A Thesaurus of Old English*, ed. J. Roberts and C. Kay, with L. Grundy, King's College London Medieval Studies 11, 2 vols. (London, 1995) I, 669–90, esp. 670 (*preost*, nos. 16.02.03 and 16.02.03.02.07), 688 (*cruc*, no. 16.02.04.18.01) and 689 (*cirice*, no. 16.02.05.02.03).

[6] *HE* I.30 (p. 106): 'ad loca quae consueuit familiarius concurrat'; cf. Wallace-Hadrill, *Commentary*, pp. 44–5.

[7] *HAR* II.ii, 189–90 (§126).

[8] P. Dronke, 'Arbor Caritatis', in *Medieval Studies for J. A. W. Bennett*, ed. P. L. Heyworth (Oxford, 1981), pp. 207–53.

Heathen gods

continental Europe in the eighth century.[9] In England, a canon in an eighth-century text probably derived from the pupils of Theodore, archbishop of Canterbury (668–90), decrees: 'If anyone makes an offering on trees or wells or stones or railings or anywhere except in the Church of God, ... this is sacrilege, that is, sacrifice to demons.'[10] An eleventh-century translation of Halitgar's *Penitential* elaborates on this prohibition as follows:

Sume men synd swa ablende þæt hi bringað heora lac to eorðfæstum stane and eac to treowum and to wylspringum swa swa wiccan tæcað and nellað under-stondan hu stuntlice he doð oððe hu se dæd[a] stan oððe þæt dumbe treow him mæge gehelpan oððe hæle forgifan, þone hi sylfe ne astyriað of þære stowe næfre. (II. 22)[11]

The late date of this translation confirms the continuing need to legislate against tree-offerings in Anglo-Saxon England. That Christians used crosses to heal the sick, however, is shown in St Willibald's *Hodoeporicon*, in which Willibald says that he was a sickly child when he grew up in Wessex (probably at the beginning of the eighth century), but recovered his health when his parents 'took their son and placed him down before the holy cross of the Lord Saviour ... as is the custom of the Saxon nation'.[12] In this respect it is worth noting some correspondences

---

[9] Witness St Boniface's attempt to destroy the 'oak of Jove' (*robor Iobis*) in Gaesmere, Hesse, in c. 723–4 (*Vitae S. Bonifatii*, ed. Levison, pp. 31 and 135); cf. also Charlemagne's destruction of *Hirminsuul*, the Old Saxon world pillar, in 772 (*Widukindi Gestarum Saxonicarum*, ed. Hirsch and Lohmann, pp. 20–1 (I.12); *Annales Regni Francorum*, ed. Pertz and rev. Kurze, p. 35).

[10] See *Ancient Laws and Institutes of England*, ed. B. Thorpe, 2 vols. (London, 1840) II, 34 (XXVII.xviii): 'Si quis ad arbores, vel ad fontes, vel ad lapides, sive ad cancellos vel ubicunque, excepto in aecclesia Dei votum voverit ... hoc sacrilegium est, vel daemoniacum.' This text is not edited in *Die Canones Theodori*, ed. Finsterwalder. On the life of Theodore, see M. Lapidge, 'The Career of Archbishop Theodore', in *Archbishop Theodore*, ed. Lapidge, pp. 1–29.

[11] *Die altenglische Version des Halitgar'schen Bussbuches*, ed. Raith, p. 29: 'Some men are so blinded that they take their offerings to a stone made firm in the earth and also to trees and wells, just as witches teach them, and such a man will not understand how stupidly he acts or how this dead stone or that dumb tree can help him or give him health, when these things, for their part, can never move from that place.'

[12] *Vita Willibaldi episcopi Eichstetensis*, ed. O. Holder-Egger, MGH, Scriptores 15.1 (Hanover, 1887), 86–106, esp. 88: 'sumentes filium suum, obtulerunt illum coram illam dominicam sanctamque crucem Salvatoris ... sicut mos est Saxanice gentis'.

between the above translation of Halitgar and *The Dream of the Rood*: the words 'that dumb tree' (*þæt dumbe treow*) imply that late Anglo-Saxon backsliders believed that their trees could talk; while at the heart of *The Dream of the Rood*, with 'then the best tree of wood began to speak' (*ongan þa word sprecan wudu selesta*, *Dream* 27), the Dreamer is given reason to believe the same; to an Anglo-Saxon miscreant in the text quoted above from Halitgar's penitential, a tree 'can help him or give him health' (*him mæge gehelpan oððe hæle forgifan*); rather as the Dreamer's cross announces that 'I can heal anyone who goes in fear of me' (*ic hælan mæg æghwylcne anra þara þe him bið egesa to me*, *Dream* 84–6). It is no wonder, therefore, that standing crosses were sometimes worshipped in open fields as if they were trees: writing to Boniface in 744, Pope Zacharias complains that the self-promoting Bishop Aldebert of Gaul, in addition to other errors, 'has put little crosses and oratories in the fields, by springs or anywhere it seemed best to him, ordering public prayers to be celebrated there'.[13] A close relationship between the cult of the cross and popular tree-superstition seems to have continued throughout the Anglo-Saxon period.

From the evidence of OE *treow*, *rod* and *beam* it is clear how easily the early Anglo-Saxons could imagine the cross as a tree. This image might have been assisted or justified with a verse on Doomsday: 'Then all the trees of the forests will rise to face the Lord' (*Tunc exsultabunt omnia ligna silvarum a facie Domini*, Ps. XCV.12–13). In his sixth-century hymn *Vexilla regis prodeunt*, Venantius Fortunatus also quotes a variant reading of Ps. XCV.10 as 'God has ruled among the nations from the tree' (*in nationibus regnavit a ligno Deus*).[14] Yet it is unlikely that this psalm or other scriptural or patristic authority furthered the *treow* conceit to the point of limiting the use of Lat *crux* in the vernacular. With this deep-rooted conceit some pre-Christian background must be sought, with the aid of analogues from the oldest traditions of Norway and Iceland. Even then it is often difficult to distinguish Anglo-Saxon traditions of common

---

[13] *Die Briefe des Heiligen Bonifatius und Lullus*, ed. M. Tangl, MGH, Epistolae Selectae 4.1 (Berlin, 1955), 102–5, esp. 104: 'fecit quoque cruciculas et oratoriola in campis, et ad fontes, vel ubicumque sibi visum fuit, et iussit ibi publicas orationes celebrari'.

[14] *Venanti Fortunati Opera*, ed. Leo, pp. 34–5, esp. 34 (lines 17–18). On the extent of the knowledge of Venantius's poems in early Anglo-Saxon England, see R. W. Hunt, 'Manuscript Evidence for Knowledge of the Poems of Venantius Fortunatus in Late Anglo-Saxon England (with an Appendix, "Knowledge of the Poems in the Earlier Period", by M. Lapidge)', *ASE* 8 (1979), 279–95, at 287–95.

Germanic origin from ninth- or tenth-century heathen imports from Scandinavia. Another problem is the uncertainty in using the references in Old Norse–Icelandic literature that must support conclusions of what Scandinavian paganism was. Yet some fragmentary motifs recur in a wide variety of Old Norse–Icelandic poems, particularly where negative and positive aspects of the world tree are concerned. The first of these aspects is the ash of Yggdrasill, the second a Norse god named Heimdallr. The following discussion of the Norse world tree is a prerequisite for my reading of an Anglian world tree on the Ruthwell cross and in *The Dream of the Rood*.

THE NORSE WORLD TREE

OIce ascr Yggdrasils

Two of the earliest references to Yggdrasill survive in *Grímnismál* and *Vǫluspá*.[15] In *Grímnismál* the god Óðinn, disguised as the traveller Grímnir, is tortured with fire in King Geirrǫðr's hall, but reveals to Agnarr, the king's son who offers him water, a catalogue of mythical and topographical knowledge which includes locating the Æsir's judgement place 'at the ash of Yggdrasill' (*at asci Yggdrasils*, *Grím* 29 and 30). Óðinn goes on to describe the three roots of this cosmic ash-tree, beneath which Hel, the frost-giants and mankind dwell (*Grím* 31). A squirrel named *Ratatoskr* ('auger-tooth') runs up and down the trunk bearing the tidings of an eagle at the top to the dragon Níðhǫggr down below (*Grím* 32). Harts gnaw at the boughs, Níðhǫggr at the roots of Yggdrasill (*Grím* 33–5), a tree which can thus be taken as synonymous with the world:

> Ascr Yggdrasils   drýgir erfiði,
>   meira, enn menn viti;   (*Grím* 35)[16]

Óðinn also says that 'the ash of Yggdrasill is the best of trees' (*ascr Yggdrasils, hann er œztr viða*, *Grím* 44).

With the syncretism of an attempt to harmonize heathen cults in the face of Christianity, the poet of *Vǫluspá* presents the world tree as the measure of the world: a 'splendid measuring tree' (*mjǫtvið mæran*, *Vsp* 2) and the home and symbol of fate:

[15] See *AR* II, 380–3 (§§583–5).
[16] 'The ash of Yggdrasill endures hardships greater than men can understand.'

Ingui's death

>   Asc veit ec standa,   heitir Yggdrasill,
>   hár baðmr, ausinn   hvítaauri;
>   þaðan koma dǫggvar, þærs í dala falla,
>   stendr æ yfir, grœnn, Urðar brunni.   (*Vsp* 19)[17]

Thus *Vǫluspá*, a creation poem of unusual imaginative intensity, seems to move away from the cyclical eschatology of *Grímnismál* and *Vafþrúðnismál*, towards the eschatology of Christianity. When the world comes to an end in *Vǫluspá*, the god Heimdallr blows his horn, fate is made known and the ash-tree groans: 'the ash of Yggdrasill trembles as it stands, the ancient tree groans' (*scelfr Yggdrasils ascr standandi, ymr it aldna tré*, *Vsp* 47).

In the 1230s Snorri quoted and enlarged on these stanzas as part of his *Gylfaginning* (chs. 15–16, 41 and 51). This part of the prose *Edda* is structured chiefly on *Vafþrúðnismál* and *Vǫluspá* with the embellishment of passages based on other Eddic poems. As Snorri augments *Vǫluspá*'s eschatology with some of his finest prose, so he gives Yggdrasill a grandeur which hides the malign meaning of its name. *Yggr* ('terror') is Óðinn's second most important name in *Grím* 54. The name *Ygg-drasill*, 'Terror-steed', probably refers to the gallows on which Óðinn hangs himself in a self-sacrifice at the core of *Hávamál*:

>   á þeim meiði,   er mangi veit,
>   hvers hann af rótom renn.   (*Háv* 138)[18]

Though Snorri refers to Óðinn as 'god of the hanged man' (*hangaguð*) in *Gylfaginning*, he does not allude to this part of *Hávamál*.[19] Nor does Snorri cite Egill's kenning for the world, *Elgjar galgi* ('Óðinn's gallows', *Sonatorrek* 15), though he probably knew this part of *Sonatorrek*.[20] Óðinn's riding the gallows, as in *Háv* 138, is probably part of the *drasill* image in *ascr Yggdrasils* (the genitive *Yggdrasils* can be taken as partitive on analogy with *Fenrisúlfr*, an alternative for the wolf's name *Fenrir*). Generally, however, the conceit in *ascr Yggdrasils* seems to have been widely known among poets: witness Þjóðólfr's kenning for hanging, 'to

---

[17] 'I know [says the sibyl] that an ash stands, called Yggdrasill, a high trunk, splashed with the white mud; from there come the dews that fall in the valleys, it stands forever green over the well of Urðr.'

[18] 'On the branch that no-one knows from whose roots it runs.'

[19] *Gylf*, p. 21 (ch. 20).   [20] *Egils saga*, ed. Sigurður, p. 251.

tame the cool horse of Signý's man [Sigmundr, a wolf: wolf's horse: gibbet]' *(temja svalan hest Signýjar vers, Ynglingatal* 12).[21]

In *Gylfaginning*, through the speaker Jafnhár, Snorri focuses on the ash of Yggdrasill as the gods' chief holy place: 'the ash is the biggest and best of all trees. Its limbs are spread over all the world and extend across the heavens. The tree's three roots hold it up and extend extremely widely'.[22] It seems that the hanging motif in the collocation *ascr Yggdrasils* was ancient even by the time it formed part of *Grímnismál*. With the exception of its revitalized role in *Vsp* 19, Yggdrasill does not occur in the poetry as a simplex and therefore probably represents a tradition older than the date of its surviving instances. As *ascr Yggdrasils* ('ash of Terror-steed'), therefore, the world tree supports Óðinn in his nine-night hanging-sacrifice and is seen as ancient, agonized and extending from heaven to hell over the whole world.

OIce Heimdallr

Heimdallr presents many puzzles and contradictions.[23] Besides being the subject of allusions which pervade the Eddic corpus, in *Gylfaginning* Heimdallr has a riddle of his own (the *Heimdalargaldr*): 'I am the boy of nine mothers, I am the son of nine sisters' *(Níu em ek mœðra mǫgr, níu em ek systra sonr)*.[24] In the *Rígsþula*, a Norse poem possibly composed in Ireland in the twelfth century, Heimdallr is identified with 'Rígr' and appears as the hero of his own poem, a mythic progenitor who spends nights with Edda ('great-grandmother'), Amma ('grandmother') and Móðir ('mother') to beget the races, respectively, of thralls, churls and earls.

As early as the end of the tenth century this legend was familiar to the poet of *Vǫluspá*, whose first sibyl begins her prophecy by ordering silence from mankind: 'all sacred creatures, the greater and the lesser, kinsmen of Heimdallr' *(allar helgar kindir, meiri oc minni, mǫgo Heimdalar, Vsp* 1). Another feminine subject in *Vǫluspá*, probably a second sibyl, is said to know of the existence of 'Heimdallr's hearing concealed beneath the holy tree-trunk which is accustomed to the bright vault' *(Heimdalar hljóð um fólgit undir heiðvǫnum helgom baðmi, Vsp* 27). Heimdallr blows his horn to

[21] *Heimskringla I*, ed. Bjarni, pp. 38–9 *(Ynglinga saga*, ch. 19).
[22] *Gylf*, p. 17 (ch. 15): 'Askrinn er allra tréa mestr ok beztr. Limar hans dreifask yfir heim allan ok standa yfir himni. Þrjár rœtr trésins halda því upp ok standa afar breitt.'
[23] *AR* II, 238–44 (§§491–5).   [24] *Gylf*, p. 26 (ch. 27: *Heimdalargaldr*).

warn the gods of the approach of the giants in Ragnarǫk, immediately before Yggdrasill, the world tree again, trembles and groans (*Vsp* 46–7). Thus at the end of the pagan period in Iceland, Heimdallr is twice associated with the ash of Yggdrasill and works as the Æsir's sentinel, listening and watching for the giants.

Heimdallr accuses Loki of drunken recklessness in Ægir's doomed party in *Lokasenna*, whereupon Loki calls him 'the gods' watchman' (*vǫrðr goða*), his backside perpetually smeared with mud (*Lok* 48). Heimdallr is also said to be *vǫrðr goða* in *Grímnismál*, this time happily drinking mead in his house in 'Heaven-hill' (*Himinbjǫrg, Grím* 13). In *Þrymskviða* (a late poem, probably of the thirteenth century) it is Heimdallr, 'whitest of the Æsir' (*hvítastr ása*), who proposes that Þórr should be dressed up as Freyja, the bride for whom the giant Þrymr has stolen Þórr's hammer (*Þrym* 15–16). In this verse sequence Heimdallr is said to know the future 'just as other Vanir' (*sem vanir aðrir*). This Vanir identity in Heimdallr might seem at first to be a late confusion, but as we have seen in the late ninth-century *Haustlǫng*, it was an old poetic licence to term all the gods as part of 'all the kindreds of the Ingvi-lord' (*allar áttir Ing{v}i-freys*).

As we have seen in ch. 8, a legend was known in Úlfr Uggason's *Húsdrápa* 2 (*c*. 985) in which Heimdallr wrestles with Loki in seal's shape for possession of a jewel:

Straightforward in counsel, the land-guardian of the powers [Heimdallr] wrests the *Singa*-stone away from the crime-cunning son of Fárbauti [Loki], famous for doing so; strong in heart, the son of eight and one mothers [Heimdallr] is first to take possession of the dazzling sea-kidney. I proclaim this in tales of glory.

This story is probably the subject of *Lok* 20 in which Loki taunts Gefjun for having slept with 'the white lad' (*sveinn inn hvíti*, possibly Heimdallr) for a jewel. As an honest guardian, Heimdallr is typified as 'land-guardian of the powers' (*ráðgegninn ragna reinvári*) in the first half-stanza; in the second, he is 'strong in heart, the son of eight and one mothers' (*móðǫflugr mǫgr átta ok einnar mœðra*).[25] The second kenning supports his identification as the 'spike-headed man' ('naddhǫfgan mann', MS *naddbǫfgan*) to whom nine giantesses give birth in *Hynd* 35–8. There, as if he is a tree to whom sacrificial offerings are made, the same son is said to be 'increased

[25] *Skj* B I, 128.

in growth with the power of earth, by the chilly-cold sea and a pig's blood' (*aukinn iarðar megni, svalkǫldum sæ ok sonardreyra, Hynd* 38).

In the third mythological scene in *Húsdrápa*, Freyr leads a wild procession of Norse gods towards the funeral pyre of Baldr. After Freyr and Óðinn comes Heimdallr:

> Kostigr ríðr at kesti,   kynfróðs þeims goð hlóðu
> hrafnfreistaðar, hesti   Heimdallr, at mǫg fallinn
>
> (*Húsdrápa* 10)[26]

Heimdallr's names *Hallinskíði* and *Heimdali* are classed among 'ram's names' (*hrúts heiti*) in the thirteenth-century *Þulur*.[27] Snorri cobbles together these and other properties of Heimdallr in *Gylfaginning*:

> He is called the white god. He is big and holy. Nine maidens bore him as their son, all of them sisters. He is also called *Hallinskíði* ('Leant-plank') and *Gullintanni* ('Golden-tooth'): his teeth were made of gold. His horse is called *Gulltoppr* ('Gold-top'). He lives by *Bifrǫst* ('Trembling-?current'), at a place called *Himinbjǫrg* ('Heaven-hill'). He is the gods' watchman and sits there, at the end of heaven guarding the bridge against mountain giants. He needs less sleep than a bird. He can see, at night just as well as day a hundred leagues off. He can also hear the grass growing on the earth or wool on the sheep and anything that makes more noise. He has the trumpet called *Gjallarhorn* ('Horn of Resounding') and his blast can be heard in all the worlds: 'Heimdallr's sword' is a name for the head.[28]

The last statement is probably the most perplexing: how can the 'head' be called 'Heimdallr's sword'? Yet two late kennings for head as 'Heimdallr's sword' show that Snorri did not invent this tradition.[29] Otherwise Snorri

---

[26] *Skj* B I, 129: 'Well-decorated Heimdallr rides on his horse to the woodpile that the gods raised up when the kinsman of the kindred-fertile tester of the raven [son of Óðinn: Baldr] fell [dead].'

[27] *Skj* B I, 670, IV aa.

[28] *Gylf*, pp. 25–6 (ch. 27): 'Hann er kallaðr hvíti Áss. Hann er mikill ok heilagr. Hann báru at syni meyjar níu ok allar systr. Hann heitir ok Hallinskíði ok Gullintanni: tennr hans váru af gulli. Hestr hans heitir Gulltoppr. Hann býr þar er heitir Himinbjǫrg við Bifrǫst. Hann er vǫrðr goða ok sitr þar við himins enda at gæta brúarinnar fyrir bergrisum. Þarf hann minna svefn en fugl. Hann sér jafnt nótt sem dag hundrað rasta frá sér. Hann heyrir ok þat er gras vex á jǫrðu eða ull á sauðum ok allt þat er hæra lætr. Hann hefir lúðr þann er Gjallarhorn heitir ok heyrir blástr hans í alla heima. Heimdalar sverð er kallat hǫfuð.'

[29] *Skj* B I, 523, 1 (s. xii?: *Heimdalls hjǫrr*); 289, 2, 7 (s. xiii?: *Heimdalar hjǫrr*).

Ingui's death

says that Heimdallr is to be called 'son of nine mothers and gods' watchman, as was written earlier, or the white god, Loki's foe, seeker of Freyja's necklace'; Snorri then alludes to kennings, the *Heimdalargaldr* and Heimdallr's role in *Húsdrápa*.[30]

Hugo Pipping made the least forced attempt to reconcile Heimdallr's diverse characteristics with each other and with the meaning of his name.[31] As he showed, the meaning of *-dallr* is problematic in Heimdallr's name. On the sole evidence of OE *deall* ('bright'), Heimdallr might be taken as a sun-god on a par with the likely phenomenon in *Ullr* and *Ullinn* (OE *wuldor*). In Old Icelandic, however, the rare word *dallr* is glossed differently: Bjørn Haldorsen in 1814 described *dallr* as a 'fruit-bearing tree or tree-trunk which puts forth shoots and branches' and a 'vessel for pouring, a measure for liquids: a bucket, measuring vessel'.[32] Sigfús Blöndal defines *dallur* as '1. tub, small wooden vat, especially for keeping spoon-food in; 2. (*öskjur*) a little wooden box with a lid for butter or dairy products'.[33] Pipping's argument was that it is 'very common for wooden tools to take their names from the type of wood from which they are most often manufactured'.[34] Focusing on the variant spelling *-dalr*, Pipping believed that Snorri's synonym equation between *dalr*, *bogi* and *ýr* (respectively, 'curve', 'bow' and 'yew') in *Skáldskaparmál* explains how a form *heim-dalr* came to replace *heim-ýr ('World-Yew') in a periphrastic substitution, 'whether this word [*dallr*] meant "yew" or "tree" (in general)'.[35] Whether or not this etymology of *heimdallr* is correct, the second element of this compound, even given the slightness of evidence

---

[30] *SnE* 264–5 (ch. 8): 'son níu mæðra, vörð goða, svá sem fyrr er ritað, eða hvíta Ás, Loka-dólg, mensækir Freyju'; *FJSnE* 98.

[31] Pipping, 'Eddastudier I', pp. 1–52; 'Eddastudier II', pp. 120–30; see further Tolley, 'Oswald's Tree', p. 157, n. 21.

[32] *Lexicon islandico-latino-danicum*, ed. B. Haldorsen (Copenhagen, 1814), s.v. 'dallr': 'arbor prolifera – Træstamme som sætter Skud og Grene'; 'vasculum distributorium, mensura liqvidorum, en Bytte, Maalekar'; J. de Vries derives *dallr* from a root **dal-* ('flowering') and suggests Heimdallr represents a spontaneous energy guarding the world, in 'Heimdallr, dieu énigmatique', *Études germaniques* 10 (1955), 257–68.

[33] Sigfús Blöndal, *Islandsk-dansk Ordbog* (Reykjavik, 1920–4), s.v. 'dallur': '1. Bøtte, mindre Trækar, is. til at gemme Søbemad i: – 2. (*öskjur*) en lille Æske af Træ med Laag til Smör el. Fedvarer.'

[34] Pipping, 'Eddastudier I', p. 8: 'mycket vanligt, att redskap av trä få namn efter det träslag, av vilket de oftast förfärdigas'.

[35] *SnE* 571 (ch. 75); *FJSnE* 203; Pipping, 'Eddastudier I', pp. 8–9: 'vare sig att detta ord betydde "idegran" eller "träd" (i allmänhet)'.

in Haldorsen and Sigfús, is more likely to be identified with some kind of 'wood' than with 'brightness'. Thus Pipping is probably right to translate *heimdallr* as 'world tree'.[36]

As *Heimdali* is never found as a nominative form of *Heimdallr*, Pipping held it likely that its weak ending was a fossil of a locative dative inflection indicating the ram's position when hung on the tree.[37] With *Hallinskíði* the same would apply, though this form is found as a nominative noun for Heimdallr. This conclusion would be confirmed by Ibn Fadlan's account of the Rus' and their hanging of the heads of sheep and cattle on posts by the Volga in 922.[38] Pipping informed the rest of his work on Heimdallr with Finno-Ugric parallels that explain how this god was imagined not only as a tree, but also as a world-pillar rearing up from the earth to the bright pole-star in heaven. Worshippers thus would have represented this axis of the constellations with a golden spike or nail.[39] *Gulltoppr*, the name of Heimdallr's horse, Pipping interpreted as the golden nail itself on which Heimdallr, if we take him to be heaven's vault here, could be seen riding. *Hallinskíði* ('leant-plank') would thus characterize Heimdallr as 'the world-axle leaning towards the north'.[40]

No identification of Heimdallr with the world tree Yggdrasill is made in Icelandic sources, though these names are cited close together in two places in *Vǫluspá*. In one case the sibyl bids her human audience to be quiet, calling them 'kinsmen of Heimdallr' (*mǫgu Heimdalar*, Vsp 1), shortly before declaring her ability to remember 'a splendid measuring tree beneath the earth' (*miǫtvið mæran fyr mold neðan*, Vsp 2): that is, the world tree when it was still a seedling in the ground. In the second case, towards the end of *Vǫluspá*, another sibylline speaker (perhaps speaking through the first) shows the world collapsing: 'measuring-fate [? or *miǫtviðr*: measuring-tree] blazes forth, at the old Horn of Resounding; loud blows Heimdallr' (*miǫtuðr kyndiz at ino gamla Giallarhorni; hátt blæss*

---

[36] Pipping, *ibid.*, p. 9: 'världsträdet'.
[37] Pipping follows Finnur Jónsson's suggestion that rams could be named in the dative *Heimdali* and *Hallinskíði* because they were sacrificed 'to Heimdallr'. See Pipping, *ibid.*, pp. 19–23, esp. 20–1.
[38] See H. M. Smyser, 'Ibn Fadlan's Account of the Rus, with some Commentary and some Allusions to *Beowulf*', in *Medieval and Linguistic Studies in Honor of Francis Peabody Magoun, Jr.*, ed. J. B. Bessinger, Jr and R. P. Creed (New York, 1965), pp. 92–119.
[39] Pipping, 'Eddastudier I', pp. 16–19.
[40] *Ibid.*, p. 19: 'den mot norr lutande världsaxeln'.

Heimdallr, *Vsp* 46). Yggdrasill begins to groan and tremble not long afterwards (*Vsp* 47), whereupon the world ends.

This connection between Heimdallr and Yggdrasill may go further. In *Vsp* 2 the sibyl remembers the ancient giants who nourished her, nine worlds and *nío íviði*, a phrase which at face value means 'nine roots'. However, two erased letters at the end of *íviði* in the *Hauksbók* text may be read also in Codex Regius through ultraviolet photography and yield the form 'íviðior' ('giantesses').[41] The form *íviðior* is unique, but would seem to mean 'giantess-roots', which, as Pipping went on to show, identifies Heimdallr's nine mothers immediately with the nine roots leading up into the one 'splendid measuring-tree'.[42] Although Yggdrasill's three roots (*Grím* 31) do divide neatly into nine, not everyone agrees with this identification.[43] Yet as the poet of *Vǫluspá* is evidently capable of effects of this kind, Heimdallr's thematic proximity to Yggdrasill might be read as an attempt to revitalize his name.

Double perspective, a key to *Lokasenna*, explains Loki's taunt to Heimdallr more effectively than before, if Heimdallr is taken to be the world tree. Heimdallr's gnomic statement that often a man 'pays no heed to the limit of his capacity' (*sína mælgi né manað*, *Lok* 47) could allude to his world-tree status as 'measuring-tree' (*mjǫtviðr*, *Vsp* 2). Secondly, Loki taunts Heimdallr as if he is habitually covered in filth:

> Þegi þú, Heimdallr!   þér var í árdaga
>   iþ ljóta líf um lagit;
> aurgo baki   þú munt æ vera
>   oc vaca vǫrðr goða.   (*Lok* 48)[44]

John McKinnell interprets Loki's meaning as an accusation that Heimdallr is either 'sleeping on the job, or at any rate lying down' on the mud; or, with reference to the whitewashed world tree in *Vsp* 19, that Heimdallr has 'acquired the mud on his back as he walked away from the tree after depositing his hearing under it'.[45] Loki would thus be accusing

---

[41] Stefán Karlsson, 'Íviðjur', *Gripla* 3 (1979), 227–8.
[42] Pipping, 'Eddastudier I', pp. 45–9.
[43] J. P. Schjødt, 'Nío man ec heima, nío íviði, miǫtvið mæran fyr mold neðan: tid og rum i Vǫluspá 2', *ANF* 107 (1992), 152–66, esp. 161.
[44] 'Be quiet Heimdallr! An ugly life was ordained for you in ancient days; with a muddy backside you will always be, staying awake as the god's watchman.'
[45] J. McKinnell, 'Motivation in *Lokasenna*', *Saga-Book* 22 (1987–8), 234–62, esp. 252–3.

Heimdallr of incompetence as the gods' sentinel. But if Heimdallr is the world tree, then his trunk is smeared with white mud, as in *Vsp* 19 or by the implication of his role as 'whitest of the Æsir' (*hvítastr ása*, *Þrym* 15) and 'the white Áss' (*hvíti Áss*, *Gylf*, p. 25), or even 'the white boy', as I have suggested, in *Lok* 20 (*sveinn inn hvíti*). McKinnell's interpretation is thus less straightforward than the idea that in *Lok* 48, as in other stanzas, Loki humiliates his opponent by making his natural phenomenon look ridiculous against the human standards of his person.[46]

Heimdallr's role as a progenitor in *Vǫluspá* and *Rígsþula* can be matched with motifs of human descent from trees here and in other sources. *Ascr* ('ash') and *Embla* ('?elm') are names for the first man and woman in *Vsp* 17–18. In the *Sonatorrek* (c. 960) the world is called '?Óðinn's gallows' (*Elgjar galgi*, st. 15), whilst Egill stylizes his lost son Bǫðvarr as a grown tree:

> Þat man ek enn,   es upp um hóf
> í goðheim   Gauta spjalli
> ættar ask,   þanns óx af mér,
> ok kynvið   kvánar minnar.   (*Sonatorrek* 21)[47]

Bǫðvarr's role as an 'ash-tree' (*askr*) in this stanza and as a 'shield-wood' (*randviðr*) that can 'ripen' (*rǫskvask*) in *Sonatorrek* 11 is part of a Norse topos: Meissner lists thirty types of tree or tree-like plant in the whole poetic records, each of which makes up the baseword of a kenning for 'man'.[48]

Where Heimdallr's house in *Himinbjǫrg* is concerned, it is worth noting that King Oswald, before his crucial battle against Cadwalla near Hexham in 634, erected a wooden cross, according to Bede, in *Hefenfeld* ('Heaven-field'), which can be said to be *Campus Caelestis* in Latin and which certainly received its name in ancient times as a presage of events to come'.[49] As Clive Tolley has pointed out, 'Hefenfeld' is reminiscent of 'Himinbjǫrg' ('heaven-hill'), where 'they say Heimdallr governs the

---

[46] See further Dronke, 'Scope of the *Corpvs Poeticvm Boreale*', pp. 104–6; also published in *Myth and Fiction*, no. V.

[47] *Egils saga*, ed. Sigurður, pp. 254–5: 'This I remember once more, that the companion of the Gautar [Óðinn] raised up into the world of the gods the ash-tree of my family, that which grew out of me, and the kindred-wood of my wife.'

[48] Meissner, *Kenningar der Skalden*, pp. 266–72.

[49] *HE* III.2 (p. 216): 'Hefenfeld, quod dici potest latine Caelestis Campus, quod certo utique praesagio futurorum antiquitus nomen accepit.'

sanctuaries' (*Heimdall qveða valda véom, Grím* 13).[50] Bede uses the name to foretell Oswald's victory, but if, as he says, the place got its name as a presage of events to come, Hefenfeld might also be regarded as an Anglian analogue of Urðr and the Norse world tree (*Vsp* 20).

In *Vǫluspá* and other sources, Heimdallr is the father of mankind, protecting, listening and warning, while Yggdrasill or *ascr Yggdrasils* is pictured as the groaning support of the world. Thus it is reasonable to suppose that the personality of this tree was emphasized, contained and then isolated in Heimdallr, while its phenomenon was largely restricted to Yggdrasill. At a stage in history earlier than the surviving Scandinavian records, older Germanic counterparts of Heimdallr and the ash of Yggdrasill may have coexisted as aspects of the world tree: positive and benign in the Heimdallr case, malign or suffering where the Yggdrasill motif was concerned. Both aspects can be found in the cross in *The Dream of the Rood*.

THE ANGLIAN WORLD TREE

Old Norse influence on *The Dream of the Rood* is unlikely, given the early date and remote north-western location of the Ruthwell cross, on which were carved four passages from a poem apparently of common ancestry with the core of *The Dream of the Rood*. Ray Page's revised opinion of the date of these runes is *c*. 650 – *c*. 750.[51] One scholarly consensus on the dating of the cross is that it was erected towards the middle of the eighth century, while the poem was carved onto its sides some time later before *c*. 750.[52] A recent qualification of this view is that the Ruthwell cross was first built as an obelisk at a time *c*. 700, with the cross-head superimposed at a later date, at which time the runic poem may have been added to reinforce this monument's defiant message of a continuing Northumbrian political presence in a British region after King Ecgfrith's defeat in

---

[50] On the heathen status of the Hefenfeld cross, exploited by St Oswald 'to bring Christianity into the hearts of his people', see Tolley, 'Oswald's Tree', pp. 154–7 and 173; Wallace-Hadrill (*Commentary*, pp. 88–9) notes that the Hefenfeld story was probably preserved in Hexham abbey.

[51] R. I. Page, *An Introduction to English Runes* (London, 1973), pp. 148–53, esp. 148.

[52] See R. Cramp, 'The Anglian Tradition in the Ninth Century', in *Anglo-Saxon and Viking Age Sculpture and its Context: Papers from the Collingwood Symposium on Insular Sculpture from 800 to 1066*, ed. J. Lang, BAR 49 (Oxford, 1978), 7–8; MacClean, 'Date of the Ruthwell Cross', pp. 68–9; Meyvaert, 'New Perspective on the Ruthwell Cross', pp. 148–51 and 164–5.

Nechtansmere in 685.[53] Ruthwell is just twenty miles west of Carlisle, which stayed in Anglian hands after Nechtansmere.[54] For theological reasons it is also plausible that the Ruthwell monument was erected, as Swanton suggests, in the aftermath of the synod held near to Ruthwell by the river Nith in 705.[55] The *c.* 700 dating of the lower cross-shaft is in keeping with Éamonn Ó Carragáin's theory that its panels, influenced by baptismal liturgy, show that conversion was still a relatively recent process in Anglian Northumbria.[56] Though the runic carving on the cross seems to be of a later date, the use of runes rather than Roman letters seems to emphasize a Northumbrian over a British or Irish Christianity; the poem from which the carver quoted, analogous to passages in *The Dream of the Rood*, was probably older than its runic transcription, with an indigenous character that looks back to an older Germanic ancestry in common with Norse paganism.

Mediterranean culture, however, was the chief prerequisite for the hybrid mixture of Italianate carving and Latin–Germanic epigraphy on the Ruthwell cross. On the lower shaft was a carefully planned theological programme, with carved panels representing scenes from the gospels on north and south faces; the crosshead has a bird in foliage and an archer taking aim.[57] On the east and west sides of the lower shaft are panels carved with a devolved style of vine with birds and fantastic animals growing out of the stem, around which the four runic passages of the Ruthwell poem were carved.[58] The connection between Northumbria and

---

[53] Suggested by F. Orton, I. Wood and J. Hill in 'Rethinking the Ruthwell Cross: Texts and Contexts – A roundtable Discussion', at the International Medieval Congress 450–1500, at Leeds, 12 July 1995.

[54] MacClean, 'Date of the Ruthwell Cross', pp. 61 and 68.

[55] R. Cramp, 'The Anglian Tradition in the Ninth Century', in *Anglo-Saxon and Viking Age Sculpture and its Context: Papers from the Collingwood Symposium on Insular Sculpture from 800 to 1066*, ed. J. Lang, BAR 49 (Oxford, 1978), 1–32, at 7–8; *The Dream of the Rood*, ed. Swanton, p. 25.

[56] É. Ó Carragáin, 'The Ruthwell Cross and Irish High Crosses: some Points of Comparison and Contrast', in *Ireland and Insular Art, AD 500–1200: Proceedings of a Conference at University College Cork, 31 October – 3 November 1985*, ed. M. Ryan (Dublin, 1987), pp. 118–28, esp. 121–2.

[57] Described and reconstructed by Howlett, 'Inscriptions and Design', pp. 72–82; *The Dream of the Rood*, ed. Swanton, pp. 11–31, esp. 13; for large illustrations of the panels and vinescroll carving, see *The Ruthwell Cross*, ed. Cassidy, esp. pp. 27–9 (and plates 1–30).

[58] Howlett, 'Inscriptions and Design', pp. 82–8.

Byzantine Italy already dated almost a century back to the Italian missionary Paulinus, who may have brought Roman books with him to Edwin's court as early as c. 619. With Wilfrid of York, Benedict Biscop went to Rome in 653. For Benedict this was the first of six journeys to Rome in search of Latin books and other cultural artefacts.[59] The church begun in Monkwearmouth in 674 was constructed by workmen whom he brought from Gaul. It was these and other masons and sculptors who subsequently enriched the monastery of Jarrow with at least twenty-five lathe-turned balusters and other church furnishings.[60] Revealing a relationship between book-painting and the vinescroll carving typical of these and other crosses, Rosemary Cramp suggests that Benedict's sculptors could have carved the Bewcastle and Ruthwell crosses after their work in Jarrow.[61] If not these sculptors, their apprentices could have carved on Northumbrian crosses at a later date.

Yet there are problems of stylistic attribution. Swanton notes that there was no monumental tradition in England and that 'the origin of the free-standing stone cross – a form of monument unique to the British Isles – is still obscure'.[62] Although Cramp implies that Bishop Aidan and the Irish introduced free-standing wooden crosses after Oswald's victory in Hefenfeld in 634, Tweddle notes 'how and why this type of monument was developed remains obscure'.[63] Another problem is the absence of contemporary Italian parallels for the vinescrolls found on Northumbrian crosses. Although there are similarities with the vinescroll found on Maximian's sixth-century throne in Ravenna and in later Italian carving, Cramp notes that the stylization of these differs from Anglo-Saxon inhabited vinescroll and that 'the animals in both areas remain distinct and indigenous'.[64]

To this extent, Northumbrian carving in an age which Cramp defines as 'stylistically volatile' became an acclimatized rather than faithful form of Italian sculpture.[65]

---

[59] Mayr-Harting, *The Coming of Christianity*, pp. 120–8.
[60] Tweddle, 'Sculpture', in 'The Church in Northumbria', pp. 147–50.
[61] Cramp, 'Anglo-Saxon and Italian Sculpture', pp. 135–7; and 'The Anglian Sculptured Crosses of Dumfriesshire', pp. 9–20.
[62] *The Dream of the Rood*, ed. Swanton, p. 24.
[63] Cramp, 'Anglo-Saxon and Italian Sculpture', p. 129; Tweddle, 'The Church in Northumbria', p. 149.
[64] Cramp, 'Anglo-Saxon and Italian Sculpture', p. 135.   [65] *Ibid.*, p. 137.

Heathen gods

Although Meyvaert does not discuss the Ruthwell vinescroll, he believes that the western face (A) of the Ruthwell cross was intended for a local lay community.[66] To the early Christians in Northumbria, vinescrolls probably signified the once-living trees from which earlier wooden replicas of the cross had been cut. The preaching cross of St Bertelin of *c.* 700, said to have been buried beneath his church in Stafford, is evidence that wooden crosses preceded stone ones.[67] Animals on a cross could have been justified as Christian symbols, but, as with prosopopoeia in some artefacts and riddles, attribution alone does not explain why this style was so popular. The need was local even if the style was not. Thus while the bird in foliage, vines, occasional grapes and fantastic animals of the Ruthwell cross are to be explained as products of Italianate culture, it might have helped if laymen saw in them images which might now be described as Anglian versions of the Norse eagle, squirrel and goats that appear about the leaves and branches of Yggdrasill in *Grímnismál*. By legitimizing a need for leaves and branches on the cross, Roman vinescroll could assist the transition from superstition to doctrine.

The fragment *dægisgæf* on the upper stone may or may not stand for [*wæp*]*dæ gisgæf*[*t*], corresponding to *Dream* 55.[68] Otherwise the words of the cross are written around the vinescrolled sides of the Ruthwell cross, rather than on the margins of the gospel scenes on its north and south faces. One line from the second runic inscription, in particular, recalls the tradition of Heimdallr:

[Ahof] ic riicnæ KyniNGc,   heafunæs H*l*afard, hælda ic ni dorstæ.[69]

More archaic than WS *hyldan* in *hyldan me ne dorste* (*Dream* 45), *hælda* of the last half-line of the second Ruthwell inscription is cognate with OIce

---

[66] Meyvaert, 'New Perspective on the Ruthwell Cross', p. 106.
[67] *The Dream of the Rood*, ed. Swanton, pp. 47–8.
[68] *Ibid.*, p. 31; supported by Howlett, 'Inscriptions and Design', p. 91; this and other inscriptions, Roman and runic, are presented and discussed in E. Okasha, *Handlist of Anglo-Saxon Non-Runic Inscriptions* (Cambridge, 1971), pp. 108–12, esp. 111 (no. 105).
[69] *The Dream of the Rood*, ed. Swanton, p. 94: 'I [lifted up] a powerful king, Heaven's Lord, I did not dare to lean down.' Howlett makes *hælda* a transitive verb and *Heafunæs Hlafard* its object complement rather than a phrase in apposition to *riicnæ Kyningc*, as is demanded by the syntax of the corresponding *Dream* 44–5; see also Howlett, 'Inscriptions and Design', p. 88.

halla ('to incline'), which is the first element of Heimdallr's name *Hallinskíði*.[70]

To some extent the Ruthwell line proceeds as a riddle: by saying 'a powerful king' the cross does not specify Christ; by saying 'I did not dare to lean down' a speaking person is suggested, thus turning the attention away from the phenomenon of *galgu* previously inscribed. This is the first clear case of prosopopoeia on the Ruthwell cross, one in which the cross confirms the implication of its vinescrolled sides by using *hælda* to identify himself as the world tree, constrained in this case to bear the weight of a sacrifice. Thus a continuity with the pre-Christian past could have been ensured.

The poet of *The Dream of the Rood*, writing probably in the first half of the eighth century, uses techniques of evasion and misdirection that, as Orton has shown, are developed from the tradition of Old English riddles.[71] Making serious puns is one of the means by which this poet celebrates Christianity. So the cross in the Dreamer's eyes is changing all the time: first a rare tree encircled with light (*Dream* 4–6); now a beacon showered with gold and with five jewels on the axlespan (*Dream* 6–9); a tree of glory adorned with vestments as well as gold and jewels (*Dream* 14–17); with blood and water flowing from its right side (*Dream* 19–20 and 22–3); then with *wendan* either revolving or changing shape with different vestments and colours (*Dream* 22). The instability of this imagery enables the poet to typify the cross in many theologically useful manifestations, blending the horror of its use with the splendour of its victory.

The cross first seems to be described as an angel in the heavenly hierarchy:

> Beheoldon þær engel Dryhtnes ealle,
> fægere þurh forðgesceaft.   Ne wæs ðær huru fracodes gealga.
> Ac hine þær beheoldon   halige gastas,
> men ofer moldan   ond eall þeos mære gesceaft.   (*Dream* 9–12)[72]

---

[70] The Ruthwell form *hælda* is cognate with a *lectio difficilior* in Snorri's description of Baldr: *SnE* 90–2 (*Gylf*, ch. 22): 'náttúra fylgir honum, at engi má *hallaz* dómr hans'; FJSnE 29.

[71] See Orton, 'Object-Personification', pp. 14–15.

[72] 'They beheld there an angel of the Lord, all those beautiful in future creation. Nor was that by any means the gallows of a criminal. But they beheld him there, holy spirits, men over the earth and all this famous creation.'

Heathen gods

As Christ has not yet appeared in this poem, *engel* in line 9 may be the cross, a usefully personified *creatura* which, with the words *syllicre treow*, is also presented as a tree (*Dream* 4). *Beama beorhtost* ('brightest of beams/rays', *Dream* 6) also resembles Heimdallr's description as 'whitest of the Æsir' (*hvítastr ása*, *Þrym* 15) and 'the white Áss' (*hvíti Áss*, *Gylf*, p. 25).

There are other indications of an old world-tree tradition in *The Dream of the Rood*. These archaic details would not conflict with the poet's Latin learning, for most hints of the world tree in this poem would have been useful only as native counterparts to motifs in patristic writing. Yet the imputed suffering of the cross in *The Dream of the Rood* recalls the immense 'hardships greater than men can understand' (*erfiði meira enn menn viti*, *Grím* 35) of the ash of Yggdrasill. Rosemary Woolf has shown how the Anglian poet could have made the cross suffer passively in order to avoid the pitfalls of two centuries of Christological debate.[73] In the Monophysite position, Christ was not fully man; in the Nestorian, not fully God; where his suffering is transferred to the cross and Christ embodies divine and human natures in keeping with the Vatican's attempt to reconcile these positions, the *communicatio idiomatum*, the poet evades these heresies.[74] Though Rosemary Woolf discounted the influence of liturgy on this poem, E. R. Anderson has shown it to be an important source of the poet's cross-imagery. In his hymns *Vexilla regis prodeunt* and *Pange lingua gloriosi proelium*, Venantius refers to the crucifixion as a battle and praises the Tree adorned with purple as noblest of trees.[75] Christ's warrior status in *The Dream of the Rood* is thus as Latinate as it is Germanic. The cross thus shares some of his Lord's suffering and refrains from crushing legionaries in obedience to his command (*Dream* 28–38 and 45–8). It trembles when Christ climbs upon it, then helps to kill his mortal body paradoxically to a greater end (*Dream* 42–5). Even the jewels, vestment and golden ornament later bestowed upon the cross can thus be seen as the rewards that a loyal thegn expects.

The cross does not openly reveal the species of tree from which it was made. He says that he was 'cut down at the end of the wood' (*aheawen*

---

[73] Woolf, 'Doctrinal Influences', pp. 142–3.

[74] *Ibid.*, p. 153: 'By the semi-identification of the cross with Christ, the poet enables his hearers to share in the imaginative recreation of Christ's sufferings, whilst the problem which bewilders the mind – the nature of Christ's consciousness – is evaded.'

[75] *Venanti Fortunati Opera*, ed. Leo, pp. 27–8 and 34–5; see Anderson, 'Liturgical Influence on *The Dream of the Rood*', pp. 293–4.

holtes on ende, Dream 29). Obliquely, the arbitrary position of the tree before it is cut down might refer to the mystery of God's grace, although it is also reminiscent of Heimdallr sitting 'there, at the end of heaven' (*þar við himins enda*).[76] Yet when the Dreamer calls him 'best tree of wood' (*wudu selesta, Dream* 27), the cross also resembles 'the most superior of the trees of the wood' (*œztr viða*) that is the ash of Yggdrasill (*Grím* 44). This identification would be of slight interest, were it not for the literal meaning of a word that most readers emend:

> Hwæt, me þa geweorþode   wuldres Ealdor
> ofer *holmwudu*,   heofonrices Weard,
> swylce swa he his modor eac,   Marian sylfe,
> ælmihtig God,   for ealle menn
> geweorðode   ofer eall wifa cynn.   (*Dream* 90–4)[77]

OE -*wudu* in the second line of this extract has a collective sense, as 'trees'; *holtwudu* is usually read here: 'trees of the forest'.[78] Yet Berkhout reads an unemended *holmwudu* as a kenning for 'ships', arguing that this poet drew from Venantius's conceit in *Pange lingua* of the cross as a ship rescuing the shipwrecked world.[79] This influence would have justified an indigenous interpretation of nominative *holmwudu* as a simple kenning for *æsc*, not only an Old English word for 'warship', but also as the common name for 'ash-tree'.

These are not the only plausible 'Germanic' readings of *miles Christus* and other Latin motifs doctrinally convenient to the poet of *The Dream of the Rood*. It is also possible that this poet was portraying the cross not only as an ash-tree but also as the 'horse' to which an Anglian counterpart of *ascr Yggdrasils* ('ash-tree (of) Terror-steed') would have alluded. Styling the cross as a horse was common in the fourteenth century and would be consistent with the doctrine of Christ doing mounted battle with Satan,

---

[76] *Gylf*, pp. 25–6 (ch. 27).
[77] 'Listen, the prince of glory, guardian of heaven's kingdom, then honoured me over the *sea-woods* [ships: ash-trees], just as he, Almighty God, also honoured before all men his mother, Mary herself, over all the tribe of women.' The topos of Heimdallr as *vǫrðr goða* ('sentinel of the gods', *Grím* 13, *Lok* 48) seems to resemble that of the Lord in *Dream* 91 as *heofonrices Weard* ('Guardian of Heaven').
[78] See B. Mitchell and F. C. Robinson, *A Guide to Old English*, 5th ed. (Oxford, 1992), pp. 256–63, esp. 261; for a more detailed discussion, see *The Dream of the Rood*, ed. Swanton, p. 132.
[79] C. T. Berkhout, 'The Problem of OE *holmwudu*', *Mediaeval Studies* 36 (1974), 429–33.

although Woolf indicated no cases of Christ as the *miles equitans in equo* before the Normans introduced cavalry to England.[80] Yet it is conceivable that an allegory of the cross as a horse could have been created earlier on the basis of the *asina* (Matt. XXI.7) on which Jesus rode into Jerusalem. In the terms of pre-Christian mythology, furthermore, this image would recall the role of *Ygg-drasill* as the (eight-legged) Sleipnir, on which, in the later Scandinavian tradition, Óðinn rides to the world of the dead.

A different light can thus be thrown on some well-known passages in *The Dream of the Rood*. After the legionaries carry the cross to Calvary and fasten it there, the cross reveals that it saw the Lord of mankind hastening 'wanting to mount me' (*þæt he me wolde on gestigan, Dream* 34). The cross admits that it dares not 'bow down or shatter against the word of the Lord' (*ofer Dryhtnes word bugan oððe berstan, Dream* 35–6), when it sees the earth shaking. These lines suggest not only Christ ascending the cross, but also a figure mounting a horse and speaking words into its ear which command it not to buck wildly at the people standing by. The patience of the cross, which says 'yet I stood fast' (*hwæðre ic fæste stod, Dream* 38), is in keeping with the master–servant relationship that Orton has shown to be characteristic of inanimate objects describing their human users in the Old English riddles.[81] Although Woolf found the motif of *crucem ascendere* in the late fourth-century writing of St Ambrose, she regarded the motif of the cross standing in position watching Christ advancing as 'the poet's own variation'.[82]

The cross typifies itself as the high gallows that Christ ascends, but then again seems to portray itself as a horse:

Bifode ic þa me se beorn ymbclypte;   ne dorste ic hwæðre bugan to eorðan,
feallan to foldan sceatum.   Ac ic sceolde fæste standan.

(*Dream* 42–3)[83]

This embracing could also refer to a lord–retainer relationship such as

---

[80] Woolf, 'Doctrinal Influences', pp. 143–5; a chivalric portrait of the cross as Jesus's horse was common in the fourteenth century and occurs in lyrics (*mi palfrey is of tre*), the Towneley crucifixion play and sermons including MS Balliol 149 (*pro equo habuit crucem super quam pependit*): see R. Woolf, 'The Theme of Christ the Lover-Knight', *RES* n.s. 13 (1962), 1–16, esp. 14–16.

[81] Orton, 'Object-Personification', pp. 11–12.

[82] Woolf, 'Doctrinal Influences', pp. 145–6.

[83] 'I trembled when the warrior embraced me; yet I did not dare to bow to the earth, fall to the ground's surfaces. But I had to stand fast.'

that which the Wanderer once enjoyed with his master (*Wan* 41–4).[84] Yet at the same time these words could be used to describe a man steadying a trembling horse in order to mount it.

The cross returns to its self-portrait as the suffering rood, unable to harm anyone and forced to watch Christ stretched out in agony (*Dream* 44–52). Darkness follows and creation weeps (*Dream* 52–6). Then Christ's disciples arrive (*Dream* 57–8). The cross is afflicted with sorrows:

>   hnag ic hwæðre þam secgum to handa,
> eaðmod elne mycle.   Genamon hie þær ælmihtigne God,
> ahofon hine of ðam hefian wite.   Forleton me þa hilderincas
> standan steame bedrifenne;   eall ic wæs mid strælum forwundod.
>
> (*Dream* 59–62)[85]

Swanton hints that the conventional translation of *steame bedrifenne* as 'drenched with moisture, i.e. blood' forces the sense.[86] Yet literally 'driven with steam' conveys an image of an animal ridden hard, one who lowers his head into the hands of warriors whose task is to take the Lord down from the saddle and leave the sweating mount to cool off. By the same token this horse conceit could also be implicit in the words [*b*]*ug*[*a*] and *h*[*n*]*ag* of the Ruthwell cross (*c.* 700).[87]

A sculptural parallel for this motif, the cross as a horse, might be found in the 'Repton rider', the relief carving of a mounted warrior found on an upper cross shaft dug up under the east window of the crypt of the church of St Wystan in Repton. This stone has been carefully described and discussed by Martin Biddle and Birthe Kjølbye-Biddle. Only two faces survive intact: A, the rider; adjacent to which is B, a carving of a serpent with a man's face devouring the heads of two men.[88] The rider has a fashionably wavy moustache but no beard and he appears to be dressed as a Germanic warrior from the waist up; from the waist down, a victorious

---

[84] H. R. Patch, 'The Liturgical Influence in the *Dream of the Rood*', *PMLA* 34 (1919), 233–57, esp. 253.

[85] 'Yet I sank down into the hands of those men, humble but with great zeal. In that place they took hold of Almighty God, lifted him from that heavy torment. Then warriors left me standing driven with steam; I was all wounded with arrows.'

[86] *The Dream of the Rood*, ed. Swanton, p. 125: 'Neither *steam* "moisture", here "blood", nor *bedrifan* "to drench, bespatter", are otherwise recorded with these senses.'

[87] Howlett, 'Inscriptions and Design', p. 86; *The Dream of the Rood*, ed. Swanton, pp. 94 and 96.

[88] Biddle and Kjølbye-Biddle, 'The Repton Stone', p. 242 (plate VI).

classical emperor carved in Romanesque style.[89] He wears cross-garters, a kilt and mailcoat without helmet but with a 'crinkly band' on his forehead, which indicates imperial status. He holds his arms raised with a target in the left hand and an obscured sword in the right. The Biddles assign the carving to eighth-century Mercia before the Viking Age. Because the rider lacks a nimbus, they argue that he represents a king, Æthelbald of Mercia (717–57), commemorated by his kinsman Offa of Mercia.[90] This is an attractive hypothesis, which is strengthened by Peter Clemoes's suggestion that the men whose heads are swallowed by the hell-mouth on face B may have represented Æthelbald's assassins.[91] In either case, the carver was attempting to illustrate fates of men in the hereafter; that King Æthelbald rides a horse to heaven appears to be the meaning of face A.

This riding to the other world may have been a pre-Christian topos: apparently to the same end, to carry his master to the underworld, a harnessed horse was buried alongside an Anglian nobleman in a sixth-century grave in Little Wilbraham, Cambridgeshire; another horse was buried likewise in Hardingstone, Northamptonshire; and at least six other horse-burials have been found adjacent to separate fifth- or sixth-century human burials in the east Midlands, East Anglia and Yorkshire; horse-images have also been found stamped on cremation-urns in East Anglia: all these finds occur in Anglian areas.[92] In the Christian period, as the 'Repton rider' seems to indicate, it is possible that the cross could have been stylized in the horse's role. So I suggest that the cross in *The Dream of the Rood* can be read as the horse both on which Christ rides to harrow hell and on which the Northumbrian Dreamer rides to paradise 'when', as he says, 'the Lord's cross will fetch me and then bring me to where there is great bliss' (*hwænne me Dryhtnes rod ... gefetige, and me þonne gebringe þær is blis mycel, Dream* 136–9).[93]

---

[89] *Ibid.*, pp. 254–64.   [90] *Ibid.*, pp. 264 and 271–2.
[91] *Ibid.*, pp. 254–8; Clemoes, *Interactions of Thought and Language*, pp. 58–67, esp. 66.
[92] Wilson, *Anglo-Saxon Paganism*, pp. 101–2 (Wanlip, Leicestershire; Marston St Lawrence, Northamptonshire; Warren Hill, Suffolk; Sporle, Norfolk; Heslerton, Yorkshire) and 151–3 (Lackford, Suffolk, and in Caistor-by-Norwich and Spong Hill, Norfolk); Carver, 'The Anglo-Saxon Cemetery at Sutton Hoo', pp. 362 and 368–9 and plate 32 (next to the 'Sutton Hoo Prince' in Mound 17).
[93] A mounted nobleman, apparently riding Sleipnir to Valhǫll or the world of the dead, can be seen on the Lillbjärs picture stone, Stenkyrka in Gotland, from the early ninth century, in Graham-Campbell, *Viking Artefacts*, pp. 141 (no. 480) and 292 (illustration).

Ingui's death

THE DYING GOD IN *THE DREAM OF THE ROOD*

In this poem the cross says that it is 'made wet with blood, poured open upon, from that man's side' (*mid blode bestemed, begoten of þæs guman sidan*, *Dream* 48–9). Furthermore, if Howlett is right in thinking that runes for 'bi[goten of þæs guman sida siþþan he his gastæ sendæ]' fill the space for forty runes left on the east border, south side of the Ruthwell cross, then it is possible that *begeotan* was used in the Ruthwell text to show Christ *se guma* as a sacrificial victim of an indigenous tradition (discussed in ch. 6 as the *geot*-aspect of the Ing-hypostasis).[94] Hilda Ellis Davidson considers it possible that some human sacrifice took place in early Anglian England, while Carver suggests that the east sector of early seventh-century Sutton Hoo, with a group of executed bodies found lying in a circle round a rootstock, can be interpreted 'as a ritual area, contemporary with the mounds and involving human sacrifice around a tree'.[95]

There are traces both on the Ruthwell cross and in *The Dream of the Rood* of sacrifice and battle combined in the death of Christ. The emphasis on sacrifice can be read at the heart of this poem:

> Weop eal gesceaft,
> cwiðdon Cyninges fyll.   Crist wæs on rode. (*Dream* 55–6)[96]

Weop eal gesceaft may survive on the upper stone of the Ruthwell cross as [*wæp*]*dæ gisgæf*[*t*].[97] This use of *weop* is thought to be based on the lamentation of nature following Christ's death. The apocryphal Gospel of Nicodemus contains this image in the words of a demon addressing Christ as he harrows hell: 'and in Thy death', the demon says, 'all creation groaned and all the stars in the firmament were shaken'.[98] Yet tears are not identical with groans: T. D. Hill admits that so far, at least, his CD-

---

[94] Howlett, 'Inscriptions and Design', p. 86.
[95] H. Ellis Davidson, 'Human Sacrifice in the Late Pagan Period', in *The Age of Sutton Hoo*, ed. Carver, pp. 331–40; Carver, 'The Anglo-Saxon Cemetery at Sutton Hoo', pp. 353–5.
[96] 'All [things of] creation wept, they lamented the King's fall. Christ was on the rood.'
[97] Howlett, 'Inscriptions and Design', p. 91.
[98] *Evangelia Apocrypha*, ed. C. Tischendorf, 2nd ed. (Leipzig, 1876), pp. 389–416, esp. 399 (*Descensus Christi ad inferos*, ch. 6): 'et in tua morte omnis contremuit creatura et universa sidera commota sunt'; reiterated by Pope Leo I, in *Sancta Leonis Magni Romani Pontificis Opera Omnia*, PL 54, 317–18 (*De passione Domini* I, 'omnia elementa tremuerunt'), 324–5 (IV), 330 (VI) and 341 (VIII).

Heathen gods

ROM search has failed to find evidence for a Latin source for the *weop* motif in *The Dream of the Rood*.[99] Thus it is still possible that *weop eal gesceaft* (or {wæp}dæ gisgæf{t}) is derived from a Germanic motif older than the coming of Latin learning to Northumbria.[100]

Weeping occurs also in the legend of the Scandinavian Baldr.[101] When Hǫðr accidentally kills Baldr with a shaft of mistletoe in this version of this story, Hel promises to release Baldr 'if everything in the world, living and dead, weeps for him'.[102] When the Æsir pass on her instructions, 'everyone did this, men and animals and the earth and the stones and trees and every kind of metal, just as you will have seen these things weeping when they come out of frost into the heat'.[103] The plan fails because Loki, in disguise as Þǫkk, a giantess, refuses to weep. Snorri here quotes a stanza from his (now-lost) source:

> Þǫkk mun gráta   þurrum tárum
> Baldrs bálfarar.
> Kyks né dauðs   nautka ek karls sonar:
> haldi Hel því er hefir.[104]

Ursula Dronke suggests that Þǫkk's identity with Loki is contained in a pun in 'Loka *áþecc*ian' ('similar unto Loki', *Vsp* 35), Loki being the figure whom the gods punish for Baldr's death.[105] Other evidence that the motif

---

[99] T. D. Hill, 'CETEDOC and the Transformation of Anglo-Saxon Studies', *Old English Newsletter* 26.1 (1992), 46–8. On further Latinate parallels, see V. L. Baird, '"Natura Plangens", the Ruthwell Cross and "The Dream of the Rood"', *Studies in Iconography* 10 (1984–6), 37–51, at 39–40.

[100] The *wopes hring* ('necklace of weeping') of Elene and everyone else on Golgotha, where they first behold the nails of the cross, might be thought similar, but Cynewulf specifies that these tears are *nalles for torne* ('not at all for grief', *El* 1131–3); Anderson, in 'Liturgical Influence on *The Dream of the Rood*', pp. 297–8, connects Cynewulf's phrase *wopes hring* in *El* 1131 and *Christ* 457–8 (which he derives from the image of overflowing cauldrons) with the gushing of water from the cross in *The Dream of the Rood*.

[101] Green, *Carolingian Lord*, pp. 21–33.

[102] *Gylf*, p. 47 (ch. 49): 'ef allir hlutir í heiminum, kykvir ok dauðir, gráta hann'.

[103] *Ibid.*: 'allir gerðu þat, mennirnir ok kykvendin ok jǫrðin ok steinarnir ok tré ok allr málmr, svá sem þú munt sét hafa at þessir hlutir gráta þá er þeir koma ór frosti ok í hita'.

[104] *Gylf*, p. 48 (ch. 49): 'Þǫkk will weep with dry tears for Baldr's funeral pyre. I got no profit from the old man's son either alive or dead: let Hel keep what she has!'

[105] Dronke, 'War of the Æsir and Vanir', p. 232, n. 38 (also published in *Myth and*

298

Ingui's death

of weeping for Baldr is datable to the period before the conversion is contained in *Vǫluspá*, in which the poet says that, in spite of Váli's vengeance for Baldr, 'Frigg yet wept on in Fen-Halls' (*enn Frigg um grét í Fensǫlum*, *Vsp* 33).

In keeping with his attempt to root the *Edda* in western Christianity, Bugge suggested that Snorri's weeping motif had come from England, but if that is so, doubt remains of what patristic authority it might have had in *The Dream of the Rood*.[106] No form of OE *bealdor* occurs in this poem. That *bealdor* is neither here nor elsewhere used in the manner of *Baldr* suggests that Baldr's name was unknown in England when *The Dream of the Rood* was composed, probably too early to have been influenced by contemporary Scandinavian legends. In ch. 6, I have argued that Baldr's name evolved separately, through a heathen emulation of the Arian Christ, from a now-lost nominal form of the epithet *balþa* ('the bold'), which would have been associated with the Gothic Enguz (cognate with Ing-, Inguz and Ingui). As the Anglii are listed among Nerthus's worshippers, it is possible that the weeping in *The Dream of the Rood* represents an Anglian analogue of the Baldr legend in which Ingui fulfilled the same role.

Most Baldr texts postdate the conversion of Iceland, yet the Þǫkk stanza cited above shows that Baldr was the captive of Hel. This corroborates Snorri's thirteenth-century evidence in *Gylfaginning*, showing that, as with Óðinn's sacrifice in *Háv* 138, Baldr dies into the world of the dead. To travel there in *Háv* 138, Óðinn hangs himself for nine nights on a branch of the world tree. In the same stanza he is 'wounded with a spear and given to Óðinn' (*geiri undaðr oc gefinn Óðni*), a line which represents hanging and stabbing as the generic means of sacrifice. Consistent with this is a twelfth-century tale in which Starkaðr ends up dedicating his friend and master Víkarr to Óðinn by hanging and then stabbing him.[107] Thus Dronke has suggested that in one of the

---

Fiction, no. VII); according to Jan de Vries, Þǫkk is Hel showing Man the limits of his self-deception: 'Mythos von Baldrs Tod', p. 45. Hauck has interpreted Loki or Þǫkk in three gold bracteates from Sievern in north Germany. See K. Hauck, *Goldbrakteaten aus Sievern: Spätantike Amulett-Bilder der 'Dania Saxonica' und die Sachsen-'Origo' bei Widukind von Corvey*, Münstersche Schriften 1 (Munich, 1970), 184–8.

[106] S. Bugge, *Studier over de nordiske Gude- og Heltesagns Oprindelse* (Christiania (Oslo), 1881–9), pp. 32–79.

[107] *Fornaldarsögur*, ed. Guðni and Bjarni III, 12–29 (*Gautreks saga*, ch. 7); *GD*,

oldest traditions known to the poet of *Vǫluspá*, Baldr's death was a sacrifice in which he was not only pierced with a spear but also hanged from the world tree: Baldr is a 'holy offering' (*heilagt tafn*) in Úlfr's *Húsdrápa* 14 (*c.* 985); and a 'blood-stained sacrifice' (*blóðugr tívurr*) in *Vsp* 31 (*c.* 1000). Both are late pagan poems in which variant traditions appear to be drawn together to create unified counter-theologies.

As I have suggested above, the meaning of the compound *Ygg-drasill* ('Terror-steed') suggests that Óðinn's self-sacrifice could be imagined as a ride to the dead using the gallows or world tree as a 'horse'. On the evidence of the kenning *haf-Sleipnir* ('sea-Sleipnir', *Húsdrápa* 14), which probably alludes to Baldr's cremation-ship as it is pushed out to sea at his funeral, the eight-legged Sleipnir, foal of Svaðilfari, was connected with Baldr's death. As Sleipnir was probably developed from the *Yggdrasill* conceit, Baldr's 'sacrifice' to which *Húsdrápa* and *Vǫluspá* refer seems to be imagined as his hanging from the world tree. Sleipnir probably carries not only Baldr to Hel (and Óðinn in *Bdr* 2) but also Hermóðr, Óðinn's son sent to negotiate for Baldr's release (*Gylf* ch. 49).[108] While Baldr is burned in his floating ship, Hermóðr on Sleipnir 'rode for nine nights' (*reið níu nætr*) through dark valleys until he comes to the Gjǫll river this side of Hel.[109] Móðguðr, the female guardian of the bridge, tells Hermóðr that, on the previous day, 'five companies of dead men rode over the bridge'.[110] When Hermóðr asks her whether she has seen Baldr along with the other dead, 'she said that Baldr had ridden at that time over the Gjǫll bridge'.[111] Although no other version of this epilogue survives, Christian motifs are unlikely to have influenced it. Instead, Baldr's horse-ride, just like Óðinn's, probably began as a stylization of his hanging for nine days. Óðinn hangs himself for nine nights in *Háv* 138 in order to ride *Yggdrasill* to the world of the dead. Baldr's hanging may thus be the subject of a pun in *Lokasenna*, when Loki taunts Frigg with his part in the death of Baldr: 'it was I who decided that you will never again see Baldr *riding* into the halls' ('ec því ræð, er þú *ríða* sérat síðan Baldr at sǫlum', *Lok* 28).

When Óðinn rides to Hel in *Bdr* 2, he is called *gautr*, whereby the poet

---

pp. 152–64 and trans. in *History of the Danes*, trans. Fisher and ed. Ellis Davidson I, 170–5 (and commentary, II, 99–102).

[108] *Gylf*, pp. 34–5 (ch. 42).   [109] *Ibid.*, p. 47 (ch. 49).

[110] *Ibid.*,: 'riðu um brúna fimm fylki dauðra manna'.

[111] *Ibid.*: 'hon sagði at Baldr hafði þar riðit um Gjallar brú'.

Ingui's death

seems to use *gautr* as an epithet for a sacrificed man. As I have suggested above, OIce *gautr* is cognate with the suffix OE *-geot*. Thus an Anglian motif of sacrifice, in the use of a participle related to *-geot*, appears to be reflected in 'mid blode bestemed, *begoten* of þæs guman sidan' ('made wet with blood, *poured open upon*, from that man's side', *Dream* 48–9); and also when the cross is first seen as '*begoten* mid golde' ('drenched with gold', *Dream* 7). Christ the *Cyning* in *Dream* 56 is a heroic topos which can be traced to the legionary taunt *rex Iudaeorum* in Luke XXIII.37 and Matt. XXVII.29, yet in keeping with the implication of *begoten* in *Dream* 7 and 49, the poet may also refer to Christ's death in a reflex of the language used of sacral kingship in the continental Anglian past. The *miles Christus* theme in this poem appears when, as if he were fighting against Satan, Christ's ordeal becomes 'that great combat' (*þæt micle gewinn*, *Dream* 65). Christ's warrior portraiture in this poem is one of the finest examples of a Latin topos, yet it could also be part of the *geot* aspect of an Ing-hypostasis, a king both sacrificed in peace and destroyed in battle.

Similarly, but emphasizing the battle over the sacrifice in the death of his king, Eyvindr skáldaspillir commemorated the death of Hákon Aðalsteinsfóstri in *Hákonarmál* first by describing Hákon's immortalization in Valhǫll (sts. 1 and 9–18), then by stylizing his loss as that of Baldr (st. 20). Although no cognate of OIce *Baldr* is found in *The Dream of the Rood*, the poet's words for the crucifixion, *þæt micle gewinn*, suggest a death on the battlefield; and the Dreamer describes the strangely mobile cross 'fetching' him from his life (*gefetige*) and 'bringing' him (*gebringe*) to a joyful retinue in heaven 'where the Lord's host is seated, at the banquet, at which there is continual bliss' (*þær is Dryhtnes folc geseted to symle, þær is singal blis*, *Dream* 141). If the poet draws his image of the *symbel* from the Parable of the Feast in Luke XIV.15 or from the *coena* of Rev. XIX.9, as Swanton suggests, his militarization of this feast with *Dryhtnes folc* also points to the indigenous Anglian warrior-paradise that is indicated by the various textual and archaeological evidence cited in ch. 4.[112] Hell is harrowed and hope renewed for the souls of the just (*Dream* 147–9):

> Se sunu wæs sigorfæst   on þam siðfate,
> mihtig ond spedig,   þa he mid manigeo com,
> gasta weorode,   on Godes rice,
> Anwealda ælmihtig,   englum to blisse

[112] *The Dream of the Rood*, ed. Swanton, p. 138.

Heathen gods

> ond *eallum ðam halgum   þam þe on heofonum ær*
> *wunedon on wuldre,*   þa heora Wealdend cwom,
> ælmihtig God,   þær his eðel wæs.   (*Dream* 150–6)[113]

This image of Christ approaching heaven 'with a multitude' (*mid manigeo*) and 'a troop of souls' (*gasta weorode*) cuts straight to the ascension and is echoed by Eyvindr's portrait of the dead Hákon nearing Valhǫll 'with a great army' (*með her mikinn*) in *Hákonarmál* 10. Also striking is the fact that a number of non-angelic beings is already awaiting Christ and his multitude as they approach heaven. This fact represents a paradox in *The Dream of the Rood*, in that 'all the holy ones' in *Dream* 154–5, presumably human souls, cannot be in heaven before Christ admits them. In contrast, it is worth noting that heaven at this point has no more than a 'troop of angels' (*engla þreat*) in *Christ* 738. Who are 'all the holy ones' in *The Dream of the Rood* who anticipate Christ and the souls of the just? A. D. Horgan identifies two of them as the prophets Enoch and Elijah, though she must add the good thief on Calvary for these to be 'all' rather than 'both'.[114] Following Horgan, Finnegan suggests that the poet gives their abode as heaven, whereas in the Gospel of Nicodemus, likely to be a major source, some pagans burn in hell and others are led by Archangel Michael to the former Eden to stay there until Christ's ascension.[115] It is not clear why the poet's doctrine is occasionally so inexact, and his Christology was praised by Rosemary Woolf.[116] But in Old Norse–Icelandic sources, it is clear that the Norse cognates of OE *halgum* were associated with deified mortals or with the *einherjar*: these dead warriors are imagined as members of a '*holy* sanctuary' in the phrase 'til vés *heilags*' in *Hynd* 1; and in *Hákonarmál* 18, Eyvindr's dead patron is immortalized in Valhǫll at the point 'when all the deciding powers bade Hákon be

---

[113] 'The Son was confirmed in victory in that expedition, powerful and successful, when he came with a multitude, with a troop of souls, into God's kingdom, almighty One-Ruler, to the bliss of angels and *of all the holy ones who had been dwelling in glory previously*, when their Ruler came, almighty God, to where his country was.'

[114] A. D. Horgan, '"The Dream of the Rood" and Christian Tradition', *NM* 79 (1978), 11–20.

[115] R. E. Finnegan, 'The Gospel of Nicodemus and *The Dream of the Rood*, 148b–156', *NM* 84 (1983), 338–43, esp. 340: 'the distinction in the Gospel between "paradise" and what I suppose we might call "heaven proper" would not have troubled our poet unduly'.

[116] Cf. Woolf, 'Doctrinal Influences', pp. 147 and 153.

welcome' ('es Hákon báðu *heilan* koma ráð ǫll ok regin'). OIce *heilagr* or *heill* can thus denote the health and prosperity of gods and deified mortals in Valhǫll. In *The Dream of the Rood*, nearly three centuries earlier than this Norse evidence, I suggest that the Northumbrian poet's doctrine was conditioned by a native Anglian version of the same Valhǫll topos as this was applied to the death of Anglian kings. The lingering influence of this native Anglian mythology may account for the poet's occasionally inexact doctrine, as well as for the unusual licence whereby he appears to describe the cross variously as a living tree, an angel, a king's thegn and a horse; and whereby he appears to present the crucifixion in the language of a myth about Ingui, a native 'dying god'.

CONCLUSION

The present chapter concerns the poetic after-effects of a pre-Christian culture on the diction of *The Dream of the Rood*. In no sense should my argument be regarded as an attempt to read this work as a heathen poem with a learned Christian veneer. On the contrary, it is clear that the poet or poets of this early Northumbrian work adapted the story of the crucifixion with a good command of Christian doctrine and knew enough about Christology, as Rosemary Woolf has shown, to evade the complexities of this debate by transferring the suffering of the Son to the cross. However, it is also clear that the poet of *The Dream of the Rood* was bound by the conventions of a formulaic Anglian vocabulary which was as yet unsuited to theological discourse. Thus he could not have presented Christian narrative and doctrine in the Anglian poetic vernacular of early eighth-century Northumbria without also including the distortions which this essentially pre-Christian vocabulary imposed on his theme. This vernacular heritage may explain why the poet of *The Dream of the Rood* describes Christ as a warrior king and his disciples as members of a *comitatus*, and why, in some ways, this poet also appears to present the manner, circumstances and aftermath of the crucifixion as if it were the sacrifice of a young Anglian hero for whom nature mourned and whose name in Northumbria may have been 'Ingui *geot*'. My argument not only suggests that an Anglian myth about Ingui's death survived into the early eighth century, despite the rapid progress of Christian learning in Northumbria, but also asks us to consider what impact Ingui may have had on the Roman mission to northern England a century earlier.

10
Paulinus and the *stultus error*: the Anglo-Saxon conversion

The conclusion of this book is focused on Bede's narrative on the Roman missions to Kent and Northumbria (*HE* I.23–III.9). Before Oswald introduced Irish Christianity to Northumbria, the Roman missionary Paulinus is already thought to have succeeded in converting Edwin and thousands more to Christianity after a dramatic scene in which Coifi, a native *pontifex*, was induced to reveal the failure of his religion and to destroy his own enclosure at Goodmanham. This was an early success for the Anglo-Saxon church, but in relating this success, Bede occasionally reveals evidence that might have told a different story. Bede, in short, appears to disguise the implications of his local source-material to conform with his information on Paulinus from Canterbury, York or Whitby. In my conclusion I shall suggest that Bede, by celebrating in this way the first Roman contribution to the diocese of York, helped to obscure the circumstances in which Woden got his role as the father of English kings.

Throughout this book I have consistently used Old Norse–Icelandic evidence to identify and interpret some remnants of pre-Christian ideology in Old English words. To reach the point where something can be gained by applying this method to Bede, however, some understanding will be needed of the different conditions in which the Roman missions were undertaken in England and Scandinavia.[1] As Germanic paganism lived on three centuries longer in Scandinavia, so it perished there in a more highly evolved form. In the first century AD, Nerthus was probably worshipped both by the Anglii, ancestors of the Angles in Britain (*Germania*, ch. 40), and by Scandinavians further north. Although it is not

---

[1] See Page, 'The Evidence of Bede', pp. 99–129.

clear how pagan cults developed in England, it is clear that in Scandinavia Nerthus's derivative, Njǫrðr, gradually lost his pre-eminence to the Æsir. By the end of the ninth century, the period in which the oldest surviving Norse poems were probably composed, it is Æsir, not Vanir, who are presented as the masters of a growing pantheon of exclusively personified gods.[2] The process by which Æsir grew and Vanir waned in Scandinavia seems to be linked with Óðinn, whom Snorri names the 'oldest of the Æsir' (*elztr Ásanna*).[3] Óðinn perhaps stands out because, as Helm suggested, this figure was imported northwards, as Mercury, across the upper Rhine in the first few centuries of this era, thence into southern and northern Germany and the Low Countries, southern England and Scandinavia.[4] Þórr seems to have grown in popularity only in the eighth century and at the beginning of the Viking Age.[5] On analogy with the relatively late growth of Óðinn and Þórr in Scandinavia, therefore, it is plausible that those gods which predominated in northern regions of seventh-century England, where there is no evidence of *Woden* or *þunor* in English placenames, were natural phenomena or *numina* of an older Vanir type. In my earlier chapters, I have suggested that the focus of these *numina* was Ingui and that the Anglian name of his religion was implicit in Bede's use of the Latin word *vanitas*. In the present chapter, and contrary to the expectations of most scholars who have studied the history of the Anglo-Saxon conversion, I shall argue that the Angles, in particular, offered no resistance to Christianity and indeed failed to perceive the difference between this new religion and their own. In other words, the scholarly axiom that Christianization involved a clash of cultures or ideologies in seventh-century England may have been conceived on the basis of the history of the Scandinavian conversion in the tenth and eleventh centuries. The differences in time, place and conversion history between England and Scandinavia, which I shall now attempt to show in more detail, may explain why there was a stronger reaction to Christianization in Scandinavia than there was in England.

HEATHEN REACTION IN SCANDINAVIA

By the ninth century, the Æsir predominated in Denmark, Sweden and Norway. Heathen reaction was not slow in coming in these places and

[2] *AR* I, 169 (§451) and II, 18 (§353). [3] *Gylf*, p. 21 (ch. 20).
[4] Helm, *Wodan*, pp. 60–71. [5] McKinnell, *Both One and Many*, pp. 57–8.

there were vigorous setbacks for Christianity in Birka in the mid ninth century, in the Trondheim region in the tenth and in Iceland at the turn of the millennium.

As ever, the first task of the church was to secure the support of local rulers. An attempted conversion in Sweden was recorded in Rimbert's *Vita S. Anskarii*.[6] According to Rimbert, a delegation purporting to come from King Bern and requesting conversion arrived in the court of Emperor Louis the Pious in Saxony (ch. 9), a meeting that is datable to *c*. 826. Louis promised a mission and called Anskar out of the abbey of Corvey to lead it. Not without trouble on the way, Anskar and his fellow monks arrived in Birka, the remote centre of Bern's kingdom and yet a north-eastern mart of international standing. Bern belatedly recognized their embassy, consulted with his advisers and gave them permission to preach the gospel, 'the freedom thus being yielded to them to seek out anyone who might want their teaching'.[7] Rimbert says that many Swedes 'spoke no words against their embassy and freely heard the teaching of the Lord'.[8] The warmth of this welcome was understandable. Rimbert says that Christians already lived as captives in Birka and rejoiced in being able to perform their sacred mysteries after so long without them. Here Rimbert admits that the message of the original Swedish delegation now seemed to be true. Not a few Swedes sought baptism, including the king's prefect, who built his own church. Yet this picture changed over the years, when an otherwise unknown Olef succeeded Bern. When Bishop Anskar, as he now was, returned to Birka:

invenit regem et multitudinem populi nimio errore confusam. Instigante enim diabolo, adventum beati viri omnimodis praesciente, contigit eo ipso tempore, ut quidam illo adveniens diceret, se in conventu deorum, qui ipsam terram possidere credebantur, affuisse, et ab eis missum, ut haec regi et populis nunciaret: 'Vos', inquam, 'nos vobis propitios diu habuistis et terram incolatus vestri cum multa abundantia nostro adiutorio in pace et prosperitate longo tempore tenuistis. Vos quoque nobis sacrificia et vota debita persolvistis, grataque nobis vestra fuerunt obsequia. At nunc et sacrificia solita subtrahitis et

---

[6] *Vita S. Anskarii*, ed. G. Waitz, pp. 30–3 and 56–8.
[7] *Ibid.*, p. 30 (ch. 11): 'concessa libertate ut quicumque vellent eorum doctrinam expeterent'.
[8] *Ibid.*: 'eorum legationi favebant et doctrinam Domini libenter audiebant'.

vota spontanea segnius offertis et, quod magis nobis displicet, alienum deum super nos introducitis.'[9]

The gods warn Olef to return to their worship with greater offerings and to reject 'the other god' (*alter deus*). Not to be thought unreasonable, however, they offer to deify 'a king of former times' (*quondam regem*), Erik for example, if it is only more gods that Olef and his people want. The Swedes had thrown out the previous Christian priests 'in a popular revolt' (*populari seditione*). Anskar enlisted King Olef's help as he had earlier enlisted Bern's, but despite his second attempt to convince them, many Swedes stayed heathen until the twelfth century. Christ was now 'a foreign god' (*alienus deus*) that Bern and Olef wanted to impose on their people (ch. 26). The god behind this Swedish reaction is most likely to have been Þórr.

King Bern's lack of recognition earlier in the *Vita S. Anskarii* shows how little surprise Anskar's first party occasioned in Birka. Some simple vocabulary also shows why Christ was not thought at first to be a *deus alienus*: OIce *Freyr* means literally 'lord', the royal god of Sweden whose name Adam of Bremen cites as *Fricco* in *c.* 1076; just as the Latin word *Dominus* in Anskar's *doctrina Domini* which the Swedes could have understood only in translation. This stage of conversion represents an initial pagan failure to perceive the difference of Christ from a local god whose epithets were the same or similar: a misunderstanding which resembles one between Bishop Wilfrid and King Aldgisl in *c.* 680, when, probably believing in a reflex of Nerthus, the Frisians were temporarily converted *en masse* after unusually big harvests and a large catch of fish.[10]

---

[9] *Ibid.*, p. 56: (ch. 26): 'he found the king and the multitude of people troubled by a great error. For, at the prompting of a devil who knew beforehand every detail of the arrival of the blessed man, it happened then too that a person came to that man [Anskar] saying that he had been present at an assembly of the gods who were believed to occupy the selfsame land [cf. OIce *bǫnd í landi*], and that he was sent from them to announce the following to the king and people: "You people", he said, "have long had our favour, and for a long time you have held the land in which you dwell with great abundance and in peace and prosperity [cf. OIce *ár ok friðr*] only with our help. The sacrifices and offerings owed to us you have also paid, and your acts of obedience have pleased us. Yet now you withdraw both the accustomed sacrifices and make your freely given offerings more slowly. And what displeases us more, you bring in a foreign god over us."' For a lively topical discussion of this episode, see L. Lönnroth, 'När vikingarna blev européer', *Fornvännen* 89 (1994), 198–201, esp. 199.

[10] *Vita S. Wilfridi*, ed. Levison, p. 220 (ch. 26).

Up in Trondheim in the first half of the tenth century, Hákon Aðalsteinsfóstri was chosen king regardless of his beliefs. His Christianity probably went unnoticed until the local farmers perceived that he had no interest in representing them to their gods with regular sacrifice. In his turn, Hákon may have relaxed his principles as soon as his peasants made it clear that they would otherwise replace him. Yet as if Hákon's power were a secondary consideration, the early thirteenth-century writer of *Fagrskinna* and, later, Snorri in *Hákonar saga góða*, present him in this affair as the conscience-stricken loser of a duel with a pagan trinity. In doing so, these authors evade the question of Hákon's apostasy, which they none the less illustrate by quoting his celebration of paganism in Eyvindr's contemporary *Hákonarmál* (c. 960).

In this poem the Norwegians have now learnt to define themselves as 'heathen', for Eyvindr says that Hákon 'went among *heathen* gods' ('fór með *heiðin* goð', *Hákonarmál* 24), borrowing a Christian term of reference that had probably come to Trondheim from England. Nor could it be forgotten that OE *hæðen* and OIce *heiðinn* are Christian words, for they show the pagan awareness of a loss of prestige in paganism. These terms, which represent calques on Lat *paganus*, could not have been adopted without an awareness of the more powerful *civitas Dei* further south. So, in a fragment from c. 990 – c. 1000, Eilífr Goðrúnarson says:

> Setbergs kveða sitja   sunnr at Urðar brunni,
> svá hefr ramr konungr remðan   Róms banda sik lǫndum.[11]

To Eilífr Christianity was apparently *urðr*, a physical law; Rome was the hub of the world and Christ its ruler; in contrast, Þórr, Óðinn, Freyr and other northern *numina* were politically impotent.

Late in the tenth century, both Eyvindr and Eilífr along with many other *skáld* were paid to immortalize Hákon Jarl 'the powerful' (*inn ríki*) as the renewer of sacrifices and victor of Hjǫrungavágr in c. 985. With their sophisticated kennings and many-layered narratives, Eyvindr's *Háleygjatal*, Einarr's *Vellekla*, Eilífr's *Þórsdrápa*, Hallfreðr's *Hákonardrápa* and other works effectively constructed a heathen theology from local superstition. In *Þórsdrápa*, in particular, Daphne Davidson has shown that Þórr's battle against the giants hints at Hákon Jarl's campaigns against the Jómsvikings and the Danes. In this political allegory within

---

[11] *Skj* B I, 144: 'Thus has the powerful king of Rome empowered himself in the lands of the stronghold of the bonds; they say he sits in the south by the well of Fate.'

Paulinus and the stultus error

Þórsdrápa, Hákon makes common cause with the peasant farmers of Norway by identifying himself with Þórr. However, by emulating Freyr in a sexually incontinent role with the same farmers' wives and daughters, Hákon took archaism too far and lost his kingdom not to a foreign Christian king, but to his own Þórr-worshipping subjects. As the expression of a late heathen reaction, the poets of Hákon Jarl provide evidence of the political anxiety underlying his doomed attempt to build an ideology against the influence of Christian kings further south.[12]

In Iceland there had been Christians from the beginning of its history in the later ninth century: Irish 'fathers' (*papar*), who disappeared when the Norwegians arrived, according to Ari's polished *Íslendingabók*, leaving 'Irish books, bells and croziers' (*bækr írskar ok bjǫlla ok bagla*) behind them. Yet unlike the authors of the less tidy *Landnámabók* recensions, Ari omits to mention the Christian faith of settlers from the British Isles including Auðr *in djúpúðga* ('the deep-minded') and Helgi *inn magri* ('the lean'). Although it is generally assumed that this Christianity died out in Iceland, Jesse Byock admits that 'it is possible that some individuals and families maintained a belief in the Christian god'.[13] Given the open nature of polytheism, this is indeed likely. According to *Landnámabók*, Helgi worshipped both Þórr and Christ, being 'greatly mixed in his faith' (*blandinn mjǫk í trú*).[14] *Vǫluspá* (c. 1000) is evidence of an Icelandic poet so familiar with Christian sermons that he incorporates some Last Days vocabulary into his heathen poem without the slightest trace of antagonism.[15] Yet this poet's knowledge of Christianity never tempted him or her to impose its monotheism on the native eschatology.[16] In Iceland there were probably heretical forms of Christianity until the first missionaries, though Roman orthodoxy was the only acceptable form of

---

[12] Davidson, 'Earl Hákon and his Poets', pp. 25–30; see also Ström, 'Poetry as an Instrument of Propaganda', pp. 440–58.

[13] Byock, *Medieval Iceland*, p. 138.

[14] *Landnámabók*, ed. Jakob, p. 250 (*Sturlubók*, ch. 218).

[15] The words *menn meinsvara oc morðvarga* ('men perjured and murderous wolves') in *Vsp* 39 echo Wulfstan's *manswōran 7 morþorwyrhtan* ('perjurers and murderers') and *ðurh morðdæda 7 ðurh mandæda* ('through murderous deeds and through criminal deeds'), in *Homilies of Wulfstan*, ed. Bethurum, pp. 273 and 264.

[16] On cyclical time in *Vǫluspá*, see J. P. Schjødt, '*Vǫluspá*: Cyklisk tidsopfattelse i gammelnordisk religion', *Danske Studier* 76 (1981), 91–5; and Dronke, '*Vǫluspá* and Sibylline Traditions', pp. 3–23, and 'War of the Æsir and Vanir', pp. 223–38 (also published in *Myth and Fiction*, resp. nos. II and VII).

Christian worship open to Christian historians. Given the choice, no Icelandic writer would damn his ancestors as heretics if they could be saved as pagans. Thus Auðr's Christianity is recorded in *Landnámabók*, her paganism admired in *Laxdœla saga*.[17] In this way it would have been odd if a living form of Christianity had not survived within Icelandic polytheism before the crisis caused by King Óláfr Tryggvason at the end of the millennium.

Íslendingabók (c. 1125–30) is the earliest record of the Icelandic conversion.[18] Although Ari probably had European models for his chronology, he based his story of the Icelandic conversion on the verbal testimony of his fosterfather Teitr Ísleifsson (d. 1110), who had an unnamed source 'who was there himself'.[19] Unlike the story so far in Birka and the Trondheim region, the *kristnitaka* ('Christianization') of the Icelanders in c. 999 was an artful compromise with its emphasis on republican independence. Several missionaries seem to have arrived in this mid-Atlantic colony from the 980s onwards, but it was Óláfr who completed their work in c. 997: first by sending Þangbrandr, a German Saxon, to convert the Icelanders, then by threatening the lives of Icelanders in Norway when it became clear that Þangbrandr's obsessive violence had turned half the population against him. If ever pagans had included Christ in their own cults in Iceland, Christianity was now disowned as a disruptive *frændaskǫmm* ('kinsmen's shame').[20] This reaction is essentially that of *Sif* ('family') in the Þórr-centred cults of the south and west. 'Have you heard', asks Steinunn *skáldkona* ('poet-woman'), quoting or creating some living mythology for Þangbrandr when his ship had been run aground in c. 998, 'that Þórr challenged Christ to a duel, and Christ didn't dare to fight with Þórr?'[21] Þangbrandr replies that Þórr

---

[17] *Landnámabók*, ed. Jakob, p. 147 (*Sturlubók*, ch. 110); *Laxdœla saga*, ed. Einar Ólafur Sveinsson, ÍF 5 (Reykjavik, 1934), pp. 12–13 (ch. 7).

[18] *Íslendingabók*, ed. Jakob, pp. 14–18 (ch. 7); discussed by D. Strömbäck, *The Conversion of Iceland*, trans. P. Foote, Viking Society for Northern Research, Text Series 6 (London, 1975), 13–37; see also Byock, *Medieval Iceland*, pp. 138–43.

[19] *Íslendingabók*, ed. Jakob, p. 15: 'es sjalfr vas þar'.

[20] *Kristnisaga*, ed. B. Kahle, Altnordische Saga-Bibliothek 11 (Halle a. S., 1905), 1–57, esp. 19; see also Hastrup, *Culture and History*, pp. 179–86.

[21] *Brennu-Njáls saga*, ed. Einar Ólafur Sveinsson, ÍF 12 (Reykjavik, 1954), 265 (ch. 102): 'Hefir þú heyrt þat, er Þórr bauð Kristi á hólm, ok treystisk hann eigi at berjask við Þór?'

Paulinus and the stultus error

would be nothing but ashes if Christ did not want him to live. Steinunn then recites two *dróttkvætt* verses which show her belief that Þórr had smashed Þangbrandr's ship.[22] Despite Þangbrandr's conversion of Hallr *á Síðu* ('of Síða') and other chieftains in the meantime, Ari reveals that 'there were however more who spoke against it and refused'.[23] Eventually Þangbrandr's mission failed and Óláfr began to round up young Icelanders in Norway. Ari says that Gizurr *inn hvíti* ('the white') went there to negotiate, returned to Iceland the following summer and quickly mustered an army. This Christian faction was soon joined by the young Hjalti Skeggjason, a Byronic figure who had been outlawed the previous summer for blasphemy, after proclaiming:

Vil ek eigi goð geyja;   grey þykki mér Freyja.[24]

According to Ari, the heathens now gathered their own forces. Gizurr and Hjalti delivered speeches on the law-rock in which, naming each other as witnesses, they formally 'declared each side illegal by the other's law, both Christian and heathen'.[25] Thereupon the Christians asked Hallr á Síðu 'that he should publicly recite the laws that might accord with Christianity'.[26] The Christians are thus presented as looking for their own courts of law. Hallr headed off a civil war by paying or bribing Þorgeirr, the official Lawspeaker, a heathen, to 'recite [the laws] in public'.[27] Ari is here ambiguous: either Hallr requested a compromise Icelandic law, or he bribed Þorgeirr to embody some Christian codes within the existing ones. After a day and night under his cloak, whether communing with the Icelandic *bǫnd* or sleeping, Þorgeirr appealed to both parties to accept one law in which Christian codes would predominate, though three *heiðni*

---

[22] *Skj* B I, 128 and in Turville-Petre, *Scaldic Poetry*, pp. 65–7.

[23] *Íslendingabók*, ed. Jakob, p. 14 (ch. 7): 'þeir váru þó fleiri, es í gegn mæltu ok neittu'.

[24] *Ibid.*, p. 15: 'I don't want to blaspheme the gods (/ to bark at the gods); Freyja seems a bitch to me.' In this line, Hjalti first appears to claim piety, then rapidly undermines this claim by applying the meaning of *goðgá* ('blasphemy') literally ('barking at the gods') and thus hinting instead that not even Hjalti (a philanderer?) wishes to encourage the sexual demands of Freyja (a bitch in heat). For another interpretation, cf. K. von See, 'Der Spottvers des Hjalti Skeggjason', *ZfdA* 97 (1968), 155–8.

[25] *Íslendingabók*, ed. Jakob, p. 16: 'sǫgðusk hvárir ýr lǫgum við aðra, enir kristnu menn ok enir heiðnu'.

[26] *Ibid.*: 'at hann skyldi lǫg þeira upp segja, þau es kristninni skyldi fylgja'.

[27] *Ibid.*: 'at hann skyldi upp segja'.

('heathen customs') should be allowed to continue: exposure of unwanted children, the eating of horseflesh and secret sacrifice.[28]

Behind Þorgeirr's plea for 'one law and one [religious] custom' (*ein lǫg ok einn sið*) is the fear of political secession, from which he deflects attention with a flattering tale of two warring kings of Denmark and Norway whose common people forced them to make peace, 'though they did not want to'.[29] Although this timely *exemplum* is fictitious, it must have strengthened the Christian cause by detaching it from royal power, for the Icelanders cannot have forgotten Óláfr's ambition behind his earlier attempt to convert them. Ari says that finally they agreed to convert, provided they could keep the three *heiðni*. Yet since paganism was nothing if not sacrifice, whether in secret or not, it is not even clear that an immediate conversion took place.[30] Þorgeirr's solution is a deception, not a compromise, for by the open terms of his three *heiðni* emendments Þórr-worshippers and Christians alike could claim a victory. Only when monotheism was slowly enforced after years of consolidation could it have dawned on the Icelandic heathens which side had won that afternoon.

THE ROMAN MISSION IN ENGLAND

In England the official conversion of the Anglo-Saxons took nearly ninety years.[31] Here, unlike later Scandinavia, there was no long acquaintance with a massed army of Christian nations advancing from a powerful papacy in Rome. Late sixth-century England lay on the fringe of a fragmented world still adjusting to the devolution of the Roman empire. Heathen reaction had no cause to grow in England as long as Christian communities here and on the Continent were isolated in large tracts of

---

[28] This episode is imaginatively discussed by Jón Hnefill Aðalsteinsson in *Under the Cloak: the Acceptance of Christianity in Iceland with Particular Reference to the Religious Attitudes Prevailing at the Time*, Acta Universitatis Upsaliensis, Studia Ethnologica Upsaliensia 4 (Uppsala, 1978), 88–126.

[29] *Íslendingabók*, ed. Jakob, p. 17: 'þótt þeir vildi eigi'.

[30] Peter Foote makes a distinction between public and private sacrifice for which it would not be easy to find proof, given that both temples and households were meant in the Icelandic *hof* placenames: see 'On the Conversion of the Icelanders', in *Aurvandilstá: Norse Studies*, ed. M. Barnes, H. Bekker-Nielsen and G. W. Weber (Odense, 1984), pp. 56–64, esp. 62; on *hof*, see Svavar, 'Átrúnaðr og örnefni', p. 247.

[31] Mayr-Harting, *The Coming of Christianity*, pp. 13–68, esp. 29.

Paulinus and the stultus error

pagan countryside and Pope Gregory (590–604) had only limited power over bishops even closer to Rome.[32] In 596 Gregory sent a mission to England with St Augustine at its head. At first Augustine and his companions were fearful and turned back, but Gregory urged them to continue and wrote to Bishop Etherius of Arles for his assistance in Gaul. Probably in the early summer of 597, Augustine and about forty other monks came ashore on Thanet, an island off Kent (*HE* I.25).

King Æthelberht of Kent

How did Æthelberht perceive Augustine and his monks? Any answer to this question depends on an interpretation of the motives and sources underlying Bede's *Historia ecclesiastica*, which in any case is not the earliest extant source for the conversion of Kent and the other Anglo-Saxon kingdoms. An earlier work is the *Vita Sancti Gregorii Magni*, written in *c.* 704–14 by an anonymous author of Whitby, but this writer's sources were sparse and only the facts of Æthelberht's status and conversion are recorded.[33] In writing his own more detailed account in *c.* 732, Bede reveals that he used records supplied to him by Abbot Albinus through Nothhelm, who later became archbishop of Canterbury.[34] Yet there were probably factual errors or misunderstandings in these Canterbury records. First, as Nicholas Brooks has suggested, Gregory of Tours's references to Ingoberga, Æthelberht's mother-in-law, show that Æthelberht had probably married Bertha, Ingoberga's daughter, as early as 575 × 581, but may not have become king of Kent until as late as *c.* 590: so that when Bede says that Æthelberht ruled for fifty-six years, it is likely that he or Albinus or an earlier Canterbury source misunderstood a statement that Æthelberht was fifty-six years old when he died.[35] Second, by revealing that Æthelberht died in 616, twenty-one years after taking the faith (*HE* II.5), Bede implies that Æthelberht had been baptized in 595, two years before Augustine arrived. Even if Æthelberht's death is dated to 616 × 618, as Brooks suggests, Bede's statement would imply that Æthelberht accepted baptism at the latest on Augustine's arrival, even though Bede makes it clear that he declined it at this time

[32] On Gregory's power, see *ibid.*, pp. 51–7.
[33] *Vita S. Gregorii*, ed. Colgrave, p. 94 (ch. 12).
[34] *HE*, pp. 2–4 (preface); Wallace-Hadrill, *Commentary*, pp. 31, 33 and 147.
[35] Brooks, 'Creation and Early Structure of the Kingdom of Kent', pp. 65–7.

Heathen gods

(*HE* I.25).³⁶ In this way, Bede's own account appears to have been confused by that of his source in Canterbury.

None the less, if we leave aside Bede's dating of Æthelberht's death (*HE* II.5), it is still possible to treat his view of Æthelberht as a pagan king as correct from the Roman Catholic point of view. Four years later, in a letter of 601 unknown to Bede, Pope Gregory chided Bertha for the fact that Æthelberht was still unbaptized.³⁷ Bede says that Bertha practised Christianity with a Frankish bishop named Liudhard in the church of St Martin in Canterbury (*HE* I.25–6). Bede therefore attempts to conceal Æthelberht's contact with Christians when he states, while he says that Æthelberht was preparing to greet Augustine in 597, that 'a rumour of the Christian religion had reached him earlier'; for by this time Bertha had been married to Æthelberht for at least sixteen years.³⁸ Although Bertha's father Charibert had died in 567, at least nine (and at most fourteen) years before his daughter's marriage with Æthelberht, it is possible that Æthelberht refused baptism from Liudhard in the early days of his marriage so as to stay free of subordination to Charibert's Merovingian successors.³⁹ Evidently it was the political source, not the religious question, of his baptism that concerned Æthelberht: in whose interest should he be baptized? First, Augustine's *Liber responsionum* (*HE* I.27) may show that Welsh bishops had converted some *Angli* before 597.⁴⁰ Second, when the anonymous author of Whitby states that Æthelberht was 'the first of all the kings of England to be *corrected* to faith in Christ', his own source may have told him that Æthelberht had already been baptized by non-Roman bishops.⁴¹ It is even possible, on analogy with Brooks's conclusion about Æthelberht's fifty-six years, that Æthelberht had been twenty-one when he was baptized (i.e. in *c*. 580 × 582). It

---

³⁶ *Ibid.*, pp. 65–6.   ³⁷ Kirby, *Earliest English Kings*, pp. 35–6.
³⁸ *HE* I.25 (p. 72): 'antea fama ad eum Christianae religionis pervenerat'.
³⁹ On this motive, see A. Angenendt, 'The Conversion of the Anglo-Saxons Considered against the Background of the Early Medieval Mission', *Settimane* 32 (1986), 747–81. Against this motive, see Brooks, 'Creation and Early Structure of the Kingdom of Kent', p. 67.
⁴⁰ R. Meens, 'A Background to Augustine's Mission to Anglo-Saxon England', *ASE* 23 (1994), 5–17. On the *Magonsæte* and *Hwicce* being 'converted from within', see Sims-Williams, *Religion and Literature*, pp. 54–76.
⁴¹ *Vita S. Gregorii*, ed. Colgrave, p. 94 (ch. 12): 'regum omnium Angulorum Edilberctus rex Cantuariorum ad fidem Christi *correctus*'.

Paulinus and the stultus error

is thus possible that Æthelberht had accepted a version of Christianity unacceptable to Rome before Augustine arrived in 597.

Whether or not Æthelberht was already baptized at this time, it is not clear that he would have been told to regard Welsh, Frankish or Roman bishops as members of the same religion, given the disunity between western Christians at the end of the sixth century. How Æthelberht perceived Augustine and his monks is thus a complex question. Rather ironically, as Bede tells the story, Æthelberht treats Augustine and his monks as if he is a Christian and they are pagans: when Augustine sends word that his God 'promised those submitting to Him everlasting joys in heaven and a future kingdom without end with the living and true God (*cum Deo uiuo et uero*) without any doubt whatsoever', Bede says that King Æthelberht ordered Augustine and his companions to stay on Thanet 'until he saw what to do with them'.[42] A few days later Æthelberht crossed over from the mainland:

et residens sub diuo iussit Augustinum cum sociis ad suum ibidem aduenire colloquium. Cauerat enim ne in aliquam domum ad se introirent, uetere usus augurio, ne superuentu suo, siquid maleficae artis habuissent, eum superando deciperent. At illi non daemonica sed diuina uirtute praediti ueniebant.[43]

This piece of information about Æthelberht's beliefs may have been modelled on a canon such as that edited by the *Discipulus Umbrensium* ('Disciple of the Northumbrians') in the first half of the eighth century on the basis of second- or third-hand knowledge of the (lost) canons of Archbishop Theodore.[44] In the Disciple's text, excommunication for the clergy, or, if secular, five years of penance, is recommended for those 'who observe auguries or auspices or dreams or any kind of divinations according to the customs of pagans, or introduce men of this kind to their

---

[42] *HE* I.25 (p. 72): 'sibi obtemperantibus aeterna in caelis gaudia et regnum sine fine cum Deo uiuo et uero futurum sine ulla dubietate promitteret'; 'donec uideret quid eis faceret'.

[43] *Ibid.* I.25 (p. 74): 'and sitting in the open air, he ordered Augustine and his companions to come to talk with him there. For he took care that they should not enter any house to see him, making use of an old prediction that if they had any knowledge of the magic art, they would deceive and overcome him by their sudden arrival. But these men came endowed with divine not demonic power.'

[44] On the date and likely development of the Disciple's text (U), see Charles-Edwards, 'The Penitential of Theodore and the *Iudicia Theodori*', pp. 147–58.

Heathen gods

houses for the purpose of investigating the art of magical acts'.[45] The source for this canon appears to be a brief decree in the Synod of Ancyra (LXIV.5) in which 'those seeking divinations after the custom of pagans' (*qui diuinationes expetunt more gentilium*) do penance for five years.[46] Since the Disciple's clause concerning wizards in houses is not found in the Ancyra canon, it is possible that he, his sources or even Theodore himself added this clause to the Ancyra text because it reflected a feature of seventh-century Anglo-Saxon paganism. Bede or his Canterbury source thus appears to give Æthelberht the correct Christian response to men whom Æthelberht, in keeping with Anglo-Saxon paganism, perceived to be wizards.

In this light, although Æthelberht's response to the Roman monks seems to be expressed in canonical language, his fear of them as magicians appears to be the truth on which this story is based. This fearful perception is odd, for it might be thought that Æthelberht had better reason to regard Augustine and his followers as officials of the Roman empire, the remains of which were still visible in Canterbury. On the other hand, it is not clear how much Æthelberht could have known of the Romans, nor of forty Romans wearing gowns, chanting Latin litanies and holding aloft a panel depicting a human face. The sixth-century man buried in female dress and jewellery with a flint nodule on his chest in Portway, Hampshire, constitutes some evidence that Æthelberht could have feared men in gowns as male witches.[47] Whether or not Augustine's monks were wearing cassocks, their outer gowns may have been white long-sleeved, collarless and ankle-length *albae* of the simple type that Gregory the Great seems to have worn.[48] Gregory of Tours, writing in *c.* 590, shows that such garments were no longer worn by the laity, only by

---

[45] *Die Canones Theodori*, ed. Finsterwalder, p. 311 (U, I.xv.4): 'Qui auguria, auspicia sive somnia vel divinationes quaslibet secundum mores gentilium observant, aut in domus suas huiusmodi homines introducunt in exquirendis aliquam artem maleficiorum.'

[46] *Sinodus Anchiritana* LXIV.5 and U I.xv.4 are both cited in Charles-Edwards, 'The Penitential of Theodore and the *Iudicia Theodori*', p. 174.

[47] Wilson, *Anglo-Saxon Paganism*, pp. 96–7.

[48] John the Deacon, *Sancti Gregorii Papae Cognomento Magni Opera Omnia*, PL 75, 72 (*Sancti Gregorii Magni Vita*, I.25): 'tanta solertia ministravit, ut in ecclesiasticae hierarchiae ministerio videretur divinis angelis non solum nitore habitus, verum etiam claritate morum probabilium quodammodo coaequari'. The ecclesiastical costume of this era is discussed in di Berardino, *Encyclopedia of the Early Church*, s.v. 'Vestments, Liturgical' (pp. 864–5).

the clergy.⁴⁹ Gregory of Tours also illustrates a contemporary suspicion of men in religious vestments in Count Palladius, who insulted Bishop Parthenius (in the court of King Sigibert of the Merovingians in *c.* 550 × 70) by asking 'Where are those husbands of yours, the ones that you live with in such disgrace and filth?'⁵⁰ Palladius was a Christian; in Roman eyes, Æthelberht was not; the burden of proof thus lies in showing that Æthelberht could not have perceived monks in general, or in particular Bishop Liudhard and many years later Augustine and his monks, as dangerous effeminates endowed with demonic power.

Æthelberht's misperception of *daemonica uirtus* in these monks suggests that male witches were familiar members of early Anglo-Saxon society and that the Kentish vernacular term for their influence may have resembled lWS *ælfsiden* ('demon-magic'). As I have attempted to show in ch. 3, *ælfsiden* is cognate with OIce *seiðr*. The Norse *seiðmenn* were also regarded as effeminate male witches and were associated with the Vanir: in *Vǫluspá*, the *seiðmenn* are represented in the person of Heiðr and in her attempt to seduce men and women away from their allegiance to the Æsir; this scene and the resulting Æsir–Vanir cult-war appear to comprise an analogue of the Greek legend of Dionysus's arrival outside Thebes.⁵¹ As with the Bacchants in the Greek legend, the Vanir *seiðmenn* in *Vǫluspá* worship a god of licence whose magic possesses them in a trance and whose demand to sober townsfolk is that he be respected along with their other gods. Heiðr, the first Van, is thus the harbinger of Ingvi-freyr:

> Heiði hana héto   þar hón til húsa kom,
> vǫlo vel spá,   vitti hón ganda.
> Seið hón kunni,   seið hón leikin,
> æ var hón angan   illrar brúðar.   (*Vsp* 22)⁵²

---

⁴⁹ *Gregorii Episcopi Turonensis Miracula et Opera Minora*, ed. B. Krusch, MGH, SRM 1.2 (Hanover, 1885), p. 309 (*De gloria confessorum*, ch. 20): 'sacerdotum ac levitarum in albis vestibus non minimus chorus et civium honoratorum ordo praeclarus'.

⁵⁰ *Gregorii Historiae*, ed. Krusch and Levison, p. 170 (IV.39): 'Ubi sunt mariti tui, cum quibus stuprose ac turpiter vivis?' This type of insult is discussed by J. M. Pizarro, 'On *Níð* against Bishops', *MScan* 11 (1982), 149–53.

⁵¹ Dronke, 'War of the Æsir and Vanir', pp. 223–38; also published in *Myth and Fiction*, no. VII.

⁵² I follow the text and base my translation on Dronke (*ibid.*, p. 225): '"Brilliant" they called her, at all the houses she came to, a prophetess of good fortune-telling – she conjured spirits to tell her. Sorcery she had skill in, sorcery she practised, possessed. She was always the darling of an evil bride.'

Heathen gods

Kentish paganism in the early seventh century might seem a long way in time and space from the Æsir–Vanir cult-war, or from the conflict between Dionysus and Pentheus of Thebes. However, three limited but unusual parallels appear between Heiðr's 'good fortune-telling' (*vel spá*) in *Vǫluspá* and the 'old prediction' (*vetus augurium*) of which Æthelberht makes use in Kent; between Heiðr's magic taking place 'at all the houses she came to' (*þar hón til húsa kom*) and Æthelberht's fear 'that they should not enter any house to see him' (*ne in aliquam domum ad se introirent*); and between Heiðr as she 'practised witchcraft, possessed' (*seið hón leikin*) and Augustine's monks being in Kentish eyes 'endowed with demonic power' (*daemonica uirtute praediti*).[53] Bede's late ninth-century Mercian translator rendered *uetere usus augurio* as *breac ealdre hælsunge* ('used an old charm').[54] More literally, however, *uetus augurium* is intangible and refers rather to a prophecy upon which, in Bede's passage, Æthelberht acted without hesitation when he heard Augustine's promise of a *Deus uiuus et uerus*.

So far in this book, I have noted three correspondences between elements of Merovingian kingship and the Old Norse–Icelandic cult of Ingvi-freyr.[55] The ethnic and cultural composition of Kent in the sixth century was complex: Saxon towards the west, Jutish in the east; with Æthelberht's family itself likely to be of Frankish origin, yet apparently having inherited its sub-Roman kingdom from Romano-British kings.[56] Nor is it a foregone conclusion that forms of Insular Christianity had ever

---

[53] For the West Saxon versions of these Latin phrases, see *Old English Ecclesiastical History*, ed. and trans. Miller, p. 58: 'breac ealdre hælsunge'; 'þy læs hie on hwylc hus to him ineodan'; 'mid deofulcræfte ... gewelgade'.

[54] *Ibid.*, p. 58. S. Lerer (*Literacy and Power in Anglo-Saxon England* (Lincoln, NA, and London, 1991), pp. 40–1) draws attention here to a shift in the focus from the monks as sorcerers to King Æthelberht's own use of magic, noting this passage as proof that pagans were apt to attribute power to signs as autonomous entities rather than as symbols of greater power.

[55] (1) The ox-drawn wagon tour of Childeric III, in *Vita Karoli Magni*, ed. Pertz and Waitz, p. 3 (I.1). (2) '*Ingo*mar' as the first son of pagan Clovis and Christian Clothild, in *Gregorii Historiae*, ed. Krusch and Levison, p. 75 (II.29). (3) Twenty-one horses buried near the pagan Childeric I (481/2): J. Werner, 'Childerichs Pferde', *Germanische Religionsgeschichte*, ed. Beck, Ellmers and Schier, pp. 229–69; to be compared with the horse-cult of Ingvi-freyr, on which see *AR* II, 188–91 (§§463–4).

[56] Brooks, 'Creation and Early Structure of the Kingdom of Kent', pp. 55–8, esp. 57, and 64.

Paulinus and the stultus error

disappeared from Canterbury.[57] Bertha's mother was called *Ingo-berga* ('?sustinence of Ingo'), although she was Christian; this name and an evident lack of communication with Æthelberht (Ingoberga had apparently forgotten her son-in-law's name on her deathbed in 588–9)[58] may partly explain how Æthelberht could have construed the royal Christian cult of Bertha as the same religion which had been practised by Bertha's, and thus also by Æthelberht's, ancestors. Above all, it is likely that Æthelberht had no learning with which to distinguish Welsh or Roman Christianity from older cults, whether these cults reflected Merovingian heathenism or the substrata of older Roman ecstatic religions, such as those of Bacchus or Mithras, that had most probably continued to be practised in Kent after the official withdrawal of Roman government from Britain in the early fifth century. Henig has shown, in the fourth-century Bacchic inscription from London (*hominibus bagis bitam*, 'I give life to wandering men') that the promise of eternal life was nothing new to late Roman pagans.[59] So Æthelberht may not have apprehended any novelty in the heavenly revels, regeneration and *uerbum uitae* ('word of life') promised him by Augustine in 597.[60] Rather, when Æthelberht treated Augustine as a magician, it is more plausible that Æthelberht, although he was still a pantheist and could be called a pagan by the church in Rome, had already been baptized as an Insular Christian and had suited Christ to the role of a dying god in his own composite Germanic–Roman heritage. This mythology would have enabled Æthelberht to rationalize the coming of Augustine and his monks as the fulfilment of a *uetus augurium* in which the harbingers of *Ingo*, the god of Bertha's ancestors, arrived from Gaul to demand his tribute in Kent.

The objection to this reading of Bede is, of course, that he could not have conceived of Æthelberht's beliefs in this way; and it is unlikely that Bede knew as much of Kentish paganism as he did of the Northumbrian paganism with which I shall conclude this book. Rather, it appears to be Bede's intention in this story to obscure the possibility that Æthelberht had been heretically or unsuccessfully baptized before the arrival of a Roman emissary from Pope Gregory. Yet because Bede also indicates that Æthelberht perceived Augustine as a demon, that is, as a figure from his

[57] J. Stevenson, 'Christianity in Sixth- and Seventh-Century Southumbria', in *The Age of Sutton Hoo*, ed. Carver, pp. 175–83, esp. 176–9.
[58] Brooks, 'Creation and Early Structure of the Kingdom of Kent', p. 66.
[59] Henig, *Religion in Roman Britain*, pp. 221–2.   [60] *HE* I.25 (p. 74).

native religion, Bede seems to have known not only the Roman perspective on the Christianization of England in the early seventh century, by which conversion must follow a clash of ideologies; but also something of the native point of view, in which the Anglo-Saxons rationalized Christianity by identifying it with cults of their own.

Heathen reaction in Kent and Essex

When Æthelberht died in 616 × 618, his son Eadbald is said to have lapsed into heathen ways, at the same time as the sons and successors of the converted King Sæberht of the East Saxons, after a misunderstanding over the eucharist, drove their bishop Mellitus out of London into Kent. According to Bede, the miraculous chastisement of Archbishop Laurentius convinced Eadbald to cast off his idols and unlawful wife and be baptized (*HE* II.6). Kirby, however, argues that Eadbald was still heathen when he sent his sister Æthelburh to Edwin in Northumbria in *c.* 619, and that he returned to Christianity only when Edwin was moving that way in *c.* 625.[61] Eadbald, like his father, may have wished to remain free of the Merovingians. Now he married another Frankish princess to strengthen his position with them. His son Eorcenberht (640–64), succeeding to part of Kent, ordered the destruction of Kentish idols, which, by implication, must have remained popular even while Augustine converted hundreds of people in Kent to Christianity. That these idols were toppled as many as two generations after 597 shows the influence that the polytheist farmers of Kent and Essex could still exert on their rulers.

Despite the claim in the St Mildthryth legend that Eadbald left his kingdom entirely to his son Eorcenberht, his older son Eormenred probably ruled the eastern part of Kent, Eorcenberht the west.[62] In this legend Eorcenberht's son Ecgberht apparently colludes in the martyrdom of his cousins, Eormenred's sons Æthelred and Æthelberht, during the archbishopric of Deusdedit, then offers part of Thanet in compensation to their sister.[63] Since Ecgberht negotiated with the pope over Deusdedit's successor, Wigheard, in 664, these murders must have occurred during the lifetime of his father Eorcenberht, who was the 'first among English

---

[61] Kirby, *Earliest English Kings*, p. 41.
[62] See Rollason, *Mildrith Legend*, p. 38: 'Kent may have been divided into two sub-kingdoms for at least part of its history.'
[63] *Leechdoms*, ed. Cockayne III, 422–8.

Paulinus and the stultus *error*

kings to order idols to be abandoned and destroyed in all his kingdom' when he succeeded Eadbald in *c.* 640.[64] Therefore it is possible that whenever Eormenred died, his nephew Ecgberht inherited his eastern part of Kent because his sons Æthelred and Æthelberht were too young to rule. Thereupon 'Thunor' martyred the boys, or rather Ecgberht may have had them killed in a reciprocal arrangement with the heathens from the farms around Canterbury: I suggest that these peasants would choose Ecgberht as the next king of eastern Kent, on condition that Ecgberht allowed them to renew their sacrifices to idols of *þunor* on the death of his uncle Eormenred. Although this resurgence would have collapsed under pressure from Wulfhere of Mercia and Deusdedit of Canterbury, the names Þ*unor* and *þunoreshlæw*, as we have seen in ch. 9, hint at the reactionary power of OE *þunor*, an early thunder *numen*, among the Jutes and Saxons of England.

King Rædwald of the eastern Angles

Visiting Æthelberht at the beginning of the seventh century was a man from a different culture: Rædwald, a rising *brytenwalda* of the eastern Angles. Augustine or an assistant baptized him:

sed frustra; nam rediens domum ab uxore sua et quibusdam peruersis doctoribus seductus est, atque a sinceritate fidei deprauatus habuit *posteriora peiora prioribus*, ita ut Samaritanorum et Christo seruire uideretur et diis, quibus antea seruiebat, atque in eodem fano et altare haberet ad sacrificium Christi et arulam ad uictimas daemonium.[65]

Rædwald's son Eorpwald made the eastern Angles Christian in *c.* 628, but there was a relapse when he was killed soon after by Ricberht, whose stepson Sigeberht, though converted in Gaul, ceded most of his kingdom to his pagan brother Ecgric.[66]

---

[64] *HE* III.8 (p. 236): 'primus regum Anglorum in toto regno suo idola relinqui ac destrui . . . praecepit'.

[65] *HE* II.15 (p. 190): 'but in vain; for when he came back home he was led astray by his wife and certain perverted teachers, and thus depraved from the earnestness of his faith, he was *in a plight worse than before*; for as in the custom of the ancient Samaritans, he was seen to serve both Christ and the gods whom he had once served, and in the same temple had both an altar for the holy sacrifice of Christ and a little altar for the sacrifice of victims to demons'.

[66] Kirby, *Earliest English Kings*, pp. 62 and 80–1.

Heathen gods

Rædwald's lapse is different from the others discussed so far. Firstly, there is neither reaction nor apostasy in this tale. Given Æthelberht's need as the reigning *brytenwalda* to impose political as well as spiritual authority on the eastern Angles, a reaction might be expected, but Rædwald's wife and friends did not expel the Christian cult. Secondly, Bede shows the errant king as *seductus* and *prauatus*, not the subject but the object of heathen activity. Thirdly, with the word *arula*, as Wallace-Hadrill says, 'Rædwald meant the pagan altar to be less prominent than his Christian altar.'[67] In these ways it is likely that Rædwald remained a pantheist but none the less considered himself to be a practising Christian for the rest of his life.

Bede does not forgive Rædwald, comparing him with the Samaritans in a reference to the worship of rightful and unrightful gods. Yet Bede's allusion to Luke XI.26 with the words *peiora prioribus* shows that Luke XI.14–26 was his source. Here Jesus drives out a demon from a man struck dumb, for which members of the crowd then accuse him of using Beelzebub's powers. Jesus refutes them with a parable, reminds them that a demon can always return and tells them another parable of the demon who returned with seven others worse than he to the man in whose mind he lived before: 'Et fiunt *nouissima* hominis illius *peiora prioribus*' ('And *the newest state* of this man becomes *worse than it was before*', Luke XI.26). In *HE* II.15 this man appears to be the model for Rædwald. In this case, given the late parallel of *ælfsiden* and demonic possession in *Lacnunga* (cf. ch. 3), the closest Germanic analogue for Rædwald's *doctores peruersi* appears to be the *seiðmenn* of the Vanir, i.e. male witches.

If gods of the Vanir type were worshipped by Rædwald alongside Jesus Christ, the evidence is lacking for their names: David N. Wilson points out that in East Anglia no placenames survive with the names of specific gods, as they do in Saxon and Jutish areas.[68] The Sutton Hoo ship of *c.* 625 may have been buried in Suffolk in memory of Rædwald by Eorpwald, his Christian son.[69] Although it contained baptismal spoons and a gold buckle that seem to be Christian, the whetstone sceptre with a stag emblem might refer to royal and popular aspects of paganism, in Ingui and a thunder *numen* respectively: one for his ancestors and the

---

[67] *Ibid.*, p. 37; Wallace-Hadrill, *Commentary*, p. 76.
[68] Wilson, *Anglo-Saxon Paganism*, pp. 5–21, esp. 16.
[69] This man was possibly not Rædwald, but rather an unknown status-seeking chieftain: see M. O. H. Carver, 'Sutton Hoo in Context', *Settimane* 32 (1986), 77–123.

other for his laws.[70] Wallace-Hadrill says of this find that 'it would perhaps be better to regard it as specifically neither Christian nor pagan'.[71] This is probably also how paganism of the Vanir type appeared to missionaries from the Jutish and Saxon kingdoms in the south.

King Edwin of Deira

In 601 the Italian Paulinus arrived in Kent as part of a second wave of missionaries from Rome; Bede next mentions him when Eadbald (some eighteen years later) gives his sister Æthelburh in marriage to Edwin of Northumbria (*HE* II.9). Working out a chronology from the timing of Pope Boniface's letters to Edwin and Æthelburh in *HE* II.10–11, Kirby estimates that Paulinus accompanied Æthelburh as her private chaplain to Northumbria in 619.[72] Bede says that Paulinus, on the way, kept his companions from lapsing while he attempted to convert local heathens: 'Sed, sicut apostolus ait, quamuis multo tempore illo laborante in uerbo, "*deus saeculi huius* excaecauit mentes infidelium, ne eis fulgeret inluminatio euangeli gloriae Christi".'[73] Bede here quotes II Cor. IV.4 in order to defend the failure so far of Paulinus to convert the people of Northumbria. Since Bede has already stated that Augustine and his monks 'began to imitate the life of the primitive apostolic church' when they arrived in Canterbury, it is clear that he intended to present the early missionaries as apostles of England; and in *HE* II.9 in particular, to present Paulinus as a hypostasis of St Paul.[74]

In this passage, Bede also appears to use the quotation from II Cor. IV.4 as a means of referring to the devil by a specifically Northumbrian name. Although *saeculum* in this quotation is a widespread word in the

---

[70] Webster and Backhouse, *The Making of England*, p. 33 (no. 17); on Þórr and whetstones, see Simpson, 'The King's Whetstone', pp. 96–101; without discussion of Þórr and Hrungnir's whetstone, M. J. Enright suggests that this sceptre was made with mostly Celtic influences in southern Scotland, whence its stone derives: 'The Sutton Hoo Whetstone Sceptre: a Study in Iconography and Cultural Milieu', *ASE* 11 (1983), 119–34, esp. 120 and 129, and 134–5.

[71] Wallace-Hadrill, *Commentary*, p. 76.

[72] Kirby, 'Bede and Northumbrian Chronology', pp. 522–3.

[73] *HE* II.9 (p. 162): 'But just as the Apostle says, although he toiled for a long time spreading the Word, *The god of this age* blinded the minds of them that believed not, lest the light of the gospel of Christ's glory should shine unto them."'

[74] *HE* I.26 (p. 76): 'coeperunt apostolicam primitiuae ecclesiae uitam imitari'.

gospels, Paul's formulation *deus saeculi huius* occurs nowhere in the Bible but here.[75] Bede's commentary on II Corinthians has not yet been edited.[76] However, Bede quotes II Cor. IV.4 in his commentary on the prodigal son in Luke XV.11–32, where the son, having spent his inheritance on whores and dissipation, ends up herding the swine of 'a certain citizen of that region' (*uni ciuium regionis illius*), a former associate (Luke XV.15); Bede calls also this figure *deus huius saeculi*:

Unus autem ciuium regionis illius cui egens adhaesit: ille est utique qui concupiscentiis terrenis merito suae peruersitatis praepositus *princeps huius mundi* a domino uocatur et de quo apostolus, '*Deus*', inquit, '*huius saeculi* excaecauit mentes infidelium.[77]

Bede furthermore interprets the complaint of the righteous son about his prodigal brother, that he squandered his wealth with prostitutes (Luke XV.30), as a metaphor for the worship of heathen gods: '"Whores" are the superstitions of pagans, and to squander one's wealth with whores is to neglect the one marriage with the word of God and to fornicate in foulest lust with a crowd of demons.'[78] Besides the sexual licence in this tale, two other details which come fortuitously close to the Norse cult of Ingvi-freyr are the pigs owned by the son's former friend, which recall the golden boar on which Freyr rides in *Húsdrápa* 7;[79] and the wealthy man's 'perversity' (*peruersitas*), which recalls the reputation of OIce *seiðr*.

Since the phrase *princeps huius mundi* refers to the devil in John XIV.30, there is no doubt that Bede refers to the devil with *deus huius saeculi* both

---

[75] *Saeculum* is found in Ps. XC.2, Eccl. III.11, Is. LXIV.4, John I.29, III.16, III.17, VI.33, X.36, XI.27, Acts III.21, XV.18, 17:24, Rom. I.8, III.6, III.19, XII.2, I Cor. I.20, I.21, I.27, I.28, II.7, II.12, III.19, IV.9, VIII.4, II Cor. I.12, IV.4, V.19, Gal. I.4, VI.14, Ephes. II.12, III.9, Phil. II.15, Coloss. I.16, I Tim. III.16, VI.17, Titus I.2, Heb. I.6, VI.5, XI.7, James I.27, II.5, IV.4, I John II.17, III.1, III.17, IV.1, IV.3, IV.4, IV.9, V.4, V.5, V.19, Rev. XVI.14.

[76] Brown, *Bede the Venerable*, p. 58.

[77] *Bedae Venerabilis Opera Exegetica*, ed. D. Hurst, CCSL 120 (Turnhout, 1960), 288 (*In Lucae evangelium expositio*): '"A certain citizen of that region" to whom "he cleaved when in need": this is especially he who, having been made foremost in earthly delights through the merit of his own perversity, is called by the Lord *prince of this world*; he of whom the Apostle said "*the god of this age* blinded the minds of them that believed not".'

[78] *Ibid.*, p. 294: '"Meretrices" sunt gentilium superstitiones cum quibus relicto uno conubio uerba Dei cum turba daemonorum cupiditate turpissima fornicari.'

[79] *Skj* B I, 129, 7.

Paulinus and the stultus error

in his commentary on Luke XV and in his story of Paulinus's initial failure to convert the Northumbrians in *HE* II.9. It is not clear, in this case, why Bede did not refer to the devil in Northumbria with a commoner term such as *diabolus* or *antiquus hostis*. Thus the use of *deus huius saeculi* in *HE* II.9 not only connects Paulinus with his apostolic namesake, but may also refer to the devil, Paulinus's adversary, as Ingui, a Northumbrian god, in that *deus huius saeculi* ('god of this age') appears to be a seventh-century analogue of Ingvi-freyr's title *veraldar goð* ('god of the world').[80]

Thus Ingui and his family, the *numina* of the natural world, appear to have frustrated Paulinus's first attempt to convert Northumbria. The Angles, partly British themselves, but in most ways isolated from the enriching influences of Gaul and further south, cannot have differed greatly from the Germanic Anglii from whom they were descended.[81] At this stage, therefore, it seems that Edwin worshipped Ingui as this god's descendant and chosen representative.

A pattern of sacral kingship in Edwin's reign is implicit in two texts. First, as we have seen in the *Vita S. Gregorii*, the anonymous author of Whitby says that Paulinus and Edwin chided Edwin's royal kinsmen before their catechizing for still being 'bound not only to paganism but also to unlawful unions'.[82] This rebuke, as we have seen in the story of the crow in ch. 7, may refer to concubinage rather than marriage within prohibited degrees of kinship; as Edwin was involved in giving this rebuke, it is possible that he, too, had had concubines in Deira before his baptism. A royal prerogative of this kind would resemble the *droit du seigneur* of Hákon Jarl with the daughters, sisters and wives of his subjects in late tenth-century Norway. Second, in *HE* II.9, Bede says that Paulinus among the Angles wanted 'to summon to the knowledge of the truth the nation to which he drew near, that he might, according to the Apostle's saying, "present her as a chaste virgin to the one true husband Christ"'.[83] In II Cor. XI.2–3, from which Bede takes this quotation, Paul imagines his congregation as a woman to be protected from the wiles of the serpent

---

[80] *Heimskringla I*, ed. Bjarni, p. 25 (*Ynglinga saga*, ch. 10); *Flat* I, 403 (ch. 323).

[81] See Kirby, *Earliest English Kings*, p. 61; Dumville, 'The Origins of Northumbria', p. 219.

[82] *Vita S. Gregorii*, ed. Colgrave, p. 97 (ch. 15): 'gentilitati non solum, sed etiam et non licitis stricti coniugiis'.

[83] *HE*, p. 162: 'ut gentem quam adibat, ad agnitionem ueritatis aduocans iuxta uocem apostoli "uni uero sponso uirginem castam exhiberet Christo"'.

that seduced Eve. Yet Bede's use of this quotation may also reveal that Paulinus failed to marry the Anglian nation as a chaste virgin to Christ, because, through Æthelburh or her predecessor Cwenburh, and through any number of other women representative of the Anglian regions, the northern Angles believed themselves to be married to Edwin.

A note in the *Historia Brittonum* (c. 829–30) claims that Edwin was converted by a certain Rhun ab Urbgen, the son of a local Welsh chieftain from Rheged.[84] Bede may or may not know this claim (which may be true), but there is no reason to discount its implication that for six years until c. 625, Paulinus faced competition for Edwin's baptism with at least one missionary from outside the jurisdiction of Canterbury. Since Rædwald helped him kill Æthelfrith in the battle of the river Idle in 616, Edwin had become the Anglian *brytenwalda* in Deira and Bernicia, expanded his borders and was no longer the exile who had sheltered in Rædwald's court nine years before.[85] To this extent, King Eadbald of Kent had little influence over his brother-in-law Edwin for which Paulinus could usefully apply through Canterbury. It was probably to strengthen this weak position that Archbishop Justus consecrated Paulinus as bishop of York on 21 July 625 (*HE* II.9).

On Easter Day in 626, Edwin survived an attempt on his life by an assassin sent from King Cwichelm of Wessex. Here and later in the story of Edwin's conversion, Bede's chief source appears to be an epic lay. This can be deduced from the character of the story and its various new names, none of which is relevant to Bede's Christian narrative. In gratitude Edwin promised to take the Christian faith, in which, Bede says, he had Paulinus baptize his newest daughter. However, having killed Cwichelm in battle, Edwin put his own baptism off again.

Bede says that Edwin was still wondering which faith to follow when Paulinus drew near and placed his hand on Edwin's head. Edwin fell almost to his knees, for he remembered the promise that he had made to a spirit in a vision eleven years earlier in Rædwald's court. About Paulinus knowing the story about the spirit, Bede seems vague – 'at length, as seems likely to be true, he learned in the soul what type of oracle had once been shown the king by the heavenly powers' – although, as

---

[84] *Historia Brittonum*, ed. Lot, pp. 203–4 (ch. 63); Kirby attributes this claim to a confusion between the mass baptism in Yeavering with Edwin's in York, in *Earliest English Kings*, pp. 78–9.

[85] Kirby, *ibid.*, pp. 83–8.

Wallace-Hadrill has shown, it is likely that Paulinus heard this story from Edwin himself.[86]

Whilst Bede relates Edwin's vision, he adapts a quotation from Vergil's *Aen*. IV.2 in which Dido burns inwardly with love for Aeneas.[87] Since Dido's story does not fit Edwin's context, it is possible that Bede quoted these words for another purpose: to render some words from a profane poem in his vernacular. At the end of the *Historia*, Bede says that he gleaned his information 'from the literature of the ancients or the tradition of my fathers or even from my own knowledge';[88] Bede would thus have been in a position to approximate, through Vergil's lines, an Anglian poem that he had once heard from his elders. Back in 616, Edwin in exile faced the prospect of Rædwald betraying him to Æthelfrith: 'Cumque diu tacitus mentis angoribus et "caeco carperetur igni", uidit subito intempesta nocte silentio adpropinquantem sibi hominem uultus habitusque incogniti; quem uidens, ut ignotum et inopinatum non parum expauit.'[89] Bede does not say who the dream visitant was (he is equally restrained in his story of Cædmon in *HE* IV.24). The anonymous author of Whitby, in the earlier account of this vision, identifies the spirit 'crowned with the cross of Christ' with Paulinus, from whom the Whitby version of this story may have come: 'they say that Paulinus, the aforesaid bishop, appeared on this first occasion'.[90] Alcuin, in his poem *De patribus regibus et sanctis Euboricensis ecclesiae*, probably follows Bede in leaving us to infer Paulinus in the vision: 'There stood a man unknown in his clothes and unfamiliar in his appearance before the young man's eyes.'[91]

---

[86] *HE* II.12 (p. 178): 'ut uerisimile uidetur, didicit in spiritu, quod uel quale esset oraculum regi quondam caelitis ostensum'. See Wallace-Hadrill, *Commentary*, p. 71.

[87] *Vergili Opera*, ed. Mynors, p. 176 (lines 1–2): 'At regina gravi iamdudum saucia cura / vulnus alit venis et *caeco carpitur igni*'.

[88] *HE* V.24 (p. 566): 'uel ex litteris antiquorum uel ex traditione maiorum uel ex mea ipse cognitione'.

[89] *Ibid*. II.12 (p. 178): 'He remained long in silent anguish of mind and "was consumed with blind fire", when suddenly, at dead of night, he saw a man silently approaching with a face and attire unknown to him; when he saw the unknown and unexpected man, he was not a little afraid.'

[90] *Vita S. Gregorii*, ed. Colgrave, pp. 98–100 (ch. 16): 'cum cruce Christi coronatus'; 'dicunt illi Paulinum prefatum episcopum primo apparuisse'.

[91] *Bishops, Kings and Saints of York*, ed. Godman, p. 12 (lines 97–8): 'vir stetit ignotus habitu vultuque repente / ante oculos iuvenis'.

Heathen gods

One reason for Bede's reluctance to name the spirit may be that he knew another version of this story which descended from Edwin, in which it was clear that Edwin had identified this spirit with *Uoden*. The anonymous author of Whitby hints that there were other, less acceptable, versions of this story.[92] In his version of the tale of Edwin's vision, Bede's use of Vergil's words without a similar context seems to indicate that he relied in this case on a profane vernacular source. It seems then likely that Edwin 'was consumed with blind fire' (*caeco carperetur igni*) because he saw Uoden approach: *Helblindi* ('Hell-?blinder', *Grím* 46), *Bileygr* ('injured-eyed', *Grím* 47), *Báleygr* ('furnace-eyed', *Grím* 47 and *Hákonardrápa* 6) and *Gestumblindi* ('the ?blind guest', *Heiðreks saga*) are all names referring to Óðinn, the Norse counterpart of Uoden or Woden, with his one burning eye.[93] Bede says that the stranger asked three times what reward Edwin would give to someone who, first, freed him from his troubles; second, assured him that his enemies would be destroyed and he would surpass in power 'not only all your forebears but also all those who were kings of the Angles before you' (*non solum omnes tuos progenitores sed et omnes, qui ante te reges in gente Anglorum fuerant*); 'third' (*tertio*), gave him counsel as to his salvation and way of life 'better and more useful than any of your parents and kinsmen ever heard' (*melius atque utilius quam aliquis de tuis parentibus aut cognatis umquam audiuit*). With these words, 'as they say' (*ut ferunt*), the spirit vanished and Rædwald was persuaded by his queen not to turn Edwin over to Æthelfrith's men.

This scene resembles three passages from Scandinavian literature. First, before a battle in the probably eleventh-century *Reginsmál*, Sigurðr's men tell him that there is a man on a headland wishing to talk to him. When the man calls himself Hnicarr (a name used by Óðinn in *Grím* 47), Sigurðr asks him, since he knows 'omens of gods and men' (*goða heill oc guma*), which are the best 'omens in the darting of swords [battle]' (*heill at sverða svipon*, *Reginsmál* 19). Óðinn answers in three stages, saying that many omens are good: first, that the company of the raven is worthy for a warrior; 'second' (*annat*), if he sees two warriors standing on the road; 'this is the third' (*þat er iþ þriðia*), if he hears a wolf howling under ash boughs. Óðinn's advice to Sigurðr is how to win the next battle.

[92] *Vita S. Gregorii*, ed. Colgrave, pp. 99 (ch. 16): 'etiam sepe fama cuiusque rei, per longa tempora terrarumque spatia, post congesta, diverso modo in aures diversorum perveniet'.

[93] *Heiðreks saga*, ed. Turville-Petre and Tolkien, pp. 36–51.

Paulinus and the stultus error

Second, in *Gesta Danorum*, King Haraldus receives a visitor the day before his battle with King Ingo of Sweden:

while Haraldus was desirous of finding out the outcome of this by oracles, an old man appeared of distinguished size but deprived of one eye, who, wrapped in a shaggy cloak and avowing himself to be Othinus and wise in the practice of war, offered Haraldus the most practical advice on the drawing up of his army in formation.[94]

Third, in *Óláfs saga Tryggvasonar*, Snorri says that while Óláfr was staying in Qgvaldsnes on his way to convert more heathens in Norway:

one evening a very loquacious old man came in with a long hood. He was one-eyed. This man could talk of all kinds of countries. He fell into a conversation with the king, who thought it was great fun talking to him and asked him many things, while the guest knew the answer to all kinds of questions, and so the king sat long into the evening.[95]

Eventually Óláfr's bishop reminds him that it is time to sleep, the guest cannot be found and Óláfr declares that 'this cannot have been a man, and must have been Óðinn'.[96]

All three passages are similar to Bede's. Yet if it is thought that, because Bede's story is three centuries earlier, the Scandinavian authors derived their visitation motif from *HE*, it should be remembered that Bede's clue about the spirit's *caecus ignis* is not so obvious that a reader of Bede such as Saxo or Snorri could have inferred or borrowed from this phrase the sudden appearance of Óðinn, the one-eyed spirit. Conversely, it is more likely that all four passages have an old vernacular motif in common in which Woden or Óðinn appears to mortal kings to offer them military advice. Thus Edwin, in his own mind, appears to have talked to Uoden eleven years before.

[94] *GD*, p. 207: 'Cuius eventum Haraldo oraculis explorare cupienti senex praecipuae magnitudinis, sed orbus oculo extitit, qui hispido etiam amiculo circumactus, Othynam se dici bellorumque usu callere testatus, utilissimum ei centuriandi in acie exercitus documentum porrexit.'

[95] *Heimskringla I*, ed. Bjarni, p. 313 (*Óláfs saga Tryggvasonar*, ch. 64): 'þar kom eitt kveld maðr gamall ok orðspakr mjǫk, hafði hǫtt síðan. Hann var einsýnn. Kunni sá maðr segja af ǫllum lǫndum. Hann kom sér í tal við konung. Þótti konungi gaman mikit at rœðum hans, ok spurði hann margra hluta, en gestrinn fekk órlausn til allra spurninga, ok sat konungr lengi um kveldit.'

[96] *Ibid.*: 'þetta myndi engi maðr verit hafa ok þar myndi verit hafa Óðinn'. The figure Gestr is similar, in *Flat* I, 349–59 (*Nornagests þáttr*).

Heathen gods

UODEN = COIFI = PAULINUS

Now Paulinus raised Edwin up and warned him to keep his promise. Yet first, as if prevaricating further, Edwin gathered his council; presumably near Goodmanham, scene of the next action.[97] First, Bishop Paulinus gave the Anglian nobles some instruction, then Coifi, their local *pontifex*, spoke up and announced that serving his gods had brought even him no reward. Now, after due reflection, he was ready to take the faith that offered more. After the unnamed Anglian counsellor's sparrow *exemplum*, Edwin publicly accepted the gospel, renounced his idols and confessed his faith in Christ. He asked Coifi, whom Bede describes as 'first among high-priests' (*primus pontificum*), which of those present should be the first to destroy the idols; Coifi put himself forward and rode out against his own shrine.

Bede's quotation from Vergil (*Aen.* II.501–2) in the next part of this story leads into a narrative with an epic structure apparent in three stages: first, in the varied repetition of Coifi's taking arms and mounting the king's stallion to destroy the idols; second, in a digression on the fact that a pagan priest was allowed to do neither of these things; and third, in greater detail, Coifi's taking a sword and spear and setting off towards the idols. This sandwich structure is a smaller version of Wiglaf preparing to help Beowulf when he sees him burning in the dragon's fire (*Beo* 2602–5); then a digression on Wiglaf's debt to Beowulf and the speech in which he recalls it (*Beo* 2606–60); then Wiglaf moving forward to help his lord (*Beo* 2661–2). Thus, in addition to Paulinus's version of events, with which Bede was provided by either a source in Whitby or Nothhelm from Canterbury nearly a century after Edwin's death in Hatfield Chase in 632, Bede's story of Coifi may be based on a vernacular poetic source.

Coifi asked Edwin to give him weapons 'and a stallion, after mounting which he then set out to destroy the idols. For it was not permitted for a priest of the sacred mysteries either to bear arms or to ride except on a mare'.[98] Tacitus says that the people in Nerthus's festival, including the

---

[97] Two possibilities are Londesborough and Market Weighton (the Roman *Delgovitia*), each nearly two miles from Goodmanham and joined to each other by a Roman road; see Ordnance Survey Market Weighton: Sheet SE 84/94, Pathfinder 675 (scale 1:25,000), 84889145 and 84889142.

[98] *HE* II.13 (p. 182): 'et equum emissarium, quem ascendens ad idola destruenda ueniret. Non enim licuerat pontificem sacrorum uel arma ferre uel praeter in equa equitare'.

continental Anglii, 'do not go to war, do not take up arms'.[99] The motif of the forbidden horse, which Bede later describes as 'the king's stallion' (*emissarium regis*), can be found in two Icelandic passages from the late fourteenth century.[100] First, in *Hrafnkels saga*, Hrafnkell gives his god Freyr a half-share in his stallion Freyfaxi, having such love for this stallion 'that he took a vow to be the death of any man who rode Freyfaxi without Hrafnkell's permission'.[101] Second, in the *Flateyjarbók* legend of Óláfr Tryggvason's attempt to convert the heathens of the Trondheim region in c. 995–8, Óláfr's ship draws near to Freyr's temple by the river:

> and when he came to shore, his men saw some studmares by the road which they said Freyr owned. The king mounted on the back of the stallion and ordered them to take the mares, and now they rode up to the shrine. The king dismounted and walked into the temple and smashed the gods down from their altars. Then he took Freyr under his arm and carried him out to the stallion, and then locked the shrine.[102]

In both Icelandic passages the stallion and mares belong jointly to Freyr and the local king or chieftain. This later material, when combined with the evidence of horse-burials in Anglian England, Hrothgar's possession of stallions and Edwin's *emissarium regis*, may show that it was Edwin's privilege across Deira to own the herds of Ingui, probably the god from whom Edwin claimed his descent.[103] This ideology appears to be implicit in the *double entendre* 'superstitio *uanitatis*' ('superstition of the *uuani'), which, as we have seen in ch. 7, is Bede's term for the set of beliefs which Coifi cast aside when he took arms and mounted the stallion.[104]

Goodmanham, probably half a day's ride east of York, lies in the East Riding not far from the source of the river Foulness, which flows into the Humber; the mound on which All Hallows Church now stands may be

---

[99] *Germania*, p. 317 (ch. 40): 'non bella ineunt, non arma sumunt'.
[100] *HE* II.13 (p. 182); see A. Liestøl, 'Freyfaxi', *MoM* (1945), 59–66.
[101] *Hrafnkels saga*, ed. Jón, p. 100 (ch. 3): 'at hann strengði þess heit, at hann skyldi þeim manni at bana verða, sem honum riði án hans vilja'.
[102] *Flat* I, 401 (*Óláfs saga Tryggvasonar*, ch. 322): 'En er hann kom a land þa sa hans menn stodhross nokkur vid ueginn er þeir sogdu at Freyr etti. konungr stæig a bak hestinum ok let taka rossin ok ridu þeir nu fram til hofsins. konungr stæig af hestinum ok gek inn j hofit ok hio nidr godin af stollunum. sidan tok hann Frey undir hond ser ok bar hann vt til hestz en byrgde sidan hofit.'
[103] Wilson, *Anglo-Saxon Paganism*, pp. 101–2.
[104] *HE* II.13 (p. 182).

the enclosed site of Coifi's shrine.[105] The fact that *Godmunddingaham* and not York was the site of the Anglian conversion might be thought odd. Edwin's presence in the area of Londesborough, Market Weighton and Goodmanham could be explained as a royal circuit or 'itineration' by which Edwin's nobles fed and entertained him.[106] The fact that Deiran Angles congregated in this area might, in addition, be related to the likelihood that the East Riding, as the 'nucleus of the kingdom of Deira', was the first region to be settled by their ancestors.[107] Although the present church in Goodmanham is Norman in its lower stages, there is an Anglo-Saxon font on the floor in its west end; according to information in the church, 'Goodmanham lies on a favourable position on a south facing slope, on the spur of the chalk wolds between two streams'.[108] Bede says that the *pontifex* Coifi did not hesitate to profane the enclosure at Goodmanham as soon as he reached it and 'threw into it the spear which he was holding' (*iniecta in eo lancea quam tenebat*, HE II.13). In the later West Saxon translation of Bede's *Historia*, this line is *þa sceat he mid þy spere*, naturally closer than the Latin to a line which describes the Æsir–Vanir cult-war in *Vǫluspá*:

> Fleygði Óðinn   oc í fólc um scaut,
> þat var enn fólcvíg   fyrst í heimi;   (Vsp 24/1–4)[109]

When Coifi rode up to the shrine, the common people, 'catching sight of this, guessed that he was mad' (*aspiciens uulgus aestimabat eum insanire*). In the later West Saxon translation of these words: *ðæt folc* ... *þa wendon heo þæt he teola ne wiste, ac þæt he wedde* ('then they thought that he was not in his right mind, and that he was mad'). There are three correspondences

---

[105] The identity of Goodmanham with *Godmunddingaham* is doubted by Wallace-Hadrill (*Commentary*, p. 73), perhaps because of the remove of this town from York; but it is defended by Wilson (*Anglo-Saxon Paganism*, p. 30).

[106] On 'itineration' as a royal institution, see T. Charles-Edwards, 'Early Medieval Kingships in the British Isles', in *The Origins of Anglo-Saxon Kingdoms*, ed. Bassett, pp. 28–39, esp. 28–33.

[107] M. L. Faull, 'British Survival in Anglo-Saxon Northumbria', in *Studies in Celtic Survival*, ed. L. Laing, BAR 37 (Oxford, 1977), 1–55, esp. 2.

[108] Ordnance Survey Market Weighton: Sheet SE 84/94, Pathfinder 675, 84859443; *East Ings Drain* looks appropriate at 84859141, but *ing* is common as a topographical name and means 'meadow' (from Old Norse *engi*).

[109] '*Óðinn* cast and *shot* into the *people*, again it was the first war of the peoples in the world.'

between this passage and the *Vǫluspá* stanza quoted above: first, Bede's *uulgus* (*ðæt folc*), which in this scene corresponds to *fólc* in *Vsp* 24; second, his word *iniecta* (*sceat*), which corresponds to *um scaut* also in this stanza; and third, the word *insanire* (*wedde*), which not only refers to the common people's perception of Coifi as 'mad', but also resembles the meaning of Óðinn, cognate with OE *Woden* ('inspired', 'maddened'). In the last case, in particular, Bede may be obscuring a legend in which the crowd 'guessed that Coifi was *Uoden*'.

As regards the status of Coifi as a *pontifex*, it is worth noting that no priesthood is mentioned in the Old Norse–Icelandic sources relating to Scandinavian paganism.[110] Other than Coifi *primus pontificum*, the only pagan Anglo-Saxon 'priest' is the Sussex 'prince of the priests of idolatry' (*princeps sacerdotum idolatriae*) or 'wizard' (*magus*) who tries to cast a spell on Wilfrid and his *comitatus* on the beach in the *Vita S. Wilfridi*.[111] This man is better explained as a local *seiðmaðr* or male witch. In Iceland priestly functions were embodied in the chieftain's role of *goði*; in the Scandinavian monarchies, apparently in the role of *konungr* or *jarl*. When he designated Coifi as a *pontifex*, in this way, it is likely that Bede imposed a priestly role from the Old Testament on a priestless Anglian society.

With *Coifi*, furthermore, Bede uses a name that is not found elsewhere. This word appears to be a noun, not a name, deriving with *i*-mutation from Lat *cofium* or *cofia*.[112] The form of Bede's *Coifi*, which Alcuin spells *Coefi* and the West Saxon translator *Cefi*, is evidence that this name came from an early vernacular rather than direct Latin source.[113] The meaning of Lat *cofium* or *cofia* is 'hood'. In his *Vita S. Radegundae* (580 × 590), Venantius Fortunatus says that when Queen Radegund became a deaconess, she gave her 'camisas, manicas, *cofias*, fibulas' ('shirts, sleeves, *hoods*, brooches') and all her gold to the altar of

---

[110] *HAR* II.ii, 189–90 (§126).

[111] *Vita S. Wilfridi*, ed. Levison, 207 (ch. 13).

[112] The sound changes of Bede's *Coifi* may be deduced along the lines of OE *ele* (Lat *olium*), as discussed by A. Wollmann in 'Early Christian Loan-Words in Old English', in *Pagans and Christians*, ed. Hofstra, Houwen and MacDonald, pp. 175–210, esp. 192–206 and 210 (§3); see also A. Campbell, *Old English Grammar* (Oxford, 1959), pp. 78 (§198) and 189 (§473, n. 3).

[113] *Bishops, Kings and Saints of York*, ed. Godman, p. 18 (lines 167–8): 'Ecce sacerdotum Coefi tunc temporis auctor / errorumque caput fuerat'; *Old English Ecclesiastical History*, ed. Miller, p. 134.

Heathen gods

St Iumer.[114] In the *De officiis divinis*, attributed to Alcuin, it is stated that only Greek bishops 'wear Greek caps, that is *cuphiae*, on their heads when they assist at the altar'.[115] From the ninth century onwards *cuphiae* were worn by western bishops as well, and the Greek spelling of *cuphia* in *De officiis divinis* shows the revival or redefinition of a Greek word previously borrowed into sixth-century France as *cofia*.[116] A *cuffie*, 'perhaps a loose-fitting hood or scarf', is left by Wynflæd to Æthelflæd among other clothes in a will from the mid tenth century.[117] In contrast with *cuphia* and *cuffie*, its likely derivative, *coifi* seems to be an early reflex of Frankish *cofia* accepted into the Anglian vernacular before the eighth century. How a Merovingian 'hood' could become a proper noun only in Bede's story of Edwin's conversion may be explained if this name is taken to be the second specific reference to Uoden in this passage: *Síðhǫttr* ('long-hood') is Óðinn's name in *Grím* 48 and an item of clothing by which he makes himself known to kings in the northern world. Coifi's name, in this case, appears to have been a by-name of Uoden.

Bede thus may have derived his story of the destruction of the shrine in Goodmanham from a now-lost Anglian poem analogous to the story of the Æsir–Vanir cult-war in *Vǫluspá*. Repudiating his belief in *uanitas*, Coifi hurled his spear into the heathen gods, just as Óðinn does in *Vǫluspá* when he renews the war against the Vanir; the name *Coifi* may be interpreted as a name for the Northumbrian version of Óðinn; and there was apparently a *uulgus* gathered about the enclosure in Goodmanham, just as there is a hostile Vanir *fólc* in *Vǫluspá*. As we have seen in earlier

---

[114] *Venanti Honori Clementiani Fortunati Presbyteri Italici Opera Pedestria*, ed. B. Krusch, MGH, Auct. Antiq. 4.2 (Berlin, 1885), 41–2 (ch. 13).

[115] *B. Flacci Albini seu Alcuini Opera Omnia*, PL 101 (Paris, 1863), 1239 (*De officiis divinis*, ch. 38): 'pileos, id est, *cuphias* gestant in capite, dum assistant altaribus'.

[116] *Mittellateinisches Wörterbuch bis zum angehenden 13. Jahrhundert*, Bayerische Akademie der Wissenschaften (Munich, 1973), s.v. 'cofia' (p. 786): '2.a. spec. de signo investiturae, dignitatis'; '*cupheo* nostro a capite dempto' (charter *anno* 1223); 'pontificum ac abbatum ordinibus congrua, inter quae *cophiam*'; 'annulum illi (episcopo) et *cophium* . . . contulerat'.

[117] *Anglo-Saxon Wills*, ed. and trans. D. Whitelock (Cambridge, 1930), no. III: '[æþelf]læde þisse hwitan hyre cincdaðenan cyrtel 7 *cuffian* 7 bindan'. OE *cuffie* is discussed by G. R. Owen in 'Wynflæd's Wardrobe', *ASE* 8 (1979), 195–222, esp. 216: 'a head-dress which enveloped the head and neck . . . but a cap or a scarf or a veil is also possible'; and in *Dress in Anglo-Saxon England*, pp. 50–3, esp. 52 (quotation in text).

chapters, a rivalry between Óðinn and the Vanir was probably traditional in the north. In *Vǫluspá*, as Ursula Dronke has shown, the Vanir win the confrontation and overwhelm the Æsir by regenerating the dead combatants of their *fólc*:

> brotinn var þá borðveggr   borgar ása,
> knátto vanir vígspá   vǫllo sporna.   (*Vsp* 24/5–8)[118]

However, in the narrative on which Bede seems to have based his story of Coifi, it appears that Uoden was said not only to bear arms, to ride a stallion and to cast his spear at the idols, but also to succeed in destroying the *uanitas* of Northumbria by burning their shrine.

Who was the man who destroyed the shrine at Goodmanham? Firstly, it appears from the name Coifi and from the other correspondences that Bede's source presented this man in Goodmanham as if he were Uoden, a heathen god, in an assault against the gods of a rival cult. Secondly, it seems from the structure of Bede's account of Edwin's vision earlier, and also from his adaptation of his phrase *caeco carperetur igni* from *Aen.* IV.2, that Edwin believed that he had made a promise to Uoden eleven years before. Since Edwin began to fulfil this promise only when Paulinus reminded him of it, it follows that Edwin may have rationalized Paulinus by identifying him with Uoden. The meaning of *Coifi* ('hood'), the name by which the Deirans could then have called Bishop Paulinus, seems to be related to his head-dress as a bishop. There is little evidence of bishops wearing the *mitra* or *infula* as a liturgical emblem until about the ninth century, but it seems that where bishops wore a hat in the early seventh century, they followed the custom of local dress.[119] For his headgear,

---

[118] 'Broken was the shield-wall of the fortress of the Æsir, Vanir by a war charm were live and kicking on the plains.' As with the idiom in *Oddr* 8: *knátti mær oc mǫgr moldveg sporna* ('daughter and son began to kick the earth-road [= were born]'); see Dronke, 'Æsir–Vanir Cult-War', p. 226 (also published in *Myth and Fiction*, no. VII).

[119] *Real-Encyklopädie der christlichen Alterthümer*, ed. F. X. Kraus, 2 vols. (Freiburg in Breisgau, 1880–3) II, 213, s.v. 'Kleidung': 'Kurz, es ist aus den ersten acht oder neun Jahrhunderten kein zuverlässiges Zeugnis dafür zu finden, dass die Kirchendiener eine liturgische Kopfbedeckung getragen hätten, und wenn das eine oder andere Zeugnis sich sollte als begründet erweisen, so war der Gebrauch einer solchen Kopfzier ein rein lokaler'; see also di Berardino, *Encyclopedia of the Early Church*, s.v. 'Vestments, Liturgical' (p. 886): 'it is probable once more that, analogously to what happened for other items of clothing, the liturgical *mitra* was derived from a hat ... much used in ordinary life'.

therefore, Bishop Paulinus could have worn a Merovingian *cofia* such as other items of luxury Merovingian clothing imported into Kent from Gaul in the fifth and sixth centuries.[120] If these identifications are accepted, then it is possible that Edwin trembled and nearly prostrated himself before Paulinus when he saw Paulinus in his episcopal regalia (*HE* II.12), when, after six years of having him at court, he realized who Paulinus was.[121] By making use of a popular conviction that he had been Uoden all along, Bishop Paulinus, alias 'Cofia' to the credulous Angles, could at last have succeeded in preparing Edwin for baptism.

Bede says that after Goodmanham Edwin had little time to build a church before his baptism on Easter Day, 12 April 627 (*HE* II.14). Thus the destruction of the Goodmanham idols seems to have coincided with a festival that, as Bede indicates in *De temporibus*, took place in April with 'joys' (*gaudia*) in honour of a 'goddess of theirs who used to be called "Eostre"' (*dea illorum quae Eostre vocabatur*).[122] The *uulgus* which Bede mentions in Goodmanham is reminiscent, furthermore, of the *vulgus innumerum* ('crowd of countless people') in Berecynthia's spring-time procession outside Autun in the story of Simplicius by Gregory of Tours.[123] So, to complete this hypothesis, I suggest that Paulinus knew from past experience that an itinerant spring festival was about to start in Goodmanham (a site near the source of the Foulness and hence near the river Humber, the estuary through which the first northern Angles arrived from Germania); King Edwin, a Deiran descendant and representative of Ingui, waited at a royal hall nearby, ready to start a festive itineration around Deira which threatened to compromise his celibacy during Lent, making his baptism impossible and delaying the wider Anglian conversion further; so, as if he were Uoden in a role expected of that god, Paulinus rode out against the idols in the midst of their festival at Goodmanham, cast a spear into their shrine and set fire to the idols inside.

Bede, by embedding these implications in a narrative that was morally

---

[120] Owen, *Dress in Anglo-Saxon England*, pp. 57–63.
[121] Cf. Mayr-Harting, *The Coming of Christianity*, pp. 67–8: 'Whatever lay behind the vision at Redwald's court, Paulinus was using his gifts now in order to play upon something in Edwin's spiritual experience or in the workings of his mind and to point to a moral which was perfectly clear.'
[122] *Bedae Opera de Temporibus*, ed. Jones, pp. 211–13, esp. 212.
[123] *Liber de gloria confessorum*, PL 71, 884 (ch. 77).

Paulinus and the stultus error

if not factually true, seems to have admired Paulinus for destroying a temple and succeeding in converting the Angles where others had failed. Bede later shows us that he knows of a biblical precedent for mistaken identity in this affair, through a scene following Acts XIV.7–9, in which SS Paul and Barnabas get a warm welcome from local people after healing a paralysed man in Lystra: 'Turbae autem cum vidissent quod fecerat Paulus, levaverunt vocem suam lycaonice, dicentes: Dii similes facti hominibus, descenderunt ad nos. Et vocabant Barnabam Iovem, *Paulum vero Mercurium*: quoniam ipse erat dux verbi.'[124] Bede devoted a few lines to this scene in his commentary on Acts, written before *HE*.[125] After etymologizing the names of these pagan gods, Bede switches from the narrative past tense to the present, in order to describe what had happened as a 'stultus error gentilium, qui omne quod supra se vident deos *putant*' ('a stupid error of the pagans, who *think* that all things they see above them are gods'). *Putant*, rather than *putabant*, suggests that Bede knew of this *stultus error* among his own people too, because he knew or suspected that it had happened less than a century earlier in Deira. Paulinus's brand of pragmatism would be admissible if it was adapted from the life of his namesake the Apostle Paul. If again it is doubted that Bede would have known of such things, his quotation from Acts XIII.48 on the very next page after his account of the scene at Goodmanham (*HE* II.14) may show that he wrote the story of Coifi with a text of Acts XIV.10–11 beside him.[126]

In days to come the paranoid Edwin probably favoured Uoden as his god. Meanwhile Paulinus baptized thousands of peasants from the interior of Deira and Bernicia. Bede waits two more chapters before he introduces an eyewitness account of Paulinus, relayed to him through Abbot Deda of Partney, from a man accustomed to refer to Paulinus as 'a man tall in stature, with a slight stoop, black hair, a thin face, a slender aquiline nose, and, at the same time he was both venerable and *terrifying in aspect*' ('uir

---

[124] Acts XIV.10–11: 'But when the crowds saw what Paul had done, they lifted up their voices in Lycaonian and said: "Like gods made for men they have come down to us." And they were calling Barnabas Jupiter and *Paul in truth Mercury*, since he was the spokesman.'

[125] *Bedae Venerabilis Expositio Actuum Apostolorum et Retractionis*, ed. M. L. W. Laistner (Cambridge, MA, 1939), p. 60; Bede dedicated his *Expositio Actuum* to Acca of Hexham not long after 709: Brown, *Bede the Venerable*, pp. 57–8.

[126] *HE* II.14 (p. 186).

longae staturae, paululum incuruus, nigro capillo, facie macilenta, naso
adunco pertenui, uenerabilis simul et *terribilis aspectu*', HE II.16). Of
Óðinn's many names in *Grímnismál*, one of the most important, as we have
seen in the previous chapter, is 'Terrifier' (*Yggr*, *Grím* 53 and 54). Another
feature of this reference to an eye witness is Bede's use of Lat *effigies*: Deda's
informant was a man 'qui etiam *effigiem* eiusdem Paulini referre esset
solitus' ('who was also accustomed to relate an *image* of the same Paulinus',
HE II.16). Nowhere else in HE does Bede use *effigies*, Vergil's word in *Aen*.
II.167 for the spear- and shield-bearing idol of Athene which Diomedes
and Ulysses are said to steal from her temple.[127] If borrowed from the
same book as his previous quotation in HE II.13 (*Aen*. II.501–2), Bede's
use of *effigies* would imply that at least one Anglian convert made an idol
to Paulinus and worshipped him as a god.

Bede echoes *Aen*. II.501–2 at the end of his story about Coifi in order
to show Coifi laying waste *quas ipse sacrauerat aras* ('the altars which he
himself had consecrated').[128] With the same meaning in the West Saxon
translation of Bede's *Historia*, Cefi *fordyde þa wigbed þe he seolfa ær gehalgode*.
It is worth noting that, in their context, both the Latin and West Saxon
phrases resemble *Woden worhte weos*, a vernacular verse-phrase whose
implications I have attempted to interpret in ch. 4. If Bede intended to
echo Vergil in order to render an Anglian verse-line analogous to *Woden
worhte weos*, it appears that the *idola* in Goodmanham included *weos*, idols
of dead ancestors.[129]

Edwin's ancestors were probably not a matter of political weight until
after he was killed six years later in the battle of Hatfield Chase against
Cadwalla and the heathen Penda of Mercia. Paulinus fled to Kent with
Edwin's widow and dependents and in 633–4 there was a wild interregnum of two heathen kings, Osric and Eanfrith. Calling this an
'apostasia *demens* regum Anglorum' ('a *demented* apostasy of English
kings'), Bede may reveal that there was now a return to a popular *ælfsiden*

---

[127] Jones, *Concordance to Historia Ecclesiastica*, s.v. 'effigies' (p. 174); *Vergili Opera*, ed. Mynors, p. 132.

[128] *Vergili Opera*, ed. Mynors II.501–2 (p. 142). These are the altars which Priam had consecrated and which were now drenched with his blood.

[129] There are two tumuli on Weighton Wold a mile or so to the south-east of Goodmanham; less than 200 yards to the south-south-east of the church are a group of mounds whose name, 'Howe Hills', also suggests a series of graves: Ordnance Survey Market Weighton: Sheet SE 84/94, Pathfinder 675, 9041 and 8942.

or *insaniae falsae* of former years in Northumbria (a regeneration of Anglian *vanitates* akin to that of the Vanir in *Vsp* 24/7–8).[130] By revealing, furthermore, that the apostates Osric and Eanfrith, Edwin's kinsmen, were erased from the list of Christian kings (*HE* III.9), Bede shows that a revision of Edwin's ancestry was undertaken when King Oswald inherited Northumbria. It is likely that this revision was assisted by Irish clergy, particularly by Bishop Aidan, whom Oswald received from Iona in 634. Aidan understood the workings of tribal aristocracy better than his predecessors. In the manner shown in ch. 4 of this book, Anglian poets would have deified Edwin, upon his warrior's death in Hatfield, as Uoden's adoptive son (*HE* II.20). So Aidan, finding Northumbria wasted after two years of dissolution and war, may have been inclined to make Edwin's adoptive father into an official one by having Uoden's name transcribed into a regnal list. It is known that the Irish clergy were ready to sanction some heathen judgements: an entry in the early eighth-century *Canones Hibernenses* alludes to Ex. XVIII.21–2, in which Moses relies on the seventy judges of Israel, in order to prove that 'if we find judgements of the heathen good, which their good nature teaches them, and it is not displeasing to God, we shall keep them'.[131] Thus Aidan could have written Uoden into a regnal list, a table of Deiran ancestors, in order to erase Edwin's descent from Ingui, the worse alternative. The long day of Nerthus was over. That Aidan did not strike out *Ingui* from the Bernician list suggests that the dynastic records of Bernicia, probably compiled orally (and even transcribed) during Oswald's exile in Iona in 616–33, were considered inviolable by Oswald's family.[132] Yet it is reasonable to suppose that Uoden became the Bernician ancestor upon or after Oswald's death in battle against Penda in 644. Warfare was common and the cult of *ese* seems to have been a growing tendency among Oswald's family: Æthelfrith, his father, resembles the Odinic Eiríkr Haraldsson when he massacres the Bangor monks

---

[130] *HE* III.9 (p. 240). See my discussion of OE *ælfsiden* in ch. 3 (above, pp. 48–56) and *vanitates* and *insaniae falsae* in Ps. XXXIX. 5 in ch. 7 (above, pp. 176–9).

[131] *The Irish Penitentials*, ed. L. Bieler, Scriptores Latini Hiberniae 5 (Dublin, 1963), 8–9 (date) and 168–9 (III.8): 'quia si inuenerimus iudicia gentium bona, que natura bona illis docet et Deo non displicet, seruabimus'. This period of Christianization is discussed by Wormald, in 'Bede, "Beowulf" and Conversion', pp. 56–63.

[132] On Oswald's 'Anglian training' besides 'Celtic education', see M. Miller, 'The Dates of Deira', *ASE* 8 (1979), 35–61, esp. 60.

Heathen gods

in Bede's account of the battle of Chester; and not only *Os*-ric and *Os*-wine, Edwin's first and second cousins, but also *Os*-wald himself, his brother *Os*-wiu and his grandsons *Os*-red and *Os*-ric all carried names with prefixes that connected them more with Uoden and the military *ese* than with the *vanitas, vani dii* and *deus huius saeculi* that had frustrated Paulinus for six years.[133] Thus for a while, after the destruction of the enclosure in Goodmanham, a piece of Christian pragmatism and a late development within Anglian paganism became one and the same.

CONCLUSION: THE LITERARY CULT OF WODEN

Goodmanham defined not only the beginnings of Christianity in Anglian Northumbria, but eventually the way in which all Anglo-Saxons remembered their paganism in its last days. A literary cult of Woden became common across the country as a whole; the political need to write Woden's name into Anglo-Saxon regnal lists, as noted in the Northumbrian cases in ch. 5 and above, probably continued until the end of the seventh century. The descent of the West Saxon line from Uoden through Bældæg, his Bernician son, suggests that Uoden's name was sanctioned in Oswald's regnal list at about the time Oswald sponsored Cynegils of Wessex in baptism *c.* 636. Out went Seaxneat, in came Uoden, in Wessex in the first half of the seventh century. All other kingdoms followed suit, with the exception of Essex (and perhaps Sussex). In the previous chapter, I have suggested that the heavenly banquet in *The Dream of the Rood* is styled on the afterlife of Anglian kings in battle. The ascension in this poem would thus illustrate the style of an elegy in memory of Edwin of Deira. Just like Hákon Aðalsteinsfóstri more than three centuries later, Edwin after Hatfield would ascend 'with a multitude, with a troop of souls' (*mid manigeo, gasta weorude*) to his own

> blis mycel,
> dream on heofonum,   þær is dryhtnes folc
> geseted to symle,   þær is singal blis;   (*Dream* 139–41)[134]

Edwin died a Christian; just like the former warrior Guthlac, whose

---

[133] Kirby, *Earliest English Kings*, p. 225; Dumville, 'Anglian Collection', pp. 30–1.
[134] 'Where there is great bliss, joy in the heavens, where the warlord's people are seated at the feast, where there is perpetual bliss.'

Paulinus and the stultus error

servant in *Guthlac* B, by hailing him as 'prince of men' (*beorna bealdor*), gives him the distinction of an Anglian prince's death:

> se selesta   bi sæm tweonum
> þara þe we on Engle   æfre gefrunen
> acennedne   þurh cildes had
> gumena cynnes,   to godes dome,
> werigra wraþu,   worulddreamum of,
> winemæga wyn,   in wuldres þrym
> gewiten, winiga hleo,   wica neosan
> eardes on upweg.   (*Guth* 1359–66)[135]

Through poetic diction of this kind, Edwin's death could have been stylized as a journey to a warrior's paradise, in elegies which encouraged the growth of Uoden's influence: from the recently privileged position of this god in Northumbrian politics to the topos of his role as a dead king's 'father' in Deiran, Bernician, East Anglian, Lindsey, West Saxon, Mercian and Kentish regnal lists; from Woden in West Saxon royal genealogy and Hákon góði's connection with Æthelstan to Óðinn's acquisition of Freyr's or Hǫlgi's role in Eyvindr's *Háleygjatal* and in the work of other late tenth-century poets of Hákon Jarl; thence to the literary cult of Óðinn in Iceland and to Snorri's Odinic bias in his mythography of the thirteenth century; onwards towards nineteenth-century romanticism, the operatic role of Wotan and beyond; and then to the Odinic emphasis of Jan de Vries, so influential in scholarship up to this day.

Where less successful heathen gods were worshipped in pre-Christian England, I have attempted in this book to show their traces in hidden and not-so-hidden places. Compared to the progress of an enquiry into the traces of indigenous heathen gods, it is clearly a less fraught business to define the evidence for heathen gods during and after the period of Scandinavian trade, invasion and settlement in England. So, in *Beowulf*, the terms *woroldrǽden*, *Scyld* and *Herebeald* may have been loan-translations from Danish terms which were made as a result of mercantile contact with Denmark. A personification of *-geot* was made, perhaps as a result of

---

[135] 'The best man between the seas of those whom we have ever heard created through childhood from the tribe of men among the Angles, he, the mainstay of the weary, the joy of friends and kinsmen, the shield of his friends, has departed to God's judgement, into the splendour of the light, to seek the dwellings of his homeland on the upwards road'.

influence from Carolingian Europe, into *Geot* or *Geat* in regnal lists in the early ninth century. From the end of this century onwards, after Danish and Norse invasions and settlement in the five Danelaw boroughs and in Yorkshire, Cheshire, the north-west and even in south-western parts of England, there may have been an awareness among the Anglo-Saxons that gods with the names *Tir*, *Þor*, *Fricg*, *Ing*, *Oðon* and *Balder* had once been worshipped or commemorated by the Scandinavian settlers.

However, if we attempt to move further back in time to the indigenous Anglo-Saxon gods, the evidence is less straightfoward. *Uoden* or *Woden* is the clearest example of any heathen god; *Tiu* or *Tig* barely survives in a couple of runic inscriptions, in glosses, in placenames and in the Old English *Martyrology*; the word *þunor* survives also in placenames and in glosses and by implication in Kent and in the Saxon kingdoms; and in mostly Anglian contexts, words for phenomena of sea, sky and earth such as I have examined in ch. 8 may also be taken as representative of elemental *numina*, of Ingui's family; the world tree *holmwudu* ('ash') becomes *engel Dryhtnes* in *The Dream of the Rood*, in which traces survive of a legend concerning Ingui as *-geot* or a 'dying god'; and by alluding to the devil uniquely as *deus huius saeculi* and his cult as *uanitas*, Bede seems to give us a glimpse of Ingui in Northumbria in the early seventh century. In connection with Ingui, in particular, it seems clear that variants or elements of what might be generally called 'sacral kingship' were widely practised as a political system in northern Europe in the first few centuries of this era. By the eighth century in England, of course, sacral kingship would have become nothing more than the memory of an earlier ideology lingering on in cryptic poetic lines (some of which were later copied into manuscripts in the late tenth or early eleventh century), but traces of the memory did survive. So did a multitude of *numina*, Ingui's family, in the more archaic nouns of Old English poetry. Their pantheon was commensurate with the world. Relatively few literary traces survive, but with due analysis and argument, they all show that God's earliest English *creaturae* were varied and widespread, and that to the heathen mind in the early seventh, if not to our own blind folly in the late twentieth century, the world was charged with their power.

Bibliography

Primary sources are listed by the (first) editor's surname, where this is known. Icelandic authors or editors are entered by forename.

Anderson, E. R., 'Liturgical Influence on *The Dream of the Rood*', *Neophil* 73 (1989), 293–304
Arntz, H., and H. Zeiss, *Die einheimischen Runendenkmäler des Festlandes* (Leipzig, 1939)
Augustine of Hippo, *Sancti Aurelii Augustini De Civitate Dei*, ed. B. Dombart and A. Kalb, CCSL 48 (Turnhout, 1955)
Baetke, W., *Yngvi und die Ynglinger: eine quellenkritische Untersuchung über das nordische "Sakralkönigtum"*, Sitzungsberichte der sächsichen Akademie der Wissenschaften zu Leipzig, philologisch-historische Klasse 98 (Berlin, 1951)
Ball, C., 'Incge Beow. 2577', *Anglia* 78 (1960), 403–10
Barlow, C. W., ed., *Martini Episcopi Bracarensis Opera Omnia* (New Haven, CT, 1950)
Bassett, S., ed., *The Origins of Anglo-Saxon Kingdoms* (Leicester, 1989)
Bately, J., *The Old English Orosius*, EETS s.s. 6 (1980)
Bately, J., ed., *MS A: a Semi-Diplomatic Edition with Introduction and Indices*, vol. III of *The Anglo-Saxon Chronicle: a Collaborative Edition*, gen. ed. D. N. Dumville and S. Keynes (Cambridge, 1986)
Beck, H., D. Ellmers and K. Schier, ed., *Germanische Religionsgeschichte: Quellen und Quellenprobleme*, Ergänzungsbände zum Reallexikon der Germanischen Altertumskunde 5 (Berlin and New York, 1992)
di Berardino, A., ed., *Encyclopedia of the Early Church*, trans. A. Walford, with foreword and bibliographic amendments by W. H. C. Frend, 2 vols. (Cambridge, 1992)
Bethurum, D., ed., *The Homilies of Wulfstan* (Oxford, 1957)
Biddle, M., and B. Kjølbye-Biddle, 'The Repton Stone', *ASE* 14 (1985), 233–92
Bjarni Aðalbjarnarson, ed., *Heimskringla I*, ÍF 26 (Reykjavik, 1941)
Heimskringla II, ÍF 27 (Reykjavik, 1944)

Bibliography

Bjarni Einarsson, ed., *Ágrip af Nóregskonunga Sǫgum. Fagrskinna – Nóregs Konunga Tal*, ÍF 29 (Reykjavík, 1985)

Bremmer, R. H., Jr., 'Hermes-Mercury and Woden-Odin as Inventors of Alphabets: a Neglected Parallel', in *Old English Runes and their Continental Background*, ed. A. Bammesberger (Heidelberg, 1991), pp. 409–19

Brodeur, A. G. 'The Climax of the *Finn* Episode', *University of California Publications in English* 3 (1943), 285–361

Brooks, N., 'The Creation and Early Structure of the Kingdom of Kent', in *The Origins of Anglo-Saxon Kingdoms*, ed. Bassett, pp. 55–74

Brown, G. H., *Bede the Venerable* (Boston, MA, 1987)

Bullough, D. A., 'What has Ingeld to do with Lindisfarne?', *ASE* 22 (1993), 93–125

Byock, J. L., *Medieval Iceland: Society, Sagas and Power* (Berkeley, CA, and London, 1988)

Campbell, A., ed., *The Chronicle of Æthelweard* (London, 1962)

Carver, M. O. H., 'The Anglo-Saxon Cemetery at Sutton Hoo: an Interim Report', in *The Age of Sutton Hoo*, ed. Carver, pp. 343–71

Carver, M. O. H., ed., *The Age of Sutton Hoo: the Seventh Century in North Western Europe* (Woodbridge, 1992)

Cassidy, B., ed., *The Ruthwell Cross: Papers from the Colloquium Sponsored by the Index of Christian Art, Princeton University, 8 December 1989*, Index of Christian Art, Occasional Papers 1 (Princeton, NJ, 1992)

Chaney, W. A., *The Cult of Kingship in Anglo-Saxon England: the Transition from Paganism to Christianity* (Manchester, 1970)

Charles-Edwards, T., 'The Penitential of Theodore and the *Iudicia Theodori*', in *Archbishop Theodore*, ed. Lapidge, pp. 141–74.

Chase, C., ed., *The Dating of 'Beowulf'* (Toronto, 1981)

Clemoes, P., *Interactions of Thought and Language in Old English Poetry*, CSASE 12 (Cambridge, 1995)

Cockayne, O., ed., *Leechdoms, Wortcunning and Starcraft of Early England*, 3 vols., Rolls Series (London, 1864–6)

Colgrave, B., ed., *Vita Sancti Gregorii Magni: the Earliest Life of Gregory the Great* (Lawrence, KA, 1968)

Colgrave, B., and R. A. B. Mynors, ed. and trans., *Bede's Ecclesiastical History of the English People* (Oxford, 1969, repr. with corrections 1991)

Cramp, R., 'The Anglian Sculptured Crosses of Dumfriesshire', *Transactions of the Dumfries and Galloway Antiquarian Society* 38 (1959–60), 9–20

'Anglo-Saxon and Italian Sculpture', *Angli e sassoni al di qua e al di là del mare*, Settimane 32 (1986), 125–40

Davidson, D. L., 'Earl Hákon and his Poets' (unpubl. D.Phil. dissertation, Oxford Univ., 1983)

Bibliography

diPaolo Healey, A., and R. L. Venezky, ed., *A Microfiche Concordance to Old English*, Publications of the Dictionary of Old English 1 (Toronto, 1980)

Dodds, E. R., *The Greeks and the Irrational* (Berkeley, CA, 1951)

Dodds, E. R., ed., *Euripides: Bacchae*, 2nd ed. (Oxford, 1960)

Dronke, U., 'Art and Tradition in *Skírnismál*', in *English and Medieval Studies Presented to J. R. R. Tolkien on the Occasion of his Seventieth Birthday*, ed. N. Davis and C. L. Wrenn (London, 1962), pp. 250–68

'The War of the Æsir and Vanir in *Vǫluspá*', in *Idee. Gestalt. Geschichte. Festschrift Klaus von See. Studien zur europäischen Kulturtradition*, ed. G. W. Weber (Odense, 1988), pp. 223–38

'The Scope of the *Corpvs Poeticvm Boreale*', *Úr Dölum til Dala: Guðbrandur Vigfússon Centenary Essays*, ed. R. McTurk and A. Wawn, Leeds Texts and Monographs n.s. 11 (Leeds, 1989), 93–111

'*Vǫluspá* and Sibylline Traditions', in *Latin Culture and Medieval Germanic Europe*, ed. North and Hofstra, pp. 3–23

'Eddic Poetry as a Source for the History of Germanic Religion', in *Germanische Religionsgeschichte*, ed. Beck, Ellmers and Schier, pp. 656–84

Myth and Fiction in Early Norse Lands: Collected Studies [pagination follows that of each collected article] (Aldershot, 1996)

Dronke, U., ed., *The Poetic Edda I: Heroic Poems* (Oxford, 1969)

Dronke, U., Guðrún P. Helgadóttir, G. W. Weber and H. Bekker-Nielsen, ed., *Speculum Norroenum: Norse Studies in Memory of Gabriel Turville-Petre* (Odense, 1981)

Duemmler, E., ed., *Epistolae Karolini Aevi*, MGH, Epist. 4, 2 vols. (Berlin, 1894)

Dumézil, G., *Archaic Roman Religion: with an Appendix on the Religion of the Etruscans*, trans. P. Krapp, 2 vols. (Chicago and London, 1966)

Dumville, D. N., 'The Anglian Collection of Royal Genealogies and Regnal Lists', *ASE* 5 (1976), 23–50

'Kingship, Genealogies and Regnal Lists', in *Early Medieval Kingship*, ed. P. H. Sawyer and I. N. Wood (Leeds, 1977), pp. 72–104

'The West Saxon Genealogical Regnal List and the Chronology of Early Wessex', *Peritia* 4 (1985), 21–66

'The West Saxon Genealogical Regnal List: Manuscripts and Texts', *Anglia* 104 (1986), 1–32

'The Origins of Northumbria: Some Aspects of the British Background', in *The Origins of Anglo-Saxon Kingdoms*, ed. Bassett, pp. 213–22

Eckhardt, K. A. and A. Eckhardt, ed. and trans. [into German], *Lex Frisionum*, MGH, FIG sep. ed. 12 (Hanover, 1982)

Ehwald, R., ed., *Aldhelmi Opera Omnia*, MGH, Auct. Antiq. 15 (Berlin, 1919)

Evans, D. A. H., ed., *Hávamál*, Viking Society for Northern Research, Text Series 7 (London, 1986)

Faulkes, A., 'Descent from the Gods', *MScan* 11 (1982), 92–125
  'Pagan Sympathy: Attitudes to Heathendom in the Prologue to *Snorra Edda*', in *Edda: a Collection of Essays*, ed. R. J. Glendinning and Haraldur Bessason (Winnipeg, 1983), pp. 283–314
Faulkes, A., ed., *Snorri Sturluson: Edda: Prologue and Gylfaginning* (Oxford, 1982)
Finnbogi Guðmundsson, ed., *Orkneyinga saga*, ÍF 34 (Reykjavik, 1965)
Finnur Jónsson, ed., *Den norsk-islandske skjaldedigtning*, 4 vols. (Copenhagen, 1912–15)
  Edda Snorra Sturlusonar (Copenhagen, 1931)
Finsterwalder, P. W., ed., *Die Canones Theodori Cantuariensis und ihre Überlieferungsformen*, Untersuchungen zu den Bussbüchern des 7, 8 und 9. Jahrhunderts 1 (Weimar, 1929)
Fisher, P., trans., and ed. H. R. Ellis Davidson, *Saxo Grammaticus: the History of the Danes: Books I–IX*, 2 vols. (Cambridge, 1979–80)
Frank, R., *Old Norse Court Poetry: the Dróttkvætt Stanza* (Ithaca, NY, 1978)
Fry, D. K., ed., *Finnsburh: Fragment and Episode* (London, 1974)
Furneaux, H., ed., *Cornelii Taciti Annalium ab Excessu Divi Augusti Libri: the Annals of Tacitus*, 2 vols. (Oxford, 1884–1907)
Gelling, M., *Signposts to the Past: Place-Names and the History of England* (London, 1978)
Gertz, M. C., ed., *Scriptores Minores Historiae Danicae Medii Aevi*, 2 vols. (Copenhagen, 1918–20)
Gillespie, G. T., *A Catalogue of Persons Named in German Heroic Literature (700–1600) including Named Animals and Objects and Ethnic Names* (Oxford, 1973)
Glob, P. V., *The Bog People: Iron Age Man Preserved*, trans. R. Bruce-Mitford (London, 1971)
Gneuss, H., 'A Preliminary List of Manuscripts Written or Owned in England up to 1100', *ASE* 9 (1981), 1–60
Godden, M., 'Biblical Literature: the Old Testament', in *The Cambridge Companion to Old English Literature*, ed. M. Godden and M. Lapidge (Cambridge, 1991), pp. 206–26
Godman, P., ed., *Alcuin: the Bishops, Kings and Saints of York* (Oxford, 1982)
Goossens, L., ed., *The Old English Glosses of MS. Brussels, Royal Library 1650, Aldhelm's De Laudibus Virginitatis* (Brussels, 1974)
Graham-Campbell, J., *Viking Artefacts: a Select Catalogue* (London, 1980)
Grattan, J. H. G., and C. Singer, ed. and trans., *Anglo-Saxon Magic and Medicine Illustrated Specially from the Semi-Pagan Text 'Lacnunga'* (London, 1952)
Green, D. H., *The Carolingian Lord: Semantic Studies on Four Old High German Words: Balder; Frô; Truhtin; Hêrro* (Cambridge, 1965)

Bibliography

Guðni Jónsson and Bjarni Vilhjálmsson, ed., *Fornaldarsögur Norðurlanda*, 3 vols. (Reykjavik, 1950)

Gutenbrunner, S., *Die germanischen Götternamen der antiken Inschriften*, Rheinische Beiträge und Hülfsbücher zur germanischen Philologie und Volkskunde 24 (Halle a. S., 1936)

Hackenberg, E., ed., *Die Stammtafeln der angelsächsischen Königreiche* (Berlin, 1918)

Halsall, M., ed., *The Old English Rune Poem: a Critical Edition* (Toronto, 1981)

Hamer, A., 'Death in a Pig-Sty: Snorri's Version of the Death of Hákon Jarl Sigurðarson', in *Latin Culture and Medieval Germanic Europe*, ed. North and Hofstra, pp. 55–69

Hastrup, K., *Culture and History in Medieval Iceland: an Anthropological Analysis of Structure and Change* (Oxford, 1985)

Heather, P., 'The Crossing of the Danube and the Gothic Conversion', *Greek, Roman, and Byzantine Studies* 27 (1986), 289–318

'Cassiodorus and the Rise of the Amals: Genealogy and the Goths under Hun Domination', *Journal of Roman Studies* 79 (1989), 103–28

Goths and Romans 332–489 (Oxford, 1991)

Heather, P., and J. Matthews, *The Goths in the Fourth Century*, Translated Texts for Historians 11 (Liverpool, 1991)

Hedeager, L., 'Kingdoms, Ethnicity and Material Culture: Denmark in a European Perspective', trans. J. Hines, in *The Age of Sutton Hoo*, ed. Carver, pp. 279–300

Iron-Age Societies: from Tribe to State in Northern Europe, 500 BC to AD 700, trans. J. Hines (Oxford and Cambridge, MA, 1992)

Helm, K., *Altgermanische Religionsgeschichte*, 2 vols. [I, II.1, II.2] (Heidelberg, 1913, 1937 and 1953)

Wodan: Ausbreitung und Wanderung seines Kultes, Giessener Beiträge zur deutschen Philologie 85 (Giessen, 1946)

Henig, M., *Religion in Roman Britain* (London, 1984)

Hessels, J. H., ed., *An Eighth-Century Latin–Anglo-Saxon Glossary* (Cambridge, 1890)

Hill, J., ed., *Old English Minor Heroic Poems* (Durham and St Andrews, 1983)

Hines, J., *The Scandinavian Character of Anglian England in the pre-Viking Period*, BAR 124 (Oxford, 1984)

'The Scandinavian Character of Anglian England: an Update', in *The Age of Sutton Hoo*, ed. Carver, pp. 315–29

Hirsch, P., and H.-E. Lohmann, ed., *Widukindi monachi Corbeiensis Rerum Gestarum Saxonicarum libri tres*, 5th ed., MGH, SRG 60 (Hanover and Leipzig, 1935)

Hofstra, T., L. A. J. R. Houwen and A. A. MacDonald, ed., *Pagans and Christians: the Interplay between Christian Latin and Traditional Germanic Cultures in Early Medieval Europe*, Germania Latina 2 (Groningen, 1995)

Bibliography

Howe, N., *Migration and Mythmaking in Anglo-Saxon England* (New Haven, CT, and London, 1989)

Howlett, D., 'Inscriptions and Design of the Ruthwell Cross', in *The Ruthwell Cross*, ed. Cassidy, pp. 71–93

Irving, E. B., Jr., ed., *The Old English Exodus* (New Haven, CT, 1953, repr. with supplementary bibliography, 1970)

Jakob Benediktsson, ed., *Íslendingabók. Landnámabók*, ÍF I. 1–2 [1 vol.] (Reykjavik, 1986)

Jente, R., *Die mythologischen Ausdrücke im altenglischen Wortschatz*, AF 56 (1921)

Johannesson, A., *Altisländisches etymologisches Wörterbuch* (Bern, 1956)

Johnson, D. F., 'Euhemerization versus Demonisation: the Pagan Gods and Ælfric's De Falsis Diis', in *Pagans and Christians*, ed. Hofstra, Houwen and MacDonald, pp. 35–69

Jón Helgason, ed., *Heiðreks saga: Hervarar saga ok Heiðreks konungs* (Copenhagen, 1924)

Jón Jóhannesson, ed., *Hrafnkels saga Freysgoða*, ÍF 11 (Reykjavik, 1950)

Jón Sigurðsson et al., eds., *Edda Snorra Sturlusonar*, Sumptibus Legati Arnamagnaeani, 3 vols. (Copenhagen, 1848–87)

Jónas Kristjánsson, ed., *Eyfirðinga Sǫgur*, ÍF 9 (Reykjavik, 1956)

Eddas and Sagas: Iceland's Medieval Literature, trans. P. Foote (Reykjavik, 1992)

Jones, C. W., ed., *Bedae Opera de Temporibus* (Cambridge, MA, 1943)

Jones, P. F., *A Concordance to The Historia Ecclesiastica of Bede* (Cambridge, MA, 1929)

Kaske, R. E., 'The Finnsburh Episode in *Beowulf*', in *Old English Poetry: Fifteen Essays*, ed. R. P. Creed (Providence, RI, 1967), pp. 285–310

Keynes, S., and M. Lapidge, trans., *Alfred the Great: Asser's Life of King Alfred and Other Contemporary Sources* (Harmondsworth, 1983)

Keyser, P., and Unger, C. R., ed., *Barlaams saga ok Josaphats* (Christiania [Oslo], 1849)

Kirby, D. P., 'Bede and Northumbrian Chronology', *English Historical Review* 78 (1963), 514–27

The Earliest English Kings: Studies in the Political History of the Anglo-Saxon Heptarchy (London, 1991)

Kirk, G. S., trans., *The Bacchae of Euripides* (Cambridge, 1979)

Klaeber, F., ed., *Beowulf and The Fight at Finnsburg*, 3rd ed. (New York and London, 1950)

Krag, C., *Ynglingatal og Ynglingesaga: en studie i historiske kilder*, Studia Humaniora 2 (Kristiansand, 1991)

Krapp, G. P., and E. van Kirk Dobbie, ed., *The Anglo-Saxon Poetic Records*, 6 vols. (New York, 1931–53)

Bibliography

Krusch, B., and W. Levison, ed., *Gregorii Episcopi Turonensis Libri Historiarum X*, MGH, SRM 1.1 (Hanover, 1951)

Kuhn, H., 'Gaut', in *Festschrift für Jost Trier zu seinem 60. Geburtstag am 15. Dezember 1954*, ed. B. von Wiese and K. H. Borck (Meisenheim, 1954), pp. 417–33

'Die gotische Mission: Gedanken zur germanischen Bekehrungsgeschichte', *Saeculum* 27 (1976), 50–65

Kleine Schriften: Aufsätze und Rezensionen aus den Gebieten der germanischen und nordischen Sprach-, Literatur- und Kulturgeschichte, 4 vols. (Berlin and New York, 1969–78)

Lapidge, M., '"Beowulf", Aldhelm, the "Liber Monstrorum" and Wessex', *Studi Medievali*, 3rd ser., 23 (1982), 151–92

Lapidge, M., ed., *Archbishop Theodore: Commemorative Studies on his Life and Influence*, CSASE 11 (Cambridge, 1995)

Lapidge, M., and M. Herren, trans., *Aldhelm: the Prose Works* (Cambridge and Totowa, NJ, 1979)

Leo, F., ed., *Venanti Honori Clementiani Fortunati Presbyteri Italici Opera Omnia*, MGH, Auct. Antiq. 4.1 (Berlin, 1881)

Levison, W., ed., *Vita Vulframni episcopi Senonici auctore Pseudo-Iona*, MGH, SRM 5 (Hanover and Leipzig, 1905)

Vitae Sancti Bonifatii Archiepiscopi Moguntini, MGH, SRG 57 (Hanover and Leipzig, 1905)

Vita Wilfridi I. Episcopi Eboracensis Auctore Stephano, MGH, SRM 6 (Hanover and Leipzig, 1913)

Liebermann, F., ed., *Die Gesetze der Angelsachsen*, 3 vols. (Halle, 1903–16)

Lindow, J., L. Lönnroth and G. W. Weber, ed., *Structure and Meaning in Old Norse Literature* (Odense, 1986)

Lindsay, W. M., ed., with an index by H. McM. Buckhurst, *The Corpus Glossary* (Cambridge, 1921)

Lot, F., ed., *Nennius et L'Historia Brittonum* (Paris, 1934)

Luetjohann, C., ed., *Gai Sollii Apollinaris Sidonii Epistulae et Carmina*, MGH, Auct. Antiq. 8 (Berlin, 1887)

MacClean, D., 'The Date of the Ruthwell Cross', in *The Ruthwell Cross*, ed. Cassidy, pp. 49–70

Malone, K., ed., *Deor*, 3rd ed. (London, 1961)

Martin, R., *Tacitus* (London, 1981)

Mayhoff, C., ed., *C. Plini Secundi Naturalis Historia*, 4 vols. (Leipzig, 1892–1909)

Mayr-Harting, H., *The Coming of Christianity to Anglo-Saxon England*, 3rd ed. (London, 1991)

McKinnell, J., *Both One and Many: Essays on Change and Variety in Late Norse Heathenism*, with an appendix by M.-E. Ruggerini (Rome, 1994)

McTurk, R., 'Sacral Kingship in Ancient Scandinavia', *Saga-Book* 19 (1974–7), 139–69

'Scandinavian Sacral Kingship Revisited', *Saga-Book* 24 (1994), 19–32

Meaney, A. L., 'Woden in England: a Reconsideration of the Evidence', *Folklore* 77 (1966), 105–15

'Bede and Anglo-Saxon Paganism', *Parergon* n.s. 3 (1985), 1–29

'Scyld Scefing and the Dating of *Beowulf* – Again', *Bulletin of the John Rylands University Library of Manchester* 71 (1989), 1–40

Meissner, R., *Die Kenningar der Skalden: ein Beitrag zur skaldischen Poetik* (Bonn and Leipzig, 1921)

Menner, R. J., ed., *The Poetical Dialogues of Solomon and Saturn* (New York and London, 1941)

Meritt, H. D., *Old English Glosses: a Collection* (New York and London, 1945)

Merkelbach, R., *Die Hirten des Dionysos: die Dionysos-Mysterien der römischen Kaiserzeit und der bukolische Roman des Longus* (Stuttgart, 1988)

Meyvaert, P., 'A New Perspective on the Ruthwell Cross: Ecclesia and Vita Monastica', in *The Ruthwell Cross*, ed. Cassidy, pp. 95–166

Miller, T., ed. and trans., *The Old English Version of Bede's Ecclesiastical History of the English People*, 2 vols., EETS o.s. 57 and 59 (London, 1890)

Moisl, H., 'Anglo-Saxon Royal Genealogies and Germanic Oral Tradition', *JMH* 7 (1981), 214–48

Mommsen, T., ed., *Romanica et Getica*, MGH, Auct. Antiq. 5, 2 vols. (Berlin, 1882)

Mynors, R. A. B., ed., *P. Vergili Maronis Opera* (Oxford, 1969, repr. with corrections, 1977)

Myres, J. N. L., *The English Settlements* (Oxford, 1986)

Neckel, G., ed., rev. H. Kuhn, *Edda: die Lieder des Codex Regius nebst verwandten Denkmälern*, 5th ed. (Heidelberg, 1983)

Nelson, J. L., 'Reconstructing a Royal Family: Reflections on Alfred, from Asser, ch. 2', in *People and Places in Northern Europe 500–1600: Essays in Honour of Peter Hayes Sawyer*, ed. I. Wood and N. Lund (Woodbridge, 1991), pp. 47–66

Charles the Bald (Harlow, 1992)

Nelson, M., 'The Rhetoric of the Exeter Book Riddles', *Speculum* 49 (1974), 421–40

Newton, S., *The Origins of Beowulf and the Pre-Viking Kingdom of East Anglia* (Cambridge and Woodbridge, 1993)

North, R., *'Jeux d'Esprit* in "Deor" 14–16: Geat and Mæðhild', *ABäG* 27 (1988), 11–24

'The Pagan Inheritance of Egill's *Sonatorrek*', in *Poetry in the Scandinavian Middle Ages. Atti del 12. Congresso internazionale di studi sull'alto medioevo*, ed. T. Pàroli (Rome, 1990), pp. 147–67

'Tribal Loyalties in the *Finnsburh* Fragment and Episode', *LSE* n.s. 21 (1990), 13–43

Pagan Words and Christian Meanings, Costerus New Series 81 (Amsterdam and Atlanta, GA, 1991)

'"Wyrd" and "wearð ealuscerwen" in *Beowulf*', *LSE* n.s. 25 (1994), 69–82

'Boethius and the Mercenary in *The Wanderer*', in *Pagans and Christians*, ed. Hofstra, Houwen and MacDonald, pp. 71–98

North, R., and T. Hofstra, ed., *Latin Culture and Medieval Germanic Europe*, Germania Latina 1 (Groningen, 1992)

Oliphant, R. T., ed., *The Harley Latin-Old English Glossary* (The Hague, 1966)

Olrik, J., and H. Ræder, ed., *Saxonis Gesta Danorum* (Copenhagen, 1931)

Olsen, M., 'Fra gammelnorsk myte og kultus', *MoM* (1909), 17–36

Orton, P., 'The Technique of Object-Personification in *The Dream of the Rood* and a Comparison with the Old English Riddles', *LSE* n.s. 9 (1980), 1–18

Owen, G. R., *Dress in Anglo-Saxon England* (Manchester, 1986)

Page, R. I., 'Anglo-Saxon Paganism: the Evidence of Bede', in *Pagans and Christians*, ed. Hofstra, Houwen and MacDonald, pp. 99–129

Pertz, G. H., ed., and rev. F. Kurze, *Annales Regni Francorum, Annales Laurissenses* and *Annales Einhardi*, MGH, SRG 6 (Hanover, 1895)

Pertz, G. H., and G. Waitz, rev. O. Holder-Egger, *Einhardi Vita Karoli Magni*, 6th ed., MGH, SRG sep. ed. 25 (Hanover and Leipzig, 1947)

Pheifer, J. D., ed., *Old English Glosses in the Epinal-Erfurt Glossary* (Oxford, 1974)

Philippson, E. A., *Germanisches Heidentum bei den Angelsachsen* (Leipzig, 1929)

Picard, E., *Germanisches Sakralkönigtum? Quellenkritische Studien zur Germania des Tacitus und zur altnordischen Überlieferung*, Skandinavistische Arbeiten 12 (Heidelberg, 1991)

Piggott, S., *Waggon, Chariot and Carriage: Symbol and Status in the History of Transport* (London, 1992)

Pipping, H., 'Eddastudier I', *SNF* 16 (1925), 7–52

'Eddastudier II', *SNF* 17 (1926), 120–30

Plummer, C., and J. Earle, ed., *Two of the Saxon Chronicles Parallel: with Supplementary Extracts from the Others*, 3rd ed., 2 vols. (Oxford, 1965)

Pokorny, J., *Indogermanisches etymologisches Wörterbuch*, 2 vols. (Bern and Munich, 1959)

Pope, J. C., ed., *Homilies of Ælfric: a Supplementary Collection*, EETS o.s. 259–60 (Oxford, 1967–8)

Raith, J., ed., *Die altenglische Version des Halitgar'schen Bussbuches (sog. Poenitentiale*

Pseudo-Ecgberti), Bibliothek der angelsächsischen Prosa 13, 2nd ed. (Darmstadt, 1964)
Robinson, R. P., ed. *The Germania of Tacitus* (Middletown, CT, 1935)
Rollason, D. W., *The Mildrith Legend: a Study in Early Medieval Hagiography in England* (Leicester, 1982)
Schier, K., 'Freys und Fróthis Bestattung', in *Festschrift für Otto Höfler zum 65. Geburtstag*, ed. H. Birkhan and O. Gschwantler (Vienna, 1968), pp. 389–409
 'Húsdrápa 2: Heimdall, Loki und die Mierniere', in *Festgabe für Otto Höfler zum 75. Geburtstag*, ed. H. Birkhan and O. Gschwantler (Vienna, 1976), pp. 577–88
Schilling, R., ed., *Fasti: Ovide: Les Fastes*, 2 vols. (Paris, 1992–3)
Schlauch, M., 'The Dream of the Rood as Prosopopoeia', in *Essays and Studies in Honor of Carleton Brown* (New York, 1940), pp. 23–34
Schmeidler, B., ed., *Magistri Adam Bremensis Gesta Hammaburgensis Ecclesiae Pontificum*, MGH, SRG 2, 3rd edition (Hanover and Leipzig, 1917)
Sedgefield, W. J., ed., *King Alfred's Old English Version of Boethius' De Consolatione Philosophiae* (Oxford, 1899)
von See, K., 'Zwei eddische Preislieder: Eiríksmál und Hákonarmál', in *Festgabe für Ulrich Pretzel, zum 65. Geburtstag dargebracht von Freunden und Schülern*, ed. W. Simon, W. Bachofer and W. Dittmann (Berlin, 1963), pp. 107–17; repr. in von See, *Edda. Saga. Skaldendichtung: Aufsätze zur skandinavischen Literatur des Mittelalters*, Skandinavistische Arbeiten 6 (Heidelberg, 1981), 318–28 and 522–5
 Mythos und Theologie im Skandinavischen Hochmittelalter, Skandinavistische Arbeiten 8 (Heidelberg, 1988)
Sigurður Nordal, ed., *Egils saga Skallagrímssonar*, ÍF 2 (Reykjavik, 1933)
 Vǫluspá, trans. B. S. Benedikz and J. McKinnell (Durham, 1980)
Simpson, J., 'The King's Whetstone', *Antiquity* 53 (1979), 96–101
Sims-Williams, P., *Religion and Literature in Western England 600–800*, CSASE 3 (Cambridge, 1990)
Sisam, K., 'Anglo-Saxon Royal Genealogies', *PBA* 39 (1953), 287–348
Skeat, W. W., ed., *Ælfric's Lives of Saints: Being a Set of Sermons on Saints' Days Formerly Observed by the English Church*, EETS o.s. 94 and 114 [2 vols.] (Oxford, 1890 and 1900, repr. [1 vol.] 1966)
Socrates and Sozomenos, *Historiae Socratis Scholastici et Hermiae Sozomeni Historia*, Patrologia Graeca 67 (1864)
Steinsland, G., *Det hellige bryllup og norrøn kongeideologi: en analyse av hierogamimyten i Skírnismál, Ynglingatal, Háleygjatal og Hyndluljóð* (Larvik, 1991)
Stevenson, W. H., ed., and rev. D. Whitelock, *Asser's Life of King Alfred: De Rebus Gestis Ælfredi* (Oxford, 1959)

Storm, G., ed., *Historia Norvegiae*, Monumenta Historiae Norvegiae (Christiania [Oslo], 1880)

Ström, F., 'Poetry as an Instrument of Propaganda. Jarl Hákon and his Poets', in *Speculum Norroenum*, ed. Dronke, Guðrún P., Weber and Bekker-Nielsen, pp. 440-58

Strömbäck, D., *Sejd: Textstudier i nordisk religionshistoria*, Nordiska texter och undersökningar 5 (Lund, 1935)

Svavar Sigmundsson, 'Átrúnaðr og örnefni', in *Snorrastefna*, ed. Úlfar, pp. 241-54

Swanton, M., ed., *The Dream of the Rood* (Exeter, 1987)

Syme, R., *Tacitus*, 2 vols. (Oxford, 1958)

Thompson, E. A., *The Visigoths in the Time of Ulfila* (Oxford, 1966)

Tolkien, J. R. R., *Finn and Hengest: the Fragment and the Episode*, ed. A. Bliss (London, 1982)

Tolkien, J. R. R., ed., *The Old English Exodus: Text, Translation and Commentary*, rev. J. Turville-Petre (Oxford, 1981)

Tolley, C., 'A Comparative Study of Some Germanic and Finnic Myths' (unpubl. D.Phil. dissertation, Oxford Univ., 1994)

'Oswald's Tree', in *Pagans and Christians*, ed. Hofstra, Houwen and MacDonald, pp. 149-73

Turville-Petre, [E. O.] G., 'Fertility of Beast and Soil in Old Norse Literature', in *Old Norse Literature and Mythology: a Symposium*, ed. E. C. Polomé (Austin, TX, 1969), pp. 244-64

Nine Norse Studies, Viking Society for Northern Research: Text Series 5 (London, 1972)

Scaldic Poetry (Oxford, 1976)

Turville-Petre, [E. O.] G., and C. Tolkien, ed., *Heiðreks saga ok Hervarar* (London, 1956)

Turville-Petre, J., 'On Ynglingatal', *MScan* 11 (1982), 48-67

Tweddle, D. 'The Church in Northumbria', in *The Making of England*, ed. Webster and Backhouse, pp. 147-50

Tylor, E. B., *Primitive Culture: Researches into the Development of Mythology, Philosophy, Language, Art and Custom*, 2 vols. (London, 1903)

Úlfar Bragason, ed., *Snorrastefna: 25.-27. júlí 1990*, Rit Stofnunar Sigurðar Nordals 1 (Reykjavik, 1992)

Unger, C. R., ed., *Flateyjarbók*, 3 vols. (Christiania [Oslo], 1860-8)

Stjórn (Christiania [Oslo], 1862)

Unterkircher, F., *Alkuin-Briefe und andere Traktate im Auftrage des Salzburger Erzbischofs Arn um 799 zu einem Sammelband vereinigt: Codex Vindobonensis 795 der österreichischen Nationalbibliothek Faksimileausgabe*, Codices Selecti 22 (Graz, 1969)

Bibliography

Vermaseren, M. J., *Cybele and Attis: the Myth and the Cult*, trans. A. M. H. Lemmers (London, 1977)

de Vriend, H. J., ed., *The Old English Herbarium and Medicina de Quadrupedibus*, EETS o.s. 286 (Oxford, 1984)

de Vries, J., *Altgermanische Religionsgeschichte*, 1st ed., 2 vols., Grundriss der germanischen Philologie 12 (Berlin and Leipzig, 1935–7)

'Der Mythos von Baldrs Tod', *ANF* 70 (1955), 41–60

Altgermanische Religionsgeschichte, 2nd ed., 2 vols. (Berlin, 1956–7)

Altnordisches etymologisches Wörterbuch, 2nd ed. (Leiden, 1961)

Waitz, G., ed., *Pauli Diaconi Historia Langobardorum*, MGH, Scriptores Rerum Langobardorum et Italicarum, saec. VI–IX (Hanover, 1878)

Vitae S. Anskarii et Rimberti, MGH, SRG 55 (Berlin, 1884)

Wallace-Hadrill, J. M., *Early Germanic Kingship in England and on the Continent* (Oxford, 1971)

Bede's Ecclesiastical History of the English People: a Historical Commentary (Oxford, 1988)

Webster, L., and J. Backhouse, ed., *The Making of England: Anglo-Saxon Art and Culture AD 600–900* (London, 1991)

Whitelock, D., M. Brett and C. N. L. Brooke, ed., *Councils and Synods: with Other Documents Relating to the English Church: Part I: 871–1066* (Oxford, 1981)

Wilson, D. N., *Anglo-Saxon Paganism* (London, 1992)

Winterbottom, M., ed. and trans., *Gildas, De Excidio Brittaniae: The Ruin of Britain and Other Works* (London, 1978)

Wolfram, H., *History of the Goths*, trans. T. J. Dunlap, 2nd ed. (Berkeley, CA, 1988)

Woolf, R., 'Doctrinal Influences on *The Dream of the Rood*', *MÆ* 27 (1958), 137–53

Wormald, P., 'Bede, "Beowulf" and the Conversion of the Anglo-Saxon Aristocracy', in *Bede and Anglo-Saxon England: Papers Given in Honour of the 1300th Anniversary of the Birth of Bede*, ed. R. T. Farrell, BAR 46 (Oxford, 1978), 32–95

Wright, T., and R. P. Wülcker, ed., *Anglo-Saxon Vocabularies*, 2 vols. (London, 1884)

Zijlstra, J., 'Onderzoek Wijnaldum: Supplement "Finns Fibula"', *Friese Bodemvondsten* 2 (Leeuwaarden, 1991), 1–30

Index

Abel, 172
Abimelech, 126
Abingdon Chronicle, see *Chronicon de Abingdon*
Abraham, 53, 63–4, 111, 117–18, 126, 132
Achilles, 208
Acoetes, 32
Acrisius, king of Argos, 35
Adam 112, 220, 251
Adam of Bremen, in *Gesta Hammaburgensis Ecclesiae Pontificum* of: Wodan, 101; Thor, 101, 236; Fricco, 30, 101, 307; deified mortals, 106–7; Hákon Jarl, 122
Adonis, 31
Aeneas, 41, 136, 153, 208, 327
Africans, 18, 104, 206
Agaue, 31
Agilan, Visigothic envoy, 152
Agnarr, son of Geirroðr, 278
Agni, 40
Ágrip, 118, 308–9
Aidan, St, missionary bishop, 178n, 289, 339
Alaric, Gothic war-leader, 144–5, 150
Alavivus, 148
Albinus, abbot, 313
Alci, 21
Alcuin, 1–2, 139; *De patribus regibus et sanctis Euboricensis ecclesiae* of, 327, 333; *De officiis divinis* of, 334; letter to Speratus of, 44, 56–7, 77, 139; letter to King Æthelred of, 173
Aldebert, bishop in Gaul, 277
Aldfrith, king of Northumbria, 114
Aldgisl, king of the Frisians, 71, 307
Aldhelm, St, x, 1; *De laudibus virginitatis* of, 52, 106; letter to Wihtfrith of, 51; letter to Heahfrith of, 51
Alemans, 150, 186
Alfred jewel, 213
Alfred, king of Wessex, 1, 53, 113, 118, 161–4, 170, 213; alleged descent from Geat of, 161–2; alleged descent from Noah of, 182
Allecto, 106n
Alrekr, 40
Amali, see Goths
Ambrose, St, bishop of Milan, 151, 294
Amma, mother of churls, 280
Anatolia, 52
Anchises, 136
Andrew, St, in *Andreas*, 218, 222
Angengeot, Bernician ancestor, 134, 143
Angles, 2, 18–19, 104, 114–15, 117, 176–9, 228, 234, 304, 325–6, 332
Anglii, 10–11, 17, 141, 214, 217, 251, 259–60, 270–1, 299, 304, 325, 331
The Anglo-Saxon Chronicle, 43, 66, 111–13, 116, 132, 134–5, 159, 161–2, 164, 182, 194, 239; common archetype (æ) of, 182–4, 191–4

355

Index

Anglo-Saxon paganism, 3; animism in, 4, 204–7, 210–13, 271 (*see also* earth, sea *and* sky *numina*); casting lots in, 68; in *Beowulf*, 172–82, 188–91, 202–3; idols in, ix, 51, 61, 89, 97, 206–7, 240, 276, 332–8; burials within, 19, 50–1, 180n, 234, 296–7, 316, 318n, 322, 323n
animism, 206; abstractions in, 207–8; two-way passage between persons and phenomena in, 207–8, 212–13; *see also* Anglo-Saxon paganism
Annales, *see* Tacitus
anses, derivation from *anseis, 136–7
Anskar, St, missionary and archbishop of Bremen, 306–7
Aphrodite, 35n, 45
Apollo, 79
Argus, 87, 230n
Ari Þorgilsson, Icelandic historian, 8, 41; *Íslendingabók* of, 8, 9n, 40–1, 309–12
Ariadne, 34–5
Arian Christians, 146, 149, 151–2, 167
Arngrímur Jónsson, 187
Árni Magnússon, 39
Arno, archbishop of Salzburg, 139
Arnobius of Sicca, 209
Arnórr Þórðarson, 91n
Askr (Ascr), 101, 185, 286
áss, *see* Æsir
Asser, bishop of Sherborne, *De Rebus Gestis Ælfredi* of, 135, 154, 161–6, 168, 259
Athalaric, Ostrogothic king of Italy, 136, 153
Athanaric, Terving *iudex*, 147–9
Athene, 338
Atlakviða, 81, 91, 104
Atlas, N. African titan, 249
Atli, king of the Huns, 92, 244
Attis (Atys), 22, 30
Auðr in djúpúðga, 309–10
Augustine, St, bishop of Hippo, 34, 208
Augustine, St, missionary bishop of Canterbury, 50, 313–19
Augustus, Roman emperor, 103–4, 153

Aurvandill, 228–30
aza, Gothic A-rune, 136
Azarias, in *Azarias*, 222, 243

Æcerbot, 247, 250–5
æg-, *see* sea *numina*
Ægir, sea-god, husband of Rán, 98, 218–21, 225, 232, 281
Ælfgiefu, 54
Ælfric, 1; derivation of name, 54; *De falsis diis* of, 81–2, 115–16, 123, 205–6, 234–5, 247, 256; *Lives of Saints* of, 89, 256
ælfsiden, 44, 48–56, 77, 177–8, 317–18, 322, 338–9
Æsir, 14, 215, 231; etymology of *áss* from *ansuz, 82, 107–8, 137; cognates of, 108 (*ese*); fight cult-war with the Vanir, 36–8, 49, 131, 317–18, 332–5; arrange Skaði's marriage, 268; entertained by Ægir and Rán, 220; sons of, 100, 108, 110; origin in Troy of, 121; and phenomena, 209; pre-eminence over Vanir of, 305
Æthelbald, king of Mercia, 296
Æthelbald, king of Wessex, 163–6, 168
Æthelberht, St, king of Kent, 89, 114, 313–22
Æthelberht, St, martyred prince of Kent, 238–40, 320–1
Æthelburh, St, wife of Edwin, 114, 323, 326
Æthelflæd, beneficiary of Wynflæd, 334
Æthelflæd, lady of the Mercians, 118
Æthelfrith, king of Northumbria, 50–1, 116–17, 326–7, 339
Æthelmær, 82
Æthelræd unræd, king of England, 82
Æthelred, king of Northumbria, 173
Æthelred, St, martyred prince of Kent, 238–40, 320–1
Æthelstan, king of Wessex and England, 13, 118, 121–2, 132, 341
Æthelweard, in *Chronicon* of, 82, 112, 124,

Index

131; and Scef, 182–5, 188–94; and Beo, 194
Æthelwold, St, 1
Æthelwulf, king of Wessex, 2–3, 112, 118; alleged descent from Geat of, 133, 135, 161–2; alleged descent from Beaw of, 182; alleged descent from Scef of, 183; and *Beowulf*, 203; journey to Rome of, 161–2; marriage of with Judith, 133–4, 160–6, 168, 170–1; death of, 184

The Bacchae, *see* Euripides
Bacchanalia, 34, 51
Bacchus, *see* Dionysus
Balder (OE), *see* Baldr
balder (OHG), 83, 128
Balderus, 128, 130, 201, 267
Baldr, x, 11, 75, 260; derivation of name of, 143, 267; cognates of, 83, 124, 126–7, 143; etymology of *bhel*, 127, 267; common ancestry of with Ingvifreyr, x–xi, 111, 128–31, 153, 171, 267–8; common ancestry of with Njǫrðr, 268; peculiar to Scandinavia, 111, 153; name of as an epithet, 129–31; parentage of, 124–5, 152, 261; as brother of Þórr, 152; childhood of, 128, 267; wagon-tour of, 128, 267; death of, 109, 125–6, 267–8, 298; death of as sacrifice, 129, 143, 152, 199–201, 299–300; arrival in Niflhel of, 108, 125, 300; in Valhǫll, 129–30; universal mourning for, 298; dwelling with Hǫðr of, 129; reincarnation of as Váli, 131; and Bældæg, 111, 124–31; influence on Herebeald in *Beowulf*, 199–200; in England (Balder), 124, 131, 342; role in genealogy of (as Balldr), 124; as Norse counterpart of Anglian Ingui, 131; syncretism of with Christ, 133, 171, 299; in *Haustlǫng*, 152; in *Húsdrápa*, 152; in *Vǫluspá*, 152
Baldrs Draumar, 84, 143, 144

baldruus, 126–8; as Ing-hypostasis, 128, 131, 143, 145
Balthi, *see* Goths
Barnabas, St, 337
Barri, 46, 196
Bartholomew, St, 97
Batavi, 126–7, 246
Battle of Brunanburh, 132
Baudihillia, 104n
Bældæg, 43, 111, 113, 115, 117–18, 340; and Baldr, 124–31; written as *Balder*, 124, 131, 342; basis of *Beldegg*, 125
Beadohild, 155, 166–7
bealdor, 124–6, 143, 153
Beaw, *see* Beow
Bede, St, ix–xii, 1, 4, 12; *De temporibus* of, 178, 227–8, 336; *In Lucae evangelium expositio* of, 324–5; *Expositio Actuum* of, 337; *Historia ecclesiastica gentis Anglorum* of, 4, 11–13, 50, 59, 116–17, 131–2, 176, 178–9, 239, 304–5, 313–42; Alfredian translation of *Historia ecclesiastica* of, 318, 332–3, 338; and Uoden, 79, 111, 116; and Bernician genealogy, 117–18
Bedwig, West Saxon ancestor, 112, 183, 187 (Beðvig), 192
Beelzebub, 322
Beldegg, 122, 125
Belial, 56–7, 77
Benedict Biscop, St, 289
Benjamin, 116–17
Benty Grange helmet, 74
Beornuc, 42
Beow(ulf), *see* Beow
Beow, 112, 180, 182, 188, 194–6, 202
Beowulf the Dane 182–3, 189
Beowulf the Geat, 175, 180–1, 196, 198–201; and Grendel's Mother, 222; and Breca, 217; and Wiglaf, 235n, 330; salvation of, 202
Beowulf, x, 2–3, 11, 27, 44, 51, 64–77, 142, 222; Anglo-Saxon paganism in, 172–82, 188–91, 202–3; Finnsburh

357

Beowulf (cont.)
  Episode in, 63, 65–77, 180, 196; date and provenance of, 174; Danish influence on, 57, 341; structural integrity of, 182–94
Berecynthia, 22, 336
Berkshire Ridgeway, 53
Bern, king of Birka, 306–7
Bertelin, St, abbot of Sithiu, 290
Bertha, wife of Æthelberht, 313–14, 319
Bewcastle cross, *see* cross
Biaf, 187
Bible: Old Testament, 150, 333: Genesis, 62–4, 117, 126, 172, 202; Exodus, 61, 339; Kings, 150; Psalms, 54, 60, 88–90, 117, 177, 179–80, 277, 324n; Deuteronomy, 56, 57; Ecclesiastes, 251, 324n; Isaiah, 117, 324n; New Testament: St Matthew, 54–5, 118, 301; St Luke, 180, 301, 322, 324; St John, 54, 324; Acts, 324n, 337; Romans, 324n; I Corinthians, 324n; II Corinthians, 56, 323, 324n, 325; Galatians, 324n; Ephesians, 324n; Colossians, 324n; I Timothy, 324n; Titus, 324n; Hebrews, 324n; James, 324n; I John, 324n; Revelations, 16, 301, 324n; Apocrypha: Gospel of Nicodemus, 297, 302
Billingr, 156
Blodmonath, 178
boar-figures, 73–5
Boethius, St, 167; *De consolatione Philosophiae* of, 53, 157, 159, 166–7, 268n; in *The Wanderer*, 82
bog-people, 23, 272n
Boniface, pope, 89
Boniface, St, missionary, 59; in Gaesmere, 234, 276n, 277
Borgný, 248
Bous (= Váli), younger brother of Balderus, 267
Bragi inn gamli Boddason, *Ragnarsdrápa* of, 7, 16, 138–9, 142, 168–9, 220, 224, 259

Bragi, minor god, 102
Breca, 217
Brennu-Njáls saga, 201
Breta sǫgur, 123
Brísingamen, Freyja's necklace, 197
Broddenbjærg oakfork figure, 23, 30, 270
Brosinga mene, 196–7
Brussels cross-reliquiary, *see* cross
Brynhildr, 92
Byggvir, 195–6
Bǫðvarr Egilsson, 137, 221, 286
bǫnd, 207, 210–12, 307n

Cadwalla, Welsh king, 286, 338
Caesar, Julius, 79, 103
Cain, 172
Canones Hibernenses, 339
Caser, king of East Anglia, 115, 118
Cassiodorus, *Historia Gothorum* of, 135–6, 144, 148–9
Cædmon, 79–81, 327; *Hymn* of, 81, 247
Ceawlin, king of Wessex, 112, 116
Celtic religion, 18, 127
Cerdic, founder of Wessex, 112
Ceres, 22, 265; and Liber, 33–4, 45, 215
Charibert, father of Bertha, 314
Charlemagne, 28, 163
Charles the Bald, king of Western Francia, 134, 163–4, 168
The Charm for a Sudden Stitch, 105–6, 249
The Charm for Unfruitful Land, *see Æcerbot*
Chatti, 116, 142
Chaucer, Geoffrey, *Troilus and Criseyde* of, 169; *The Merchant's Tale* of, 169–70
Childeric I, 263n
Childeric III, 47
Chilperic, 152
Christ: human ancestry of, 118; birth of, 257–8; works of, 55–7, 273, 322; and herbal medicine, 87–8; vision of sea-bed of, 222; crucifixion of, 272–3; ascension of, 301–2; *stephanus* of, 244; as morning star, 228–9; as *Christus miles*, 150, 293, 303; the King, 301, 303, 308; nations

Index

as consorts of, 16, 326; and Christology, 292, 302–3; and Arian Christ, 133, 147, 149, 151–3; syncreted with Enguz, 152, 171; syncreted with Freyr, 307; compared with Hinieldus, x, 56; worshipped within Anglian paganism, 322; in *The Dream of the Rood*, 292–7, 301–3; not named in *Beowulf*, 71, 172, 175; example of followed by Hrethel, 198; Baldr as emulation of, 125–6; hypostatized in *Vǫluspá*, 200; worshipped within Icelandic paganism, 309–10
The Christian Ritual against Elves, 54–5, 77
Christianization: of England, x–xi, 312–40; of Scandinavia, xi, 118–19, 305–12; of the Goths, 146–53
Chronicon de Abingdon, 189–91
Circe, 87
Claudian, 145
Claudius, emperor, 34
Cleopatra, 35n
Clothild, Merovingian queen, 72n
Clovis, Merovingian king, 72n
Coifi, 11, 12n, 304, 330, 332–8; derivation of *coifi*, 333–4
Constantine I, 146, 149–50, 274
Constantius II, 149
Criseyde, 169–70
Cronos, 233
cross: invention of true, 274; stylized as a tree, 273–8, 303 (*arbor*, 275; *beam*, 275, 277; *gealga*, 275; *lignum*, 277; *rod*, 275, 277; *treow*, 275, 277; *wudu*, 277); as an angel, 291–2, 303; as a thegn, 294–5, 303; as a horse, 293–6, 303; *Hefenfeld* cross, 286–7; Ruthwell cross monument, 274, 287–91, 295, 297–8; Bewcastle cross, 289; cross of St Bertelin, 290; 'Repton Rider' upper cross-shaft, 295–6; Brussels cross-reliquiary, 274; in the *Riddles*, 274; in *The Dream of the Rood*, 273–4, 277–8, 287; etymology of OE *cruc*, 275

Cwenburh, wife of Edwin, 326
Cwichelm, king of Wessex, 326
Cybele, 2, 21–2, 31, 34, 45, 50n, 214
Cynegils, king of Wessex, 114, 340
Cynewulf, 89
Cynric, 112

Dagr, 40
Dan, eponym of the Danes, 185
Danes, 57, 180, 234, 308
Daniel, 60, 243
David, 118, 126
De temporibus, see Bede
Deda, abbot of Partney, 337–8
Demeter, 31, 33, 215
demons, *see ælfsiden*
Deor, 153–71, 196, 258–9; date and provenance of, 165; as political satire, 133–70
Deor, 161, 166, 170
deus huius saeculi, see Ingui
Deusdedit, St, archbishop of Canterbury, 239–40, 320–1
devil, 2, 54–6, 77, 95, 174–5, 180–2, 220, 240, 293, 324–5
Dido, queen of Carthage, 327
Dietrich von Bern, 160–1
Diomede, 338
Dionysus (Bacchus), 26, 30–6, 38, 45, 48–9, 51n, 56, 109n, 146, 179, 215, 267n, 270, 317–19
Discipulus Umbrensium, 315–16
Dómaldi, king of the Swedes, 264–6
Domitian, emperor, 136, 141
Domneva, St, mother of Mildthryth, 238–9
Donar, 127
*drauhtins, 150
Dream of the Rood, 3, 272–4, 277–8, 287–8, 290–9, 301–3, 340
dryads, 52

Eadbald, king of Kent, 238–9, 320, 326
Eadred, king of England, 118

359

Index

Eafe, *see* Domneva
eagor, *see* sea *numina*
Ealhstan, bishop of Sherborne, 164
Eanfrith, apostate Northumbrian king, 338
Eanwulf, ealdorman of Somerset, 164
earth *numina*, 246–71; *eorþan modor*, 204, 246–7, 250–5; *firgen-*, 222, 246–50; *fold fira modor*, 247, 251, 255; *frige*, 204, 246–7, 255–9; *geunnan*, 204, 246–7, 252–5; *grund*, 222, 258–9; stones, 207n; trees, 207n
Ebroin, Frankish duke, 71
Ecgberht, king of Kent, 238–40, 320–1
Ecgberht, king of Wessex, 112, 161
Ecgfrith, king of Northumbria, 118, 287
Ecgric, king of eastern Angles, 321
Edda (poetic), 6–11, 299
Edda (prose), *see* Snorri Sturluson; meaning of name, 8
Edda, mother of slaves, 280
Eddius Stephanus, *see* Stephen of Ripon
Edmund, king of England, 118
Edward, king of Wessex, 118
Edwin, St, king of Deira: presumed descent from Ingui of, 331; vision of Uoden in exile of, 80, 326–9; sacral kingship of, 259, 270, 325–6; ownership of horse-herds of, 331; marriage to Æthelburh of, 114, 320, 323; entreated to renounce idols by Pope Boniface, 89; converted by Rhun ab Urbgen, 326; survives attempt on life by Cwichelm, 326; mistakes Paulinus for Uoden, 326; favours Uoden as his god, 337; council near Goodmanham, 330; itineration in spring festival, 332; catechized by Paulinus, 176–7, 179, 325; baptized by Paulinus, 11, 304, 320, 326; killed in Hatfield Chase, 338–9; ancestry of revised, 339
Egill Skalla-Grímsson, 49; and *landvættir*, 212; *Sonatorrek* of, 137, 199, 220–1, 279, 285

Egils saga Skalla-Grímssonar, *see* Snorri Sturluson
Egyptians, 58, 60–4, 218
Eilífr Goðrúnarson, 120; *Þórsdrápa* of, 215–16, 240–1, 243n, 308–9; Christian fragment of, 308
Einarr skálaglamm Helgason, 91n, 120; *Vellekla* of, 98–101, 110, 145n, 308
Einhard, biographer of Charlemagne, 47
einherjar, 102, 107, 109–10, 125, 129, 302
Eiríkr blóðøx Haraldsson, 50, 99, 102, 118–19, 212, 339; in *Eiríksmál*, 106–7, 129–30
Elene, 126, 222
Eleusius, 97
Elijah, 302
elves, 44, 52–5, 77; *see also ælfsiden*
Embla, 101, 185, 286
Enguz, Gothic rune-name, 29, 139, 146–7 (*Inggws*); derivation of from *inggws* (*gutané*), 140–1; cognates of, 133, 139, 299; *gáut-* as an aspect of, 140–1; *balþa* as an aspect of, 145, 152, 299; wagon-tour of, 147–8; syncreted with Arian Christ, 133, 150–2, 171, 267; identified with Theodosius I, 148–9
Enoch, 302
Eorcenberht, king of Kent, 238, 320
eorendel, *see* sky *numina*
Eormanric: in *Deor*, 155, 161, 166; in *Beowulf*, 196; in *Widsith*, 197; *see also* Ermanaric *and* Jǫrmunrekkr
eormen-, 28, 51
Eormenred, king of Kent, 238–9, 320–1
Eorpwald, king of eastern Angles, 321–2
eorþan modor, *see* earth *numina*
Eostre, *see* sky *numina*
Erce, 250
Erik, deified Swedish king, 106, 110, 307
Erinis, 106n
Ermanaric, king of Greuthungi, 154, 161, 167; *see also* Eormanric *and* Jǫrmunrekkr
ese, 108, 136, 339–40
Etherius, bishop of Arles, 313

Index

Euric, Visgothic king of Toulouse, 151
Euripides, *The Bacchae* of, 31–3, 35–8, 45, 55
Eurydice, 158
Eurynis, 106n
Eusebius Pamphilus, 146n
Eve, 220, 326
Exodus, 2, 44, 57–64, 77, 211, 218; historical allegory in, 58–9, 64
Eyrbyggja saga, 220
Eysteinn Valdason, poem on Þórr of, 243n
Eyvindr skáldaspillir Finsson, 7, 120, 308; *Hákonarmál* of, 7, 91, 102–3, 106–7, 110, 129–31, 181, 301–3, 308; *Háleygjatal* of, 7, 39–40, 42, 111, 120–4, 260, 308

Fabricius, *alias* Weland, 53
Fagrskinna (also known as the prose *Nóregs Konunga Tal*), 99, 118, 308
Færeyinga þáttr, see *Flateyjarbók*
Fenrir, cosmic wolf, 130, 231
Finn Folcwalding, 65–73, 75, 181
Finnr skjálgi, chieftain of Hálogaland, 121
Finnsburh Episode, *see Beowulf*
firgen-, *see* earth *numina*
Fjǫlnir, 39–41
Fjǫlsvinnsmál, 217
Fjǫrgyn, *see* Jǫrð
Fjǫrgynn, Norse titan, 247–50, 261
Flateyjarbók, 25, 33, 77, 94, 267; *Færeyinga þáttr* in, 261; *Gunnars þáttr helmings* in, 25, 128, 267; *Nornagests þáttr* in, 329n; *Þorleifs þáttr Jarlaskálds* in, 95–6, 100–101, 108, 110; *Óláfs saga Tryggvasonar* in, 93, 110, 331
Folcwalda, 73
fold fira modor, *see* earth *numina*
Fornjótr, 9–10
Franks Casket, 53
frauja, 150
Fravitta, 140n
Fræ æ, *see* Freyja
Frea, wife of Godan, 108, 255; *see also* Frigg

Frealaf, 112–13
Fredegar, Frankish historian, 41
Freyfaxi, 77n, 331
Freyja: etymology of name, 256; provenance of name, 32–3, 257; as daughter of Njǫrðr, 14; as sister of Freyr, 14, 254, 256; regenerative power of, 37; incest of with Freyr, 254; teaches Æsir *seiðr*, 85, 108; chooses partners with Óðinn for Valhǫll, 14, 107; as hypostasis of Skaði, 122–3; as Gefn, 204, 222–6; her *Brísingamen* stolen, 197, 254; blasphemed by Hjalti, 311; in England (Fræ æ), 257
Freyr, *see* Ingvi-freyr
Friagabi, 255; *see also* Frigg
Fricco, 30, 236, 307
Fricg, *see* Frigg
Frig, *see* Frigg
frige, *see* earth *numina*
Frigg, 1 (Frig), 14; cognates of, 83 (Friia), 255 (Friagabi, Frea, Friia), 257; as daughter of Fjǫrgyn(n), 250, 261; as wife of Óðinn, 220; as mother of Baldr, 125, 129, 200, 261, 299–300; as prostitute (Frigga), 257–8; as controller of marriages, 127; as a phenomenon, 204, 209; in England (Fricg), 256, 342
Frigga, *see* Frigg
Friia, *see* Frigg
Frisians, 18, 65–77, 180, 307
Fritigern, 148
Frø, 128n, 267, 269
Froda, 40
Fróði, king of Denmark, 40, 57
Frothi, 187
Frotho, 57, 194
Froy, 41
Fructuosus, bishop of Braga 205

Gabiae, 221, 223, 226; *see also* Gefjun, Gefn and *geofon*
Gambrivii, 26, 29
Gangleri, *see* Óðinn

Index

Gapt, 133, 171; cognates of, 133–5, 138, 171; derivation of, 133, 135, 138–9, 142, 148, 153; role in genealogy of, 135–6, 153, 159, 171; dynastic influence in England of, 154, 171; human status of, 137; deified status of, 259; wagon-tour of, 148; and Wodan, 138
garsecg, see sea *numina*
Garulf, 67
Gauls, 29, 79
Gausus, 135, 154, 171
Gaute, 157
Gauti, 157, 160
gautr, 138–45, 153, 259 (*her-*), 300
Gautr, see Óðinn
Geat, 2–3, 112, 133–5, 154, 171, 182, 341–2; in *Geates frige*, 255–9
Gefjun, 204, 221–6, 249; derivation of, 223
Gefn, see Freyja
Gefwulf, 67
Geirrøðr, giant, 216, 240–1
Geirrøðr, king and torturer of Óðinn, 278
geneorð, see sea *numina*
Genesis B, 60, 211, 220, 222
Geoffrey of Monmouth, *Historia regum Britanniae*, 123
geofon, see sea *numina*
-geot, 2, 133–5, 139, 142–3, 153, 171, 301; derivation of, 134
Geot, see Geat
Gepids, 150–1
Gerðr, partner of Ingvi-freyr, 8, 30, 46, 52, 123, 139, 142, 160, 171, 253–5, 261, 264
Germania, see Tacitus
Geta, a slave, 134–5, 163
Getica, see Jordanes
geunnan, see earth *numina*
Gibbon, Edward, 149n
Gildas, St, in *De Excidio Britanniae*, 16, 68n
ginehord, see sea *numina*

Giuta, 134, 153
Gizurr inn hvíti Teitsson, 311
Gizurr Ísleifsson, bishop, 40
Godan (Lombardic), 108, 123
Goodmanham, 11–12, 176, 228, 330–9
Goths, 15n, 48, 112, 133, 138–41, 146, 148–54, 161–3, 166–8, 171, 196; Gothones, 29n, 135n, 141; Tervingi, 146–50; Greuthungi 148–50; Amali, 135–6, 144, 160, 171; Balthi, 144; Visigoths, 135n, 145, 151–2; Ostrogoths, 135n, 145, 153, 161
Gratian, western emperor, 148
Grauballe man, 272n
Gregory the Great, St, pope, 59, 89, 275, 313–14, 316, 319
Gregory, St, bishop of Tours, *Historiae*, 152, 313; *De gloria confessorum*, 22, 316–17, 336
Grendel, 64, 174–5, 180
Grendel's Mother, 64, 180, 222
Greuthungi, see Goths
Grímnir, see Óðinn
Grímnismál, 6n, 110, 123, 128, 131, 137, 278–81, 287, 338
Gróa, wife of Aurvandill, 229–30
grund, see earth *numina*
Guðmundr Oddsson, 91n
Guðrún Gjúkadóttir, 92, 244
Guðrún lundasól, 262
Guilden Morden boar image, 74
Gull-Haraldr, 119
Gullinbursti, boar, 75; *see also* Ingvi-freyr
Gullintanni, see Heimdallr
Gulltoppr, see Heimdallr
Gullveig, 37–8
Gunnarr Gjúkason, king of the Burgundians, 92–3
Gunnarr helmingr, in *Gunnars þáttr helmings*, 24–5
Gunnhildr, 49, 119, 212
Gunnlǫð, partner of Óðinn, 14, 96
Guthlac, St, in *Guthlac* 126, 211, 340–1
Guthlaf, 70

362

Index

Gyða, concubine of Haraldr hárfagri, 264
Gylfaginning, see Snorri Sturluson
Gylfi, king in Sweden, 6, 96, 224–5; and *gjálfr*, 225
Gymir, giant and father of Gerðr, 253

Hadingus, 48, 268–9
Hákon góði Aðalsteinsfóstri Haraldsson, king of Norway: fostered by King Æthelstan, 13, 118, 341; returns to rule Norway, 13–14, 118; his Christianity, 118; abandons conversion of Norway, 119, 308; dies in battle of Storð, 99, 102, 130; arrival in Valhǫll, 102–3, 110, 301–2, 340; likened to Baldr, 130; and influence of West Saxon Woden on Óðinn, 118–19, 124, 261
Hákon Hákonarson, king of Norway, 5–6
Hákon Jarl Grjótgarðsson of Hlaðir, 123
Hákon Jarl inn ríki Sigurðarson of Hlaðir and Norway, 14; exiled in Denmark, 119; begins rule in Norway, 119; forced baptism of by Otto II, 119; apostatizes and returns to Norway, 119–20; wins battle of Hjǫrungavágr, 120, 145n, 262, 308; revives paganism, 99–100, 110; patron of poets, 99, 120–3, 215, 308–9, 341; worships idol Þorgerðr, 95, 261–2; creates Þorgarðr to kill Þorleifr, 95, 108; sexual incontinence of, 120, 262–4, 309, 325; death of, 120, 309
Hákonardrápa, see Hallfreðr vandræðaskáld
Hákonarmál, see Eyvindr skáldaspillir
Haldanus, 187
Háleygjatal, see Eyvindr skáldaspillir
Hálfdanr Gamli, father of Gylfi, 224
Hálfr, in *Hálfs saga ok Hálfsrekka*, 92, 93
Halitgar's *Penitential*, 276–7
Hallfreðr vandræðaskáld Óttarsson, 120; *Hákonardrápa* of, 262–4, 266, 308, 328
Hallinskíði, *see* Heimdallr
Hallr á Síðu Þorsteinsson, 311
Hallr Þórarinsson, 8
Hama, 182, 196–8

hamadriads, 52
Hamðir, 8, 138, 143, 167
Hame, 197
Haraldr Gormsson, king of Denmark, 119
Haraldr gráfeldr Eiríksson, 119
Haraldr hárfagri Hálfdanarson, king of Vestfold and Norway, 4, 9, 13, 50, 118, 121, 264
Haraldus, king of Denmark, 329
Hariasa, 104n
Harimella, 104n
Harthgrepa, 268–9
Háttatal, see Snorri Sturluson
Haustlǫng, see Þjóðólfr of Hvinir
Hávamál: structure of, 156; Óðinn in, 14, 84, 87, 90–3, 101–2, 154, 156–7, 160, 279
Hávi, *see* Óðinn
Hæthcyn, 142, 181–2, 198–202
Hæklingr, 94
Heahfrith, 51
Heardingas, 48
Heathobards, 56
Heðinn, lover of Hildr, 91n, 168
Heðinn Sigmundarson, 74
Hefenfeld, 286–7; *see* Heimdallr
Heiðr, witch of the Vanir, 37, 49, 317–18
Heiðrekr, 74–5
Heimdallr, 98, 280–6, 290; meaning of name of (Hallinskíði, Gullintanni), 283–4; other names of, 282, 284, 291; identity of with Rígr, 280; as son of nine mothers, 280–1, 283; lives in Himinbjǫrg, 281, 286–7; sits at the end of heaven, 282, 293; horse Gulltoppr of, 283; as *hvítastr Ása*, 226, 281, 285; tells the future, 48, 281; as sentinel of gods, 281, 293n; at Baldr's funeral, 282; wrestles with Loki, 197, 226, 281; blows horn, 279–80, 284–5; common ancestry of with Norse world tree (Yggdrasill), 278, 283–5, 293; *see also* tree
Heime, Heimir, 197

363

Index

Heimskringla, see Snorri Sturluson
Hel, death-place and -goddess, 125, 128, 267, 299–300
Helena, St, empress, 274
Helgakviða Hjǫrvarðssonar, 74
Helgakviða Hundingsbana I, 93, 220
Helgi Hjǫrvarðsson, 220
Helgi inn magri Eyvindarson, 309
Helgi Sigmundarson, 74, 141
hell, 104, 107
hendinos, 147n
Hengest, 65–72, 75–7, 180
Hengistus, 66, 70
Heoden, 168, 170
Heorrenda, 155, 168, 170
Heracles, see Hercules
Hercules, 210, 212, 270; as *baldruus lobbonus macusanus*, 126, 143, 246
Herebeald, 181–2, 198–202, 341; death of as sacrifice, 199–200; see also Baldr
Heremod, 112, 181–3, 185–7, 191–2, 202–3; see also Hermóðr
Heriafǫðr, see Óðinn
Herinis, 106n
Hermes, 79, 87–8, 230n
Herminiones, 26, 28, 113, 246
Hermione, 52
Hermóðr, warrior and minor god, 102, 110, 125, 181, 187 (*Heremóð*), 200, 300
Hermunduri, 116, 142
Heruli, 150, 152
Hetele, 169
Hiarrando, 169
hieros gamos, 16–17, 139, 270–1; see also Baldr, Ingui, Ingvi-freyr, Nerthus, Njǫrðr
Hildeburh, 65, 67–8, 70, 76
Hildr Hǫgnadóttir, 168
Hincmar, bishop of Rheims, 164
Hinieldus, x, 44, 56–7, 77, 173
Hirminsul, 28, 113, 276n
Historia Brittonum, 27n, 41n, 42–3, 66, 70, 134, 153–4, 259, 326
Historia Ecclesiae Gentisque Anglorum, see Bede

Historia Langobardorum, see Paulus Diaconus
Historia Norvegiae, 41, 265–6
Hithinus, 169
Hjalti Skeggjason, 311
Hjarrandi, 168–9
Hlǫðyn, see Jǫrð
Hnæf, 65–7, 69–70
Hoginus, 169
Holofernes, 126
Homer, 87–8
Hœnir, 36, 185, 252
Hôrant, 169
horse burials, 180n, 296, 318n, 331
Hotherus, 128, 130, 201
Hrafnkell Freysgoði Hallfreðarson, 77, 331
Hrethel, king of the Geats, 126, 180–1, 198–202
Hróðólfr, missionary bishop, 9
Hrothgar, king of the Danes, 27, 51, 174, 186, 196; ancestry of, 176, 181; praise of God of, 175–6, 179; friendship with Ingui of, 64–5, 180–1
Hrungnir, giant, 229, 323n
Hrunting, 189
Hulmul, Gothic ancestor, 160
Hundingr, 92
Huns, 48, 148, 151n, 161
Hversu Nóregr byggðisk, 9
Hwætberht, St, abbot of Monkwearmouth-Jarrow, 274
Hygebald, abbot of Lindisfarne, 57
Hygelac, 181
Hymir, giant, 216, 232–3, 249–50
Hymiskviða, 98, 237, 249
Hyndla, 108
Hǫðr, 129, 198; etymology of name of, 125, 128; influence on *Hæthcyn* of, 201
Hǫgni Gjúkason, 91n
Hǫgni, father-in-law of Heðinn, 168
Hǫlgi of Hálogaland, 122, 124, 261–2
hǫpt, 210–12
Hǫskuldr Hvítanessgoði Þráinsson, 201

Iceland: first vernacular writing in, 8;

364

conversion of, 309–12; literature of, 4–9, 11
Ida, king of Bernicia, 42, 56
idols: biblical, 61, 89–90, 97, 274; Roman, 89, 208–9, 338; Gallo-Roman, 22; Anglo-Saxon, ix, 51, 61, 89, 97, 206–7, 240, 276, 332–8; Old Saxon, 28, 276; Danish, 30, 89, 174–6, 270; Swedish, 24, 100–1, 236; Norwegian, 90–100, 110, 237–8, 261–2; Gothic, 134–5, 147–8, 151; Slavic, 100
Iðunn, fertility goddess, 204, 250, 252–5, 264; as a phenomenon, 253, 266; as an aspect of Gerðr, 254–5; embrace of brother's killer, 254, 266
Iffley, Oxon., 189–90
in(c)ge, 2, 33, 57; in Exodus, 44, 58–64; in Beowulf, 44, 64–77, 172; in compounds: (-folc, 60, 62, 77; gold, 65, 70, 72, 77; -here, 60–2; laf, 61, 75; -men, 60, 62–3; -steald, 72–3; -þeod, 60, 63–4)
Ine, king of Wessex, 112, 114
Ing, in The Old English Rune Poem, 2, 30, 36, 43–8, 77, 227–8; as a man, 48; relation to Nerthus of, 33, 45, 271; wagon-tour of, 45, 48n, 147
Ing-hypostasis, 2–3, 26–7, 32–3, 38, 45, 77, 139, 215, 299; etymology of *inguaz, 30, 32; as baldruus, 128, 131; marriage with Terra Mater of, 214–15, 260, 266–73; death of, 260, 266–73, 297, 301
Ingaevones, see Ingvaeones
Ingeld, 56, 173
Ingellus, 56
inggws, see Enguz
Ingibrand, 42n, 43
Ingibrand, Bernician ancestor, 134
Ingild, 112
Ingo, king of Sweden, 329
Ingo, presumed Merovingian deity, 319
Ingoberga, mother of Bertha, 313, 319
Ingomar, 72
Inguec, 42–3

Ingui, 2–3; cognates of, 57, 299; family of, 204, 342; marriage of, 143, 270–2; death of, 143, 271–2, 297–303; role in genealogy of, 17, 30, 38, 42–3, 110; erased from regnal lists, 339; relation to Nerthus of, 26, 33; cult of, 44, 271; association with the devil of, 56–7, 63, 77; geot as an aspect of, 133, 139, 142–3, 153, 171; as woroldræden, 75–7, 342; as deus huius saeculi, 323, 325, 340; as an Anglian counterpart of Baldr, 131; and Sutton Hoo sceptre, 322; in Exodus, 57–64; in Beowulf, 64–77, 172, 179–81, 195, 202
Ingunar, 122
Ingunar-Freyr, see Ingvi-freyr
Inguz, Frisian god, 27, 29, 72, 139, 141, 299
Ingvaeones, 17, 26–30, 43, 64, 133, 246, 270–1
Ingvi-freyr, xi, 38–42, 53, 260, 308; as Ingunar-Freyr, 27, 42, 121, 195–6; cognates of ingvi, 26–7, 29–30, 42, 61, 72n, 179; meaning of freyr, 25, 32, 269, 307; kindreds of, 42, 63, 138, 260, 271, 281; childhood of, 128, 267; parentage of, 14, 38; divine role of, 17n, 73; gautr as an aspect of, 138–9, 140–2, 153; baldruus as an analogue of, 128, 131, 246; common ancestry of with Baldr, x–xi, 128–31, 152–3, 267–8; as priapic god, 30, 141; wagon-tour of, 24–5, 33, 35, 128; and coercion of Gerðr, 8, 30, 46, 128, 139, 160, 171, 196, 253–5, 262; as vaningi, 52, 267; as veraldar goð, 75–6, 195, 325; and elves, 48, 53, 267; and seiðr, 317, 324; boar-cult of, 73–5, 324; horse of, 83, 128; horse-cult of, 77, 331–2; and stags, 51, 234; sword of, 75; idols of, 30 (Fricco), 94–5, 331; as leader of hosts, 73; at Baldr's funeral, 75, 282; role in Ragnarǫk of, 51; burial of, 73, 267; role of in genealogy, 38–9, 120–3, 260, 264; and Merovingian

Ingvi-freyr (*cont.*)
  royal custom, 47–8, 72n, 180n, 318; in *Háleygjatal*, 120–3; in *Gunnars þáttr helmings*, 25, 128, 147, 267; influence on OE *frea* in *Beowulf*, 195
Ingwine, 27, 51, 64, 180–1, 203
Irminsul, *see* Hirminsul
Irpa, 95, 108
Isaac, 63
Isidore, St, bishop of Seville, in *Etymologiae*, 92n
Isis, 210, 212
Íslendingabók, *see* Ari Þorgilsson
Israelites, 58, 61–4, 116, 202
Istaevones, 26, 28, 246

Jacob, 111, 115–18
Jafnhár, 280
January (in *The Merchant's Tale*), 169
Jeconiah, 118
Jón Qgmundarson, bishop
Jordanes, *Getica* of, 135–7, 140, 144–5, 148–9, 154, 159–60, 230, 259
Joseph, son of Jacob, 62
Judith, daughter of Charles the Bald, 134, 160–6, 168, 170–1
Judith, in *Judith*, 53, 126
Julian Valens, Arian Gothic priest, 151
Juliana, St, in *Juliana*, 89, 126, 258; in *Passio S. Juliana*, 142
Juno, consort of Jupiter, 223
Jupiter, 79, 139, 146, 234, 237, 337; Latiaris, 210
Justus, St, archbishop of Canterbury, 326
Jutes, 65–70, 234, 265; paganism of, 180; and giants, 67; in Kent, 66n
Jǫrð, 14, 261; as Fjǫrgyn, 247–50, 261; as Hlǫðyn, 261
Jǫrmunrekkr, king of the Goths, 8, 138–9, 143–4, 161, 167, 220; *see also* Eormanric and Ermanaric

Ketill Jörundarson, 124
Ketill Þorsteinsson, bishop of Hólar, 40

kindins, 147n
Kormákr Qgmundarson, *Sigurðardrápa* of, 50, 85, 109
Kudrun, in *Kudrun*, 169
Kvasir, 36

Lacnunga, 54, 105n, 226n, 322
Lactantius, 208
Laȝamon, *Brut* of, 257
Landnámabók, 9n, 98, 211–12, 309–10
landvættir, 211–12
Laurentius, St, archbishop of Canterbury, 320
Laxdœla saga, 310
Leo I, pope, 297n
Leo IV, pope, 161–3, 170
Leuvigild, Visigothic king of Spain, 152
Lex Frisionum, 71
Liber, 26, 32, 48, 77; and Libera, 34; and Ceres, 33, 34, 38, 45, 179, 215
Liudhard, St, 314, 317
Livy, 28, 137
lobbonus, 127–8; *see baldruus*
Lóðurr, 185
Lofn, 127
Lokasenna, 7, 27, 49, 122, 216, 225–6, 250, 252, 254, 266, 285, 300
Loki: as *agent provocateur*, 7; steals Iðunn for Þjazi, then returns her, 252; castrates himself to amuse Skaði, 22n; brings about Baldr's death, 125; as Þǫkk, refuses to weep, 126, 298; accuses Óðinn of *seiðr*, 49; accuses Frigg, 258; taunts Frigg, 200; accuses Njǫrðr of vice, 216–17; soothed by Gefjun, 249 (as Loptr); accuses Gefjun of prostitution, 225; warned of her wrath, 226; accuses Iðunn, 254; altercation with Byggvir, 195–6; punished for Baldr's death, 298
Lombards, 133, 135, 150, 154, 163, 171
Loptr, *see* Loki
Lotherus, 185–6
Louis the Pious, emperor of Saxony, 306

Index

Lucretius, 33, 210

macusanus, 127–8; *see also baldruus*
Magna Mater, 2, 21–2, 45
Magnhildur, 157, 160
Magnild, 157
Mahabharata, 36
maiads, 52
Mannus, 26–7, 113, 269–71
Mark Antony, 35n
Mars, 79, 101, 210, 212, 227, 230–1; and Mercury, 104; Gothic Mars, 230; the planet, 232
Marsi, 29
Martin, bishop of Braga, *De correctione rusticorum*, 81, 115, 176, 204–6, 247
Martin, St, bishop of Tours, 81, 235, 256
Mary, the blessed Virgin, St, 257–8
Masyos, king of the Semnones, 22n, 141, 210
matres (matronae), 223, 227
Maxentius, 146
Maximian, 289
Maxims (Exeter Book), 78, 85, 88, 90, 212, 219, 221, 226, 244, 246
mægðegsa, *see* sea *numina*
Mæthhild, 154–60, 259
Medicina de quadrupedibus, 248
Mellitus, St, bishop of London and archbishop of Canterbury, 59, 89, 114, 275, 320
Mercury (Mercurius) 2, 78–9, 81–2, 112, 115–16, 210, 212, 235, 305; and Mars, 104, 142; and Atlas, 249; and St Paul, 337
Messalina, empress, 34–5
Michael, St, archangel, 302
Mildthryth (Mildred), St, 238–40, 320
Mímir, 36
Mimmingus, 130
Minerva, 79
mistletoe, 125, 128
Mithras, 153n, 319
Móðguðr, guardian of Hel, 200, 300

Móðir, mother of earls, 280
modranect, 227
moon, *see* sky *numina*
Moses, 59, 61, 63, 257, 339
Muhammad, 96

naiads, 53
Namatius, 218
Nanna, consort of Baldr, 128, 201, 267
Narses, Byzantine general, 161
Nægling, 189
Nennius, 41n; *see Historia Brittonum*
Neorth, 41
Nerthus, x, 2, 27; Celtic cognate of, 214; cult of, 17, 19–25, 29, 46, 72, 304, 307, 330–1; as Terra Mater, 11, 19–20; sex-change of, x, 20; masculinity of, 21–2, 45; hypostasis of, 30, 32–5, 45, 77; Anglian reflex of, 17; Norse reflex of, 23, 259; Frisian reflex of, 71; marriage of with Terra Mater, 47, 204, 214–15, 260; wagon-tour of 47, 107, 147; phenomenon of, 214–15, 217; *see also* Baldr, Ing-hypostasis, Ingui, Ingvi-Freyr, Njǫrðr
Níðaðr, king of the Niárar, 92, 252
Níðhǫggr, 87, 278
Niflhel, 108
The Nine Herbs Charm, 78, 85–8, 211, 226n, 244
Nithhad, 155
Njǫrðr, x, 11, 14, 40–2, 122; and Nerthus, 40–2, 259, 305; and *njǫrðungar*, 215; wagon of, 24; role of, 17n, 36, 215; as hostage of the Æsir, 14, 215; marriage with Skaði of, 23–4, 48, 121, 123, 139, 261, 268–70; children of, 14, 32–3, 37, 42, 215, 254; wealth of, 11, 73, 195; phenomenon of, 214–17
Noah, 63, 112, 182–3, 191–2, 222
Norðrsetudrápa, 10
Nóregs Konunga Tal (prose), *see Fagrskinna*
Nóregs konungatal, 39
Nornagests þáttr, *see Flateyjarbók*

367

Index

Nothhelm, St, archbishop of Canterbury, 313
numen, 208–10; *see also* earth, sea, sky *numina*

nymphs, 52
Oceanus, 19, 24, 26–7, 29
Oddrún, 248
Odin, *see* Óðinn
Óðinn, x, 11, 14–15, 78, 308; cognates of, 78; cult of, 13; southern provenance of (Wodan), 79, 152, 246, 305; and *Semnonenhain*, 141–2; rising importance of, 119n; as *áss*, 82, 305; as *gautr*, 84, 137, 139, 153, 300–1; perversity of, 49; witchcraft of, 78, 83–5; and the mead of poetry, 80, 96, 157; makes man and woman (Askr and Embla) with Hœnir, 185; makes stars from Þjazi's eyes, 230; shamanism on the world tree of, 83–5, 88, 143, 279–80, 299–300; rides to Hel, 300; in Niflhel, 108; in Valhǫll, 102–10; role of in Æsir–Vanir cult-war, 36–8, 332–5; opposition to Ingvi-freyr of, 120; dependence on Vanir of, 84–5; loss of Baldr of, 125, 199–200; fathering of Váli by, 109, 157; revenge on Hǫðr by, 198; influenced by Woden, 118–24, 131; genealogical role of, 13–14, 111, 120–4, 187 (Voden); father of Skjǫldr, 187; names of (Alfǫðr, 14, 122; Báleygr, 263, 328; Bileygr, 328; Elgr, 279; Gangleri, 96; Gauta spjalli, 286; Gautr, 96–7, 137–8, 140, 142, 153, 160; Gestumblindi, 328; Gestr, 329n; Grímnir, 278; Hangaguð, 279; Hávi, 156; Helblindi, 328; Heriafǫðr, 110, 131; Hiálmberi, 199; Hnicarr, 328; *karl*, 199; Síðhǫttr, 334; Sigtyr, 81; Váfǫðr, 91; Valfǫðr, 80, 104, 110, 131; Viðrir, 199; Viðurr, 199; Yggr, 50, 85, 101, 279, 338; Þriði, 263); consorts of (Frigg, 220, 258; *Billings mær*, 156–7; Gunnlǫð, 14, 96; Rindr, 14, 50, 85, 157; Jǫrð, 261; Skaði, 121); and Starkaðr, 181, 299; appears to Sigurðr, 328; appears to Óláfr Tryggvason, 329; in England (Oðon), 81–2, 115, 235, 342; horse of, 84; idol of (Wodan), 101, 236; acquisition of other gods' roles by, 123, 153, 160; in *Sonatorrek* 221; in *Háleygjatal*, 131, 260, 341; in *Hávamál*, 14, 84, 87, 90–3, 101–2, 154, 156–7, 160, 299–300
Oðon, 81–2, 115; *see also* Óðinn
Odysseus, 82, 87, 208, 338
Offa the Great, king of Mercia, 118, 296
Oglala Sioux, 206
Ohthere (Óttarr), Norwegian skipper, 162
Óláfr trételgja, 40
Óláfr Tryggvason, king of Norway, 94, 96, 120, 262, 310–12, 329, 331
Óláfs saga Tryggvasonar, see *Flateyjarbók*
The Old English Martyrology, 231, 342
The Old English Rune Poem, 2, 33, 36, 43–4, 77, 82, 227–8
Olef, king of Birka, 306–7
Ollerus, 244–5
On Arthour and Merlin, 158
Ongentheow, king of Swedes, 142, 181
oreads, 52
Orendel, 228
Orkneyinga saga, 9–10, 96
Orosius, *Historia adversus paganos*, 162
Orpheus, 158
Osburh, Alfred's mother, 162–4
Oslac, Alfred's maternal grandfather, 162
Oslaf, 70
Osred, grandson of Oswald, 340
Osric, apostate Northumbrian king, 338–40
Osric, grandson of Oswald, 340
Ostrogoths, *see* Goths
Oswald, St, king of Northumbria, 113n, 114, 115, 286–7, 339–40
Oswine, second cousin of Edwin, 340
Oswiu, brother of Oswald and king of Northumbria, 117, 239, 340

Index

Othinus: exiled from Byzantium and replaced with Ollerus, 244–5; animates his own statue, 90; appears to King Haraldus, 329; and Rinda, 85, 244; revenge for Balderus, 85, 244; *see also* Óðinn

Otto II, emperor of Saxony, 119

Ovid, *Fasti*, 35n; *Metamorphoses*, 32, 35, 38

Palladius, Frankish count, 317

Pandarus, 169–70

Parthenius, Merovingian bishop, 317

Paul, St, 56, 323–4, 337

Paulinus, missionary, bishop of York and Rochester, 3; arrives in Kent, 323; accompanies Æthelburh to Edwin, 323; may have brought books to Northumbria, 289; first attempt to convert Angles, 323, 325; consecrated bishop of York, 326; mistaken for Uoden by Edwin, 330, 335–6; converts Edwin, 11, 304; as *Coifi*, destroys heathen enclosure in Goodmanham, 330–8; idol made to, 337–8; orders Edwin's nobles to abandon 'unlawful unions', 176, 259, 325; choice of a Psalm by, 177; lesson from about the crow, 179; flees Northumbria to Kent, 338; conveys tale of Edwin's vision, 327

Paulinus, St, bishop of Nola, 209

Paulus Diaconus, *Historia Langobardorum*, 108, 123

Penda, heathen king of Mercia, 338–9

Pentheus, king of Thebes, 31–3, 35–7, 45, 318

Peter, St, 163

Pharaoh, 58, 61–4

Philostorgius, 150

Phol, 83; *see also* Baldr

Picts, 18, 104

Pietroasa neck-ring, 140, 142, 144, 147, 149

Pirmin, St, abbot of Reichenau, 205

Pliny the Elder, 144; *Historia Naturalis*, 27, 29

Plutarch, 35n

Portway transvestite skeleton, 50, 316

Posidonius, 28

Priapus, 51

Prose Dialogue of Solomon and Saturn, 240–1

Proserpina, 51

Radagaisus, Gothic war-leader, 149

Radegund, St, Merovingian deaconness, 333

Ragnarr Loðbrók, 94

Ragnars saga Loðbrókar, 93, 96, 101, 110

Ragnarsdrápa, see Bragi Boddason

Ragnarǫk, 14, 51, 101

Rällinge bronze figure, 30

Rán, wife of Ægir, 220; phenomenon of, 220–1

Randvér Jǫrmunrekksson, 167

Ratatoskr, cosmic squirrel, 278

Rædwald, king of eastern Angles, 321–3, 326

regen-, 210–11; *Regenmælde*, 211; *regnþeofas*, 211

regin, 210–12

Reginn the Smith, 211

Regnilda, 268–9

Repton Rider, *see* cross

Resen, P. H., 39

Rheda, *see* sky *numina*

Rhun ab Urbgen, prince of Rheged, 326

Ricberht, king of eastern Angles, 321

Riddles (Exeter Book), 212, 274, 291

Rígr, 280; *see also* Heimdallr

Rígsþula, 280, 285

Rimbert, *Vita S. Anskarii*, 106–7, 306–7

Rindr, 14, 50, 85, 157

Rothari, 153

Ruthwell cross, *see* cross

Rǫgnvaldr Óláfsson, king of Grenland, 9–10, 39–40

Rǫgnvaldr réttilbeini Haraldsson, 50

Rǫskva, wife of Þjálfi, 237

sacral kingship, x, 15, 17, 29, 141; Norwegian, 259–69; Anglian, 204, 259, 269–71, 259–60, 270–1, 325–6
Salvian, priest of Marseilles, 151
Sarah, 53
Satan, *see* devil
Satapatha-Brahmana, 36
Sathiel, 240
Saturn 234–5
Saul, 116
Saxnôt, 113
Saxo Grammaticus, 7; *Gesta Danorum* of, 7, 48, 56, 90, 128–30, 169, 173–4, 181, 185–7, 194, 201, 244–5, 267–9, 329
Saxons: in England, 18, 68n, 114–15, 234; Old Saxons, 59, 113; pirates, 218–19
Sæberht, king of Essex, 114, 320
Sæmingr, 121–2
Sæmundr inn fróði Sigfússon, 40
Sceaf(a) (Scef), 112, 182–94, 196, 203; foundling legend of, 184; Norse cognate of, 185
Sceldius, Sceldwea, *see* Scyld Scefing
Scioldus, *see* Skjǫldr
Scyld Scefing, 112, 122, 180–94, 196, 202–3, 341; variant forms of (Sceldwea, 183n, 188; Scyldwa, 185, 192; Sceldius 188; Norse forms of (*skjald-* (in *skjaldblœtr*), Skuld, 122); Scialdun 187); as phenomenon, 184, 188–91, 193–4, 196, 203, 212
Scyldwa, *see* Scyld Scefing
Scythians, 151
sea *numina*, 214–26; *æg-*, 220; *eagor*: *garsecg*, 214, 217–19, 221, 246; *geneorð* (*ginehord*), 214; *geofon*, 204, 214, 221–6, 246; *mægðegsa*, 214, 217, 219–21, 246
Seaxneat, 13, 111, 113–14, 340
The Second Merseburg Charm, 83, 128, 255
seiðr: as carnality, 49; as perversity, 49–50; as regenerative magic, 108, 131, 168; practicioners of, 50–1, 317–18, 322, 333; relation to *ælfsiden* of, 55, 85, 108, 317–18; and Óðinn, 84–5, 108

Semele, 31
semideus, 130, 136–7
Semnones: king Masyos of, 22n, 141, 210; grove of, 29n, 141–2, 208, 210
Septimius Severus, emperor, 104
sex, 8, 16–17, 30, 45–7, 51, 94–5, 126, 128, 139, 143, 160, 171, 176–8, 196, 210–12, 235–5, 246, 254, 257–8, 261–4, 266, 270–1, 324–5, 336
Sextus, St, martyr, 231
sibb (OE), 235n; *see also* Sif
Síðhǫttr, *see* Óðinn
Sidonius Apollinaris, bishop of Clermont, 151, 218–19
sidsa, 55; *see also ælfsiden*
Sif, wife of Þórr, 235, 242, 310
Sigeberht, St, martyr, 321
Siggeot, Deiran ancestor, 134, 143
Siggi, 122
Sigibert, Merovingian king, 317
Sigmundr Vǫlsungsson, 102, 110, 280
Signý Vǫlsungsdóttir, 280
Sigtýr, *see* Óðinn
Sigurðardrápa, *see* Kormákr Ǫgmundarson
Sigurðr Jarl Hákonarson, 121, 123
Sigurðr Sigmundarson, 92, 211, 328
Silius, partner of Messalina, 34
Simplicius, bishop of Autun, 22, 336
Sinhtgunt, 83
Skaði, xi, 22n; cognates of name of, 123, 261; death of father of, 215, 268; marriage with Njǫrðr of, 23–4, 139, 215, 270; marriage with Óðinn of, 122–4; hypostasis of, 122; in *Háleygjatal*, 120–2
Skáldskaparmál, *see* Snorri Sturluson
Skiold(us), *see* Skjǫldr
Skírnir: etymology of name of, 255; in *Skírnismál*, 6n, 8, 30, 38, 46, 52, 55, 57, 142, 250, 252–3, 264–7
Skjǫldr, 122, 185–8
Skjǫldunga saga, 187
Skuld (a Norn), 202n
Skuld, *see* Scyld

Skúli Jarl, regent of Norway, 6
sky *numina*, 226–46; *eorendel (earendel, earendil, oerendil)*, 226, 228–30, 246; Eostre, 3, 178, 226–8, 246, 336; moon, 205, 207n; Rheda, 227–8; sun, 205, 207n; stars, 205; Tiu (Tig, Tiw), 226, 230–3, 246, 342; *wuldor*, 204, 226, 241–6; *þunor*, 3, 204, 213, 226, 232–5, 237–41, 246, 322, 342
Sleipnir, 144, 200, 300
Snorri goði Þorgrímsson, 220
Snorri Sturluson, 6–9, 14, 51, 218, 341; *Edda* of, 6–7 (Prologue, 6, 121–2, 187–8, 261; *Gylfaginning*, 6, 14–15, 48, 73, 96, 101, 106, 108, 123, 125, 199–200, 207, 209, 213, 224, 226, 237, 242–3, 247, 255, 267, 279–82, 299–300, 305; *Skáldskaparmál*, 6, 24, 36, 67, 168–9, 215–16, 224, 229, 241, 268–9; *Háttatal*, 6); *Heimskringla* of, 6–7, 14n, 121 (*Ynglinga saga*, 14, 36, 49, 73, 83, 85, 96, 224, 265–6, 267; *Hákonar saga góða*, 118–19, 308; *Óláfs saga Tryggvasonar*, 99n, 212, 329; *Óláfs saga Helga*, 121); and *Egils saga Skalla-Grímssonar*, 7, 14, 123
Socrates Scholasticus, 145
Solomon, 63
Sozomenos, 145n, 147
Speratus, 2, 56–7, 77, 173
Starkaðr, 181, 299
stars, *see* sky *numina*
Steinunn skáldkona, 211, 310–11
Stephen of Ripon, *Vita S. Wilfridi*, 71, 333
Stilicho, 145
Stuf, 162
Suaevi, 79
Suebi, 18 (Suebians), 19, 26, 27, 29, 141
sun, *see* sky *numina*
Sunna, 83
Surtr, a fire-giant, 92
Sutton Hoo, 19, 297; sceptre of, 51n, 234, 322, 323n; spoons and buckle of, 322

Svanhildr, daughter of Guðrún, 8, 167, 220
Sváva, 74
Sven Aggesen, 186–7
Sǫrli, 8, 138, 143–4, 167

Tacitus, x, 1, 23–4, 28, 207; debt to Caesar of, 79; priestly role of, 45; praetorship of, 141; and Masyos, 141; *Annales* of, 34–5, 104n; *Agricola* of, 103; *Germania* of, x, 2, 10–11, 17, 19–27, 30, 38, 43, 45–7, 79, 86, 107, 113, 135n, 139, 141, 204, 208–10, 215, 246, 250–1, 259, 269, 330–1
Tartarus, 159
Tatwine, St, archbishop of Canterbury, 274
Tætwa, 112, 183
Teiresias, 33, 35, 48
Teitr Ísleifsson, fosterfather of Ari, 310
Tellus Mater, 21n, 22
Terence, 135
terpen, 68
Terra Mater, x, 19, 20–2; bronze-age provenance of, 20; cults of, 246, 250–1; Norse reflex of, 23; marriage of, 47, 204, 214–15; washing of, 208, 215; phenomenon of, 215; *see also* Nerthus
Tervingi, *see* Goths
Theoderic, Ostrogothic king of Italy, 136, 153–4, 160–1, 167, 171
Theodore, St, archbishop of Canterbury, canons of, 276, 315–16
Theodosius I, 148–9, 151
Theodric (*Deor*), 155, 160, 166–7
Thespius, 127
Thietmar, bishop of Merseburg, 100
Thor, *see* Þórr
Thunaer, 113
Thunor, Kentish thegn, 1, 232, 235, 238–40, 321; *see also* þunor
Tibullus, 33
Tig, *see* sky *numina*
Tindr Hallkelsson, 120

371

Index

Tir, *see* Týr
Tisifone, 106n
Tiu, Tiw, *see* sky *numina*
Totila, Gothic war-leader in Italy, 161
tree: and superstition, 275–7; as metonym for the cross, 273–8; as synonym for 'man' in Scaldic kennings, 286; Norse world tree Yggdrasill, 273, 278–80, 292–3, 299; and Heimdallr, 278, 280–7; Anglian world tree, 273, 287–96, 342
Troilus, 169–70
Trondheim region, 8, 14, 39, 94–5, 118–21, 261, 308–10
Trøndelag, *see* Trondheim region
Tuisto, 21, 26–9, 113, 246, 247n, 260; etymology of, 269–70
Tyrfingr, 189
Týr, 39, 128, 230–2; in *The Old English Rune Poem* (Tir), 231–2, 342; loses hand in Fenrir's mouth, 231; friend of Þórr, 232–3
Týz, Gothic rune, 230

Ubii, 104
Uegdæg, *see* Wegdæg
Úlfljótr, laws of, 211
Úlfr Uggason, *Húsdrápa* of, 152, 197, 200, 226, 281, 300, 324
Ullr, minor god, 242–5; cult of, 243, 245; as phenomenon, 204, 209, 235, 243, 283
Ulysses, *see* Odysseus
Um þat hvaðan ótrú hófst, 205–6
Unuuona, bishop of Leicester, 57, 177
Uoden, *see* Woden
Urðr, 202n, 287, 308
Uuodan (OHG), 78–9; in *The Second Merseburg Charm*, 83

Váfǫðr, *see* Óðinn
Vagdavercustis, 104n
Valens, emperor, 146, 147
Valfǫðr, *see* Óðinn

Valhǫll, 14, 102–110, 129–31, 181, 302–3
Váli, son of Óðinn, 98, 109, 157; derivation of name of, 108; reincarnation of Baldr in, 131; *see also* Bous
valkyries, 105–6, 108
Vandals, 108, 150–1
Vandilii, 26, 29
Vanir, 14, 33; cognates of, 138; cult-war with the Æsir of, 36–8, 49, 131, 317–18, 332–5; regeneration of, 37–8, 131, 339; ancient pre-eminence of, 42; wisdom of, 48; as demons, 52; *seiðr* of, 108, 168; teaching of Óðinn by, 84–5; loss of status to Æsir of, 305; and *vanitas*, 178–9, 241
vanitas, 52, 177–8, 241, 305, 331, 339–40, 342; *see also* Vanir
Varro, *De lingua Latina*, 34n
Varus, 142n
vé, 97–9, 103; definition of, 98–9; association of with Óðinn, 97; making of kings into, 103–4, 106–7, 110
Végeirr of Sogn, 98
Veggdegg, 122
Veleda, 141n
Vellekla, *see* Einarr skálaglamm Helgason
Venantius Fortunatus, St, bishop of Poitiers, *Vexilla regis prodeunt* of, 277, 292; *Pangue lingua* of, 292; *Vita S. Radegundae* of, 333–4
Venus, 34, 106, 136, 256; the planet, 229
Verðandi, 202n
Vergil, 33; in *Aeneid*, 208, 327, 330, 335, 338
Victoria, St, 52
Víðarr, son of Óðinn, 98
Vidigoia, 160
Vihansa, 104n
Víkarr, 299
Vikings, x, 18, 57, 118, 164–5, 219, 275
Vísburr, 265
Visigoths, *see* Goths

372

Index

Vita S. Anskarii, see Rimbert
Vita S. Gregorii Magni, 176–9, 259, 313–14, 327
Vita S. Vulframni, 72
Vita S. Wilfridi, see Stephen of Ripon
Vitalian, pope, 117
Voden, see Óðinn
Volla, 83
Vortigern, 70–1
Vǫlsunga saga, 197
Vǫlundr, 53–4
Vǫluspá, 7, 36–8, 49, 80, 101, 108, 110, 129, 185, 278–9, 285–7, 300, 309, 317–18, 332–5, 339

Wade, 169–70
Walahfrid Strabo, De imagine Tetrici of, 171
Walbrook marble statuette, 51n, 319; see also Dionysus
The Wanderer, 82
wanseoc, 52, 178
Wate, 169
Wayland's Smithy, 53
Wægbrand, 42n, 43
Wealhtheow, 196, 235n
Wecta, 118
Wegdæg, king of Deira, 115, 118
Weland, 53–4, 197; as Welund, 155, 166–7
weos, 97–8, 110, 338
Weoþulgeot, Mercian ancestor, 115, 118, 143
Widia (Wudga), 160–1, 167, 197
Widsith, 12, 154n
Widukind, Gestae Saxonicae, 28, 113n
Wigheard, archbishop of Canterbury, 239, 320
Wiglaf, 235–6n, 330
Wihtfrith, 51
Wihtgar, 162
Wijnaldum, W. Frisia, 68n, 72, 139
Wilfrid, St, bishop of York and missionary, 289, 307, 333

William of Malmesbury, De gestis regum Anglorum of, 188–90
Willibald, St, missionary and bishop of Eichstätt, 276
Winnili, 108, 123
Winta, 118
Wodan (OS), 113
Wodan, see Óðinn
Woden, x–xi, 1–2, 11–13, 74n, 132; cognates of, 78; derivation of name of, 79; variant names of: Oðon, 81–2; Vuoddan, 82; Wothen, 82; growth in England of, 341; heathen cult of, 78–83, 131; in place-names, 79–80, 233; and Bede, 79–80; and Cædmon, 80–1; role in genealogy of, 17, 78–9, 111–24, 133–4, 304; literary cult of, 15–16, 340–1; witchcraft of, 78, 85–8, 90, 103, 110–11, 115; and weos, 88–90, 244; and wuldor, 244–6; and wuldortanas, 85–8, 244, 246; and a warriors' paradise, 110; appears to Edwin in court of Rædwald, 328–9; written into Deiran regnal list, 339; parity with Jacob of, 114–17, 132, 203; parity with Abraham of, 117–18, 132, 203; influence on Óðinn of, 118–24, 131–2, 261; in The Nine Herbs Charm, 85–8, 244, 246; in Maxims I, 88–90; as os in The Old English Rune Poem, 82; in Beowulf, 181; in The Wanderer, 82
Wotan, 15, 341
Wudga, see Widia
wuldor, see sky numina
wuldorbeag, 244; see also wuldor
wuldorgeflogene, 244; see also wuldor
wuldortanas, 86–8, 244; see also wuldor
Wulfhere, king of Mercia, 114, 321
Wulfila, missionary bishop, 146, 150, 151
Wulfred, Anglo-Saxon missionary, 236
Wulfstan, St, archbishop of York, 1, 234; De falsis deis of, 81, 205, 235; Sermo Lupi ad Anglos of, 106, 309n; Cnut's Laws of, 206–7

Index

Wynflæd, 334
wyrd, 3, 4n, 202n

Yeavering, 15n, 18, 327n
Yggdrasill, see tree
Yggr, see Óðinn
Ynglinga saga
Ynglingar, 26, 39
Ynglingatal, see Þjóðólfr of Hvinir
Yngvi Tyrkjakonungr, 40–1
Yngvi, a dwarf, 42
Yngvi-freyr, see Ingvi-freyr

Zacharias, St, pope, 277
Zeus, 31, 109n, 230, 233, 270
Zosimus, 148, 149n

Þangbrandr, German missionary, 211, 310–11
Þiðreks saga af Bern, 197
þiudans, 147n, 149
Þjálfi, servant of Þórr, husband of Rǫskva, 216, 237
Þjazi, father of Skaði, 215, 230, 252, 268
Þjóðólfr of Hvinir, 7, 120; *Ynglingatal* of, 7, 9–10, 39–42, 120–1, 260, 265–6, 279–80; *Haustlǫng* of, 7, 10, 42, 63, 124, 138, 152, 229, 237–8, 243, 250, 252–4, 259–60, 271, 281
Þorbjǫrn dísarskáld, Þórr-fragment of, 101
Þorgarðr, 'tree-man', 95–6, 100, 110

Þorgeirr Þorkelsson, lawspeaker, 311–12
Þorgerðr Hǫlgabrúðr, 93, 108, 123; as *Hǫrðabrúðr*, 95, 261–2
Þorkell Gíslason, *Búadrápa* of, 100
Þorlákr, St, bishop of Skálholt, 40
Þorleifr Jarlaskáld, 95–7
Þorleifs Þáttr Jarlaskálds, see *Flateyjarbók*
Þórr: cult of, 236, 305, 308–12; parentage of, 124, 235, 247–8, 261; as husband of Sif, 235; as phenomenon, 204, 209; in drag, 281; travels to Geirrøðr, 216, 240–1; travels to Hymir, 232–3; challenges Christ to duel, 311; smashes Þangbrandr's ship, 211, 311; as friend of Týr, 232–3; as kinsman of Ullr, 242–3; fights in Ragnarǫk, 101; associated with Hercules, 127; idol of (Thor), 101; equipment of, 237, 241; in England (Þor), 235, 240–1, 342; in Sweden, 101, 307; in Iceland, 309–12; in *Haustlǫng*, 124, 229, 237–8, 243, 259; in *Þórsdrápa*, 215–16, 240–1, 243n, 308–9; in *Alvíssmál*, 102
Þórsdrápa, see Eilífr Goðrúnarson
Þórsteinn rauðnefr, 211
Þrymr, giant, 281
þunor, see sky numina
Þunores hlæw, 239–40; see also *þunor*
þunorrad, 237–8; see also *þunor*
Þǫkk, 125–6, 129, 199, 298–9

Ǫgmundr inn danski, 94

For EU product safety concerns, contact us at Calle de José Abascal, 56–1°,
28003 Madrid, Spain or eugpsr@cambridge.org.

www.ingramcontent.com/pod-product-compliance
Lightning Source LLC
LaVergne TN
LVHW091528060526
838200LV00036B/520